LEVANT SUPPLEMENTARY SERIES
VOLUME 9

CULTURE, CHRONOLOGY AND THE CHALCOLITHIC

THEORY AND TRANSITION

Edited by J. L. Lovell and Y. M. Rowan

OXBOW BOOKS
Oxford and Oakville

Published jointly by
the Council for British Research in the Levant
and
Oxbow Books, Oxford, UK

ISBN 978-1-84217-993-2

Cover image:
Wheel of Fortunate Archaeologists
by Chris Schofield

This book is available direct from:

Oxbow Books, Oxford, UK
(Phone: 01865-241249; Fax: 01865-794449)

and

The David Brown Book Company
PO Box 511, Oakville, CT 06779, USA
(Phone: 860-945-9329; Fax: 860-945-9468)

or from our website

www.oxbowbooks.com

A CIP record for this book is available from the British Library

Library of Congress Cataloging-in-Publication Data

Culture, chronology and the Chalcolithic : theory and transition / edited by J. L. Lovell and Y. M. Rowan.
p. cm. -- (Levant supplementary series ; vol. 9)
"Published jointly by the Council for British Research in the Levant and Oxbow Books."
Includes bibliographical references and index.
ISBN 978-1-84217-993-2
1. Copper age--Middle East. 2. Middle East--Antiquities. I. Lovell, Jaimie L. II. Rowan, Yorke M.
GN778.32.M628C85 2011
939'.4--dc22
2011010633

Printed and bound in Great Britain by
Short Run Press, Exeter

Contents

List of Figures and Tables

List of Figures

List of Tables

Acknowledgements

Numerous people and institutions made this volume possible. We would like to thank the organizers and hosts of the ICAANE conference, in particular. Generous funding support to YMR was made possible by The University of Notre Dame and to JLL by the Council for British Research in the Levant to attend the conference in Madrid. Much of the work for this volume was made possible while YMR was a Fulbright Research Scholar in Jordan (2006–7) and a CAORC Scholar at the American School of Oriental Research in Amman; the support of both institutions is gratefully acknowledged. JLL completed work on the volume while employed by the Council for British Research in the Levant.

List of Contributors

The editors

JAIMIE L. LOVELL
Department of Archaeology
School of Philosophical and Historical Inquiry, A14
University of Sydney
NSW 2006
Australia
jaimie.lovell@sydney.edu.au

YORKE M. ROWAN
The Oriental Institute
University of Chicago
1155 East 58th Street
Chicago IL 60637
United States of America
ymrowan@uchicago.edu

The authors

NILS ANFINSET
Department of Archaeology, History, Culture and Religious Studies
University of Bergen
P.O. Box 7800
N-5020 Bergen
Norway
nils.anfinset@ahkr.uib.no

EDWARD B. BANNING
Department of Anthropology
University of Toronto
Ontario M5S 3G3
Canada
ted.banning@utoronto.ca

ELIOT BRAUN
P.O. Box 21
Har Adar 90836
Israel
ebraun@netvision.net.il

MARGIE BURTON
San Diego Archaeological Centre
16666 San Pasqual Valley Road
Escondido CA 92027-7001
United States of America
mburton@sandiegoarchaeology.org

MARIE-AGNÈS COURTY
CNRS, Muséum National d'Histoire Naturelle
UMR-7194-Histoire naturelle de l'Homme préhistorique
1, rue René Panhard
75013 Paris
France
courty@mnhn.fr

GENEVIÈVE DOLLFUS
CNRS, Paléorient
Maison René Ginouvès
21 Allée de l'Université
F-92023, Nanterre Cedex
France
dollfus@mae.u-paris10.fr

PETER FABIAN
P.O. Box 271
Omer
Beer Sheva 84965
Israel
fabian@israntique.org.il

KEVIN GIBBS
Archaeology, Mansfield Cooper Bdg
The University of Manchester
Oxford Road, Manchester M13 9PL
United Kingdom
kevin.gibbs@manchester.ac.uk

ISAAC GILEAD
Archaeological Division
Ben-Gurion University of the Negev
Beer Sheva
Israel
gilead@bgu.ac.il

CHRISTOPHER J. GOHM
Department of Near and Middle Eastern Civilizations
University of Toronto
4 Bancroft Avenue
Toronto, ON M5S 1C1
Canada
christopherj.gohm@utoronto.ca

Amir Golani
Israel Antiquities Authority
P.O. Box 586
Jerusalem 91004
Israel
golani@israntique.org.il

Seiji Kadowaki
The University Museum
The University of Tokyo
7-3-1 Hongo, Bunkyo
Tokyo 113-0033
Japan
kadowaki@um.u-tokyo.ac.jp

Zeidan A. Kafafi
Yarmouk University
Irbid
Jordan
zeidan@yahoo.com

Thomas E. Levy
University of California-San Diego
9500 Gilman Drive
La Jolla CA 92093-0532
United States of America
tlevy@ucsd.edu

Ofer Marder
Israel Antiquities Authority
P.O. Box 586
Jerusalem 91004
Israel
oferm@israntique.org.il

Ianir Milevski
Israel Antiquities Authority
P.O. Box 586
Jerusalem 91004
Israel
ianir@israntique.org.il

Yossi Nagar
Israel Antiquities Authority
P.O. Box 586
Jerusalem 91004
Israel
yossi@israntique.org.il

Graham Philip
Department of Archaeology
Durham University
South Road
Durham, DH1 3LE
United Kingdom
graham.philip@durham.ac.uk

Steve Rosen
Archaeological Division
Ben-Gurion University of the Negev
Beer Sheva
Israel
rosen@bgu.ac.il

Valentine Roux
CNRS, Université de Paris-Ouest – La Defense
Maison René Ginouvès
21, Allée de l'Université
F-92023, Nanterre Cedex
France
valentine.roux@mae.u-paris10.fr

Aaron N. Shugar
Art Conservation Department
Buffalo State College
Rockwell Hall 230
1300 Elmwood Ave
Buffalo, NY 14222
United States of America
shugaran@buffalostate.edu

Hamdan Taha
Department of Antiquities
Palestinian Authority
P.O. Box 870
Ramallah
Palestine
Htaha99@yahoo.com

Edwin C. M. van den Brink
Israel Antiquities Authority
P.O. Box 1230
Tel Aviv 61012
Israel
edwin@israntique.org.il

Yehad Yasine
Department of Antiquities and Cultural Heritage
Palestinian National Authority
P.O. Box 870
Ramallah
Palestine
jehah-yasine@yahoo.co.uk

Mohammad al-Zawahra
Department of Antiquities and Cultural Heritage
Palestinian National Authority
P.O. Box 870
Ramallah
Palestine
mohammadalzawahra@hotmail.com

1. Introduction: Culture, Chronology and the Chalcolithic

Yorke M. Rowan and Jaimie L. Lovell

... an archaeological culture is an arbitrary division of the space-time-cultural continuum defined by reference to its imperishable content and whatever of 'common social tradition' can be inferred therefrom. (Phillips and Willey 1953, 617)

Introduction

The Near East constitutes a core region for understanding fundamental changes in human existence such as the domestication of plants and animals, the formation of hierarchical social organization and the rise of urbanism and city states. The long history of archaeological research in the region has been both enriched and coloured by these research interests. Those working in later prehistoric periods, which appear to bridge deep prehistory and 'history', often find themselves operating with perspectives vastly different from one another. Scholars of all periods will recognize parallel issues in their own fields of research. This volume challenges entrenched models and hopes to highlight new directions for research.

One of the greatest frustrations with Near Eastern archaeology is the plethora of chronological divisions and sometimes contradictory terminology developed over the course of two centuries of exploration and engagement. These form roadblocks to discussions of people and their lives in the past. We want to understand and describe more about people than the wiggly lines on their pots, but somehow existing paradigms have roped us into the accepted order of progressive changes in material culture. In the southern Levant (Israel, Palestine and Jordan) the Chalcolithic period (4700/4500–3700/3600 cal BC) is a particularly good example of this because it falls between two major traditions in scholarship: the archaeology of the biblical world and the fundamental prehistoric shifts in human adaption. To some, the Chalcolithic, as the first period with metallurgy, large sprawling villages, rich mortuary offerings and cult centres, represents a developmental stage on the road to the urban Bronze Age, the 'dawn of history' (Bar-Adon 1980, preface). Others have called it 'the end of prehistory' (Joffe *et al.* 2001). More recent scholarship has focused upon the diversification of economy, elaborated craft production and expanded networks for resource acquisition. For general syntheses of the Chalcolithic see Levy (1998, for Israel), Bourke (2001, for Jordan) and Rowan and Golden (2009).

The Chalcolithic period encompasses some of the most remarkable and visually striking discoveries made to date in the region – the Nahal Mishmar hoard, the Nahal Qanah gold rings, Peqi'in cave, the Teleilat Ghassul wall paintings – partially animating this last period of prehistory and leaving one with the sense that the ancient inhabitants themselves are within reach. But this in itself does not explain the continual search for discrete prehistoric cultural groups in the record. Explicit engagement with and critique of culture history has been a long time coming in the scholarship of the southern Levant (but see Sharon 2001; Whiting 2007 for studies of the Iron Age, where ethnicity and culture are perhaps more obviously pressing concerns); there is still a vast swathe of research in the region that completely ignores these issues and considers theory to be irrelevant. One has the impression that the political realities of the region (including a predilection for biblical archaeology) have left a large proportion of archaeologists in the region, including prehistorians, lost without a map. Today's Chalcolithic specialists were in many cases taught by biblical archaeologists such that the culture history paradigm remains deeply embedded. Students and scholars of the Chalcolithic will therefore find this volume a useful guide to the ugly academic facts behind the more synthetic representations of the late prehistoric Levant.

The advent of radiocarbon dating promised resolution of many chronological problems (Willey and Phillips 1958, 46). Even the wealth of assays generated in the heady days of the 1980s and 1990s, however, have not brought about consensus. At the beginning of the 21st century differences of opinion concerning southern Levantine prehistory lie just as often with divergent perspectives as with disparate datasets. It is clear, in trying to unravel the origins of these conflicting viewpoints, that many scholars view cultural interactions in late prehistory from distinct and different theoretical perspectives.

Despite intensive research and excavation of the Chalcolithic (Figure 1.1), its internal sequencing, particularly the initial and final phases, remains contentious. In archaeology 'transitions' between periods are often quite arbitrary divisions between implicitly defined sets of material culture which shift up and down absolute radiocarbon scales as an increasing number of samples are submitted to labs across the globe. However, just as scholars are prisoners of their conceptual frameworks, outmoded datasets still hold sway, preserving models which are often reliant upon fairly gross fluctuations in type fossils, in turn generated by the same 'legacy data'. It seems to be extremely difficult for archaeologists to disengage from templates that derive from old excavations.

In the southern Levant this problem is perhaps more acute because of the intensity of archaeological investigations since the 18th century. Many of those excavations were conducted for reasons that would be judged as outmoded and even unethical in today's scientific and research-focused environment, but they nonetheless generated data that continue to shape and colour current archaeological frames of reference. The few Chalcolithic assemblages that exist from tell sites unfortunately often derive from an early period of archaeological field research, when methods were coarse and horizontal exposure of basal [prehistoric] layers was minimal. Other sequences come from short-lived single-period sites with few radiocarbon dates. The combined effect is one of a poor understanding of regional and site-based data which has led to scholarly debate on the precise ordering of and relationships between these assemblages. More recent excavation has improved our resolution, but the sequencing of the Early Chalcolithic remains deeply problematic. For summaries of the Late Neolithic see Gopher (1998, for Israel) and Rollefson (2001, for Jordan).

To some the Late Chalcolithic appears to end abruptly. Considerable scholarship has been expended on identifying the elusive 'missing link' between a potential terminal Chalcolithic phase and the first period of the Early Bronze Age. Since this lacuna was first widely discussed (Braun 1989; 2000; Hanbury-Tenison 1986) there have been advances, but the rarity of transitional sites demonstrates that the problem is not just a conceptual one.

Culture as an archaeological and anthropological construct

Culture is a primary concept for this volume because almost all scholars use the term, although sometimes in highly variable ways. The reason that this concept is of such relevance to the papers contained herein is that they deal with periods for which there are no written records, and for which anthropology and ethnography are powerful disciplinary and explanatory platforms. The place of culture within anthropological scholarship has shifted and evolved (Kuper 1999), and became the central concern of American anthropologists only in the 1940s (Kroeber and Kluckhohn 1952). Just as there are a multitude of definitions and uses of the term 'culture' within anthropological literature (for a recent review see Brumann 2002), there are also a number of ways in which the term is pressed into service by archaeologists (Parkinson 2006), who seem to see it as an expedient abstraction. Meanwhile, anthropology is grappling with the very real possibility of discarding the culture concept altogether, such that hard questions are being asked: 'Is anthropology sustainable without it – or, for that matter, would anthropology have been better all along without it?' (Fox 1999). Archaeologists may not readily recognize the relevance of such statements to their own discipline, but if some anthropologists doubt the utility of the concept, then the ontological basis for much of archaeological description rests on some potential minefields:

> ... the more one considers the best modern work on culture by anthropologists, the more advisable it must appear to avoid the hyper-referential word altogether, and to talk more precisely of knowledge, or belief, or art, or technology, or tradition, or even ideology (though similar problems are raised by that multivalent concept). There are fundamental epistemological problems, and these cannot be solved by tiptoeing around the notion of culture, or by refining definitions. The difficulties become most acute when (after all the protestations to the contrary have been made) culture shifts from something to be described, interpreted, and even perhaps explained, and is treated as a source of explanation in itself. (Kuper 1999, x–xi)

Ultimately archaeologists may define the term culture to serve their own analytical and narrative purposes, but if we do not push towards consensus then we will be talking past one another. If archaeologists employ the concept differently from anthropologists, how might this bear upon different perspectives and reconstructions of the past? Despite denials and qualifications, researchers often employ an implicit equation of material culture and cultural complexes (pots = people), although numerous cautionary tales (*e.g.*, Hodder 1978; 1982; Moore and Romney 1994) demonstrate that archaeologists are generally aware that a 1:1 correspondence between material culture and self-identified ethnic groups is rare in the present or ethnographic past (Renfrew 1987; Shennan 1989; 1991; Ucko 1969). Cultural anthropologists also maintain that the relationships between cultural practices, material culture

Figure 1.1 Map of all sites relevant to all chapters

and language are neither direct nor simple. Studies indicate that geographic propinquity often plays a fundamental role in village assemblages of material culture (Gosselain 2000; Welsch *et al.* 1992), sometimes with little correlation to language (*cf.* Moore and Romney 1994).

Indeed, culture may be the single most criticized concept within contemporary archaeology (Miller 2005, 8) and archaeologists of various theoretical stripes express doubts that cultures constitute useful units of study (Hodder 1982; Renfrew 1978; Shennan 1978; Trigger 1968; 2003). However, the widespread faith that 'complexes', 'cultures' or 'phases' accurately represent ancient entities belies a continued empirical belief in a 'true' classification. Debates concerning classification (or 'taxonomy', to some) have occupied archaeological discussions for decades and sometimes appear to be intractable problems. In effect, classification is devised according to analytical goals and is only as good as its ability to meet those objectives (Adams and Adams 1991, 4–5) – and it remains an artificial construct, a tool, not an 'objective' reflection of reality (see discussions of empirical versus cultural types in Phillips *et al.* 1951).

Culture: materialization and identification

The fact that culture is so often defined by ceramic groupings which are divorced from their rich material-culture context is a difficult problem to overcome given the strength of archaeology's relationship with the sherd. One could argue that the emphasis on ceramic studies is partly due to the fact that 'ceramic production is an additive process, a pot embodies many of the choices made in the production sequence' (Chilton 1999, 2), choices that are 'elected in a rich context of tradition, value, alternatives, and compromises' (Rice 1996, 140). Nevertheless, all too frequently in our region ceramics are viewed as the best indicators for ancient groups, via more superficial studies of vessel morphology, shape and decoration, the latter serving as a source of 'social information'. Ethnoarchaeological research indicates that pots and their decoration *may* express cosmological or religious ideas and thus contain connections between style and cultural perceptions (David *et al.* 1988). When studying ancient groupings archaeologists often preference decorative techniques on ceramics because they are thought to be temporally sensitive and also to form straightforward subjects for quantitative studies. However, superficial and easily imitated decorative techniques may spread quickly regardless of culture, ethnicity or language. Such techniques are highly receptive to borrowing and, as a consequence, fluctuate through time and space, reflecting the more situational and temporary aspects of identity (Gosselain 2000, 209). This predilection for studies of decoration is not confined to culture historians (Chilton 1999, 45), but is, at least implicitly, shared by processual archaeologists as well (*e.g.*, Binford 1965, 208). As a result, at times archaeologists consider stylistic boundaries the equivalent of ethnic boundaries (Stark 1999, 25–6).

By contrast, 'roughing out' (Courty and Roux 1995) or 'fashioning techniques' (Gosselain 2000) are arguably more resistant to change because they depend upon motor habits acquired through repeated practice. These techniques are deeply ingrained early on, and therefore do not change with the same ease as decorative schemes. Gosselain (2000) argues that some manufacturing techniques, such as coiling, correspond to social boundaries defined by cultural closeness and affiliation that supersede geographical proximity. The nature of stylistic variation and its relationship to social boundaries is complex and therefore long debated (Conkey 1990; Sackett 1977; 1982; 1985; 1986; 1991; Wiessner 1983; 1984; 1985; Wobst 1977; 1999). Arguments have particularly concentrated on the merits of grouping variables versus objects (Cowgill 1982; Doran and Hodson 1975; Hodson 1982). The proliferation of such studies suggests that much of archaeological intuition concerning style is wrongheaded (Wobst 1999, 119). Thus ethnoarchaeological studies have moved the discussion beyond cautionary tales and highlighted the fact that the dichotomies between style and function are blurred and, in fact, style and function are intertwined (Stark 1999, 42).

Approaching the Chalcolithic data

Intractable problems are not new to archaeology. Conflicts between anthropological and culture historical approaches confront archaeologists in many regions. Prehistoric archaeology is also not immune, and is perhaps more insidiously affected. This is an old argument that will be all too familiar to anthropologists. However, archaeologists working in the southern Levant have been slower than their European or North American counterparts to grapple with the problematic, intertwined aspects of cultural change, chronology and geographic variability and have commonly generated a series of conflicting models without explicit reference to theory. Instead, scholarly discussion has often prioritized the definition and redefinition of 'archaeological cultures', and matters of chronology and terminology.

This edited volume grew out of a similarly titled workshop held at 5ICAANE in Madrid (2006). We realized that it would be fruitless to expect a single workshop to resolve complex chronological issues, so our goal with this volume was to invert the problem by encouraging researchers to engage with their underlying conceptual assumptions. In thinking about how different material culture related in time and space across the landscape, scholars need to be clear about how they envisage material culture operating, and how it is described in their analyses and reports.

We see this volume as an opportunity to ask key scholars to engage with their material while explaining their data in terms of broader and more current theoretical and pragmatic concerns. This is a particularly timely challenge, as previous researchers have been reflexive about the difficulties faced in setting up frames of reference (*e.g.*, Gopher and Gophna 1993, 303, 339). There has been, however, a general lack of engagement with some theoretical concepts. Terminology is often at the heart of disagreements, yet different terminology may belie vast gulfs between theoretical perspectives and classification schemes. In addition, we each approach the problem, seated like yogis, on different datasets, making discussions of apples and apples quite unachievable.

In the workshop we asked participants to explore archaeological 'culture' in the light of their data, and challenged them to consider how their concept of archaeological culture is situated within archaeological theory. Each scholar had a different emphasis, and we do not seek to iron out the differences here, but rather to expose and explore the various different ways of approaching data and interpretation. This also allows us to elucidate important divergences which fuel deep disagreements about datasets.

At times traditions of scholarship are divorced from theoretical debate, and it is uncommon for individual scholars to acknowledge their own theoretical background. Because theoretical discourse is undervalued, incorporation of theoretical concerns from the global discourse is minimized. Furthermore, this lack of theoretical engagement has produced an almost active pride of place for the status quo. In contrast to Euro-western traditions, it is rare to find a post-processualist in the southern Levant; and true processualists are by no means the majority. Instead, the majority are culture historians operationalizing their archaeology (purportedly) through an atheoretical lens.

Dominant paradigms

> Acceptable field work can perhaps be done in a theoretical vacuum, but integration and interpretation without theory are inconceivable. (Willey and Phillips 1958, 1)

Culture history formed the dominant paradigm for archaeological analyses throughout much of the world during the 20th century. The culture concept, initiated in part to describe spatial variation, was particularly strong in North American anthropology and archaeology, inspired by Franz Boas as part of the rejection of unilinear evolution and the effort to trace historical movements of tribes (Jones 1996; Trigger 2003). In Europe an emphasis on identifying ethnic groups reflected growing nationalism and, in turn, a focus upon geographical and chronological variation of the archaeological data (Trigger 2003, 53). Yet perceptions of archaeological cultures soon diverged: Trigger (2003, 54) suggests that in North America regional cultural chronologies cross-cut geographical variation, whereas in Europe geographical variability of cultures supplemented developed cultural sequences. A series of regional cultural chronologies produced for North America remained dependent on stereotypes of Native Americans formulated in an earlier time that considered most change as the result of diffusion and migration. Such explanations were ill-equipped to explain cultural change and development (Willey and Sabloff 1974, 133–4), and much of archaeology in North America concentrated on taxonomic debates with little connection to the people who produced the material culture.

Even with processual approaches, which eschewed the emphasis on descriptive historical reconstructions in favour of delineating law-like generalizations about processes, the importance of culture chronologies was maintained. The traditional culture unit survived among processual archaeologists as a necessary empirically descriptive convenience, without which social explanations and interpretation would not be possible (Renfrew 1972, 17; Jones 1996, 1998, 27–8). Dobres notes that our notions of seeing the archaeological record are taught skills and that the 'culture history emphasis on building up regional-scale spatio-temporal frameworks from site specific findings' characterizes much of archaeology today, where the goal is 'identifying, describing, and tracking both regional and extra regional culture complexes through typological studies' (Dobres 1999, 11–12).

One of the primary critiques of culture history is based upon how (and, often, whether) we are able to differentiate functional variations in archaeological assemblages from non-functional (ethnic, cultural) variation (Jones 1998, 107). Within processual approaches, only some facets of artefact variability are considered to be related to cultural or ethnic identity. Jones (1998, 111–12) notes that although studies of ethnicity were not typically the focus of processual studies, the distinction between style and function remained similar to that found in culture historical models.

Although ethnicity is a separate phenomenon that most contributors to this volume do not explicitly consider central to their case studies, the analytical units for examining such a concept are similar and present similar obstacles and challenges of interpretation to the archaeologists. Just as processual archaeologists were reacting against the standard assumption among traditional culture history proponents that material culture reflected social norms and could be equated with ethnic groups, so post-processualists objected to the processualist interpretations that emphasized the functional role of culture as an adaptive mechanism (Hodder 1982, 4–5). Rejection of the neo-evolutionary models and environmental determinism that were so fundamental to the formation and growth of New Archaeology did not necessarily lead to a cohesive new paradigm or unified theory (for critiques of processual archaeology see Trigger 1989, 294–328; Willey and Sabloff 1993, 214–311). In fact, post-processualists include those who question the modern socio-political construction of ethnic and national identity (Trigger 1984), thereby challenging the empirical basis of interpretations regarding ethnicity, cultures and identity formation.

Even where identifying ethnicity is not the express goal, many an archaeologist is satisfied with referencing Clarke's definition and relying on the vague distinction of an archaeological culture rather than culture *per se*.

Culture: Specific cultural assemblage; an archaeological culture is a polythetic set of specific and comprehensive artifact-type categories which consistently recur together in assemblages within a limited geographical area.
Entity: An integrated ensemble of attributes forming a complex but coherent and unitary whole at a specific level of complexity. A special class of system. (Clarke 1968, 666)

This seminal definition of archaeological cultures is frequently cited by archaeologists, as noted above (although Phillips and Willey (1953, 617) had defined archaeological culture in a similar fashion), but Clarke too argued that culture-history frames of reference are inadequate because of the need to understand the functional elements of archaeological assemblages; archaeological distributions, he argued, cannot be easily equated to ethnic groups because functional variations might be misunderstood as ethnic differences (Jones 1998, 107). Clarke also decried the misuse of the archaeological culture concept based on, for example, 'So-called cultures composed almost entirely from single aspects of material culture' (Clarke 1968, 232).

Gopher and Gophna (1993) approach the Neolithic–Chalcolithic transition by borrowing Clarke's view of an archaeological culture 'based on the assumption that repetitiveness and similarities of assemblages largely represent group identity and that we are dealing with social units' (Gopher and Gophna 1993, 340). Their seriation study led them to propose a chrono-cultural framework built on a variety of 'local adaptions' (Gopher and Gophna 1993, fig. 17) (despite the concept of adaption, this still sits within a culture-historical framework). In building a culture-historical framework for the Beer Sheva basin, Gilead also references Clarke's definition of archaeological cultures (Gilead 1990). Despite repeated reference to Clarke's seminal work, however, southern Levantine scholarship remains firmly entrenched in the culture-historical mould. Right up to the present, the focus has been on refining regional chronological schemes without significant challenge to the culture-historical base (Garfinkel 1999).

The impact of the New Archaeology has been widely felt, and most archaeologists in the southern Levant have been quick to see the value of new scientific techniques. In particular, radiocarbon dates offered potential resolution to chronological sequencing – a particular concern for cultural historians. This has been particularly true in the case of the Late Neolithic–Chalcolithic transition, where radiocarbon dates promised further refinements (Blackham 2002; Joffe and Dessel 1995; Lovell 2001; Burton and Levy 2000). Even with improved and diverse datasets, there continues to be strong disagreement over chronological issues. Blackham's statistical study was based upon a combination of legacy data and small-scale excavations (Blackham 2002); and, while Joffe and Dessel (1995) and Burton and Levy (2000) were widely discussed, they were ultimately unable to provide the necessary contextual linkages between different sequences. The revision of radiometric data from better-stratified sequences has had wider impact, but arguments continue and real engagement with the new data is only just beginning (Banning 2002; Bourke and Lovell 2004; Banning 2007; Lovell *et al.* 2007).

Tom Levy exploded the anthropological bomb on Chalcolithic archaeology. Drawing upon survey and excavations in the northern Negev in the 1980s, Levy developed a model of chiefdoms which challenged earlier conceptions of Chalcolithic life. Through a series of articles (Levy 1983; 1992) he posits that hierarchically arranged, ranked societies (chiefdoms) were first organized in response to the need for risk management of increasingly scarce resources, particularly with regard to the conflicting needs of specialized transhumant pastoralists and settled agriculturalists. Like many processualist models, Levy's emphasized the adaptive role of culture in response to environmental conditions, and focused on functional and evolutionary interests rather than building chronological sequences. This shift in interests resulted in conflict between cultural historians and processualists that mirrors similar conflict elsewhere (*e.g.*, Dobres 1999 on the Magdalenian).

Strangely, Levy's processualist challenge does not seem to have encouraged others. Many have taken up the chiefdom model, but those that do subscribe to it largely on the basis of impressive objects rather than demonstrable broader patterns of socio-economic relationships (Gal *et al.* 1999, 14*; Gopher and Tsuk 1996, 234).

Just as processual archaeology had minimal impact on late prehistoric archaeology in the southern Levant, post-processualism has also failed to take hold in Chalcolithic discourse. Kerner's work on differential frequencies of ceramic decorative schemes fits more within the processual school than with any cognitive approach (Kerner 2001). Even discussions of symbolism have been firmly rooted in art-historical traditions (Elliott 1978; Epstein 1978; Fox 1995; Merhav 1993). The constant cycling back through the culture-historical foundation no doubt reflects important discrepancies in datasets, but it also results in stasis – where the same arguments are constantly recycled. In order to avoid this we wanted participants in this volume to engage more directly with their theoretical base while presenting their data. We felt this was more likely to encourage fresh approaches.

Current context: political confines and professional constraints

The impact of the current political situation on archaeology in the southern Levant deserves some further comment. The political and economic fractures through the region inhibit (if not totally prevent) regular and free contact across the region – especially between local archaeologists. Given the continuing tragic situation in the occupied Palestinian territories it is extraordinary that any new archaeology has been carried out at all. Certainly, renewed foreign excavations in Gaza have been very much curtailed in the last few years (for the most recent excavations, see Humbert 2000; de Miroschedji and Sadeq 2001; Steel *et al.* 2004). While there has been more research in the Palestinian Autonomous (PA) areas (*e.g.*, Nigro and Marchetti 1998) there have been few legal excavations, so in this respect we are pleased that this volume includes a contribution from the Palestinian–Norwegian team recently working near Jericho in the PA (Anfinset *et al.*, this volume). Fresh contributions are emerging from a new generation of Palestinian scholars, but the political realities of the region mean that these scholars frequently receive training in foreign universities and consequently their datasets are sometimes limited to Jordan (Ali 2005; Hourani 2002; Sayej 2004).

Compounding the difficulties presented by different traditions, national approaches and political and economic realities, there is also a disparity between research-driven programmes and rescue excavations. Much current archaeology in the region is practised in the context of 'rescue' from development. In Israel and the occupied territories this is especially true and is reflected in a number of contributions to this volume (*e.g.*, Golani *et al.*, this volume). Basic procedural decisions regarding, for example, the processing of material and broad versus deep exposures in this context will be necessarily different to those taken by archaeologists operating in a research-driven project (*e.g.*, Banning *et al.*, this volume), although some of the same pressures can still exist. The fact that archaeologists working for government agencies manage to do any research at all is a minor miracle, but many of these excavations are the ones that will, in the end, contribute the most to our understanding of the basic character of the periods under consideration, and some will form the lynchpins of future work (van den Brink, this volume).

Contributions to this volume

Our backgrounds are influenced by different traditions, national perspectives and schools of archaeology. As editors neither of us view ourselves as one type of archaeologist or another (processualist or culture historian, for example). Perhaps in the sense that we are both open to a variety of theoretical perspectives, we might be considered post-processualist. We suspect that many of our contributors would feel a similar reluctance to be cast as one 'type' of archaeologist. Perhaps this reluctance reflects the general low level of theoretical engagement in the region for late prehistory.

It was for this reason that we see our role as provocateurs, to kick-start a dialogue about how to move beyond culture history and chronology in order to re-engage with larger theoretical discourses. Theory is not interesting simply for its own sake – there is a danger of continually adding new sites and assemblages to the culture-history list without engaging with the ancient social landscape, which is what gives our discipline relevance to the scientific community and indeed the general public. Culture history is fundamental to the discipline, but in other parts of the world social processes are approached from more recent theoretical standpoints that possess greater explanatory potential. If we wish to avoid relegation to the position of stamp collectors of southern Levantine late prehistory, then demonstrating how and why 'site X' contributes to our knowledge of how people in the past interacted becomes critical.

Contributors to this volume all agree that culture history is the platform upon which current archaeological research is discussed, but differ in the degree of emphasis that they place on previously defined entities/phases/'chrono-cultural' blocs. Delineating levels of difference and similarity between temporal boundaries is critical in this process. Readers of this volume will detect contrasting approaches reflected in the structure of individual papers: some discuss their data in strictly sequential (vertical), chronological order, while others emphasize more horizontal, cultural entities supported by radiometric dates. At the transition between periods different, and sometimes conflicting, points are emphasized.

Differences in interpretation are not solely confined to cultural facies but also extend to the tin tacks of the data themselves. Analysing and understanding radiocarbon data has become more complicated rather than less, and it is clear that not all practitioners understand good practice to mean the same thing – some argue that one must average dates, others that it is sacrilege to do so. All participants of the workshop were asked to carefully consider and present their radiocarbon data and the context from which it came. Precise radiocarbon data is important because the Late Neolithic–Chalcolithic and the Chalcolithic–Early Bronze Age transitions are imprecisely dated and both are critical to the understanding of cultural and socio-economic change in late prehistory.

The most eloquent proponent of a continued culture history approach, Gilead, argues in Clarkean terms in favour of cultural entities. He argues for retaining taxonomic definitions for regional and temporal groupings – *e.g.*, the Ghassulian, the Besorian and so on – on the basis that their use 'simplifies complex archaeological expressions' (p. 13). Further, he notes that using period definitions in preference to cultural entities can be equally problematic and reminds us that accurate dating of sites is a prerequisite for discussions of inter-site interaction.

Banning, Gibbs and Kadowaki argue for a gradual transition from the Late Neolithic to the Chalcolithic based upon detailed elaboration of stratified ceramic and lithic data from Tabaqat al-Bûma (Wadi Ziqlab). Their radiocarbon dates support continuity in ceramic and lithic traditions over the course of approximately 1400 years. In the context of the current debate on the Wadi Rabah horizon the paper offers a well-dated assemblage from the northern Jordan Valley which fleshes out our understanding of the geographic spread and temporal extent of a particular sub-set of material culture.

Today's research-driven agenda is producing more and more data of higher and higher quality, and this in turn drives newer questions. It is axiomatic that yesterday's datasets will not be sufficient for today's investigations and the contributions in this book highlight the difficulties involved with integrating legacy data and newly excavated sequences. Exemplying this, Kafafi attempts to contextualize legacy data from Mellaart's excavations at Ghrubba with his more recently excavated sequences at Abu Thawwab and Abu Hamid.

Anfinset, Taha, al-Zawahra and Yasine acknowledge that the culture concept has a long history in anthropology, but argue that archaeology has developed its own distinct definition. However, they point out that archaeologists' use of the concept remains static and unrelated to social processes. It is for this reason that they prefer the term 'society' over that of 'culture'. They contend that multiple scales of analysis will make social aspects more accessible.

Rosen's terminology (preferring the terms 'complexes' or 'units' to 'cultures') reflects his grounding in processual archaeology. He makes the point that, despite the considerable influence of post-processualism elsewhere, 'culture systematics' remain fundamentally important to the discipline. What is clear, when we are dealing with transitions, is that our understanding of how Timnian pastoralists in arid zones managed and responded to significant shifts in lifeways is dependent upon our understanding of how material culture and culture itself are interrelated and connected. Rosen accepts the environment as a major force for cultural difference but stresses that the maintenance of separate identities over the long term is culturally driven. To him the interplay between geography and culture is an issue that applies even where environmental contrasts are less striking.

New excavations often promise overhauls of ingrained constructs. This is particularly true of the extensive rescue excavations at Modi'in (central Israel), where there is a rare continuous stratigraphic sequence from the Late Chalcolithic to the Early Bronze Age. Van den Brink contextualizes this sequence and builds a picture of continuity that challenges arguments for a dramatic break in settlement at the end of the Chalcolithic.

Braun revisits his previous research on the 'missing link' (1989; 2000) in this volume. He too stresses continuity and seeks to redress an 'imbalance in comprehension of the archaeological record' (p. 160). With the additional data available to him today from the excavations in the Shephelah (*e.g.*, Modi'in) and Ashkelon/Afridar he confidently closes the perceived gap between the Late Chalcolithic and the Early Bronze Age I (hereafter EB I). For Braun, the reason that a transitional phase is apparently not widespread is because scholars have not yet developed the tools and/or the assemblages to detect such rapid change.

Golani and Nagar explore the possibility that Chalcolithic traditions of burial continued into the Early Bronze Age. Their data comes from a cist grave cemetery west of the EB I site of Ashkelon Barnea. They argue that the presence of intramural child burials at the site of Ashkelon Barnea itself is an indication of a Chalcolithic tradition carried through into the EB I. By contrast, the cemetery contained no child burials, but does have Chalcolithic building techniques, as seen at Palmahim. The authors acknowledge the problematic nature of their data, and one may dispute the dating of the various elements. Their reconstruction of the Chalcolithic–Early Bronze Age shift envisages archaeological artefacts as reflecting two or more *ethnic* groups.

New ways of working with material evidence following the French school and the *chaîne opératoire* approach are featured here by Roux, Courty, Dollfus and Lovell. They find that social groups may be better identified via differential techniques of manufacture. Skills required to maintain a traditional practice are less resistant to change and act as 'fixers' of culture. Such a study shows the efficacy of combining technological techniques with more traditional typological approaches. In the final analysis, local studies of fashioning techniques provide broader relevance when they are integrated with statistical data based on multiple assemblages.

Shugar and Gohm also combine techniques from material sciences with seriated radiometric assays to investigate the dating of metallurgical techniques. By moving metallurgical studies beyond issues of specialization and exchange, they challenge the intuitive notion that the use of native copper preceded that of complex metals. As copper is the defining material for the period, understanding the development of its technology is particularly pertinent to reconstructing cultural change.

This theme is also picked up by Milevski, Fabian and Marder, who make the case for greater flexibility in temporal frames applied to type fossils. They illustrate the difficulty of disengaging sequences, local or regional, from the hegemony of the type fossil. They treat Canaanean technology as a mode of production, the nascent phase of which probably pre-dates the Early Bronze Age.

Several contributors in this volume see the Chalcolithic and the EB I as temporally overlapping. Yet radiocarbon data does not support this argument. Burton and Levy note that rigid conceptualization of chrono-cultural entities serves to solidify our own taxonomic frameworks of spatial and temporal boundaries, thereby undermining our reconstruction of socio-economic changes. Instead, they propose methodical examination of the degree of connectedness between Chalcolithic and EB I sites and regions in order to better understand periods of transition. Their innovative paper illustrates that the necessary challenge to culture-history approaches proves most effective when analysis is data driven.

Concluding remarks

The strength of this volume lies in its recognition that the 'data ladder', constructed by generations of culture historians, continues to form the core that all scholars in the region work with. The two themes of this volume

– culture and chronology – combine the need for theoretical engagement with the establishment of broader and more precise empirical data using explicit classificatory schemes. These might appear to be contradictory aims, but this is, essentially, the rock and the hard place where much archaeological debate is centred and as such the volume will have resonance for scholars of other periods and regions.

There is, of course, more than one way to do archaeology in the 21st century. With that in mind, and with an awareness that there continues to be disagreement among our colleagues and friends on how to resolve conflicting models for understanding the 5th to 4th millennia BC in the southern Levant, this volume cannot insist upon a single programmatic statement. Rather, there is a need for reflexive culture history (as a platform for more diverse and multi-faceted theoretical approaches), if only because so much field archaeology in the region is data driven and descriptive, rather than connected to the problematization of broader social issues. With this in mind, we asked Graham Philip to offer some thoughts on the issues and approaches raised by the contributions here and how we might consider new directions in research in late prehistoric archaeology in the region.

This volume does not seek to cover all of the issues pertinent to current research in the Chalcolithic. Instead, it is our abiding interest to push research forward in a more theoretically reflexive way. Transitions are difficult. They require energy and new perspectives. Chalcolithic archaeology is in a good position – there is a wealth of securely dated, well-excavated material – but significant and meaningful progress will only result if practitioners are willing to rework and reframe their data. We trust that readers will find within this volume the basis for new directions in research.

Acknowledgements

We would also like to thank Ian Kuijt and an anonymous reviewer for insightful critical comments.

References

Adams, W. Y. and Adams, E. W. (1991) *Archaeological Typology and Practical Reality*. Cambridge: Cambridge University Press.

Ali, N. (2005) *The Development of Pottery Technology from the Late Sixth to the fifth millennium BC in Northern Jordan. Ethno- and Archaeological Studies: Abu Hamid as a Key Site*. Oxford: BAR Int. Ser. 1422.

Banning, E. B. (2002) Consensus and debate on the Late Neolithic and Chalcolithic of the southern Levant. *Paléorient* 28/2, 148–55.

Banning, E. B. (2007) Introduction: Time and tradition, problems of chronology in the 6th–4th millennia in the Levant and Greater Mesopotamia. *Paléorient* 33/1, 11–14.

Bar-Adon, P. (1980) *The Cave of the Treasure. The Finds from the Caves in Nahal Mishmar.* Judean Desert Studies. Jerusalem: IES.

Binford, L. R. (1965) Archaeological systematics and the study of culture process. *American Antiquity* 31, 203–10.

Blackham, M. (2002) *Modeling Time and Transition in Prehistory: The Jordan Valley in the Chalcolithic (5500–3500 BC)*. Oxford: BAR Int. Ser. 1027.

Bourke, S. J. (2001) The Chalcolithic period. Pp. 107–62 in B. MacDonald, R. Adams and P. Bienkowski (eds), *The Archaeology of Jordan*. Sheffield: Sheffield Academic Press.

Bourke, S. J. and Lovell, J. L. (2004) Ghassul, chronology and cultural sequencing. *Paléorient* 30/1, 179–82.

Braun, E. (1989) The transition from the Chalcolithic to the Early Bronze Age in northern Israel and Transjordan. Is there a missing link? Pp. 7–28 in P. de Miroschedji (ed.), *L'urbanisation de la Palestine à l'âge du Bronze ancien: bilan et perspectives des recherches actuelles* (Actes du Colloque d'Emmaüs, 20–24 octobre 1986). Oxford: BAR Int. Ser. 527 {1}.

Braun, E. (2000) Area G at Afridar, Palmahim Quarry 3 and the earliest pottery of Early Bronze I. Part of the missing link. Pp. 113–28 in G. Philip and D. Baird (eds), *Breaking with the Past. Ceramics and Change in the Early Bronze Age of the Southern Levant*. Sheffield: Sheffield Academic Press.

Brumann, C. (2002) On culture and symbols. *Current Anthropology* 43/3, 509–10.

Burton, M. and Levy, T. E. (2000) The Chalcolithic radiocarbon record and its use in southern Levantine archaeology. *Radiocarbon* 43/3, 1223–46.

Chilton, E. S. (1999) One size fits all. Typology and alternatives for ceramic research. Pp. 44–60 in E. S. Chilton (ed.), *Material Meanings: Critical Approaches to the Interpretation of Material Culture*. Salt Lake City: University of Utah Press.

Clarke, D. (1978) [1968] *Analytical Archaeology*. London: Methuen.

Conkey, M. W. (1990) Experimenting with style in archaeology: some historical and theoretical issues. Pp. 5–17 in M. W. Conkey and C. A. Hastorf (eds), *The Uses of Style in Archaeology*. Cambridge: Cambridge University Press.

Courty, M.-A. and Roux, V. (1995) Identification of wheel throwing on the basis of ceramic surface features and micro-fabrics. *Journal of Archaeological Science* 22/1, 1–29.

Cowgill, G. (1982) Clusters of objects and associations between variables: two approaches to archaeological classification. In E. S. Chilton (ed.), *Material Meanings: Critical Approaches to the Interpretation of Material Culture*. Salt Lake City: University of Utah Press.

David, N., Sterner, J. and Gavua, K. (1988) Why pots are decorated. *Current Anthropology* 29/3, 365–89.

Dobres, M.-A. (1999) Of paradigms and ways of seeing: artifact variability as if people mattered. Pp. 7–23 in E. S. Chilton (ed.), *Material Meanings: Critical Approaches to the Interpretation of Material Culture*. Salt Lake City: University of Utah Press.

Doran, J. E. and Hodson, F. R. (1975) *Mathematics and Computers in Archaeology*. Cambridge, MA: Harvard University Press.

Elliott, C. (1978) The Ghassulian culture in Palestine. Origins, influences and abandonment. *Levant* 10, 37–54.

Epstein, C. (1978) Aspects of symbolism in Chalcolithic Palestine. In R. Moorey and P. Parr (eds), *Archaeology in the Levant: Essays for Kathleen Kenyon*. Warminster: Aris and Phillips.

Fox, N. S. (1995) The Striped Goddess from Gilat: Implications for the Chalcolithic Cult. *Israel Exploration Journal* 45, 212–25.

Fox, R. G. (1999) Editorial: culture – a second chance? *Current Anthropology* 40/S1, Si–Sii.

Gal, Z., Smithline, H. and Shalem, D. (1999) New iconographic aspects of Chalcolithic art: preliminary observations on finds from the Peqi'in cave. *'Atiqot* 37, 1–16.

Garfinkel, Y. (1999) *Neolithic and Chalcolithic Pottery of the Southern Levant*. Qedem 39, Jerusalem Institute of Archaeology, The Hebrew University of Jerusalem.

Gilead, I. (1990) The Neolithic–Chalcolithic transition and the Qatifian of the northern Negev and Sinai. *Levant* 22, 47–63.

Gopher, A. (1998) Early pottery-bearing groups in Israel, the Pottery Neolithic period. Pp. 205–25 in T. E. Levy (ed.), *Archaeology of Society in the Holy Land*. Leicester: Leicester University Press.

Gopher, A. and Gophna, R. (1993) Cultures of the eighth and seventh millennia BP in the southern Levant: a review for the 90s. *Journal of World Prehistory* 7/3, 297–353.

Gopher, A. and Tsuk, T. (1996) Conclusion. Pp. 209–43 in A. Gopher (ed.), *The Nahal Qanah Cave: Earliest Gold in the Southern Levant*. Monograph Series of the Institute of Archaeology 12. Tel Aviv: Tel Aviv University.

Goren, Y. (1990) The 'Qatifian Culture' in southern Israel and Transjordan: additional aspects for its definition. *Mitekufat Haeven* 23, 100*–112*.

Goring-Morris, A. N. and Belfer-Cohen, A. (2003) *More than Meets the Eye: Studies on Upper Paleolithic Diversity in the Near East*. Oxford: Oxbow Books.

Gosselain, O. (2000) Materializing identities: an African perspective. *Journal of Archaeological Method and Theory* 7(3), 187–217.

Hanbury-Tenison, J. (1986) *The Late Chalcolithic to Early Bronze I Transition in Palestine and Transjordan*. Oxford: BAR Int. Ser. 311.

Hodder, I. (1978) Simple correlations between material culture and society: a review. Pp. 3–24 in I. Hodder (ed.), *The Spatial Organization of Culture*. Pittsburgh, PA: University of Pittsburgh Press.

Hodder, I. (1982) *Symbols in Action: Ethnoarchaeological Studies of Material Culture*. Cambridge: Cambridge University Press.

Hodson, F. R. (1982) Some aspects of archaeological classification. Pp. 21–9 in R. Whallon and J. A. Brown (eds), *Essays in Archaeological Typology*. Evanston, IL: Center for American Archaeology Press.

Hourani, F. (2002) Le cadre paléographique des premiè res sociétés agricoles dans la vallée du Jourdain: Etude de l'impact des événements de l'Holocène ancien sur le dynamique du peuplement humain. Unpublished PhD thesis, Institut National Agronomique Paris-Grignon.

Humbert, J.-B. (2000) *Gaza méditerranéenne: histoire et archéologie en Palestine*. Paris: Errance.

Joffe, A. H. and Dessel, J. P. (1995) Redefining chronology and terminology for the Chalcolithic of the southern Levant. *Current Anthropology* 36, 507–18.

Joffe, A. H., Dessel, J. P. and Hallote, R. (2001) The 'Gilat Woman': female iconography, Chalcolithic cult, and the end of southern Levantine prehistory. *Near Eastern Archaeology* 64, 8–23.

Jones, S. (1996) Discourses of identity in the interpretation of the past. Pp. 62–80 in P. Graves-Brown, S. Jones, and C. Gamble (eds), *Cultural Identity and Archaeology: The Construction of European Communities*. London/NY: Routledge.

Jones, S. (1998) *The Archaeology of Ethnicity. Constructing Identities in the Past and Present*. New York: Routledge.

Kerner, S. (2001) *Das Chalkolithikum in der südlichen Levante. Die Entwicklung handwerklicher Spezialisierung und ihre Beziehung zu gesellschaftlicher Komplexitat*. Rahden/Westf.: Verlag Marie Leidorf BmbH.

Kroeber, A. and Kluckhohn, C. (1952) *Culture*. New York: Meridian Books.

Kuper, A. (1999) *Culture: The Anthropologists' Account*. Cambridge, MA: Harvard University Press.

Levy, T. E. (1983) The emergence of specialized pastoralism in the southern Levant. *World Archaeology* 15, 15–36.

Levy, T. E. (1992) Transhumance, subsistence, and social evolution. Pp. 65–82 in O. Bar-Yosef and A. Khazanov (eds), *Pastoralism in the Levant*. Madison, WI: Prehistory Press.

Levy, T. E. (1995; repr. 1998) Cult, metallurgy and rank societies – Chalcolithic period. Pp. 226–44 in T. E. Levy (ed.), *Archaeology of Society in the Holy Land*. London: Leicester University Press.

Lovell, J. L. (2001) *The Late Neolithic and Chalcolithic Periods in the southern Levant: New Data from Teleilat Ghassul, Jordan*. Oxford: BAR Int. Ser. 974.

Lovell, J. L., Dollfus, G. and Kafafi, Z. (2007) Abu Hamid and the burnished tradition *Paléorient* 33/1, 50–75.

Merhav, R. (1993) Sceptres of the divine from the Cave of the Treasure at Nahal Mishmar. Pp. 21–42 in M. Heltzer, A. Segal and D. Kaufman (eds), *Studies in the Archaeology and History of Ancient Israel in Honour of Moshe Dothan*. Haifa: Haifa University Press (Hebrew).

Miller, D. (2005) Materiality: an introduction. Pp. 1–50 in D. Miller (ed.), *Materiality*. Durham, NC: Duke University Press.

de Miroschedji, P. and Sadeq, M. (2001) Les fouilles de Tell es-Sakan (Gaza): Nouvelles données sur les contacts egypto-cananéens aux IVe–IIIe millenaires. *Paléorient* 27/2, 75–104.

Moore, C. C. and Romney, A. K. (1994) Material culture, geographic propinquity, and linguistic affiliation on the north coast of New Guinea: a reanalysis of Welsch, Terrell, and Nadolski (1992). *American Anthropologist* 96/2, 370–96.

Nigro, L. and Marchetti, N. (1998) *Scavi a Gerico, 1997: relazione preliminare sulla prima campagna di scavi e prospezioni archeologiche a Tell es-Sultan, Palestina*. Rome: Universita di Roma 'La Sapienza'.

Parkinson, W. A. (2006) Tribal boundaries: stylistic variability and social boundary maintenance during the transition to the Copper Age on the Great Hungarian Plain. *Journal of Anthropological Archaeology* 25, 33–58.

Phillips, P. and Willey, G. R. (1953) Method and theory in American archaeology: an operational basis for culture-historical integration. *American Anthropologist* 55, 615–33.

Phillips, P., Ford, J. A. and Griffin, J. B. (1951) *Archaeological Survey in the Lower Mississippi Alluvial Valley 1940–1947*. Papers of the Peabody Museum 25. Cambridge: MA.

Renfrew, C. (1972) *The Emergence of Civilisation: The Cyclades and the Aegean in the third millennium BC*. London: Methuen and Co.

Renfrew, C. (1978) Space, time and polity. Pp. 89–92 in J. Friedman and M. J. Rowlands (eds), *The Evolution of Social Systems*. Pittsburgh, PA: University of Pittsburgh Press.

Renfrew, C. (1987) *Archaeology and Language. The Puzzle of Indo-European Origins*. London: Jonathan Cape.

Rice, P. M. (1996) Recent ceramic analysis: I. Function, style, and origins. *Journal of Archaeological Research* 4, 133–63.

Rollefson, G. (2001) The Neolithic period. Pp. 67–105 in B. MacDonald, R. Adams, and P. Bienkowski (eds), *The Archaeology of Jordan*. Sheffield: Sheffield Academic Press.

Rowan, Y. and Golden, J. (2009) The Chalcolithic period of the southern Levant: a synthetic review. *Journal of World Prehistory* 22, 1–92.

Sackett, J. R. (1977) The meaning of style in archaeology: a general model. *American Antiquity* 42/3, 369–80.

Sackett, J. R. (1982) Approaches to style in lithic archaeology. *Journal of Anthropological Archaeology* 1, 59–112.

Sackett, J. R. (1985) Style and ethnicity in the Kalahari: a reply to Weissner. *American Antiquity* 50, 154–60.

Sackett, J. R. (1986) Style, function, and assemblage variability: a reply to Binford. *American Antiquity* 51/3, 628–34.

Sackett, J. R. (1991) Style and ethnicity in archaeology: The case for isochrestism. Pp. 32–43 in M. W. Conkey and C. A. Hastorf (eds), *The Uses of Style in Archaeology*. Cambridge: Cambridge University Press.

Sayej, G. J. (2004) *The Lithic Industries of Zahrat adh-Dhra '2 and the Pre-Pottery Neolithic Period of the Southern Levant*. Oxford: BAR Int. Ser. S1329.

Sharon, I. (2001) Philistine bichrome painted pottery: scholarly ideology and ceramic typology. Pp. 555–609 in S. R. Wolff (ed.), *Studies in the Archaeology of Israel and Neighboring Lands in Memory of Douglas L. Esse*. Chicago, MI: Oriental Institute of the University of Chicago.

Shennan, S. (1978) Archaeological 'cultures': an empirical investigation. Pp. 113–39 in I. Hodder (ed.), *The Spatial Organisation of Culture*. London: Duckworth.

Shennan, S. (1989) Introduction: Archaeological approaches to cultural identity. Pp. 1–32 in S. Shennan (ed.), *Archaeological Approaches to Cultural Identity*. London: Unwin Hyman.

Shennan, S. (1991) Tradition, rationality, and cultural transmission. In R. Preucel (ed.), *Processual and Postprocessual Archaeologies: Multiple Ways of Knowing the Past*. Center for Archaeological Investigations Occasional Paper No. 10, Southern Illinois University of Carbondale.

Stark, M. T. (1998) Technical choices and social boundaries in material culture patterning: an introduction. Pp. 1–11 in M. Stark (ed.), *The Archaeology of Social Boundaries*. Washington DC: Smithsonian Institution Press.

Stark, M. T. (1999) Social dimensions of technical choice in Kalinga ceramic traditions. Pp. 24–43 in E. S. Chilton (ed.), *Material Meanings: Critical Approaches to the Interpretation of Material Culture*. Salt Lake City, UT: University of Utah Press.

Steel, L., Clarke, J., Sadeq, M., Manley, W. P., McCarthy, M. and Munro, R. N. (2004) Gaza research project. Report of the 1999 and 2000 seasons at al-Moghraqa. *Levant* 36, 37–88.

Trigger, B. (1968) *Beyond History: The Methods of Prehistory*. New York: Holt, Rinehart & Winston.

Trigger, B. (1984) Alternative archaeologies: nationalist, colonialist, imperialist. *Man* 19, 355–70.

Trigger, B. (1989) *A History of Archaeological Thought*. Cambridge: Cambridge University Press.

Trigger, B. (2003) *Artifacts and Ideas: Essays in Archaeology*. New Brunswick, NJ: Transaction Publishers.

Ucko, P. (1969) Ethnography and archaeological interpretation of funerary remains. *World Archaeology* 1, 262–80.

Welsch, R. L., Terrell, J., and Nadolski, J. A. (1992) Language and culture on the north coast of New Guinea. *American Anthropologist* 94/3, 568–600.

Whiting, C. (2007) *Complexity and Diversity in the Late Iron Age Southern Levant: The Investigation of 'Edomite' Archaeology and Scholarly Discourse*. Oxford: BAR Int Ser 1672.

Wiessner, P. (1983) Style and ethnicity in the Kalahari San projectile point. *American Antiquity* 48, 253–76.

Wiessner, P. (1984) Reconsidering the behavioural basis for style: A case study among the Kalahari San. *Journal of Anthropological Archaeology* 3, 190–234.

Wiessner, P. (1985) Style or isochrestic variation? A reply to Sackett. *American Antiquity* 50, 160–5.

Willey, G. R. and Phillips, P. (1958) *Method and Theory in American Archaeology*. Chicago: University of Chicago Press.

Willey, G. R. and Sabloff, J. A. (1974) *A History of American Archaeology*. London: Thames & Hudson.

Willey, G. R. and Sabloff, J. A. (1993) *A History of American Archaeology*, 3rd edn. New York: W. H. Freeman.

Wobst, M. (1977) Stylistic behaviour and information exchange. Pp. 317–42 in C. E. Cleland (ed.), *For the Director: research essays in honour of the late James B. Griffin*. Ann Arbor: University of Michigan.

Wobst, M. (1999) Style in archaeology or archaeologists in style. Pp. 118–32 in E. S. Chilton (ed.), *Material Meanings: Critical Approaches to the Interpretation of Material Culture*. Salt Lake City: University of Utah Press.

2. Chalcolithic Culture History: Ghassulian and Other Entities in the Southern Levant

Isaac Gilead

Introduction

The term 'Ghassulian culture', intensively used since the 1930s (Albright 1932), occurs less frequently in the current discourse on the Chalcolithic period. Other cultural taxons are unpopular too. It is more common nowadays to divide the period into temporal phases such as 'Early', 'Middle' and 'Late'. Joffe and Dessel (1995, 507) state that the developed material culture of the period is '... *sometimes* called "Ghassulian" ...' (emphasis mine), and they do not use the term 'Ghassulian' in the new terminology they suggest. Sometimes, the entire period is discussed as one whole, implying that material-culture attributes cross-cut its entire temporal and spatial ranges. This is probably due also to the impact of New Archaeology, which prefers the anthropological approach rather than the historical (Trigger 1989, 312–19). The eclipse of the term 'culture' in Levantine Chalcolithic research is also due, probably, to the impact of the trend in anthropology that rejects the use of the term 'culture' and even suggests its complete abandonment: 'It may be true that the culture concept has served its time' (Clifford 1988, 274).

The first part of this paper is devoted to terminology, especially to the terms 'culture' and 'material culture'. It is argued that 'culture' is a proper concept in terms of the classification, clustering and interpreting of archaeological data and that attempts to understand social and economic facets of the Chalcolithic period are either biased or impossible without the recognition of cultural entities, *i.e.* without establishing an elementary culture history of this time span. In the second part, cultural entities will be discussed with special reference to their radiometric chronology and their place in the Chalcolithic period.

The concept of culture

The editors regard culture as a primary concept of this volume and I will therefore start with this term. The concept of culture, from the perspective of both anthropology and archaeology, has been debated extensively during the last decades (see below). However, since the aim of the present paper is to discuss 5th-millennium BC archaeology, my comments on 'culture' will be brief. Archaeologists working in the Levant and elsewhere apply names to artefact assemblages that are similar to each other, are geographically delineated and are of the same time span. It is impossible to discuss the end of the Palaeolithic period in the southern Levant without names such as 'Natufian', and no one suggests eliminating them. The question now is what the term Natufian means. Garrod, in reporting and defining the Natufian for the first time, referred to it as both an 'industry' and a 'culture' (Garrod 1932, 257, 267 respectively). Currently, however, the Natufian is perceived almost unanimously as representing a culture (*e.g.*, Bar-Yosef 1998) or a cultural entity (Belfer-Cohen 1989). This is also true for other names used to cluster assemblages that share common features, such as 'Yarmoukian' and 'Ghassulian'.

Archaeologists of the southern Levant follow implicitly (in most cases), but sometimes explicitly, Childe's (1927) and Clarke's (1978) definitions of culture. Gilead (1981, 339; 1985; 1995, 475) and Gopher and Gophna (1993, 340) use Clarke's approach. Henry (1989, 79–83) adopts Clarke's classificatory hierarchy but modifies it. His archaeological entities are 'assemblage', 'phase/facie', 'industry' and 'complex'. He correlates them respectively with socioeconomic entities such as 'occupation', 'culture', 'cultural group' and 'technocomplex'. Lovell (2001, 50–1) regards the term culture as 'unnecessary' and suggests replacing it with the term 'tradition'. According to Lovell, traditions are groups of villages found in different ecological zones (*e.g.*, Negev or Golan) that are similar in aspects of material culture but are adapted to the area they inhabit. Thus Lovell's 'tradition' is equivalent to Clarke's (1978, 252–3) 'regional sub-culture'. So, why not use labels associated with the term 'culture' so commonly used by archaeologists working in the southern Levant (Bar-Yosef 1998; Garfinkel 1993; Gopher and Gophna 1993)?

During recent decades a number of anthropologists and archaeologists have developed a critique of the concept of culture which probably originates in deconstructionist and poststructuralist thought (Brumann 1999: S1 and references therein). Fox (1999), for one, wonders if anthropology would be better all along without it; is it 'spurious', as suggested by Sapir (1924)? The question is therefore whether this critique should have an impact on the terminology of Levantine prehistory. I suggest that this trend is of little relevance to the way archaeologists conceive culture. Sapir did not reject the ontological existence of culture, but regarded as 'spurious' its nature in modern industrial societies. Moreover, he accepted the term as used by ethnologists and culture historians but, for the clarity of his argument, preferred to call it 'civilization' (Sapir 1924, 402–3).

'Writing for Culture', by Brumann (1999), is a recent and relevant basis for the examination of archaeological cultures in a broader context. Brumann defines culture as:

> ... the set of specific learned routines (and/or their material and immaterial products) that are characteristic of a delineated group of people; sometimes these people are tacitly or explicitly included. The existence of such culture presupposes that other sets of routines shared by other groups of people, thus constituting different cultures. (Brumann 1999, S6)

Cultures consist of a cluster of traits, many of which are shared by many individuals. Not every trait is necessarily present in each and every member or product of the culture. Some of the traits in a culture are not mutually exclusive and can be shared by different cultures (Brumann 1999, S6–S8). This perception of culture is very similar to the archaeological culture of Clarke (1978, 247), mentioned above:

> ... an archaeological culture is a polythetic set of specific and comprehensive artifact-types which consistently recur together in assemblages within a limited geographic area. In ethnological terms, archaeological cultures were produced by people 'with a largely homogeneous tribal organization, language systems and breeding population' ... (Clarke 1978, 369).

Culture as such is a hypothetical entity that could be real, but, even if not so, it is still a powerful and much-needed concept since it simplifies complex archaeological expressions (Clarke 1973). That a similar idea of cultures is shared by archaeologists of the 1960s, their successors and by anthropologists nowadays indicates that culture is not an outmoded term and supports my assertion that there is no contradiction between the way in which archaeologists and anthropologists conceive culture and that it is a viable concept for studying ancient societies.

The methodology used below for reconstructing the culture history of the Chalcolithic period is based on comparative typo-technological observations combined with ^{14}C dates in order to define cultural entities in time and space. The discussion will concentrate on entities that post-date Late Neolithic entities such as Wadi Rabah (Gopher and Gophna 1993) and the Qatifian (Gilead 1990; Kuijt and Chesson 2002). All the dates mentioned in this paper are calibrated BC dates unless otherwise stated (see Burton and Levy 2001, Appendix, and Joffe and Dessel 1995, Table 2.1, for detailed radiocarbon lists. When newer dates are mentioned, they are referenced below). Generally, the Chalcolithic cultural sequence presented here is based on Clarke's classificatory system discussed above. To define the cultural entities temporally, ^{14}C dates are grouped into clusters that are statistically similar and may be averaged by using the software OxCal version 3.10 (Bronk Ramsey 2001).

Inter-cultural heterogeneity

The Ghassulian culture

The Ghassulian is the most important culture of the Chalcolithic period. The name '*Ghassoulien*', after the name of the site Teleilat Ghassul, was introduced by Neuville (1930), and Albright (1932, 10), acknowledging this, frequently uses the combination 'Ghassulian culture' in his discussion of the 'Chalcolithic Age'. Being used by his followers (*e.g.*, Wright 1937, 23), it gained popularity and has been in use since. The sets of Ghassulian artefact-types are too well known to be listed in detail. One can, however, attribute to the Ghassulian culture assemblages that include all or many of the recognized artefact-types such as V-shaped bowls, churns, cornets, vessels with lug handles and/or red painted bands, narrow-backed sickle blades, microliths, clay ossuaries, basalt bowls, copper artefacts, broad room architecture and off-site community cemeteries. Geographically, the Ghassulian is limited to the southern Levant, mainly to the northern Negev, the Dead Sea basin, the southern and central coastal plain, the Shephella and the Jordan valley (Figure 2.1).

At the type-site Teleilat Ghassul (Mallon *et al.* 1934) the stratigraphy of the Ghassulian culture is clear and detailed; it is underlain by pre-Ghassulian layers referred to by Lovell (2001, 49) as Late Neolithic. Beside the differences in pottery assemblages, a very clear marker of the Ghassulian is seen in the section between phases J–G and A–F (Figure 2.2). While in the latter architectural remains are obvious and common, in the lower levels (excluding two instances in upper phase G), there is practically no evidence of buildings. This is probably the best stratigraphic section available now for illustrating the cultural distinction, although the same phenomenon can be observed in sections AXI, AII and AIII (Lovell 2001, 97–101). This distinction between the Ghassulian and earlier entities is also apparent in the Beer Sheva area too (see below).

The AXI section is also of importance since its ^{14}C

Years BC (cal)	Period	Southern Levant cultural entities: North and centre		Southern Levant cultural entities: South and east
4000/3900		Late Ghassulian		Late Ghassulian
4250	Chalcolithic	Golanian**		
4500		Early Ghassulian		Early Ghassulian
4700	Neolithic–Chalcolithic transition	Natzur 4, Tsafian	Pre-Ghassulian	Besorian, Teleilat Ghassul G/H–J
5000				Qatifian
				Timnian*
	Late Neolithic (Pottery Neolithic)	Wadi Rabah		
5600		Lodian		Lodian
		Yarmoukian		

* The Timnian of the southern Negev and Aravah and eastern Sinai yielded ^{14}C dates that cover the Late Neolithic to Early Bronze Age periods.

** The Golanian yielded ^{14}C dates that cover the second half of the 5th millennium and early 4th millennium. Its place in the table does not imply it links Early and Late Ghassulian.

Table 2.1 The Late Neolithic and Chalcolithic of the southern Levant: periodization and cultural entities

dates demonstrate that at Teleilat Ghassul the Ghassulian culture started at about 4500 BC (Gilead 2003). This date is supported also by a profusion of ^{14}C dates from other sites in the southern Levant, and especially from the northern Negev (Gilead 1994; Gilead 2007). The new dates from Teleilat Ghassul and elsewhere are incompatible with the assumption that the 'Ghassulian Chalcolithic' started at about 5000 BC (Joffe and Dessel 1995, 511). The termination of the Ghassulian fell at about 4000–3900 BC (Gilead 1994; Mellaart 1979). The suggestions of Joffe and Dessel (1995, 512) that the end of their Ghassulian Chalcolithic dated to *c.*3500 BC and of Burton and Levy (2001, 1237) that the Chalcolithic activities at Shiqmim ended at about 3300 BC are both unlikely, as there are Early Bronze Age (EBA) dates which indicate very clearly that the EBA began not later than around 3500 BC (Braun 2001, 1280–3) and probably earlier (Golani and Segal 2002). Moreover, new dates from Teleilat Ghassul, the Nahal Mishmar Cave and Shiqmim also indicate that the Ghassulian terminated earlier than previously thought. The new set of dates from Teleilat Ghassul suggests to Bourke *et al.* (2004, 419) that the final occupation of the site is at *c.*3900/3800 BC. The six new dates from the Nahal Mishmar Cave, all in the 5th millennium, indicate that the two old 4th-millennium dates obtained in the 1960s cannot be accepted as valid (Aardsma 2001, 1251–3). Another confirmation of the relatively early end of the Ghassulian comes from Shiqmim (Burton, this volume). The 13 new dates for Stratum I suggest to Burton that the settlement at Shiqmim terminated at *c.*3800 BC, but given that only 1 of the 13 dates (Beta-161867) is early in the 4th millennium, the new set seems to support the previous estimate (Gilead 1993; Gilead 1994; Mellaart 1979) that the Ghassulian ended at about 4000/3900 BC. The nature and time of the transition between the Ghassulian and the EBA is currently debated, but it is possible that it took place in the first half of the 4th millennium, earlier than previously thought (see the papers of Brown and of Golani *et al.* in this volume).

The Golanian culture

The Chalcolithic sites of the Golan Heights (Figure 2.1) lack many of the Ghassulian artefact-types and have a markedly different ceramic repertoire and a distinct architectural feature, namely the chain house (Epstein 1998). It is evident that the bulk of the pottery is manufactured of local sediments, as there are local basalt minerals in the matrix (Epstein 1998, 159). A number of typical Ghassulian vessel-types (*e.g.*, cornets and churns) are totally missing and the V-shaped bowl, a hallmark of the Ghassulian and its most common vessel, '… is by no means common and many small bowls are seldom found' (Epstein 1998, 164). Another clear difference between the

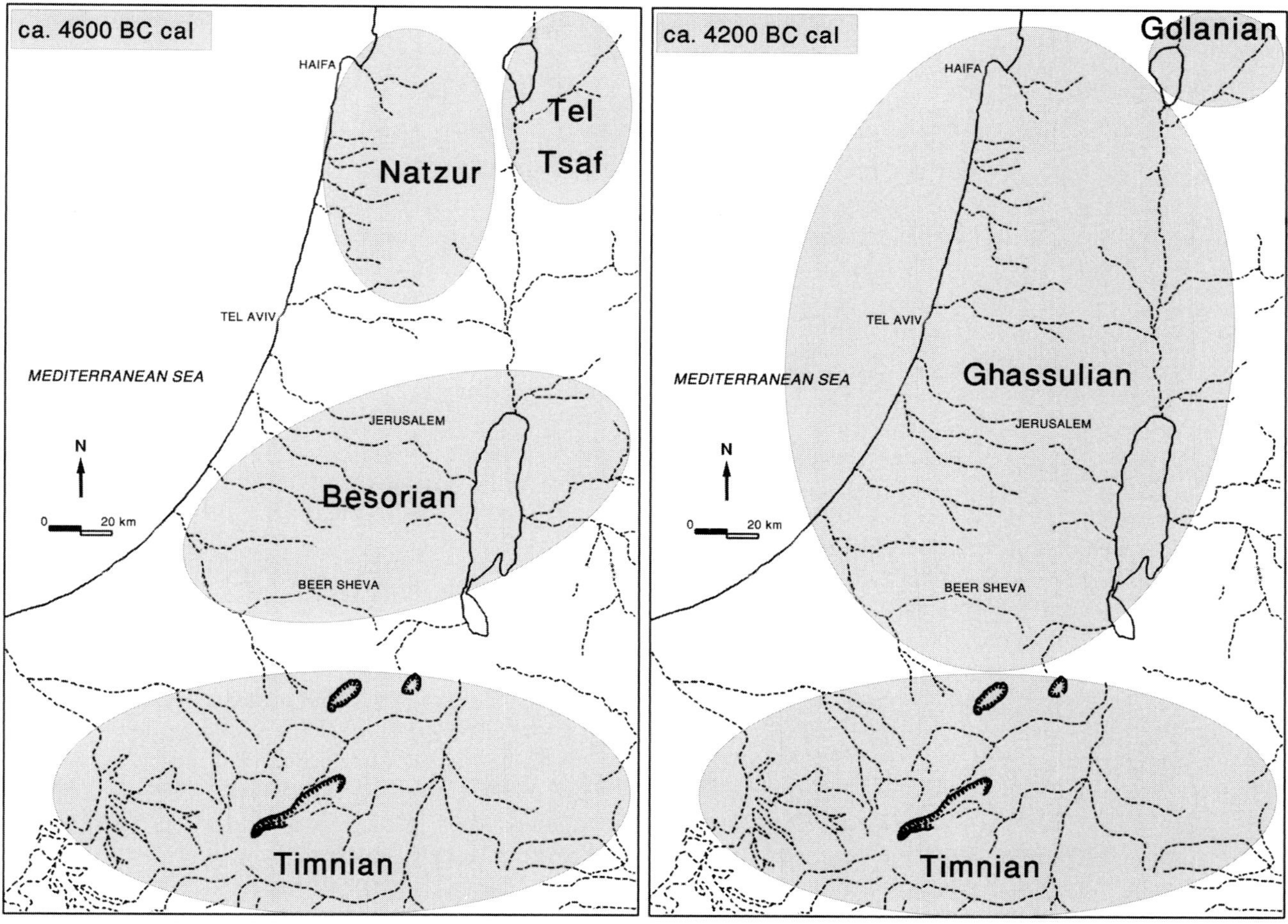

Figure 2.1 Chalcolithic entities in the southern Levant

Golanian and the Ghassulian is the use of red pigments for decoration. While it is most common in the Ghassulian, in the Golanian '… wash is not used, while painted decoration does not occur, except in the South Golan …' (Epstein 1998, 160). The impressed rope patterns, punctuated dots and incised lines so common in the Golanian are rare in the Ghassulian (Epstein 1998, 160–2). Garfinkel (1999, 206–90) further outlines the differences by distinguishing between 'Ghassulian ware' and 'Golan ware'. In addition, the flint industry of the Golanian (Noy 1998) is different in that it features numerous perforated tools, many of them bifacially knapped. These tools are found at all the Golan sites, but are rare or absent from most Ghassulian sites (Noy 1998, 277–83).

There are six ^{14}C dates for the Golanian: four from the site of Rasm Harbush, one from the 'Silo site' and one from Daliyyot (Carmi and Segal 1998, tables 1–2). The dates from the 'Silo site' and Daliyyot are practically identical and indicate that these sites were settled in the third quarter of the 5th millennium, around 4400 BC. The interpretation of the four Rasm Harbush dates is more complicated. While two similar dates indicate that the site was settled approximately in the 200 years surrounding 4000 BC, the other two dates, again similar to one another, suggest that settlement occurred during the 200 years around 3700 BC. Carmi and Segal (1998), however, mention that the latest date (RT-1866, 4810 ± 90 BP) and the earliest date (RT-525, 5279 ± 40 BP) come from the same sampling, and therefore the later date should be rejected in light of the other dates from the site. On the basis of the six dates Epstein (1998, 336) suggests that the Golanian sites existed between 4500 and 3650 BC. This suggestion is difficult to accept, considering the shallow occupation deposits in the habitation structures. It seems more probable that the early Golanian sites are of the third quarter of the 5th millennium, while the later sites are of the last quarter of that millennium, and that the settlement at the Golan ended at about 4000 BC. Thus, the date of about 4000 BC, which correlates well with other sites in the country, seems to be appropriate for the end of the Golanian settlement.

Epstein (1998, 334) is very explicit about the unique nature of the Golan sites and consistently labels them 'the Golan Chalcolithic'. She separates the Golan Chalcolithic from 'Ghassul-Beer Sheba', a taxon she regards as too extensively used and inappropriate in conjunction with the Golan sites. As mentioned above, the difference in shapes and matrix between Golanian and Ghassulian vessels is most obvious, and it is therefore easy to trace sites, mainly in the eastern Galilee, where such indicative vessels are present, albeit in small quantities (Shalem 2003, 82–8). The fact that Golanian vessel types are found at Ghassulian sites, such as Tel Te'o (Eisenberg 2001) and the burial cave of Peqi'in (Gal *et al.* 1997), probably as exotic items, proves the Ghassulian–Golanian contemporaneity in the Galilee. The presence of so-called 'Hula ware' (Garfinkel 1999, 291–5) and/or 'Galilean ware' (Shalem 2003, 80–2) suggests that there are more cultural entities, probably of a lower order, that still await recognition and definition in time and space.

The Timnian culture

The southernmost Ghassulian site, Nahal Zalzal, is known from the dissected plain north-west of the central Negev highlands. It features typical Ghassulian elements such as a churn and a 'Cream ware' amphoriskos (Cohen 1999, 15–36; Goren 1999). Other Chalcolithic sites from the central Negev reported by Cohen seem to be Timnian; worth noting is the site of Kvish Harif (Rosen 1984). This area is probably the boundary zone between the Ghassulian and the Timnian cultures (Figure 2.1). The Timnian is spread mostly in the deserts of eastern Sinai (Eddy *et al.* 1999; Kozloff 1974) and the southern Negev and Aravah (Avner 2002; Henry 1995, 353–74). Since the paper of Rosen (this volume and bibliography therein) is devoted to the Timnian culture, I will limit myself here to brief notes concerning its main cultural attributes and chronology in relation to the Ghassulian.

Timnian architecture consists of what seem to be pens and attached rooms, features unknown in the Ghassulian. There are also open shrines, mazzeboth sites and burial sites, including *nawamis* tombs (Avner 2002, 140–2 and bibliography therein). The pottery of the Timnian differs radically from the rich repertoire of pottery shapes and decorations characterizing the Ghassulian; pottery is extremely scarce at most Timnian sites and there is an overwhelming dominance of holemouth jars in the meagre assemblages (Avner 2002, 14; Avner *et al.* 1994, 280). In the Timnian flint assemblages it is worth noting the presence of small arrowheads, practically unknown in the Ghassulian, and the importance of fan-scrapers (Rosen, this volume).

Desert sites, most of them Timnian, have by now yielded 171 radiometric dates that cover the span of the 6th to 3rd millennia. It is therefore obvious that the Timnian has a very long duration and it is partially contemporaneous with the Ghassulian. Intra-cultural changes are also apparent (Rosen, this volume). There are 52 5th-millennium dates, of which 22 cover the time span of the Ghassulian culture, *c.*4500–4000 BC (Avner 2002, table 1, fig. 3). While contemporary cultural entities to the north of the Ghassulian are similar to it in certain ways, to the south the Timnian is a cultural entity with a very different way of life and economy. The Timnian probably represents a pastoral nomadic society quite different from the farming–herding Ghassulian society in the northern Negev and beyond. As illustrated above, the central Negev was one of the boundary zones between the two cultural entities which were in contact. This is indicated by a few Ghassulian pottery sherds found in Timnian sites in the southern Negev (Avner 2002, 141). Copper and metalworking could have been of mutual interest to the two populations, but it is important to note that there are no Ghassulian sites, and practically no Ghassulian pottery sherds, at the two locales where copper could have been mined, Timna and Faynan. These places are located well within typical the Timnian territories. Thus the possibility that native copper was an exchange commodity controlled by pastoral nomads (Gates 1992), Timnians in our case (Gilead 1992, 39; Rosen 1993, 50–1), cannot be excluded.

The Besorian culture

The Besorian was first defined by Gilead and Alon (Gilead 1990; Gilead and Alon 1988) in the late 1980s. The definition was based on the results of a new sounding carried out in part of site D in Wadi Ghazzeh excavated in the late 1920s by Macdonald (1932; and see Roshwalb 1981) and a re-evaluation of the artefact assemblages of other sites in the Nahal Besor area. In the 1990s it was argued that there is no such entity, and that it is either Qatifian (Garfinkel 1999, 199) or 'a minor variation' of a regional culture that was not specified (Bourke 1997, 397). New sites excavated in the early 1990s and new radiometric dates from sites already known do indicate that the Besorian is a cultural entity rather than a 'minor variation', however (Figure 2.1).

The site of Ramot Nof was discovered and excavated in 1991 (Nahshoni *et al.* 2002). It is located on the hilly part of Beer Sheva, *c.*4 km north of the Nahal Beer Sheva channel where the Ghassulian sites are situated. The site consists of a series of pits, but mudbrick fragments found in the pits suggest that there were structures too. The pottery assemblage of Ramot Nof is typologically different from the Beer Sheva Ghassulian assemblages: neither churns nor bowls were discovered, and the dominant vessel type is a holemouth jar with large loop handles – the Beth Pelet jar (Gilead and Alon 1988, 127*), which is unknown in Ghassulian assemblages. Moreover, the petrography of these vessels indicates that an important component of the assemblage is made of Motza marl or clay with crushed calcite. Such a matrix comes probably from the Shephella area. It is also known from the Besor sites but is extremely rare in the Negev Ghassulian assemblages (Nahshoni *et al.* 2002, 12*). The flint assemblage also accords better with the Besor flint assemblages than with those of the Nahal Beer Sheva sites. Nahshoni *et al.* note that the frequency distributions of debitage and the tool types of Ramot Nof are more similar to those of the Qatifian and the Besorian sites further to the west than to sites in the Negev, like

Ramot Nof. Worth noting, too, is the high frequency of bladelet cores and retouched bladelets in Ramot Nof, and their relative rarity at the Beer Sheva sites (Nahshoni *et al.* 2002, 16*–21*). Ramot 3 was discovered in 1997 several hundred of metres north of Ramot Nof (Fabian *et al.* 2004). No structures or pits have been unearthed at this site, and the pottery assemblage is meagre. The shapes and petrography of the vessels, however, are very indicative. The Beth Pelet jars as well as the use of Motza marl show that Ramot 3 and Ramot Nof are components of the same cultural entity.

These are the first Chalcolithic sites in the Beer Sheva area discovered beyond the immediate vicinity of the Nahal Beer Sheva channel (Gilead and Fabian 2010). The ^{14}C date of Ramot Nof adds weight to the claim that Ramot Nof and the Nahal Beer Sheva sites represent different entities. At 5715±75 BP (ETH-8828), with a 2 sigma calibrated range of 4730–4440 BC, the site is *c.*4600–4500 BC, significantly earlier than the Nahal Beer Sheva sites, which are dated to *c.*4200–4000 BC (Gilead 1994).

The excavators recognized in the field that the nature of the sites and especially their pottery assemblages clearly differ from the Ghassulian sites adjacent to the Nahal. On the basis of comparative analysis of artefact assemblages from Ramot 3 and Ramot Nof, the excavators concluded that they are similar to each other and to the Besor sites A, B, D and M, and that they are to be associated with the Besorian (Fabian *et al.* 2004, 77–9; Nahshoni *et al.* 2002, 21*–22*). Briefly stated, the Besorian pottery assemblages consist of the following main components: 1) jars and holemouth jars with loop handles and thick bases, the 'Beth Pelet jars'; 2) bowls with straight wall, the precursors of V-shaped bowls; and 3) large basins with vertical thumb decoration and rims similar in thickness to the walls (Fabian *et al.* 2004, 78). In these they contrast with the Ghassulian sites near Nahal Beer Sheva.

Dissimilarities between the Besorian and the Ghassulian in the Beer Sheva area are not restricted to pottery. The Ghassulian sites of Abu Matar, Bir es-Safadi and Horvat Beter feature very similar cultural traits that include underground structures, broad rooms with lower courses of walls built of stone, and copper and ivory industries, none of which is found in the Ramot sites. The nature of the Ramot sites and the broad spectrum of pottery and flint artefact-types found at them negate the option that these are specialized activity loci of people coming from the nearby large Ghassulian sites.

The excavators noted in the 1990s that the petrography and typology of the pottery vessels from Ramot Nof are similar to those of vessels found at the site of Gilat (Nahshoni *et al.* 2002, 12*, 22*). Now, after the petrography of the Gilat pottery has been published (Goren 2006), it is clear that there is a Besorian component at Gilat. It is best to use Goren's statements in order to illustrate this point:

> The pottery of Gilat cannot be treated any more as a homogeneous whole. It should be separated into early and late … the one-to-one comparison of the Gilat assemblage with the developed Chalcolithic 'cultic' assemblages … is seemingly meaningless (Goren 2006, 380), In conclusion, 'Besorian' pottery assemblages from north-eastern Sinai, the northern Negev and the lower Shephela all illustrate a petrographic situation that is similar to that of Gilat but differs significantly from the later Developed Chalcolithic assemblages in the same area. (Goren 2006, 381)

The typological study of the Gilat ceramics by Commenge (2006) is orientated towards aspects of function and cognition. However, even in her limited discussion of the place of Gilat ceramics in the later local prehistory she mentions the pottery of Gilat as being 'Early Chalcolithic' and suggests that Gilat is earlier than the Beer Sheva sites (Commenge 2006, 347).

That Gilat contains a component that is earlier than the Ghassulian and may partially correspond to the Besorian in general and the Ramot sites in particular can also be substantiated radiometrically. The eight ^{14}C dates from Gilat (Levy and Burton 2006) cover a very long time span, from the first half of the 5th millennium to the end of the 4th millennium. A closer examination of the, however, dates suggests that they form three different clusters. Dates RT-2058 and RT-860B are similar but significantly later than the rest, falling in the first half of the 4th millennium. This cluster is clearly within the Early Bronze Age and does not seem to be related to the Chalcolithic cultural assemblages discussed here, as admitted by the excavators (Levy and Burton 2006, 866). Dates RT-860B, OxA-4011 and Beta-131729 represent another temporal episode, and their most probable 2 sigma averaged range is 4460–4330 BC. The third set of dates, OxA-3555, Beta-131730 and OxA-3566, is earlier, and the most probable 2 sigma averaged range is 4690–4490 BC. The range of these dates in the first half of the 5th millennium (Figure 2.3) accords with the previously proposed date of the Besorian (Gilead 1994, 11), and is close to the date obtained from the site of Ramot Nof discussed above.

Lovell (2001, table 6.1) divides the stratigraphic sequence of Teleilat Ghassul into four units: Late Neolithic (J–H), Early Chalcolithic (G), Middle Chalcolithic (F–D) and Late Chalcolithic (C–A and A+). She suggests that '… the Late Neolithic material from Teleilat Ghassul may relate to the "Besorian"', and that 'The lowest phases at Teleilat Ghassul represent a Late Neolithic phase that might be associated, in part, with the "Besorian"' (Lovell 2001, 46, 49 respectively). This designation seems justified considering the fact that many ceramic parallels to these phases presented by Lovell are from the Besorian Site DII (Gilead and Alon 1988). I suggest elsewhere (Gilead 2003, 222–3) that phase G, or most of it, should be regarded as part of the lower J–H Besorian-like complex. This is based, among other things, on Lovell's (2001, 49) observation that 'The most significant shift in terms of architecture occurs between phase G and phase F.' I have shown above (and see Figure 2.2) that the intensive construction activities at phases F–A+ are a defining attribute of the Ghassulian and clearly illustrate the sharp cultural division between the Besorian and the

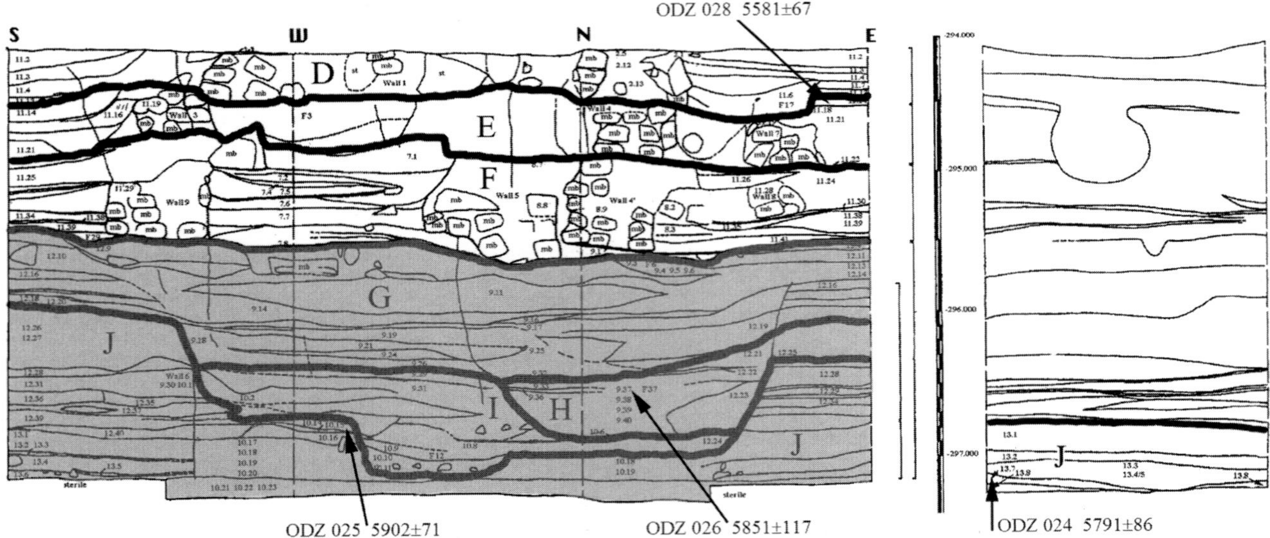

Figure 2.2 Teleilat Ghassul, section AXI. Shaded part – Besorian or Besorian-like; unshaded – Ghassulian (after Lovell 2001, fig. 3.2 and data in Appendix A)

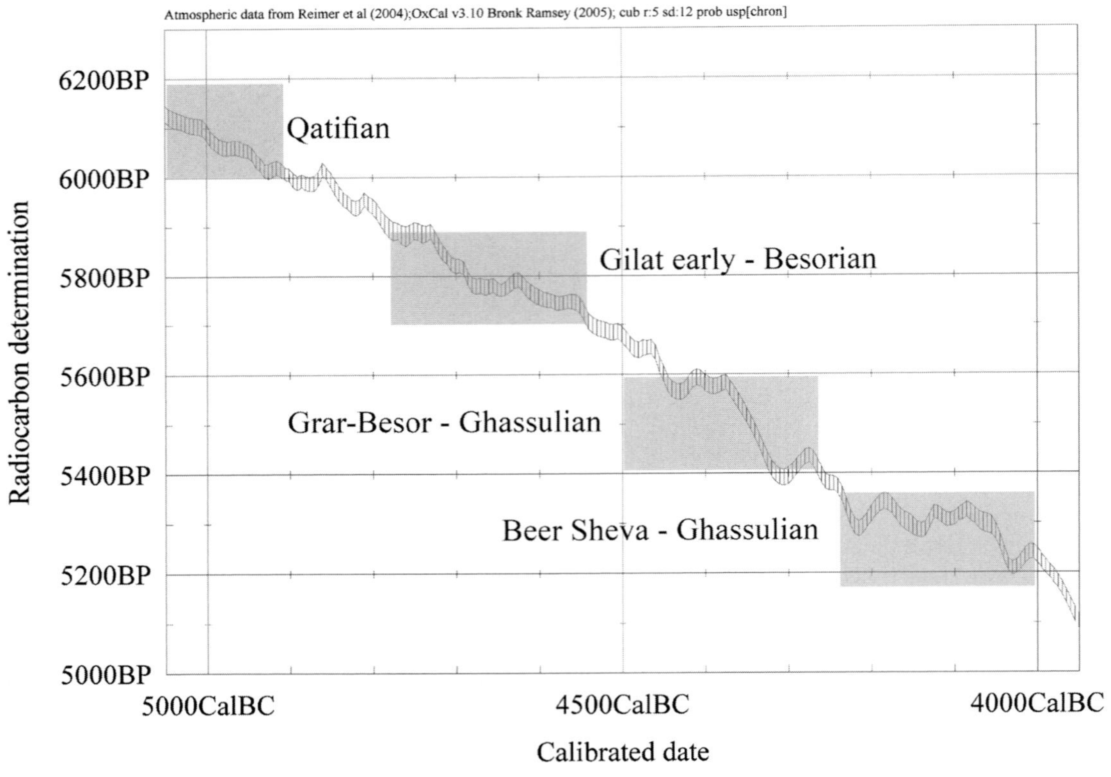

Figure 2.3 14C chronology of major Chalcolithic entities

Ghassulian. Teleilat Ghassul also furnished ^{14}C dates that are relevant to the Besorian–Ghassulian dichotomy.

It is clear now that the problematic early dates of Teleilat Ghassul (SUA 732–739) are erroneous (Bourke *et al.* 2001, 1219). With new dates from the deepest levels of the site, the chronology of the site can be put into a clearer perspective (Bourke *et al.* 2001, table 2). There are three dates from the earliest phases: two from Phase J (OZD 024 – 5791±86; OZD 025 – 5902±71), and one from Phase H (OZD 026 – 5851±117). The dates are similar and their average marks the earliest settlement at Teleilat Ghassul: the most probable 2 sigma calibrated range is 4840–4580 BC. These dates accord well with the range of the Besorian site Ramot Nof and that of Gilat, discussed above. Date OZD 028 from this section and additional dates for the Ghassulian phases at Teleilat Ghassul are discussed below.

To conclude, the formal status of the Besorian, in terms of Clarke's system of entities, is not easily determined. Is it an independent culture which was transformed into the Ghassulian or is it a formative state of the Ghassulian cultural system? When the Besorian was defined we tended to regard it as an early variant of the Ghassul–Beer Sheva assemblages (Gilead and Alon 1988, 129*). Now, with more assemblages and better chronological control, it seems that the possibility of the Besorian being a 'culture' cannot be excluded. There is a continuity of flint knapping techniques and a few types of pottery into the Ghassulian, but the richness in shapes and types of decoration in the Ghassulian pottery assemblages gives the impression of a profound technological, typological and aesthetic change after the Besorian. The small size of the Besorian sites and the meagre construction activities evident at them set these two entities further apart and support their division into independent cultures. It is worth noting in this context that a new Besorian site was excavated near Menuha, north of Qiryat Gat, in early 2005. The site, with pits, mudbricks and a fragment of a mudbrick wall, yielded a typical Besorian pottery assemblage: jars with loop handles and vessels with crushed calcite as temper (P. Nahshoni and E. Aladgem, pers. comm.).

The Natzur and the Tsafian cultures

The possible geographical distribution of the Besorian north of the Besor–Ghassul line is unclear, and the work carried out since the 1990s in northern Israel suggests that post-Wadi Rabah and pre-Ghassulian entities were present there too. The site of Natzur 4, excavated by Yannai (forthcoming), probably represents a cultural entity in the northern half of Israel that is contemporary with the Besorian. Yannai suggests that the assemblages at the site form a cultural entity, which he has termed 'Natzur 4 Culture' (Figure 2.1), the pottery, flint and stone vessels of which suggest to Yannai a post-Wadi Rabah and pre-Ghassulian date. Typologically and chronologically it is regarded by him as a northern counterpart of the Besorian. At the site of Horvat Uza in western Galilee, excavated by Getzov *et al.* (2009), a sequence of pre-Ghassulian layers has been uncovered between layer 20 (Wadi Rabah) and layer 15 (Ghassulian). Of these, it is probable that layer 16 is contemporaneous with Natzur 4. Unfortunately there are no radiometric dates for these sites and their exact chronological position cannot be ascertained.

As indicated above, the Besorian covers most of the second quarter of the 5th millennium, in the later part of the period referred to by Garfinkel (1999, 309–10) as 'Middle Chalcolithic', which started in his opinion at about 5300 BC. Layer Ib at Tel 'Ali yielded four radiocarbon dates that cover the second quarter of the 5th millennium. It is therefore contemporary with the Besorian, although no cultural attribution is mentioned beyond the fact that the ware common in the pottery assemblage is the 'Beth Shean ware'. With additional sites and radiometric dates, the cultural attribution of sites such as Tel 'Ali 1b will hopefully become possible.

Tel Tsaf in the Jordan valley was first excavated by Gophna and Sadeh (1989). The site yielded a pottery assemblage that includes numerous fragments decorated in a style known as Tel Tsaf, which consists of the painting of black or red geometric patterns on white wash. Garfinkel's renewed excavations at the site in 2004–6 yielded an exotic fragment, probably from northern Syria, with a Late 'Ubaid decoration style. New radiocarbon dates from Tel Tsaf suggest that the Tsafian assemblages, here and at a number of adjacent sites, are to be dated to the second quarter of the 5th millennium, about 1000 years later than the previous ^{14}C date suggested (Y. Garfinkel, pers. comm.). The unique Tel Tsaf decoration is limited to several sites in the central Jordan valley (Garfinkel 1999, 186–8). It therefore represents an entity which is contemporary with the adjacent Tel 'Ali Ib and the distant Besorian sites in the south, but is clearly distinct culturally (Figure 2.1).

Intra-cultural variability

Although in terms of artefact-types the Ghassulian is a homogeneous entity, there is still variation signifying sub-cultures, most probably geographic sub-cultures, to use Clarke's (1978, 249–61) terminology again. The existence of two different sub-cultures is most apparent in the northern Negev (Gilead 1989, 390–2; 1995, 473–6). The first consists of sites along the Nahal Beer Sheva such as Nevatim (Gilead and Fabian 2001), Abu Matar, Bir es-Safadi (Perrot 1955, 1984) and Shiqmim (Levy 1987). Sites of the second sub-culture, the Besor-Grar sub-culture, are found to the north and west of the Nahal Beer Sheva sites and include Grar (Gilead 1995) segments of Gilat (Levy 2006), sites E and O in the Besor (Macdonald 1932; Roshwalb 1981), and probably Gat Guvrin (Perrot 1961 and Peter Fabian, pers. comm.).

Cultural distinctions between the two sub-cultures begin with the fact that stone was used to construct the lower rows of walls in the Beer Sheva sub-culture, a rare feature in the Besor-Grar sub-culture, where bricks were used. Two of the best known crafts of the Beer Sheva sub-culture, copper metallurgy and ivory carving, were not practised in the sites of the Besor-Grar sub-culture. The cornet, one of the typical pottery vessels of the Chalcolithic period, is restricted in distribution to the Besor-Grar sub-culture and is hardly found in the large sites of the Beer Sheva sub-culture. The dichotomy between the two sub-cultures is also expressed in the flint industry. In most cases, the frequency of sickle blades is higher in the Besor-Grar sub-culture than in the Beer Sheva sub-culture. Finally, a major disparity between the two sub-cultures is the fact that pigs were raised in the Besor-Grar sub-culture, whereas they are not found in the faunal assemblages of the Beer Sheva sub-culture. Although this dissimilarity could have been a result of different ecological settings (Grigson 1995, 254–6), the fact that one group raised pigs and the other did not, in addition to the other differences listed above, is to be regarded as reflecting behavioural, cultural and socio-economic differences between the members of these two sub-cultures.

The chronological relation between the two sub-cultures is a complex issue (Gilead 1989, 390–2; 1995, 473–6), but recent dates from Gilat (Levy and Burton 2006) and Teleilat Ghassul (Bourke *et al.* 2001; Bourke *et al.* 2004) suggest a possible solution. As described above, the three earliest dates from Gilat (OxA-3555, Beta-131730, OxA-3556) are clearly within the range of the Besorian, in the second quarter of the 5th millennium. The above-mentioned presence of Besorian characteristics in the pottery assemblages further supports the suggestion that the early phase at Gilat is Besorian (see also Goren 2006, 381–4). The three dates of the second set (RT-860A, OxA-4011, Beta-131729) are younger and different from the first. The combined 2 sigma date range is between 4460 and 4330 BC (Figure 2.3).

There is a new series of 19 dates from the Ghassulian phases at Teleilat Ghassul (G–A) (Bourke *et al.* 2001, table 3; Bourke *et al.* 2004, table 3). The only date of phase G–F in the 2004 published set, 5870 ± 40 BP (OZF421), falls within the range of the H–J dates and supports my contention, above, that phase G is Besorian. The date from phase E in section AXI, 5581 ± 67 BP (OZD028), is from a considerably higher point in the section, above the Besorian phases J–H. Its most probable 2 sigma calibrated range is 4550–4320 BC, definitely later than phases H–J discussed above. The other dates are from phases D–A from other areas in the site, and most of them cluster around 4400–4300 BC. Two dates attributed to A–D seem to be outliers: 5750 40 BP (OZF418), probably a 'residual material from an earlier stratum' (Bourke *et al.* 2004, 320), and 5100 ± 50 BP (OZG251), probably too late. The fact that about a quarter of the E–A dates cluster at about 4400–4300 BC suggests that the main phase of occupation at Teleilat Ghassul is contemporary with the Ghassulian occupation at Gilat and probably with the Besor-Grar sub-culture. This phase may be termed 'Early Ghassulian' since it is earlier than the major phase of the settlement in the Beer Sheva region, the 'Late Ghassulian'. This is based on the 21 ^{14}C dates available now from sites near Beer Sheva: Abu Matar, Bir es-Safadi, Horvat Beter (Gilead *et al.* 2004, table 1) and Tel Sheva (courtesy of Yael Abadi-Reiss). The 2 sigma combined average of the entire set ranges between *c.*4200 and 4000 BC (Figure 2.3).

The set of dates from Shiqmim, until recently the most dated Chalcolithic site (Burton and Levy 2001), seems to contradict the above reconstruction. Shiqmim is a typical member of the Beer Sheva sub-culture, but the dates from the site feature a temporal distribution which differs remarkably from the other dated sites of the Nahal Beer Sheva basin. While the latter dates mostly cover the span of two or three centuries, the dating of Shiqmim 'suggests continuity of settlement probably occurring within temporal boundaries of about 5500–3300, conservatively speaking' (Burton and Levy 2001, 1236). The problem of accepting such a long span of occupation for what seems to be one cultural entity has already been addressed (Gilead 1994). The cultural sequence of Teleilat Ghassul is less than half than that of Shiqmim, although it features a complex cultural variability, including the Besorian yet unknown in Shiqmim. Structurally and culturally Shiqmim is similar to Bir es-Safadi, which was occupied for perhaps two centuries. Burton and Levy's claim that Shiqmim represents more than 2000 years of Chalcolithic history cannot therefore be maintained.

Inter and intra-site culture variability: the Gilat case

The inter- and intra-culture heterogeneity presented above should play a dominant role in interpreting the archaeological evidence. The current view on the place of Gilat in the culture and cult of the northern Negev may illustrate this point. Alon and Levy (1989; Levy 2006, 831–46) suggest that Gilat is a central shrine that served the sites in the northern Negev and beyond. In their opinion the shrine was run by a priestly segment of the society and was used to accommodate pilgrims in a religious behaviour that is analogous to pilgrimage in biblical times. Religious facets of this interpretation have been discussed elsewhere (Gilead 2002; Joffe *et al.* 2001) and the discussion below concentrates on aspects of material culture, cultural entities and chronology.

Levy (2006, 833) assumes that Gilat is contemporary with all of the other major northern Negev sites, although the pottery and the ^{14}C dates clearly indicate that this is not the case. Since the artefact-types of Gilat are clearly distinct from those of the Nahal Beer Sheva sites, and the site is earlier than the sites of Nahal Beer Sheva, Gilat could not have been a ritual centre for the Ghassulian sites in the Beer Sheva area, which had not yet been settled then. Gilat, however, at least in chronological terms, could have been a centre for sites in the north-western Negev, such as the Besor-Grar sites. Now the issue is whether the archaeological records of sites such as Besor E, O, Grar and, maybe, Gat Guvrin support the idea of a social complexity that results in the rise of priesthood.

Periodization and the Neolithic–Chalcolithic transition

Until now the discussion has focused on cultural entities of different scales and the issue of periodization has been mentioned only briefly. The discussion below will concentrate on issues of defining the Chalcolithic as a period. While it is becoming a consensus that the

Chalcolithic period ended at about 4000–3800 BC, the beginning of the period is still an open issue. It is best illustrated by comparing, by way of example, the opinions of Garfinkel and Lovell. Garfinkel (1999, 6–7, 303–10) dates the beginning of his 'Early Chalcolithic' to about 5800 BC and the end of his 'Late Chalcolithic' to about 3600 BC. For Lovell (2001, 49), 'Early Chalcolithic' starts at about 4600 BC and the 'Late Chalcolithic' terminates at about 3600 BC. Thus the Chalcolithic of Garfinkel is more than twice as long as that of Lovell.

Both scholars, explicitly or implicitly, base their periodization mainly on estimates of how similar or dissimilar to the Ghassulian are ceramic assemblages they study. Since 'Wadi Rabah Ware reveals more similarities to the pottery of the subsequent phase ... the Wadi Rabah has been defined here as the Early Chalcolithic period' (Garfinkel 1999, 6). The question is, what 'Chalcolithic' is there in the subsequent phase? Garfinkel's subsequent phase ('Middle Chalcolithic') is also 'Chalcolithic' since it 'represents a gradual transition from the Wadi Rabah to the Ghassulian Chalcolithic' (Garfinkel 1999, 305–6). Lovell is not less familiar with pottery assemblages but she does not see the kind of similarity or gradual transition that warrants labelling Wadi Rabah, and even the Besorian-like assemblages of Ghassul, as Chalcolithic. She prefers to regard them as Late Neolithic and she is not alone; most authorities (*e.g.*, Banning 1998; Gopher and Gophna 1993) regard Wadi Rabah as 'Late Neolithic'.

It is preferable to define cultural entities and to relate to them, rather than to periods, whenever possible. When, for example, the 'Natufian culture' is discussed, the fact that it is commonly dated to the 'Late Epipalaeolithic' is of little consequence. However, since period names are in use, and they are sometimes useful, the term 'Chalcolithic' will undoubtedly stay with us. In order to free it from subjective estimates of similarity between artefact assemblages, it is preferable to characterize it on the basis of its original definition and its current common use. It is evident that Albright's (1932) definition of the 'Chalcolithic Age' was driven primarily by the discovery of the Ghassulian culture at Teleilat Ghassul, although he refers to a number of the Besor sites as 'Early Chalcolithic'. However, since the term 'Early' is problematic, as demonstrated above when comparing Garfinkel's and Lovell's ideas of Early Chalcolithic, it is suggested that the Chalcolithic period should be basically equated with the Ghassulian.

> In the history of archaeological research in Palestine, various cultures have been named 'Chalcolithic', confusing its designation. In this chapter, I shall not use ambiguous terms such as 'Early Chalcolithic' or 'Late Chalcolithic.' The main culture of the Chalcolithic period is the Ghassulian Culture; this latter term will be used here in its most comprehensive framework – including regional variants (Mazar 1990, 59).

It is suggested here that Mazar's general statement that almost everything Chalcolithic is Ghassulian, excluding a relatively few sites that are different owing to either geographical or temporal circumstances, should be followed (*e.g.*, The Golanian, and see Table 2.1). No less importantly, the Ghassulian is Chalcolithic in producing and using copper artefacts along with an elaborate flint industry, attributes fully compatible with the copper–flint dichotomy embedded in the name of the period. Beyond the artefacts, the distribution of sites and aspects of inter- and intra-site variability, such as off-settlement community cemeteries, are also essential attributes of the Ghassulian and thus of the Chalcolithic period as a whole. Assemblages that are prior to the Ghassulian – that is, prior to *c.*4500 BC – are therefore 'Neolithic', excluding, however, the Besorian and its contemporaries, which are mostly of the second quarter of the 5th century. Assemblages that immediately precede the Ghassulian, the 'pre-Ghassulian', are to be regarded as 'Transitional' or 'Intermediate Neolithic–Chalcolithic' entities (Table 2.1).

Conclusions

A cluster of similar artefact types and similar assemblages, a patterned set, must always be labelled. This enables a specific pattern to be distinguished from other patterns, be it 'cornet', 'churn', 'Ghassulian', 'Timnian' and so on. Named cultural entities should be explicitly defined in terms of material-culture constituents, mainly the artefact types, assemblages, spatial distribution and chronology. It is not always an easy task and the application of a name to many assemblages is sometimes debated (*e.g.*, for the case of the Natufian see Belfer-Cohen 1989). Philip (2006) explicitly attempts to avoid defining cultural entities, or at least higher level cultural entities. He prefers to think of 'communities' like 'nodes' within a 'web', terms the meaning of which he does not explicitly define. I presume that his 'web' is not a World Wide Web since, for example, the so-called Badarian of Egypt or the Cucuteni-Tripolje of south-eastern Europe are not part of it. Thus, in order to define a spatial–temporal 'web' it has to be defined and named in order to differentiate it from other webs. The same goes for 'nodes' within a web. Since nodes are by definition different, they will, again, have to be described and named. Once Philip presents his names and definitions of 6th- to 4th-millennia 'webs' and 'nodes', many – or, at least, some – of us will adopt them. However, studying 'webs' and 'nodes' is practically tantamount to Clarke's attempts to define what he calls 'phase pattern regularities', 'time pattern regularities', 'processes' and 'procedures' that relate to entities. What are 'webs' and 'nodes' if not cultural entities? There is only a short distance from 'web' and 'node' to material-culture entities in the Clarkeian sense.

The concept of culture and its archaeological correlates form a sensible and practical framework for analysing and interpreting archaeological assemblages. The application of this concept entails two main corollaries: that several archaeological entities existed in the southern Levant during the 5th millennium and that the use of the term 'Chalcolithic' as a denominator of cultural or social attributes is misleading. The most important entity of the Chalcolithic period is the Ghassulian culture of *c.*4500–4000/3900 BC. At the same time the Timnian culture existed to the south. The Timnian consists of totally different cultural assemblages and is associated with a pastoral nomadic way of life. In the north, the Golanian culture represents a different cultural entity which had contact with Ghassulian settlements in the Galilee. Prior to the Ghassulian, the Besorian, dated to the second quarter of the 5th millennium, was the main cultural entity in southern Israel and Jordan. It was contemporary with an earlier phase of the Timnian and a group of cultural entities in central and northern Israel, one of them probably the Tsafian. Since the Besorian features elements in the material culture that seem to be associated later with the Ghassulian, it is best to regard it, as well as other entities of the second quarter of the 5th millennium, as entities of the Neolithic–Chalcolithic transition.

In recent decades numerous assemblages and ^{14}C dates pertinent to the issue of the transition from the Late Neolithic to the Chalcolithic have been accumulated from southern Israel and Jordan. This relative wealth of data enables a fine-resolution treatment of a variety of aspects. The crucial problem is the contribution of the sequence in the south to a better understanding of the Late Neolithic–Chalcolithic development in the northern half of Israel and Jordan. The sites in the north which are dated to Qatifian–Besorian times are usually referred to as Wadi Rabah culture or its variants and they are different from the southern cultures (Gopher and Gophna 1993, 326–39). In the pottery, the variety of shapes, the intensity of painting and the application of plastic decorations are much more pronounced in the north. Since one of the typical characteristics of the Ghassulian everywhere is the intensity of decoration, it seems that northern entities were an important factor in the emergence of the Ghassulian. The process through which northern and southern traditions merged and the reasons behind the impressive developments of the Ghassulian in the south will undoubtedly be a major topic of future research.

Acknowledgements

I would like to thank the editors for inviting me to participate in the ICANNE workshop and to contribute to the present volume. Angela Davidzon, Steve Rosen and Jacob Vardi read the draft of the text. They made valuable comments, but I alone am responsible for the remaining mistakes.

References

Aardsma, G. E. (2001) New radiocarbon dates from the reed mat from the Cave of the Treasure. *Radiocarbon* 43, 1247–54.

Albright, W. F. (1932) The Chalcolithic age in Palestine. *Bulletin of the American Schools of Oriental Research* 48, 10–13.

Alon, D. and Levy, T. E. (1989) The archaeology of cult and the Chalcolithic sanctuary at Gilat. *Journal of Mediterranean Archaeology* 2, 163–221.

Avner, U. (2002) Studies in Material and Spiritual Culture of the Negev and Sinai Populations, During the 6th–3rd Millennia BC. Unpublished PhD thesis, The Hebrew University.

Avner, U., Carmi, I. and Segal, D. (1994) Neolithic to Bronze Age settlement of the Negev and Sinai in light of radiocarbon dating: a view from the southern Negev. Pp. 265–300 in O. Bar-Yosef and R. S. Kra (eds), *Late Quaternary Chronology and Paleoclimates of Eastern Mediterranean.* Radiocarbon and Peabody Museum. Cambridge, MA: Harvard University.

Banning, E. B. (1998) The Neolithic period: triumphs of architecture, agriculture and art. *Near Eastern Archaeology* 61, 188–237.

Bar-Yosef, O. (1998) The Natufian culture in the Levant, threshold to the origins of agriculture. *Evolutionary Anthropology* 6, 159–77.

Belfer-Cohen, A. (1989) The Natufian issue: a suggestion. Pp. 297–307 in O. Bar-Yosef and B. Vandermeersch (eds), *Investigations in South Levantine Prehistory*. Oxford: BAR Int. Ser. 497.

Bourke, J. S. (1997) The 'pre-Ghassulian' sequence at Teleilat Ghassul: Sydney University excavations 1975–1995. Pp. 395–417 in H. G. K. Gebel, Z. Kafafi and G. O. Rollefson (eds), *The Prehistory of Jordan, II. Perspectives from 1997*, Studies in Early Near Eastern Production, Subsistence and Enviroment, vol. 4. Berlin: ex oriente.

Bourke, J. S., Lawson, E., Lovell, J. L., Hua, Q., Zoppi, U. and Barbetti, M. (2001) The chronology of the Ghassulian Period in the southern Levant: new ^{14}C determinations from Teleilat Ghassul, Jordan. *Radiocarbon* 43, 1217–22.

Bourke, J. S., Zoppi, U., Meadows, J., Hua, Q. and Gibbins, S. (2004) The end of the Chalcolithic period in the south Jordan valley: new ^{14}C determinations from Teleilat Ghassul, Jordan. *Radiocarbon* 46, 315–23.

Braun, E. (2001) Proto, Early Dynastic Egypt, and the Early Bronze Age I–II of the southern Levant: some uneasy ^{14}C correlations. *Radiocarbon* 43, 1279–95.

Bronk Ramsey, C. (2001) Development of the radiocarbon program OxCal. *Radiocarbon* 43, 355–63.

Brumann, C. (1999) Writing for culture, why a successful concept should not be discarded. *Current Anthropology* 40, S1–S29.

Burton, M. and Levy, T. E. (2001) The Chalcolithic radiocarbon record and its use in southern Levantine archaeology. *Radiocarbon* 43, 1223–46.

Carmi, I. and Segal, D. (1998) ^{14}C dates from the Chalcolithic sites in the Golan. Pp. 343 in C. Epstein (ed.), *The Chalcolithic Culture of the Golan.* Israel Antiquities Authority Reports 4. Jerusalem.

Childe, V. G. (1927) *The Dawn of European Civilization*, 2nd edn. London: Kegan Paul, Trench, Trubner.

Clarke, D. (1973) Archaeology: the loss of innocence. *Antiquity* 47, 6–18.

Clarke, D. (1978) *Analytical Archaeology*, 2nd edn. London: Methuen & Co.

Clifford, J. (1988) *The Predicament of Culture: Twentieth-Century Ethnography, Literature and Art.* Cambridge, MA: Harvard University Press.

Cohen, R. (1999) *Ancient Settlements of the Central Negev. Volume 1, the Chalcolithic Period, the Early Bronze Age and Middle Bronze Age I.* Israel Antiquities Authority Reports 6. Jerusalem (Hebrew).

Commenge, C. (2006) Gilat's ceramics: Cognitive dimensions of pottery production. Pp. 394–506 in T. E. Levy (ed.),

Archaeology Anthropology and Cult: The Sanctuary at Gilat, Israel. London: Equinox.

Eddy, F. W. and Wendorf, F. (1999) *An Archaeological Investigation of the Central Sinai*. Boulder, CO: The American Research Center in Egypt and University Press of Colorado.

Eisenberg, E. (2001) Pottery from strata VII–VI, the Chalcolithic period. Pp. 105–16 in E. Eisenberg, A. Gopher and R. Greenberg (eds), *Tel Te'o, A. Neolithic, Chalcolithic, and Early Bronze Age site in the Hula Valley*. Israel Antiquities Authority Reports 13. Jerusalem.

Epstein, C. (1998) *The Chalcolithic Culture of the Golan*. Israel Antiquities Authority Reports 4. Jerusalem.

Fabian, P., Hermon, S. and Goren, Y. (2004) Ramot 3: a Pre-Ghassulian open-air site in the northern Be'er-Sheva' basin. *'Atiqot* 47, 57–80.

Fox, R. G. (1999) Editorial: culture a second chance? *Current Anthropology* 40, S1.

Gal, Z., Smithline, H. and Shalem, D. (1997) A Chalcolithic burial cave in Peqi'in, Upper Galilee. *Israel Exploration Journal* 47, 145–54.

Garfinkel, Y. (1993) The Yarmukian culture in Israel. *Paléorient* 19, 115–35.

Garfinkel, Y. (1999) *Neolithic and Chalcolithic Pottery of the Southern Levant*. Qedem 39, Jerusalem Institute of Archaeology, The Hebrew University of Jerusalem.

Garrod, D. A. E. (1932) A new Mesolithic industry: the Natufian of Palestine. *The Journal of the Royal Anthropological Institute of Great Britain and Ireland* 62, 257–69.

Gates, M.-H. (1992) Nomadic pastoralists and the Chalcolithic hoard from Nahal Mishmar. *Levant* 24, 131–9.

Getzov, N., Lieberman-Wander, R., Smithline, H. and Syon, D. (2009) *Hurvat 'Uza. The 1991 Excavations Vol. 1. The Early Periods*. Jerusalem: Israel Antiquities Authority Reports 41.

Gilead, I. (1981) Upper Paleolithic tool assemblages from the Negev and Sinai. In J. Cauvin and P. Sanlaville (eds), *Préhistiore du Levant*. Paris: CNRS.

Gilead, I. (1985) Chalcolithic and accompanying terms: On the need for definition of terms in archaeological research. Pp. 65–74 in M. Cogan (ed.), *Beer Sheva*, vol. II. Jerusalem: The Magness Press (Hebrew).

Gilead, I. (1989) Grar: a Chalcolithic site in Nahal Grar, northern Negev, Israel. *Journal of Field Archaeology* 16, 377–94.

Gilead, I. (1990) The Neolithic–Chalcolithic transition and the Qatifian of the northern Negev and Sinai. *Levant* 22, 47–63.

Gilead, I. (1992) Farmers and herders in southern Israel during the Chalcolithic period. Pp. 29–41 in O. Bar-Yosef and A. Khazanov (eds), *Pastoralism in the Levant: Archaeological Materials in Anthropological Perspectives*. Madison, WI: Prehistory Press.

Gilead, I. (1993) Sociopolitical organization in the northern Negev at the end of the Chalcolithic period. Pp. 82–97 in A. Biran and J. Aviram (eds), *Biblical Archaeology Today, Supplement*. Jerusalem: Israel Exploration Society.

Gilead, I. (1994) The history of the Chalcolithic settlement in the Nahal Beer Sheva area: The radiocarbon aspect. *Bulletin of the American Schools of Oriental Research* 296, 1–13.

Gilead, I. (1995) *Grar, A. Chalcolithic Site in the Northern Negev. Beer-Sheva VII*. Beer Sheva: Ben-Gurion University Press.

Gilead, I. (2002) Religio-magic behavior in the Chalcolithic period of Palestine. Pp. 103–28 in S. Ahituv and E. D. Oren (eds), *Aaron Kempinski Memorial Volume, Studies in Archaeology and Related Disciplines*. Beer Sheva, vol. 15. Beer Sheva: Ben-Gurion University of the Negev Press.

Gilead, I. (2003) Review of *The Late Neolithic and Chalcolithic Periods in the Southern Levant* by J. L. Lovell. *Mitekufat Haeven – Journal of the Israel Prehistoric Society* 33, 218–23.

Gilead, I. (2007) The Besorian: a pre-Ghassulian cultural entity. *Paléorient* 33, 33–49.

Gilead, I. and Alon, D. (1988) Excavations at proto-historic sites in the Nahal Besor and the Late Neolithic of the northern Negev. *Mitekufat Haeven – Journal of the Israel Prehistoric Society* 21, 109*–130*.

Gilead, I. and Fabian, P. (2001) Nevatim: a site of the Chalcolithic period in the northern Negev. Pp. 67–86 in A. M. Maeir and E. Baruch (eds), *Settlement, Civilization and Culture: Proceedings of the Conference in Memory of David Alon*. Ramat-Gan: Bar-Ilan University (Hebrew).

Gilead, I. and Fabian, P. (2010) Pre-Ghassulian sites in the Ramot neighborhood, Beer Sheva: chronological and cultural perspectives. Pp. 89–107 in S. Yona (ed.), *Or Le-Mayer*. Beer Sheva: Ben-Gurion University Press.

Gilead, I., Marder, O., Khalaily, H., Fabian, P., Abadi, Y. and Yisrael, Y. (2004) The Beit Eshel Chalcolithic flint workshop in Beer Sheva: a preliminary report. *Mitekufat Haeven – Journal of the Israel Prehistoric Society* 34, 245–63.

Golani, A. and Segal, D. (2002) Redefining the onset of the Early Bronze Age in southern Canaan: new evidence of ^{14}C dating from Ashkelon Afridar. Pp. 135–54 in E. C. M. van den Brink and E. Yannai (eds), *In Quest of Ancient Settlements and Landscapes, Archaeological Studies in Honour of Ram Gophna*. Tel Aviv: Ramot Publishing – Tel Aviv University.

Gopher, A. and Gophna, R. (1993) Cultures of the eighth and seventh millennia B.P. in the southern Levant: a review for the 1990s. *Journal of World Prehistory* 7, 297–352.

Gophna, R. and Sadeh, S. (1989) Excavations at Tel Tsaf: an early Chalcolithic site in the Jordan valley. *Tel Aviv* 15–16, 3–36.

Goren, Y. (1999) Petrographic analysis of the ceramic finds from the Nahal Zalzal Cave. Pp. 5*–6* in R. Cohen (ed.), *Ancient Settlements of the Central Negev, Volume 1: The Chalcolithic Period, the Early Bronze Age and Middle Bronze Age I*. Israel Antiquities Authority Reports 6. Jerusalem.

Goren, Y. (2006) The technology of the Gilat pottery assemblage. Pp. 369–93 in T. E. Levy (ed.), *Archaeology, Anthropology and Cult, The Sanctuary at Gilat, Israel*. London: Equinox.

Grigson, C. (1995) Plough and pasture in the early economy of the southern Levant. Pp. 245–68 in T. E. Levy (ed.), *The Archaeology of Society in the Holy Land*. London: Leicester University Press.

Henry, D. O. (1989) *From Foraging to Agriculture: The Levant at the End of the Ice Age*. Philadelphia, PA: University of Pennsylvania.

Henry, D. O. (1995) *Prehistoric Cultural Ecology and Evolution. Interdisciplinary Contributions to Archaeology*. New York: Plenum Press.

Joffe, A. H. and Dessel, J. P. (1995) Redefining chronology and terminology for the Chalcolithic of the southern Levant. *Current Anthropology* 36, 507–18.

Joffe, A. H., Dessel, J. P. and Hallote, R. S. (2001) The 'Gilat Woman': female iconography, Chalcolithic cult and the end of southern Levantine prehistory. *Near Eastern Archaeology* 64, 9–23.

Kozloff, B. (1974) A brief note on the lithic industries of Sinai. *Museum Ha'aretz Yearbook* 15/16, 35–49.

Kuijt, I. and Chesson, M. S. (2002) Excavations at 'Ain Waida', Jordan: new insights into Pottery Neolithic lifeways in the southern Levant. *Paléorient* 28, 109–22.

Levy, T. E. (ed.) (1987) *Shiqmim I, Studies Concerning Chalcolithic Societies in the Northern Negev Desert*. Oxford: BAR Int. Ser. 356(i).

Levy, T. E. (ed.) (2006) *Archaeology, Anthropology and Cult, The Sanctuary at Gilat, Israel*. London: Equinox.

Levy, T. E. and Burton, M. (2006) Radiocarbon dating of Gilat. Pp. 863–6 in T. E. Levy (ed.), *Archaeology, Anthropology and Cult The Sanctuary at Gilat, Israel*. London: Equinox.

Lovell, J. L. (2001) *The Late Neolithic and Chalcolithic Periods in the Southern Levant: New Data from the Site of Teleilat Ghassul, Jordan*. Oxford: BAR Int. Ser. 974.

Macdonald, E. (1932) *Prehistoric Fara, Beth Pelet II*. London: The British School of Archaeology in Egypt.

Mallon, A., Koeppel, R. and Neuville, R. (1934) *Teleilat Ghassul I*. Rome: Institut Biblique Pontifical.

Mazar, A. (1990) *Archaeology of the Land of the Bible: 10,000–586 BCE*. The Anchor Bible Reference Library. New York: Doubleday.

Mellaart, J. (1979) Egyptian and Near Eastern chronology: a dilemma? *Antiquity* 53, 6–18.

Nahshoni, P., Goren, Y., Marder, O. and Goring-Morris, N. A. (2002) A Chalcolithic site at Ramot Nof, Beer-Sheva. *'Atiqot* 43, 1*–24* (Hebrew).

Neuville, R. (1930) Notes de préhistore Palestinienne. *The Journal of the Palestine Oriental Society* 10, 193–221.

Noy, T. (1998) Flint artifacts. Pp. 269–332 in C. Epstein (ed.), *The Chalcolithic Culture of the Golan*. Israel Antiquities Authority Reports 4. Jerusalem.

Philip, G. (2006) Subsistence, resource procurement and manufacture in the southern Levant *c.*5000–3000 BC: Tell esh-Shuna its regional context. Paper presented at Culture, Chronology and the Chalcolithic: Transitions in the Late Prehistory of the Southern Levant, Workshop at the 5th International Conference on the Archaeology of the Ancient Near East, Madrid, April 2006.

Philip, G. and Baird, D. (eds) (2000) *Ceramics and Change in the Early Bronze Age of the Southern Levant*. Sheffield: Sheffield Academic Press.

Perrot, J. (1955) The excavations at Tell Abu Matar near Beersheba. *Israel Exploration Journal* 5, 17–40, 73–84, 167–89.

Perrot, J. (1961) Notes and news: Gat-Guvrin. *Israel Exploration Journal* 11, 76.

Perrot, J. (1984) Structures d'habitat, mode de la vie et environment: les villages souterrains des pasteurs de Beershéva dans le sud d'Israël, au IVe Millénaire Avant l'ère Chrétienne. *Paléorient* 10, 75–92.

Rosen, S. (1984) Kvish Harif: preliminary investigations at a Late Neolithic site in the central Negev. *Paléorient* 10, 111–21.

Rosen, S. (1993) Metals, rocks, specialization, and the beginning of urbanism in the northern Negev. Pp. 41–56 in A. Biran and J. Aviram (eds), *Biblical Archaeology Today, 1990, Proceedings of the Second International Congress on Biblical Archaeology, Supplement*. Jerusalem: Israel Exploration Society.

Roshwalb, A. F. (1981) Proto-history in the Wadi Ghazzeh: A Typological Study Based on the Macdonald Excavations. Unpublished PhD thesis, University of London.

Sapir, E. (1924) Culture, genuine and spurious. *The American Journal of Sociology* 29, 401–29.

Shalem, D. (2003) The Chalcolithic Period Sites in the Mountains of the Galilee – Settlement Distribution and Ceramic Characteristics. Unpublished MA dissertation, Haifa University (Hebrew).

Trigger, B. G. (1989) *A History of Archaeological Thought*. Cambridge: Cambridge University Press.

Wright, G. E. (1937) Palestine in the Chalcolithic age. *Bulletin of the American Schools of Oriental Research* 66, 21–5.

Yannai, E. (forthcoming) *Nazur – An Early Chalcolithic Site in the Northern Coastal Plain – Israel*. Israel Antiquities Authority Reports. Jerusalem.

3. Ghrubba: Ware or Culture?

Zeidan Kafafi

Introduction

The editors have invited the contributors to this volume to discuss chronological and terminological problems relating to the Chalcolithic period in southern Levant in the context of their own datasets. They ask us to engage with our conceptual assumptions. As a local archaeologist in Jordan I am fortunate to have excavated several of the key well-stratified Late Neolithic and Chalcolithic pottery assemblages: Abu Thawwab (Kafafi 2001; Obeidat 1995), Abu Hamid (Dollfus and Kafafi 1988; Dollfus and Kafafi 1993; Lovell *et al.* 1997), Ain Ghazal (Kafafi 1990; 1995) and Wadi Shu'eib (Simmons *et al.* 1989; 2001). In addition, I have worked on numerous other Pottery Neolithic assemblages such as Khirbet edh-Dharih (Bossut and Kafafi 2005) and Ain Rahub (Kafafi 1989). It is clear to me that the culmination of data over the last 20 years allows a reassessment of a cultural phase not recognized in the literature (for a summary of habitually discussed 'cultural phases' see Gopher and Gophna 1993). This paper presents a study of a pottery assemblage excavated a long time ago: Ghrubba, near Tell el Shuna (South), which has parallels with other, more recently excavated collections at better-dated and better-stratified sites. Here I explore the possibility that a particular ceramic ware group can be an indicator of a Pottery Neolithic 'culture'.

Excavations at Ghrubba were limited and the publication is brief (Mellaart 1956), but a fuller understanding of the assemblage is now possible as a result of more recent excavations of other assemblages, especially Abu Hamid Phase I (Lovell *et al.* 1997) and Jebel Abu Thawwab (Obeidat 1995), which have produced parallel ceramic material to that found at Ghrubba, specifically in levels 5–16 (Mellaart 1956). A reliable series of ^{14}C dates from Abu Hamid Phase I also allow us to assign the Ghrubba material to its proper place.

The concept of culture is much debated in anthropological research and the relationship between material culture and actual culture is not simple (see Rowan and Lovell, this volume). Ceramics are not the only factor in identifying a 'culture' during the Late Neolithic in the southern Levant. However, the similarity of the Ghrubba ceramics to those from the better-stratified Abu Hamid Phase I is striking to me, and forms the focus of this paper. It is hoped that this paper will prompt discussions rather than provide absolute answers.

Pottery as an indicator of culture

As noted above, the concept of culture is debated among anthropologists and archaeologists. As archaeologists we study the remnants of past behaviour, and various aspects of that behaviour may reflect past cultural traits. Thus culture is best studied from several material-culture sets, and in order to convincingly define a culture all these materials must be discussed (Clarke 1978). Nonetheless, in discussions of the Pottery Neolithic period in the south of the Levant, ceramics remain the dominant dataset for defining cultures because, with a pottery vessel, the researcher may study several aspects: the manufacturing techniques, surface treatment, fabric and morphology. As Chilton puts it, pottery vessels have implicit and explicit information, which can aid explanations of different styles and/or cultures (Chilton 1999a). Moreover, it has been argued that pottery decoration may be approached 'through analogy with ornament of the person, another transform of culture' (David *et al.* 1988, 365). Thus researchers argue that decoration (and other aspects of artefact form) can be a means sending messages (Wobst 1977). But understanding how these messages work, who will read the sent messages, and who is transmitting to whom, are more complicated questions, which anthropologists have sought to address via studies of contemporary ethnic groups (David *et al.*

1988; Chilton 1999a; Wobst 1999). Thus we are returned to the problem of understanding social interaction through objects: is it best understood via the artefacts or via the makers and users of these same artefacts?

Nevertheless, the pattern of material culture is symbolic and serves to transmit culture. Material culture encodes, mediates and enforces a pattern of social relations (David *et al.* 1988). A certain mode of pottery production thus may be passed down via a lineage of one family, but may also represent aspects of a broader culture (both in the temporal and the geographic sense). Chilton notes that typologies and classifications of material culture form the core of archaeological interpretation and that they provide a means of expressing time–space relationships in material culture (1999b, 44). It is precisely those time–space relationships that concern us when we are building cultural chronologies.

Wobst argues that 'the number of production steps is virtually invisible when an artefact is finished and placed into use' (1999, 123). However, the technical aspect of pottery manufacturing is accessible and is one way to explore the identification of cultures (Ali 2005). Thus, we argue that pottery production may be seen as a cultural aspect, but that an assemblage of vessels may not represent a distinct and defined group of people: in studying ancient pottery production in Jordan and Palestine scholars commonly use terms such as local and regional, or Ghassulian or Beer es-Saba' Ware (for the Chalcolithic), or Esdraelon and Khirbet Kerak Ware (for the Early Bronze Age) (Amiran 1969), but they rarely refer specifically to ethnic groups. Actually, it is only during the last few decades that scholars have directly attributed pottery assemblages excavated at historical sites to ethnic groups (Golden 2004, 229).

The excavations at Ghrubba

In 1953 Mellaart excavated the site of Ghrubba, Jordan, located on the southern side of Wadi Nimrin, about 2 km west of the police station in the town Shunah South (see Figure 1.1), on the main Amman–Jerusalem road (Mellaart 1956). The extent of the site has not been determined. The excavated pottery sherds and flint tools were uncovered in a pit exposed in the cut made by Wadi Nimrin (Mellaart 1956, fig. 3, reproduced here as Figure 3.1). Mellaart assigned part of the contents of this pit to the Pottery Neolithic period.

At the time the sounding at Ghrubba was published it was the only Neolithic site to produce such a pottery type, and thus it was thought that this type of pottery was limited to this site. However, as stated above, recent archaeological excavations conducted at the sites of Abu Hamid, Abu Thawwab and 'Ain Ghazal produced similar pottery sherds. I argue here that because similar pottery assemblages to those found at Ghrubba are found at a significant number of sites in the southern Levant it may be argued that this represents an archaeological culture in which people at several sites used the same forms of vessels, rather than a pottery tradition found at just one or two villages.

Stratigraphy

Soundings were made at the site in 1953 by J. Mellaart (1956). In 1976 the site was resurveyed by the Jordan Valley Survey team (Yassine *et al.* 1988) and the collected material studied by the author (Kafafi 1982). In his sounding Mellaart recognized 16 layers. Layers 1–4 had been partially disturbed by a modern burial and produced an assemblage of pottery sherds related to the Ghassulian culture. Sealed by these layers was a feature described/drawn as a pit dug through a layer of gravel down to the underlying soft limestone. The 'pit' has an oval shape and measuring approximately 5 m × 3 m, and is 1.80 m deep. Inside this, 12 layers (5–16) which consisted of ash and gravel were identified. Only one floor (Layer 15a) was found (Figure 3.1). The nature of the deposits suggests that they hold greater integrity than those of a refuse pit. It is possible that the pit represents some kind of dwelling pit similar to those more recently excavated at the site of Abu Hamid where several pits, some deep, have been excavated from contemporary levels (Dollfus and Kafafi 1993, 244; Lovell *et al.* 1997, fig. 3). Ghrubba probably contains other unexcavated archaeological structures and materials.

The pottery excavated in Layers 5–16

The pottery excavated in Layers 5–16 by Mellaart was mostly hand-made and painted (Figure 3.2–3.6). The excavator distinguished four categories:

1) Plain or coarse ware: in this collection, bowls with knobs and with flaring sides, as well as small jars with lug handles, were recognized. Straw temper was visible only in the case of a few coarse white bowls (Mellaart 1956, 30). Bow-rim jars similar to those found in Munhata, Wadi Rabah and Jericho VIII were encountered in Layers 12, 14, and 16 at Ghrubba (Mellaart 1956, figs 4.40–4.42; an example is reproduced here as Figure 3.2.2). This may indicate that bow-rims appear as earlier in the Pottery Neolithic.
2) Painted and incised ware: this group is characterized by a red or brown paint or wash covering the pots (Figure 3.2.3), as well as incised decoration which consists of a horizontal band below the rim of the bowls or at the base of the neck of jars. In the case of jugs the decoration passed through the opening of the loop handles. Usually zigzag or herringbone decorations appear with the horizontal band (Figure 3.3.1).
3) Burnished ware: this type of pottery is very rare. The excavator notes only one burnished sherd, a bowl fragment (Mellaart 1956, 32, fig. 4.16).
4) Painted ware: The painted ware is the most common at Ghrubba. It was hand-made and well fired. The surface of the vessels is puff, pink, or whitish. The painted

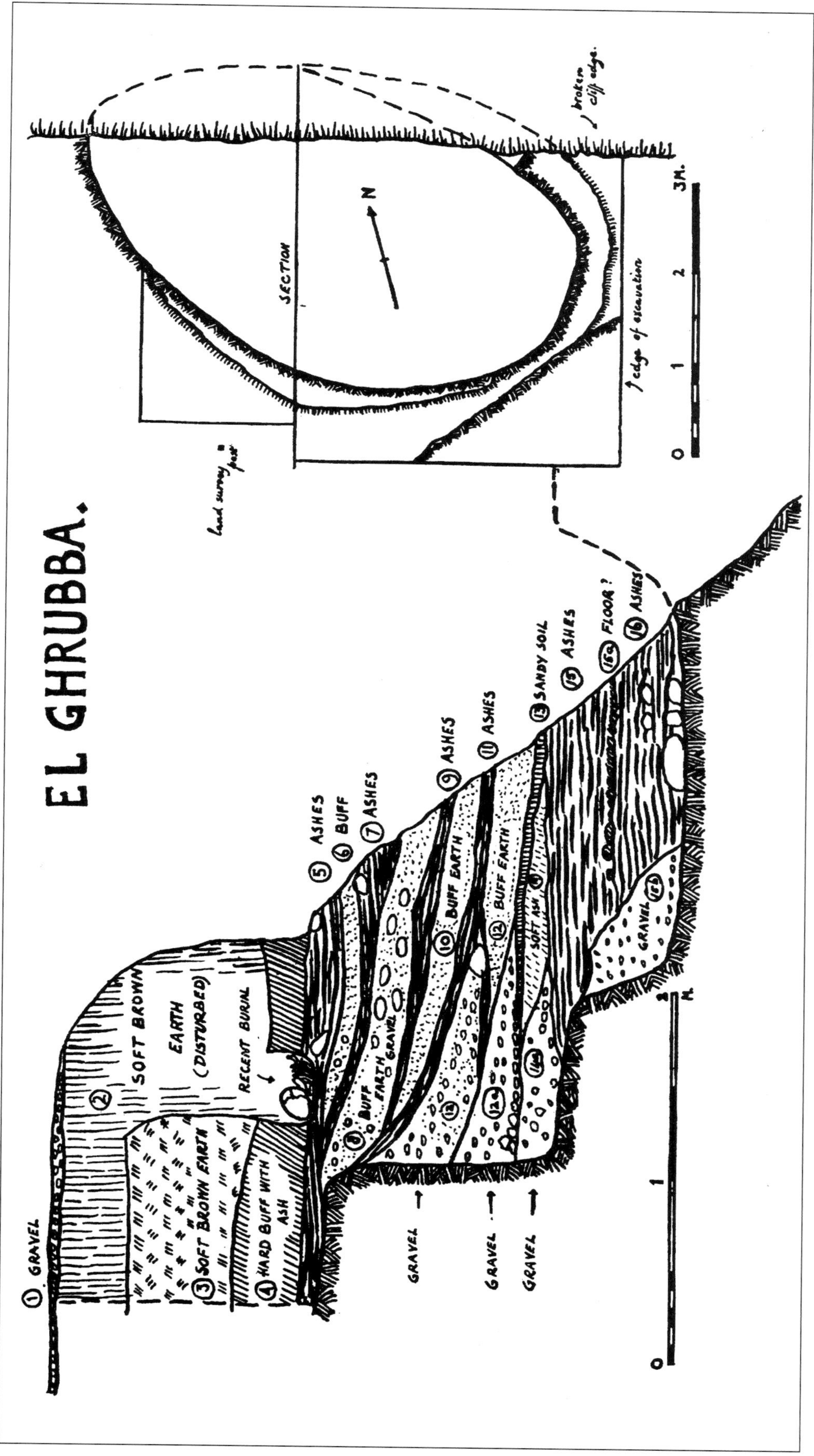

Figure 3.1 Stratigraphy at Ghrubba (after Mellaart 1956, fig. 3)

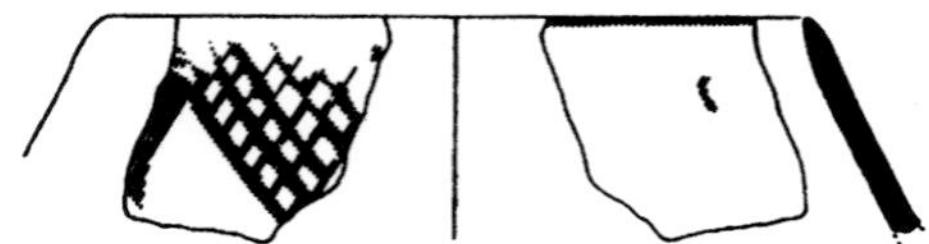

1. Abu Hamid

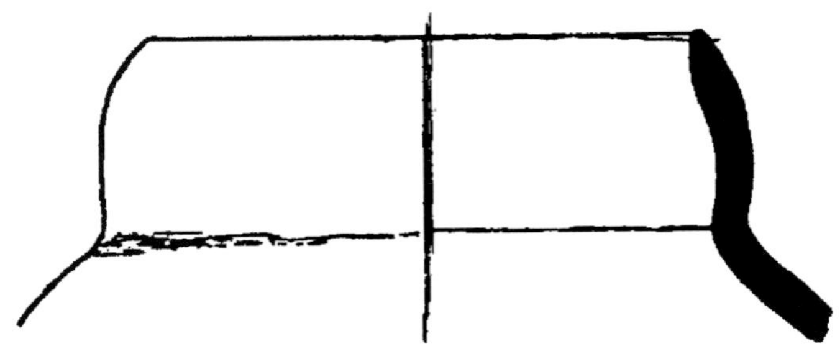

2. Ghrubba

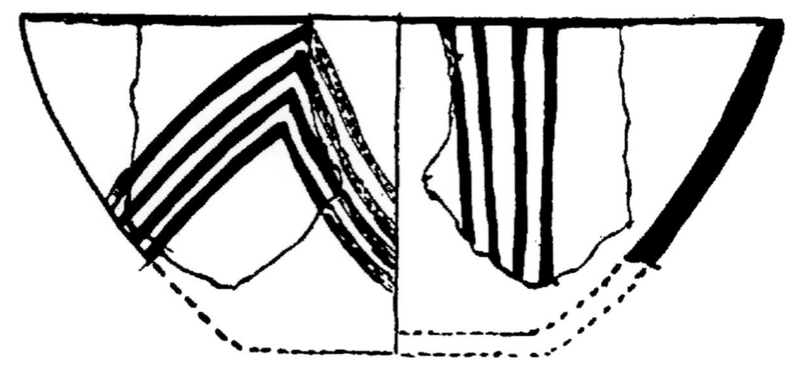

3. Ghrubba

4. Abu Hamid

Figure 3.2 Ghrubba ware from Ghrubba, Abu Hamid and Abu Thawwab (Ghrubba pieces after various items from Mellaart 1956, figs 4–6): Ghrubba ware jars

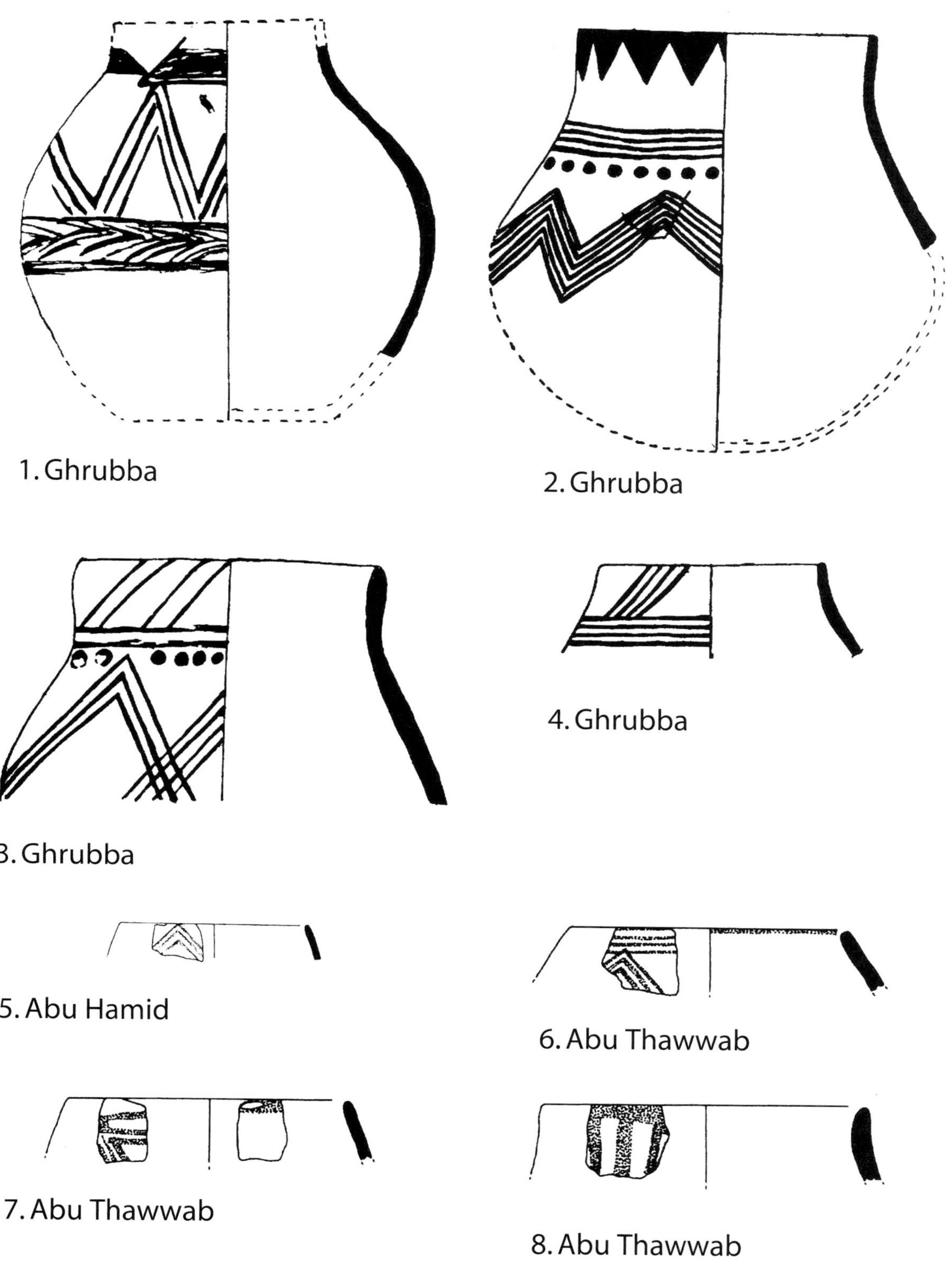

Figure 3.3 Ghrubba ware from Ghrubba, Abu Hamid and Abu Thawwab (Ghrubba pieces after various items from Mellaart 1956, figs 4–6): Ghrubba ware jars

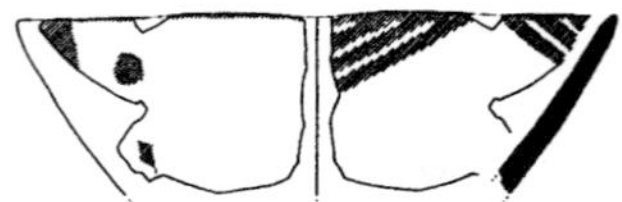

Figure 3.4 Ghrubba ware from Ghrubba, Abu Hamid and Abu Thawwab (Ghrubba pieces after various items from Mellaart 1956, figs 4–6): Ghrubba ware deep bowls

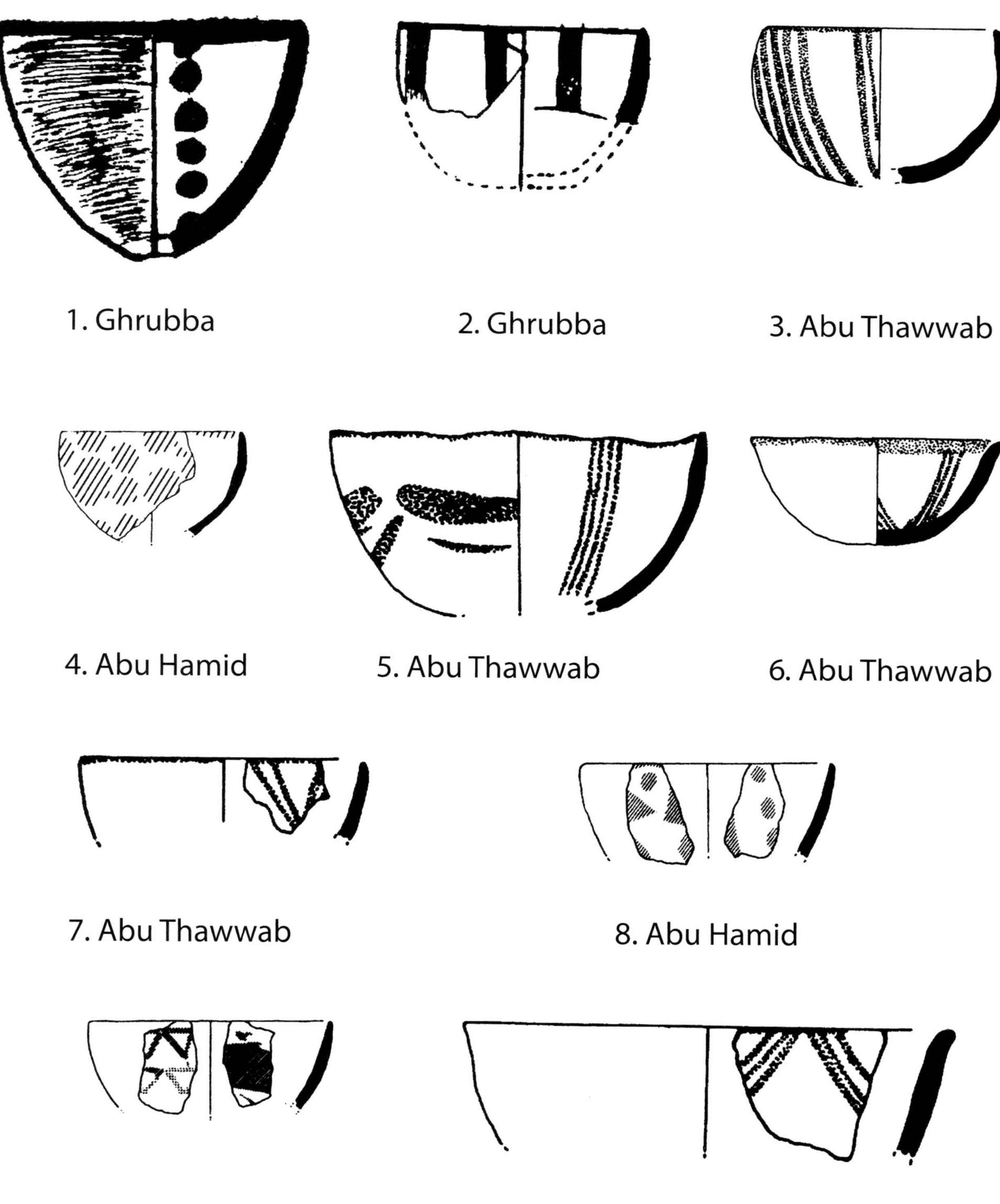

Figure 3.5 Ghrubba ware from Ghrubba, Abu Hamid and Abu Thawwab (Ghrubba pieces after various items from Mellaart 1956, figs 4–6): Ghrubba ware cups and small bowls

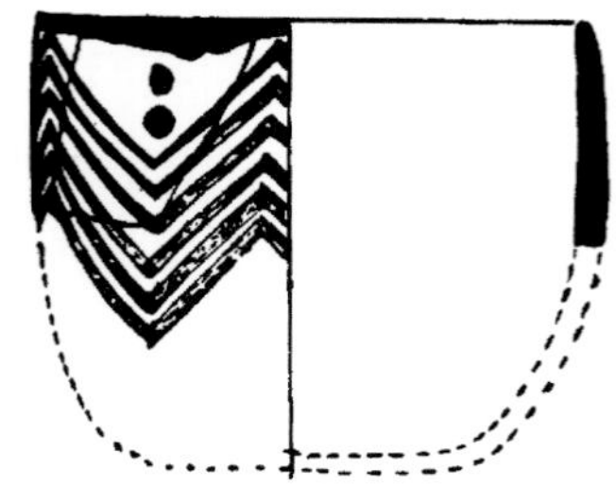

1. Ghrubba

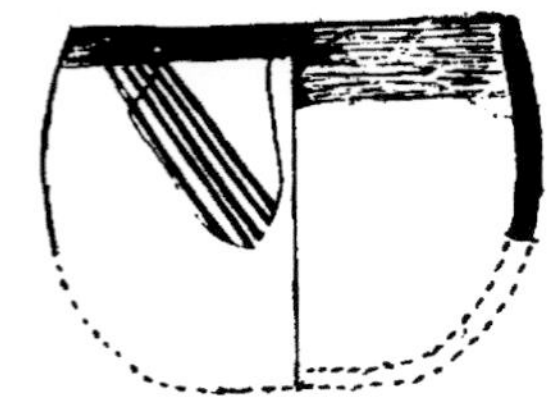

2. Ghrubba

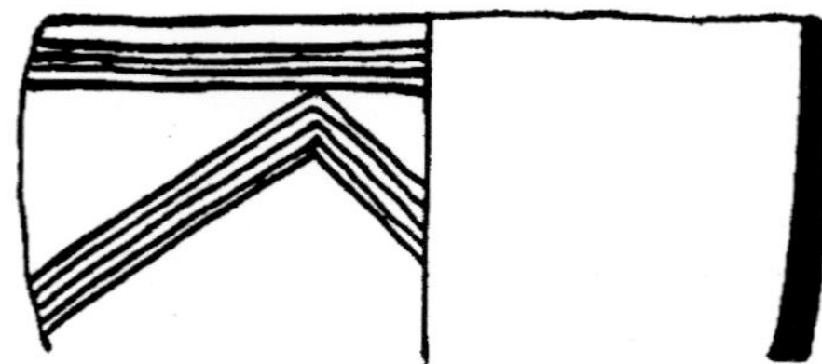

3. Ghrubba

4. Abu Thawwab

5. Abu Thawwab

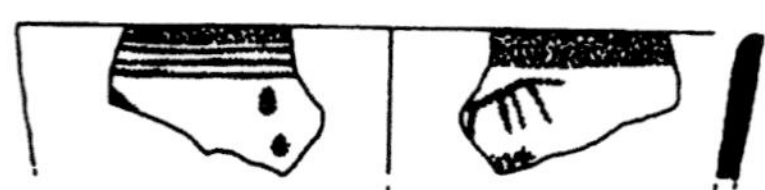

6. Abu Thawwab

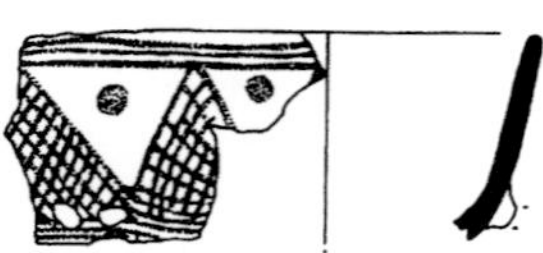

7. Abu Thawwab

Figure 3.6 Ghrubba ware from Ghrubba, Abu Hamid and Abu Thawwab (Ghrubba pieces after various items from Mellaart 1956, figs 4–6): Ghrubba ware deep bowls

decorations consist of triangles (Figures 3.3.1–2, 3.5.8), chevrons (Figures 3.2.3–4; 3.3.3, 5–6), diagonal parallel lines (Figures 3.3.4; 3.5.5), intersected lines (Figures 3.3.3; 3.4.1; 3.6.5, 7), zig-zags (Figure 3.3.1–2; 3.6.1) and dots (Figures 3.3.2–3; 3.5.1, 4, 8; 3.6.1). In many cases a combination of several decorative elements was painted (Figures 3.3.2; 3.5.8; 3.6.1, 7). The vessel forms include cups (Figures 3.2.4; 3.5.1–2), bowls (Figures 3.4; 3.5.3; 3.6.4–6) and jars, including necked (Figures 3.3.2–4) and holemouth (Figures 3.2.1; 3.3.5–7) types. The excavator judged that this Ghrubba material represented a different pottery tradition from that of Jericho IX, comparing it with Hassuna Archaic painted ware (Mellaart 1956, 31). He noted that similar painted pottery vessels were also encountered at Al Amuq B, Mersin and other sites in Cilicia in Turkey (Mellaart 1956, 32). The vessel forms include the bow-rim jars similar to those from Jericho, Wadi Rabah, Byblos (Jubail), and sites in the Beqa' region in Lebanon such as Tell el-Jisr, Tell 'Ain Nfaikh and Tell Ard Tleili (Copeland and Wescombe 1966; Kirkbride 1969). However, more recent work within the Jordan valley has shown that similar painted decoration is known from sites like Abu Hamid, Beth Shan and in the mountains ranges at Jebel Abu Thawwab (see parallels featured on Figures 3.2–3.6). There are also parallels with material from Tell Zaf (Garfinkel 1999, pl. XIX.7; *cf.* Lovell 2001, 46).

'Ghrubba' ware and other cultural traits

The ceramic assemblage from the Basal Levels at Abu Hamid, or Phase I, is studied and preliminarily published (Lovell *et al.* 1997). The material was excavated from two trenches transecting, the first measuring 1.50 × 20m (running north–south), and the second measuring 2 × 30 m (east–west) (Dollfus and Kafafi 1993, 242). A wide variety of decorated sherds parallel those excavated at Ghrubba (Lovell *et al.* 1997, 366). The results of the excavation in those trenches indicated that the site was first inhabited during the second half of the 6th millennium BC. The archaeological remains relating to this period consisted of pits, a series of floors often covered by a thin layer of ashes, fireplaces, an elliptical structure and other materials such as pottery, flints and bones (Lovell *et al.* 1997). Abu Hamid can therefore be considered a key site, producing well-stratified material dated to the 6th and 5th millennia in Jordan (Figure 3.7), and the Phase I assemblage can be used as a reference for other parallel pottery collections.

Both at Abu Hamid and at Ghrubba the ceramic material appears to come from pit dwellings; as noted above, the Ghrubba ceramics appear to come from layers within a large pit feature (Figure 3.1). Although the nature of the publication and the small size of the excavation make it impossible to be sure at Ghrubba, this is certainly the case at Abu Hamid (Lovell *et al.* 1997, 363, fig. 1).

Dating

Mellaart proposed that the Ghrubba pottery assemblage found in Layers 5–16 should be attributed to a period earlier in date than Jericho IX and the Yarmoukian. Moore, on the other hand, suggested that Ghrubba should be related to the Early Chalcolithic period and not the Neolithic, stressing that the pottery Mellaart published strongly resembles the Ghassulian (Moore 1973, 60). I have previously argued that Ghrubba pottery is to be considered Late Neolithic rather than Chalcolithic (Kafafi 1982, 200; 1987, 37). Furthermore, based on similarities with assemblages found in better stratigraphic positions (Abu Hamid and Abu Thawwab), I argued that the material be placed within the Late Neolithic 1 (*c.*5500–5000 BC), contemporaneous with Jericho IX/PNA and the Yarmoukian traditions (Kafafi 1998, 132).

As we have seen, at Abu Hamid similar painted material is found in Phase I (Lovell *et al.* 1997), and Obeidat (1995, 86) found that Ghrubba ware was found in Yarmoukian levels at Abu Thawwab and dated it to the same period. Garfinkel therefore argues that Ghrubba ware should be attributed to the Neolithic and treats it the same as Yarmoukian/Sha'ar Hagolan rather than a separate pottery tradition:

> Small changes in the proportion of painted and incised decoration cannot be used as cultural marks in the Pottery Neolithic period (Garfinkel 1999, 103).

However, the question of dating is more problematic than this: if Ghrubba-type sherds are part of the Yarmoukian repertoire, how can we explain the fact no classic incised Yarmoukian sherds were found with 'Ghrubba' sherds at Abu Hamid (Dollfus and Kafafi 1993; Kafafi and Dollfus 1997; Lovell *et al.* 1997)? This suggests to me that Ghrubba ware belongs to a phase distinct from the Yarmoukian phase. As stated above, the Abu Hamid Phase I material is well-dated, providing dates ranging from 5300–5000 BC (calibrated) (see Figure 3.7), entirely consistent with my earlier statements (Kafafi 1998, 132). Thus, although we still require ^{14}C dates from levels belonging to the Ghrubba phase, the above dates are sufficient to provide a general range.

Given that the argument here rests largely on the presence of a particular painted pottery style, it is important to address the question of Beth Shan and Tell Zaf wares, which are sometimes linked with Ghrubba ware. Garfinkel published painted pottery sherds found at the sites of Beth Shan and Tell Zaf (dated by him to the Middle Chalcolithic, *cf.* Braun 2004, see also Gophna and Sadeh 1989) that appear similar to those found at Ghrubba (Garfinkel 1999, XIX 4, 7). These sherds were excavated from pits and the excavator considered them similar to those from Stratum XVIII at Beth Shan (Fitzgerald 1935, pl. III, 17); they thus make up the phase termed 'Stratum XVIII and pits' (Tzori 1977, cited in Garfinkel 1999, 183).

The excavations at Abu Hamid and Abu Thawwab have confirmed that Ghrubba ware is distinct from that of Jericho

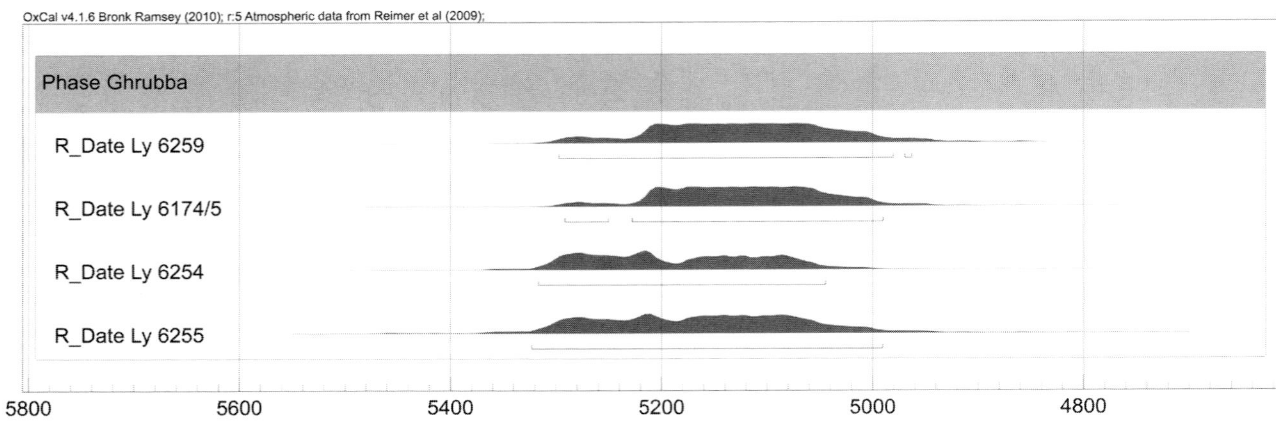

Figure 3.7 ¹⁴C dates from Abu Hamid

IX/PNA and the Yarmoukian. Ghrubba's closest contacts appear to be with sites located in the northern part of the Jordan valley: Abu Hamid, Beth Shan. In addition, the site of Jebel Abu Thawwab, located on the Amman–Irbid highway, also produced a good collection of Ghrubba ware vessels.

Conclusion

During the second half of the 6th millennium BC, several pottery assemblages were in use: the Jericho PNA/IX, the Yarmoukian and Ghrubba. This might be explained in different ways: first, that there were three different groups of people, each one of which had its own pottery manufacture; and, second, that the Ghrubba ware 'diffusion' represents the movements of several ethnic groups that lived during the same period of time in this region. Either way, there may have been a very diverse archaeological culture (social groups?) in this part of the Levant. It is true that we can not define a culture only by pottery grouping and it may not be acceptable to give assemblages such an ethnic weight. However, as we stated above, pottery production, including 'style' (Wobst 1999), reflects cultural aspects and can therefore be an important indicator for a culture.

During the Late Neolithic southern Levantine ceramics were diverse (three traditions) and produced in a wide variety of social and ecological contexts, but all have followed the same manufacturing techniques. Therefore, the technical approach is perhaps not warranted or useful. Instead, an attribute analysis of surface treatment has been preferred as a means to highlight the main choices available for Jordan's Late Neolithic potters. As a result of the focus on decoration, vessels are shown to provide information about subsistence, settlement, political organization, social integration and social boundaries.

Ghrubba ware, as is evident from this paper, had a wider distribution across the Jordan valley, and into the highlands, than has previously been recognized. If Mellaart's associations are correct then it may also have extended into southern Anatolia and perhaps had contact with northern Iraq – but this would suggest that it was more of a cultural phase rather than a part of the Yarmoukian or Jericho PNA. Nevertheless, it is possible that the Ghrubba phase and the Yarmoukian coincide to a degree, with the Yarmoukian beginning slightly earlier and overlapping with the Ghrubba phase, which is dated at Abu Hamid from *c.*5500 BC cal. Although the term 'culture' has very wide meanings and includes and reflects several human behavioural aspects and thoughts, in this case the wide distribution of a pottery ware in several geographic regions might be considered an indicator of human interactions (trade relationships, human movements and transfer of ideas). In this sense, the argument is no less sound than that put forward for Halaf and 'Ubaid ceramics as indicators of cultures.

Acknowledgements

Sincere thanks are due to Yorke Rowan for reading the text, making the necessary comments and editing the English language, and to Jaimie Lovell for presenting the lecture in Madrid on my behalf and helping to edit this paper. I am also grateful to Susanne Kerner and Nabil Ali for reading the text and commenting on it, and to Sandra Rosendahl for assistance with the figures.

Note regarding the plates

The illustrations are produced with sherds represented at only approximately equivalent scales because of the quality of the early publications.

References

Ali, N. (2005) *The Development of Pottery Technology from the Late Sixth to the fifth millennium BC in Northern Jordan. Ethno- and Archaeological Studies: Abu Hamid as a Key Site*, Oxford: BAR Int. Ser. 1422.

Amiran, R. (1969) *Ancient Pottery of the Holy Land*. Jerusalem: Massada Press.

Bossut, P. and Kafafi, Z. (2005) Foulles de Khirbet edh-Dharih, II. Un site néolithique à céramique (PNA) en Jordanie du sud (DH 49/WHS 524). *Syria* 82, 5–48.

Braun, E. (2004) *Early Beth-Shan (Strata XIX–XIII). G. M. Fitzgerald's Deep Cut on the Tell*. University Museum Monograph 121. Philadelphia, PA: University of Pennsylvania Museum of Archaeology and Anthropology.

Chilton, E. (ed.) (1999a) *Material Meanings. Critical Approaches to the Interpretation of Material Culture*. Salt Lake City, UT: University of Utah Press.

Chilton, E. (1999b) One size fits all. Typology and alternatives for ceramic research. Pp. 44–60 in E. Chilton (ed.), *Material Meanings. Critical Approaches to the Interpretation of Material Culture*. Salt Lake City, UT: University of Utah Press.

Clarke, D. (1978) *Analytical Archaeology*. London: Methuen.

Copeland, P. J. and Wescombe, P. J. (1966) Inventory of stone-age sites in Lebanon. *Mélange de l'Université Saint-Joseph de Beyrouth* 42, 1–174.

David, N., Sterner, J. and Gavua, K. (1988) Why pots are decorated. *Current Anthropology* 29/3, 365–89.

Dollfus, G. (1993) Recent researches at Abu Hamid. *Annual of the Department of Antiquities of Jordan* 37, 241–62.

Dollfus, G. and Kafafi, Z. (eds) (1988) *Abu Hamid, village du 4e millénaire de la vallée du Jourdain*. Amman: Economic Press.

Fitzgerald, G. M. (1935) The earliest pottery of Beth-Shean. *The Museum Journal* 24, 6–7.

Garfinkel, Y. (1999) *Neolithic and Chalcolithic Pottery of the Southern Levant*. Qedem 39, Jerusalem Institute of Archaeology, The Hebrew University of Jerusalem.

Golden, J. M. (2004) *Ancient Canaan and Israel. New Perspectives*. Santa Barbara, CA: ABC CLIO.

Gopher, A. and Gophna, R. (1993) Cultures of the eighth and seventh millennia BP in the southern Levant: A review for the 1990s. *Journal of World Prehistory* 7, 297–353.

Gophna, R. and Sadeh, S. (1989) Excavations at Tel Tsaf: an early Chalcolithic site in the Jordan Valley. *Tel Aviv* 15/16, 3–36.

Kafafi, Z. (1982) The Neolithic of Jordan (East Bank). Unpublished PhD thesis, Frei Universität Berlin.

Kafafi, Z. (1987) The Pottery Neolithic in Jordan in connection with other Near Eastern regions. Pp. 33–9 in A. Hadidi (ed.), *Studies in the History and Archaeology of Jordan* 3. Amman: The Department of Antiquities of Jordan.

Kafafi, Z. (1989) Late Neolithic 1 pottery from Ain Rahub. *Zeitschrift des Deutschen Palästina-Vereins* 105, 1–17.

Kafafi, Z. (1990) Early pottery contexts from Ain Ghazal, Jordan. *Bulletin of the American Schools of Oriental Research* 280, 15–31.

Kafafi, Z. (1995) Decorative elements on the excavated pottery at 'Ayn Ghazal. Pp. 545–55 in K. 'Amr, F. Zaydine and M. Zaghlul (eds), *Studies in The History and Archaeology of Jordan* 5. Amman: The Department of Antiquities of Jordan.

Kafafi, Z. (1998) The Late Neolithic in Jordan. Pp. 127–39 in D. O. Henry (ed.), *The Prehistoric Archaeology of Jordan*. Oxford: BAR Int. Ser. 705.

Kafafi, Z. (2001) *Jebel Abu Thawwab (Er-Rumman), Central Jordan. The Late Neolithic and Early Bronze Age I Occupations*. Bibliotheca Neolithica Asiae Meridionalis et Occidentalis and Yarmouk University Monograph of the Institute of Archaeology and Anthropology 3. Berlin: ex oriente.

Kafafi, Z. and Dollfus, G. (1997) Abu Hamid, Tell. Pp. 402–3 in A. M. Meyers (ed.), *The Oxford Encyclopedia of Archaeology in the Near East*. Oxford: Oxford University Press.

Kirkbride, D. (1969) Early Byblos and the Beqa'. *Mélange de l'Université Saint-Joseph de Beyrouth* 45, 43–60.

Lovell, J. L. (2001) *The Late Neolithic and Chalcolithic Periods in the Southern Levant. New Data from the Site Teleilat Ghassul, Jordan*. Oxford: BAR Int. Ser. 974.

Lovell, J. L., Kafafi, Z. and Dollfus, G. (1997) A preliminary note on the ceramics from the basal levels of Abu Hamid. Pp. 361–70 in H. G. K. Gebel, Z. Kafafi and G. Rollefson (eds), *The Prehistory of Jordan, II. Perspectives from 1997*. Studies in Early Near Eastern Production, Subsistence, and Environment 4. Berlin: ex oriente.

Mellaart, J. (1956) The Neolithic site of Ghrubba. *Annual of the Department of Antiquities of Jordan* 3, 24–40.

Moore, A. M. T. (1973) The Late Neolithic in Palestine. *Levant* 5, 36–68.

Obeidat, D. (1995) *Die neolitiische Keramik aus Abu Thawwab, Jordanien*. Studies in Early Near Eastern Production, Subsistence, and Environment 2. Berlin: ex oriente.

Simmons, A., Kafafi, Z., Rollefson, G. and Moyer, K. (1989) The excavations at Wadi Shu'eib. A major Neolithic settlement in central Jordan. *Annual of the Department of Antiquities of Jordan* 33, 27–42.

Simmons, A., Rollefson, G. O., Kafafi, Z., Mandel, R. D., al-Nahar, M., Cooper, J., Köhler-Rollefson, I. and Durand, K. R. (2001) Wadi Shu'eib, a large Neolithic community in central Jordan: final report of test excavations. *Bulletin of the American Schools of Oriental Research* 321, 1–39.

Tzori, N. (1977) Beth-She'an in the Chalcolithic period. *Eretz Israel* 13, 76–81.

Wobst, H. M. (1977) Stylistic behavior and information exchange. Pp. 317–42 in C. E. Cleland (ed.), *Papers for the Director: Essays in Honor of James Griffen*. Ann Arbor, MI: University of Michigan Museum of Anthropology Anthropological Papers 61.

Wobst, H. M. (1999) Style in archaeology or archaeologists in style. Pp. 118–32 in E. S. Chilton (ed.), *Material Meanings. Critical Approaches to the Interpretation of Material Culture*. Salt Lake City, UT: The University of Utah Press.

Yassine, K., Ibrahim, M. and Sauer, J. (1988) The east of Jordan Valley Survey, 1976. Pp. 189–207 in K. Yassine (ed.), *Archaeology of Jordan: Essays and Reports*. Amman: Department of Archaeology, University of Jordan.

4. Changes in Material Culture at Late Neolithic Tabaqat al-Bûma, in Wadi Ziqlab, Northern Jordan

Edward B. Banning, Kevin Gibbs and Seiji Kadowaki

The transition from the Neolithic to the Chalcolithic in the southern Levant has been a major research problem among Near Eastern archaeologists since the 1950s. One of the early debates was whether the southern Levantine Chalcolithic was a result of cultural intrusion from the north (Perrot 1955; de Vaux 1966; Kenyon 1979) or indigenous development from local Neolithic cultures (Moore 1973). More recent syntheses (Garfinkel 1999; Gilead 1988) and publication of material from 'pre-Ghassulian' assemblages (*e.g.*, Bourke 1997; Lovell 2001; Lovell *et al.* 1997; 2004) have focused on indigenous development and attempted to fit the growing body of evidence into the cultural systematics of those early years through reference to 'Wadi Rabah' (Kaplan 1959) and other cultural entities. However, this task suffers not only from a lack of consensus on the nature of these entities (Banning 2002), but also from a growing awareness that the old systematics are outdated and unrealistic models of cultural variation around this transition (Banning 2007; Lovell *et al.* 2004, 263–4; *cf.* Campbell 2007 for Halaf). A better alternative is to study how the material culture varies over time and space with well-dated sequences from many sites and with recognition that material culture at these sites did not change in unison or necessarily in the same ways.

In this paper we present evidence for some of the changes in material culture over a millennium or so at the small Late Neolithic settlement of Tabaqat al-Bûma, in northern Jordan, and attempt to place them in the wider context of the 6th millennium cal BC. The successive occupations of farmsteads at this site provide small but relatively well-dated assemblages for investigation of these changes and their socio-economic implications. Because the sample sizes for many categories of artefact are so small, the focus will be on pottery and chipped-stone artefacts. Attention to the stratigraphy of the site and site-formation processes in each level allows us to identify gradual transitions that defy traditional assignment to entities such as 'Yarmoukian' or 'Wadi Rabah'.

The stratigraphic and occupational sequence at Tabaqat al-Bûma

In 1987, subsurface survey of a small stream terrace in Wadi Ziqlab discovered a previously unsuspected site with Epipalaeolithic and Neolithic artefacts when a 3 m × 1 m test trench intersected a slab-covered cist grave (Banning *et al.* 1989). On the floor of this cist grave were the poorly preserved skeletal remains of two adults (Shafiq 1996, 12–15) along with a small group of ceramic and stone vessels, a stone palette or grinding slab and a pierced stone disk or spindle whorl. Both Epipalaeolithic microliths (mainly narrow, backed bladelets) and distinctively Neolithic tools were found in this trench (Area A) and in a 1 m × 1 m square (Area B) south of it. Subsequent excavations at the site in 1990 and 1992 exposed about 350 m^2 of the site's uppermost levels, uncovering fairly well-preserved architecture belonging to what appeared to be a small Late Neolithic farmstead (Banning *et al.* 1994). Smaller areas of deeper levels, down to less than 25 m^2 of the Epipalaeolithic levels, were uncovered.

Stratigraphic analysis of the site by Blackham (1994; 1997), with revisions by Kadowaki (2007), provides the basis for the subdivision of the Late Neolithic use of the site into five phases that are mainly distinguished by episodes of construction and demolition of structures. Blackham originally identified four such phases, numbered 1 to 4, but his phase 1 included two quite distinct uses of the site, leading us to subdivide it. To clarify this renumbering of the phasing, we add the prefix LN to those phases that belong to the Late Neolithic. An earlier

Phase	Locus	Locus type	Date BP	±1σ	Comments
LN4	E3319	Outdoor sediment	6190	70	
	E3314	Room fill between two floors	6350	70	
	D3516	Wall collapse	6590	70	Residual?
LN3	G3418	Ashy deposit in a hearth	6380	70	
	E3326	Outdoor sediment	6490	70	
	E3431	Outdoor sediment	6630	80	
	F3417	Outdoor sediment	6670	60	
	E3326	Outdoor sediment	6900	70	Residual
LN1	F3426	Burial	7350	160	
	A05	Burial	7800	70	
	F3426	Burial	7830	670	Omitted

Table 4.1 Radiocarbon dates from phases LN1 to LN4 from Tabaqat al-Bûma

Epipalaeolithic (Kebaran) phase at the site and a much later and ephemeral occupation of the site in classical times are not the focus on the present paper (Banning 1993; Blackham 1997, 358). Finally, the last phase of occupation at the site prior to our excavations consisted of tent sites and associated livestock enclosures of the 1980s (Banning 1993) and the use of the site by the Jordanian army in the late 1960s and 1970s.

We pursued a conservative strategy in the field in that, whenever context was ambiguous or uncertain, we assigned a bag either to the uppermost of alternative loci, or to locus 001 (the uppermost context), or locus 000 (no context), depending on the degree of uncertainty. This ensured that any contamination, insofar as we were able to control it, was always in an upper direction, and thus consistent with the expected effect of residuality on a site where pit-digging was a common activity. Unlike Garfinkel (1992a, 19; 1999, 5), we do not claim to have isolated 'pure' or 'unmixed' deposits because, on any long-lived or repeatedly occupied site, we would expect site occupants to redeposit earlier artefacts on later surfaces and in later fills. Despite our practice and that of the site's prehistoric occupants, we do, however, assume that (apart from the appearance of Late Neolithic material in the Roman–Byzantine levels) residual artefacts constitute a fairly small proportion of the artefacts in any phase, giving the impression of 'lag-time' in any changes in material culture. Our conservative practice has had the unfortunate effect, however, of placing some very interesting artefacts in a stratigraphic category of more limited usefulness; notably, many sherds that probably come from Late Neolithic contexts have been assigned to the Roman–Byzantine phase.

Phase LN1

Following an erosional period that probably removed some of the Epipalaeolithic deposits (Field 1993), the first Neolithic use of the site appears to have been as a cemetery. Our excavations uncovered two graves belonging to this phase, both stone-lined cists covered by large, flat limestone slabs (Banning *et al.* 1989; 1994). Because our exposure of this phase is much smaller (*c.* 10 m^2) than that of later phases, it is unlikely that our small sample of the site intersected the only LN1 graves there. The excavations found no traces of domestic occupation in this phase.

The grave in Area A, which was subsumed under Area J33 after the site grid was established in 1990, was the larger of the two, and the shallow depth of deposit above the cover slabs has made it difficult to connect it stratigraphically with other parts of the site except insofar as it, like the other one (in Area F34), was constructed in a pit dug into the Kebaran deposits. We found no Neolithic material in deposits cut by this pit.

The other grave, locus 026 in Area F34, enclosed the remains of a subadult and an infant, but contained no grave goods except for dentalium-shell beads associated with the infant's skeleton (Shafiq 1996, 17–18). The shallow mound of earth (locus F34.024) that covered this cist's cover slabs contained Epipalaeolithic artefacts, which were probably derived from material removed during excavation of the grave pit. This slight mound was lined with an oval of small cobbles (F34.025), and probably constituted a sort of tumulus. An LN2 wall (locus F34.023) cut into the mound. No traces of a tumulus were preserved at the Area A cist, where erosion and recent activities had removed most of the overlying deposits. Overall, the LN1 graves have similarities to cist graves at Byblos (Dunand 1973, 30–2, 100, 136), some of which are roughly contemporary with the Tabaqat al-Bûma graves, and to those at the somewhat later site of Neve Yam (Galili *et al.* 1998a; 1998b).

We have three plausible dates for this phase, although the error on one is large (Table 4.1). A fourth, much later, date, from fill infiltrated into the Area A cist but well above the cist floor, is intrusive. The small sample of two good dates do not allow a very precise estimate of the age of LN1 unless we constrain them in a Bayesian analysis by published dates on Pre-Pottery Neolithic C (PPNC) from Ain Ghazal (Rollefson *et al.* 1992, table 1) and, rather more loosely, by our dates from LN3. This leads to an estimated beginning of 6686–6563 cal BC and end of 6306–5902 cal BC (68% confidence).

Phase LN2

The excavations exposed very little of this phase (*c.* 17 m^2), which probably represents the first domestic occupation of the site, and later construction activities have destroyed or disturbed its architecture. Short segments of walls that probably originally belonged to two or three buildings occur in Areas F34 and E35, and are sometimes preserved by their incorporation into later terrace walls. As noted above, one of these walls, F34.023, cut into the low tumulus of an earlier cist grave.

We have no radiocarbon samples from this phase, but its position between LN1 and LN3 suggests a date *c.*5900–5700 cal BC.

Phase LN3

This is the first well-preserved phase of domestic occupation at the site, and the excavations uncovered some 123 m^2 of it, an area that probably constitutes a high percentage of the site's total area. Two small clusters of rooms in this phase may have constituted a farmstead with two or three small residences (Banning *et al.* 1994; Blackham 1997; Kadowaki 2007). Spatial analysis of finds suggests that some activities, including tool production and use and food preparation, took place in common areas, especially the open space between the structures (Kadowaki 2007), as we might expect if the occupants of the site belonged to an extended household or other closely cooperative social unit.

Using the revised stratigraphic analysis, it is difficult to estimate the date of the beginning of the phase, since no dates from LN2 are available to constrain it, and one apparent outlier of 6900 ± 70 BP (found in exactly the same context as one of 6490 ± 70 BP) is probably on residual charcoal. However, Bayesian analysis of the radiocarbon evidence allows an estimate of 5706–5542 cal BC (68% confidence), if we omit the 6900 BP date, for the phase's beginning. The estimated date for the end of LN3, assuming that it coincides with the beginning of LN4, is 5426–5287 cal BC (68% confidence).

Phase LN4

This phase, exposed over an area of 210 m^2, saw the addition of one new structure in E33/F33 and the abandonment and partial collapse of two of the buildings of LN3. This phase shows more compartmentalization of space, while more activities, including food preparation, storage, and the production and maintenance of tools, took place in segregated spaces (Kadowaki 2007).

As just mentioned, Bayesian analysis of the radiocarbon dates from this phase suggests that it began *c.*5426–5287 cal BC. This follows omission of the oldest date from this phase as a probable residual (it has a posterior probability of 69% of being an outlier), so a somewhat earlier date is possible. The end of the phase is more difficult to specify, as we currently have no radiocarbon determinations from LN5 and, in any case, it is likely that the site was abandoned, if only briefly, prior to the LN5 occupation. A Bayesian model with a gap between LN4 and the earliest occupation of a nearby Chalcolithic site, Tubna, whose assemblage contains no artefacts similar to those of LN4 or LN5, leads to an estimated end of LN4 about 5276–5072 cal BC at 68% confidence, but this probably underestimates the age of the LN4 abandonment.

Phase LN5

The final Neolithic occupation of the site, exposed over 228 m^2, involved construction of two new structures on its north-eastern and south-western extremities, apparently after at least a brief episode of site abandonment (Banning 2007; Banning *et al.* 1994; Kadowaki 2007). Once again, two distinct residential groups appear to have occupied the site and, although they performed many activities in open areas, each of these groups had its own distinct spaces for tool production and use, food preparation and area maintenance (Kadowaki 2007). In other words, they do not appear to have shared space for most of their domestic activities, and it is likely that they constituted different households.

The current lack of any dates from this phase or an overlying one, except for the much later Roman–Byzantine phase, makes it particularly difficult to date this phase precisely. Assuming that it occupies the gap between LN4 and the earliest phase at Tubna (Banning *et al.* 1998), a rough estimate for the LN5 occupation of Tabaqat al-Bûma is about 5100–5000 cal BC.

Ceramics from Tabaqat al-Bûma

During the excavation of Tabaqat al-Bûma, a large proportion of deposits were screened through 4-mm mesh, certain loci were selected for flotation or micro-refuse analysis and all recognizable ceramics were recovered. This led to retention of a significant number of very small ceramic fragments from which little information concerning pottery typology or fabric can be gathered. The following analysis includes only those sherds with a maximum dimension of 10 mm or greater. This includes approximately 19,000 sherds from phases LN1 to LN5 and an additional 10,000 sherds that have been attributed to the Roman–Byzantine phase or that cannot be accurately assigned to any particular phase. As mentioned below, many of the latter are clearly of Late Neolithic origin, with forms and fabrics similar to the specimens from phases LN1 to LN5.

Most sherds from phases LN1 to LN5 are body sherds with no visible surface treatment or decoration. Only 1440 sherds, including rims, handles, bases, spouts and body sherds with any kind of surface treatment or decoration, including slip or burnish, were identified as diagnostic. The diagnostic sherds also include body sherds exhibiting an obvious carination, sherds that are clearly from the neck or shoulder of a jar, and ceramic disks or spindle whorls. Very few vessels recovered by these excavations exhibit a complete profile and most of these are from the LN1 cist grave in Area A.

The statistics presented here probably under-estimate the actual number of diagnostics in the assemblage, especially slipped and burnished sherds. Much of the Late Neolithic pottery from Tabaqat al-Bûma is partially or completely encrusted with carbonate that obscures the identification of slip and burnish, and even of more invasive surface treatments such as incised or impressed decoration. The generally friable nature of the pottery has hindered our attempts to remove this carbonate.

High fragmentation of the pottery also means that the majority of sherds, including rims, are small, complicating the identification of vessel form in two ways. First, small rims, especially ones derived from hand-built pots with irregular lips, are more difficult to stance accurately than large ones. Second, even if a rim can be stanced with confidence, it can be difficult to distinguish the original vessel form if the preserved profile is short. Many sherds identified as 'cups' or 'bowls' could actually be the rims of necked jars, including bow-rim jars, which are otherwise absent from the Tabaqat al-Bûma collections. However, if bow rims were common, we might expect to find at least some clear examples of the join between the neck and shoulder (see below, LN3). When relying on small rim sherds, it can also be difficult to distinguish bowls with an inverted or restricted rim, such as Garfinkel's (1999, 115) 'incurving' and 'closed carinated bowls' (Early Chalcolithic types B1 and B3) or Blackham's (2002, 117, 123) HB 'holemouth bowl' from a holemouth jar. In addition, base sherds from round-based vessels may be misidentified as body sherds.

A fabric analysis of the Tabaqat al-Bûma pottery is ongoing but the prevalence of light colours, including pale brown, reddish-yellow and pink, is notable. Inclusions are mainly limestone with smaller amounts of flint, quartz, and a hard black grit that is probably basalt. Small red flecks indicating the presence of iron oxides often occur with, and probably derive from, the limestone inclusions.

Throughout this section we make reference to Garfinkel's (1992a; 1999) pottery typology as an accessible source with terminology for consistent comparison of assemblages. However, while this is convenient for archaeologists' use, it is unlikely that Late Neolithic potters would have recognized such 'types', and we would argue that using rigid typologies to define cultural units may obscure subtle yet significant variation.

Phase LN1

The small group of vessels from the Area A cist grave (Figure 4.1) includes two complete jars, one probable jar neck, three deep bowls and two small shallow bowls that might have served as lids for the jars. Garfinkel (1999, figs 98 and 102) assigns most of these vessels to his chapter on the Middle Chalcolithic. Despite the lack of overlying LN2–LN5 deposits in Area A, where the proximity of LN1 to the modern surface is due to post-Neolithic erosion, we are confident that this group pre-dates the other LN material at the site and is broadly contemporary with the Yarmoukian. Because most vessels of the group are complete and heavily encrusted with carbonate, we are unable to report their fabrics or surface treatments. The complete vessels are now on display at the Irbid Museum.

One of the jars (Figure 4.1.3) is typologically comparable to Garfinkel's (1999, 43–7) Late Neolithic type D1 Sha'ar Hagolan jar. However, the loop handles are on the shoulder, rather than on the inflexion between neck and shoulder, and the neck is vertical or even slightly inverted, while D1 jars are more often slightly everted at the neck. However, 'vertical' necks reportedly make up 43.7% of jar necks at Munhata 2b (Garfinkel 1992a, 50). The jar's concave base has parallels with a jar from Munhata 2b (Garfinkel 1992a, fig. 71.1), while the somewhat triangular section of the handles recalls examples from Sha'ar Hagolan (Garfinkel 1992b, fig. 75.16) and Nahal Qanah Cave (Gopher and Tsuk 1996, figs 3.5.2, 3.8.4).

The other small jar (Figure 4.1.2) could also be considered an exemplar of the type D1 Sha'ar Hagolan jar. Its neck conforms better to the slightly everted shape typical of Yarmoukian necked jars, although it does bow slightly on one side. Its flat strap or 'tubular' handle falls within the Yarmoukian repertoire (Garfinkel 1999, 59), as does the concave base. Removal of some carbonate concretions after the jar had stabilized revealed incised and punctate decoration over much of the body, a form of decoration that occurs, for example, at Jebel Abu Thawwab (Kafafi 2001, fig. 16.38; Obeidat 1995, fig. 48.23).

One sherd of a flaring rim (Figure 4.1.1) is probably from a jar similar to a Jericho IX example from Jericho (Kenyon and Holland 1982, fig. 215.3; Garfinkel 1999, fig. 58.5) or the flaring-rim jars of Wadi Rabah (Garfinkel 1999, 135–7), although it could be from an everted bowl similar to ones found, for example, at Abu Zureiq (Garfinkel and Matskevich 2002, fig. 3.7–10). Jars with such everted necks are also known from Néolithique Ancien at Byblos (Dunand 1973, 50, 57).

The two small shallow bowls, or possibly jar lids, are somewhat similar to examples from Pella (McNicoll *et al.* 1982, pl. 103.8), Jebel Abu Thawwab (Obeidat 1995, fig. 59.50), and Sha'ar Hagolan (Garfinkel 1992b, fig. 74.18). They are perhaps most similar to shallow stone bowls and small ceramic cups from Néolithique Ancien and Moyen at Byblos (Dunand 1973, 39, 53, 102).

The other three bowls have concave bases and a somewhat S-shaped profile, but without any flaring at the rim. They are broadly similar to Garfinkel's (1999, 115–17) B1 Wadi Rabah incurving bowl. However, the present examples have rather thicker walls and more carinated profiles, and one (Figure 4.1.8) has 'tubular' handles just below the rim. By contrast, B1 bowls lack handles

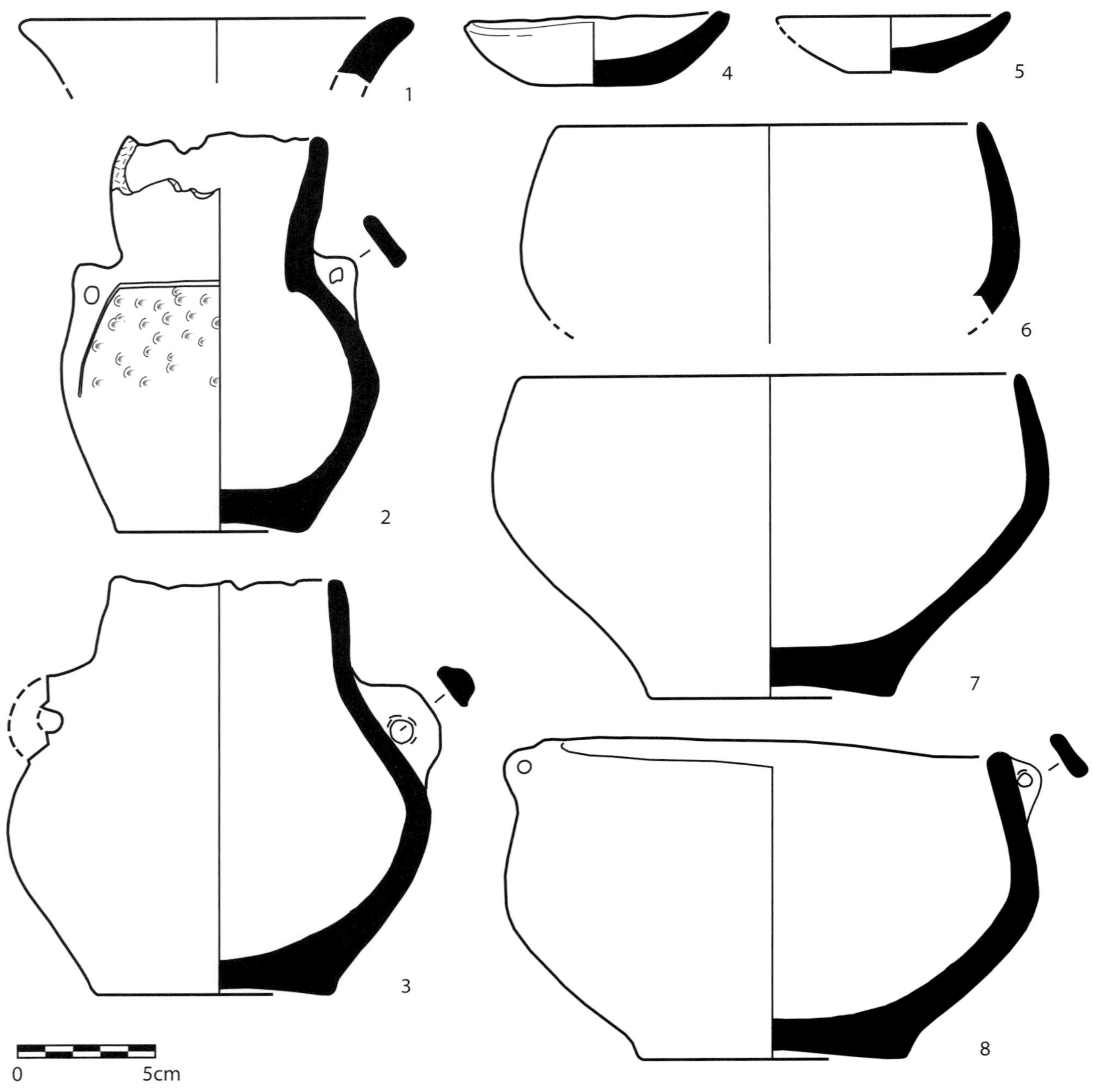

		Inclusions	Ext. Surface Colour	Slip Colour	EVE	Comments
1	WZ200.A.72.10	Limestone	7.5YR 7/6		7	
2	WZ200.A.72.6	Limestone and/or flint	5YR 6/6		50	Each side has a field of punctates surrounded by three incised lines. Tubular handle.
3	WZ200.A.72.4	Limestone, quartz	5YR 6/6		100	
4	WZ200.A.72.8	Not available	5YR 6/6		80	
5	WZ200.A.72.22	Not available	not available		100	Shallow bowl possibly recycled from body sherd with handle attachment serving as base.
6	WZ200.A.72.5	Not available	not available		n/a	
7	WZ200.A.72.1	Not available	not available		100	
8	WZ200.A.72.3	Not available	5YR 6/6		100	Possible red slip near lip. Tubular handle.

Figure 4.1 Pottery from phase LN1

and are usually burnished fine wares. They may also be similar to Garfinkel's (1999, 78, 81) type C7 Jericho IX 'hemispherical bowls,' none of which have their lower profiles preserved but, somewhat like one example from Tabaqat al-Bûma, have loop handles at the rim.

Where they are preserved, all the ceramic vessels from this cist grave except one of the shallow bowls have concave bases. Concave bases (called 'convex') constitute 3.8% of bases in Munhata 2b (Garfinkel 1992a, 52) and account for 4.3% of bases from Sha'ar Hagolan (Garfinkel 1999, 59). Concave and ring bases also occur at Ain Rahub and Jebel Abu Thawwab, accounting for 10% of base sherds at the latter (Kafafi 1989, fig. 5.57–58; 2001, fig. 17.52; Obeidat 1995, 49–50, fig. 32.22).

Typologically, this small group of vessels seems to bridge aspects of assemblages conventionally assigned to Yarmoukian and Wadi Rabah 'cultures', while also having some unusual features of its own.

Phase LN2

Our very limited exposures of this level have left us with a very small sample of confidently assigned diagnostic sherds (n = 47) (Figure 4.2). Most are red-slipped body sherds that tell us little about vessel form. Combed decoration and black burnish (*e.g.*, Figure 4.2.1) both appear.

Phase LN3

This is the first phase for which we have a reasonable sample of diagnostic pottery (n = 319). As in the preceding phases, most sherds are light in colour, sometimes with a distinct, darker core. The most common surface treatment is red slip, which occurs over all or the upper portion of the exterior, and either all, or in a band near the rim, of the interior, especially on bowls (Figure 4.3). Burnish is hard to discern, but, when identifiable, generally occurs over the slipped portion of the vessel and rarely on unslipped sherds. A small number of sherds have incised, combed or impressed decoration and a single sherd is painted with two thin, wavy lines.

Pithoi (Figure 4.4.7, 8) and bowls include deep carinated bowls (type A2, Garfinkel 1999, 111–12), as well as inverted bowls and slightly carinated ones with an S-profile (Figure 4.3.11, 12). The last appear similar in form to a red-slipped bowl from Jericho (Kenyon and Holland 1982, fig. 76.10). A cup (Figure 4.3.7) is similar to ones from Tel Te'o (Sadeh and Eisenberg 2001, fig. 5.2.6) and Abu Zureiq (Garfinkel and Matskevich 2002, fig. 3.1).

Jars are mainly simple holemouths (type E3, Garfinkel 1999, 131–3) with rounded or flattened rims. Handles are uncommon, but include a broad ledge handle, knob-like lugs, and strap handles with broad or oval sections (Figure 4.4.2, 3). One possible candidate for a bow-rim jar (see discussion above) is the upper part of a shoulder with the beginning of a neck that seems to curve outward somewhat like a bow rim (Figure 4.4.4).

Bases of this phase are primarily flat or disk bases, sometimes exhibiting mat-impressions, with rare examples of concave, ring and pedestal (Figure 4.4.11) bases. One poorly preserved base may have pebble impressions similar to examples with rounded impressions on the base from 'Ain Rahub (Kafafi 1989, fig. 5.79), Munhata 2a (Garfinkel 1992a, fig. 132.5), Neve Yam (Prausnitz 1977, fig. 1.12), Pella (McNicoll *et al.* 1982, pl. 103.11) and Tel Te'o (Sadeh and Eisenberg 2001, figs 5.4.9, 5.5.1). At least one base appears to belong to a rectangular or subrectangular vessel.

Phase LN4

This phase yielded a sample of 408 diagnostic ceramics, again with fabrics similar to those of the preceding phase and inclusions of limestone and, more rarely, flint, quartz and black grit.

Incurving bowls (Figure 4.5.6) might belong to type B1 (Garfinkel 1999, 115–17), while others may fit Garfinkel's A1 or B3 carinated bowl (Figure 4.5.2, 5; Garfinkel 1999, 115–18), or do not conform well to the Garfinkel types. There are no clear examples of shallow, inverted carinated bowls or flaring-rim bowls.

Platters from this phase (Figure 4.5.16), unlike Garfinkel's type B7 (Garfinkel 1999, 122–3), have walls that do not flare outward and do not exhibit burnish (but *cf.* Garfinkel 1992a, fig. 101.8, 12, 15). Basins of Garfinkel's (1999, 119–20) type B4 are present in this level (Figure 4.5.15).

Holemouths are illustrated in Figure 4.6. Handles are infrequent, but include small lugs (Figure 4.8.2) and broad or oval loop handles. As in the previous phase, bases are flat or disk bases (Figure 4.7), with only a few examples of concave, ring and round bases. A single mat-impressed base was found.

Incised and impressed decoration includes spatula – or 'fingernail' – impression (Figure 4.8.1), simple incision with no particular pattern and a single sherd with a band of herringbone incision that is undoubtedly a residual from the Yarmoukian use of the site (Figure 4.8.6). Red slip, sometimes with burnish, as well as combed, incised and impressed decoration all occur. Phase LN4 has the highest proportion of black-burnished sherds, which make up 8.6% of all sherds with diagnostic surface treatment in this phase.

Phase LN5

LN5 provides a greater sample size, with 648 diagnostics. Fabrics continued to be light-coloured with the same range of inclusions.

Some small and medium bowls (Figure 4.9.5) could belong to Garfinkel's type A4 flaring-rim bowls (1999, 111, 114), but we found no examples retaining the sharp inflection at the shoulder. Thus it seems more likely that they belong to simple open bowls similar to ones that

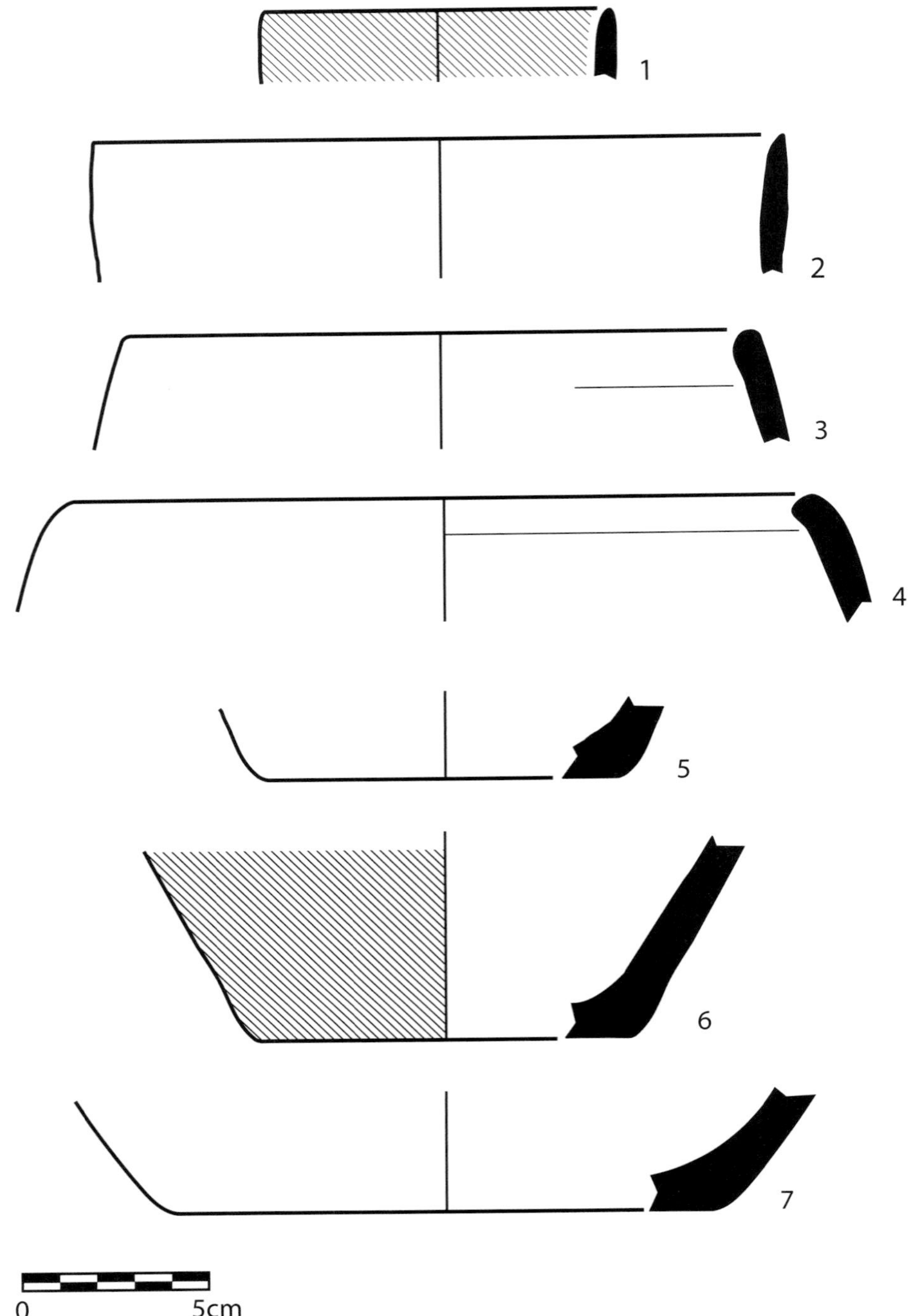

		Inclusions	Ext. Surface Colour	Slip Colour	EVE	Comments
1	WZ200.F34.70.4	Limestone	2.5Y 2.5/1		6	Black burnished.
2	WZ200.F34.22.25	Limestone	5YR 7/4		5	Very few inclusions.
3	WZ200.F34.50.11	Limestone, black grit, iron oxide	n/a		n/a	
4	WZ200.F34.47.1	Not available	7.5YR 7/6		n/a	Stance and diameter are estimates.
5	WZ200.F34.50.5	Not available	10YR 7/4		11	
6	WZ200.F34.50.18	Limestone	10YR 7/4	10R 5/6	22	
7	WZ200.F34.22.24	Limestone, hematite	7.5YR 7/6		n/a	Diameter is an estimate.

Figure 4.2 Pottery from phase LN2

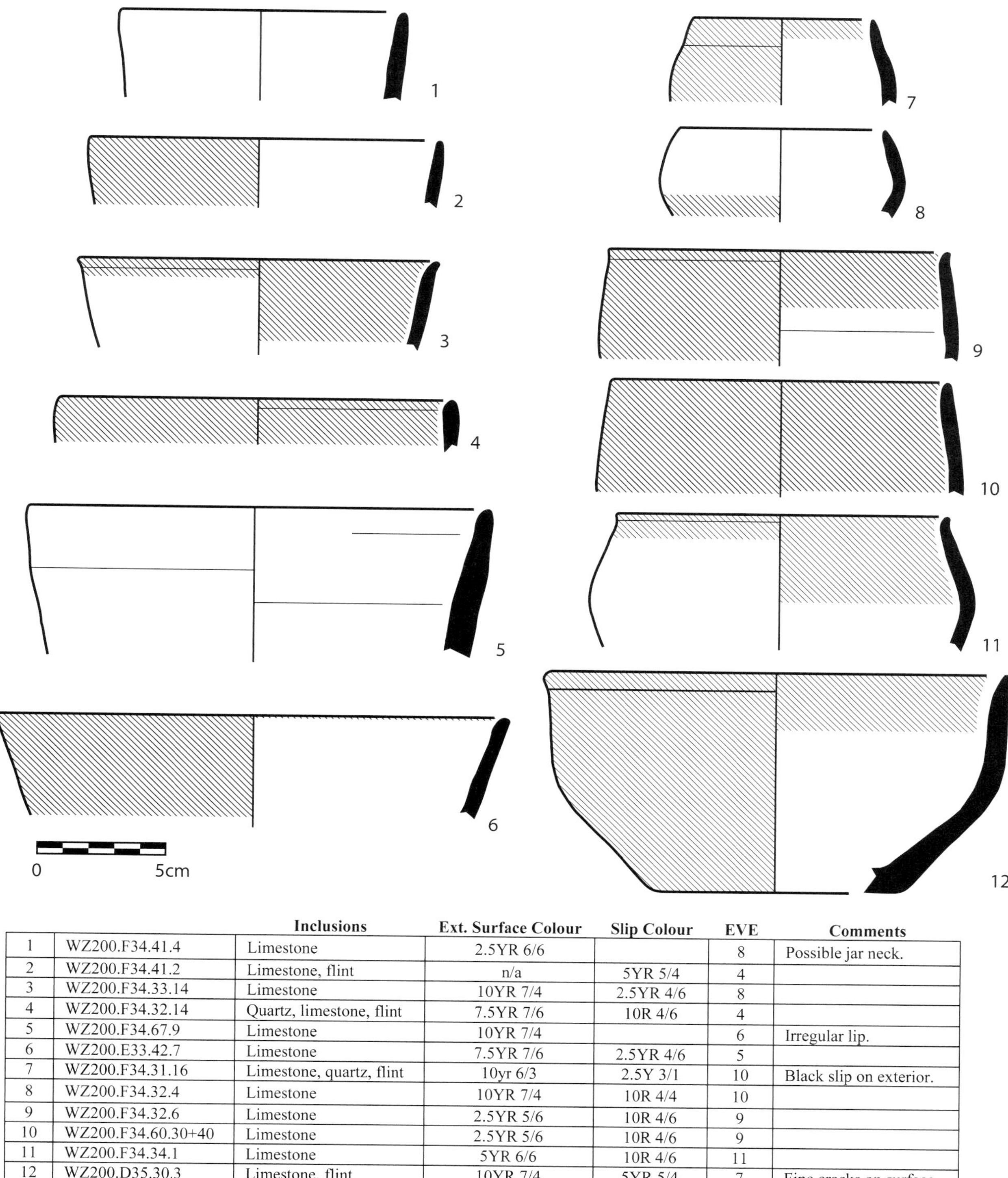

		Inclusions	Ext. Surface Colour	Slip Colour	EVE	Comments
1	WZ200.F34.41.4	Limestone	2.5YR 6/6		8	Possible jar neck.
2	WZ200.F34.41.2	Limestone, flint	n/a	5YR 5/4	4	
3	WZ200.F34.33.14	Limestone	10YR 7/4	2.5YR 4/6	8	
4	WZ200.F34.32.14	Quartz, limestone, flint	7.5YR 7/6	10R 4/6	4	
5	WZ200.F34.67.9	Limestone	10YR 7/4		6	Irregular lip.
6	WZ200.E33.42.7	Limestone	7.5YR 7/6	2.5YR 4/6	5	
7	WZ200.F34.31.16	Limestone, quartz, flint	10yr 6/3	2.5Y 3/1	10	Black slip on exterior.
8	WZ200.F34.32.4	Limestone	10YR 7/4	10R 4/4	10	
9	WZ200.F34.32.6	Limestone	2.5YR 5/6	10R 4/6	9	
10	WZ200.F34.60.30+40	Limestone	2.5YR 5/6	10R 4/6	9	
11	WZ200.F34.34.1	Limestone	5YR 6/6	10R 4/6	11	
12	WZ200.D35.30.3	Limestone, flint	10YR 7/4	5YR 5/4	7	Fine cracks on surface.

Figure 4.3 Bowls and cups from phase LN3

Garfinkel assigns to the Middle Chalcolithic (*e.g.*, Garfinkel 1999, figs 95–96, 99). Vessels of this shape are also known from Wadi Rabah assemblages, such as Munhata 2a (*e.g.*, Garfinkel 1992a, fig. 101.1–4, 12–15) and Tel Te'o (Sadeh and Eisenberg 2001, fig. 5.1.1–7). One bowl is painted with groups of vertical lines between a painted band on the rim and another painted band on the carination (Figure 4.10.7). Rims with somewhat everted but fairly straight profiles (Figure 4.9.1–4) probably belong to small carinated cups of Garfinkel's type B3 (Garfinkel 1999, 115, 118).

Of the jars, several small and medium inverted jars whose lips flare slightly outward (Figure 4.11.1–3) are somewhat similar to Garfinkel's type E2 (Garfinkel 1999, 129, 132), but the flaring is more subtle (*cf.* Garfinkel 1992a, figs

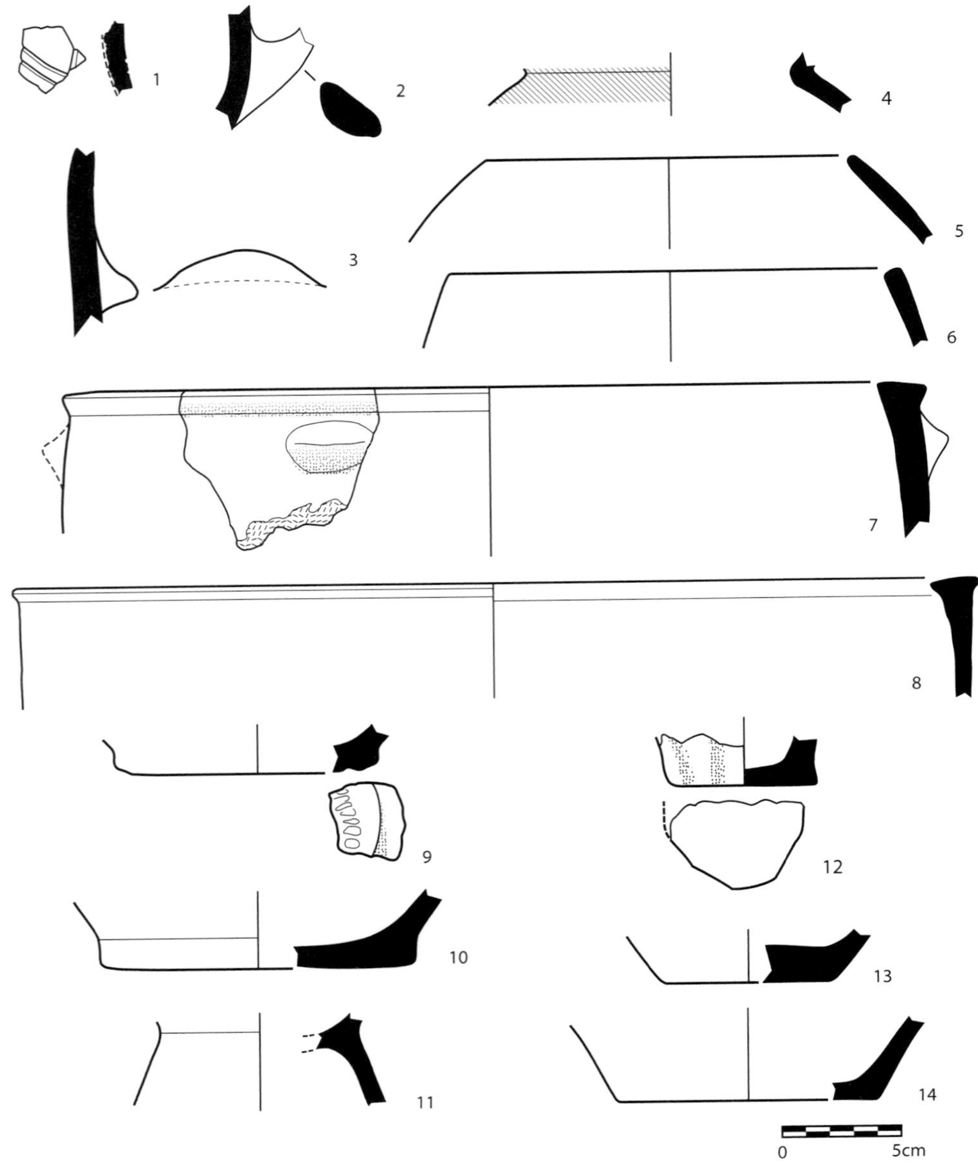

		Inclusions	Ext. Surface Colour	Slip Colour	EVE	Comments
1	WZ200.F34.46.18	Limestone, iron oxide	10YR 7/4			Incised. Interior surface not preserved.
2	WZ200.E35.21.4	Limestone	2.5YR 6/6			Strap handle
3	WZ200.F34.30.10	Limestone, flint	10YR 7/4			Lug handle.
4	WZ200.E33.42.6+12	Limestone	10YR 3/1	5YR 4/4		Necked jar. Stance and diameter are estimates.
5	WZ200.F32.25.63	Limestone, flint, black grit	5YR 7/6		5	
6	WZ200.F34.30.4	Limestone	10YR 5/2		7	
7	WZ200.F35.37.1	Limestone, flint, iron oxide	5YR 6/6		8	Pithos. Lug handle.
8	WZ200.F35.39.1	Flint, quartz, iron oxide	5YR 7/6		6	Pithos. Not to scale. Diameter of vessel orifice is 48cm.
9	WZ200.G35.64.7	Flint, quartz, limestone	5YR 6/4		12	Mat-impressed base.
10	WZ200.G35.50.1	Limestone, flint	7.5YR 7/6		17	
11	WZ200.F32.26.4	Flint	10YR 7/3			Pedestal base. Orientation, and stance are estimates.
12	WZ200.F35.30.11	Limestone, flint, black grit	7.5YR 7/6		40	Irregular shaped base. Stippling indicates surface depression.
13	WZ200.F32.27.19	Limestone, iron oxide	2.5YR 7/6		20	
14	WZ200.G35.50.3	Limestone	10YR 6/2		14	

Figure 4.4 Pottery from phase LN3

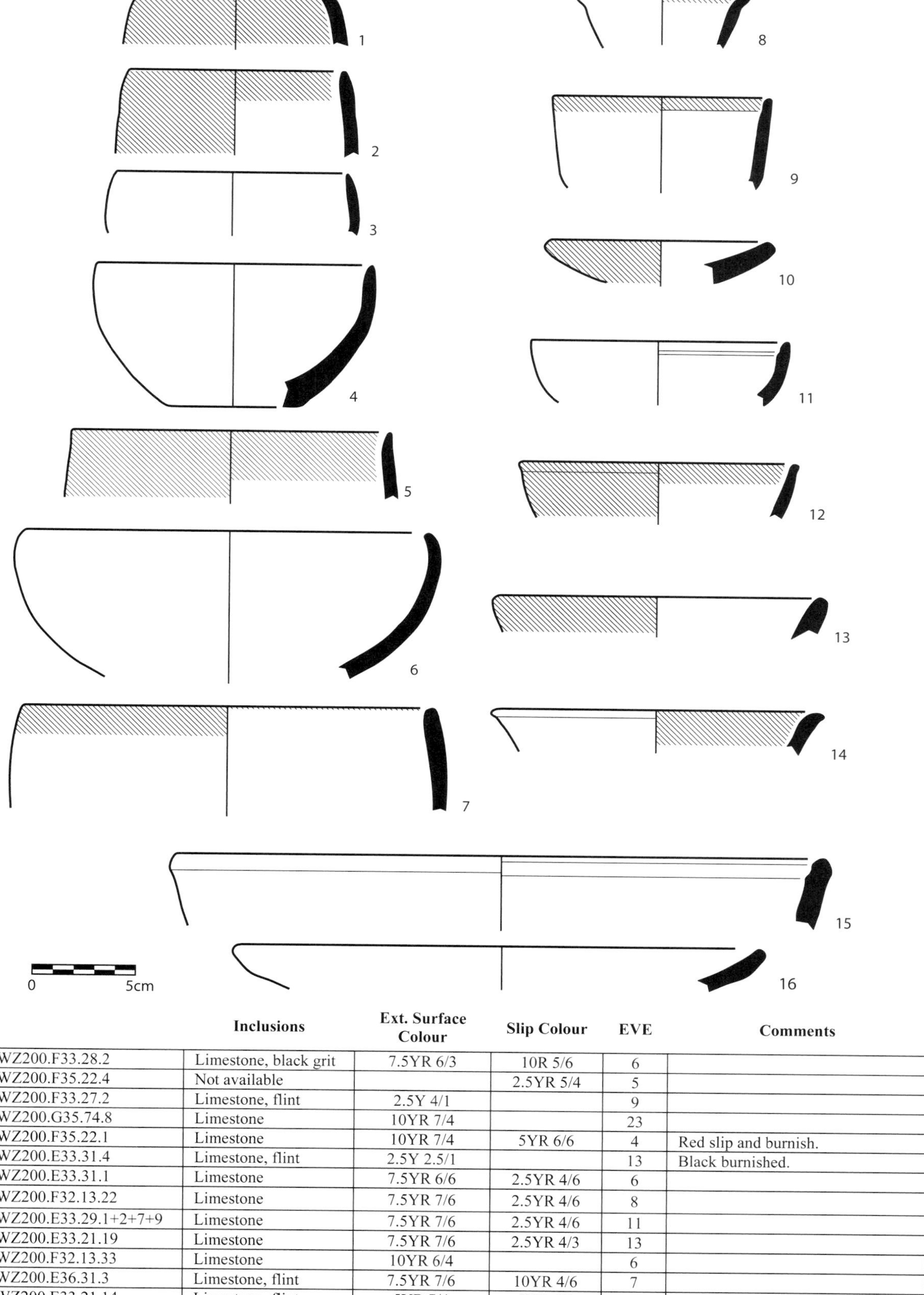

		Inclusions	Ext. Surface Colour	Slip Colour	EVE	Comments
1	WZ200.F33.28.2	Limestone, black grit	7.5YR 6/3	10R 5/6	6	
2	WZ200.F35.22.4	Not available		2.5YR 5/4	5	
3	WZ200.F33.27.2	Limestone, flint	2.5Y 4/1		9	
4	WZ200.G35.74.8	Limestone	10YR 7/4		23	
5	WZ200.F35.22.1	Limestone	10YR 7/4	5YR 6/6	4	Red slip and burnish.
6	WZ200.E33.31.4	Limestone, flint	2.5Y 2.5/1		13	Black burnished.
7	WZ200.E33.31.1	Limestone	7.5YR 6/6	2.5YR 4/6	6	
8	WZ200.F32.13.22	Limestone	7.5YR 7/6	2.5YR 4/6	8	
9	WZ200.E33.29.1+2+7+9	Limestone	7.5YR 7/6	2.5YR 4/6	11	
10	WZ200.E33.21.19	Limestone	7.5YR 7/6	2.5YR 4/3	13	
11	WZ200.F32.13.33	Limestone	10YR 6/4		6	
12	WZ200.E36.31.3	Limestone, flint	7.5YR 7/6	10YR 4/6	7	
13	WZ200.E33.21.14	Limestone, flint	5YR 7/4	5YR 4/6	6	
14	WZ200.E33.20.4	Limestone, iron oxide	n/a	2.5YR 4/6	3	Elongated voids in break.
15	WZ200.E33.28.9	Limestone, quartz	7.5YR 6/6		3	Groove running below interior lip.
16	WZ200.G35.75.59	Limestone, iron oxide	5YR 6/6		5	

Figure 4.5 Bowls, a basin, and a platter from phase LN4

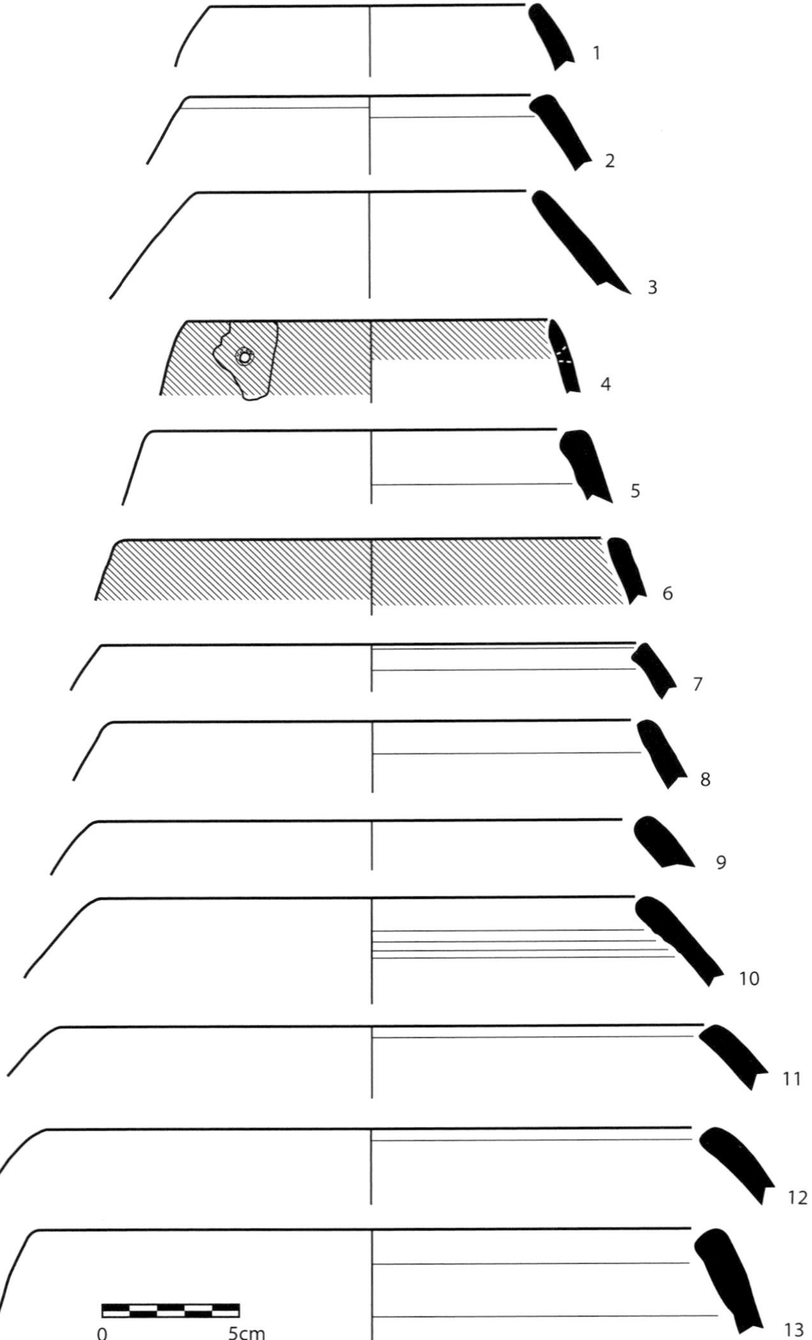

		Inclusions	Ext. Surface Colour	Slip Colour	EVE	Comments
1	WZ200.E33.16.7	Limestone	10YR 3/1		11	
2	WZ200.F35.10.6	Not available	7.5YR 7/4		5	
3	WZ200.E36.47.39	Limestone	10YR 7/3		8	
4	WZ200.G35.67.23	Black grit	n/a	10R 4/8	3	Perforated. Very few inclusions.
5	WZ200.E33.31.2	Flint, limestone	10YR 7/4		5	
6	WZ200.G35.68.1	None visible	10YR 7/4	2.5YR 5/6	8	Well levigated.
7	WZ200.G33.12.6	Limestone, flint	10YR 7/4		3	
8	WZ200.E33.21.10	Limestone, flint	10YR 7/3		2	
9	WZ200.F34.13.18	Limestone	10YR 7/3		3	
10	WZ200.E33.25.2	Limestone, quartz	10YR 7/4		3	Irregular interior surface
11	WZ200.E33.16.5	Limestone	7.5YR 7/6		6	
12	WZ200.E33.16.9+20	Flint, limestone	7.5YR 7/6		5	
13	WZ200.E33.26.5	Flint, limestone	5YR 6/6		6	

Figure 4.6 Holemouth jars from phase LN4

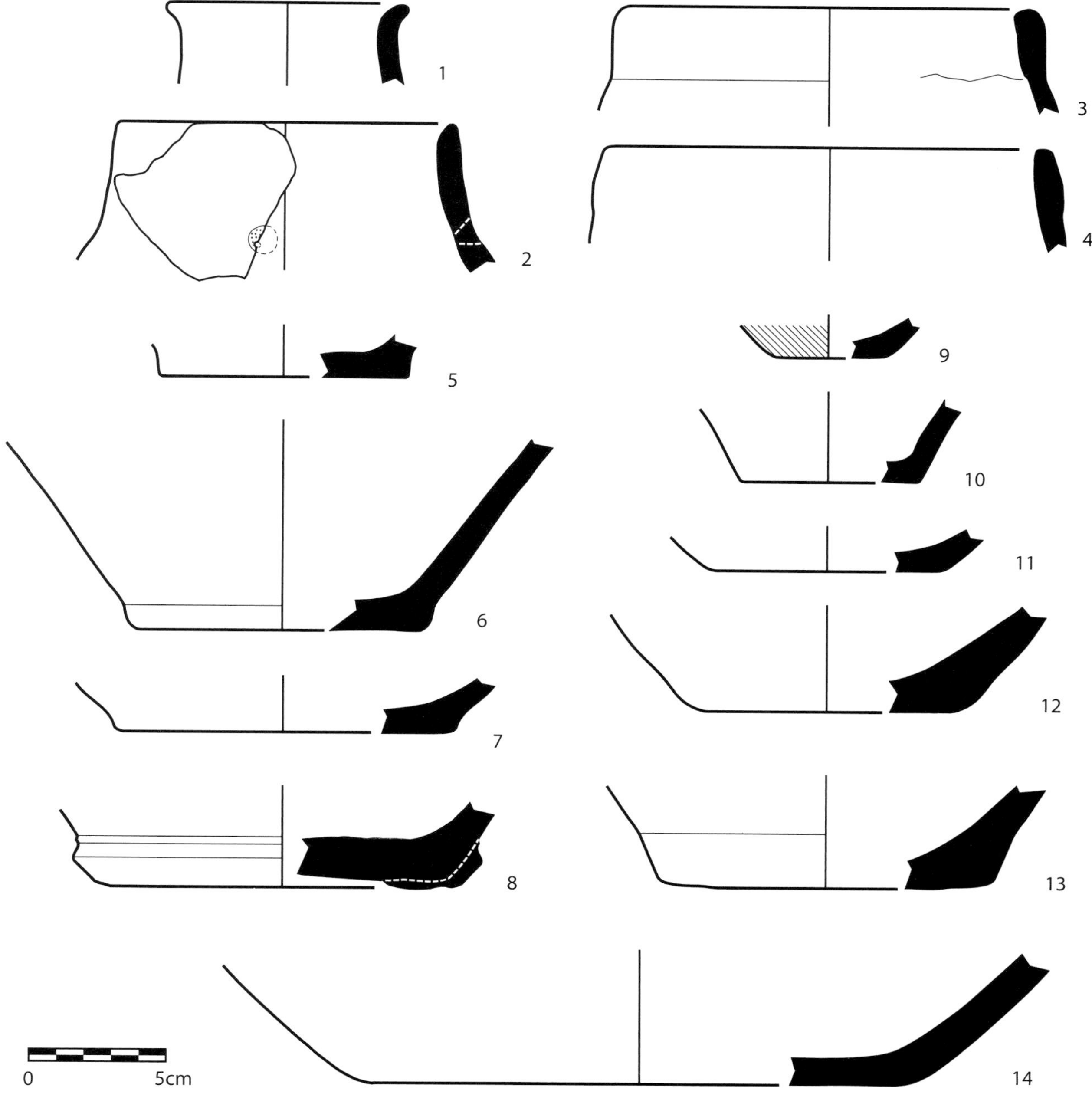

		Inclusions	Ext. Surface Colour	Slip Colour	EVE	Comments
1	WZ200.E36.31.1	Limestone	5YR 7/6		13	
2	WZ200.E33.20.10	Limestone	10YR 8/2		5	Perforation.
3	WZ200.G35.68.2	Limestone, quartz, chert	10YR 7/4		4	
4	WZ200.F35.22.3	Black grit, limestone	7.5YR 7/4		7	
5	WZ200.F35.22.7	Limestone, quartz, iron oxide	7.5YR 7/6		7	
6	WZ200.F35.33.1	Limestone, flint, quartz, black grit	10YR 7/4		13	
7	WZ200.F32.20.3	Limestone	10YR 6/4		7	
8	WZ200.E33.45.1	Limestone, quartz	5YR 6/6		25	Flat base with extra clay adhering to it.
9	WZ200.E33.28.12	Limestone	5YR 7/6	2.5YR 4/6	18	Red slip is also found on bottom of base.
10	WZ200.I34.13.2	Limestone	10YR 6/4		13	
11	WZ200.F35.22.13	Limestone, quartz	10YR 7/4		18	
12	WZ200.G35.74.1	Limestone, flint	7.5YR 7/3		10	Chaff impressions on exterior surface.
13	WZ200.F34.14.1	Limestone, flint	5YR 6/6		8	
14	WZ200.G35.74.9	Limestone, quartz	10YR 7/4		15	

Figure 4.7 Jars and bases from phase LN4

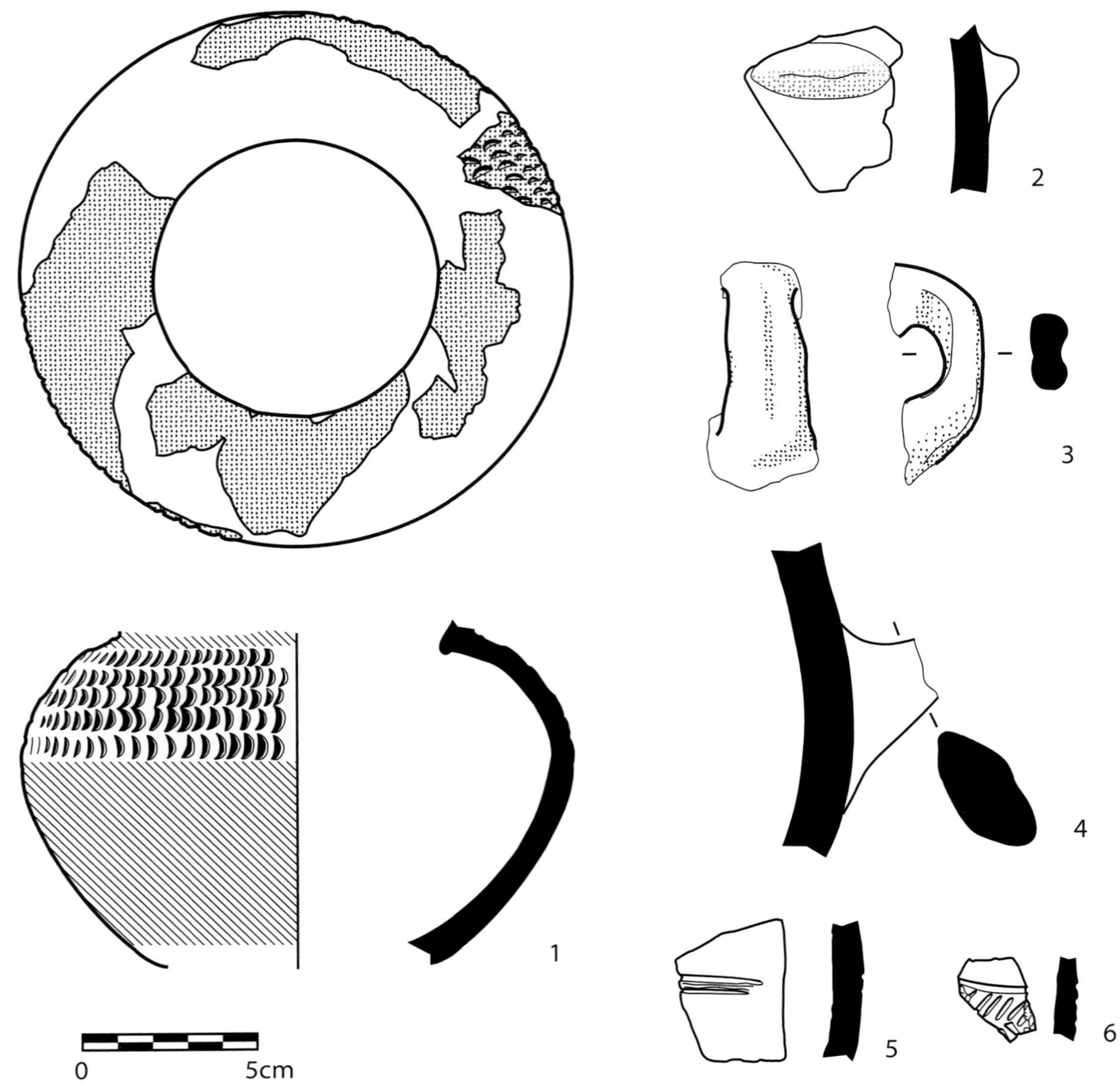

		Inclusions	Ext. Surface Colour	Slip Colour	EVE	Comments
1	WZ200.G35.67.24	Limestone, iron oxide	10YR 7/3	10R 4/6	35	Band of "thumbnail" impressions. Black and red slip and burnish.
2	WZ200.G35.73.6	Black grit	5YR 7/6			Small ledge handle.
3	WZ200.E32.22.1	Limestone, quartz, black grit	5YR 7/6			Concave strap handle.
4	WZ200.I34.17.10	Limestone, quartz	10YR 7/4			Strap handle.
5	WZ200.G35.67.22	Limestone, flint	10YR 7/3			Incised lines.
6	WZ200.I34.16.9	Black grit	10YR 7/3	7.5YR 7/3		Herringbone incision. Burnished exterior.

Figure 4.8 Handles and decorated sherds from phase LN4

116.3–4, 116.11–13; Sadeh and Eisenberg 2001, fig. 5.4.3). This makes them similar to later Chalcolithic examples from Abu Hamid, Ghassul and Tell el-Mafjar (*e.g.*, Garfinkel 1999, 173–5; Hennessy 1969, fig. 9a.3; Leonard 1992, pls 3.20, 3.22; Lovell 2001, fig. 4.6.5–7; Lovell *et al.* 2004, fig. 6.9), but similar rims also occur as early as the Yarmoukian (*e.g.*, Garfinkel 1992a, fig. 78.2–6).

Decoration occurs on only 4% of the diagnostic pieces (not including slip or burnish) and consists either of combing (Figure 4.12.7) or the painting of a band along the rim (*e.g.*, Figure 4.10.10), a horizontal band on the body (Figure 4.10.3), or, as mentioned above, groups of vertical lines.

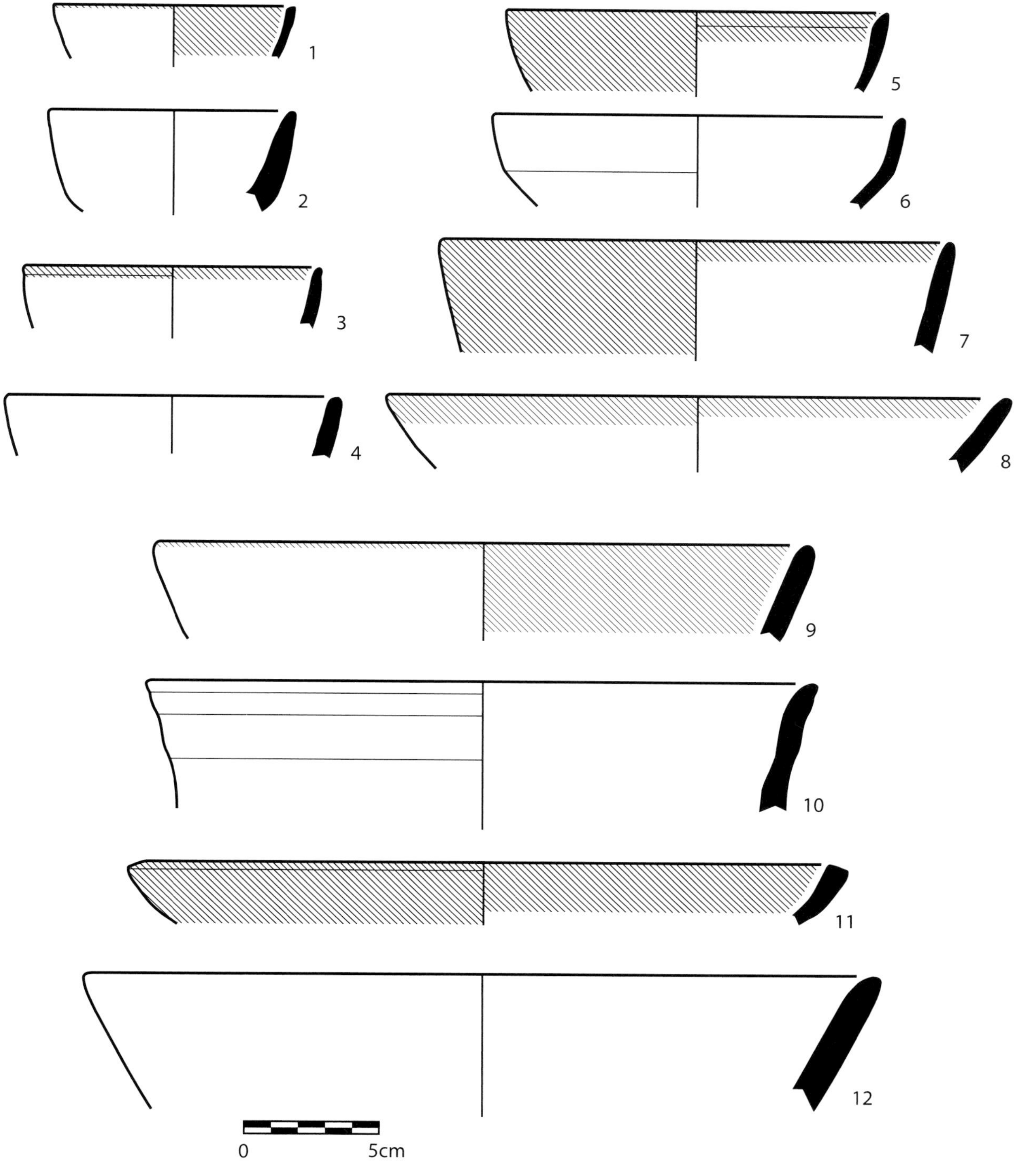

		Inclusions	Ext. Surface Colour	Slip Colour	EVE	Comments
1	WZ200.E35.5.7	Limestone	7.5YR 7/6	2.5YR 4/6	6	
2	WZ200.F35.20.21	Limestone	2.5YR 6/6		12	
3	WZ200.F34.15.1	Limestone	5YR 6/6	10R 3/6	8	
4	WZ200.A.103.1	Limestone	2.5Y 8/2		3	
5	WZ200.E35.5.9	Limestone, iron oxide	7.5YR 7/6	5YR 5/4	7	
6	WZ200.E35.5.6	Limestone	10YR 7/4		3	Diameter is an estimate.
7	WZ200.F32.5.4	Limestone, black grit, iron oxide	5YR 7/6	10R 4/6	3	
8	WZ200.E33.6.37	Black grit	5YR 7/6	10R 4/8	5	Few inclusions.
9	WZ200.E33.4.2	Limestone, flint	10YR 6/4	7.5YR 3/2	4	Black slip. Diameter is an estimate.
10	WZ200.F34.17.4	Limestone	5YR 6/6		8	
11	WZ200.F33.26.6	Limestone, quartz	10YR 7/3	5YR 5/3	5	
12	WZ200.E36.10.2	Limestone	7.5YR 6/6		4	Diameter is an estimate.

Figure 4.9 Everted bowls from phase LN5

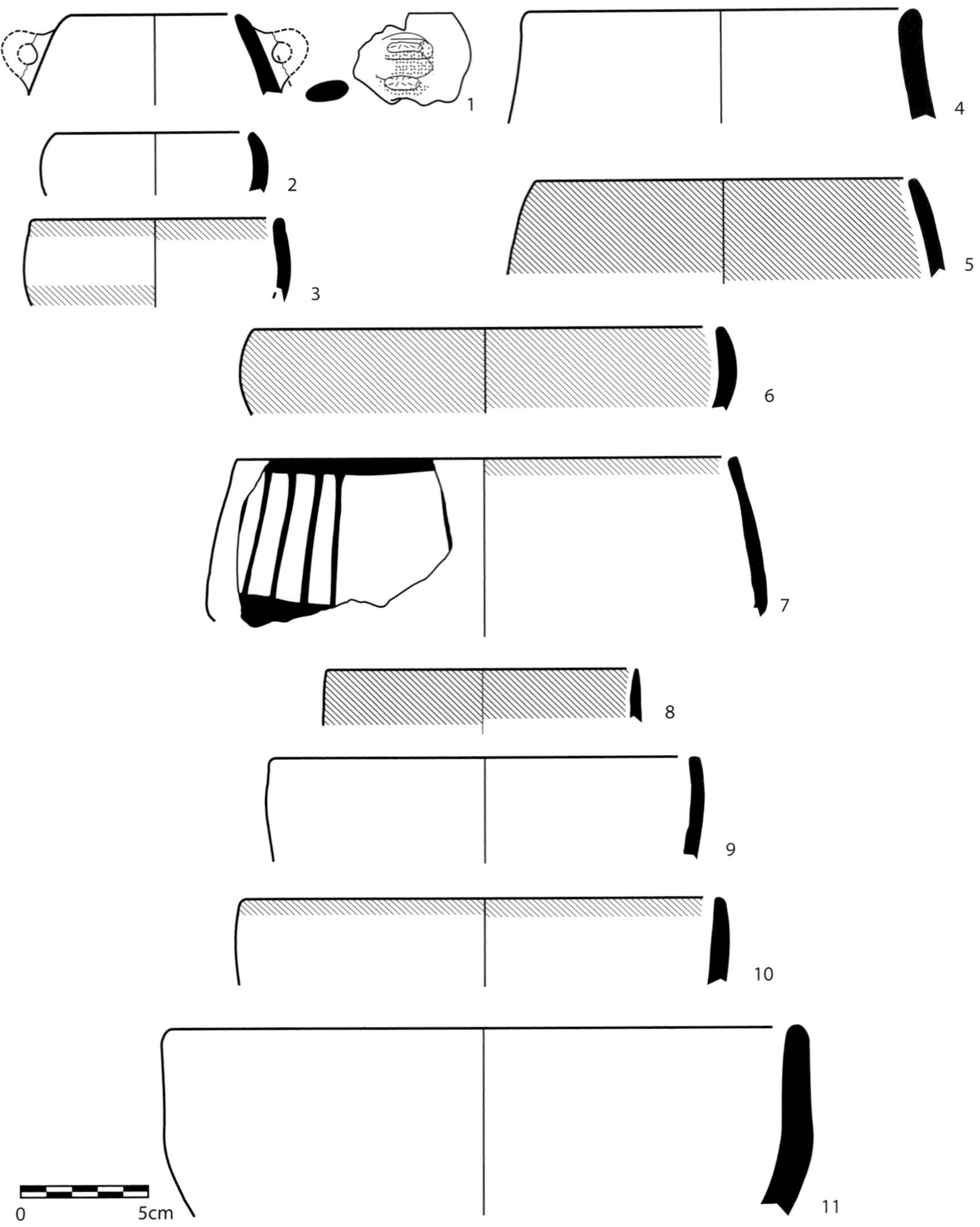

		Inclusions	Ext. Surface Colour	Slip Colour	EVE	Comments
1	WZ200.F32.8.79	None visible	7.5YR 7/6		8	Small strap or pierced lug handle.
2	WZ200.E33.4.26	Limestone	5YR 6/6		8	
3	WZ200.F32.8.80	Limestone	7.5YR 7/6	10R 3/4	10	Slip in two bands.
4	WZ200.E33.4.3+11	Limestone	10YR 7/4		12	
5	WZ200.E35.5.5	Limestone	n/a	2.5YR 6/6	6	
6	WZ200.E33.8.2	Limestone, iron oxide	10YR 7/3	7.5YR 4/3	4	
7	WZ200.G35.54.3	Limestone	10YR 7/4	2.5YR 5/4	13	Painted decoration.
8	WZ200.E35.70.1	Limestone, iron oxide	n/a	10R 4/8	7	Burnished. Interior surface and exterior lip are black slipped.
9	WZ200.E33.3.33	Limestone	10YR 7/4		3	
10	WZ200.F35.20.20	Limestone, iron oxide	7.5YR 6/6	7.5YR 4/4	4	
11	WZ200.F34.17.9+11	Black grit	10YR 7/4		5	Well levigated.

Figure 4.10 Incurving and vertical bowls from LN5

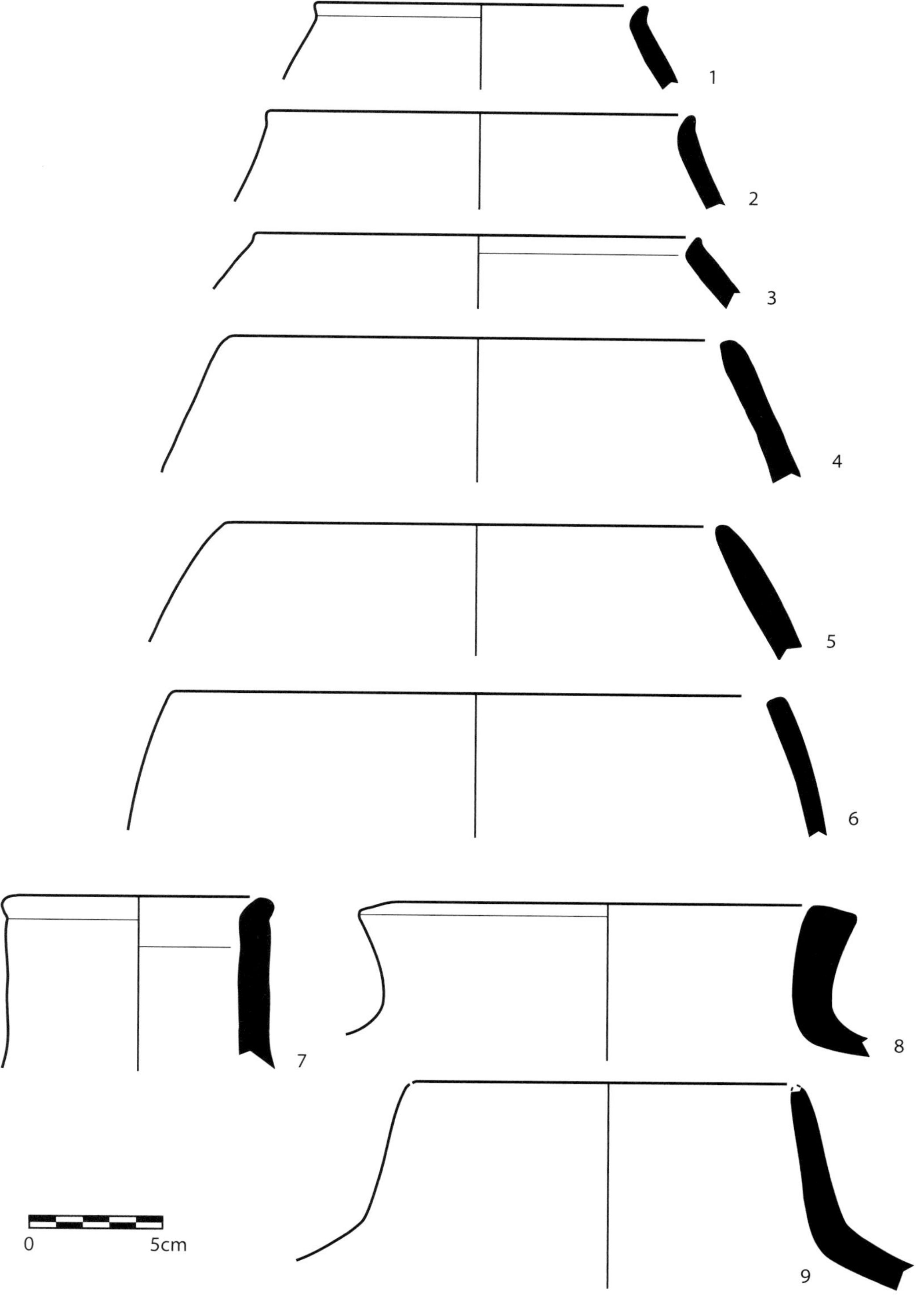

		Inclusions	Ext. Surface Colour	Slip Colour	EVE	Comments
1	WZ200.E36.12.5	Limestone, iron oxide	10YR 6/4		8	
2	WZ200.E33.10.13	Limestone	7.5YR 7/6		3	Diameter is an estimate.
3	WZ200.E33.3.42	Limestone, black grit	10YR 7/4		4	
4	WZ200.E36.10.1	Limestone	5YR 7/6		7	Few inclusions.
5	WZ200.G34.20.7	Limestone, iron oxide	5YR 7/6		7	
6	WZ200.E35.5.10	Limestone, flint	10YR 7/4		6	
7	WZ200.E33.8.11	Limestone, black grit	7.5YR 7/6		30	
8	WZ200.H35.8.4	Limestone, black grit, quartz	5YR 7/6		16	
9	WZ200.E32.18.1	Limestone	7.5YR 7/6		9	Stance is an estimate. Well levigated.

Figure 4.11 Jars from LN5

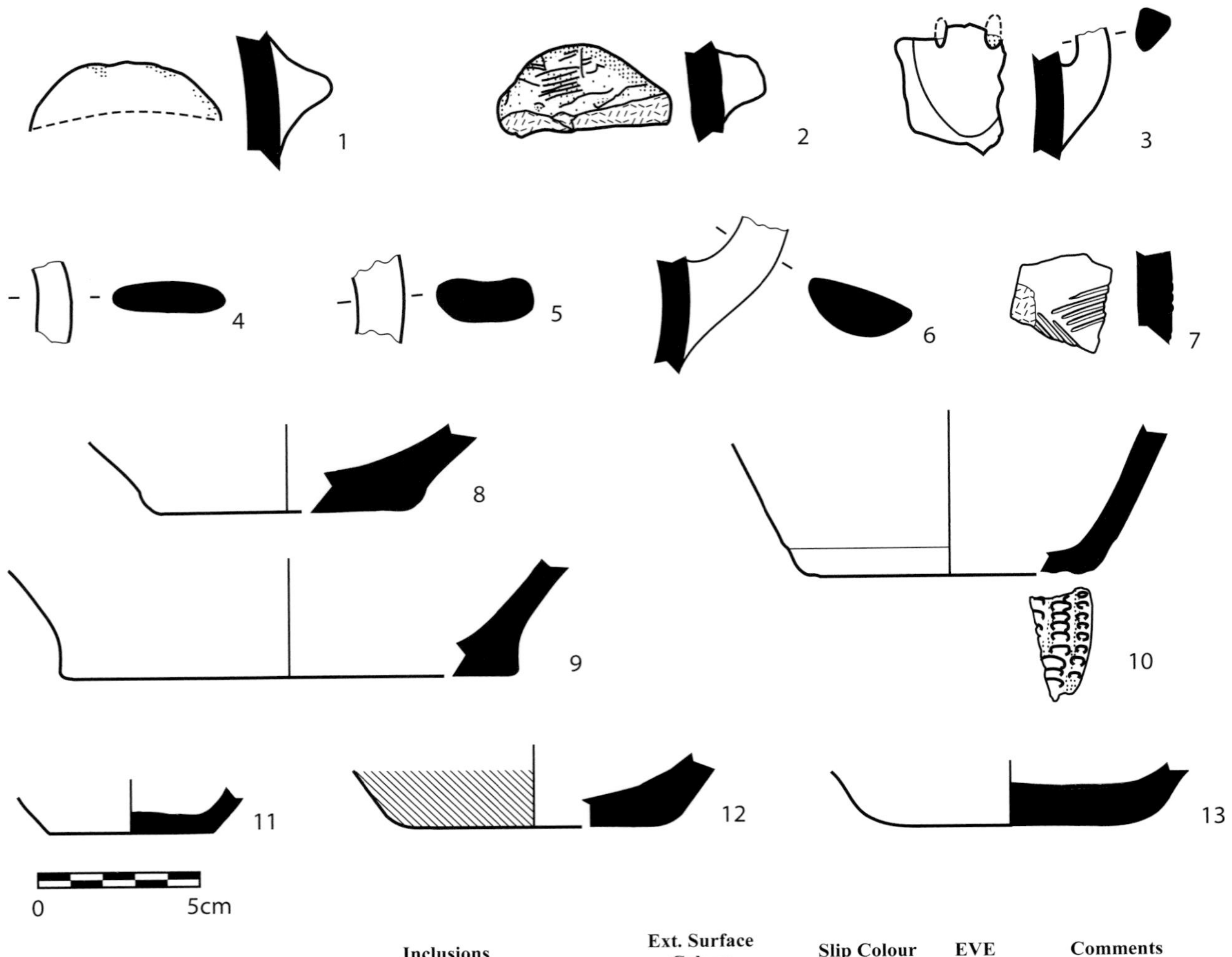

		Inclusions	Ext. Surface Colour	Slip Colour	EVE	Comments
1	WZ200.F32.3.3	Limestone, iron oxide	5YR 7/6			Small ledge handle.
2	WZ200.A.46.1	Limestone, iron oxide	5YR 7/4			Lug handle.
3	WZ200.E35.5.2	Limestone	5YR 7/6			Pierced lug handle.
4	WZ200.I34.6.1	Quartz, flint, limestone	5YR 7/6			Strap handle.
5	WZ200.E33.9.16	Limestone, iron oxide	10YR 7/4			Strap handle.
6	WZ200.E35.75.12	Limestone, black grit	5YR 6/6			Strap handle.
7	WZ200.I33.18.4	Limestone, flint	10YR 7/3			Combed incisions.
8	WZ200.E34.5.3	Limestone	5YR 6/4		22	
9	WZ200.F35.30.7	Not available	5YR 6/6		7	
10	WZ200.F35.20.18	Limestone	5YR 7/6		16	Mat-impressed base.
11	WZ200.E35.36.2	Limestone, quartz	5YR 6/6		30	
12	WZ200.E33.6.4	Limestone	7.5YR 7/6	2.5YR 3/4	13	
13	WZ200.E35.5.11	Limestone, quartz, flint, black grit	5YR 7/6		16	

Figure 4.12 Handles, bases, and a combed sherd from LN5

Residual Neolithic sherds from the Roman–Byzantine phase and uncertain contexts

Although we cannot be certain in which phase they originated, a fairly large sample of sherds in upper deposits and deposits that were disturbed or considered uncertain by their excavator clearly derive from LN2–LN5. Because of its proximity to the surface, a large proportion of these probably originated in LN5. Given the mixed nature of this collection, its sample statistics are of doubtful utility; however, individual sherds are worthy of illustration, description and comment, particularly as some of these provide excellent parallels with other Late Neolithic sites.

Surface treatment and decoration on these sherds include slip and burnish, paint, and combed and applied decoration. A sherd with a group of vertical painted lines extending down from a painted lip (Figure 4.13.11) is similar to one from phase LN5 (Figure 4.10.7). A painted net-pattern (Figure 4.13.26) has parallels at Munhata 2a (Garfinkel 1992a, fig. 140.2), Ain el Jarba (Kaplan 1969, fig. 9.2–4)

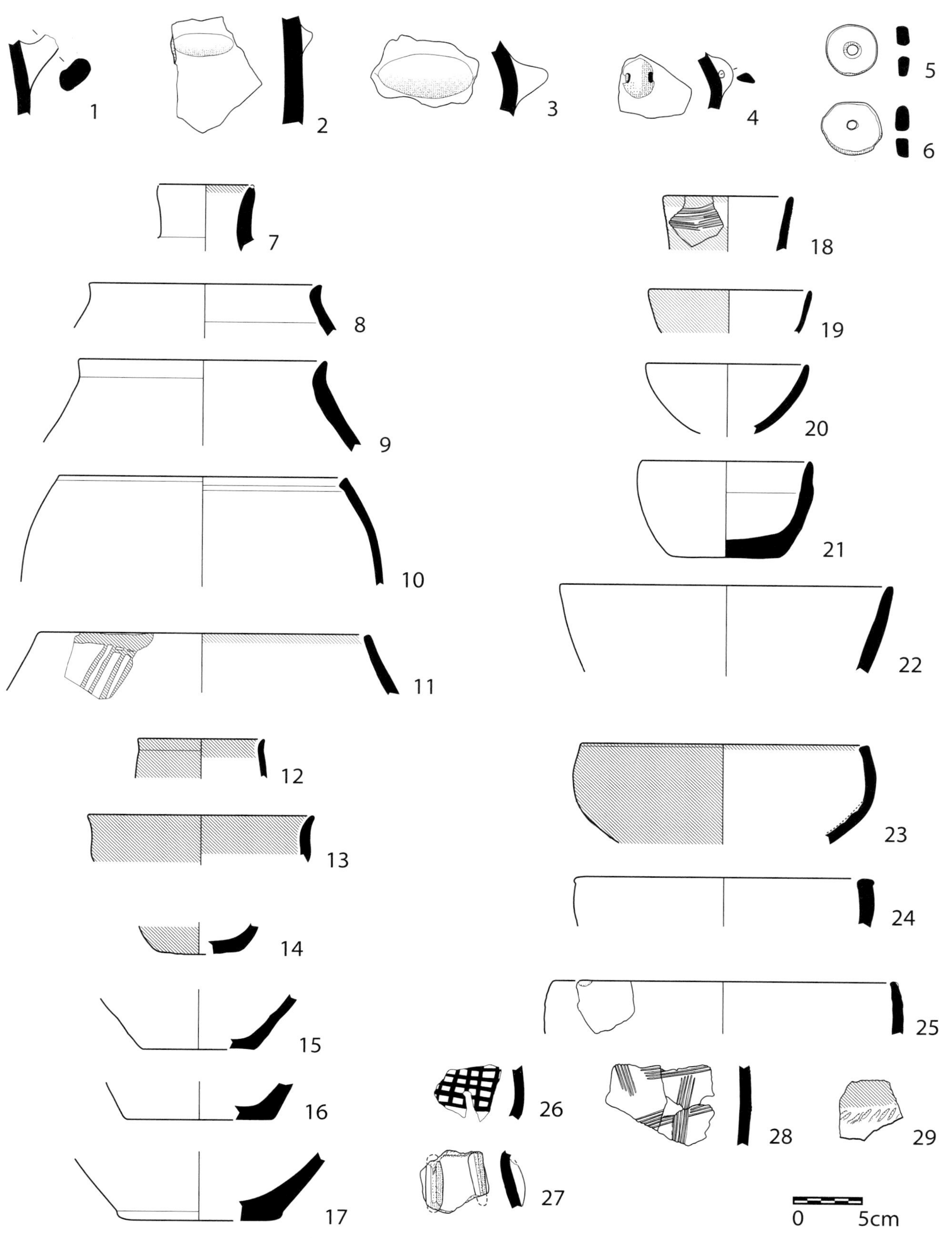

Figure 4.13 Residual Late Neolithic pottery from phase RB. See next page for the table

See previous page

		Inclusions	Ext. Surface Colour	Slip Colour	EVE	Comments
1	WZ200.D31.5.1	Limestone, chert, iron oxide	10YR 7/4			Strap handle.
2	WZ200.E35.71.1	Limestone, iron oxide	7.5YR 7/6			Lug handle.
3	WZ200.H35.5.3	Limestone	10YR 7/4			Small ledge handle.
4	WZ200.F33.4.2	None observed	5YR 6/6			Pierced lug handle. Possible red slip on exterior not illustrated.
5	WZ200.D31.2.1	Limestone	7.5YR 5/6			Pierced disk fashioned from potsherd.
6	WZ200.D31.2.2	Limestone	7.5YR 7/6			Pierced disk fashioned from potsherd.
7	WZ200.E32.8.5	Flint, limestone	5YR 6/6	2.5YR 4/6	30	Lip damaged; stance an estimate.
8	WZ200.E32.8.2	Limestone	10YR 7/4		9	
9	WZ200.E34.65.3	Limestone, iron oxide	7.5YR 8/3		12	
10	WZ200.E32.1.3	Not available				
11	WZ200.E34.2.3	Limestone, iron oxide		10YR 8/4	6	Red paint on a white slip.
12	WZ200.F33.6.4	Limestone, iron oxide		2.5YR 4/4	10	Lip damaged; stance an estimate.
13	WZ200.H34.6.4	Not available		not available		
14	WZ200.E34.2.5	Limestone		2.5YR 4/6	17	Red slip also on exterior bottom of vessel.
15	WZ200.E35.7.1	Limestone, flint	10YR 7/4		27	
16	WZ200.H34.4.5	Limestone, flint	10YR 7/4		18	Possibly mat-impressed.
17	WZ200.E32.8.3	Limestone	7.5YR 5/6		15	
18	WZ200.D36.2.7+8	Limestone		10R 4/4		Red slip with combed incisions in reserved band.
19	WZ200.F33.12.5	Limestone		2.5YR 4/4	3	
20	WZ200.F33.6.1	Limestone	10YR 7/4		20	
21	WZ200.D35.4.11	Flint, limestone	10YR 7/4		8	
22	WZ200.E32.1.26	Not available				
23	WZ200.F33.12.1	Limestone, flint		2.5YR 5/8	15	Burnished on exterior.
24	WZ200.F34.4.1	Limestone, flint	5YR 7/6		6	
25	WZ200.E35.3.1	Limestone	5YR 7/4		3	
26	WZ200.D35.4.75	None observed	7.5YR 6/4			Painted decoration 5YR 4/6.
27	WZ200.F33.5.3	Limestone		7.5YR 4/4		Applied decoration. Slip not shown on drawing.
28	WZ200.J33.2.16+17+24	Limestone, flint, quartz	10YR 7/3			Bands of combed incisions.
29	WZ200.A.67.3	Limestone, flint	10YR 6/3	10YR 2/1		Dark slip with burnish. Incised lines.

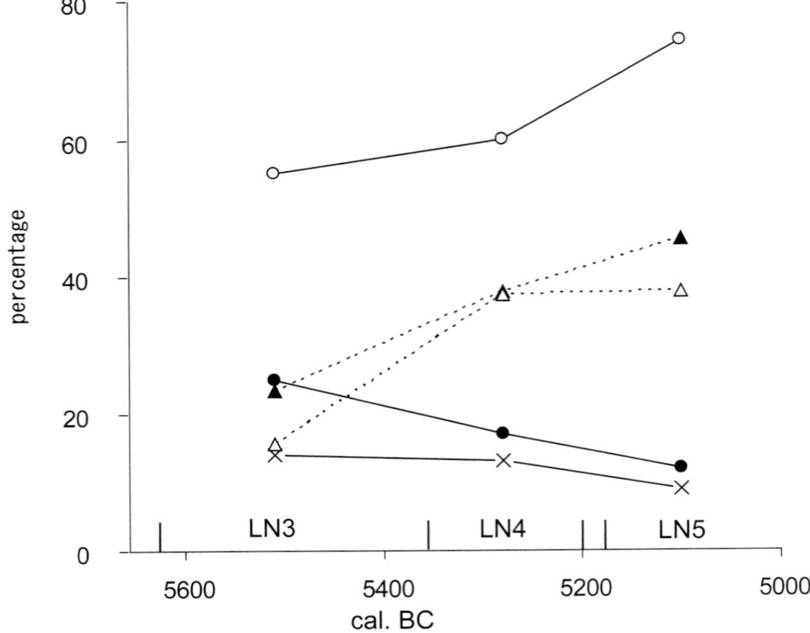

—○— unburnished slipped sherds (among sherds with surface treatment)

—●— slipped and burnished sherds (among sherds with surface treatment)

—×— combed, incised, and impressed sherds (among sherds with surface treatment)

···▲··· Type C/E sickle elements (among sickle elements of identifiable types)

···△··· sickle elements made on blades (among all sickle elements)

Figure 4.14 Trend lines showing changes in pottery and lithic attributes during three Late Neolithic phases at Tabaqat al-Bûma. Plots are positioned at estimated mid-points of calibrated dates of phases. Approximate boundaries of phases are shown on the x-axis

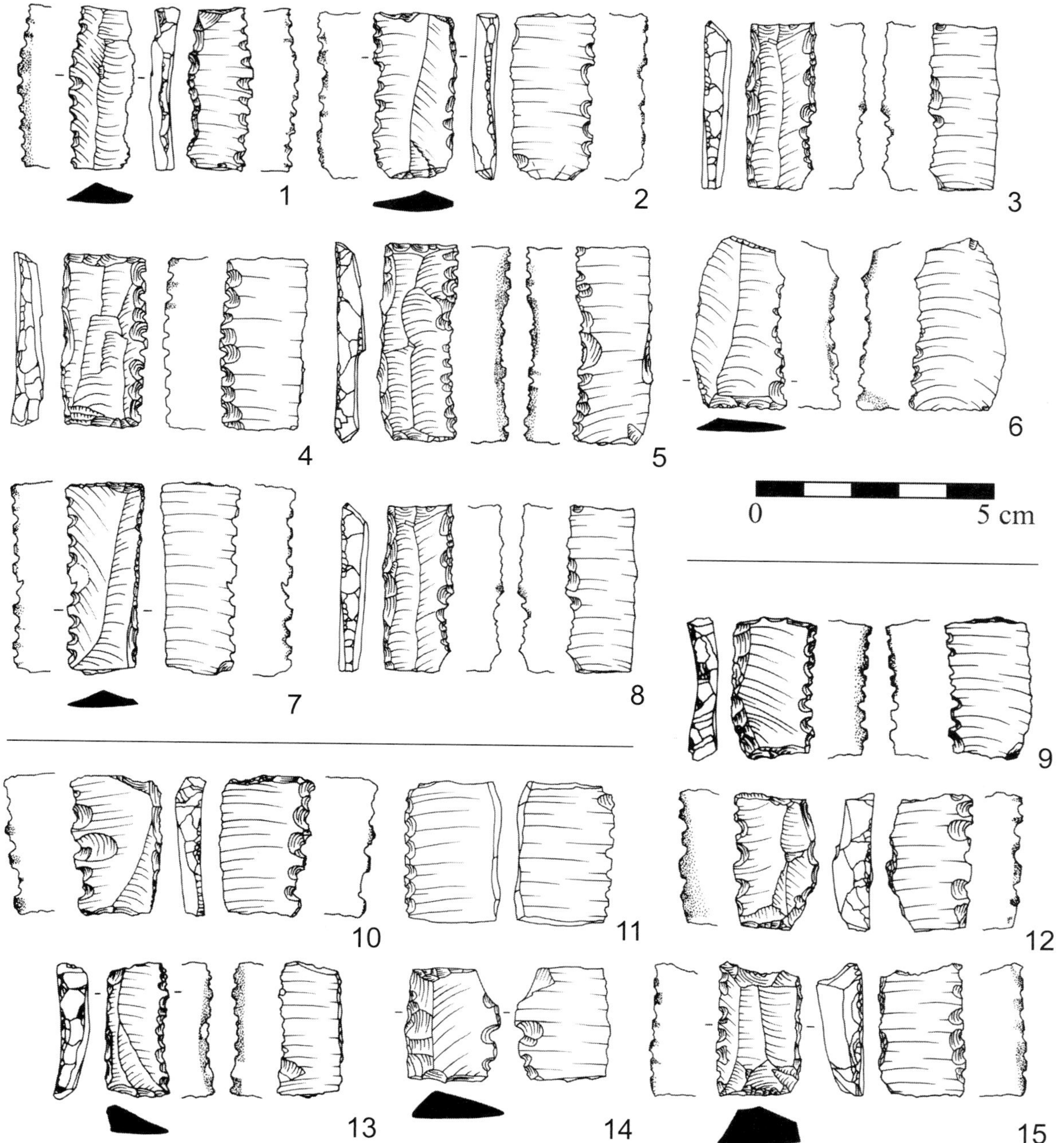

Figure 4.15 Late Neolithic sickle elements from Tabaqat al-Bûma. Type C/E: Phase 3 (6: E35.20.6), Phase 4 (3: F34.14.21, 5: F34.15.5, 7: E32.25.68, 8: F34.14.21), Phase 5 (1: H33.20.12, 2: E35.9.9, 4: F33.26.29). Type D: Phase 3 (11: E35.20.4, 14: F32.25.4, 15: G35.50.16), Phase 4 (12: G35.66.32), Phase 5 (9: E35.82.13, 10: G35.47.3, 13: E33.15.69)

and Abu Hamid I (Lovell *et al.* 1997, fig. 3.2). A number of sherds with bands of straight, overlapping combed decoration (*e.g.*, Figure 4.13.28) are probably from the same vessel as a combed sherd from phase LN5 (Figure 4.12.7) One red-slipped rim has horizontal combing in a reserved band below the lip.

Summary of ceramics and ceramic change over LN1–LN5

Throughout the sequence, at least from LN2 on, the majority of sherds have light-coloured fabrics, sometimes with a distinct core, and limestone remains the most abundant inclusion. This probably indicates a continued preference for local calcareous clays for pottery production (*cf.* Goren 1991). However, even given the small sample sizes and fragmentary evidence, we can recognize some changes in other aspects of the ceramics.

Forms are fairly consistent over time except that necked jars are more common in phases LN1 and LN2, where they comprise 23% and 17% of all vessels with identifiable forms, compared with 3–5% for phases LN3 to LN5. Despite the small-sample effect, this change parallels the decrease in necked jars at Munhata from the Yarmoukian to the Wadi Rabah phases (Garfinkel 1992a, figs 11, 25). While the small sample precludes statistical significance, 'raised-rim' holemouths (Garfinkel's type E2, Garfinkel 1999, 129, 173) occur in our samples from LN4 and LN5, but not earlier.

LN1 stands out as having concave bases (83%, compared to 0–4% for the later phases). Sample size alone is unlikely to account for this large difference. Mat-impressed bases are rare throughout the sequence and do not occur until LN3.

Handles are rare in all periods but tubular handles occur only in LN1, while pierced lug handles, so typical of Chalcolithic sites, appear only in LN5.

Surface treatment at the site consists of slipped sherds, sometimes with burnish, as well as combed, incised, impressed and painted decoration. Sample size generally precludes identification of trends in phases LN1–LN2, and the proportion of slipped vessels is fairly constant for phases LN3–LN5 (77–86%). Sherds with slip and burnish, however, exhibit a decline from 25% in LN3 to 17% in LN4 and 12% in LN5 (Figure 4.14). If combed, incised and impressed sherds are combined, there is also decline, from 14% in LN3 to 13% in LN4 and 9% in LN5. However, the distinctive 'cross-combed' or 'weave-combed' surface treatment (Figure 4.12.7; Garfinkel 1999, fig. 90.5, photo 71.2) seems to occur only in our LN5. Black-burnished pottery is rare in all phases, and does not occur at all in LN1.

In summary, for the most part, the Tabaqat al-Bûma ceramic assemblages are quite consistent, with the most obvious parallels in assemblages conventionally attributed to the Wadi Rabah culture. LN1 stands out as the most distinct phase at the site and, not surprisingly, has more parallels with ceramics attributed to the Yarmoukian culture. However, there are subtle changes over the whole sequence and even LN1 has features that preclude easy assignment to any well-recognized cultural entity.

Trends in lithic artefacts, LN3 to LN5

As the sample sizes for lithics of LN1 and LN2 are so small, the only meaningful trends we can attempt to analyse are among the later phases. Expedient flake tools dominate the chipped-stone assemblages from all Late Neolithic phases at the site, while formal tools include sickle elements, cortical scrapers and axes/adzes (Banning and Siggers 1997; Siggers 1997). The distribution of formal tool types, particularly the near-absence of arrowheads, is similar to that in lithic assemblages conventionally attributed to the Wadi Rabah culture (Barkai and Gopher 1999; Gopher and Gophna 1993; Gopher 1995; Finlayson *et al.* 2003). In addition, most sickle elements from the Late Neolithic phases at Tabaqat al-Bûma have rectangular forms shaped by abrupt backing retouch and truncations on both ends (Figure 4.15). These attributes of sickle elements generally characterize Wadi Rabah chipped-stone assemblages (Barkai and Gopher 1999; Gopher 1989; Gopher and Rosen 2001; Kadowaki 2005).

Sickle elements show some clear temporal trends, including consistent increase in their proportions among retouched tool types from 21% in LN3 through 24% in LN4 to 26% in LN5. This accompanies morphological changes. According to Gopher's typology (1989; Barkai and Gopher 1999), type C/E sickle elements are usually thin and narrow with a trapezoidal cross-section formed by semi-abrupt backing retouch, while those of type D are relatively thick and wide with a triangular cross-section formed by abrupt backing retouch. Type D elements are more common at Tabaqat al-Bûma than at 'normative' Wadi Rabah sites such as Munhata 2a, Nahal Zehora I or Abu Zureiq (Kadowaki 2005, 72–3). However, the initial dominance of type D in LN 3 declined as the proportion of type C/E increased in subsequent phases (Figure 4.14). There is also a trend towards more elongated forms of sickle elements, with an increase in the ratio of length to width of complete sickle elements from LN3 to LN5.

Changes in the morphology of sickle elements were probably related to changes in blank form. Preferential use of blades, rather than other tool types, for the production of sickle elements at Tabaqat al-Bûma (Kadowaki 2007, Appendix B) appears to have increased over time (Figure 4.14). The proportion of sickle elements made on blades increased from 16% in LN3 to 37% in LN4 before levelling off (38% in LN5). In order to identify blank forms reliably, determination was made only for sickle elements with relatively marginal retouch, but the unidentifiable pieces were included in the calculation of the proportions of sickle elements made on blades so that the blade proportions are not overrepresented. Blank forms were identified according to their shape, thickness and cross-sectional form and the straightness of ridges. Blades were more elongated and thinner, had a trapezoidal cross-sectional form and showed straight ridges.

The increasing use of blades for the production of sickle elements accompanies the growth of blade production. The relative frequencies of blades increased from 5% in LN3 through 6% in LN4 to 7% in LN5, while an increase in unidirectional flaking and overhang-removals during core reduction, observable more frequently on blades than flakes at Tabaqat al-Bûma (Kadowaki 2007), also indicates an increase in blade production. In addition, blades became longer and wider from LN3 to LN5.

The lithic data indicate several interrelated diachronic trends: a proportional increase in sickle elements among retouched tools; morphological change in sickle elements (increasing proportion of type C/E and more elongated forms); the more frequent use of blades for sickle elements; and an increasing number and size of blades among debitage. It may seem obvious to attribute these changes to increased demand for blades for the production of sickle elements. However, the frequent use of flakes for the production of sickle elements during the Late Neolithic (Gopher 1989), even at Tabaqat al-Bûma, makes it obvious that blades were not strictly necessary. Thus, we must consider what conditions may have led to the increasing production and use of blades.

Technological requirements for the production of sickle elements entail greater costs than for the production of many other retouched tools because of the need for standard blank forms and multiple stages of retouch, including backing, truncation and denticulation (Kadowaki 2005). Flakes require a greater modification to achieve these standardized forms, often through extensive backing that creates thick, triangular cross-sections that are less suitable for hafting. Consequently, although blades were not mandatory, their use made it easier to retouch sickle elements into standardized forms that met the mechanical requirements of composite cutting tools (Kadowaki 2005; Peros 2000).

On the other hand, the production of blades usually has greater technological requirements than does that of flakes (Inizan *et al.* 1992). Although the blade technology at Tabaqat al-Bûma was not complicated, it still entailed greater investment than flake production, such as the more frequent use of fine-grained flint and core-trimming techniques (Kadowaki 2007). Blade production may not be cost-effective unless these costs are rewarded by subsequent use.

In light of these considerations, the increase in the production and use of blades for sickle elements in LN 4 suggests that either the cost of blade production decreased, the cost of retouching sickle elements increased, or both. Any increase in the production of sickle elements will incur greater costs for retouch, but the production of greater numbers of blades reduces the unit cost of products (Costin 1991, 39).

Implications

These observations on the chipped-stone technology at Tabaqat al-Bûma have broader implications for general trends in Late Neolithic and early Chalcolithic lithic production. First, morphological change in sickle elements at Tabaqat al-Bûma may represent the initial part of the long-term process of type C/E replacing type D. According to recent studies of Late Neolithic and Chalcolithic lithic assemblages in the southern Levant (Barkai and Gopher 1999; Garfinkel and Matskevich 2002; Gopher 1989; Gopher *et al.* 2001; Kadowaki 2005; Rosen 1997), types D and C/E account for most of the sickle elements in Wadi Rabah assemblages, while type C/E dominates those of the Chalcolithic period (Gopher 1989; Gopher *et al.* 2001; Gopher and Rosen 2001, 56; 'backed truncated segments' in Rosen 1997, 44–60). Comparison of Wadi Rabah and later Chalcolithic assemblages from multi-layered sites such as Munhata (Gopher 1989), Hagoshrim (Gopher *et al.* 2001) and Tell Te'o (Gopher and Rosen 2001) broadly supports this techno-morphological transition. However, evidence from Tabaqat al-Bûma indicates that this change may not have been a sudden transformation but rather a gradual process during the 6th millennium cal BC.

Second, the increasing use of blades for sickle elements and development of blade production during the successive phases at Tabaqat al-Bûma are consistent with general technological trends from the Late Neolithic to the Chalcolithic. For example, stratigraphic evidence at Hagoshrim shows increasing use of blades for sickle elements from the Lodian–Jericho IX to the Wadi Rabah levels and similar developments in the morphology of blades used for sickle elements from the Wadi Rabah to the Chalcolithic levels. Gopher *et al.* (2001, 419) suggest that the blanks used for sickle elements from the Wadi Rabah stratum are thick and relatively short blades, while those from the Chalcolithic are narrower, longer blades.

Changes in chipped-stone technology at Tabaqat al-Bûma are thus consistent with broader trends in lithic technology from the Late Neolithic to the Chalcolithic in the southern Levant, but suggest that such change was gradual. Growing demand for sickle elements, probably due to increasing intensity of agricultural production, was among the factors that influenced these trends.

Conclusions

The five Neolithic phases of occupation at Tabaqat al-Bûma entail changes in site function and the repertoire of material culture at an important transition to the Chalcolithic in the southern Levant.

Although our exposed area is very small for phase LN1, the evidence points to the site's use as a specialized cemetery. The pottery from the only cist grave to yield substantial grave goods is unusual in a number of respects but appears to have its closest similarities with ceramics from Yarmoukian assemblages, especially for the small jars. If our interpretation of this phase is correct, the site is quite significant for providing a rare glimpse into the use of cemeteries in this early period.

Phase LN2 appears to mark the first construction of domestic structures at the site. Our evidence for this phase is scant, and consists mainly of several wall segments built either directly on old Kebaran deposits or cut into the tumulus over the F34 cist grave. Our sample of artefacts of this phase is too small for any generalizations, but the pottery appears to have more in common with the phases above than with the vessels from LN1.

Phases LN3 and LN4 mark the substantial use of the site for settlement, probably by two or three farming households that, initially at least, appear to have cooperated in some domestic and economic activities, or at least carried them out in shared outdoor areas. Over time, these households appear to have become more 'private' in their operation, with more distinct domestic areas (Kadowaki 2007). LN5 appears to continue this trend, but after a brief period of site abandonment.

The material culture of these last phases appears to have much in common with 'Wadi Rabah' assemblages such as those from Abu Zureiq (Garfinkel and Matskevich 2002), Munhata 2a (Garfinkel 1992a; Gopher 1989) or Nahal Beset I (Gopher *et al.* 1992), but with some unusual features of its own. There was little change in ceramic technology or the distribution of pottery fabrics, but apparently some change in the relative abundance of some morphological features of pottery. Among surface treatments, the abundance of burnished slip declined. Among lithics, the technology, although mainly based on expedient flakes, became increasingly blade-orientated as sickle elements in general, and type C/E ones in particular, gained in importance.

Overall, the assemblages suggest not an abrupt change from the Late Neolithic to the Chalcolithic, but a gradual transition, with some material features (and probably also social and economic ones) already presaging Chalcolithic developments that would culminate in the Ghassulian many centuries later. Although some of the proportional changes that we described above (*e.g.*, Figure 4.14) may seem too subtle to be meaningful, a series of statistical tests indicate that the differences among phases are significant (Kadowaki 2007, Appendix B). For example, while the increase in the proportion of sickle elements (including unfinished ones) among the retouched tools may seem small, even it is significant at the 0.1 critical level ($Z = 1.36$, one-tailed $p<0.09$). Similarly, the overall proportional decline in burnished slip from LN3 to LN5 is also significant ($Z = 3.51$ and one-tailed $p<0.001$). At the same time, it seems unlikely that the gradual nature of the trends is due only to the effects of residual artefacts, even though we would expect the lag from such residuals to soften the apparent changes somewhat.

The evidence from Tabaqat al-Bûma also accentuates the diversity of 'Wadi Rabah-related' assemblages, which has led to considerable disagreement over the definition of Wadi Rabah and indeed over whether such classifications are even meaningful (Banning 2007; Bourke and Lovell 2004; Lovell *et al.* 2007). Cultural variation during this period was more complex than the old classifications are able to capture and, although it may not always have involved the gradual changes we have identified, forcing our data into these classifications tends to obscure evidence for transitions while emphasizing discontinuities.

Acknowledgements

Excavations at Tabaqat al-Bûma and analysis of the finds were supported by grants from the Social Sciences and Humanities Research Council of Canada, and we would also like to thank the Department of Antiquities of Jordan, and its past Directors-General, Adnan Hadidi and Ghazi Bisheh, for permits to carry out the excavations and to export much of the material to Canada for analysis. Excavation crews at the site from 1987 to 1992 included Anita Buehrle, Margaret Darmanin, Robin Dodds, Adam Ford, Ian Kuijt, N. Claire Loader, Sandra Low, Stephen Monckton, Dan Rahimi, Sally Randell, Bruce Routledge, Rula Shafiq, Peter Sheppard, Julian Siggers, John Triggs and Hikmat Ta'ani, who also served as Antiquities Representative. We thank them all for their careful attention to excavation and recording of the contexts used for this paper. Mark Blackham carried out the difficult job of analysing the stratigraphy and resolving stratigraphic contradictions in the initial Harris matrix. We would also like to thank the many volunteers and work-study students who have helped us process and analyse the material, with special mention to Jo Bradley and N. Claire Loader, who so ably organized the materials in the field and in the lab in Toronto. Original illustrations of artefacts are by Julia Pfaff, with new illustrations and digitization of originals by Kevin Gibbs and Raïna Stebelsky. S. Maltby was our conservator.

References

Banning, E. B. (1993) Where the wild stones have been gathered aside: pastoralist campsites in Wadi Ziqlab, Jordan. *Biblical Archaeologist* 56/4, 212–21.

Banning, E. B. (2002) Consensus and debate on the Late Neolithic and Chalcolithic of the southern Levant. *Paléorient* 28, 148–55.

Banning, E. B. (2007) Wadi Rabah and related assemblages in the southern Levant: interpreting the radiocarbon evidence. *Paléorient* 33/1, 77–101.

Banning, E. B. and Siggers, J. (1997) Technological strategies at a Late Neolithic farmstead in Wadi Ziqlab, Jordan. Pp. 319–31 in H. G. K. Gebel, Z. Kafafi and G. O. Rollefson (eds), *The Prehistory of Jordan, II. Perspectives from 1997*. Studies in Early Near Eastern Production, Subsistence, and Environment 4. Berlin: ex oriente.

Banning, E. B., Dods, R. R., Field, J. J., Maltby, S. L., McCorriston, J., Monckton, S., Rubenstein, R. and Sheppard, P. (1989) Wadi Ziqlab Project 1987: a preliminary report. *Annual of the Department of Antiquities of Jordan* 33, 43–58.

Banning, E. B., Blackham, M. and Lasby, D. (1998) Excavations at WZ121, a Chalcolithic site at Tubna, in Wadi Ziqlab. *Annual of the Department of Antiquities of Jordan* 42, 141–59.

Banning, E. B., Rahimi, D. and Siggers, J. (1994) The Late Neolithic of the southern Levant: hiatus, settlement shift or observer bias? The perspective from Wadi Ziqlab. *Paléorient* 20/2,151–64.

Barkai, R. and Gopher, A. (1999) The last Neolithic flint industry: A study of the technology, typology and social implications of the lithic assemblage from Nahal Zehora I, A Wadi Rabah (Pottery Neolithic) site in the Menashe Hills, Israel. *Journal of the Israel Prehistoric Society* 29, 41–122.

Blackham, M. (1994) Chronological Correlations of Archaeological Stratigraphy: An Intrasite Test at Tabaqat al-Bûma, Jordan. Unpublished MSc dissertation, Department of Anthropology, University of Toronto.

Blackham, M. (1997) Changing settlement at Tabaqat al-Bûma

in Wadi Ziqlab, Jordan: a stratigraphic analysis. Pp. 345–60 in H. G. K. Gebel, Z. Kafafi and G. O. Rollefson (eds), *The Prehistory of Jordan, II. Perspectives from 1997*. Studies in Early Near Eastern Production, Subsistence, and Environment 4. Berlin: ex oriente.

Blackham, M. (2002) *Modeling Time and Transition in Prehistory: The Jordan Valley Chalcolithic (5500–3500 BC)*. Oxford: BAR Int. Ser. 1027.

Bourke, S. (1997) The 'Pre-Ghassulian' sequence at Teleilat Ghassul: Sydney University excavations 1975–1995. Pp. 395–417 in H. G. K. Gebel, Z. Kafafi and G. O. Rollefson (eds), *The Prehistory of Jordan, II. Perspectives from 1997*. Studies in Early Near Eastern Production, Subsistence, and Environment 4. Berlin: ex oriente.

Bourke, S. J. and Lovell, J. L. (2004) Ghassul, Chronology and Cultural Sequencing. *Paléorient* 30/1, 179–82.

Campbell, S. (2007) Rethinking Halaf chronologies. *Paléorient* 33/1, 103–36.

Costin, C. L. (1991) Craft specialization: issues in defining, documenting, and explaining the organization of production. Pp. 1–56 in M. B. Schiffer (ed.), *Archaeological Method and Theory*, vol. 3. Tucson, AZ: University of Arizona Press.

Dunand, M. (1973) *Fouilles de Byblos*, vol. 5. Paris.

Field, J. (1993) Rainfall patterns and landscape changes in Wadi Ziqlab, Jordan. Pp. 257–9 in R. W. Jamieson, S. Abonyi, and N. Mirau (eds), *Culture and Environment: A Fragile Coexistence*. The Archaeological Association of the University of Calgary. Calgary: Chacmool.

Finlayson, B., Kuijt, I., Arpin, T., Chesson, M., Dennis, S., Goodale, N., Kadowaki, S., Maher, L., Smith, S., Schurr, M. and McKay, J. (2003) Dhra' Excavation Project, 2002 Interim report. *Levant* 35, 1–38.

Galili, E., Sharvit, Y. and Nagar, A. (1998a) Nevé Yam – underwater survey. *Hadashot Arkheologiyot – Excavations and Surveys in Israel* 18, 35–6.

Galili, E. (1998b) Nevé Yam – underwater survey (Hebrew). *Hadashot Arkheologiyot – Excavations and Surveys in Israel* 18, 54–6.

Garfinkel, Y. (1992a) *The Pottery Assemblages of the Sha'ar Hagolan and Rabah Stages of Munhata (Israel)*. Paris: Centre de Recherche Français de Jérusalem.

Garfinkel, Y. (1992b) The Material Culture of the Central Jordan Valley in the Pottery Neolithic and Early Chalcolithic Periods. Unpublished PhD thesis, Jerusalem, The Hebrew University of Jerusalem.

Garfinkel, Y. (1999) *Neolithic and Chalcolithic Pottery of the Southern Levant*. Qedem 39, Jerusalem Institute of Archaeology, The Hebrew University of Jerusalem.

Garfinkel, Y. and Matskevich, Z. (2002) Abu Zureiq, a Wadi Rabah site in the Jezreel valley: final report of the 1962 excavations. *Israel Exploration Journal* 52/2, 129–66.

Gilead, I. (1988) The Chalcolithic Period in the Levant. *Journal of World Prehistory* 2/4, 397–443.

Gopher, A. (1989) *The Flint Assemblages of Munhata-Final Report*. Paris: Association Paléorient.

Gopher, A. (1995) Early pottery-bearing groups in Israel – The Pottery Neolithic period. Pp. 205–25 in T. E. Levy (ed.), *The Archaeology of Society in the Holy Land*. London and Washington DC: Leicester University Press.

Gopher, A. and Gophna, R. (1993) Cultures of the eighth and seventh millennia BP in the southern Levant: a review for the 1990s. *Journal of World Prehistory* 7/3, 297–353.

Gopher, A. and Rosen, S. (2001) Lithics of Strata XIII–III, the Pre-Pottery Neolithic–Early Bronze Age. Pp. 49–82 in E. Eisenberg, A. Gopher and R. Greenberg (eds), *Tel Te'o, A. Neolithic, Chalcolithic, and Early Bronze Age Site in the Hula Valley*. Israel Antiquities Authority Reports 13. Jerusalem.

Gopher, A. and Tsuk, T. (1996) *The Nahal Qanah Cave: Earliest Gold in the Southern Levant*. Tel Aviv: Tel Aviv University.

Gopher, A., Sadeh, S. and Goren, Y. (1992) The pottery assemblage of Nahal Beset I: a Neolithic site in the Upper Galilee. *Israel Exploration Journal* 42, 4–16.

Gopher, A., Barkai, R. and Asaf, A. (2001) Trends in sickle blades production in the Neolithic of the Hula valley, Israel. Pp. 411–25 in I. Caneva, C. Lemorini, D. Zampetti and P. Biagi (eds), *Beyond Tools: Redefining the PPN Lithic Assemblages of the Levant*. Berlin: ex oriente.

Goren, Y. (1991) The Beginnings of Pottery Production in Israel: Technology and Typology of Proto-Historic Ceramic Assemblages in Eretz-Israel (6th–4th Millennia BCE). Unpublished PhD thesis, Jerusalem, the Hebrew University in Jerusalem.

Hennessy, J. B. (1969) Preliminary report on a first season of excavations at Teleilat Ghassul. *Levant* 1, 1–24.

Inizan, M.-L., Roche, H. and Tixier, J. (1992) *Technology of Knapped Stone*. Meudon: CREP.

Kadowaki, S. (2005) Design and production technology of sickle-elements in Late Neolithic Wadi Ziqlab, northern Jordan. *Paléorient* 31/2, 69–85.

Kadowaki, S. (2007) Changing Community Life at a Late Neolithic Farmstead: Built Environments and the Use of Space at Tabaqat al-Bûma in Wadi Ziqlab, Northern Jordan. Unpublished PhD thesis, University of Toronto, Department of Anthropology.

Kafafi, Z. (1989) Late Neolithic 1 pottery from 'Ain er-Rahub, Jordan. *Zeitschrift des Deutschen Palästina-Vereins* 105, 1–18.

Kafafi, Z. (2001) *Jebel Abu Thawwab (Er-Rumman), Central Jordan. The Late Neolithic and Early Bronze Age I Occupations*. Bibliotheca Neolithica Asiae Meridionalis et Occidentalis and Yarmouk University Monograph of the Institute of Archaeology and Anthropology 3. Berlin: ex oriente.

Kaplan, J. (1959) The Neolithic pottery of Palestine. *Bulletin of the American Schools of Oriental Research* 156, 15–18.

Kaplan, J. (1969) 'Ein el Jarba: Chalcolithic remains in the Plain of Esdraelon. *Bulletin of the American Schools of Oriental Research* 194, 2–39.

Kenyon, K. M. (1979) *Archaeology in the Holy Land*, 4th edn. London: E. Benn.

Kenyon, K. M. and Holland, T. A. (1982) *Excavations at Jericho, Volume Four. The Pottery Type Series and Other Finds*. London: British School of Archaeology in Jerusalem.

Leonard, A. (1992) *The Jordan Valley Survey, 1953: Some Unpublished Soundings Conducted by James Mellaart*. Annual of the American Schools of Oriental Research 50. Winona Lake, IN: Eisenbrauns.

Lovell, J. L. (2001) *The Late Neolithic and Chalcolithic Periods in the Southern Levant. New Data from the Site of Teleilat Ghassul, Jordan*. Oxford: BAR Int. Ser. 974.

Lovell, J. L., Kafafi, Z. and Dollfus, G. (1997) A preliminary note on the ceramics from the basal levels of Abu Hamid. Pp. 361–70 in H. G. K. Gebel, Z. Kafafi and G. O. Rollefson (eds), *The Prehistory of Jordan II. Perspectives from 1997*.

Studies in Early Near Eastern Production, Subsistence, and Environment 4. Berlin: ex oriente.

Lovell, J. L., Dollfus, G. and Kafafi, Z. (2004) The middle phases at Abu Hamid and the Wadi Rabah horizon. Pp. 263–74 in F. al-Khraysheh, K. 'Amr, H. Taher and S. Khouri (eds), *Studies in the History and Archaeology of Jordan* 8. Amman: The Department of Antiquities of Jordan.

Lovell, J. L., Dollfus, G. and Kafafi, Z. (2007) The ceramics of the Late Neolithic and Chalcolithic: Abu Hamid and the burnished tradition. *Paléorient* 33/1, 50–75.

McNicoll, A., Smith, R. H. and Hennessy, B. (1982) *Pella in Jordan 1*. Canberra: Australian National Gallery.

Moore, A. M. T. (1973) The Late Neolithic in Palestine. *Levant* 10, 36–68.

Obeidat, D. (1995) *Die Neolithische Keramik aus Abu Thawwab, Jordanien*. Studies in Early Near Eastern Production, Subsistence and Environment 2. Berlin: ex oriente.

Peros, M. (2000) Sickle blade design and hafting strategies at Tabaqat al-Bûma, a Late Neolithic farmstead in Wadi Ziqlab, Northern Jordan. *Neo-Lithics* 2/3, 2–4.

Perrot, J. (1955) The excavations at Abu Matar, near Beersheva. *Israel Exploration Journal* 5, 17–40.

Prausnitz, M. W. (1977) The pottery at Newe Yam. *Eretz-Israel* 13, 272–6.

Rollefson, G. O., Simmons, A. H. and Kafafi, Z. (1992) Neolithic vultures at 'Ain Ghazal, Jordan. *Journal of Field Archaeology* 19, 443–70.

Rosen, S. A. (1997) *Lithics After the Stone Age: A Handbook of Stone Tools from the Levant*. Walnut Creek, CA: AltaMira Press.

Sadeh, S. and Eisenberg, E. (2001) Pottery of strata X–VIII, the Pottery Neolithic period. Pp. 83–104 in E. Eisenberg, A. Gopher, and R. Greenberg (eds), *Tel Te'o, A. Neolithic, Chalcolithic, and Early Bronze Age Site in the Hula Valley*. Israel Antiquities Authority Reports 13. Jerusalem.

Shafiq, R. (1996) Histological Investigation of Late Neolithic Agriculturist Settlement in Northern Jordan. Unpublished MSc dissertation, Department of Archaeological Sciences, University of Bradford.

Siggers, J. (1997) The Lithic Assemblage from Tabaqat al-Bûma: A Late Neolithic Site in Wadi Ziqlab, Northern Jordan. Unpublished PhD thesis, University of Toronto, Department of Anthropology.

Vaux, R. de (1966) Palestine during the Neolithic and Chalcolithic periods. Pp. 498–538 in I. E. S. Edwards, C. J. Gadd and N. G. L. Hammond (eds), *The Cambridge Ancient History*, vol. 1. London: Cambridge University Press.

5. Continuity and Change – Cultural Transmission in the Late Chalcolithic–Early Bronze Age I: A View from Early Modi'in, a Late Prehistoric Site in Central Israel

Edwin C. M. van den Brink

Introduction

> The Late Prehistory of the southern Levant is understood as a continuum of human occupation of the region during which there is an observable sequence of recognizable entities archaeologists are wont to call cultures or cultural horizons. To assign one particular point on a continuum the status of a boundary between cultures is the prerogative of archaeologists. It is also a subjective exercise in arbitrary determination and it remains for the reading public to judge the degree of subjectivity and validity of such perceptions. (Braun and Gophna 2004, 225)

The disparities between the Late Chalcolithic (henceforth LC) to the Early Bronze I (henceforth EB I), and the links that associate them, have been discussed at some length (Braun 1989a; 1996; 2000; this volume). The debate has suffered from a lack of data from well-excavated sequences that document the LC–EB I transition. Thus there is considerable disagreement about just where the break in cultural continuity lies, about the very nature of this break and about how acute it was. Therefore, excavations at Modi'in which yielded strong evidence for a transitional phase *linking* the LC to the EB I provide a rare opportunity to reappraise our understanding of this poorly known transitional period. This paper is a response to the editors' call for debate and discussion on the concepts of culture and transition in light of archeological data from the southern Levant which is based on fieldwork at Modi'in, Central Israel (map ref. New Israel Grid 2010.6420) between the years 2003 and 2006.

Elements of change or innovation

The major elements of change or innovation that define and distinguish the LC from the EB I are observable in the archaeological record in four major areas: 1) settlement patterns, 2) mortuary behaviour, 3) domestic architecture and 4) objects of portable material culture, with particular emphasis on crafts, craft specialization and/or modes of production (Table 5.1). These aspects indicate some kind of major disruption in continuity at the end of the Beer Sheva facies of the LC, which can be detected throughout the rest of the southern Levant.

Settlement patterns

A noted disruption of settlement patterns at the end of the LC (*e.g.* Gophna and Portugali 1988) appears slightly less radical in the south than in the north of the southern Levant, but is characterized in both regions by almost total abandonment during the LC of settlements and burial sites, many of which were never to be resettled or reused. Possible factors that could account for such a disruption include drastic changes in climatic–environmental conditions, epidemics and an influx of newcomers resulting in overpopulation with stress arising from utilization of limited and probably inadequate natural resources. Whatever the cause or causes may have been, it has been noted that there is a 'significantly lesser break in continuity' (Braun 1996, 4) between the LC and the EB I in the south than there is in the north. Data concerning selected sites with an LC–early EB I sequence, outlined in Table 5.2, reflect this.

In both regions, excavated early EB I settlements are few in number, are located at considerable distances from one another, and suggest no real continuity with the LC. In the northern Negev, for instance, up to 120 known Chalcolithic sites were abandoned by the end of the LC, a number sharply contrasting with only two known early

	LC	*Early EB I*
Settlement density	High density of known settlements and burial sites	Paucity of known settlements and an even smaller number of known burial sites
Architectural traditions	Rectilinear dwellings	Curvilinear dwellings
Burial customs	Multiple cave burials in clay and stone ossuaries	Multiple cave burials without clay or stone ossuaries
Ceramics	For example, v-shaped bowls, churns, cornets, ossuaries, cream-ware, lug handles with triangular sections	For example, hemispherical bowls, carinated bowls with and without knobs (GBW)
Metallurgy	Copper tools and copper prestige items	Copper tools, but absence of copper prestige items
Flints	Bifacials (adzes and axes), backed sickle blades	Absence of bifacials; presence of 'Canaanean' blades
Ground stone	Flat-based and pedestalled basalt bowls	Flat-based basalt bowls, absence of pedestalled basalt bowls
Other crafts; iconographic and plastic arts	Stone and ivory carving, wall paintings	Virtual lack of iconography and plastic art throughout EB I

Table 5.1 Comparative listing of general LC and early EB I traits indicative of change or innovation

Settlement sites in the north	*Settlement sites in the south*	*Burial sites/cave sites*
Tel Te'o Stratum VI (LC) – [gap] – Stratum V (early EB I; curvilinear structures and GBW)	Tel Halif Terrace, silo site, strata IV (LC)/III (early EB I; no curvilinear structures, no GBW)	Sha'ar Efrayim, caves 1, 3 and 4 (LC and early EB I [GBW])
Ain Asawir Stratum IV (LC) – [gap] – Stratum III (early EB I; curvilinear structures and GBW)	Afridar, Area G, strata 2 (LC)/2 (early EB I; curvilinear structures but no GBW)	Shoham (north) cave 4 (LC and early EB I [GBW])
Meser Stratum III (LC) – [gap] – Stratum II (early EB I; curvilinear structures and GBW)	Palmahim Quarry, strata 3 (LC)/3 (early EB I; curvilinear structures and GBW)	Modi'in-Buchman, Cave F3346 (LC and early EB I [but no GBW])
Horvat Usa Stratum 15 (LC) – [gap] – Stratum 14 (early EB I; GBW)	Modi'in-Buchman, strata 4 (LC)/3 (early EB I; NB no curvilinear structures, no GBW)	
	Tel Aviv, Ha-Masger Stratum, Reused pits (LC and early EB I; GBW)	

(GBW = [presence of] Gray Burnished Ware)

Table 5.2 Selected sites with a LC – Early EB I sequence

EB I sites in the same area, Wady Ghazzeh Site H and Taur Ikbeineh (Alon and Yekutieli 1995, 184).

However, the southern sites resettled in the early EB I appear to be slightly earlier than those in the north. A southern site like Tel Halif Terrace 'Silo Site', Stratum III, for instance, is attributed by Alon and Yekutieli (1995, 183, table 1) to the *earliest* Early Bronze Age IA, as opposed to a northern site such as Tel Te'o, Stratum V, attributed by the excavator to the *late* EB IA (Eisenberg *et al.* 2001, 211, Table 14.1). The few LC sites resettled during the early EB I in the north thus far fail to show continuity in traditions of material culture and so are represented in Table 5.2 as having a 'gap' in occupation. Based foremost on the study of relevant pottery assemblages, the earliest vestiges of EB I occupation at these sites belong indeed to an already chronologically advanced – that is, non-initial

– stage of this period. Primarily this notion flows from comparisons with sites such as Tel Te'o, Strata VI to V, which does contain an LC–early EB I corpus. However, in the south, similarities between LC and early EB I potting traditions at relevant sites seem to exist (*e.g.* Ashkelon, Afridar Strata-2/2 and Palmahim Quarry Strata-3/3; see Braun and Gophna 2004, 228).

Mortuary practices

The custom of secondary burials in decorated ceramic ossuaries often accompanied by fenestrated and V-shaped pottery bowls, one of the hallmarks of Chalcolithic mortuary behaviour that expresses itself mainly in the context of multiple burial caves, does not seem to have survived the transition to the early EB I. In other words, it appears that the production of ceramic or stone ossuaries, as well as fenestrated and straight-sided, flat based, wheel-fashioned bowls ceased prior to the onset of the EB I.

Architecture

The Chalcolithic tradition of building rectilinear domiciles (inherited from Neolithic forebears) was temporarily replaced in both the north and the south during the early EB I by a marked preference for curvilinear dwellings (Braun 1989a; 1989b).

Material culture/crafts and craft specialization/modes of production

Ceramics

Chalcolithic diagnostic pottery types or features that did not survive the transition to the early EB I include cornets and churns as well as lug handles that are triangular in section. Roux (2008) notes that the demand for, and thus the production of, straight-walled, wheel-fashioned bowls also ceased at the end of the LC. Some of the new pottery shapes initiated and/or reintroduced during the early EB I include hemispheric and carinated bowls. Many of these last have flattened protrusions and belong to a specialized class of vessels generally referred to as Gray Burnished Ware.

Ground stone and chipped stone (flint)

The fenestrated pedestalled basalt bowl, another hallmark of Chalcolithic craft, does not survive the transition to the early EB I (see, *e.g.*, Braun 1990); nor does its distinctive decoration of incised chevrons. Region-specific items such as the basalt pillar figurines of the Golan (Epstein 1998, 230–3) ceased to be produced and, indeed, the extraordinarily high artistic output of the Chalcolithic period is unmatched in the EB I (at least in the case of durable materials). Either EB I people produced most of their art in non-durable materials, or they produced far less. Characteristic Chalcolithic flint tools such as bifacial adzes and axes also are unknown in the lithic tool kit of the early EB I, while prismatic or so-called 'proto-Canaanean' blades make what may be their first appearance at the very end of the LC (see Milevski *et al.*, this volume). Significantly, they are not found in the Beer Sheva facies of the LC sites.

Elements of continuity

The various changes noted above notwithstanding, both horizons do share certain characteristics that, as the archaeological record is increasingly revealed, seem to grow in number. As Braun (this volume) has noted: 'Given [a] constant human presence, no chrono-cultural entity recognized by archaeologists (*i.e.*, cultures, periods, phases, horizons, etc) was devoid of contacts with those [entities] immediately preceding and succeeding it.'

Life after the LC continued on the level of small villages with subsistence economies still based on mixed farming/husbandry. Knowledge of olive tree cultivation and domestication of olive trees in the Chalcolithic period (Epstein 1993; Meadows 2004; Lev-Yodi *et al.* in press) was transmitted to the early EB I populace (see, *e.g.*, Liphschitz 2004, 309). Multiple burials in caves away from settlements was a common practice during the LC (see van den Brink 1998; 2005a) and continued into the early EB I (see Braun 1996, 23–4), although secondary burials were no longer deposited in clay or stone ossuaries. Sometimes the same caves were used during the LC and the early EB I and, in at least one case, the early EB I utilizers of a cave (Cave 1 in Sha'ar Efrayim; van den Brink 2005b) seem to have made special arrangements for preserving the integrity of LC burials by screening off part of the cave with a stone wall before interring their dead.

Direct contacts established between bearers of the Beer Sheva facies of the LC and a Lower Egyptian Maadi-Buto populace as evinced by the findings at Tell el-Fara'in/Buto I in the north-west Nile Delta (Faltings 2002; Commenge and Alon 2002) continued during early EB I. They are known from finds from Maadi, near Cairo (Hartung 2004; Braun and van den Brink 2008, 649–50). The presence of specimens of imported Nilotic *Chambardia rubens arcuata* (formerly identified as *Aspatharia rubens*) in both LC and EB I contexts further demonstrates that contacts between Predynastic Egypt and the southern Levant during these periods continued. *Chambardia rubens arcuata* was favoured in the Chalcolithic period for the production of pendants. However, while these shells continued to make their way to early EB I people, they seem to have otherwise remained unaltered. They are found as shells rather than artefacts (Sharvit *et al.* 2002; Bar-Yosef Mayer 2002; Braun and van den Brink 2008, 646–8). Sparse remains of the Nilotic fish *Synodontis schall* are found in both LC and early EB I contexts (Braun and van den Brink 2008, 649). The continued occurrence of Nilotic shells and fish in the southern Levant shows that foreign traders maintained contact with the populace after the LC.

Traits of material culture shared by both LC and early EB I assemblages are detailed in the four sections below.

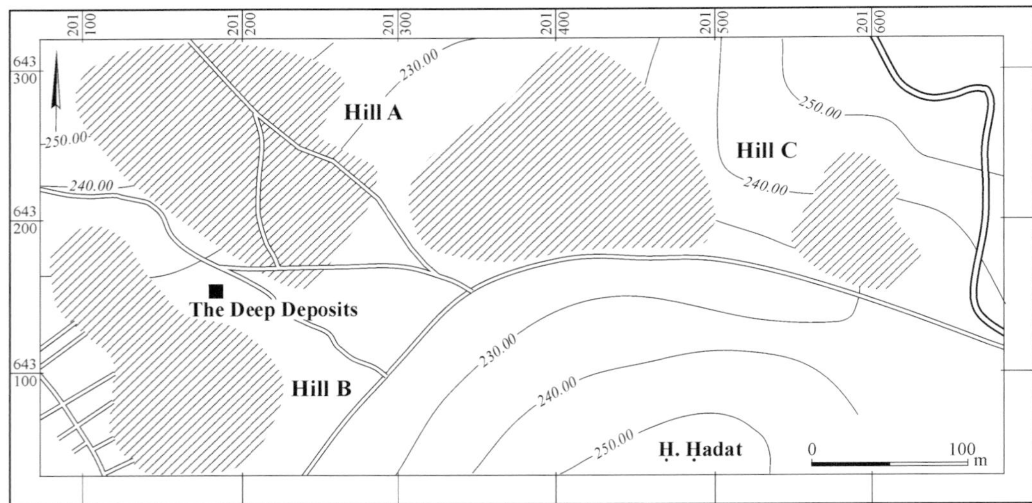

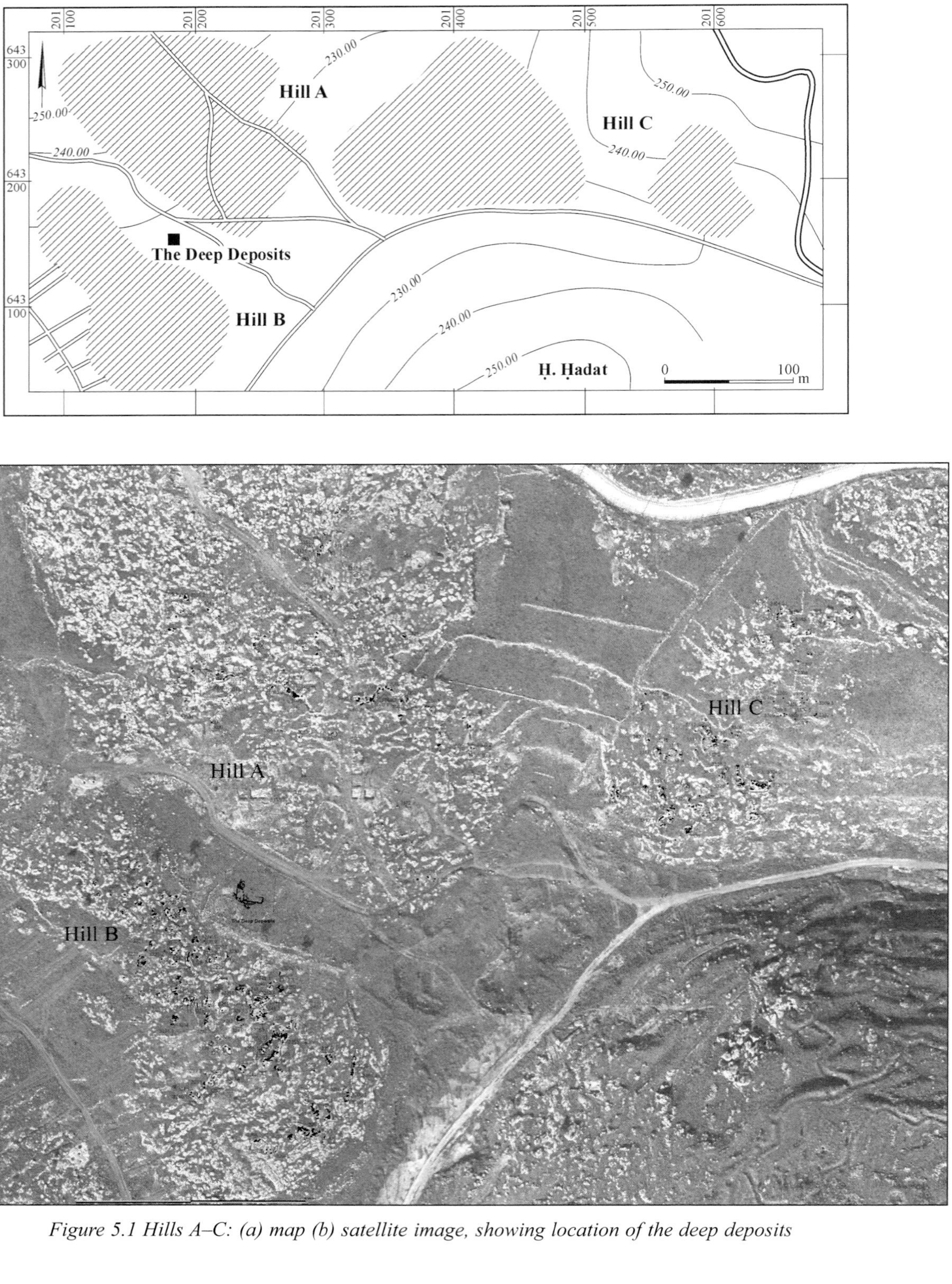

Figure 5.1 Hills A–C: (a) map (b) satellite image, showing location of the deep deposits

Ceramics

Recent excavation of LC burial caves at Shoham North (Commenge 2005, 55, figs 6.29:1 and 6.32:1–6) and Mazor (I. Milevski pers. comm.; Braun, this volume), both located in the central Shephela (internal plain and piedmont) of Israel, as well as at another site, Horvat Qarqar South (P. Fabian, pers. comm.), just south of Qiryat Gat near the northern periphery of the Negev, have clearly shown that small ledge handles with indented edges (long considered to have been an exclusive hallmark of the EB) made their first appearance during the LC. Ceramic bowls on fenestrated stands are present in the LC as well as the early EB I, albeit with different fabrics, overall shapes and surface treatments (*cf.* Amiran 1969, 24, photos 11 and 12).

Ground stone

Although fenestrated pedestalled basalt bowls seem to have ceased to be produced, flat-based EB I basalt bowls apparently developed out of Chalcolithic prototypes, keeping a stone-working tradition alive (Braun 1990).

Flint tools

The tabular (sometimes called 'fan' or 'tongue-shaped') flint scraper, struck from a large flat nodule, one side of which remained covered by cortex, is common to both the LC and EB horizons. However, incised cortex examples seem to be exclusively dated to the EBA (EBA) (Rosen 1997, 75). As for the earliest appearance of 'Canaanean' blades, one of the alleged hallmarks of the EBA, recent finds at a number of Chalcolithic sites in the central region indicate the possibility of their presence as early as the LC. These sites include Shoham North (Marder 2005, 145–7), Horvat Qarqar South (P. Fabian, pers. comm.) and Yesodot (author's pers. observ.; I. Paz and A. Nativ, pers. comm.), a small, newly discovered site just north of Beth Shemesh. This information is interesting in the light of earlier finds at Gilat (Rowan 2006) and furthers a debate (Rowan and Levy 1994) as to whether or not their so-called 'proto-Canaanean' blades, more recently also described as prismatic blades (Rowan 2006) should be considered a component of the LC tool kit (*cf.* Milevski *et al.*, this volume). Finds from the recent excavations at Fazael 2 (Bar and Winter 2010) add weight to the affirmative case.

Metallurgy

Prestige or cultic copper artefacts such as maceheads and so-called 'scepters' and 'crowns', hallmarks of LC metallurgical craftsmanship (*cf.*, *e.g.*, Bar-Adon 1980), were apparently no longer produced after the demise of the LC culture; they are unknown in EB I contexts. However, production of copper *tools* did continue in the EB I, as evidenced by the presence of a crucible fragment with traces of copper and a number of copper axeheads (*e.g.*, Shalev and Braun 1997, 93) from secure early EB I contexts. Notably, their morphology is similar to that of Chalcolithic axeheads, although Braun and Shalev have suggested that the later examples tend to be shorter and thicker. These finds indicate that, even though metal production was now apparently restricted to copper tools, 'there does not appear to be any change in the production process with this passage of time. It would seem that there is continuity evident in the choice of metal in the early EB I, probably reflecting the utilization of the same resources of ore exploited during the Chalcolithic' (Shalev and Braun 1997, 96). This observation is now further corroborated by excavation results from Ashkelon Afridar Area E (Golani 2004, 45).

A view from early Modi'in in central Israel

Plans to extend an area of modern Modi'in to the south included a major enlargement of the Buchman neighbourhood at the expense of pristine countryside, endangering archaeological remains in that area. That led to trial and salvage excavations conducted by the author on behalf of the Israel Antiquities Authority (IAA) between the years 2003 and 2006 (van den Brink 2005c; 2007a; 2007b; in press). Excavations on three adjoining hills that slope down gently and then steeply from north to south and west to east, at elevations between 260 and 240 m above sea level (Figure 5.1; van den Brink 2005c), uncovered evidence of extensive occupation and utilization of the area in the LC period.

In 2004, archaeological deposits spread over several terraces encountered on the eastern inclines of adjoining Hills A and B were located and probed. They revealed the presence of a remarkably well-preserved *tell*-like series of superimposed deposits located in what had once been a deep longitudinal depression between these hills. Its excavation yielded a sequence of archaeological deposits over 3 m in depth and consisting of eight strata, seven yielding remains of stone-built architecture (Figure 5.2). Two of these strata are dated by an array of 10 ^{14}C assays (Table 5.3) taken from samples of olive wood and carbonized olive stones. Botanical identification of the ^{14}C samples was carried out by N. Liphschitz. Six samples derive from Stratum 5, two from Stratum 6 and one each from Strata 7 and 2. They were processed by G. Bonani and L. Hajdas at the Institute of Particle Physics in Zurich, Switzerland, for ^{14}C-AMS dating. The calibrated (dendrocorrected) ages are 2σ-ranges (95% confidence limit) and were calculated using the program CalibETH (Bonani *et al.* 1992). Notably, Stratum 5 in particular was rich in organic content; its excavation yielded more than 1200 carbonized olive stones in a single cache (Lev-Yadun *et al.* in press).

But for natural bedrock, Stratum 8 and Stratum 7 dating to the Middle Chalcolithic, the material culture of the lowest four strata (7–4) is LC, or more or less equivalent to that of Ghassul III and IV and Beer Sheva cultural horizons, while the upper three strata (3–1) are associated with the early EB I horizon. Thus, this site records, in an apparently very fine-tuned time scale, the transition from the latest Chalcolithic to the earliest EB I.

The LC–early EB I deep deposits (Strata 4 and 3)

In order to understand how LC Stratum 4 compares to early EB I Stratum 3, it is first necessary to describe how Stratum 4 relates to underlying deposits in LC Strata 5

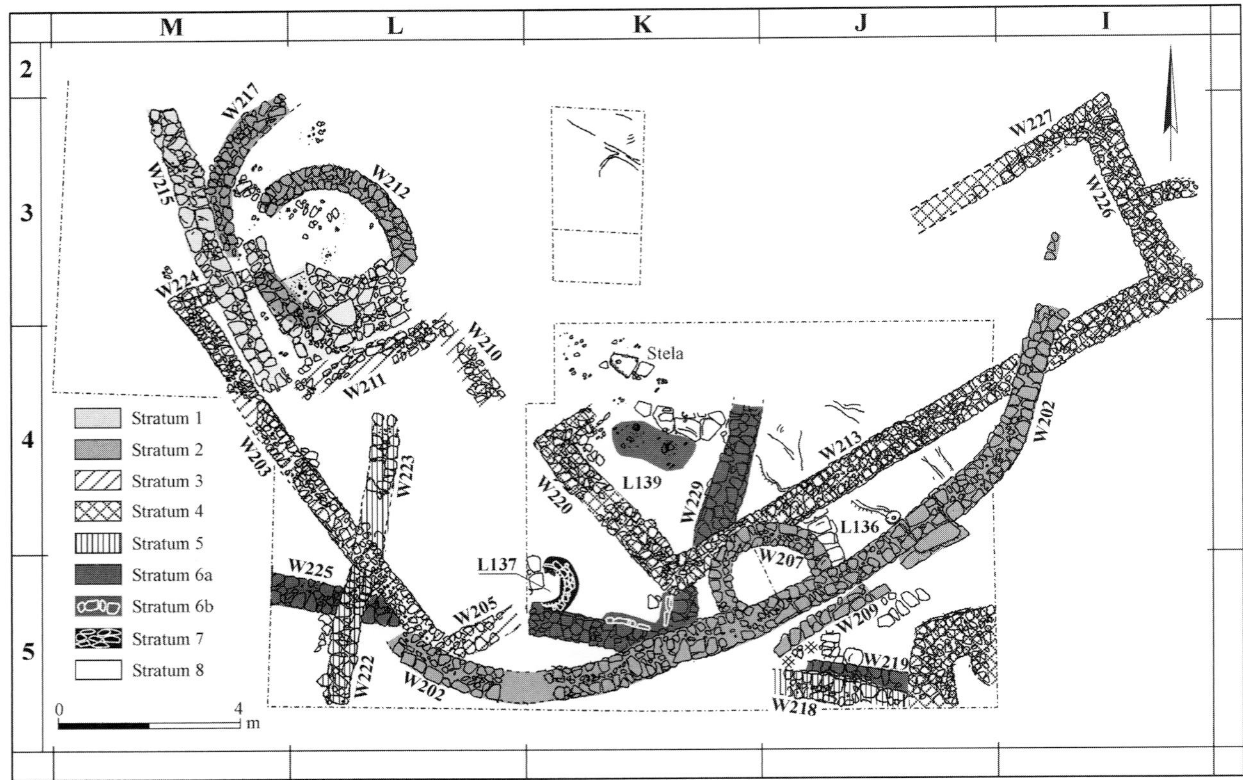

Figure 5.2 Early Modi'in: the deep deposits. Strata 7–1, compilation of exposed architectural remains

and 6, and how Stratum 3 relates to early EB I Stratum 2 above. Structures of Strata 5 and 6 share a single orientation and evince the same rectangular style of architecture well known in LC contexts. The stone foundations of the Stratum 5 building rest directly on the stone wall remains of the underlying Stratum 6 structure. The Stratum 4 structure is a broadroom, however, physically separated from the remains of the Stratum 5 building by *c.*0.5 m of fill. Moreover, the orientation of the Stratum 4 building differs significantly from the orientation of the Strata 5 and 6 buildings (see Figure 5.2). These differences undoubtedly indicate a hiatus in occupation between Strata 5 and 4, which seems corroborated by perceptible changes in pottery styles (van den Brink in press).

In contrast, occupation of the site during Strata 4 and 3 seems to have been continuous. There is no substantial fill separating these two strata and the building orientation and styles (rectangular broadroom structures) in these occupations are virtually identical. However, differences in portable aspects of material culture between these strata are significant, as at other LC and EB I sites.

Occupational continuity from Stratum 3 is indicated by the physical proximity of the Stratum 2 buildings just above. However, in Stratum 2 curvilinear architecture replaced the rectilinear building mode that prevailed throughout the settlement from Stratum 6 through to Stratum 3.

The claim that the LC–EB I transition fell between Stratum 4 and Stratum 3 is broadly outlined below in a brief discussion of the major elements which determine the ascription of these two occupations to disparate cultural horizons. These elements are architecture, ceramics and ground stone and chipped-stone artefacts (*i.e.*, flint tools).

Architecture

The presence in Stratum 3 of a *rectilinear* broadroom associated with definitively early EB I elements of material culture is surprising; one might more readily expect a curvilinear structure. Instead, this structure seems to have its roots in the preceding stratum; it is in close proximity to and shares the orientation of the broadroom of the preceding occupation in Stratum 4 (Figure 5.2). That associated artefacts which indicate that this Stratum 3 building should be assigned to the EB I horizon were not deposited in a secondary utilization of an LC building cannot be excluded *a priori* but seems unlikely (van den Brink in press).

Remains of a large curvilinear structure with a well-defined doorway, stone pavement and door socket still *in situ* do, however, make their appearance in the following early EB I Stratum 2 (Figure 5.2). An unexpected detail of that enclosure is found in the presence at the entrance of an orthostat (Figure 5.2–3), which can be related by its morphology to similar specimens found in LC burial

Laboratory number	*Sample number*	*Material*	*AMS-14C age (years BP)*	*δ13C (‰)*	*Cal age (BC)*
ETH-30317	B4300 d	Wood	5355 ± 60	-26.4 ± 1.2	BC 4332–4265 (18.6%)
					BC 4265–4041 (80.9%)
ETH-30318	B4264 a	Olive stone	5200 ± 60	-19.3 ± 1.2	BC 4222–4188 (8.6%)
					BC 4164–4117 (10.2%)
					BC 4113–3936 (72.9%)
					BC 3864–3804 (7.5.%)
ETH-30319	B4264 b	Olive stone	5230 ± 60	-21.3 ± 1.2	BC 4219–4199 (13.7%)
					BC 4158–4149 (5.2%)
					BC 4142–4126 (9.7%)
					BC 4050–3965 (69.6%)
ETH-30320	B4264 c	Olive stone	5175 ± 60	-21.3 ± 1.2	BC 4220–4197 (4.5%)
					BC 4160–4123 (5.0%)
					BC 4052–3892 (68.9%)
					BC 3882–3798 (19.5%)
ETH-30321	B4264 i	Olive stone	5265 ± 60	-21.5 ± 1.2	BC 4238–3965 (100.0%)
ETH-30322	B4264 j	Olive stone	5360 ± 60	-20.9 ± 1.2	BC 4333–4042 (100.0%)
ETH-30323*	B4289 h	Wood	4720 ± 60	-24.2 ± 1.2	BC 3638–3487 (58.5%)
					BC 3473–3370 (41.5%)
ETH-30324	B4495 f	Wood	5290 ± 60	-20.4 ± 1.2	BC 4249–3978 (98.3%)
ETH-30325	B4501 e	Wood	5740 ± 55	-26.2 ± 1.2	BC 4713–4459 (99.8%)
ETH-30326	B4514 g	Olive stone	5385 ± 55	-22.3 ± 1.2	BC 4338–4217 (54.3%)
					BC 4202–4155 (17.9%)
					BC 4131–4046 (23.8%)

* sample ETH-30323 derives from Stratum 2, samples ETH-30317–ETH 30322 derive from Stratum 5, samples ETH-30324 and ETH-303026 from Stratum 6, and ETH-30325 from Stratum 7

Table 5.3 Radiocarbon dates from the deep deposits, Strata 5 and 2

contexts in Shoham North (Rowan 2005, 116–17, figs 19.19–19.20) and Horvat Qarqar South (author's pers. observ.; P. Fabian, pers. comm.). It, therefore, probably concerns secondary utilization of an LC *matzava* (stela).

Ceramics

A preliminary study of a small sample of pottery from Strata 4 and 3 carried out by Valentine Roux shows that there is technical continuity between the LC (Stratum 4) and early EB I (Stratum 3), corroborating similar observations made concerning the early EB I ceramic artefacts from Afridar Area G, and Palmahim Quarry Stratum 3 (Braun and Gophna 2004, 228). This continuity is found in the utilization of a wheel for fashioning small open bowls. According to Roux the wheel was used in a more heterogeneous manner in Stratum 4 than in Stratum 3, suggesting different modalities of ceramic production. In addition, the presence of small ledge handles with indented edges even in the earliest LC strata at early

Figure 5.3 Early Modi'in: the deep deposits. Stratum 2, orthostat at entrance to curvilinear structure

Modi'in further corroborates the observation (noted above) that such handles appear in secure LC contexts (*e.g.*, Commenge 2005, 55, figs 6.29:1, 6.32:1–6), although they are more common in the following EB I period. At early Modi'in there are numerous examples of this type of small ledge handle on vessels decorated externally by combing, probably with a wooden object.

Stone implements

Although in-depth analysis of the flint materials from the early Modi'in site has not yet started, the presence of so-called 'Canaanean' blades seemingly associated with Stratum 4 was noticed in the field. If this association is substantiated, then this information will become relevant to any debates concerning the appearance of this tool type in the LC (see also Bar and Winter 2010). A piriform limestone macehead, reminiscent of LC specimens in copper, was found in Stratum 3. Thus there is a suggestion, at least in terms of morphology, of continuity in this type of object.

Conclusions

The focus of this paper has been on selected remains of the material culture of two of eight strata superimposed of the deep deposits, the LC Stratum 4 and the early EB I occupation of Stratum 3 at Modi'in. Although radiocarbon assays are unavailable for these strata (owing to a lack of samples), calibrated ^{14}C dates from Strata 5 and 2 indicate a lower and an upper limit within a time range of *c.*400 years for the duration of Strata 4 and 3 (Table 5.3). That is to say that *grosso modo*, Stratum 4 post-dates 4000 BC and Stratum 3 pre-dates 3600 BC. Since there seems to have been an hiatus in occupation between Strata 5 and 4, but none between Strata 4, 3 and 2 (the transitional LC–EB I trajectory), Stratum 4 is likely to be dated significantly later than Stratum 5, perhaps to a time span rather late in the 4th millennium BC. The early Modi'in site is, of course, not the only site in the region that reveals an LC–early EB I sequence (see Table 5.2); various sites both in the north and south of the country provide 'snap shots' of phases within what is basically a continuum.

Modi'in Strata 4 and 3 are remarkable because they demonstrate a very close proximity in time and material culture between the LC and the EB I, although in the end they may be shown to be the extreme end of the former and the extreme beginning of the latter cultural horizon. Notably, Modi'in Stratum 3, with its rectilinear structure, seems to be a last gasp of an ancient tradition of rectilinear house construction that is replaced early on in the EB I by a curvilinear tradition in Stratum 2. The impression gained from a preliminary study of the material culture of Strata 4 and 3 is one of accelerated cultural transmission and progression. The spatial and apparent temporal proximity of LC and early EB I communities living, as it were, side by side in the Modi'in area at large is also palpable in various other (mainly cave-related) contexts in the area of Modi'in that are beyond the scope of this paper (but *cf.* van den Brink 2007b, Caves 2 and 3). Differences in material culture notwithstanding, continuity between Strata 4 and 3 is observed in terms of subsistence, building traditions and transmission of certain potting and perhaps flint-knapping techniques.

Acknowledgements

This paper would not have been possible without colleagues' generosity in providing me with information on their fieldwork and research. I am thankful to Peter Fabian (IAA) for showing me his excavation at Horvat Qarqar South, to Ianir Milevski (IAA) for allowing me to view the materials from his excavation at Mazor, to Yitzhak Paz and Assaf Nativ (Tel Aviv University) for inviting me to their excavation at Yesodot and to all these scholars for their permission to mention materials from their sites that are relevant to this paper. Thanks are also due to Valentine Roux (Centre Nationale de Recherche Scientifique) for sharing her observation on the pottery from Modi'in Strata 4 and 3 and for her permission to quote from her unpublished notes and observations on it. Basic elements of this paper were presented during a workshop on 'Techniques and People: Anthropological Perspectives on Technology in the Archaeology of the Proto-historic and Early Historic Periods in the Southern Levant', under the auspices of the Centre de Recherche Français de Jérusalem, organized by Valentine Roux and Steve Rosen, Jerusalem, 14–16 November 2006. I would like to thank both Valentine Roux and Steven Rosen (Ben Gurion University of the Negev) for providing me an opportunity to present this material, and for their permission to include this paper in this volume. Eliot Braun read and commented on earlier drafts of this paper. His input is much appreciated, as are as his editorial skills, which significantly improved both the style and structure of this paper.

References

Alon, D. and Yekutieli, Y. (1995) The Tel Halif Terrace 'Silo Site' and its implications for the Early Bronze Age I. *`Atiqot* 27, 148–89.

Amiran, R. (1969) *Ancient Pottery of the Holy Land. From its Beginnings in the Neolithic Period to the End of the Iron Age.* Jerusalem: Masada Press Ltd.

Bar, S. and Winter, H. (2010) Canaanean Blades in Late Chalcolithic context and the possible onset of the transition to the Early Bronze Age: A case study from Fazael 2. *Tel Aviv* 37, 33–47.

Bar-Adon, P. (1980) *The Cave of the Treasure. The Finds from the Caves in Nahal Mishmar.* Judean Desert Studies. Jerusalem: IES.

Bar-Yosef Mayer, D. E. (2002) Egyptian–Canaanite interaction during the fourth and third millennia BCE: the shell connection. Pp. 129–35 in E. C. M. van den Brink and T. E. Levy (eds),

Egypt and the Levant. Interrelations from the 4th through the Early 3rd Millennium BCE. London: Leicester University Press.

Bonani, G., Ivy, S. D., Hajdas, I., Niklaus, T. R. and Suter, M. (1992) Calib ETH. *Radiocarbon* 34, 483–92.

Braun, E. (1989a) The transition from the Chalcolithic to the Early Bronze Age in northern Israel and Transjordan: Is there a missing link? Pp. 7–28 in P. de Miroschedji (ed.), *L'urbanisation de la Palestine a l'age du Bronze ancient.* Oxford: BAR Int. Ser. 527.

Braun, E. (1989b) The problem of the apsidal house: new aspects of Early Bronze I domestic architecture in Israel, Jordan and Lebanon. *Palestine Exploration Quarterly* 121, 1–43.

Braun, E. (1990) Basalt bowls of the EBI horizon in the southern Levant. *Paléorient* 16, 87–95.

Braun, E. (1996) Cultural Diversity and Change in the Early Bronze I of Israel and Jordan: Towards an Understanding of the Chronological Progression and Patterns of Regionalism in Early Bronze I Society. Unpublished PhD thesis, Tel Aviv University.

Braun, E. (2000) Area G at Afridar, Palmahim 3 and the earliest pottery of the Early Bronze Age I: part of the missing link. Pp. 113–28 in G. Phillip and D. Bairds (eds), *Breaking with the Past: Ceramics and the Change in the Early Bronze Age of the Southern Levant.* Sheffield: Sheffield Academic Press.

Braun, E. and Gophna, R. (2004) Excavations at Ashqelon, Afridar – Area G. *`Atiqot* 45, 185–241.

Braun, E. and Brink, E. C. M. van den (2008) Appraising south Levantine–Egyptian interaction. Recent discoveries from Israel and Egypt. Pp. 643–88 in B. Midant-Reynes and Y. Tristant (eds), with the collaboration of J. Rowland and S. Hendrickx, *Predynastic and Early Dynastic Egypt. Origin of the State 2.* Orientalia Lovaniensia Analecta. Leuven: Peeters Publishing.

Brink, E. C. M. van den (1998) An index to Chalcolithic mortuary caves in Israel. *Israel Exploration Journal* 48/3–4, 165–73.

Brink, E. C. M. van den (2005a) Excursus 1: Chalcolithic burial caves in coastal and inland Israel. In E. C. M. van den Brink and R.Gophna (eds), *Shoham (North). Late Chalcolithic Burial Caves in the Lod Valley, Israel*, 175–89. Israel Antiquities Authority Reports 27. Jerusalem.

Brink, E. C. M. van den (2005b) Sha'ar Efrayim. *Journal HA/ESI* 117. http://www.hadashot-esi.org.il/report_detail_eng.asp?id=170&mag_id=110 (accessed 22 November 2009).

Brink, E. C. M. van den (2005c) Modi'in. *Journal HA–ESI* 117. http://www.hadashot-esi.org.il/report_detail_eng.asp?id=280&mag_id=110 (accessed 22 November 2009).

Brink, E. C. M. van den (2007a) Modi'in, Horbat Hadat and Be'erit (A). *Journal HA–ESI* 119. http://www.hadashot-esi.org.il/report_detail_eng.asp?id=484&mag_id=112 (accessed 22 November 2009).

Brink, E. C. M. van den (2007b) Modi'in – Horbat Hadat and Be'erit (B). *Journal HA–ESI* 119. http://www.hadashot-esi.org.il/report_detail_eng.asp?id=535&mag_id=112 (accessed 22 November 2009).

Brink, E. C. M. van den (2008) A new *fossile directeur* of the Chalcolithic landscape in the Shephelah and Samarian and Judean Hill countries: stationary grinding facilities in bedrock. *Israel Exploration Journal* 58/1, 1–23.

Brink, E. C. M. van den (in press) *Material Aspects of Transitional Late Chalcolithic to Early Early Bronze Age I Occupations and Landscape Exploitation at Modi'in (Buchman South/Moriah Quarter) in Central Israel.* Israel Antiquities Authority Report. Jerusalem.

Commenge, C. (2005) The Late Chalcolithic pottery. Pp. 51–97 in E. C. M. van den Brink and R. Gophna (eds), *Shoham (North). Late Chalcolithic Burial Caves in the Lod Valley, Israel.* Israel Antiquities Authority Reports 27. Jerusalem.

Commenge, C. and Alon, D. (2002) Competitive involution and expanded horizons: exploring the nature of interaction between northern Negev and Lower Egypt (*c*.4500–3600 BCE) Pp. 139–53 in E. C. M. van den Brink and T. E. Levy (eds), *Egypt and the Levant. Interrelations from the 4th through the Early 3rd Millennium BCE.* London: Leicester University Press.

Eisenberg, E., Gohper, A. and Greenberg, R. (2001) *Tel Te'o. A Neolithic, Chalcolithic, and Early Bronze Age Site in the Hula Valley.* Israel Antiquities Authority Reports 13. Jerusalem.

Epstein, C. (1993) Oil production in the Golan Heights during the Chalcolithic period. *Tel Aviv* 20, 133–46.

Epstein, C. (1998) *The Chalcolithic Culture of the Golan.* Israel Antiquities Authority Reports 4. Jerusalem.

Faltings, D. A. (2002) The chronological frame and social structure of Buto in the fourth millennium BCE. Pp. 165–70 in E. C. M. van den Brink and T. E. Levy (eds), *Egypt and the Levant. Interrelations from the 4th through the Early 3rd Millennium BCE.* London: Leicester University Press.

Golani, A. (2004) Salvage excavations at the Early Bronze Age site of Ashqelon, Afridar-Area E. *`Atiqot* 45, 9–62.

Gophna, R. and Portugali, Y. (1988) Settlement and demographic processes in Israel's coastal plain from the Chalcolithic to the Middle Bronze Age. *BASOR* 269, 11–28.

Hartung, U. (2004) Rescue excavations in the predynastic settlement of Maadi. Pp. 337–56 in S. Hendrickx, R. F. Friedman, K. M. Cialowicz and M. Chlodnicki (eds), *Egypt at its Origins. Studies in Memory of Barbara Adams. Proceedings of the international Conference 'Origin of the State. Predynastic and Early Dynastic Egypt', Kraków, 28th August–1st September 2002.* Orientalia Lovaniensia Analecta 138. Leuven/Paris/Dudley.

Lev-Yadun, S., Inbar, M. and Brink, E. C. M. van den (in press) Two 6,000-year-old Chalcolithic olive stone hoards from Modi'in, Israel. Pp. tbc in E. C. M. van den Brink (ed.) *Material Aspects of Transitional Late Chalcolithic to Early Early Bronze Age I Occupations and Landscape Exploitation at Modi'in (Buchman South/Moriah Quarter) in Central Israel.* Israel Antiquities Authority Report. Jerusalem.

Liphschitz, N. (2004) Archaeobotanical remains from Ashqelon, Afridar. *`Atiqot* 45, 305–10.

Marder, O. (2005) The flint assemblages. Pp. 141–8 in E. C. M. van den Brink and R. Gophna (eds), *Shoham (North). Late Chalcolithic Burial Caves in the Lod Valley, Israel.* Israel Antiquities Authority Reports 27. Jerusalem.

Meadows, J. (2004) Early Farmers and their Environment: Archaeobotanical Research at Neolithic and Chalcolithic Sites in Jordan. Unpublished PhD thesis, La Trobe University.

Rosen, S. A. (1997) *Lithics After the Stone Age. A Handbook of Stone Tools from the Levant.* London: Altamira Press.

Roux, V. (2008) Evolutionary trajectories of technological traits and cultural transmission: a qualitative approach to the emergence and disappearance of the ceramic wheel-fashioning technique in the southern Levant during the fifth to third millennia BC. Pp. 82–104 in M. Stark, B. Bowser and L. Horne (eds), *Cultural Transmission and Material Culture: Breaking down Boundaries.* Tucson, AZ: Arizona University Press.

Rowan, Y. M. (2005) The groundstone assemblages. Pp. 113–39 in E. C. M. van den Brink and R. Gophna (eds), *Shoham (North). Late Chalcolithic Burial Caves in the Lod Valley, Israel*. Israel Antiquities Authority Reports 27. Jerusalem.

Rowan, Y. M. (2006) Gilat's ground stone assemblage: stone fenestrated stands, bowls, palettes and related objects. Pp. 507–74 in T. E. Levy (ed.), *Archaeology, Anthropology, and Cult: The Sanctuary at Gilat, Israel*. London: Equinox.

Rowan, Y. M. and Levy, T. E. (1994) Proto-Canaanean blades of the Chalcolithic period. *Levant* 26, 167–74.

Shalev, S. and Braun, E. (1997) The metal objects from Yiftah'el II. Pp. 92–6 in E. Braun (ed.), *Yiftah'el. Salvage and Rescue Excavations at A Prehistoric Village in Lower Galilee, Israel*. Israel Antiquities Authority Reports 2. Jerusalem.

Sharvit, J., Galili, E., Rosen, B. and Brink, E. C. M. van den (2002) Predynastic maritime traffic along the Carmel coast of Israel: a submerged find from north Atlit Bay. Pp. 159–66 in E. C. M. van den Brink and E. Yannai (eds), *In Quest of Ancient Settlements and Landscape. Archaeological Studies in Honour of Ram Gophna*. Tel Aviv: Ramot Publishing, Tel Aviv University.

6. Desert Chronologies and Periodization Systems

Steven A. Rosen

Introduction

Chrono-cultural frameworks defining periods and cultures for the proto-historic periods in the Levantine Mediterranean zone have been constructed using variation in archaeological remains (material culture, settlement patterns, architecture, *etc.*) over time and geographic space (*e.g.*, Gilead 1988; 1990; Gopher and Gophna 1993; Amiran 1969; Stager 1992; Garfinkel 1999; Greenberg 2002; Joffe 1993; Lovell 2001; Philip and Baird 2000; Yekutieli 2002; Burton and Levy 2001; Levy and Holl 1995). Although the specifics of some of the terminologies are still debated, especially as concerning some of the higher-level entities and periodization schemes (see arguments over the term 'Chalcolithic', this volume), there is general agreement on the basic components of cultural entities such as the Ghassulian, the Wadi Rabah culture of the Pottery Neolithic, and the early stages of the Early Bronze Age. At the very least, it is possible to classify material-culture assemblages into these cultural units, and indeed sub-units, and to place them into general absolute and relative chronological frameworks. In distinct contrast, the regions south of the Beer Sheva basin – the Negev Highlands, the southern Negev, southern Jordan and Sinai (Figure 6.1) – encompass a fundamentally different cultural system, dubbed originally by Rothenberg the 'Timnian', with several additional industries defined as well (Rothenberg and Glass 1992; Ronen 1970; Kozloff 1974; 1981). In contrast to the sedentary village agricultural systems of the Mediterranean zone, Timnian subsistence was based on pastoralism (and gathering), and can be characterized as mobile and tribal.

The social and economic contrasts aside, the Timnian complex within the general framework of Levantine archaeological culture systematics reflects a cultural trajectory distinct from its northerly cousins both in its span and in its internal morphology. Furthermore, the basic tools used to construct Timnian culture history contrast with those of the north, the Timnian being based primarily on lithic industries (but see Rothenberg and Glass 1992), as opposed to the ceramics of the northern regions. These distinctions, on a range of different scales of time and space, seem strong enough to warrant the suggestion that the desert regions constitute a discrete culture area, with all the anthropological implications concerning issues such as ethnicity and core–periphery relations that such distinctions bring to mind. Furthermore, hints of similarities with other archaeological entities in the

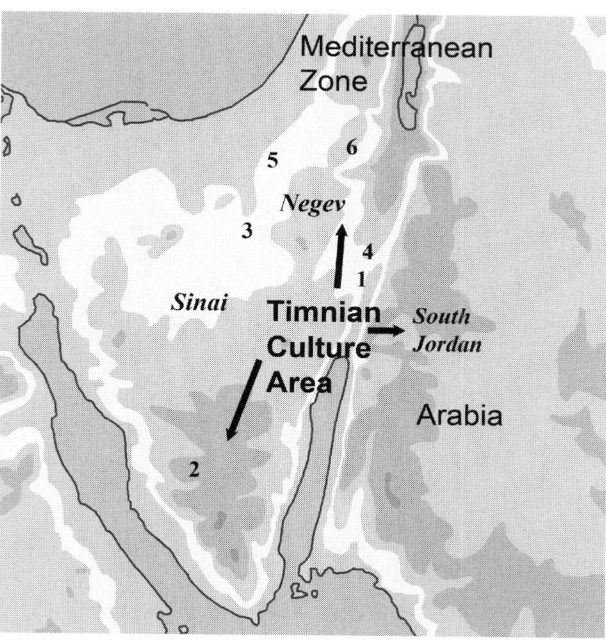

Figure 6.1 Map of Timnian culture region and sites mentioned in the text. 1. Timna; 2. Feiran; 3. Qadesh Barnea; 4. Beer Ada; 5. Nahal Tsafit

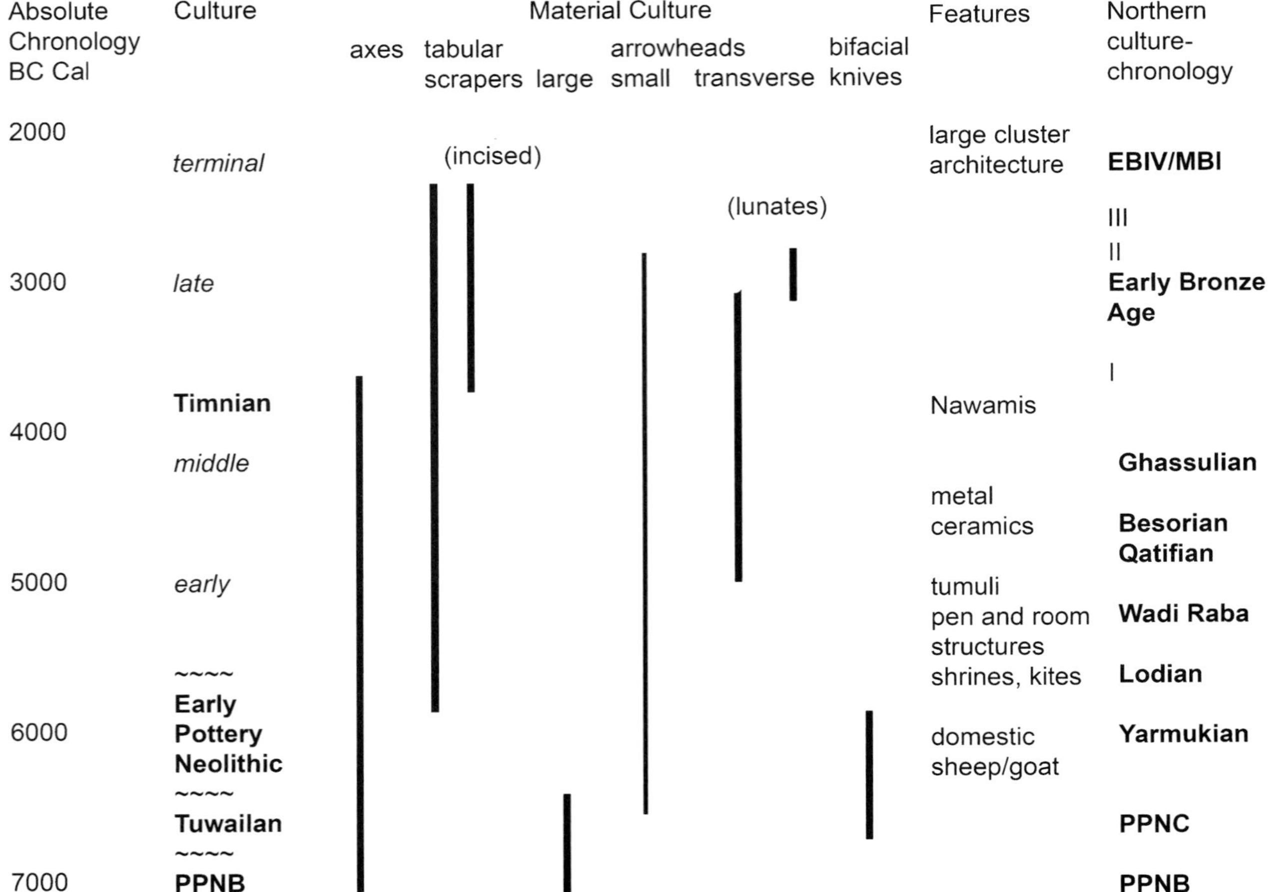

Figure 6.2 A chrono-cultural framework for the Timnian Complex and the southern desert regions of the Negev, southern Jordan and Sinai

Saharo-Arabian desert belt suggest linkages on the level of a general Saharo-Arabian pastoral complex.

The Timnian framework

Although originally defined on the basis of materials found in the Timna valley, the geographic extent of the Timnian culture varied in its different phases. In general, the culture extended throughout the regions of the southern Negev, central and southern Sinai and southern Jordan/northern Arabia (Figure 6.1). Although its northern extent varied with external relations, extending into the steppe zones of the central Negev and Jordan during some phases, the Timnian is a southern entity. There is little evidence for its presence in the Mediterranean zone.

The earliest definition of the Timnian culture based on material culture (Kozloff 1974; also Rothenberg and Glass 1992) characterized it as small flake industry with amorphous cores and high proportions of knapping errors (hinge fractures). Kozloff also noted the relatively high numbers of steep endscrapers resembling bladelet cores, the presence of various other kinds of scrapers in the tool assemblage, smaller numbers of fan scrapers (in contrast to the Eilatian), small numbers of tools in the celt family, borers, and drills, and a general absence of Levallois elements. It was specifically contrasted with the Eilatian culture, which is characterized as a 'chunky' flake industry (Kozloff 1974, 47) with varying proportions of tabular scrapers and use of tabular flint, high proportions of endscrapers and the readoption of the Levallois technique. Although not stated explicitly as chronological, the organization of Kozloff's paper indicates that the Eilatian be placed in the period immediately following the Pre-Pottery Neolithic B (PPNB) – in absolute terms, roughly the 7th millennium cal BC. It is noted to be reminiscent of Palaeolithic industries. In a study of several collections from Sinai Ronen (1970) had previously defined the Wadi Feiran and East Coast industries, suggesting that they be dated to the 4th millennium BC and linking the Wadi Feiran industry to the Egyptian Peasant Neolithic on the basis of morphological similarities among specific tool types. More recently, Goring-Morris (1993) has suggested a new culture-industry, dubbed the Tuwailan,

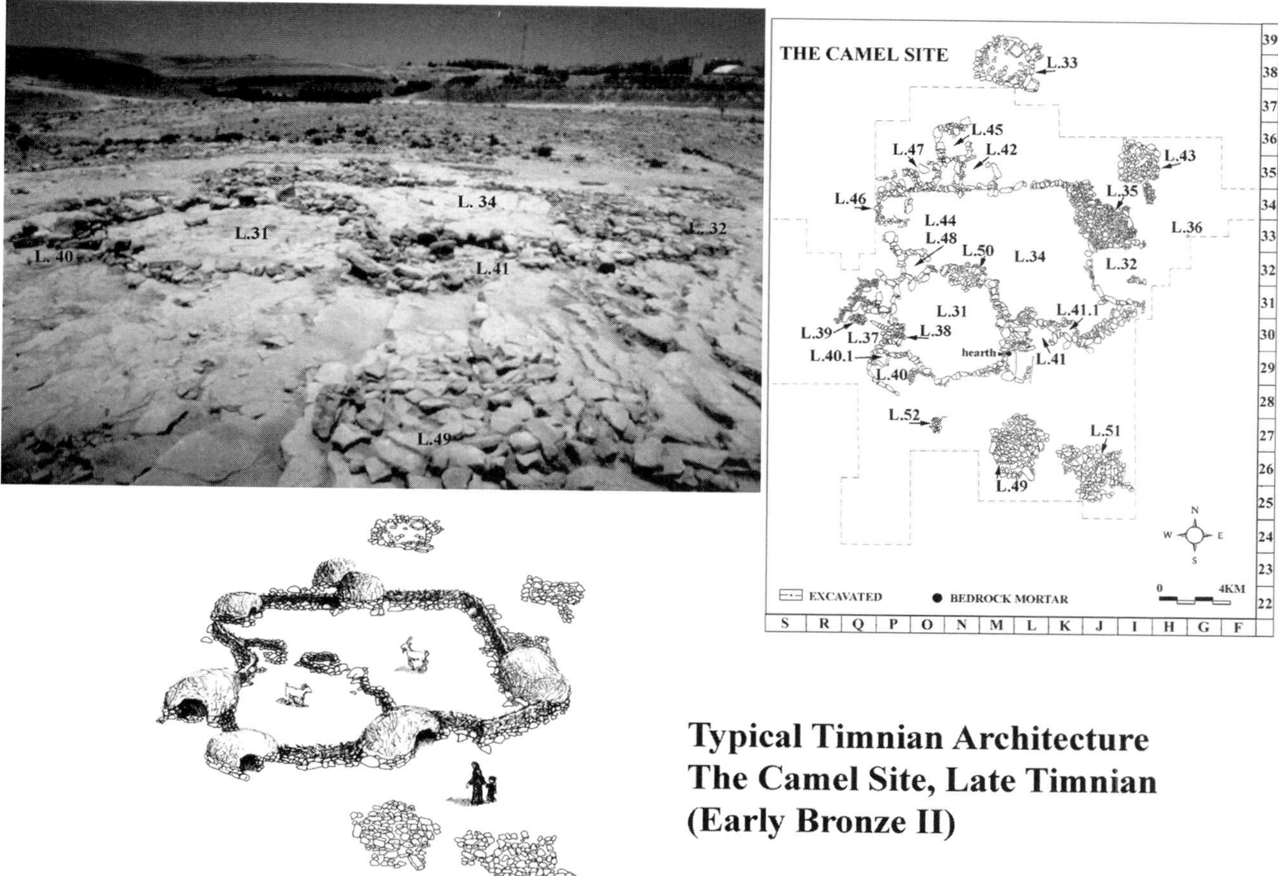

Figure 6.3 The pen-and-attached-room architecture at the Camel Site, an Early Bronze Age II, Late Timnian site in Mitzpe Ramon, Central Negev: (a) photograph of site looking north; (b) site plan; and (c) artist's reconstruction (drawing by H. Sokolskaya, plan by P. Kaminsky)

whose index fossil is the bifacial knife, and which is chronologically more or less parallel to the Pre-Pottery Neolithic C (PPNC) in the north, and is dated to the first half of the 7th millennium cal BC. This industry is known primarily from quarry sites (Goring-Morris *et al.* 1994). The Timnian was placed immediately after the Eilatian in the original desert sequence, equivalent in its early stages to the Pottery Neolithic, but extending considerably forward in time through the Early Bronze Age II, *c.*3000 cal BC. Rothenberg suggested chronological division of the Timnian into early, middle and late phases, based on ceramic petrography, typology and rare imported ceramic fossil indices.

I propose here the re-examination and reorganization of the Timnian and associated complexes based on the accumulated studies of numerous lithic assemblages and sites and combined with radiocarbon determinations and other components of the archaeological record. A preliminary framework is presented in Figure 6.2. Salient characteristics are reviewed below.

Cultural features and definitions

Currently the earliest direct evidence for the penetration of domestic herd animals, sheep and goat, into the central Negev dates to *c.*6000 cal BC (Rosen *et al.* 2005), although Goring-Morris (1993) suggests that the Tuwailan, dating to the 7th millennium cal BC, is a pastoral culture. Domestic animals are not known from PPNB occurrences in the Negev and Sinai (but see Albert and Henry 2004 for possible early presence in southern Jordan). By the middle of the 6th millennium cal BC a complex of architectural features emerged, including pen and attached room structures (in contrast to the clustered or honeycomb PPNB architecture) (Figure 6.3), elaborate mortuary structures (tumuli and later *nawamis*) organized in fields (*e.g.*, Bar-Yosef *et al.* 1986; Haiman 1993; Rosen and Rosen 2003) (Figure 6.4), shrines with cosmological symbolism (some of which are megalithic in conception) (Figure 6.5), and desert kite hunting traps (Figure 6.6). Although perhaps not originating simultaneously (there is debate on the date of the earliest desert kites (*e.g.*, Helms and Betts 1987; Meshel 1980), the features seem to converge to form a stable system around this time.

Figure 6.4 Tumuli from Ramat Saharonim, an early Timnian cult centre in the Makhtesh Ramon, Central Negev

Similarly, one can trace the emergence of a new material-culture complex, consisting primarily but not exclusively of lithics (Figure 6.7), at the same time. It comprises the following components: 1) a large flake industry, initially reflected in the earlier (Tuwailan culture) bifacial knives, but primarily expressed in tabular and fan scrapers, 2) a small arrowhead assemblage, including low quantities of small points (Herzliya, Nizzanim, and Haparsa points (Gopher 1994, 41)) and increasing numbers of transverse points of various shapes, and 3) a dominant ad hoc small flake and blade technology from which a range of tools was produced, almost always on-site. Other material culture is rare, especially in the earlier stages of the complex, but the use of beads from seashells and ostrich eggshells is common (Bar-Yosef 1997). Ceramics occur later in the sequence and are dominated by holemouth vessels. Finally, a complex sequence of rock art (Rothenberg 2001; Anati 1986), still incompletely analysed, also suggests continuities within what Anati (1986, 88–99) refers to as the Bronze Age Complex, but which corresponds readily to the Timnian.

Chronology and development

Defining the beginning of the Timnian culture is difficult owing both to a scarcity of good data as well as the general issue of defining origins in transitional periods. In terms of source region, one can trace settlement continuities from the PPNB through the beginning of the Timnian throughout the southern parts of the region under discussion: south Sinai, southern Jordan and the southern Negev. The central Negev becomes Timnian only later in the sequence. Chronologically, as above, Goring-Morris (1993) has defined an early-7th-millennium industry with high proportions of bifacial knives as Tuwailan, essentially a transitional industry between the Pre-Pottery and Pottery Neolithic periods. Following the Tuwailan, sites such as Qadesh Barnea 3, dated to the late 7th millennium cal BC and attributed to the early Pottery Neolithic period (Bar-Yosef 1981) do not yet reflect the Timnian architectural complex of pen and attached rooms. Goring-Morris (1993) has noted a 6th-millennium cal BC example of this architectural type at Beer Ada (also see Kozloff 1981), and there are a number of dates placing desert courtyard shrines in the late 6th millennium cal BC (Avner and Carmi 2001; Avner 2002; Avner *et al.* 1994; Rothenberg and Glass 1992; Eddy and Wendorf 1998; 1999). Kozloff

Figure 6.5 Shrine 1 at Ramat Saharonim, with an orientation matching the azimuth of the setting sun of the summer solstice

(1974; 1981) also suggested a later-6th-millennium cal BC date for the beginning of the complex based on a set of radiocarbon dates from Timnian occupation sites (published in Rothenberg and Glass 1992). Although tabular scrapers (as opposed to the bifacial knives of the Tuwailan industry) appear in PPNC industries in northern Israel (*e.g.*, Khalaily 2006), in the south they are not common until the 6th millennium cal BC. Similarly, small arrowheads appear in the middle 7th millennium BC, but they are still accompanied by large arrowheads, which do not drop out until the near the end of the millennium. Transverse arrowheads appear only in the late 6th or 5th millennium BC. Thus, summing up the transitional period prior to the crystallization of the Timnian complex, the Tuwailan and the Early Pottery Neolithic periods in the 7th and early 6th millennia BC show some of the elements later to become diagnostic of the Timnian, but the package which defines the complex has not yet formed prior to *c.*5500 cal BC.

It is difficult to divide the Timnian into discrete sub-periods, but fossil indices allow the construction of a general sequence of early–middle–late phases. Figure 6.2 summarizes some of the basic data. Key points include:

1) Chipped-stone axes disappear at some point in the first half of the 4th millennium cal BC (Rosen 1997, 41).

2) Incised tabular scrapers, those with patterns cut into the cortices, appear only post-4000 cal BC, perhaps several hundred years later (Rosen 1997, 41). Additionally, one can trace a decrease in the dimensions of these pieces from the earlier stages to the later, based on the materials from south Sinai (Figure 6.8; Rosen and Gopher 2003). This decrease has not been checked for other regions, and may reflect some process of local quarry exhaustion: in early stages large cores are exploited but, by later stages of use, only smaller nodules remain, resulting in smaller final products.

3) As above, transverse arrowheads appear somewhat later than small arrowheads. The microlithic lunate version (virtually indistinguishable from the Late Natufian and Harifian type (Rosen 1983a)) appears only *c.*3100 cal BC, perhaps marginally earlier, and continues in the first half of the 3rd millennium cal BC. Triangular types are earlier,

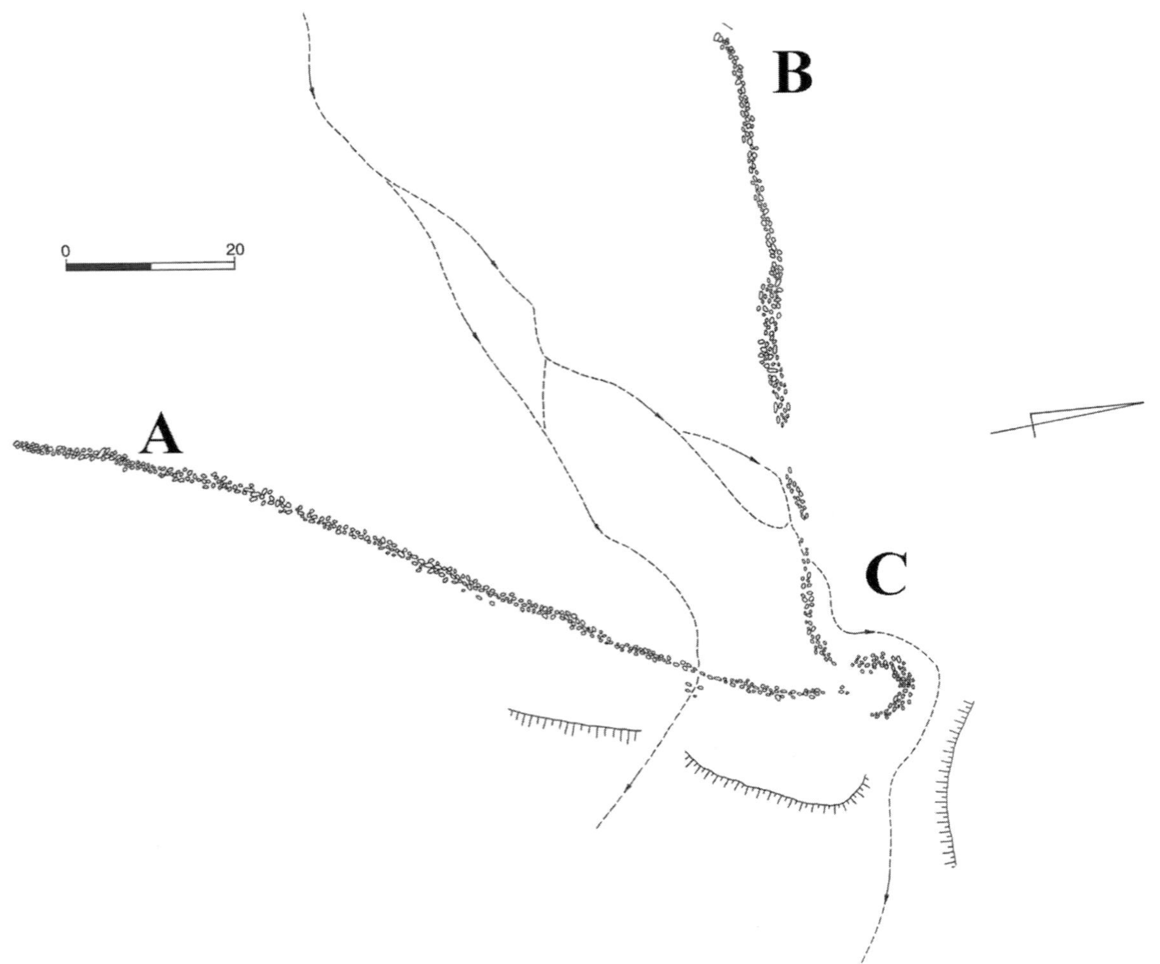

Figure 6.6 Desert kite in the Makhtesh Ramon

and rectangular types may be intermediate (Figure 6.9). Data are still incomplete.

4) Both types of tabular scrapers, as well as all types of chipped-stone arrowheads, disappear from the material-culture repertoire toward the end of the 3rd millennium cal BC. The terminal phase is marked by basic technological and typological continuities in the small flake and blade tools such as the continued presence of arched-backed blades on technologically simple blades. Analyses of microlithic drills hint at possible chronological distinctions,

desert culture-stratigraphic scheme makes inherent sense, and is empirically demonstrable, as hopefully illustrated in the preceding review. Attaching meaning beyond mere distinction is the greater challenge.

Starting with Clarke (1978), we may indeed conclude that the Timnian constitutes a culture, a long-term evolution of shared features (Clarke's polythetic set) which we translate to related groups with shared perceptions of how the world works and how to live in it. For archaeology, material culture – artefacts, constructions and technologies – carries symbols (*e.g.*, Wobst 1977; Wiessner 1983; 1984). It has been shown to play an active role in negotiations of group identity and membership. Commonalities in material culture, especially in those aspects which imply intent, choice and some investment – for example, arrowhead styles as opposed to ad hoc tools – suggest shared perceptions and values, shared ways of doing things. Shared symbols, as reflected in, for example, similar or identical mortuary behaviours – tumuli, *nawamis* – are even more powerful reflections of ethnic affiliation. The peoples living adjacent to the Timnians, those in the Mediterranean zone Neolithic, Chalcolithic and Early Bronze Age, or the Egyptians over the same span, did things differently and saw things differently, at least as reflected in their symbols, technologies and basic cultural organization. The Timnian is a distinct culture, an ethnic entity.

The difficulty here lies in the idea that we can really trace a 'culture' over the course of more than three millennia. In this sense, over the long term, the Timnian really constitutes a cultural lineage, a long-term evolution. If in Clarke's sense cultures must have some minimum set of shared features, it is not clear that the two ends of the Timnian chronological sequence actually fit the definition. Nevertheless, like animal species over great geographic distances whose constituents at the ends of their spectrum in fact cannot mate and produce fertile offspring, the early and terminal phases of the Timnian are nevertheless part of a single lineage, a single long-term cultural trajectory.

In this context, and it is perhaps a statement of the obvious when considering the long-term interactions between the settled communities and their desert counterparts, the maintenance of a distinct Timnian identity is not an obvious conclusion. Although one could argue that the environmental contrasts between desert and sown were the primary determinants of cultural division, and indeed at some level they probably were, at another level this does not lessen the fact that over the course of three millennia the Timnians did *not* adopt the ways and means of Mediterranean, or Egyptian, culture, even when they could have done so without environmental conflict. For example, Canaanean blade technology, the pan-Near Eastern technology for blade production in the late 4th and 3rd millennia BC, did not penetrate the desert, even among those populations who used sickles. Rather, the Timnians continued to make flint tools, bury their dead, worship their deities and engage in their basic subsistence practices in a cultural trajectory different from that of their settled cousins. Whether the ultimate cause is environmentally determined or not, the proximate cause is cultural. This issue of long-term dynamics is significant for archaeologists. In the absence of informants who might tell us about identity, the fact that cultural transmission in the desert continued along a separate path over the long term reflects identity in practice.

The Timnian system extends over a span of some three millennia. While the Mediterranean zone in this long period sees a dynamic spectrum of cultures and societies in what appears as a cumulative march to social complexity, the apparent stability of the Timnian is illusory. If the desert imposes constraints on social evolution, nevertheless analysis of the Timnian shows fluctuations in geographic extent, demography, technology, economy and political organization. Expansions and contractions in the overall geography of the complex can be traced, along with regional variation. Thus, the Timnian expansion into the steppe zone during the late 5th/early 4th millennium BC (Chalcolithic Early Bronze I), as evidenced clearly at the site of Nahal Tsafit, constitutes a major geographic fluctuation over previous periods. Similarly, the rise of pastoral nomadism proper (*sensu* Khazanov 1984) out of herding–gathering, with its implications of economic asymmetry in ties to a sedentary and agricultural core region, can be traced during the late phase of the Timnian, resulting from intensification of relations with the northern zone. If the tempo of change and variation does not coincide with the northern zone, this does not mean that the desert is stagnant. There are interesting hints, in the form of parallels in architectural types and some kinds of material culture, that the southern Levantine deserts are integrated at some level into some wider Saharo-Arabian desert system (see Zarins 1990; 1992; Wendorf and Schild 1998 for comparative materials), as well as linked to the Levant. The history of the desert is different from the history of the sown, but it is history.

Acknowledgments

I am grateful to Yorke Rowan and Jaimie Lovell for inviting me to participate in the ICAANE session on Chalcolithic chronologies and systematics, and for their comments and encouragement concerning the final version of this paper. I am also indebted to Itzik Gilead, Beno Rothenberg, Kobi Vardi and Benjamin Saidel for their comments on earlier versions of both the lecture and the manuscript.

References

Adams, W. Y. (1979) On the argument from ceramics to history: a challenge based on evidence from medieval Nubia. *Current Anthropology* 20, 727–44.

Albert, R. and Henry, D. O. (2004) Herding and agricultural activities at the early Neolithic site of Ayn Abu Nukhayla (Wadi Rum, Jordan). The results of phytolith and spherulite analyses. *Paléorient* 30/2, 81–92.

Amiran, R. (1969) *Ancient Pottery of the Holy Land.* Tel Aviv: Massada Press.

Anati, E. (1986) *The Mountain of God.* New York: Rizzoli.

Avner, U. (1984) Ancient cult sites in the Negev and Sinai Deserts. *Tel Aviv* 11, 115–31.

Avner, U. (1990) Ancient agricultural settlement and religion in the Uvda Valley in southern Israel. *Biblical Archaeologist* 53, 125–41.

Avner, U. (1998) Settlement, agriculture, and paleoclimate in 'Uvda Valley, southern Negev Desert, 6th–3rd millennia BC. Pp. 147–202 in A. Issar and N. Brown (eds), *Water, Environment and Society in Times of Climatic Change.* Amsterdam: Kluwer.

Avner, U. (2002) Studies in the Material and Spiritual Culture of the Negev and Sinai Populations, During the 6th–3rd Millennia BC. Unpublished PhD thesis, Hebrew University.

Avner, U. and Carmi, I. (2001) Settlement patterns in the southern Levant deserts during the 6th–3rd millennia BC: A revision based on ^{14}C dating. In H. J. Bruins, I. Carmi and E. Boaretto (eds), Near East chronology: archaeology and environment. Proceedings of the 17th International ^{14}C Conference. *Radiocarbon* 43, 1203–16.

Avner, U., Carmi, I. and Segal, D. (1994) Neolithic to Bronze Age settlement of the Negev and Sinai in light of radiocarbon dating: a view from the southern Negev. Pp. 26–300 in O. Bar-Yosef and R. Kra (eds), *Late Quaternary Chronology and Paleoclimates of the Eastern Mediterranean. Radiocarbon.* Tucson and Cambridge: University of Arizona and the American Schools of Prehistoric Research.

Barth, F. (1969) *Ethnic Groups and Boundaries.* Boston: Little Brown.

Bar-Yosef, D. M. E. (1997) Neolithic shell production in southern Sinai. *Journal of Archaeological Science* 24, 97–111.

Bar-Yosef, O. (1981) Neolithic sites in Sinai. Pp. 217–35 in W. Frey and H.-P. Uerpmann (eds), *Contributions to the Environmental History of Southwest Asia.* Biehefte Zum Tubinger Atlas der Vorderen Orient, Reihe A, Nr. 8.

Bar-Yosef, O., Belfer-Cohen, A., Goren, A., Herskovitz, I., Mienis, H., Sass, B. and Ilan, O. (1986) Nawamis and habitation sites near Gebel Gunna, southern Sinai. *Israel Exploration Journal* 36, 121–67.

Beit-Arieh, I. (1986) Two cultures in south Sinai in the third millennium BC. *Bulletin of the American Schools of Oriental Research* 263, 27–54.

Beit-Arieh, I. and Gophna, R. (1976) Early Bronze II Sites in Wadi el-Qudeirat (Kadesh Barnea). *Tel Aviv* 3, 142–50.

Bordes, F. (1972) *A Tale of Two Caves.* New York: Harper and Row.

Burton, M. and Levy, T. E. (2001) The Chalcolithic radiocarbon record and its use in southern Levantine archaeology. *Radiocarbon* 43, 1223–46.

Clarke, D. L. (1978) *Analytical Archeology.* New York: Columbia University Press.

Cohen, R. (1978) Ethnicity: problem and focus in anthropology. *Annual Review of Anthropology* 7, 379–403.

Eddy, F. W. (1999) *An Archaeological Investigation of the Central Sinai, Egypt.* Boulder: The American Research Center in Egypt and the University Press of Colorado.

Eddy, F. W. and Wendorf, F. (1998) Prehistoric pastoral nomads in Sinai. *Sahara* 10, 7–20.

Garfinkel, Y. (1999) *Neolithic and Chalcolithic Pottery of the Southern Levant.* Qedem 39, Jerusalem Institute of Archaeology, The Hebrew University of Jerusalem.

Gilead, I. (1988) The Chalcolithic period in the Levant. *Journal of World Prehistory* 2, 397–443.

Gilead, I. (1990) The Neolithic–Chalcolithic transition and the Qatifian of the northern Negev and Sinai. *Levant* 27, 47–63.

Gopher, A. (1994) *Arrowheads of the Neolithic Levant.* Winona Lake, IN: Eisenbrauns.

Gopher, A. and Gophna, R. (1993) Cultures of the eighth and seventh millennia B.P. in the southern Levant: a review for the 1990s. *Journal of World Prehistory* 7, 297–353.

Goring-Morris, A. N. (1993) From foraging to herding in the Negev and Sinai: the Early to Late Neolithic transition. *Paléorient* 19/1, 65–89.

Goring-Morris, A. N., Gopher, A. and Rosen, S. A. (1994) The Tuwailan cortical knife industry of the Negev, Israel. Pp. 511–24 in H. G. Gebel and S. K. Kozlowski (eds), *Neolithic Chipped Stone Industries of the Fertile Crescent.* Studies in Early Near Eastern Production, Subsistence, and Environment 1. Berlin: ex oriente.

Greenberg, R. (2002) *Early urbanization in the Levant: a regional narrative.* London: Leicester University Press.

Haiman, M. (1992) Sedentism and pastoralism in the Negev highlands in the Early Bronze Age: results of the western Negev highlands emergency survey. Pp. 93–105 in O. Bar-Yosef and A. M. Khazanov (eds), *Pastoralism in the Levant: Archaeological Materials in Anthropological Perspective.* Madison, WI: Prehistory Press.

Haiman, M. (1993) An Early Bronze Age cairn field at Nahal Mitnan. *'Atiqot* 22, 49–61.

Helms, S. W. and Betts, A. V. G. (1987) The desert 'kites' of the Badiyat esh-Shaur and North Arabia. *Paléorient* 13, 41–67

Henry, D. O. (1992) Seasonal movements of fourth millennium pastoral nomads in Wadi Hisma. *Studies in the History and Archaeology of Jordan* 4, 137–41. Amman: The Department of Antiquities of Jordan.

Henry, D. O. (1995) *Prehistoric Cultural Ecology and Evolution.* New York: Plenum.

Henry, D. O. and Turnbull, P. (1985) Archaeological and faunal evidence from Natufian and Timnian sites in southern Jordan with notes on pollen evidence. *Bulletin of the American Schools of Oriental Research* 257, 45–64.

Joffe, A. H. (1993) *Settlement and Society in the Early Bronze I and II in the Southern Levant.* Sheffield: Sheffield Academic Press.

Jones, S. (1997) *The Archaeology of Ethnicity.* London: Routledge.

Khalaily, H. (2006) Lithic Traditions During the Late Pre-Pottery Neolithic B and the Question of the Pre-Pottery Neolithic C in the Southern Levant. Unpublished PhD thesis, Ben-Gurion University, Beersheva.

Khazanov, A. M. (1984) *Nomads and the Outside World.* Cambridge: Cambridge University Press.

Kozloff, B. (1974) A brief note on the lithic industries of Sinai. *Museum Ha'aretz Yearbook* 15/16, 35–49.

Kozloff, B. (1981) Pastoral nomadism in Sinai: An ethno-archaeological study. *Production pastorales et societe: bulletin d'ecologie et d'anthropologie des societies pastorales* 8, 19–24.

Levy, T. E. and Holl, A. F. C. (1995) Social change and the

archaeology of the Holy Land. Pp. 2–8 in T. E. Levy (ed.), *The Archaeology of Society in the Holy Land*. London: Leicester University Press.

Lovell, J. L. (2001) *The Late Neolithic and Chalcolithic Periods in the Southern Levant: New Data from Teleilat Ghassul, Jordan*. Oxford: BAR Int. Ser. 974.

Marx, E. (1977) The tribe as a unit of subsistence: nomadic pastoralism in the Near East. *American Anthropologist* 79, 343–63.

Meshel, Z. (1980) Desert kites in Sinai. Pp. 265–88 in Z. Meshel and I. Finkelstein (eds), *Sinai in Antiquity*. Jerusalem: Israel Society for the Protection of Nature and the Israel Exploration Society.

Perrot, J. (1955) Excavations at Tell Abu Matar, near Beersheva. *Israel Exploration Journal* 5, 17–40, 73–84, 167–89.

Philip, G. and Baird, D. (2000) *Ceramics and Change in the Early Bronze Age of the Southern Levant*. Sheffield: Sheffield Academic Press.

Quintero, L., Wilke, P. and Rollefson, G. (2002) From flint mine to fan scraper: the late prehistoric Jafr industrial complex. *Bulletin of the American Schools of Oriental Research* 327, 17–48.

Ronen, A. (1970) Flint implements from south Sinai: preliminary report. *Palestine Exploration Quarterly* 102, 30–41.

Rosen, S. A. (1983a) The microlithic lunate: an old-new tool type from the Negev, Israel. *Paléorient* 9, 81–3.

Rosen, S. A. (1983b) The tabular scraper trade: a model for material culture dispersion. *Bulletin of the American Schools of Oriental Research* 249, 79–86.

Rosen, S. A. (1993) Lithic assemblages from Nahal Mitnan. *`Atiqot* 22, 62–9.

Rosen, S. A. (1997) *Lithics After the Stone Age: A Handbook of Stone Tools from the Levant*. Walnut Creek, CA: AltaMira Press.

Rosen, S. A. (2001) The lithic assemblage from 'Uvda Valley site 917 and its spatial implications. *`Atiqot* 42, 109–19.

Rosen, S. A. (2002) The evolution of pastoral nomadic systems in the southern Levantine periphery. Pp. 23–44 in E. C. M. van den Brink and E. Yannai (eds), *Quest of Ancient Settlements and Landscapes*. Tel Aviv: Ramot Publishing, Tel Aviv University.

Rosen, S. A. and Gopher, A. (2003) Flint tools from the survey. Pp. 184–95 in I. Beit-Arieh (ed.), *Archaeology of Sinai, The Ophir Expedition*. Tel Aviv University Institute of Archaeology Monograph Series 21. Tel Aviv.

Rosen, S. A. and Goring-Morris, A. N. (in press) Har Qeren XV. In A. N. Goring-Morris (ed.), *Prehistoric Investigations Around the Haluza Dunes*. Jerusalem: Israel Antiquities Authority.

Rosen, S. A. and Rosen, Y. J. (2003) The shrines of the setting sun. *Israel Exploration Journal* 53, 1–19.

Rosen, S. A., Savinetsky, A. B., Plakht, Y., Kisseleva, N. K., Khassanov, B. F., Pereladov, A. M. and Haiman, M. (2005) Dung in the desert: preliminary results of the Negev Holocene ecology project. *Current Anthropology* 46, 317–27.

Rosen, S. A., Hermon, S., Vardi, J. and Abadi, Y. (2006) The chipped stone assemblage from Be'er Resisim in the Negev highlands: a preliminary study. Pp. 133–44 in S. Gitin, J. E. Wright and J. P. Dessel (eds), *Confronting the Past: Archaeological and Historical Essays in Honor of William G. Dever*. Winona Lake, IN: Eisenbrauns.

Rothenberg, B. (2001) Rock drawings in the ancient copper mines of the Arabah – new aspects of the region's history. *Institute for Archaeo-Metallurgical Studies* 21, 4–9.

Rothenberg, B. and Glass, J. (1992) The beginnings and development of early metallurgy and the settlement and chronology of the western Arabah from the Chalcolithic period to the Early Bronze IV. *Levant* 24, 141–57.

Rothenberg, B. and Merkel, J. (1995) Late Neolithic copper smelting in the Arabah. *Institute for Archaeo-Metallurgical Studies* 19, 1–7.

Saidel, B. A. (2002) Pot luck? Variation and function in the ceramic assemblages of pre-camel pastoralists in the Negev Highlands, Israel. *Journal of the Israel Prehistoric Society* 32, 175–96.

Shennan, S. (1989) *Archaeological Approaches to Cultural Identity*. London: Unwin-Hyman.

Stager, L. E. (1992) The periodization of Palestine from Neolithic through Early Bronze Age Times. Pp. 22–41 in R. Ehrich (ed.), *Chronologies In Old World Archaeology*. Chicago, MI: University of Chicago.

Vardi, J. (2005) The Analysis of the Lithic Assemblage from Ein Ziq, An Early Bronze IV (2300–2000 BCE) Site in the Negev Highlands. Unpublished MA dissertation, Ben-Gurion University (Hebrew).

Wendorf, F. and Schild, R. (1998) Nabta Playa and its role in northeastern African prehistory. *Journal of Anthropological Archaeology* 17, 97–123.

Wiessner, P. (1983) Style and social information in Kalahari Projectile Points. *American Antiquity* 48, 253–76.

Wiessner, P. (1984) Reconsidering the behavioral basis for style: a case study among the Kalahari San. *Journal of Anthropological Archaeology* 3, 190–234.

Wobst, M. (1977) Stylistic behavior and information exchange. Pp. 317–42 in C. Cleland (ed.), *Papers for the Director: Research Essays in Honor of James B. Griffin*. Papers of the Museum of Anthropology 61. Ann Arbor, MI: University of Michigan.

Yekutieli, Y. (2002) Settlement and subsistence patterns in north Sinai during the fifth to third millennia BCE. Pp. 422–33 in E. C. M. van den Brink and T. E. Levy (eds), *Egypt and the Levant. Interrelations from the 4th through the Early 3rd Millennium BCE*. London: Leicester University Press.

Zarins, J. (1990) Early pastoral nomadism and settlement of lower Mesopotamia. *Bulletin of the American Schools of Oriental Research* 280, 31–65.

Zarins, J. (1992) Pastoral nomadism in Arabia: Ethnoarchaeology and the archaeological record – a case study. Pp. 219–40 in O. Bar-Yosef and A. M. Khazanov (eds), *Pastoralism in the Levant: Archaeological Materials in Anthropological Perspective*. Madison, WI: Prehistory Press.

7. Newly Discovered Burials of the Chalcolithic and the Early Bronze Age I in Southern Canaan – Evidence of Cultural Continuity?

Amir Golani and Yossi Nagar

Introduction

With the advent of numerous new excavations and a wealth of accompanying radiometric data, the transition between the Chalcolithic and the Early Bronze Age I (EB I) periods in the southern Levant has recently come into new focus. Recent studies of the initial stage of the EB I period during the 4th millennium BC have revealed continuity with the preceding Chalcolithic culture of the northern Negev that thrived in the late 5th millennium BC. This continuity may be seen as representing a transitional period, yet the bulk of the material culture associated with it points to a cultural association that in most respects is more akin to the EB I than to the Chalcolithic. Consequently, the early EB I occupation at Ashkelon has been proposed as representing the material culture of Chalcolithic cultural groups that had relocated northwards to the southern coastal plain after the collapse of the Chalcolithic geo-cultural sphere of the northern Negev (Golani 2004; in press a; Golani and Segal 2002).

New evidence now suggests further cultural continuity and may imply an ethnic continuity as well. In the southern Levant, infant burials are usually found within domestic settlements during the Chalcolithic period, while adults and sub-adults were generally accorded secondary burials in clay or stone ossuaries in caves or burial structures outside sites. Primary burials are usually not the norm and, when they occur, may represent a preparatory stage to the more common secondary burial stage. In contrast, during the EB I both infants and adults are usually found with burial goods in primary and possibly also secondary burials in caves or cemeteries, all outside the habitational sites.

Recent excavations at the EB I site of Ashkelon Barnea (Golani 2005; 2007; in 2008b) have revealed numerous intra-site infant burials, generally uncommon for this period, in jars and within small mudbrick cists. In addition, a rare form of secondary burial of adults in small stone cists attached to one another in 'ladder' form was revealed adjacent to the site (Golani 2005). Similar burials have also been found at a Chalcolithic burial ground near Palmahim, also in the coastal plain (Gorzalczany 2006a; 2006b; forthcoming a). The practice of intra-site infant burials associated with the EB occupation at Ashkelon and common at Chalcolithic sites as well, in addition to secondary adult cist 'ladder' burials at both Ashkelon and Palmahim, suggests a cultural continuity between these two periods that may be attributed to the fact that the same cultural and ethnic group resided in the southern part of the southern Levant during the Chalcolithic and into the EB I. These findings contrast with those from more northerly portions of the southern Levant, where a more distinct break in burial customs, and other elements of material culture, is apparent.

The material culture retrieved from a growing number of excavated EB I sites in the southern coastal plain appears to indicate continuity with the preceding Chalcolithic culture of the northern Negev (Baumgarten 2004; Braun 2000a; Braun and Gophna 2004; Golani 2004; 2008a; Golani and Segal 2002; 2004). This continuity is interpreted as an expression of a cultural transition between these two periods, in which 'Chalcolithics' of the northern Negev may have moved northwards at the turn of the millennium, resettling and developing into what may be defined as the earliest EB I facies in the area (Golani 2004; in press a; Golani and Segal 2002). This transitional stage, characterized by an EB I material culture with numerous Chalcolithic attributes, may be dated to the middle of the 4th millennium BC, possibly beginning even within its first half, after which a fully developed EB material culture and the impact of Egyptian influence can be recognized.

This reconstruction, though admittedly simplistic and certainly fraught with numerous problems, is proposed as a new avenue for research in the transition between the Chalcolithic and the EB I periods. This article presents new data concerning two aspects of burial practices that appear to bolster the theory of a direct cultural continuity between the Chalcolithic and EB I in the south of the southern Levant. The first aspect is the similar burial patterns of infants under three years of age, which are always found interred within dwelling areas (as opposed to juveniles and adults outside the settlements). The second aspect is a certain seemingly unique mode of burial that is so far known only from these two periods. Because they are more ritualized aspects of human behaviour, burial fashions are less likely to change than other elements of material culture directly affected by functional needs. Burial practices are often held to be a specific marker of cultural or even ethnic identity, so that the discovery of similar burial customs between the two periods implies a cultural and/or ethnic continuity.

The transition between the Chalcolithic and the Early Bronze Age in the southern Levant

The periodization of the proto-historic periods in the southern Levant has generally been reliant on the classification of material cultural remains and their association with a relative chronology. In the last decades of archaeological research, radiocarbon dating has provided a useful tool for more precise and absolute dating. Owing to the lack of historical sources, ^{14}C dating is the main, if not the sole, means for structuring an absolute chronology for this time period.

The transition between the Chalcolithic and the EB in the southern Levant is often vague; the non-committal term 'EB–Chalcolithic' is still used and reflects our own indecisiveness when confronted with material culture remains that often bear many similarities. The dissipation of the well-known Ghassulian and northern Negev Chalcolithic cultures at the end of the 5th millennium BC is evident from the general lack of reliable ^{14}C dates from the first half and especially the middle of the 4th millennium BC (Bourke *et al.* 2001; Levy and Burton 2006, table 2; Gilead 1994; Joffe and Dessel 1995) and, on this basis, sites of both these cultures are apparently abandoned by the first half of the 4th millennium BC (*c.*4000–3700 BC), if not earlier, at the very end of the 5th. At the same time, on the basis of Egyptian chronological synchronizations and ^{14}C dating, the onset of the EB I has been dated to the latter half of the 4th millennium (Joffe and Dessel 1995; Stager 1992, 27). The gap of 400–500 years between the terminal and initial dating of each period has caused uneasiness among some scholars (Braun 2001). While some regard this gap as an expression of the total break between the Chalcolithic and the EB I in the south (Braun 2003; Gilead 1993; 1994), others have tried to bridge it by invoking the 'Terminal Chalcolithic' (Joffe and Dessel 1995), a shaky construct based on a very few and somewhat uncertain ^{14}C dates.

In the past decade, numerous and reliable ^{14}C dates have come to fill this gap, shedding new light on the transition in the south (Golani and Segal 2002). These dates, all associated with a southern EB I material culture, indicate that the beginning of the EB I should be pushed back earlier than thought, giving birth to the term 'Initial Southern EB I' (Braun 1996), seen as the 'missing link' between the end of the Chalcolithic and the beginning of the EB I (Braun 2000a). However, while the EB I identification of the material-culture remains associated with the ^{14}C samples at Ashkelon is acknowledged, the *validity* of the dates themselves and especially their association with a southern EB I material-culture facies has been disputed (Braun 2003, Braun and Gophna 2004, 221–5). Though these dates push back the beginning of the EB I by several hundred years and distance it from commonly accepted synchronizations with the first Egyptian dynasty, the underlying problem is that the transition between the Chalcolithic and the EB I in the south has generally been defined by the differences between these two periods, while common elements have generally not been regarded as expressing continuity.

Characteristics of the material culture of the initial southern EB I – change and continuity in a transitional period

The initial southern EB I, as revealed at Ashkelon Afridar and more recently at Ashkelon Barnea (see below) may be characterized by many affinities or 'holdovers' with the previous Chalcolithic culture of the Northern Negev alongside new innovations which find further development in the succeeding southern EB I (see Braun 2000a; Golani and Segal 2002). The ceramic assemblage of the EB I at Ashkelon Afridar features a variety of forms made by manufacturing and decorative techniques that have direct antecedents in the Chalcolithic potting tradition. This allows Chalcolithic *fossile directeurs* such as cornets and churns, albeit in small quantities, in addition to V-shaped bowls and globular high-necked store jars, to co-exist alongside ledge-handled store jars and hemispherical bowls, for example. The flint assemblage is characterized by the dominance of large Canaanean blades alongside tabular scrapers and backed blades of the Chalcolithic tradition. In addition, Canaanean flint blades, generally held to be indicative of the EB, have also recently been found associated with Chalcolithic cultural remains in the south (Bar and Winter 2010; I. Paz, pers. comm.; Milevski, this volume) The ground stone assemblage is characterized by the continuation of Chalcolithic forms alongside new variants, with a preference for functional and utilitarian items. In contrast to the Chalcolithic, a substantial percentage of basalt during the EB I may indicate increased trade contacts. The developed metallurgical industry of the EB shows use of the same copper sources, with a preference for utilitarian and functional items over the well-crafted cultic or non-utilitarian items that are well known in the Chalcolithic. The faunal assemblage presents evidence of a well-based and fully sedentary subsistence economy with exploitation of sheep/goats, cattle and pigs instead of primarily sheep/goat, as in the Chalcolithic. A significant presence of donkeys in the EB I (*e.g.*, at Ashkelon) suggests their use as pack animals for trade. At Ashkelon, all these elements of material culture are found in occupational strata associated with the southern EB I cultural horizon and exhibit a large degree of continuity with the Chalcolithic material culture of the same area.

New evidence from burials at Ashkelon Barnea

The continuity between the Chalcolithic and the early EB I in the south may also be inferred from burial practices. Rescue excavations have recently uncovered extensive portions of a large, and previously unknown, EB I site located north of modern-day Ashkelon, in a region now undergoing development and here termed 'Ashkelon Barnea' (Golani 2005; 2007; 2008b). Prior to its discovery, numerous excavations within present-day Ashkelon to the south of this site, in the region of the Afridar neighbourhood and the marina of Ashkelon, revealed remains of a large and sporadic settlement beginning in the early Early Bronze Age IA and continuing into the Early Bronze Age IB periods (Baumgarten 2004; Braun and Gophna 2004; Golani 2004; Khalaily 2004).

In contrast to the non-nucleated occupation at Afridar, at least three strata spanning the late EB IA to the end of the EB IB were identified at the main settlement at Ashkelon Barnea. Large-scale excavations exposed nearly 1 hectare of this occupation, enabling the identification of different activity areas at the site (Figure 7.1), which reached its zenith of 5.5 hectares during Stratum III of the EB IB, when a certain measure of pre-meditated planning, evidenced by the construction of walled domestic and industrial compounds that were separated by alleyways and open spaces, was identified. In the south-eastern portion of the settlement a public area was defined, while the central portion of the site included several walled compounds of domestic or industrial nature separated by planned alleys and open spaces. Adult and juvenile burials only were identified strictly outside the region of the settlement in distinct cemeteries (Figure 7.1).

Adjacent to and south of the site, 20 stone-built rectangular cists were located in Area E, all oriented on the same south-west–north-east axis, parallel to the sea coast. The cists were all dug into the sterile earth and were built of local kurkar stones (Figure 7.2), occasionally incorporating mudbricks similar to those uncovered within the EB strata at the site. Only two of these cists were excavated; they were devoid of any finds. Although the rest were incompletely investigated, the location, orientation and size of these features strongly suggest that they could have been intended for burial, probably adult burial. Although none of these features had any indicative finds, their proximity to the site and the similar construction materials and technique (compared to architectural features within the site) indicates a probable EB date.

West of and adjacent to the site, excavations in Area F revealed 10 small burial cists found connected in 'ladder' fashion (Figure 7.3). These were built and sealed with stone kurkar slabs. Within each cist between one and three secondary burials were found, the bones carefully arranged with the skulls in the western portion of the cist and facing west (Figure 7.4). In total, 19 individuals, consisting of adults and juveniles (but no infants), were identified. No chronologically indicative finds were associated with these burials and none of the bones or teeth contained enough collagen for ^{14}C dating. Having been dug into the sterile earth outside the settlement area, these burials were not physically associated with any of the EB settlement strata at the site, yet their proximity to the site and the lack of any other occupation in the immediate vicinity makes their association with one or more of the EB strata at the site highly probable.

While adult and juvenile burials appear to have been located outside yet adjacent to the settlement at Ashkelon Barnea, only infants were buried within the site. Nearly 30 infant burials were excavated throughout the site, all of whom may be associated with Strata IV, III or II, dated to the late EB IA–early EB IB (Stratum IV) and throughout the EB IB period (Strata III–II). Throughout all these strata the burials were located beneath surfaces, sometimes next to walls or embedded within earlier walls that had gone out of use, always in open (unroofed) spaces and usually within ceramic vessels or covered by ceramic vessel fragments (Figure 7.5). The burials of Stratum II, however, were particularly diverse, the infants also being found within or relating to architectural remains of the previous settlements. The burials include examples within jars partially dug into walls or positioned within structures that had gone out of use (Figure 7.6). In a few cases, mudbrick cists that were dug into the ground were also used (Figure 7.6).

Infant versus adult and child burials in the Chalcolithic and EB I

Though a high infant mortality rate is characteristic of ancient populations, during the Chalcolithic period infants up to three years of age are absent in burial caves or in any defined cemetery outside dwelling areas (Nagar and Eshed 2001). Despite differential preservation of skeletal remains favouring adults and often causing bias in the anthropological analysis of human skeletal populations (Guy *et al.* 1997; Walker and Johnson 1988), numerous Chalcolithic infant burials *have* been excavated so far and all have been found within dwelling areas (see Table 7.1; Nagar and Eshed 2001). Thus, their absence in burial caves or other burial installations must be the result of cultural rather than demographic or taphonomic phenomena. While this attitude towards small children may be the result of their

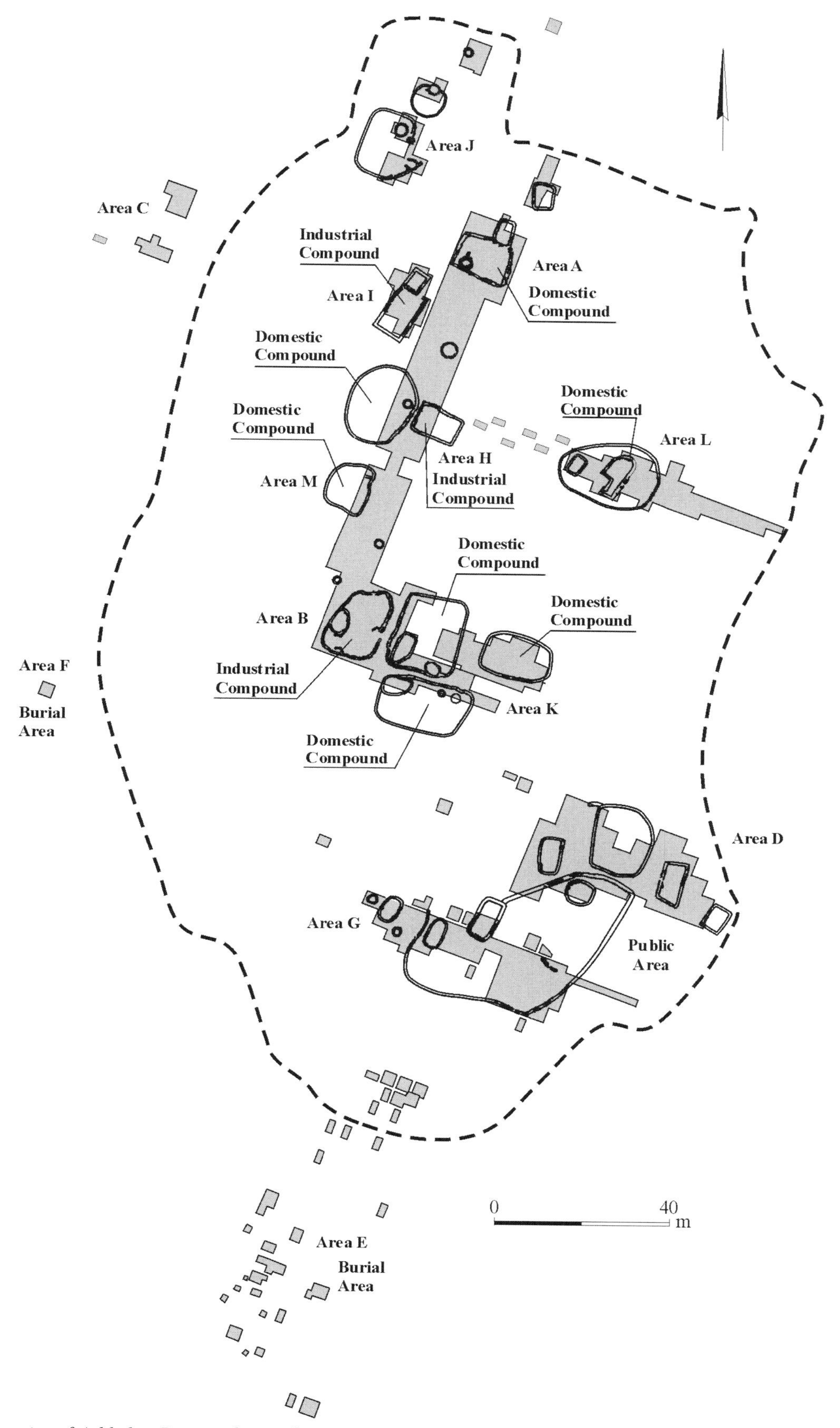

Figure 7.1 The site of Ashkelon Barnea during Stratum III: maximal extent of site, location of excavated areas and definition of activity areas. The grey shading indicates the excavated area of the site

Figure 7.2 One of the rectangular cists uncovered in Area E at Ashkelon Barnea

Figure 7.3 The stone cist 'ladder' burials in Area F at Ashkelon Barnea

Figure 7.4 Close-up picture of some of the stone cists. Note that the skulls are all at one end

Figure 7.5 An infant jar burial

Figure 7.6 Ashkelon Barnea, Stratum II. An infant burial within a mudbrick cist and another burial within a jar positioned above a circular mudbrick silo of Stratum III that had gone out of use

special importance or status, with on-site burial possibly implying a ritual significance (Mallon *et al.* 1934), it has also been suggested that the lack of infant burials in caves or cemeteries is the result of their being seen as 'left-behinds' of lesser importance (Nagar and Eshed 2001, 32).

In contrast to the Chalcolithic, during the EB period the opposite holds true where large skeletal populations within burial caves from the northern and central areas of Israel and Jordan have been recovered and studied: in all burial caves or cemeteries outside settlements, infant burials occur along with older children and adults (Table 7.2). In this respect, the infant burials uncovered so far within the dwelling area at EB I Ashkelon Barnea indicate an affinity to Chalcolithic burial practices.

As for older children and adults, numerous burials with offerings are known from burial caves and cemeteries of the Chalcolithic period throughout the country (Table 7.1). These are usually secondary burials. Burials of adults and sub-adults within dwelling sites are rare during the Chalcolithic period (see Table 7.1). Those primary burials that have been excavated may represent a preparatory stage for secondary interment outside the settlement *e.g.* as suggested at Nahal Komem (Nagar 2005). In contrast, during the EB I in the south infants and adults are usually found in primary and less often secondary burials in caves with burial goods or in cemeteries, though, as with the situation in the Chalcolithic, all are found outside the habitational sites (Table 7.2).

At EB I Ashkelon Barnea, secondary burials of older children and adults were found outside and adjacent to the settlement in Area F as interconnected cists, while more burials may have been located in Area E, adjacent to the south of the site. However, when the 'ladder' burials from Area F (described above) were first excavated, their uniqueness, the absence of any associated and datable finds and the lack of physical connection with any of the excavated EB I strata at the site made their chronological and cultural association problematic. The location of both burial grounds adjacent to the settlement and the lack of any other occupation to which these burials may be attributed makes their association with one or more of the EB strata at the site likely if not probable.

It should be emphasized that no clear remains of a Chalcolithic settlement have been located at Ashkelon

Type of burial ground	*Site*	*Sample size*	*Primary burial*	*Secondary burial*	*Individuals <3 years old*
Cemetery/burial cave removed from dwelling area	Peqi'in	453	-	+	0
	Castra	27	?	+	0
	Nazur IV	7	+	-	0
	Ain Asawir (Nagar and Winocur 2007)	1	?	?	0
	Ma'barot	58	-	+	0
	Sha'ar Ephraim	4	?	?	0
	Nahal Qanah	23	?	+	0
	Azor	6	-	+	0
	Shoham	4	-	+	0
	Shoham North	11	-	+	0
	Horvat Zur (Nagar and Sklar-Parnes, in	16	-	+	0
	Ben Shemen	39	-	+	0
	Palmahim (Gorzalczany forthcoming a; b)	14	-	+	0
	Kissufim	54	-	+	1*
	Nahal Mishmar	21	+	-	0
	Horvat Hor	7	?	?	0
	Shiqmim cemetery	48	+	+	0
	A. P. C. Necropolis	13	+	+	0
Total		**806**	**In 4 of 18 sites**	**In 13 of 18 sites**	**0***
Burials within dwelling area	Byblos	30	+	-	3
	Kfar Kana (Nagar 2001)	1	?	?	0
	Ein Hashomer (Nagar 2003)	1	?	?	1
	Tel Kitan	1	+	-	1
	Abu Hamid	2	+	-	2
	Giv'at ha-Oranim	16	+	-	1
	Tel Aviv Pinkas St. (Nagar 1999)	1	+	-	0
	Teleilat Ghassul	28	-	+	21
	Grar	5	+	-	0
	Nahal Besor	3	+	?	2
	Beer Sheva (Bir es-Safadi)	5	-	+	2
	Beer Sheva (Neve Noy)	11	+	+	1
	Beer Sheva (Tell Abu Matar)	12	+	+	2
	Horvat Beter	2	?	?	1
	Shiqmim Village	30	+	+	8
	Tel Te'o (Eisenberg *et al.* 2001, 33)	3	+	+	0
Total		**151**	**In 11 of 16 sites**	**In 6 of 16 sites**	**45**

Table 7.1 Burials in Chalcolithic sites (unless indicated otherwise, the data published here comes from various reports which are fully referenced in Nagar and Eshed 2001)

Barnea or in its immediate vicinity. In addition, none of the numerous excavations within Ashkelon itself, or its surroundings, have yielded remains of a definite, exclusively Chalcolithic settlement, nor has any Chalcolithic site been identified to date in Ashkelon or its vicinity by archaeological survey or any other means. Thus the Chalcolithic ceramic remains found within the EB I strata at the site of Ashkelon Barnea and in other excavations that uncovered remains of the EB I at Ashkelon are here interpreted as representing a Chalcolithic element *within* the material culture of the early EB I at Ashkelon. This is to be expected when a large degree of cultural continuity can be recognized in the transition between these two periods, and does not necessarily indicate Chalcolithic-period habitation at this site or in its vicinity.

New evidence from burials near Palmahim

More recently, a rescue excavation was carried out near the seashore on a low kurkar, or fossilized sandstone ridge near

Type of burial ground	*Site*	*Sample size*	*Primary burial*	*Secondary burial*	*Individuals <3 years old*
Cemetery/ burial cave removed from dwelling area	Ain Asawir (Nagar and Winocur 2007)	106	?	?	30
	Barkai-South (Nagar and Winocur 2007)	125	?	?	2
	Horvat Gilan-South (Nagar 2010)	93	?	?	23
	Sha'ar Ephraim (Nagar 2002)	40	?	?	5
	Rasm en-Nuqur (Zelin 2001)	12	?	?	1
	Bab edh-Dhra Tombs A11, 110, 111, 112, 113, 114, C11 (Frohlich and Ortner 1982)	52	+	?	25
	Bab edh-Dhra Charnel House G1 (Ortner 1982)	112	+	?	At least 5
	Ashkelon Barnea	19	-	+	0
Total		**559**	**Unclear**	**Unclear**	**91**
Within dwelling areas	Nizzanim (Yekutieli and Gophna 1994, 166-167)	3	+?	-	3?
	Ashkelon Tayassim (Ashkelon Afridar Area M) (Golani 2008a)	1	+	-	1
	Ashkelon Afridar Area G (Braun and Gophna 2004, 198, n. 19)*	2	?	?	?
	Ashkelon Barnea	29	+	-	29
	Tel Kabri (Faerman 1992)	4	+	+	1
	Tel Te'o (Eisenberg, Gopher and Greenberg 2001, 39)	3	+?	-	3
	Beth Yerah (Maisler, Stekelis and Avi-Yonah 1952, 229)**	1	+	-	1
Total		**43**	**In 6 of 7 sites**	**In 1 of 7 sites**	**34**

* Though the excavator reports two jar burials that apparently preceded the construction of the earliest structures of Stratum II in this area, the osteological remains from these jars were so limited that a definite age determination of whomever or whatever was interred in these jars is questionable at best.
** More infant jar burials from the EB I levels at this site are known and will soon be published by R. Greenberg.

Table 7.2 Burials in Early Bronze Age I sites

Figure 7.7 The cemetery at Palmahim, general view

Figure 7.8 Stone burial cists within a rounded structure at Palmahim

kibbutz Palmahim, located some 25 km south of Tel Aviv and 30 km north of Ashkelon. A. Gorzalczany, on behalf of the Israel Antiquities Authority (Gorzalczany 2006a; 2006b; forthcoming a), uncovered a cemetery dated to the Chalcolithic period that included nearly 50 burial structures (Figure 7.7). The burial structures were all constructed of the indigenous kurkar stone and are circular or rectangular with rounded corners in plan; the walls are built in corbelled fashion to create a structure resembling a squat or flattened igloo similar to the well-known *nawamis* structures found in the Sinai (Goren 1980). The Palmahim structures were not randomly positioned yet appear to have been arranged in several parallel lines on a north-west–south-east axis. A typical structure has walls 0.6 m thick and an overall diameter of 1.5–3.0 m with a doorway facing north, in the direction of the nearby Soreq river.

Within the structures a pavement of flat kurkar slabs was usually found, upon which were stone ossuaries, some of which were sealed. The ossuaries were of two types: a rectangular or trapezoidal tub hewn from one large stone block and a rectangular cell built of kurkar stone slabs (Figure 7.8). All the structures contained at least one such tub or cell; most had even more. The stone-built cells were often found as singular cists, some of which were built free-standing while others were dug into the ground or hewn into the rock. In several instances these cists were also revealed inter-connected in 'ladder-fashion' (Figure 7.9), as at Ashkelon Barnea. Several such 'ladders' were found within the tomb structures, while others were found in stratigraphical positions below some of the tomb walls, indicating that these stone-built cists also pre-dated the construction of the main tomb structures revealed at the cemetery. Within the cists, the osteological remains were poorly preserved, yet appear to indicate secondary burials of at least 14 individuals, all above the age of 15–20 years.

Within the tomb structures and alongside the burials cornets, store jars, flint tools and stone pendants were found, all of which are well known from the Ghassulian or northern Negev Chalcolithic culture. No positive indications of an EB I presence were noted at this burial site, though a large habitational site of the early stage of the EB IA period has been excavated in the nearby region at the Palmahim Quarry (Braun 2000a; Braun 2000b).

Cist burials and 'ladder'-like structures in the Chalcolithic and Early Bronze Age of the southern Levant

Burials in stone-built cists are not uncommon in the southern Levant and are known during the Chalcolithic period at Shiqmim (Levy and Alon 1987, 333–7) and in the region east of the Dead Sea, as at Adeimeh (Stekelis 1935; Mallon *et al.* 1934, 153, pl. 59b; see Levy and Alon

Figure 7.9 Stone cist 'ladder' burials at Palmahim

1987, 334, for more sites in the same region). At Shiqmim, the size and construction of several oval cists (up to 2 m in length and oriented east–west), which were similar to the rectangular cists found in Area E at Ashkelon Barnea, would have enabled the interment of an entire body. Though burial goods were found within the cists at Shiqmim, no bones were identified, leading the excavators to suggest that the cists were used as receptacles for decaying bodies, the bones of which were later collected and accorded a secondary burial (Levy and Alon 1987, 337). At Adeimeh, one of the cists included the remains of a skeleton with the skull to the west yet turned facing east (Mallon *et al.* 1934, 153, pl. 59b).

East of the Jordan and near the northern end of the Dead Sea, burials in stone-lined cists continue to be used during the EB I period, as at Ala-Safat in Jordan (Stekelis 1960–61), where they commonly appear within dolmens. In the region of the Golan and Galilee the phenomenon of megalithic cist-like structures also begins during the EB period (Vinitsky 1992).

Burials in interconnected cists or 'ladder'-like structures are less common, yet also appear in the Chalcolithic and EB I as well. At Adeimeh, Stekelis (1935, 51–65) reports over 160 stone cists, usually formed by several large stone slabs set on their narrow end and roofed over by other stone slabs. Nearly all these cists were singular, but cist no. 31 was double (Stekelis 1935, 53). Most were surrounded by a circle of stones or covered by a tumulus. The majority are oriented east–west. Osteological remains were very few and fragmentary, and it is unclear whether the cists contained specifically primary or secondary burials, though they were rather small to have housed an extended primary burial (0.55–0.95 × 1.05–1.52 m). The finds associated with these burials appear to indicate a Chalcolithic date. At the same cemetery, yet outside the area investigated by Stekelis, Mallon (*et al.* 1934, 153–4) reports over 200 visible tombs, most of them cist tombs that were sometimes found interconnected in a series of 2, 3 or even 10 cists in a row (Mallon *et al.* 1934, pl. 59c). The published photograph suggests that a 'ladder burial' consisting of 10 interconnected cists was excavated, but no mention is made of any finds within the cists themselves. North of the Adeimeh necropolis more alignments of cist tombs with rows of 6, 8, 10 and up to 13 interconnected cists are known from Wadi Ain Musa (Mallon *et al.* 1934, 154, and see map on p. 148). The date of these cists, which remain unexcavated, is still unclear; they may be of Chalcolithic date, as are some of the features excavated by Stekelis, or they may date to the EB I, as do some tumuli and possibly several dolmens in the same region.

Of the dolmens excavated at nearby Ala-Safat, the earliest are probably to be dated to the EB I. Most of these dolmens contained single cists although one (no. 38) featured two cists separated by a wide partition which may have been a cist itself, thus forming three interconnected cists (Stekelis 1960–61, 107). Several other tombs (nos 83, 117, 73, 164 and 167; see Stekelis 1960–61, 110, 112–14) featured two adjacent cists.

Burial in stone cists appears to have been a common practice during the Chalcolithic and EB I in the southern Levant and yet is but one of the varied burial customs found in these two periods (Ilan 2002; Joffe 2003). Though the osteological evidence is meagre, the available finds suggest that the larger cists, such as those found at Shiqmim and, potentially, Ashkelon Barnea Area E, may have been used for the initial interment and decay of the body, the bones being removed later to a secondary burial nearby. The latter appears to have taken place in smaller cists, which in the Chalcolithic period often appear as ossuaries. Interconnected cists, or 'ladder burials', appear to have been a common phenomenon east of the Jordan River near the northern end of the Dead Sea, now also found at

Ashkelon Barnea and Palmahim, and are just one aspect of Chalcolithic/EB I burial practice in the southern part of the southern Levant. The distinctiveness of this practice, occurring during both periods at Palmahim, Ashkelon Barnea and the Transjordanian sites as well, suggests a certain measure of continuity in mortuary practices between these two periods that is so distinctive as to hint at more than just a common cultural trait, and may provide a clue to an ethnic continuity as well.

Conclusions

The evidence unearthed in the past decade has added much to our understanding of the transition between the Chalcolithic and the EB I and it is our intent to highlight a new avenue of research concerning the nature of this transition. While the full range of burial customs associated with the Chalcolithic and the EB I periods is diverse, and presently beyond the scope of this paper, we have focused on those that appear to bear on our premise that the Chalcolithic population of the northern Negev continued to exist in the EB I period in the south. We suggest that the early EB I occupation at Ashkelon comprises some of the material culture of Chalcolithic cultural groups that relocated to the southern coastal plain after the collapse of the Chalcolithic geo-cultural sphere of the northern Negev. This is reflected not only in the continuation of material-culture elements such as ceramics, flint and the ground stone industry, especially as revealed in the EB I occupation at Ashkelon Afridar and Ashkelon Barnea, but also in the burial customs at Ashkelon Barnea that represent a direct continuation from the Chalcolithic, when infants contined to be buried within dwelling areas while older children and adults were moved out of the settlement. The discovery of 'ladder' burials, a distinct and rare expression of interment in interconnected cists associated with Chalcolithic Palmahim and possibly also southern Jordan, in EB I occupation at Ashkelon Barnea is a case in point. Such a distinct mortuary practice, within the varied and diverse milieu of Chalcolithic and EB I burial customs in the southern Levant, suggests association with a specific, previously 'Chalcolithic', ethnic group that resided at Ashkelon in the EB I.

Elements of continuity in the material culture of EB I Ashkelon with the preceding Chalcolithic period of the northern Negev and Dead Sea region now suggest that the Chalcolithic culture did not completely disappear, but actually survived into the EB I period in a different geographical and ecological setting. The reason for this may be population growth, the influx of new populations or over-exploitation of the environment along with climatic changes that caused the area of the northern Negev and eastern Jordan to become more arid, much as it is today. As a result, Chalcolithic cultures that thrived in these regions during moister conditions were forced to abandon these areas, moving northwards to more temperate settings. In doing so they abandoned their traditional homes and created a new lifestyle. The archaeological expression of this is the great deal of continuity in material culture from the Chalcolithic period, reflecting the emergence of a fully sedentary society producing utilitarian tools and with far-ranging and developed trade contacts.

Acknowledgements

The authors would like to expresss their gratitude to A. Gorzalczany for making the Palmahim information and the acccompanying photographs available.

References

Bar, S. and Winter, H. (2010) Canaanean flint blades in Chalcolithic context and the possible onset of the Early Bronze Age: A case study from Fazael 2. *Tel Aviv* 37(1), 33–47.

Baumgarten, Y. (2004) An excavation at Ashqelon, Afridar – Area J. *`Atiqot* 45, 161–84.

Bourke, S., Lawson, E., Lovell, J., Hua, Q., Zoppi, U. and Barbetti, M. (2001) The chronology of the Ghassulian Chalcolithic period in the southern Levant: New ^{14}C determinations from Teleilat Ghassul, Jordan. *Radiocarbon* 43/3, 1217–22.

Braun, E. (1996) Cultural Diversity and Change in the Early Bronze I of Israel and Jordan. Unpublished PhD thesis, Tel Aviv University.

Braun, E. (2000a) Area G at Afridar, Palmahim Quarry 3 and the earliest pottery of Early Bronze Age I: part of the 'missing link'. Pp. 113–28 in G. Philip and D. Baird (eds), *Ceramics and Change in the Early Bronze Age of the Southern Levant.* Levantine Archaeology vol. 2. Sheffield: Sheffield Academic Press.

Braun, E. (2000b) Post mortem: a late prehistoric site at Palmahim Quarry. *Bulletin of the Anglo-Israel Archaeological Society* 18, 17–30.

Braun, E. (2001) Proto, early Dynastic Egypt, and Early Bronze I–II of the southern Levant: Some uneasy ^{14}C correlations. *Radiocarbon* 43/3, 1279–89.

Braun, E. and Gophna, R. (2004) Excavations at Ashqelon, Afridar – Area G. *`Atiqot* 45, 185–242.

Eisenberg, E., Gopher, A. and Greenberg, R. (2001) *Tel Te'o: A Neolithic, Chalcolithic, and Early Bronze Age Site in the Hula Valley.* Israel Antiquities Authority Reports No. 13. Jerusalem.

Faerman, M. (1992) Excursus – the human remains from Tel Kabri, Area B. The Early Bronze I tombs. Pp. 21–2 in A. Kempinski and W.-D. Niemeier (eds), *Excavations at Kabri: Preliminary Report of 1991 Season * 6.* Tel Aviv: Tel Aviv University.

Frohlich, B. and Ortner, D. J. (1982) Excavations of the Early Bronze Age cemetery at Bab edh-Dhra, Jordan, 1981, a preliminary report. *Annual of the Department of Antiquities of Jordan* 26, 249–65.

Gilead, I. (1993) Sociopolitical organization in the northern Negev at the end of the Chalcolithic period. Pp. 82–97 in A. Biran and J. Aviram (eds), *Biblical Archaeology Today 1990 Proceedings of the Second International Congress on Biblical Archaeology. Pre-Congress Symposium: Population, Production and Power. Jerusalem 1990. Supplement.* Jerusalem.

Gilead, I. (1994) The history of the Chalcolithic settlement in the

Nahal Beer Sheva area: The radiocarbon aspect. *Bulletin of the American Schools of Oriental Research* 296, 1–13.

Golani, A. (2004) Salvage excavations at the Early Bronze Age Site of Ashqelon Afridar – Area E. *`Atiqot* 45, 9–62.

Golani, A. (2005) Ashqelon Barnea' B–C. *Journal HA–ESI* 117. http://www.hadashot-esi.org.il/report_detail_eng.asp?id=134&mag_id=110 (accessed 22 November 2009).

Golani, A. (2007) Ashqelon Barnea' B, C. *Journal HA–ESI* 119. http://www.hadashot-esi.org.il/report_detail_eng.asp?id=533&mag_id=112 (accessed 22 November 2009).

Golani, A. (2008a) The transition from the Chalcolithic to the Early Bronze Age: illuminating a dark period. *Proceedings of the 4th ICAANE at Berlin, 2004.*

Golani, A. (2008b) Ashqelon Barnea' B–C. *Journal HA–ESI* 120. http://www.hadashot-esi.org.il/report_detail_eng.asp?id=805&mag_id=114 (accessed 10 August 2010).

Golani, A. (in press) Rescue excavations at the Early Bronze Age site of Ashqelon Afridar – Area M. *`Atiqot* 60, 19–51.

Golani, A. and Segal, D. (2002) Redefining the onset of the Early Bronze Age in the southern Canaan: new evidence of ^{14}C dating from Ashkelon Afridar. Pp. 135–54 in E. C. M. van den Brink and E. Yannai (eds), *In Quest of Ancient Settlements and Landscapes Archaeological Studies in Honour of Ram Gophna*. Tel Aviv: Ramot Publications.

Goren, A. (1998) The nawamis of southern Sinai. Pp. 59–85 in S. Ahituv (ed.), *Studies in the Archaeology of Nomads in the Negev and Sinai*. Lahav: Joe Alon Center.

Gorzalczany, A. (2006a) Palmahim. *Journal HA–ESI* 118. http://www.hadashot-esi.org.il/report_detail_eng.asp?id=312&mag_id=111 (accessed 22 November 2009).

Gorzalczany, A. (2006b) A Chalcolithic burial ground at Palmahim. *Qadmoniot* 132, 87–97 (Hebrew).

Gorzalczany, A. (forthcoming a) Chalcolithic burial patterns: new evidence from Palmahim (North), in the central coastal plain of Israel. *`Atiqot.*

Guy, H., Masset, C. and Baud, C. (1997) Infant taphonomy. *International Journal of Osteoarchaeology* 7, 221–9.

Ilan, D. (2002) Mortuary practices in Early Bronze Age Canaan. *Near Eastern Archaeologist* 65/2, 92–104.

Joffe, A. H. (2003) Slouching toward Beersheva: Chalcolithic mortuary practices in local and regional context. *Annual of the American Schools of Oriental Research* 58, 45–68.

Joffe, A. and Dessel, J. P. (1995) Redefining chronology and terminology for the Chalcolithic of the southern Levant. *Current Anthropology* 36, 507–18.

Khalaily, H. (2004) An Early Bronze Age site at Ashqelon, Afridar – Area F. *`Atiqot* 45, 121–60.

Levy, T. E. and Alon, D. (1987) Excavations in Shiqmim Cemetery 3: Final report on the 1982 excavations. Pp. 333–55 in T. E. Levy (ed.), *Shiqmim I: Studies Concerning Chalcolithic Societies in the Northern Negev Desert, Israel (1982–1984).* Oxford: BAR Int. Ser. 356 (i).

Levy, T. E. and Burton, M. (2006) Appendix 2: Radiocarbon dating at Gilat. Pp. 863–6 in T. E. Levy (ed.), *Archaeology, Anthropology and Cult. The Sanctuary at Gilat, Israel.* London: Equinox.

Maisler, B., Stekelis, M. and Avi-Yonah, M. (1952) The excavations at Beth Yerah (Khirbet el-Kerak) 1944–1946. *Israel Exploration Journal* 2, 165–73.

Mallon, A., Koeppel, R. and Neuville, R. (1934) *Teleilat Ghassul I, 1929–32.* Rome: Pontificial Biblical Institute.

Nagar, Y. (1999) Anthropological report – Tel Aviv Pinkas St. Jerusalem, Israel Antiquities Authority Archives.

Nagar, Y. (2001) Anthropological report – Kfar Kana. Jerusalem, Israel Antiquities Authority Archives.

Nagar, Y. (2002) Anthropological report – Sha'ar Ephraim. Jerusalem, Israel Antiquities Authority Archives.

Nagar, Y. (2003) Anthropological report – 'Ein Hashomer. Jerusalem, Israel Antiquities Authority Archives.

Nagar, Y. (2005) Anthropological report – Nahal Komem. Jerusalem, Israel Antiquities Authority Archives.

Nagar, Y. (2010) Human Skeletal Remains from Tomb 80 in the `En Asur cemetery. *`Atiqot* 64 (in press).

Nagar, Y. and Eshed, V. (2001) Where are the children? Age-dependant burial practices in Peqi'in. *Israel Exploration Journal* 51, 27–35.

Nagar, Y. and Sklar-Parnes, D. (forthcoming) Horvat Zur (Rogalit) anthropological report.

Nagar, Y. and Winocur, E. (forthcoming) The skeletal remains from Assawir and Barkai South: reconstruction of some demographic parameters. In E. Yannai (ed.), *'Ein Assawir'. Excavations at a Proto-historic Site and Adjacent Cemeteries in the Coastal Plain, Israel.* Jerusalem: Israel Antiquities Authority Reports.

Ortner, D. J. (1982) The skeletal biology of an Early Bronze IB charnel house at Bab edh-Dhra, Jordan. Pp. 93–5 in A. Hadidi (ed.), *Studies in the History and Archaeology of Jordan* 1. Amman: Department of Antiquities of Jordan.

Stager, L. E. (1992) The periodization of Palestine from Neolithic through Early Bronze times. Pp. 22–41 in R. W. Ehrich (ed.), *Chronologies in Old World Archaeology*, vol. I, 3rd edn. Chicago, MI: University of Chicago Press.

Stekelis, M. (1935) *Les Monuments Mégalithiques de Palestine.* Archives de l'Institute de Paléontologie Humaine, Memoire 15. Paris: Masson.

Stekelis, M. (1960–61) La necrópolis megalítica de Ala-Safat, Transjordania. *Ampurias* 22–23, 49–128.

Vinitsky, L. (1992) The date of the dolmens in the Golan and the Galilee – a reassessment. *Tel Aviv* 19, 100–12.

Walker, P. L. and Johnson, J. R. (1988) Age and sex biases in the preservation of human skeletal remains. *American Journal of Physical Anthropology* 76, 183–8.

Yekutieli, Y. and Gophna, R. (1994) Excavations at an Early Bronze Age site near Nizzanim. *Tel Aviv* 21, 162–85.

Zelin, A. (2001) Rasm en-Nuqur. *Hadashot Arkeologiyot* 113, 126 (Hebrew).

8. Societies in Transition: Contextualizing Tell el-Mafjar, Jericho

Nils Anfinset, Hamdan Taha, Mohammed al-Zawahra and Jehad Yasine

Introduction

This paper contextualizes the results of two successive excavation seasons at the site of Tell el-Mafjar. We situate the site within a larger chronological framework and discuss what kind of settlement the site represents. This requires a discussion of culture and transitional chronological periods. Finally, we situate Tell el-Mafjar within a larger culture-historical framework and emphasize that the fundamental changes which occurred in the Late Neolithic/Chalcolithic periods framed these societies.

Late Neolithic or Middle Chalcolithic?

Different and sometimes conflicting chronological frameworks and nomenclature are applied to the late prehistoric archaeological assemblages of the southern Levant (the late 6th to the late 4th millennium BC – that is, the period between the Pre-Pottery Neolithic and the beginning of Early Bronze I, or in chronological terms between 5500/5200 and 3800–3600 BC (see Table 8.1). In the 1960s de Vaux noted great confusion in the application of the terms Neolithic and Chalcolithic (de Vaux 1966, 520), and this remains true. The confusion is probably even greater today as new terms and phases have been introduced (*e.g.*, Joffe & Dessel 1995; Finkelstein 1996; Garfinkel 1999a, table 1, and other authors).

The confusion is due to the long history of research (making incorporation of new information with legacy data a challenge), conflicting scholarly traditions and the spread of the total archaeological assemblage across national boundaries, all of which makes an overview of chronology and nomenclature extremely difficult. In addition, the Pottery Neolithic has fallen between two traditions: some researchers are trained in deep prehistory, while another group is primarily interested in the Chalcolithic and Bronze Age (Bar-Yosef 1992, 31). Meanwhile, one's own chronology is often heavily influenced by one's choice of comparative material. Garfinkel's (1999a) work is currently the most comprehensive, although it focuses only on the pottery traditions. The lack of radiocarbon dates from Late Neolithic strata reflects the fragmentary archaeological material from this period and is a serious problem for researchers.

Using the term Chalcolithic to refer to time periods as early as 5800 BC (Garfinkel 1999a) to 4500 BC should really be questioned, as there is no evidence of either copper artefacts or smelting and mining before this time. Therefore we would for the time being prefer to use the term Late Neolithic (*e.g.*, Rosen 1997; Lovell 2001; Blackham 2002; Levy 2007) for the period *c.*5500–4600/4500 BC, and Chalcolithic for the succeeding period down to *c.*3600/3500 BC. We see the introduction of metalworking as particularly significant in this later period, as is greater specialization in food production, agro-technology and animal husbandry (*e.g.*, Levy 1983; Burton and Levy 2006; Burton 2007). These are elements that are fundamental to social change. If we believe that changes in culture and society are reflected in the broad chronological shifts we identify (*i.e.*, periodization), then we should be able to move beyond clusters of radiocarbon dates and pottery to give this periodization a social content. In this way we treat the conditions motivating economic and political changes as significant, and break away from specific periods (Sherratt 1995).

Culture, archaeology and society

Culture is one of the most fundamental and debated

Moore (1982)	*Ben-Tor (1992)*	*Rast (1992)*	*Garfinkel (1993) Jordan Valley*	*Joffe & Dessel (1995)*	*Finkelstein (1996)*	*Rosen (1997)*	*Levy (1998)*	*Garfinkel (1999)*	*Lovell (2001)*	*Levy (2007)*
Archaic Neolithic, stage 1 and 2 8500–6000 BC							PPN (A,B,C) 8300–5500/5200 BC			PPN *c.*10000–5500 BC
Developed Neolithic, stage 3 and 4 6000–3750 BC	PN 6000/5800–5000/4800	Neolithic Period 8000–4500 BC			Formative Period III ? – 5000 BC	Later Pottery Neolithic ? – 4500 BC	Late Neolithic 5200(?)–4500 BC	PN 6400–5800 BC	Late Neolithic ? – 4800	Pottery Neolithic *c.*5500–4500 BC
	Early Chalcolithic 5000/4800–4200/4000 BC	Early Chalcolithic 4500–3800 BC	Early Chalcolithic 5000–4600 BC	Early Chalcolithic ? 4500 BC	Early Chalcolithic 5000–4500 BC	Chalcolithic 4500–3500/3400 BC	Chalcolithic 4500–3500 BC	Early Chalcolithic 5800–5300 BC	Early Chalcolithic 4600–4300 BC	Chalcolithic *c.*4500–3600 BC
	Middle-Late Chalcolithic 4200/4000–3200/3000 BC	Late Chalcolithic 3800–3300 BC	Middle Chalcolithic 4600–4000 BC	Developed Chalcolithic (I–III) 4500–3700 BC	Middle Chalcolithic 4500–3800 BC	EB I 3500/3400–2900 BC	EB I A–B 3500–3000 BC	Middle Chalcolithic 5300–4500 BC	Middle Chalcolithic 4300–4000 BC	
	EB I 3200/3000–2950/2900 BC	EB IA–IB 3300–3000 BC	Late Chalcolithic 4000–3200 BC	Terminal Chalcolithic 3700–3500 BC	Late Chalcolithic 3800–3100 BC			Late Chalcolithic 4500–3600 BC	Late Chalcolithic 4000–3800 BC	
								EB I 3600–3100 BC	Terminal Chalcolithic 3800–3500? BC	EB I *c.*3600–2900 BC

Table 8.1 Major chronological divisions of periods relevant for the text (from Anfinset 2010)

concepts in archaeology (see Thomas 1996; Shanks 2001; Trigger 2006, 232–5, for recent reviews and discussions). It is an anthropological concept which is intimately related to development and the growth of imperialism and nationalism in the 19th and early 20th centuries, and was developed in the context of encounters between European travellers and 'foreign' ideas, values and modes of social organization. Thomas (1996, 11–16) has argued that archaeological inferences of culture have been heavily influenced by the works of Descartes and the Enlightenment in gradually developing a division between nature and culture. Structured oppositions came to dominate western thought, where binary pairs became a method of classification also reflected in the epistemology and ontology of the culture concept (Thomas 1996; Kuper 1999). The result is often a strong historical particularistic approach focusing on superiority and origin without considering similarities and interconnections in larger geographical areas.

Time, space and diagnostic artefacts are the central elements, relating archaeological cultures to processes of diffusion and migration as reasons for cultural change. The focus on differences is central, and this is exactly how archaeologists most often define and locate transitions or more specific cultural change. Ethnicity, with its focus upon 'the other', is delicately interlinked with culture, but has rarely been explicitly used as an analytical concept in the prehistoric archaeology of the southern Levant. However, in other periods pottery has been used to argue for the presence of different (ethnic) groups, and there is a tendency to use pottery as a substitute for written texts in this effort, although one can never assume a one-to-one correlation (Laughlin 2000, 45). Equally, one cannot focus on one single type of artefact or category in order to define a society. Such definitions are too narrow – social groups never define themselves via a single artefact alone (Bernbeck 1995, 11).

However, it is one thing to identify change in the archaeological record; it is quite another to explain these changes in terms of social and cultural developments. No one would doubt that archaeological material is a reflection of culture, but the central issue is how we relate archaeological material to the larger social and prehistoric setting. Our perception of prehistory is formulated in a present context but this does not exclude us from understanding past cultures. Although the concept of culture is an abstraction, it is sometimes 'materialized', as we will see below.

The discussion of culture in social anthropology has a long history (Kroeber and Kluckhorn 1952). Recent discussion within the anthropological literature (see Abu-Lughod 1991; Brumann 1999; Borofsky *et al.* 2001) reflects increased scepticism regarding the use of the culture concept. The main criticism relates to applications of the culture concept, rather than the concept itself (Brumann 1999, S1). Both Brumann and Barth point out that we use 'culture' to abstract innumerable items from observed instances of thought and behaviour where people act in complex social and physical contexts (Brumann 1999, S6; Barth 2001). Following Mead (1937, 17), Brumann points out that one must distinguish between 'culture in a general and culture/s' in a specific sense, where culture in general refers to the potential of human beings to share feeling, modes of thought and interaction with other individuals with whom they are in social contact and/or to the products of that potential. In a particular sense, 'culture is the set of specific learned routines (and/or their material and immaterial products) that are characteristic of a delineated group of people; sometimes these people are tacitly or explicitly included' (Brumann 1999, S6). However, the use of the culture concept creates differences that are not necessarily real (Barth 2001).

What is the archaeological concept of culture and, if it is different from anthropological concepts, how is it different? Of course anthropologists are able to observe people in action, although culture as such is an abstraction, and therefore not directly visible. However, repeated observations and changes in these observations over time, from one pattern to another, may indicate a social change (Barth 1967, 662). Identifying the drivers of these changes may be more problematic. However, the archaeologist, possessed of a long-term perspective, has an advantage here: in the archaeological record it is possible to trace these events, changes or transitions on a cumulative basis – and this allows us a window on social/cultural change.

Archaeology has thus developed its own meaning and practice of the culture concept. Despite the fact that many archaeologists argue that their use of the concept differs from anthropological antecedents, however, it is still true to say that differences in material culture are implicitly equated to different cultural groups. Further, there is a tendency in archaeological research to view archaeological assemblages or 'cultures' in a vacuum. The most notable use of the culture concept as an explanatory mechanism in southern Levantine prehistoric periods comes from Gopher's study of the various lithic and pottery assemblages from the Pottery Neolithic period: the Yarmoukian culture, the Lodian culture and the Wadi Rabah culture (Gopher 1998). These culture assemblages have no relation to culture in the dynamic sense, but are purely viewed as static entities with no explanation or consideration of social interaction.

We argue here that we need to focus on social aspects in order to understand human behaviour. Furthermore, we argue that one of the main factors for understanding past social changes is the nature of the society. We prefer the term 'society' because it implies a more dynamic view of people as they once *lived*: society is regarded as the total number of social relations and structures both when considering groups of groups or a system of systems. This allows us to study relations on a micro level as well as on a macro level. In other words, we may conduct very detailed studies of a specific site or a specific type of artefact (at the micro level), but it is important to apply this at a larger scale – that is, on a regional or interregional (macro) level (see Dobres 1999, 19–21, for a discussion of scale). The scale of the analysis is only meaningful if our systematic observations produce insight into the potential causes of new patterns. As Barth has emphasized, this is also a matter of continuity and how we conceptualize change (1967, 664–5). All societies are reproduced and recreated continuously (involving constant cultural change) and events/social transformations must be contextualized within a wider social setting.

As archaeologists, we detect changes in activities and identify the reasons for these changed circumstances. With reference to the Late Neolithic and Chalcolithic periods, if we consider changes in burial practice as a reflection of values, and the introduction of new artefacts and materials in certain contexts as a reflection of changes in household economy, we may then be able to move beyond the innovation to the mechanisms of the change itself. For example, the introduction of copper metallurgy in the Chalcolithic was an innovation, and consideration of how the metal is incorporated into the population allows comment on the ancient social world. With this in mind we will turn to the question of material culture itself.

Material culture in the making

Material culture as a general concept can be only briefly addressed here. Processual archaeology led to an increased focus on human behaviour (Schiffer 1976) and the role of artefacts in both cultural and non-cultural processes. Recently there has been an increased interest and significant developments in material culture studies (Chilton 1999; Schiffer 1999), focusing not only on the production, use and abandonment of artefacts, but also on how this connected the identity of both makers and users, and on the role of material culture in communication. For decades now, from Spier's (1973) and Lechtman's (1977) early studies on material culture and technology, material culture studies have made an impact on archaeological theory and interpretation. Here linkages between technological systems and sets of thoughts, styles, identities and ethnicity have been developed and refined by a number of researchers (Sackett 1977; 1982; 1986; 1990; Wiessner 1985; Lemonier 1986; 1993; Gell 1988; Conkey and Hastorf 1990; Childs 1991; Hegemon 1992; Hosler 1995; Dobres and Hoffman 1999; Stark 1999 *etc.*). Dobres' work on the Magdalenian period highlights the need to recognize artefact variability:

> Normative researchers put site-specific patterns of artefact variability to use in describing regional (ethnic) Magdalenian lifeways; processualists looked at individual sites as little more than points on the ground but functionally differentiated locales where subsistence strategies making up the regional settlement system were variously played out. (Dobres 1999, 13)

This can also be applied to the southern Levant and the periods under discussion here, in terms of how variability in pottery and subsistence strategies are understood and connected to regional difference (see Schiffer and Skibo 1997).

Following Appadurai, material culture is connected to social life, and has itself a social life (Appadurai 1986) – but there has been very little uptake of these theoretical perspectives within Near Eastern archaeology. However, when analysing aspects of style and technology the scale must be appropriate and connected to a larger social context. Spier has argued that:

> Material culture and technology, like the rest of culture, are changing. Because they are part of culture, their dynamics may be examined in the same way as the rest of culture (Spier 1973, 19).

It is precisely the possibility of identifying culture-specific choices in the production of objects which enables a window on the social world of the artefacts. We now turn briefly to the archaeological material of Tell el-Mafjar, before turning back to the significance of this site and its assemblage on a large level.

Tell el-Mafjar: initial discovery and recent excavations

Today, Tell el-Mafjar is located within the oasis of Jericho and therefore the site must be regarded as part of Jericho. The oasis consists of one major spring, Ain Sultan, where Tell es-Sultan is located, in addition to several other smaller springs, including Ain Duik, Ain Nueima and Ain Quelt. The presence of these springs would have been beneficial for cultivation and pastureland, and may have also attracted a number of wild species. Within the oasis, the Late Neolithic and Chalcolithic are poorly understood (North 1982; Garfinkel 1999b), but a number of smaller and larger sites exist within Jericho (*e.g.*, Porëe 1995). The site was first discovered in 1953 by James Mellaart (Mellaart 1962), who recognized the value of Tell el-Mafjar, describing it as an important Chalcolithic site that should be watched (Mellaart 1962, 156–7). The site is located only a few hundred metres south of Khirbet al-Mafjar, an important Umayyad building excavated by Hamilton in the 1950s. In the south, towards the wadi, the site is heavily eroded and in the north intensive agriculture is practised. In the west it is probably partially cut by the road to Khirbet al-Mafjar and in the east there is a recent water reservoir. There is little doubt that the site has undergone severe damage since Mellaart visited it in 1953.

Mellaart's earlier excavations

Mellaart conducted a small excavation in what he assumed to be the centre of the site, reaching virgin soil at a depth of 2 m (Leonard 1992, 9). The trench revealed a sequence of three pits and parts of a possible wall on the western edge of the trench which he proposed may have been used as seasonal shelters, comparing them to the 'stepped entryways' formed by the pits he discovered at Tell Abu Habil during the same survey (Leonard 1992, 9, 64–8). Mellaart divided the stratigraphy of the test excavation into six different layers (1–6). The assemblage of just over 100 sherds revealed that the main corpus was hand-made (less than 10% was 'wheel-made' according to Leonard (1992, 9ff)) and that red slip decorated only a few sherds, either on the entire surface or just on the rim. Other sherds have a line of incisions or slashes, impressed cord decoration applied at or just below the rim, or a combination of these elements. The pottery shapes are, according to Leonard, straight or V-shaped bowls either plain or with red wash, as well as a few cups that are either plain or covered with a red-brown slip on the exterior and sometimes on the rim. Holemouth jars of many shapes and sizes are the most common type; some may derive from large pithoi, others from a bag-shaped vessel (Leonard 1992, 14–15). In addition, there are two marked necks and two fragments of stands. Handles fall into three categories: lug, ledge and loop, all with variations (Leonard 1992, 16–17). Mellaart's small finds and lithic material included three terracotta animal figurine fragments with four legs, four stone vessels, two spindle whorls and eight chipped tools. The lithic material included three backed sickle blades with blunted backs, two polished axes, two chisels and a side scraper. The bone tools included eight polished objects, probably awls, borers or gravers.

Although Leonard (1992, 18) pushes the date of the site to the very end of the Chalcolithic or the beginning of the Early Bronze Age, there were, with hindsight, several indications that the site may in fact be earlier. More recently, Garfinkel (1999a, 156), in a comprehensive and detailed study of the pottery of the 5th and 4th millennia BC, suggests that Tell el-Mafjar should be regarded as 'Middle Chalcolithic' – that is, between 5300 and 4500 BC. As this very brief survey shows the site was dated on the basis of the material culture (in this case, largely ceramic), but there was no attempt to discuss any other aspects of the site. Nevertheless, this basic background information forms part of the contextual frame through which we view the wider setting of the site and, thus, we have already partially placed the site within a framework, without giving it any specific 'cultural' content. We now turn to a more detailed presentation of new data from the site.

The more recent excavations at Tell el-Mafjar

The more recent excavation project at Tell el-Mafjar was part of a larger multi-disciplinary research project focused on both competence-building in terms of field practice and training, and major research themes connected to the cultural history and the ecology of the Jordan River Basin and the Central Hills (Bøe 2004; Tmeizeh 2004). In particular, the project focused on soil and water management, as well as a reconstruction of the changes over several millennia to the management of spring water, harvesting, storing, distribution and agricultural techniques. This included major studies (both in the highlands and in the lowlands) from archaeological, anthropological and historical perspectives. The joint Palestinian–Norwegian excavation of Tell el-Mafjar was a collaboration between Birzeit University, the Palestinian Department of Antiquities and the University of Bergen. The major goals of the excavations were to contribute to the local and regional understanding of the Late Neolithic and Chalcolithic periods (especially focusing upon the possible relationships with other contemporary sites) and to explore the nature of the site, its extent and its successive phases. The first season of excavation was initiated in October/November 2002 (Taha *et al.* 2004; Anfinset 2006), with an additional season in August/September 2003. The main aim is descriptive, with a focus on typology and chronology – an aim which may be regarded as quite processual and perhaps even culture historical (especially as regards the ceramic studies). However, as part of a larger interdisciplinary project, research questions beyond the mere classification of the objects have been set within an interdisciplinary theoretical framework and this approach is the frame through which we view past society, culture and cultural change.

Stratigraphy and architecture

Stratigraphy and architecture are aspects which will be dealt with in greater detail in the forthcoming publication; thus broad outlines only are considered here. Figure 8.1 illustrates the major areas of excavation in 2002 and 2003. Field A is located on the western slope of the tell near the road to Khirbet el-Mafjar (it is believed that the road partly cut the tell). In Field B (not pictured) a silo was restored in 2002. Field C was excavated in 2003, from the bottom of the tell towards the top, while Field D refers to the area excavated to the west of the road.

In Field A, the topsoil was deepest in Square 6, at the bottom of the slope. In this square most of the sediment (and associated artefacts) had the character of fill or debris, although the remnants of part of a mudbrick wall were uncovered. This wall crossed in a north–south direction into Square 5, where it was cut by another mudbrick wall running more or less east–west. A pit containing small stones and scattered pieces of pottery and animal bones cut into the wall. In Squares 10 and 11 a single row of mudbricks was found, with one stone identified as a door-socket in association. Square 11 also consisted of several successive thin layers of charcoal mixed with brown soil and mudbricks, as well as pebble surfaces. In this square a human foetus and a skull fragment of an adult were found below a floor. The foetus was covered with a large pot sherd, a common PPN practice (Garfinkel 1994; Kuijt 1996). Forty neonatal and child burials are known from Ghassul, either in jars or large storage jar sherds (Bourke 2002, 14). Square 24 was located almost on the top of the tell and consisted mainly of compact brown

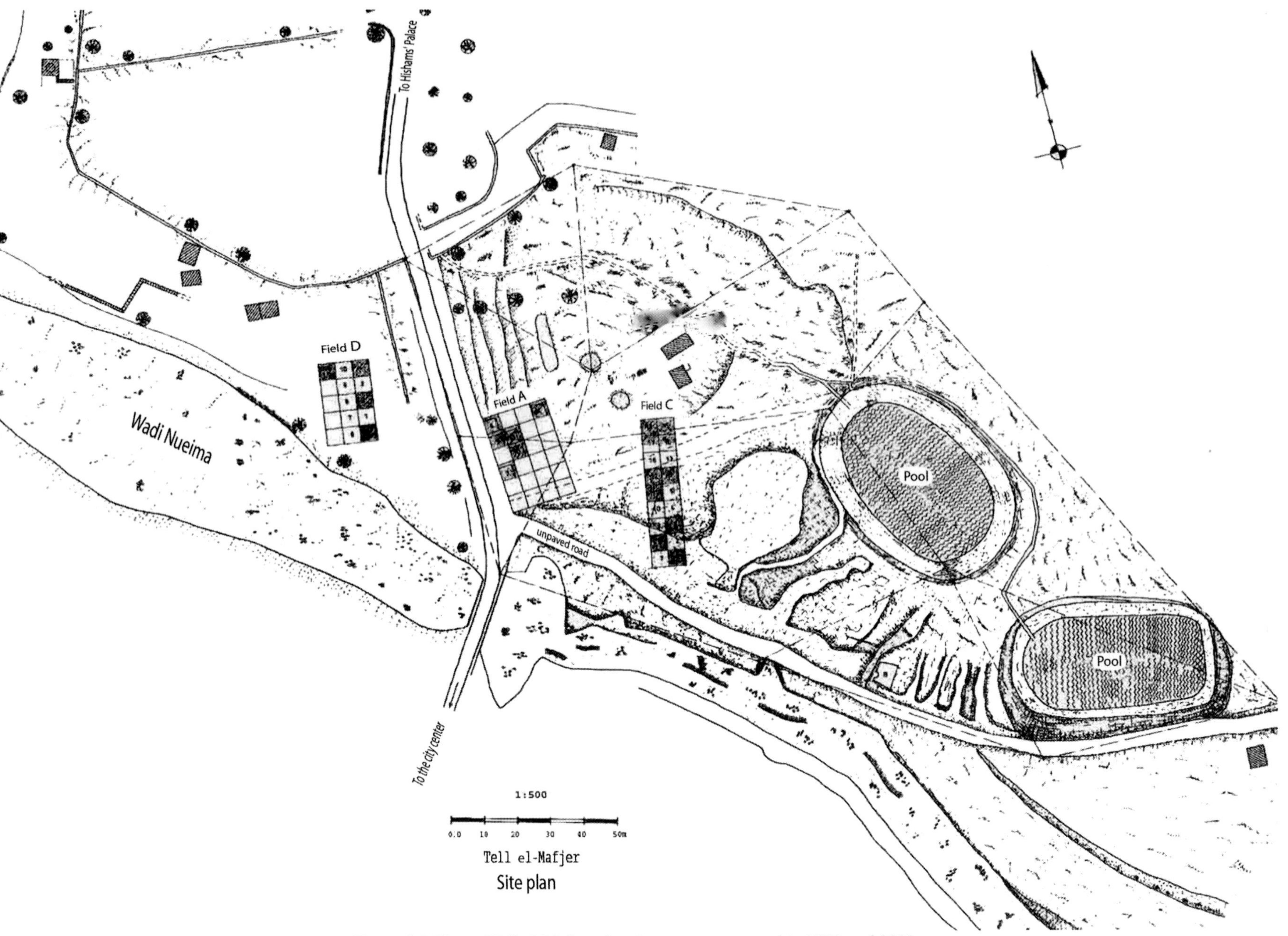

Figure 8.1 Plan of Tell el-Mafjar, showing areas excavated in 2002 and 2003

soil with occasional bone fragments, pottery and flint. A row of stones was discovered, though it is doubtful if this belongs to any architectural remains. Square 3 was the southernmost square, excavated in 2002, and consisted of several thin layers of charcoal often mixed with brown heavy soil. This square was dug down to virgin soil, where a hearth was discovered.

In 2003, a major effort was made to delimit the site both on the wadi side, to the south, and to the west, on the opposite side of the road. This latter area formed Field D, where four squares were opened. Three of these consisted mainly of deposits from the excavation at Khirbet el-Mafjar, although one had a row of stones on virgin soil which may be connected to either a fence or part of an irrigation canal of unknown date. One square, however, contained a few sherds and lithic artefacts similar to those found in the other areas of the tell. These are associated with a surface connected to occupation in the vicinity.

Field C was the most intensively excavated area, and one of the central aims here was to establish a long stratigraphic sequence from the top of the tell down to the plain next to the wadi in a north–south direction. Here the dearth of cultural material from the lower squares clearly illustrated that this area was not used for habitation. Several squares were dug deep down into virgin soil, where the stratigraphy revealed repeated flooding of the wadi. The squares at the foot of the tell, and on the southern slope, consisted largely of eroded material from the top of the tell, indicated both by the stratigraphy and by several small erosional channels dug out by water running down the slope. Towards the top of the slope excavations revealed larger pits of charcoal, possibly connected to dumping areas. The deposits excavated in the squares towards the top had a completely different character than those further down the slope. In the upper part of the tell we found scattered mudbricks mixed with hard brown soil. In Square 18 a row of larger stones forming a line, possibly part of a wall, was discovered. However, due to time constraints, it was not possible to explore this further in 2003.

Pottery

A detailed analysis of the pottery and its chronological and typological connections is still under preparation. No complete pots have been recovered; as a result the following discussion is based upon sherds alone. At this stage it is not possible to determine clear typological correlations with other site, although we can point to some broad similarities in the pottery assemblage. Major types include deep and shallow bowls, carinated bowls, small and large holemouth jars, swollen-neck jars and pithois. There are no indications of 'wheel-made' pottery. Red slip appears to dominate the assemblage. There are at least two different types of handles, including loop handles with broadening at the ends and lug handles. A large number of the bases have mat-impressions which can be divided into two basic types: circular impressions (both circular and oval) and

Figure 8.2 Pottery from Tell el-Mafjar

linear impressions (straight). Several decorative techniques are found: some large holemouth jars and pithois have rope decoration generally applied by thumb impression and a number of sherds have red paint on the exterior rim, mainly in thick stripes. Some of the rim sherds also have painted geometric decoration, particularly triangles with a thick line above and below, in addition to a net-pattern bounded above and below by a thick line.

The painted pottery at Mafjar has parallels with Garfinkel's Beth Shean ware (Garfinkel 1999a, 153ff; *cf.* Braun 2004,) and to other pottery with thumb impressions and rope decoration (Figure 8.2). In addition, there are also similarities to Tel Tsaf, further to the north in the Jordan valley (Gophna and Sadeh 1989, 9–32, fig. 6–8), as well as Phase II at Abu Hamid (see Lovell *et al.* 2007). According to Garfinkel's (1999a) periodization this would indicate that the site belongs to the 'Middle Chalcolithic', contradicting Leonard (1992, 18; see above).

Chipped stone

Rosen's (1997) lithic terminology is used here in order to standardize and broaden the comparative utility of the lithic assemblage from Tell el-Mafjar. In general, the lithic material from the site is scarce compared with that from contemporary sites. Inhabitants of Tell el-Mafjar appear to have utilized the small and medium-sized wadi flint pebbles originating in the hills to the west, although tool production at the site was not substantial. The total number of flint artefacts was 3742, most of which are defined as various kinds of waste material (96.1%, n = 3597); only a small number are classified as tools (3.9%, n = 145, see Figure 8.3 and Table 8.2). The flint tools have been classified according to their attributes, shape and function; some categories indicate functions of which we cannot be certain.

In the course of the first two seasons of excavations at Tell el-Mafjar, a total of 58 retouched flakes and pieces

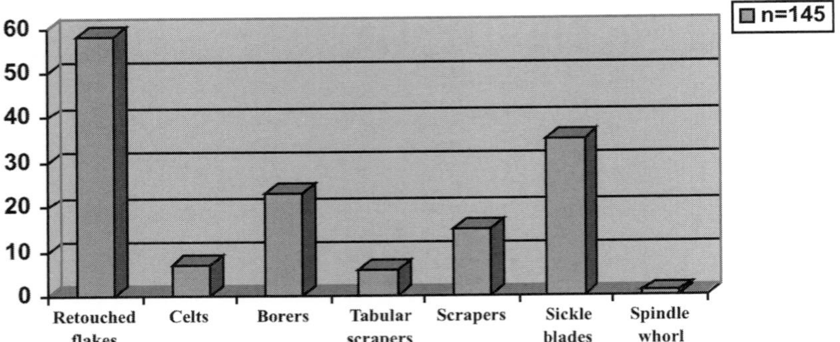

Figure 8.3 Relative frequency of flint artefacts at Tell el-Mafjar

was recovered, primarily with straight or convex retouch on one side, although bilateral retouching on two sides also occurs. At Tell el-Mafjar seven celts were recovered from excavations, with two more found while surveying the site. Of the seven found in context, three are butt fragments of necks (it has not been possible to determine the typological features), two are adzes, one is a chisel and one a roughout. Twenty-three borers were found, including microlithic drills, drills, miscellaneous points and tips only. A total of seven tabular scrapers was found in context, of which six have been classified as fan scrapers and the remaining one as an irregular tabular scraper. Fifteen scrapers were found and classified as side scrapers, tongue-shaped end scrapers, steep scrapers, scrapers and end scrapers. The majority of sickle blades have been classified as being backed, truncated segments. In addition, one single complete flint spindle whorl was recovered. There is no clear chronologically diagnostic lithic material from Tell el-Mafjar, and the flint material may be dated between the Late Neolithic and the Middle Bronze I.

In addition to the flint material, two pieces of obsidian were recovered during the excavation; both were found in the same square and locus. As indicated by Rosen (1997, 33), obsidian is rare but not totally unknown in the southern Levant – in the Chalcolithic it appears at Gilat (Yellin *et al.* 1996, 361–7).

Ground stone and clay objects

Within the ground stone repertoire pestles, mortars, grinding stones, polishing stones and stones with small crushed areas or cup-marks – often of a rectangular shape reminiscent of a small ashtray – have been identified. Additional objects made from basic limestone and basalt, classified as bowls, chalices and dishes, are all fragments and have been only tentatively classified according to the presumed shape or function. Altogether 11 objects have been classified as stoppers based on the shape, although the exact function is unknown.

Twenty-three objects of unbaked clay with cork-like or conical shapes have been interpreted as tokens (*cf.* Schmandt-Besserat 1992). Several have a small depression on the presumed top, where the diameter is larger than at the bottom, and some could, alternatively, be interpreted as fragments of animal figurines or small stamps.

Figure 8.4 Animal figurine from Tell el-Mafjar (TM.02. A.11.15.o)

Figurines of animals and humans are not uncommon in the Middle East generally and figurines of baked and unbaked clay occur at various sites. Thirty-three figurines and figurine fragments were discovered at Tell el-Mafjar (Figure 8.4). All the figures classified as animals had either one or several broken legs, one had clear male genitals and several had either a complete or a partial head. One seems to have a head with two horns, although the rest of the body is missing. Similar animal figurines were also found by Mellaart (Leonard 1992, 17, pl. 5)

Twenty-three bone tools have been found in context and most of these have been classified as complete or fragments of bone awls. In addition, one straight fragment, 130 mm long and 4 mm thick, polished on both sides and possibly originating from a rib bone, has been classified as a bone shuttle. Altogether, 60 beads of various materials, sizes and shapes were discovered. Most of the beads are broken, with half or less remaining. It has not been possible to identify the raw material of a large number of the beads. However, some are made of clay, while several are made of limestone, carnelian or turquoise.

During the two excavation seasons, 36 objects were classified as spindle whorls based on their size and

a. retouched flakes and pieces					
Object no.	*Reference*	*Material*	*Artefact type*	*No.*	*Comments*
43	TM.02.A.3.5.d	Flint	Retouched flake	1	Straight backing on two sides, truncation at one side, triangular cross section, two different colours on the flint
58	TM.02.A.5.3.c.1	Flint	Retouched flake	1	Retouch on the ventral side, straight fine retouch or possible edge damage
70	TM.02.A.5.3.aa	Flint	Retouched flake	1	Straight retouch on the ventral side, partly cortex
114	TM.02.A.3.6.h	Flint	Retouched flake	1	Slightly concave retouch, abrupt
130	TM.02.A.3.5.ap	Flint	Retouched flake	1	Straight retouch on one edge
136	TM.02.A.3.5.ah	Flint	Retouched flake	1	Ridge flake, slightly concave retouch
139	TM.02.A.3.9.i	Flint	Retouched flake	2	
141	TM.02.A.24.2.h.	Flint	Retouched flake	1	Backed and retouched on two edges
143	TM.02.A.24.3.a	Flint	Retouched flake	1	Straight retouch
146b	TM.02.A.3.7.o.6	Flint	Retouched flake	1	Convex retouch
160	TM.02.A.24.k.1	Flint	Retouched flake	1	Straight retouch on one edge
193	TM.02.A.3.9.o1	Flint	Retouched flake	1	Slightly curved retouch on one edge
199	TM.02.A.3.12.c2	Flint	Retouched flake	1	Look like CTE
202	TM.02.A.10.16.b1	Flint	Retouched flake	1	Small, no bulb of percussion (K)
210	TM.02.A.3.10.k3	Flint	Retouched flake	3	2 with straight retouch, 1 with slightly concave retouch
222	TM.02.A.6.3.a1	Flint	Retouched flake	1	Straight retouch
232	TM.02.A.3.10.n1	Flint	Retouched flake	2	Both have straight retouch on one edge
249	TM.02.A.24.3.p1	Flint	Retouched flake	1	Straight to slightly convex retouch
256	TM.02.A.3.15.b1	Flint	Retouched flake	1	retouch on two edges
272	TM.03.A.24.3.t.3	Flint	Retouched flake	1	
279	TM.02.A.3.15.h1	Flint	Retouched flake	1	Straight retouch on one edge
330	TM.02.A.5.9.b2	Flint	Retouched flake	1	Straight retouch on one edge
349	TM.03.C.3.1.b.2	Flint	Retouched flake	2	Both have straight retouch on one edge
403	TM.03.C.3.2.a.1	Flint	Retouched flake	1	Straight and slightly concave retouch
438	TM.03.C.3.2.a.2	Flint	Retouched flake	1	Straight retouch on one edge, probably part of a scraper
448	TM.03.C.11.4.c.2	Flint	Retouched flake	1	Straight retouch on one edge
454	TM.03.C.6.7.a.1	Flint	Retouched flake	1	Straight to concave retouch
517	TM.03.C.6.7.a.1	Flint	Retouched flake	1	Convex retouch on one edge, the other slight convex retouch
533	TM.03.C.7.7a.1	Flint	Retouched flake	1	Convex retouch on one edge
536	TM.03.C.15.2.a.2	Flint	Retouched flake	2	Both have straight retouch on one edge
543	TM.03.C.14.4.e.4	Flint	Retouched flake	3	All have straight retouch on one edge
596	TM.03.C.14.4.o.2	Flint	Retouched flake	1	Straight retouch on one edge
625	TM.03.C.14.4.o.4	Flint	Retouched flake	1	Straight retouch on one side
634	TM.03.C14.7.a.4	Flint	Retouched flake	2	Both have straight retouch on one edge
638	TM.03.C.14.6.a.2	Flint	Retouched flake	1	Slightly convex retouch
648	TM.03.C.17.2.a.3	Flint	Retouched flake	1	Straight retouch on one edge
652	TM.03.C.17.6.c.2	Flint	Retouched flake	2	2 with straight and slightly convex retouch
666	TM.03.C.17.5.a.1	Flint	Retouched flake	1	Straight retouch on two edges
669	TM.03.C.15.4.a	Flint	Retouched flake	1	Backed and retouched on two edges
672	TM.03.C.15.6.a.1	Flint	Retouched flake	1	Straight retouch
678	TM.03.C.17.10.b.2	Flint	Retouched flake	1	Straight retouch on one edge
683	TM.03.C.15.6.a.1	Flint	Retouched flake	1	Straight to slightly convex retouch
761	TM.03.C.17.10.b.2	Flint	Retouched flake	2	Both have straight retouch on one edge
783	TM.03.C.17.11.a.1	Flint	Retouched flake	2	Both have straight retouch on one edge, one slightly concave
788	TM.03.C.17.14.a.3	Flint	Retouched flake	1	Straight retouch on one edge
202	TM.02.A.10.16.b.1	Flint	Retouched piece	1	Small, no bulb of percussion (K)
Total				**58**	

Table 8.2 a–g Chipped stone artefacts from Tell el-Mafjar (and over the next three pages)

b. celts						
Object no.	*Reference*	*Material*	*Artefact type*	*No.*	*Comments*	*Rosen (1997) type*
41	TM.02.A.11.4.d	Flint	Chisel	1	Edge polished on both sides	L.4
73	TM.02.A.3.5.y	Flint	Fragment	1	Neck, either adze or axe	
98	TM.02.A.11.6.d	Flint	Adze	1	Partly polished towards the broken edge	L.3
140	TM.02.A.11.11.a	Flint	Miscellaneous	1	Roughout, could be natural	L.6.a
295	TM.02.A.24.3.x	Flint	Adze	1	Straight edges, one side slightly polished	L.3
329	TM.02.A.9.b.1	Flint	Fragment	1	Neck, probably celt or adze	
518	TM.03.C.7.a.2	Flint	Fragment	1	Neck, rounded or lens-shaped cross section	
Total				7		

c. borers						
Object no.	*Reference*	*Material*	*Artefact type*	*No.*	*Comments*	*Rosen (1997) type*
79	TM.02.A.3.5.u	Flint	Miscellaneous point	1	Long and narrow point, miscellaneous type	E.4
94	TM.02.A5.11.b	Flint	Microlithic drill	1	Double shoulders, retouched all around, tip broken	E.3.b
96	TM.02.A.3.7.b	Flint	Drill	1		E.2
142	TM.02.A.24.2.i	Flint	Microlithic drill	1	Narrow shoulders	E.3.d
208	TM.02.A.3.k.1	Flint	Miscellaneous point	1	Possibly natural, miscellaneous type, tip broken	E.4
258	TM.02.A.3.15.b.3	Flint	Drill	1	Two shoulders	E.2
283	TM.02.A.3.15.h.5	Flint	Drill	1	Long and narrow with two unclear shoulders, gloss visible	E.2
308	TM.02.A.3.15.k.3	Flint	Drill	1	Long and narrow, no shoulders, tip broken, possible microlithic drill	E.2 E.3.c, *cf.* Rosen 1997 fig. 3.27, no. 14
315	TM.02.A.11.21.c.2	Flint	Drill	1	Long and narrow, with two unclear shoulders, tip broken	E.2
350	TM.03.C.3.1.b.3	Flint	Borer	1	Complete, long and narrow, with retouch on all edges: W: 1.1cm, Th: 0.9 cm	Not identified by Rosen
414	TM.03.D.4.7.d.1	Flint	Microlithic drill	1	Miscellaneous	E.3
428	TM.03. C.3.2.a.2	Flint	Microlithic drill	1	Miscellaneous, drill bit	E.3
434	TM.03.C.6.3.b.1	Flint	Microlithic drill	1	Miscellaneous	E.3
523	TM.03.C.14.4.a.1	Flint	Borer	1	Tip	
535	TM.03.C15.2.a.1	Flint	Borer	1	Tip	
626	TM.03.C.14.4.o.5	Flint	Microlithic drill	3	Miscellaneous	E.3
631	TM.03.C.14.7.a.1	Flint	Awl	1	Complete	E.1
637	TM.03.C.14.6.a.1	Flint	Microlithic drill	1	Double shoulders	E.3.a
685	TM.03.C.15.6.a.3	Flint	Miscellaneous point	1		E.4
704	TM.03.C.17.7.a.1	Flint	Drill	1		E.2
787	TM.03.C.17.14.a.2	Flint	Drill	1		E.2
Total				**23**		

shape. The raw materials include sherds of pottery, limestone, sandstone and flint. The spindles are all relatively standardized both in shape and weight, regardless of material, with either a flat or slightly elliptical shape. Furthermore, 10 loomweights have been classified, although they are less standardized than the spindle whorls and are generally made of limestone. In addition, there are three pendants made of greenstone, clay and turquoise, all with a small hole on the top. Lastly, two fragments of malachite have been found.

Bone and shell

A relatively large assemblage of bones was recovered during

d. tabular scrapers						
Object no.	*Reference*	*Material*	*Artefact type*	*No.*	*Comments*	*Rosen (1997) type*
128	TM.02.A.3.5.be	Flint	Fanscraper	1		F.4
182	TM.02.A.6.2.a.3	Flint	Fanscraper	1		F.4
257	TM.02.A.3.15.b.2	Flint	Irregular tabular scraper	1	Irregular type, broken, retouched almost all the way around	F.6
284	TM.02.A.3.15.h.6	Flint	Fanscraper	1		F.4
437	TM.03.C.3.2.a.1	Flint	Fanscraper	1	Oval	See Rosen 1997, fig. 3.31.4
541	TM.03.C.14.4.e.2	Flint	Fanscraper	1	Partly broken	
Total				**6**		

e. scrapers						
Object no.	*Reference*	*Material*	*Artefact type*	*No.*	*Comments*	*Rosen (1997) type*
171	TM.02.A.3.12.c.1	Flint	Tongue-shaped endscraper	1	Convex retouch	I.1.b
273	TM.02.A.6.5.a.12	Flint	Steep scraper	1		I.3
274	TM.02.A6.8.c	Flint	Sidescraper	1	With gloss and convex retouch on one edge	I.2
300	TM.02.A.5.3.d.1 (northern bulk)	Flint	Steep scraper	1	Small	I.3
305	TM.02.A.3.15.k	Flint	Sidescraper	1		I.2
341	TM.03.C.3.1.b.1		Tongue-shaped endscraper	1		I.1.b
348	TM.03.C.1b.1	Flint	Tongue-shaped endscraper	1	Convex retouch, partly tongue shaped	I.1.b
366	TM.03.C.3.2.a.2	Flint	Sidescraper	2	2 with convex retouch, patinated, 1 small, 1 large	
367	TM.03.C.2.a.3	Flint	Scraper	1	Small convex retouch	
376	TM.03.C.6.2.a.1	Flint	Sidescraper	1	Convex retouch	
423	TM.03.C.6.4.2.b.1	Flint	Endscraper	1	Convex retouch on one edge	I.1.a
431	TM.03.C.3.2.a.5	Flint	Sidescraper	2	2 with convex retouch, 1 small, 1 large	I.2
542	TM.03.C.14.4.e3	Flint	Scraper	1	Slightly convex retouch on one edge	
Total				**15**		

the first season of excavation; the second season yielded a much smaller assemblage. The material is currently under analysis and will be mentioned only briefly here. In spite of relatively good preservation of bones at the site, no other organic material has been found. Species identified so far include sheep, goat, cattle, pig, gazelle, cervidae and dog. There are probably both wild and domestic species of sheep, goat and pig. Cattle seem to have been killed at an old age; extra bone growth between the joints which may indicate extra stress as a result of pressure and weight suggests their possible use for traction. This is also reflected by the striation marks on some of their joint bones (Al-Zawahra 2003). Grigson has pointed out that the general pattern of the southern Levant indicates a predominance of cattle with sheep/goat in second place, although there are some regional differences (Grigson 1998, fig. 6a–c). The faunal spectre from Tell es-Sultan seems to indicate a change from sheep/goat towards more sedentary animals such as cattle and pig (*cf.* Grigson 1998, 251, fig. 8). This seems to indicate a sedentary economy, but with an important component derived from pastoral products produced either for exchange and/or local consumption.

The most distinctive feature of the assemblage is the large proportion of pig specimens. Pigs need shelter and humidity, a condition which is in fact evidenced by the landsnails present at the site. Most of the pigs seem to have been slaughtered young and the bones have a number of cut marks definitely related to meat production. Their bones have mostly unfused ends and the skulls and the mandibles have at least one milk tooth remaining. No equid bones could be detected within the assemblage.

In summary, it appears likely that pigs were raised and consumed at the site and that sheep/goat were exploited for their secondary products, while cattle were raised

f. sickle blades						
Object no.	*Reference*	*Material*	*Artefact type*	*No.*	*Comments*	*Rosen (1997) type*
22	TM.02.A.3.2.e	Flint	Sickle blade	1	Broken prox. end, slightly crescent shaped, fine retouch, L:44 mm, W:2 mm, Th:4 mm	
28	TM.02.A.5.1.c	Flint	Sickle blade	1	Arched backed, slightly crescented retouch L: 44 mm, W: 12 mm, Th: 4 mm	B.3.b
39	TM.02.A.3.3.g	Flint	Sickle blade	1	Broken, backed, two straight edges, one side partly truncated, L: 40 mm, W: 6 mm, Th: 4 mm	B.1.a
44	TM.02.A.10.1.e	Flint	Sickle blade	1	Backed, tapezoid cross section, L: 33 mm, W: 14 mm, Th: 4 mm	B.1.a
91	TM.02.A.3.5.m	Flint	Sickle blade	1	Simple blade, fine retouch on one edge, L: 31 mm, W: 10 mm, Th: 3 mm	B.3.c
133	TM.02.A.3.5.aw	Flint	Sickle blade	1	Backed and truncated, L: 46 mm, W:11 mm, Th: 5 mm	B.1.a
155	TM.02.A.3.9.c	Flint	Sickle blade	1	L: 21 mm, W: 6 mm, Th: 2 mm	B.3.c
198	TM.02.A.3.12.c.1	Flint	Sickle blade	1	Flake-blade, rectangular, trapezoid cross section, L: 27 mm, W: 14 mm, Th: 3 mm	B.4.d
372	TM.03.C.11.2.b.1	Flint	Sickle blade	1	Backed and arched, steep abrupt retouch on one edge, partly retouch on the other	B.3.b
429	TM.03.C.3.2.a.3	Flint	Sickle blade	1	Backed and arched	B.3.b
439	TM.03.C.3.2.a.3	Flint	Sickle blade	1		
461	TM.03.C.11.2.a.3	Flint	Sickle blade	1	Backed and truncated	B.1.a
527	TM.03.C.11.4.b.1	Flint	Sickle blade	1	Backed and truncated	B.1.a
540	TM.03.C.14.4.e.1	Flint	Sickle blade	3	All are backed and truncated, 1 broken and mended, 1 small	B.1.a
568	TM.03.C.15.2.a.1	Flint	Sickle blade	1	Slightly concave retouch, backed truncated	B.1.a
594	TM.03.C.14.4.o.1	Flint	Sickle blade	1	Broken, backed and truncated	B.1.a
622	TM.03.C.14.4.o.1	Flint	Sickle blade	1	Simple sickle blade, unbacked	B.3.c
633	TM.03.C.14.7.a.3	Flint	Sickle blade	2	1 is broken, 1 is arched and backed	B.3.b
640	TM.03.C.14.6.a.4	Flint	Sickle blade	2	1 is arched and backed, 1 is miscellaneous	B.3.b and B.5
643	TM.03.C.17.2.e.1	Flint	Sickle blade	1	Arched and backed, rectangular shape	B.3.b
646	TM.03.C.17.2.a.1	Flint	Sickle blade	1		
680	TM.03.C.17.10.b.4	Flint	Sickle blade	2	Both are broken, backed and truncated	B.1.a
684	TM.03.C.15.6.a.2	Flint	Sickle blade	2	2 backed and truncated, 1 complete, 1 fragment	B.1.a
701	TM.03.C.14.8.a.1	Flint	Sickle blade	1	Geometric, trapezoid	B.4.d
709	TM.03.C.17.6.b.1	Flint	Sickle blade	1	Backed and truncated, segment	B.1.a
732	TM.03.C.18.9.a.1	Flint	Sickle blade	1	Backed and truncated, segment	B.1.a
760	TM.03.C.17.10.b.1	Flint	Sickle blade	2	Backed and truncated, segment	B.1.a
786	TM.03.C.17.14.a.1	Flint	Sickle blade	1	Backed and truncated, segment	B.1.a
Total				**35**		

g. spindle whorl						
Object no.	*Reference*	*Material*	*Artefact type*	*No.*	*Comments*	*Rosen (1997) type*
699	TM.03.C.18.4.b	Flint	Spindle whorl	1	Complete, D: 35 mm, Dh: 7 mm, Th: 8 mm	Not mentioned by Rosen
Total				**1**		

Lab No.	*Context*	*Uncalibrated (BP)*	*Calibrated (BC) 2 Sigma*	*Material*	*Excavation year*
B-174987	TM.02.A.10.7.e	5740 ± 40	4700–4480 BC	Charcoal	2002
B-174988	TM.02.A.3.9.b	5860 ± 40	4800–4660 BC and 4640–4620 BC	Charcoal	2002
B-191789	TM.03.C.6.7.c	6330 ± 40	5450–5410 BC and 5390–5290 BC	Charcoal	2003
B-191790	TM.03.C.17.6	6240 ± 60	5320–5040 BC	Bone	2003

Table 8.3 Radiocarbon dates from Tell el-Mafjar

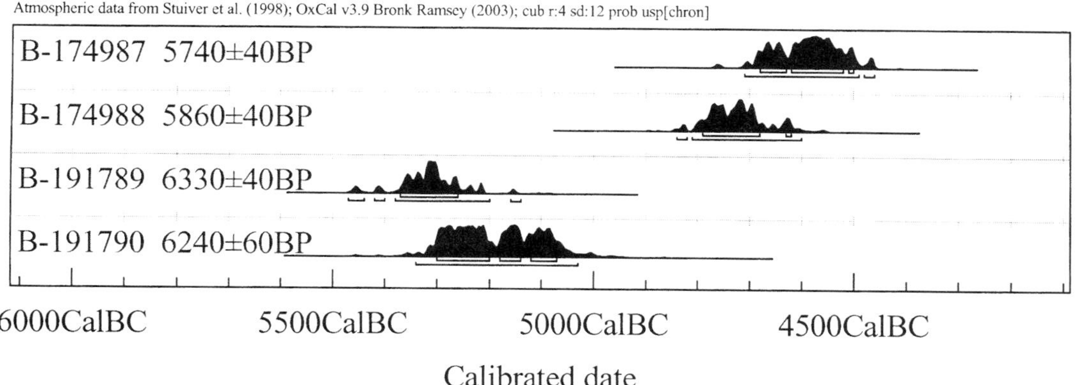

Figure 8.5 Radiocarbon assays from Tell el-Mafjar

for traction and other agricultural works. There are also indications of the utilization of wild species, such as gazelle, cervidae, fox and tortoise, but their low ratios indicate that hunting played a minor role in subsistence, as the inhabitants were mostly dependent on domesticates.

Recovered shells, of both marine and fresh-water molluscs and land snails, have been identified as *Cardidae*, *Cassidae* and *Glycymerididae* families. The majority of the shells are of fresh-water species such as *Thiaridae* and *Unionidae*, which have their natural habitat in the vicinity of the site. Interestingly, there are also shells from the Mediterranean and Red Sea, which were primarily used here as necklaces and ornaments, pointing towards exchange and interregional contacts.

Botanical material

Two sample types were collected for botanical analysis: soil samples from selected contexts and pot sherds with seed imprints. Soil samples primarily contain macrobotanical remains of cereals and lentils. The cereals have been identified as bread wheat (*Triticum aestivum*), emmer wheat (*Triticum dicoccum*) and barley (*Hordeum vulgare*). Although the samples are small, the implications that the people living at Tell el-Mafjar during the Late Neolithic–Chalcolithic period may have practised irrigation agriculture or floodwater farming using water from Ain Nueima are clear. The fields to the south and east must have been especially well suited for this practice. Along the Wadi Nueima the conditions for agriculture would have been good when the ground water was near the surface. With a continuous flow of water from Ain Nueima, the location of Tell el-Mafjar must have been a great advantage. Across the Jordan River at Ghassul both wheat and barley are attested, and Bourke (2002, 9) argues that barley increases in importance from the early Chalcolithic. This may correspond to the climatic optimum in the 5th millennium (Hassan 1997, 4; Hole 1997, 42), when agricultural technologies and practices suited for this environment developed.

The pulses are basically of two types, lentils (*Lens esculenta* or *Lens culinaris*) and peas (*Pisum sativum*), both typical components of early agricultural history together with wheat and barley. The cultivation of pulses is accepted as a good combination with cereals, either by rotation or mixing, in order to maintain high fertility of the soil (Zohary and Hopf 2000, 92). It is noteworthy that peas were the principle non-meat protein food source. They are well adapted to both the warm Mediterranean climate and cool temperate conditions (Zohary and Hopf 2000, 101). At Ghassul there is evidence of peas, vetches and chickpea, although lentils seem to be the most dominant legume (Bourke 2002, 9). Again, the material from Tell el-Mafjar fits into the overall picture of an established agricultural village society based on a few main crops that had already been used for millennia in the region.

Radiocarbon dates

Four radiocarbon dates are available (Figure 8.5): two from

the first season of excavation in 2002 and two from 2003 (Table 8.3). The samples from the first season fit fairly well with the archaeological material and expectations of the Late Neolithic or the beginning of the Chalcolithic period. The samples are taken from well-defined levels and contexts, but the last two samples are slightly later than expected. The earlier samples are both from the western edge of the tell, one from a hearth (locus 9) at the bottom of square 3, the other from a pit of loose ashy soil (locus 10) in square 10. One of the samples from 2003 is from charcoal from an ashy layer (locus 7) almost on the top of the tell in square 6, while the other was from a bone fragment also from an ashy layer (locus 6) from square 17.

We will present further details on the stratigraphy and ceramics in the forthcoming publication of the site. However, while it is difficult to make unequivocal statements, the lithics, pottery and other finds very much support a Late Neolithic/Middle Chalcolithic date in line with the 2002 radiocarbon assays; and, in fact, all the dates fall within the 'Middle Chalcolithic' as defined by Garfinkel (1999a). Therefore, a preliminary dating between 5400 and 4500 BC (late 6th millennium to mid 5th millennium BC) stands for the time being.

Contextualizing Tell el-Mafjar within the Jordan valley

The 5th and 4th millennia of Jericho are poorly understood in comparison to other sites and regions like Ghassul and Beer Sheva. Tell es-Sultan has revealed relatively scarce material from the 5th and 4th millennia BC, although Garfinkel (1999b) has recently suggested a Chalcolithic Ghassulian presence there. North (1982), on the other hand, has stressed the lacuna at Jericho, which may be more apparent than real, reflecting questions of terminology and chronology. Despite this, there are a number of sites in the lower Jordan valley and adjacent regions which are more or less contemporary and, further afield, several well-excavated sites like Ghassul, Pella, Tell es-Shuna North, Abu Hamid and Shiqmim provide overlapping occupation sequences.

Tell Tsaf, further to the north in the Jordan valley with striking similarities in location, has similar material. The site was first noted in the late 1950s (Tzori 1958), and was excavated in the late 1970s (Gophna and Sadeh 1989). More recently, renewed excavations have revealed substantial architecture (Garfinkel and Rowan 2005; Garfinkel *et al.* 2007), in contrast to the earlier excavations which revealed smaller walls of mudbricks with stone foundations, scattered mudbricks and smaller installations made of brick and mud filled with ash and small stones (interpreted as hearths or ovens). A single radiocarbon date of 4770 ± 460 BC (6720 ± 460) is regarded as problematic.

The earlier excavators interpreted the site as a permanent agricultural settlement consisting of a number of household groups scattered over the region, with open areas between them (Gophna and Sadeh 1989, 33). The botanical material included a number of domesticated species cultivated by the inhabitants, such as naked wheat, emmer, naked barley, six-row barley, lentils, peas, figs and olive (Gophna and Sadeh 1989, 33, n.5). The lithic material is also strikingly similar to that from Tell el-Mafjar, both in relative quantity and the tools represented (Gopher 1989, 37–45). Although the bone sample from Tel Tsaf was relatively small, it included domesticated sheep, goat, cattle, equids and pig, as well as gazelle, birds and molluscs (Hellwing 1989). Study of the Tell el-Mafjar bone assemblage is still underway, but its composition seems similar. There are striking similarities in the archaeological material, location, adaptation and organization of Tel Tsaf when compared with Tell el-Mafjar. It is significant that sites like Tell el-Mafjar, Tel Tsaf and others are located along major wadis with good arable land nearby, situations probably connected to both specialization in food production as well as increased population.

Societies in the making or making societies

More generally in the Late Neolithic–Chalcolithic societies are continually 'recast' owing to technological changes including changes in adaptive strategies, which also lead to changes on a social level. During these millennia there are profound alterations which must be seen in the context of important and widespread changes in agriculture, transportation technology and animal husbandry known as the 'Secondary Products Revolution' (Sherratt 1981). This brought substantial modifications to social organization, gender roles, modes of subsistence and exchange. In the southern Levant this is reflected in a rich symbolic repertoire represented on pottery, clay animals and figurines, and later the development of metallurgy. This suite of changes argues for a growing and specialized adaptation to the environment owing to population growth and for the increased exploitation of resources via, for example, the development of specialized pastoralism (Levy 1983; Anfinset 2004), and may also involve exchanges of metal, fruits and secondary products between mobile and sedentary groups (Sherratt 1999, 15–16; Anfinset 2005). The point is that the archaeology reflects a number of social shifts framing increased social complexity (Levy 1986; Golden 1998) and increased emphasis on ritualization (including persons organized for ritual purposes), and a number of social identities, within Late Neolithic and Chalcolithic societies.

In summarising the material from Tell el-Mafjar we concluded that this material is reminiscent of that excavated at Tel Tsaf's 'Middle Chalcolithic' phase as defined by Garfinkel (1999a), so can we speak of a 'Middle Chalcolithic' culture? As we stated above, culture is not a particularly useful concept because in archaeology it invokes something static – and we prefer to approach the material with a perspective on the social dynamics of prehistory. People living at Tell Tsaf may have regarded themselves as fundamentally different from those living at Tell el-Mafjar. They may have also shared a number of common beliefs and values, reflected by the similarities in the material. We must address what constitutes a society and the factors that make up a society. In other words, the analytical focus should include immaterial aspects, even if this is based on reasoning from the material that we have excavated in comparison with similar contemporary material. In focusing on technological changes we seek to understand how transitions are effected on the social level.

Regional social groups reflect both local adaptations to the environment and local and interregional contact on a variety of levels. They must have involved various social identities and organizations, where specialized sedentary groups interacted with mobile groups, exchanging commodities as well as manifesting their identities; this would have required an exchange network and a level of symbiosis between groups of different adaptive strategies. While large parts of the southern Levant may be seen as part of the same culture area, where general ideas are shared and manifested, at a regional level different social groups create a bricolage with a common basis of shared ideas, values and meaning.

Concluding remarks

Drawing comprehensive conclusions from the excavation material from Tell el-Mafjar at this stage would be premature. Nonetheless, there are several indications on both a local and an interregional level for interregional contacts of particular significance to our understanding of the Late Neolithic and Chalcolithic societies of the southern Levant. Tell el-Mafjar clearly represents a society based on agriculture and animal husbandry, an economic basis that has long traditions in the Levant in general. The people living at Tell el-Mafjar in the late 5th millennium were well aware of obsidian, turquoise and carnelian from distant points. Growing economic specialization and intensification, and increased demands for these products, led to increasing differences between people and growing social complexity. This may also relate to the increased focus on tokens and animal figurines (see above).

The discussion of culture is important, despite the fact that earlier researchers probably had a significantly different idea of the term. We argue here that we must move beyond pottery and radiocarbon dates to the social mechanisms connected with behaviour and resources in order to understand transitions. In the Late Neolithic and the Chalcolithic of the southern Levant there was great variation in local traditions of pottery, adaptation, technology, behaviour and so on, which may indicate several cultures, but it is exactly this variation that makes up the 'culture' of the southern Levant during these millennia.

Acknowledgements

We thank the staff at the General Directorate of Antiquities and Culture Heritage who have been engaged in the project and the excavation, those engaged in the NUFU project 'Lower Jordan River Basin Programme' and, in particular, Professor Randi Haaland (University of Bergen) and Professor Kamal Abdulfattah (Birzeit University). Melanie Wrigglesworth has kindly corrected grammatical errors in the manuscript. The editors Jaimie Lovell and Yorke Rowan were patient and provided much information, comments and insight throughout the revision of this article, which has been much appreciated.

References

Abu-Lughod, L. (1991) Writing against culture. Pp. 137–62 in R. G. Fox (ed.), *Recapturing Anthropology: Working in the Present*. Santa Fe, NM: Schools of American Research Press.

Al-Zawahra, M. (2003) The faunal remains from Tell el-Mafjar, Jericho. Unpublished report.

Anfinset, N. (2004) Metallurgy and pastoral nomads in the Chalcolithic period of the southern Levant. Pp. 61–73 in T. Oestigaard, N. Anfinset and T. Saetersdal (eds), *Combining the Past and the Present. Archaeological Perspectives on Society*. Oxford: BAR Int. Ser. 1210.

Anfinset, N. (2005) Secondary Products, Pastoral Nomads and the Introduction of Metal: The 5th and 4th Millennia in the Southern Levant and Northeast Africa. Unpublished PhD thesis, University of Bergen.

Anfinset, N. (2006) Aspects of excavation, cooperation and management: The joint Palestinian–Norwegian excavation at Tell el-Mafjar, Jericho. Pp. 61–82 in L. Nigro and H. Taha (eds), *Tell es-Sultan/Jericho in the Context of the Jordan Valley. Site Management, Conservation and Sustainable Development*. Rome: University 'La Sapiensa'.

Anfinset, N. (2010) *Metal, Nomads and Culture Contact. The Middle East and North Africa*. New Approaches to Anthropological Archaeology. London: Equinox.

Appadurai, A. (1986) Introduction: commodities and the politics of value. Pp. 3–63 in A. Appadurai (ed.), *The Social Life of Things. Commodities in Cultural Perspective*. Cambridge: Cambridge University Press.

Barth, F. (1967) On the study of social change. *American Anthropologist* 69, 661–9.

Barth, F. (2001) Rethinking the object of anthropology. *American Anthropologist* 103, 435–7.

Bar-Yosef, O. (1992) The Neolithic period. In A. Ben-Tor (ed.), *The Archaeology of Ancient Israel*. New Haven, CT: Yale University Press.

Bernbeck, R. (1995) Lasting alliances and emerging competition: economic developments in early Mesopotamia. *Journal of Anthropological Archaeology* 14, 1–25.

Blackham, M. (2002) *Modeling Time and Transition in Prehistory: The Jordan Valley Chalcolithic (5500–3500 BC)*. Oxford: BAR Int. Ser. 1027.

Bøe, J. B. (2004) *Farming Will Always Remain the Best Job. It Was the First Love*. Ramallah/Bergen: Birzeit University/Centre for Development Studies, University of Bergen.

Borofsky, R., Barth, F., Schweder, R. A., Rodseth, L. and Stoltzenburg, N. M. (2001) A conversation about culture. *American Anthropologist* 103, 432–46.

Bourke, S. J. (2002) The origins of social complexity in the southern Levant: new evidence from Teleilat Ghassul, Jordan. *Palestine Exploration Quarterly* 134, 2–27.

Braun, E. (2004) *Early Beth Shan (strata XIX–XIII): G. M. Fitzgerald's Deep Cut On The Tell*. Philadelphia, PA: University of Pennsylvania Press.

Brumann, C. (1999) Writing for culture. Why a successful concept should not be discarded. *Current Anthropology* 40, Supplement, S1–S13.

Burton, M. (2007) Biomolecules, bedouin and the bible: Reconstructing ancient foodways in Israel's northern Negev. Pp. 215–39 in S. Malena and D. Miano (eds), *Milk and Honey. Essays on Ancient Israel and the Bible in Appreciation of the Judaic Studies Program at the University of California, San Diego*. Winona Lake, IN: Eisenbrauns.

Burton, M. and Levy, T. E. (2006) Organic residue analysis of selected vessels from Gilat – Gilat torpedo jars. Pp. 849–62 in T. E. Levy (ed.), *Archaeology, Anthropology and Cult: The Sanctuary at Gilat, Israel*. London: Equinox.

Childs, S. T. (1991) Transformations: iron and copper production in Central Africa. *Recent Trends in Archeo-Metallurgical Research, MASCA Research Papers in Science and Archaeology* 8, 33–46.

Chilton, E. S. (ed.) (1999) *Material Meanings. Critical Approaches to the Interpretation of Material Culture*. Salt Lake City, UT: The University of Utah Press.

Conkey, M. and Hastorf, C. (1990) Introduction. In M. Conkey and C. Hastorf (eds), *The Uses of Style in Archaeology*. Cambridge: Cambridge University Press.

Dobres, M.-A. (1999) Of paradigms and ways of seeing: artifact variability as if people mattered. Pp. 7–23 in E. S. Chilton (ed.), *Material Meanings. Critical Approaches to the Interpretation of Material Culture*. Salt Lake City, UT: The University of Utah Press.

Dobres, M.-A. and Hoffmann, C. R. (eds) (1999) *The Social Dynamics of Technology. Practice, Politics and World Views*. Washington DC: Smithsonian Institutional Press.

Finkelstein, I. (1996) Toward a new periodization and nomenclature of the archaeology of the southern Levant. Pp. 103–23 in J. Cooper and G. M. Schwartz (eds), *The Study of the Ancient Near East in the Twenty-First Century. The William Foxwell Albright Centennial Conference*. Winona Lake, IN: Eisenbrauns.

Garfinkel, Y. (1993) Jordan valley. Neolithic and Chalcolithic periods. Pp. 811–14 in E. Stern, A. Lewinson-Gilboa and J. Aviram (eds), *The New Encyclopaedia of Archaeological Excavations in the Holy Land*. Jerusalem: Israel Exploration Society and Carta.

Garfinkel, Y. (1994) Ritual burial of cultic objects: The earliest evidence. *Cambridge Archaeological Journal* 4, 159–88.

Garfinkel, Y. (1999a) *Neolithic and Chalcolithic Pottery of the Southern Levant*. Jerusalem: Institute of Archaeology, the Hebrew University of Jerusalem.

Garfinkel, Y. (1999b) Ghassulian Chalcolithic presence at Jericho. *Levant* 31, 65–9.

Garfinkel, Y. and Rowan, Y. (2005) Tel Tsaf. *Hadashot Arkheologiyot* 117 (accessible online via: www.hadashot-esi.org.il).

Garfinkel, Y., Ben-Shlomo, D., Freikman, M. and Vered, A. (2007) Tel Tsaf: the 2004–2006 excavation seasons. *Israel Exploration Journal* 57, 1–33.

Gell, A. (1988) Technology and magic. *Anthropology Today* 4, 6–9.

Golden, J. M. (1998) Dawn of the Metal Age. Social Complexity and the Rise of Copper Metallurgy during the Chalcolithic of the Southern Levant, circa 4500–3500 BC. Unpublished PhD thesis, University of Pennsylvania.

Gopher, A. (1989) The flint industry from Tel Tsaf. *Tel Aviv* 15–16, 37–45.

Gopher, A. (1998) Early pottery-bearing groups in Israel – the Pottery Neolithic period. Pp. 205–25 in T. E. Levy (ed.), *The Archaeology of Society in the Holy Land*. London: Leicester University Press.

Gophna, R. and Sadeh, S. (1989) Excavations at Tel Tsaf: an early Chalcolithic site in the Jordan valley. *Tel Aviv* 15–16, 3–36.

Grigson, C. (1998) Plough and pasture in the early economy of the southern Levant. Pp. 245–68 in T. E. Levy (ed.), *The Archaeology of Society in the Holy Land*. London: Leicester University Press.

Hassan, F. (1997) Nile floods and political disorder in early Egypt. Pp. 1–23 in H. N. Dalfes, G. Kukla and H. Weiss (eds), *Third millennium BC Abrupt Climate Change and Old World Collapse*. Berlin: Springer.

Hegemon, M. (1992) Archaeological research on style. *Annual Review of Anthropology* 21, 517–36.

Hellwing, S. (1989) Animal bones from Tel Tsaf. *Tel Aviv* 15–16, 47–51.

Hole, F. (1997) Evidence for mid-Holocene environmental change in the Western Khabur Drainage, northeastern Syria. Pp. 39–66 in H. N. Dalfes, G. Kukla and H. Weiss (eds), *Third millennium BC Abrupt Climate Change and Old World Collapse*. Berlin: Springer.

Hosler, D. (1995) Sound, color and meaning in the metallurgy of ancient west Mexico. *World Archaeology* 27, 100–15.

Joffe, A. H. and Dessel, J. P. (1995) Redefining chronology and terminology for the Chalcolithic of the southern Levant. *Current Anthropology* 36, 507–18.

Kroeber, A. L. and Kluckhorn, C. (1952) *Culture: A Critical Review of Concepts and Definitions*. Cambridge, MA: The Museum.

Kuijt, I. (1996) Negotiation equality through ritual: a consideration of Late Natufian and Prepottery Neolithic A period mortuary practices. *Journal of Anthropological Archaeology* 15, 313–36.

Kuper, A. (1999) *Culture. The Anthropologists' Account*. Cambridge, MA: Harvard University Press.

Laughlin, J. C. H. (2000) *Archaeology and the Bible*. London: Routledge.

Lechtman, H. (1977) Style in technology – some early thoughts. Pp. 3–20 in H. Lechtman and R. Merill (eds), *Material Culture. Styles, Organization and Dynamics of Technology*. St. Paul, MN: West Publishing Co.

Lemonnier, P. (1986) The study of material culture today: toward an anthropology of technical systems. *Journal of Anthropological Archaeology* 5, 147–86.

Lemonnier, P. (1993) Introduction. Pp. 1–35 in P. Lemonnier (ed.), *Technological Choices. Transformation in Material Cultures since the Neolithic*. London: Routledge.

Leonard, J. A. (1992) *The Jordan Valley Survey, 1953: Some Unpublished Soundings Conducted by James Mellaart.* Winona Lake, IN: Eisenbrauns.

Levy, T. E. (1983) The emergence of specialized pastoralism in the southern Levant. *World Archaeology* 15, 15–36.

Levy, T. E. (1986) Archaeological sources for the study of Palestine: the Chalcolithic period. *Biblical Archaeologist* 49, 82–108.

Levy, T. E. (1998) Preface. Pp. x–xvi in T. E. Levy (ed.), *The Archaeology of Society in the Holy Land.* London: Leicester University Press.

Levy, T. E. (2007) *Journey to the Copper Age – Archaeology in the Holy Land.* San Diego, CA: San Diego Museum of Man.

Lovell, J. L. (2001) *The Late Neolithic and Chalcolithic Periods in the Southern Levant. New data from the site Teleilat Ghassul, Jordan.* Oxford: BAR Int. Ser. 974.

Lovell, J. L., Dollfus, G. and Kafafi, Z. (2007) The ceramics of the late Neolithic and Chalcolithic: Abu Hamid and the burnished tradition. *Paléorient* 33/1, 51–76.

Mead, M. (1937) *Cooperation and Competition among Primitive Peoples.* New York: MacGraw-Hill.

Mellaart, J. (1962) Preliminary report on the archaeological survey in the Yarmouk and Jordan valleys. *Annual of the Department of Antiquities of Jordan* 6–7, 126–57.

Moore, A. M. T. (1982) A four-stage sequence for the Levantine Neolithic, *c.*8500–3750 BC. *Bulletin of the American Schools of Oriental Research* 246, 1–34.

North, R. (1982) The Ghassulian lacuna at Jericho. Pp. 59–66 in A. Hadidi (ed.), *Studies in the History and Archaeology of Jordan* 1. Amman: Department of Antiquities of Jordan.

Porëe, B. (1995) Implantation humine dans l'oasis de Jèricho: les sites nèolithiques, chalclolithiques et de l'âge du Bronze dècouverts lors de la campagne 1994 de prospections archèologiques dan le Territoire. *Orient Express* 3, 93–4.

Rast, W. (1992) *Through the Ages in Palestinian Archaeology. An Introductory Handbook.* Philadelphia, PA: Trinity Press International.

Rosen, S. A. (1997) *Lithics After the Stone Age. A Handbook of Stone Tools from the Levant.* Walnut Creek, CA: Alta Mira Press.

Sackett, J. R. (1977) The meaning of style in archaeology: a general model. *American Antiqutiy* 42, 369–80.

Sackett, J. R. (1982) Approaches to style in lithic archaeology. *Journal of Anthropological Archaeology* 1, 59–112.

Sackett, J. R. (1986) Style and ethnicity in the Kalahari: a reply to Wiessner. *American Antiquity* 50, 154–9.

Sackett, J. R. (1990) Style and ethnicity in archaeology: the case of isochrestism. Pp. 369–80 in M. Conkey and C. Hastorf (eds), *The Uses of Style in Archaeology.* Cambridge: Cambridge University Press.

Schiffer, M. B. (1976) *Behavioral Archaeology.* New York: Academic Press.

Schiffer, M. B. (1999) *The Material Life of Human Beings. Artifacts, behavior, and communication.* London: Routledge.

Schiffer, M. B. and Skibo, J. M. (1997) The explanation of artifact variability. *American Antiquity* 62, 27–50.

Schmandt-Besserat, D. (1992) *Before Writing. From Counting to Cuneiform.* Austin, TX: University of Texas Press.

Shanks, M. (2001) Culture/archaeology: The dispersion of a discipline and its objects. Pp. 284–305 in I. Hodder (ed.), *Theoretical Archaeology Today.* Cambridge: Polity Press.

Sherratt, A. G. (1981) Plough and pastoralism: Aspects of the secondary products revolution. Pp. 261–301 in I. Hodder, G. Isaac and N. Hammond (eds), *Pattern of the Past: Studies in Honour of David Clarke.* Cambridge: Cambridge University Press.

Sherratt, A. G. (1995) Reviving the grand narrative: archaeology and long-term change. *Journal of European Archaeology* 3, 1–32.

Sherratt, A. G. (1999) Cash-crop before cash: organic consumables and trade. Pp. 13–34 in C. Gosden and J. Hather (eds), *The Prehistory of Food. Appetites for change.* London/New York: Routledge.

Spier, R. F. G. (1973) *Material Culture and Technology. Basic Concepts in Anthropology.* Minneapolis, MN: Burgess Publishing Company.

Stark, M. T. (1999) Social dimensions of technological choice in Kalinga Ceramic Traditions. Pp. 24–43 in E. S. Chilton (ed.), *Material Meanings. Critical approaches to the Interpretation of Material Culture.* Salt Lake City, UT: The University of Utah Press.

Taha, H., Anfinset, N., Yasin, J. and Zawahira, M. (2004) Preliminary report on the first season of the Palestinian–Norwegian excavation at Tell el-Mafjar 2002, Jericho. *Orient Express* July, 40–4.

Thomas, J. (1996) *Time, Culture and Identity. An Interpretive Archaeology.* London/New York: Routledge.

Tmeizeh, A.-H. A. M. (2004) *Water Rights and Uses in Midland Palestine.* Ramallah/Bergen: Birzeit University/Centre for Development Studies, University of Bergen.

Trigger, B. G. (2006) *A History of Archaeological Thought.* Cambridge: Cambridge University Press.

Tzori, N. (1958) Neolithic and Chalcolithic sites in the Valley of Beth-Shan. *Palestine Exploration Quarterly* 90, 44–51.

Vaux, R. de (1966) Palestine during the Neolithic and Chalcolithic periods. Pp. 498–538 in I. E. S. Edwards, C. G. Gadd and N. G. L. Hammond (eds), *Cambridge Ancient History*, vol. 1. Cambridge: Cambridge University Press.

Wiessner, P. (1985) Style or isocherstic variation? A reply to Sackett. *American Antiquity* 50, 160–6.

Yellin, J., Levy, T. E. and Rowan, Y. M. (1996) New evidence on prehistoric trade routes: the obsidian evidence from Gilat, Israel. *Journal of Field Archaeology* 23, 361–8.

Zohary, D. and Hopf, M. (2000) *Domestication of Plants in the Old World. The Origin and Spread of Cultivated Plants in West Asia, Europe and the Nile Valley.* Oxford: Oxford University Press.

9. A Techno-Petrographic Approach for Defining Cultural Phases and Communities: Explaining the Variability of Abu Hamid (Jordan Valley) Early 5th Millennium cal BC Ceramic Assemblage

Valentine Roux, Marie-Agnès Courty, Geneviève Dollfus and Jaimie L. Lovell

Introduction

In archaeology, the term 'culture' encompasses two main concepts: a 'cultural phase' and a 'cultural group'. The first concept, also called a chrono-cultural complex, cultural horizon or tradition (Gopher and Gophna 1993), is proper to archaeology. It defines a period of time characterized, in a certain area, by recurring assemblages of artefacts, marked by a beginning and an end, and affecting different domains (material culture, economy, sociology, religion, natural resources) (Clarke 1978; Renfrew 1972). The second concept derives from anthropology and refers to sociological entities whose definition varies according to the scale of observation (*e.g.*, Stark 1998). Contrary to the old belief that cultural phases are monolithic and represent homogenous social entities, recent research, particularly in the domain of technology, indicates that a cultural phase, as defined above, can include different socio-cultural groups, interacting at a certain level but characterized by diverse assemblages (*e.g.*, technological variability within the Beer Sheva–Ghassulian tradition). The more a period comprises socio-cultural entities that differ from each other in terms of material culture, the more difficult it is to characterize a 'cultural phase' and to assign assemblages to that phase. This is particularly pertinent to transitional periods, which are often marked by a wide variability of stylistic features at the macro-regional level. If variability is analysed in terms of presence and absence by reference to type fossils (Philip and Baird 2000), as when seeking to assign assemblages to periods such as the Late Neolithic–Chalcolithic, intense debates may follow (Banning 2002; Gopher and Gophna 1993; Gilead 1990; Lovell *et al.* 2004).

The oft-proffered solution to correlating such assemblages is to refine both the typological links and the radiocarbon sequences in order to clear up the chronological discrepancies and enable us to assign each assemblage to a given period (Banning 2002; 2007; Lovell *et al.* 2007). The problem with this approach is twofold. Firstly, it presupposes that a 'cultural phase' will include assemblages with close typological links – that is, the repertoire will exhibit a certain degree of formal homogeneity. However, one should consider the fact that a cultural phase can comprise, on the synchronic axis, assemblages quite different from one another, representing the coexistence of various different groups standing apart from each other, even though interacting; and, on the diachronic axis, assemblages originating from the same cultural group but presenting morphological and/or stylistic variability due to evolution over time (*e.g.*, Mayor 1994). Secondly, when radiocarbon assays are analysed carefully in the light of the stratigraphic sequence (Banning 2002; 2007; Lovell *et al.* 2007; Manning 2007), they can date a cultural phase. However, given methodological constraints, they can rarely be used to precisely estimate the temporal relationship between different short-lived sequences (Banning 2007; Burton and Levy 2001). It follows that it is difficult, on the basis of dates alone, to correlate assemblages at a macro-regional level.

In order to define both cultural phases and cultural groups, we suggest here that the techno-petrographic approach holds great heuristic value. This approach combines analysis of ceramic assemblages in terms of both technological traditions and clay fabrics (Roux and Courty 2005; 2007). These combined data express the technical behaviours reproduced by social entities in landscapes made up of material resources that evolve over time. Active landscapes, continuously shaped by environmental processes, offer the great advantage of displaying significant environmental changes at more or less similar time scales as cultural changes. In addition to the record provided by high resolution soil-sedimentary sequences, the effects of environmental changes can also be traced in well-stratified archaeological contexts by significant modifications of anthropogenic materials collected from various natural sources (Courty 2001). This direct reading of environmental changes in archaeological sequences thus allows a correlation with cultural periods which is independent of radiometric dating. As a consequence, an integrated study of clay materials and technical behaviour, within a high-resolution temporal frame, offers great potential for assigning ceramic assemblages both to cultural phases and cultural groups.

The techno-petrographic approach is applied here to the Abu Hamid ceramic assemblage. Abu Hamid is located in the central Jordan valley. It has provided a long occupation sequence dated from the middle of the 6th to the late 5th/beginning of the 4th millennium cal BC (Dollfus and Kafafi 1988; 1993; Lovell *et al.* 2007). In this paper we propose to analyse the ceramics belonging to Phase II (*i.e.*, levels 3a–e, dated to the first half of the 5th millennium). These precede Phase III, which is allocated to the same relative chronological horizon as the Beer Sheva–Ghassulian tradition on the basis of the presence of 'classic' cultural features (*e.g.*, wheel-shaped bowls, violin figurines, stone and hematite maceheads, basalt bowls, fenestrated vessels, churns and so on; Dollfus and Kafafi 1988). The objective is, firstly, to characterize the period prior to the Beer Sheva–Ghassulian tradition, which remains the subject of much debate as a result of the variability of ceramic assemblages assigned to the so-called 'Middle Chalcolithic' phase and the discrepancy of dates (Blackham 2002; Garfinkel and Miller 2002; Kafafi 2001; Kerner 2001; Lovell 2001); and, secondly, to assess the diversity of the cultural groups that have occupied the Jordan valley during this period.

Before presenting and discussing our results we elaborate on the importance of the techno-petrographic approach for highlighting cultural phases and groups, and present the archaeological context and the methodology followed.

The techno-petrographic approach

The techno-petrographic approach consists of classifying ceramic assemblages according to a hierarchical order that distinguishes technological, petrographic and morpho-stylistic groups, in that order, in relationship to one another (Roux and Courty 2005). We use the term 'techno-petrographic' because it emphasizes the specific sorting we use, as distinct from the traditional sorting where vessels are classified first according to shape or fabric (or a combination of both). Morpho-stylistic groups are defined on the basis of both morphological and decorative attributes. The techno-petrographic classification aims to highlight techno-petrographic groups that correspond to particular *chaînes opératoires* – that is, a sequence encompassing the different operations according to which raw material is transformed into a finished product (Creswell 1996). Techno-petrographic groups recurring over time correspond to distinct traditional *chaînes opératoires*. They are considered to be particularly relevant criteria by which to identify social groups because of the universals pertaining to the mechanisms of learning and transmission of technical tasks (Roux 2007). These mechanisms come into play at the individual and collective level.

At the individual level, any cognitive or motor skill is learned through apprenticeship according to a model. In other words, apprentices learn according to what the master shows or teaches. They never learn by inventing, whatever the context of apprenticeship (Bril 2002). When there is 'invention' in the process of learning it does not affect the technique, the method or the related skills, only the different values a technical operation can take, and these do not imply new specific skills (*e.g.*, invention in painting design, Dietler and Herbich, 1998). At the end of the apprenticeship process the skills necessary for reproducing the tradition, and only these skills, are literally 'embodied'. These skills then participate directly in the maintenance of the tradition, in the sense that it becomes difficult for the subject to foresee the making of things according to 'other ways', because the cognitive and motor skills they have developed then act as 'fixers' of world views. In other words, a technical tradition is reproduced through the apprenticeship process, and this fixes the tradition at the individual level.

Individuals are part of social groups (of whatever size or nature). At the collective level these groups ensure the reproduction of the tradition through transmission networks, understood here as networks favouring vertical and/or horizontal transmission. Distinct transmission networks express social boundaries that can correspond to different social entities: ethnic and ethno-linguistic groups, class, caste, tribe, gender and so on (*e.g.*, Degoy 2006; Dietler and Herbich 1998; Gallay 2007; Gosselain 2000; Livingstone Smith 2000; Shennan 1989; Stark 1998). The fact that different technical traditions exist side by side indicates, primarily, that the apprenticeship process took place within different social groups, or else within different 'communities of practice', a term coined by Lave and Wenger (1991) that refers to social groups who have 'the same way of doing things'. Such a concept is appropriate because it does not refer to a specific social entity, but instead to the community within which a technical tradition takes place (for use of this concept in ethnoarchaeology, see Gosselain 2008). Depending upon contextual and/or spatio-quantitative data, such communities can, in some cases, be interpreted more precisely – for example, in ethnic terms (Gallay 2007).

By definition, techno-petrographic traditions endure for a certain span of time, even though these traditions can present a certain degree of variability given continuous evolution over time (*e.g.* Shennan and Wilkinson 2001). From one period to another the material resources can remain stable or change simply as a result of triggers independent of cultural factors. The synchrony between changes in technological traditions and changes in material resources provides an ideal use of the clay fabric itself as a relative time marker of successive chrono-cultural periods with distinctive techno-petrographic traditions. This is most effective when exploitation is of clay resources from superficial soils that have been constantly reactivated by geomorphic changes. This is the case in the southern Levant, as shown by extensive palaeogeographical studies (Courty 1994; Hourani and Courty 1997). As a consequence, the southern Levant in the 5th millennium cal BC offers an ideal context to test the potential of the techno-petrographic approach for characterizing the ceramic assemblages belonging to the phase prior to the Beer Sheva–Ghassulian horizon.

Chrono-cultural context

The Abu Hamid sequence has been divided in three main phases on the basis of stratigraphy (Dollfus and Kafafi *et al.* 1993; Lovell *et al.* 2007). Radiocarbon assays provide absolute dates for the levels containing artefacts related respectively to the Beer Sheva–Ghassulian horizon (Phase III), the Wadi Rabah horizon (Phase II) and the Late Neolithic (Phase I). Phase I, levels 5–4, is dated to the end of the 6th millennium/beginning of the 5th millennium cal BC; phase II, levels 3a–e, is dated to the early–mid 5th millennium cal BC; phase III, levels 2–1, is dated to the late 5th/early 4th millennium cal BC (Lovell *et al.* 2007).

The techno-petrographic study has been conducted on the ceramics belonging to Phase II (levels 3a–e). Phase II has been recognized in the northern area of the site over 300 m^2, and in the south over 250 m^2. Architectural structures reveal houses characterized by rectangular rooms with hearths, platforms and small storage rooms; in the courtyards, small pits – both firing pits often filled with stones and plastered/clay-coated basins – have been excavated. The excavators associated the ceramic material from Phase II with the Wadi Rabah assemblage, as defined by Kaplan (1958, 1972), on the basis of the burnished and impressed ware (Dollfus and Kafafi *et al.* 1993, 254).

Methodology

Corpus

From levels 3a–e 15,485 sherds have been collected, of which 9697 come from reliable stratigraphic contexts. These have been the subject of a typological analysis (Lovell *et al.* 2007). The techno-petrographic study was carried out on a total of 933 sherds considered exemplars of significant morphological and/or stylistic attributes (as selected by Jaimie Lovell). Of these, about 400 formed the basis of a technological study. Half of these were subjected to petrographic examination. The results presented here bear on 175 sherds that were selected on two criteria: the legibility of their surface features and their possible interpretation in terms of manufacturing technique; and the integrity of their archaeological context. The majority of these sherds belong to levels 3a and 3b. Our observations on the diversity and variability of surface features and fabrics during phase II were later tested by the random sampling of body sherds.

Technological analysis

A technological analysis is aimed at the identification of technological groups – that is, groups of sherds presenting recurrent technological practices and, in this regard, representative of communities. By definition, each vessel is the output of a technological practice. Therefore, study of technological practices seeks to examine each vessel in terms of manufacturing techniques, tools, gestures, quality and 'know-how'. For this purpose, surface features, visible on both the outer and inner faces of the clay walls, are recorded. Manufacturing techniques and tools are identifiable on the basis of diagnostic attributes highlighted as such by experimental and/or ethnoarchaeological studies (*e.g.*, Roux and Courty 1998; Gelbert 2003; Ali 2005; Rye 1981); gestures are indicated by the orientation of the visible forming and/or finishing surface features; quality is expressed by the surface aspect of the clay walls; 'know-how' is suggested by the regularity of the wall and rim morphology.

Petrographic analysis

Petrographic examination under the binocular microscope commences with an estimate of the petrographic variability within, and between, each technical group. At the same time the petrographic variability is considered against the landscape context, which is now well understood from previous palaeogeographic studies (Hourani and Courty 1997; Hourani 2002). Extensive survey of soil landscapes formed during the 6th–4th millennia cal BC in the southern Levant and nearby regions has allowed us to identify a gradual change from highly humid conditions with extensive swamps along flood plains at the beginning of the second Holocene optimum to more concentrated rainfall, higher temperature, and a more incised landscape due to a significant erosional increase (Hourani and Courty 1997; Hourani 2002). Clay-rich materials, preferentially collected for ceramic fabrication in low-lying depositional and flood-plain basins, are therefore directly reflecting this palaeoenvironmental evolution. Clay materials with a higher clay content and with clay-fabrics typical of waterlogging are expected to be dominant in the ceramic assemblage of the 6th millennium. Samples with high clay content and pedogenic fabrics typical of soil stabilization can be associated with sources exploited during the phase prior to the Beer Sheva–Ghassulian phase. For this latter phase the greater proportion of coarse components resulting from repeated surface runoff is expressed in local to micro-regional specificities. This means that identification of clay provenance at a micro-regional and regional level for the 6th- to 5th-millennium cal BC ceramic assemblage in the Near East requires greater subtlety when compared with the transition from the 5th–4th millennia cal BC, which is more clearly defined owing to a more highly contrasted mosaic of landscapes. At this stage of the techno-petrographic study, the variability observed for the 5th-millennium ceramic assemblage cannot, therefore, be directly elucidated in terms of distinctive provenance. This would require an extensive study of the soil landscapes of the period, which is beyond the scope of the research presented here.

Results

The technological groups

The ceramic assemblage belonging to Phase II Abu Hamid is both highly diverse and homogeneous, depending on the scale of observation. The diversity is expressed mainly at the level of the finishing operations and the quality of the finished product. Homogeneity is expressed at the level of the forming technique. All of the vessels (large or small, open or closed) are made by coiling. The coils are progressively joined on the inner face either with fingers (uneven surfaces) or hard tools (even surface).

The finishing operations encompass the surface treatment operations aimed at regularizing the clay walls, and the decoration operations. The studies of surface treatment allow us to identify two main groups of vessels, *A* and *B*. In the former, after the rim has been fashioned and the pot partially dried, the external face of the body is coated with clay paste and then smoothed with a tool or with the moistened palm of the hand. The result is a surface with a lumpy aspect created by the coarse fraction of the coating applied on the leather-hard clay walls. The coarse fraction is covered by a thin clay layer created while smoothing the external walls with a moistened tool/hand. After a drying stage, slip, red painting or decoration (impressed, appliqué) can follow.

Variations in the lumpy aspect of the external clay wall suggest different ways in carrying out the surface treatment. These variations are expressed according to the following descriptive parameters: prominence of the coarse fraction – differences in the prominence of the coarse fraction indicates differential use of water when smoothing the clay walls; coating of clay – the coating of clay over the coils can be homogeneous or heterogeneous; striations on the external walls – the morphology and orientation of the striations indicate differences in the tools used for smoothing the external wall as well as different smoothing gestures.

The inner clay walls of vessels *A* are regularized either with the fingers or a hard tool while still humid. As a result, the coarse fraction is uncovered though damped into the clay (it is not prominent, contrasting with the external faces). When it has been smoothed with the fingers the aspect of the clay wall is slightly lumpy.

The surface treatment of Vessels *B* is carried out on humid clay. It consists of regularizing the clay walls either with fingers or with a hard tool. Finishing with fingers is achieved either with or without the use of a rotary movement. Use of a rotary movement is suggested by concentric parallel striations visible on the rim and upper part of the vessels. These striations are edged by rillings formed when adding water to regularize the clay walls while the pot was rotating. The rotary movement may have been achieved with an instrument rotating, or not, around an axis. Surface treatment on humid clay can be followed by decoration operations either on humid clay (impressed or incised decoration), or on leather-hard clay (application of a red slip which may or may not be burnished).

Vessels A

The vessels finished with surface treatment *A* present three main fashioning qualities which distinguish three groups of vessels: low-quality vessels *A1*, medium-quality vessels *A2* and higher-quality vessels *A3*. These qualities of vessel have been differentiated on the basis of the following technological attributes: the microtopography of the clay walls (from extremely uneven, bumpy, with fissures and cracks to even surfaces with no flaw), the regularity of the rim and the body (regular or irregular) and the prominence of the lumps (low, medium, high) (Table 9.1). These attributes reflect the know-how of the potters as well as the care taken in the course of the

<table>
<tr><td colspan="3">Uneven microtopography</td><td>A1</td></tr>
<tr><td rowspan="3">Even microtopography</td><td colspan="2">Irregular morphology</td><td rowspan="2">A2</td></tr>
<tr><td rowspan="2">Regular morphology</td><td>Prominence Medium</td></tr>
<tr><td>Prominence Low</td><td>A3</td></tr>
</table>

Table 9.1 Classification of the vessels belonging to the technological group A on the basis of their quality of fashioning

manufacturing process. Within each of these three groups there is a strong variability in the values of the parameters describing the fashioning or finishing operations. These values are on a continuum which means that these groups can also overlap.

Low-quality vessels – A1

The low-quality vessels (Figure 9.1) represent 29% of our corpus (Table 9.2). They are mainly characterized by uneven, bumpy clay walls, irregular rims, major faults such as drying cracks or fissures, and external faces with a strong lumpy aspect. The coarse fraction is prominent, covered unevenly by a clay slip whose differential thickness creates uneven surfaces. Visible striations, following either a horizontal or a vertical direction, indicate the smoothing of the external wall with the hand or a soft tool.

Despite these common technological features, there is also a certain variability expressed:

- in the visible properties of the fabric – the colour of the clay and the colour, size and quantity of the coarse fraction;
- in the treatment of the inner face, which can be smoothed either with the fingers or with a tool;
- in the unevenness of the superficial layer of the external clay wall, owing to different degrees of care in the coating process;
- in the degree of irregularity of the vessels, originating from the forming stage or the finishing stage, while smoothing the clay walls;
- in the faults of the vessels: some vessels present fissures, others drying cracks, others traces of joins of coils.

The range of decoration is quite limited. Most of the low-quality vessels present no decoration. However, some present a red slip or red bands on outer and inner rim and/or horizontal or oblique red bands on the body. Blackish-grey firing traces are present on most of the vessels on the body or next to the rim.

The low-quality vessels include large and small open and closed vessels. They are bowls, basins, holemouth jars and jars. Each morphological category includes different types characterized by the orientation of the walls (straight or rounded) and the shape of the rims (Table 9.3). Vessels *A1* are distributed in the different levels of Phase II.

Medium-quality vessels – A2

Medium-quality vessels (Figure 9.2) represent 39% of our corpus (Table 9.2). They present clay walls that are more even than those of vessels *A1*. They are not bumpy, reflecting more care or more know-how at the forming stage. The lumpy aspect is less prominent and more homogeneous, suggesting more control in the coating and/or smoothing operations. However, morphological features such as rims are not all regular, reflecting some awkwardness in the fashioning process. Variability within this group is much stronger than within *A1*. It can be described in terms of the visible properties of the fabric, the density of the network of the lumps (which can be more or less tight) and, lastly, the covering of the coarse fraction (which can be partial or complete). The inner faces are smoothed either with a hard tool or with fingers.

Most of these vessels present a red slip and/or red bands on outer and inner rim and/or a red wash decoration (less than half of the vessels are not slipped). Some of the non-slipped vessels present an impressed or an applied decoration. Some vessels present firing traces.

The morphological categories include bowls, basins, holemouth jars and jars of different dimensions and types (straight or rounded walls, rims of different shapes) (Table 9.3). Vessels *A2* are distributed in the different levels of Phase II.

Higher-quality vessels – A3

The higher-quality vessels (Figure 9.3) constitute 23% of our corpus (Table 9.2). These vessels present regular, even clay walls, reflecting care at the forming and finishing stage. The external walls are hardly lumpy; the coarse fraction does not stand out and is covered evenly by a clay layer despite the fact that it remains important either in size or in quantity. The inner faces are finished either with a hard tool or with fingers. Most of the so-called higher-quality vessels have received a uniform red slip,

Corpus	*Total*	*Group A1*	*Group A2*	*Group A3*	*Group B*
2/3a	17	3	7	5	2
3a	78	26	28	17	7
3b	31	11	13	3	4
3c	20	6	8	4	2
3d	8	1	3	3	1
3e	6	1	3	2	
3-	6		3	2	1
Transitional 3/4	9	2	3	4	
Total	**175**	**50**	**68**	**40**	**17**

Table 9.2 Number of vessels from phase II according to technological groups and stratigraphic level

Figure 9.1 Low quality vessels – A1

Stratigraphic level	*Vessels A1*	*Vessels A2*	*Vessels A3*
2/3a	B2a2	A1a7 B1a1	A1b5, A2b2
	D2b3	D2b3, D2b7, D1b2 E2a5	D1c2
			H1b
3a	A1a4, A2b3	A1b2, A1b3, A1b5, A1c2, A2b2, A2b3	A1b2, A1c2
	B1A7		
	D1a1, D1a3, D1a5, D1b2, D1b3,D1c2, D2a6, D2b1, D2c2,	D1a6, D1c3, D2b2, D2b3, D2c2, D2c6, D3	D1a1, D1c5, D1c7
	E1b5, E1b2, E3	E1a3, E1a5, E1b2, E1c3, E2a3	E1a5, E1b5, E1e5 E2a2, E2e3
3b	A1a5, A1b3	A1b2, A1b3, A1b5, A2b2, A2b4	
		B2a1	
	D1c3, D1a5, D2c6 E2d7	D1c4	C3 D1c5 E1a3
3c		A1b2, A1c1	A1c1
	D1c3, D1c5, D2c3, D2c5		D1c3, D2b1
		E1a3, E1e5	
		H1c	
		J3	
3d	D2c4	A1b2	A1b2
		E2a3	E1a2
3e	A2c1		
	D1c3		D1c2
		E1a3, E2b5	E1a2
3/4			A2b2, A1b5
		D1c3 E1a5	D1c2
		H1g	H1b

Table 9.3 Distribution of morphological types among the different ceramic groups A. (A = bowl, B = basin, C = churn, D = holemouth, E = jars, H = base, J = platter; 1 = straight-sided, 2 = round-sided; the full morphological codes correspond to those published in Lovell et al. 2007)

paintings (geometric motifs, red bands, red wash) and/or an applied, incised or impressed decoration. Some very rare vessels have a black slip which has been polished. Vessels without decoration are rare. Clay material colour varies. In this regard, the group of higher-quality vessels is as heterogeneous as the *A2* group.

The higher-quality group includes bowls, basins, holemouth jars, jars and churns. Within each category types are varied in terms of the profile of the walls and the rims (Table 9.3). Vessels *A3* are distributed in the different levels of Phase II.

Vessels B

Vessels *B* (Figure 9.4) are very much in the minority, representing less than 10% of our corpus (Table 9.2). They include different technical groups: two are defined on the basis of the use of the rotary movement for shaping the rim and/or the upper part of the vessels.

Vessels B1

Vessels *B1* have been regularized on humid clay with the help of a rotary movement. Unlike vessels *A*, the *B* vessels have a clay body that is quite fine, with a low quantity of coarse fraction. Vessels *B1* includes vessels with and without decoration. Those with decoration present a red

Figure 9.2 Medium quality vessels – A2

Figure 9.3 Higher quality vessels – A3

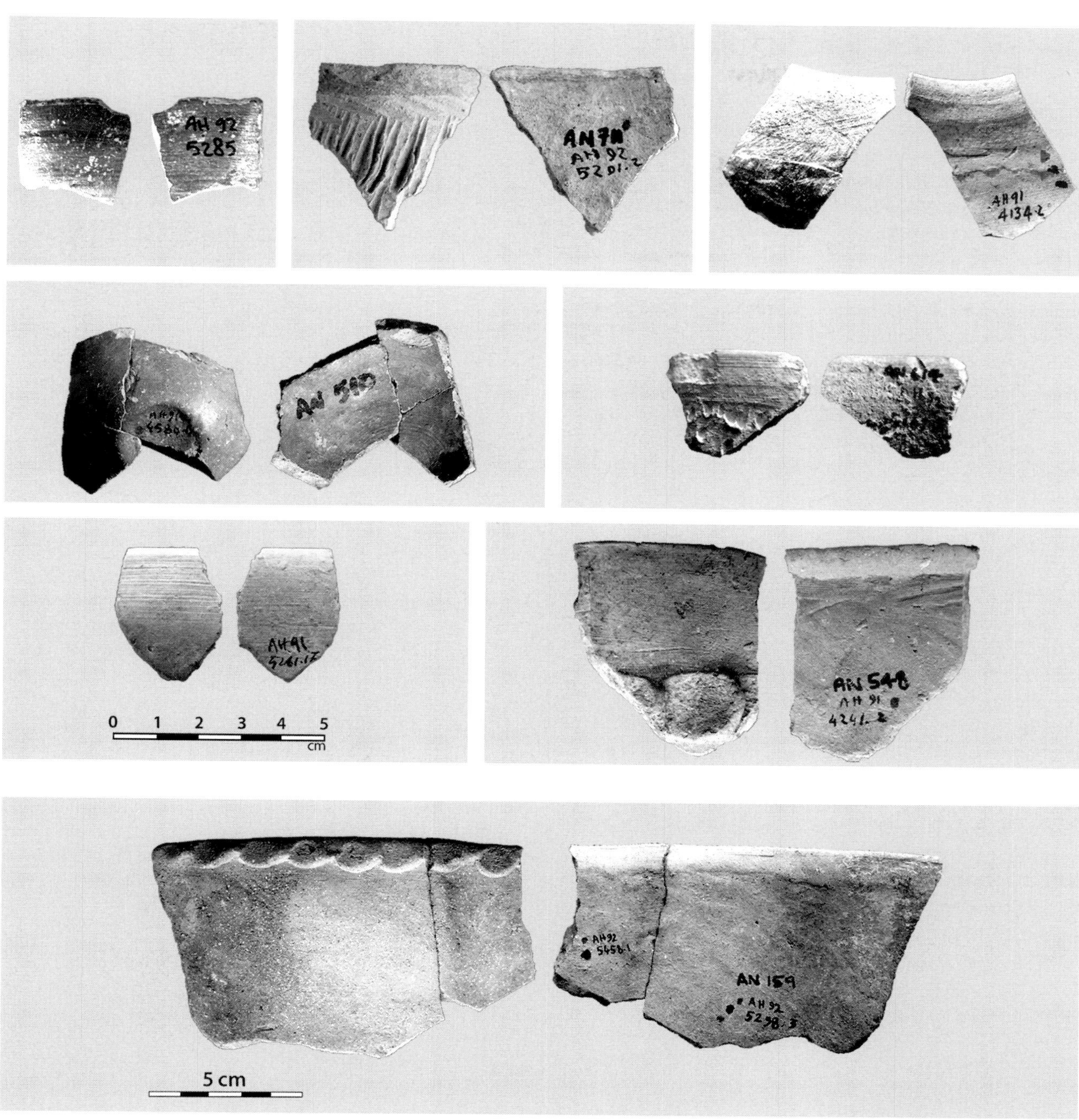

Figure 9.4 Vessels B

slip, one vessel displaying a burnished red slip. One vessel, without slip, presents an impressed decoration.

Vessels *B1* are mainly bowls, and also small holemouth jars, as exemplified by one specimen. They are found in levels 3a and 3b, which indicates that, in the southern Levant, the use of the rotary movement for regularizing rims and/or the upper part of vessels dates back to at least the first half of the 5th millennium cal BC.

Vessels B2

Vessels *B2* are characterized by clay walls whose surface aspect is not lumpy, but smooth and evened. This group is not homogeneous and presents high variability in terms of the smoothing gestures and tools and the decoration operations (red slip, burnishing, impressed or appliqué decoration). One should distinguish between the small vessels (bowls) with a red burnished slip and the vessels including small and large open vessels (bowls and basins) with or without decoration, which includes rims with a red band along with a vertical incised decoration on the body, rims with a thumb-print decoration, and thumb-print bands applied on the body. Vessels *B2* are distributed in the different levels of Phase II (3a, b, c).

Petrographic analysis: general classification of clay sources

At first, the binocular examination shows a predominance of very fine-textured raw materials that appears to reflect the widespread availability of clay-rich flood deposits throughout the Near East in flood plains, small valleys or even depositional basins. However, upon closer inspection, the comparison of the petrography and particle size composition of the coarse components, in addition to a rough estimate of the clay mineralogy based on its colour and its textural aspect, reveals the great heterogeneity of the 5th-millennium cal BC ceramic assemblage in terms of provenance. This is more particularly reflected by the difficulty in obtaining more than a very few sherds within each petrographic class of raw materials, and even to clearly define classes of strictly identifiable raw materials. Nonetheless, it seems difficult to reconcile this variability with the widely accepted assumption that, *a priori*, a settlement ceramic assemblage comprises a majority of locally made ceramics – that is, whose clay sources are located within a 10-km radius (*e.g.*, Arnold 1985). There are some roughly categorized classes of raw material within the assemblage which may, upon further study, allow more precise provenance. A few of them strongly resemble specific fabrics of the transitional 5th- to 4th-millennium cal BC ceramic assemblage as previously defined (Roux and Courty 2005). Their provenance can thus be suggested on the basis of results of our previous studies based on the similarities of the coarse fraction added to the clay materials; rock sources have remained unchanged from the 5th to the 4th millennium. However, this overall geological stability should not be confused with the high reactivity of soil landscapes to short-scale environmental changes, exemplified by modifications of the clay materials themselves, and to a lesser extent by morphology and abundance of the coarse fraction. By way of example, a group from Abu Hamid made with finely sorted crushed calcitic angular fragments within weakly prepared calcareous fine clay strongly resembles a distinctive clay material found at late 5th to early 4th millennium cal BC sites. This group originated in the Ajlun mountains and therefore possibly had a similar provenance in the earlier period.

Petro-technological classification

As we noted above, vessels *A* and *B* are distinct from a technological point of view but the difference in fabric is even more marked (Figures 9.5, 9.6, 9.7). Vessels *B* are dominated (>90%) by very fine clay (VFC) and sandy clay (SC) which, by contrast, are only minor components of vessels *A* (<5%). The majority of vessels *B2* (~60%) and the minority of vessels *B1* (30%) belong to the SC type (with a remarkable petrographic homogeneity and a range of particle sizes that matches low-energy flood deposits). This SC is likely to come from within the Jordan valley itself, which was, at the time, a wide, regularly flooded alluvial plain with a meandering channel. The majority of vessels *B1* (70%) and the minority of vessels *B2* (40%) are made of very fine clay (VFC) with a significant mineralogical variability of the clay fraction and major variations in the amount and type of the coarse fraction. This reflects a great heterogeneity in terms of provenance and, in contrast, a striking homogeneity with respect to the great care in clay preparation.

As with the technological classification, the lower-quality vessels (*A1*) (Figure 9.6) appear to form a coherent petrographic group when compared with medium-quality vessels (*A2*) and higher-quality vessels (*A3*) (Figure 9.7). This coherence is expressed by the predominance of fine clay mixed with an angular, coarse fraction crushed from various types of limestones (80%), with a particular type represented by crushed pure calcite, and another one by crushed bioclasts. This petrographical range indicates multiple provenances from the plateau regions with their distinctive limestone outcrops. The medium-quality vessels (*A2*) and the higher-quality vessels (*A3*) are both characterized by heterogeneity in raw materials (expressed in terms of variability in morphology, petrography and abundance of the coarse fraction). The predominance of weakly sorted sub-rounded calcareous grains matches a provenance from the small tributaries flowing along the colluvial piedmonts on both sides of the Jordan Valley before merging into the mainstream. The lack of distinctive petrographic classes, and the overall impression of a continuum between poorly sorted to well-sorted, and well rounded to sub-angular, calcareous grains, seems to reflect the inherent variability of flood deposits along colluvial piedmonts at the meso-regional scale. This would suggest an occasional exploitation of raw materials collected from various places and not always from the same provenance.

Discussion

The techno-petrographic approach, as applied to the Phase II ceramic assemblage from Abu Hamid, enables us to highlight a large range of technological practices originating from various places and characterize the material resources used during the period prior to the Beer Sheva–Ghassulian horizon and posterior to the 6th millennium cal BC. In this respect, the techno-petrographic approach proves to be particularly relevant to the interpretation of ceramic assemblages in terms of both period and communities ('cultural groups').

Techno-stylistic variability and communities

The techno-petrographic analysis of Abu Hamid ceramics has shown that vessels can be divided into two main techno-petrographic groups, *A* and *B*.

Group *B* is very much in a minority, and is restricted to a limited range of vessels, mainly small vessels (bowls).

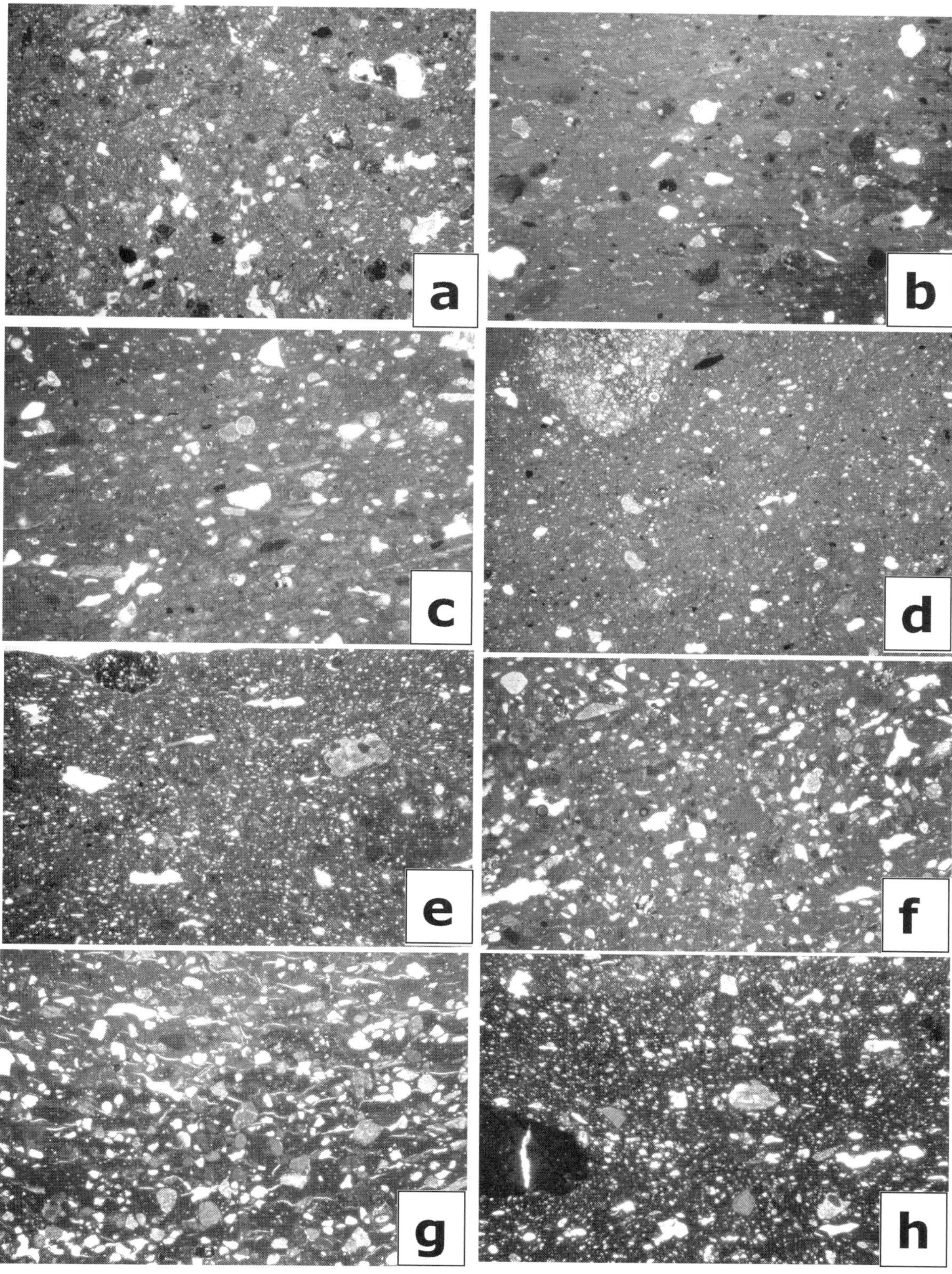

Figure 9.5 Vessels B: Illustration of the different petrofacies. Frame width for all the photos: 4 mm
(a) Yellowish-brown very fine calcareous clay with subrounded calcareous fine sands; (b) dull orange very fine calcareous clay with well-rounded calcareous fine sands; (c) pale yellow very fine calcareous clay with subangular to sub-rounded chalky fine sands; (d) pale yellow very fine calcareous clay with rare subrounded coarse clasts of chalky limestones; (e) yellowish-brown calcareous sandy clay with poorly sorted subrounded micritic fine sands; (f) yellowish-brown calcareous very fine clay with weakly sorted subrounded micritic fine sands; (g) yellowish-brown calcareous sandy clay with well-sorted well-rounded micritic fine sands of alluvial origin; (h) yellowish-brown calcareous coarse sandy clay with poorly sorted subrounded micritic fine sands

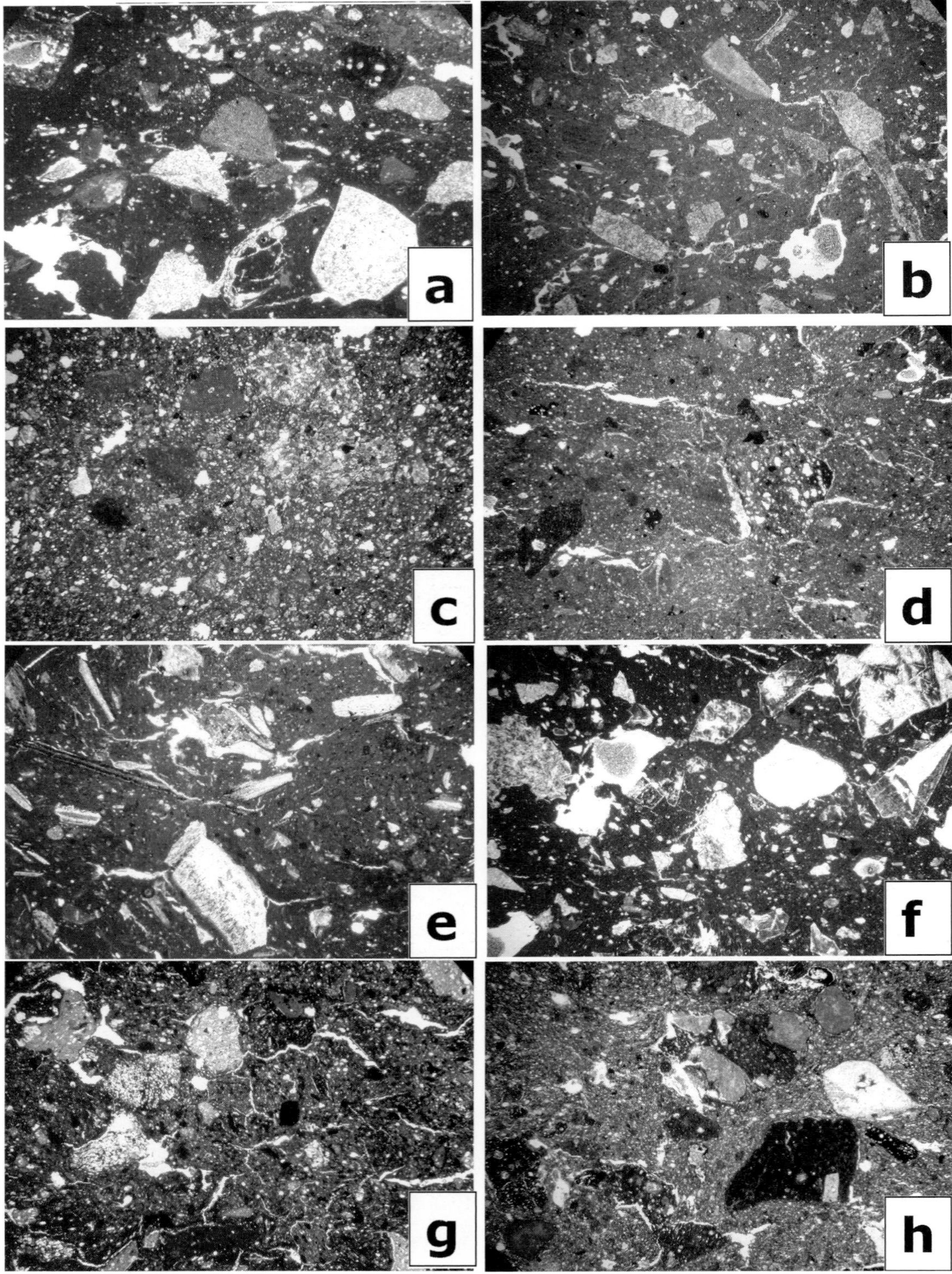

Figure 9.6 Vessels A, low quality: illustration showing the high variability of the different petrofacies derived from the plateaus. Frame width for all the photos: 5 mm

(a) Brownish-yellow calcareous clay with subangular to subrounded limestone coarse grains; (b) pale yellow fine calcareous clay with angular limestone coarse grains; (c) reddish sandy clay with poorly sorted coarse grains of micritic limestones and fine quartzitic sandstones; (d) reddish-yellow calcareous silty clay with rare subrounded soil relicts; (e) yellowish-red calcareous clay with finely crushed Ostrea fragments derived from fossiliferous Cenomanian marls of the Ajlun mountains; (f) brownish-yellow calcareous clay with finely crushed angular limestone coarse grains; (g) reddish-brown ferruginized sandy clay with subangular clasts (gypsum, clayey clasts, ferruginized concretions); (h) greyish-yellow deferruginized sandy clay with subangular clasts (micritic limestone, ferruginized concretions)

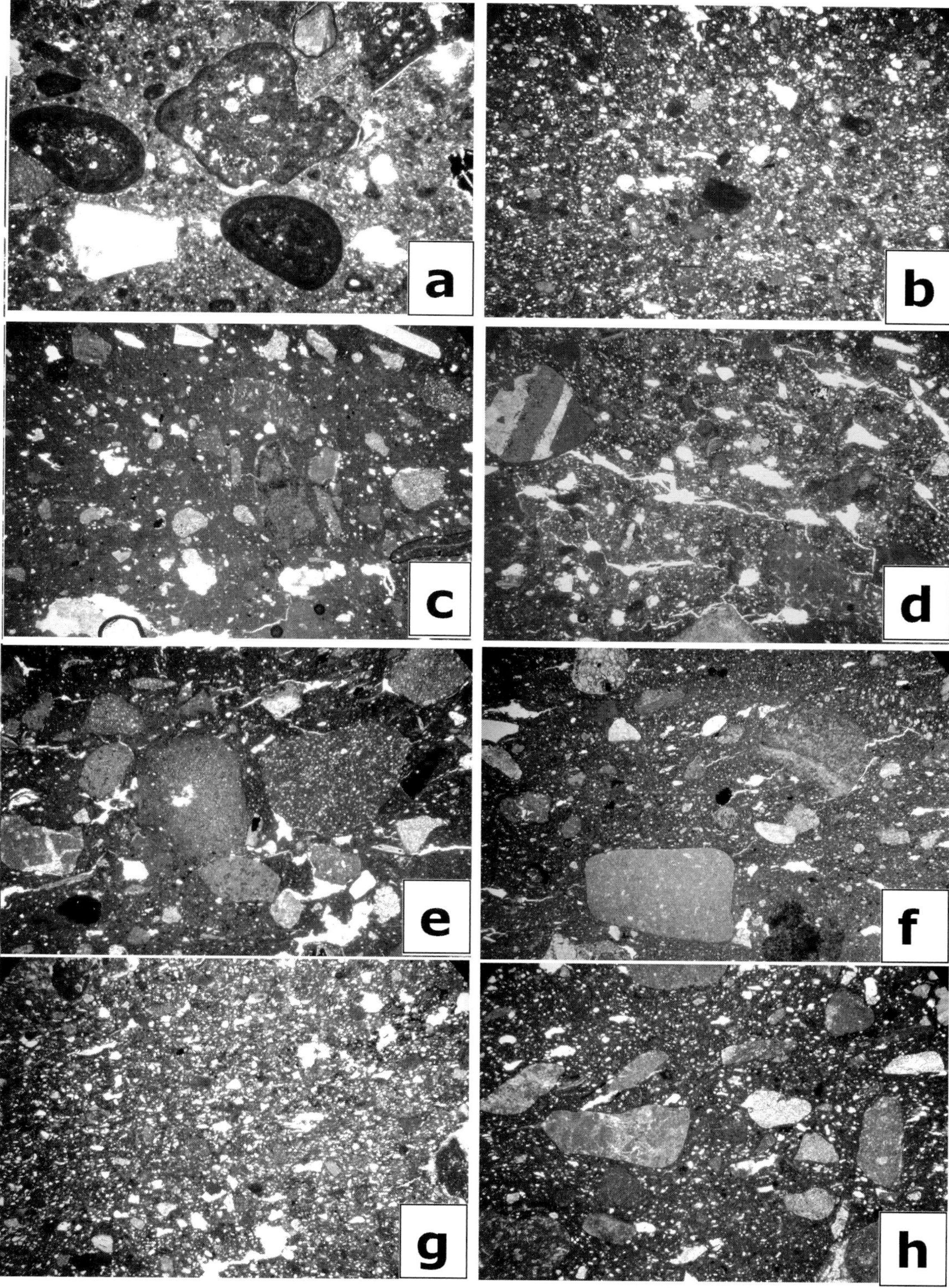

Figure 9.7 Vessels A, medium to high quality: illustration showing the wide range of petrofacies within a rather coherent group reflecting the geological homogeneity of the colluvial piedmonts at a meso-regional scale. Frame width for all the photos: 5 mm

(a) Brownish-yellow sandy clay with abundant weakly sorted subrounded coarse carbonate concretions; (b) brownish-yellow coarse sandy clay; (c) brownish-yellow very fine clay with weakly sorted subangular to subrounded, limestone coarse grains; (d) brownish-yellow clay with weakly sorted subangular to subrounded, limestone coarse grains; (e) brownish-yellow fine clay with abundant poorly sorted subrounded limestone coarse grains; (f) brownish-yellow fine clay with weakly sorted rounded limestone coarse grains; (g) brownish-yellow sandy clay with well-sorted angular micritic fine sands; (h) Reddish-brown sandy fine clay with well-sorted subrounded limestone coarse sands

Figure 9.8 Holemouth jars, straight-sided (type D1c3): from top left, strata 3e, 3c, 3c; from bottom left, 3/4, 3b, 3a. One morphological type can include different techno-petrographic groups and, in this regard, not be indicative of the different related units of production

These few vessels present varied specific stylistic features and, in this regard, correspond to quite unique pieces. They include the ones whose rim and/or upper part have been shaped with the help of rotary movement, fine small red or black burnished slip vessels, and vessels with impressed or thumb-band decoration. They originate from the Jordan valley and elsewhere. That vessels *B* are in a strong minority, that some are finished according to a new technique (the rotary movement), and that a narrow range of morphological types, all carefully made, is presented, suggests that we are probably dealing with a production whose function (in the large sense of the word, including symbolic function) is specific, and is distinct from that of vessels *A*. In other words, the technological practices which divide groups *B* and *A* express different functional categories, and perhaps different groups of producers.

Group *A* is in the majority. Within this group technological attributes have allowed us to distinguish three sub-groups on the basis of the degree of know-how involved, from low to high. These three groups do not correspond to a functionally diversified production; rather, each of them comprise a comparable range of morphological types (*e.g.*, in level 3a, each technological group presents both bowls and jars) as well as same types of vessels (Figure 9.8). Moreover, they include vessels made out of clay materials whose sources are found in distinct landscapes – the Jordan plateau versus piedmonts of the Jordan valley.

The manufacture of the lower-quality vessels (*A1*)

conveys awkwardness. Such awkwardness can be interpreted as the production of unskilled potters making a few pots per year (*e.g.*, ethnographic examples in Ali 2005). In favour of this hypothesis, the morphological data indicate that, within group *A1*, each meta-type includes a wide range of types, and each type has a strong metric variability; while ethnoarchaeological data have demonstrated that the less practice the potter has, the less standardized the vessels are (Roux 2003). In other respects, the techno-petrographic variability suggests that the potters were collecting clay in an opportunist way within a circumscribed environment, the Jordanian Plateau. It means that there was not a centre of production, but various units of production collecting clay in various places when needed. This lack of a centre of production is also supported by the technological variability characterizing the *A1* vessels. In summary, our data suggest that vessels *A1* were manufactured by various groups from the Jordanian Plateau who produced very few ceramics, probably mainly for culinary functions (as suggested by the firing traces located outside and inside the vessels). The technological similarities between the *A1* vessels suggest that these various groups were interacting at a certain level.

The medium- and higher-quality vessels *A2* and *A3* convey a better control over the manufacturing process, while their clay materials originate from different sources located in the piedmonts of the Jordan valley. This implies, firstly, that the producers of the *A2–A3* vessels had a higher rate of production and were different from the producers of the *A1* vessels. They produced a large range of functional vessels, as shown by morphological and technological features (some *A2–A3* vessels also present firing traces outside and inside the vessels, suggesting culinary functions). Secondly, techno-petrographic features suggest that *A2* and *A3* vessels were made by different communities. Indeed, technological variability is higher than within the group *A1*, in the sense that it encompasses a wider array of technical traditions, found in the surface treatment and decoration level. This variability is found throughout level 3 and cannot be correlated with any stylistic evolution over time. In addition, despite a better control over the manufacturing process and, therefore, probably, a higher rate of production, morphological and metric variability within groups *A2–A3* is as strong as that within the *A1* group. Petrographic analysis suggests a variability of the clay sources found at the level of each vessel. In this regard, the ceramic production of *A2–A3* appears as originating from different units of production distributed over a meso-region (beyond a radius of 10 km; Roux and Courty 2005), whose identities are more strongly expressed than in the case of the *A1* ceramics. Let us recall here that social interactions between master/mistress and apprentice during the pre- and post-learning process imply a certain techno-stylistic homogeneity at the settlement level as well as the continuation of a tradition over a significant period of time. This anthropological mechanism means that techno-petrographic and morpho-metrical variability between households and between communities are of a different order of magnitude. At Abu Hamid, the variability observed not only does not correspond to the sort of variability expected between households, but in addition does not match any specific spatial distribution. Strong techno-petrographic variability is observed within the same spatial units. In this regard, it cannot be explained in terms of inter-household variability or evolution over time, whatever the bias of the sampling.

In brief, the diversity of the techno-petrographic groups characterizing Abu Hamid ceramic assemblage suggests that the latter comprises in the majority productions originating from communities moving in different geographical zones with different experiences in pottery-making, and coming over time to Abu Hamid. The local production is very much in the minority. Let us recall that during the Beer Sheva–Ghassulian period, Abu Hamid was a place where communities came from all over the southern Levant. Apparently this phenomenon existed, on a smaller scale, in the previous period, raising once again the question of the function of the site (Roux and Courty 2007). More techno-petrographic studies are now to be conducted on the sites presenting Wadi Rabah techno-complexes in order to assess if such a phenomenon could not be related as well to the high degree of mobility of these communities.

Techno-stylistic variability and cultural phase

The material resources used during Phase II reflect a particular moment in the evolution of the palaeoenvironment which is well placed in terms of relative chronology. These resources are different from the ones used during Phase I and Phase III and are distinctive, in this regard, of the early 5th millennium. The marked differences in material resources between Phase II and Phases I and III are also found at the level of the technological practice and the morphological type.

Ceramics belonging to Phase I are characterized by a higher homogeneity in terms of technical practices (Ali 2005) and morphological types (Lovell *et al.* 1997). Vessels are formed by coiling and their surface treatment is largely the same as that of the lower-quality vessels of Phase II (*A1*). Generally speaking, their manufacture is awkward and reveals a low rate of production. Morphological types consist mainly of simple, straight-sided bowls, cups with button bases, holemouths with simple or slightly bevelled rims and tall-necked jars (Lovell *et al.* 1997, 366).

By contrast, ceramics belonging to Phase III are characterized by a high level of know-how as well as a techno-petrographic diversity revealing communities originating from all over the southern Levant (Roux and Courty 2005; 2007). The technological variability observed in the ceramics belonging to Phase III is different from the diversity observed in the Phase II material: it corresponds to variants of a similar technological tradition (Roux and Courty 2005) and not to distinct technological traditions. In this regard, it expresses a certain phenomenon of homogenization. By reference to ethnographic situations, such a phenomenon occurs when cultural groups interact with each other, the subsequent learning networks creating communities of practices and therefore the homogenization of technological traditions through the borrowing of technological traits (*e.g.* Livingstone Smith 2002; Gosselain 2008).

The diversity of the techno-petrographic groups of Phase II, observable in our corpus at the level of the vessel, suggests that, in the southern Levant, distinct social units were visiting Abu Hamid repeatedly, and indicates interactions between the communities living on the plateau and in the valley. Such relationships were probably part of the general evolutionary process from which the Beer Sheva–Ghassulian culture emerged. In this regard, the transitional period corresponding to Phase II can be considered as a key period, as suggested by Gilead (1990).

Such a techno-petrographic diversity might also explain why each site found on this horizon (the so-called Wadi Rabah Horizon) does not present strictly comparable ceramic assemblages (*e.g.*, Braun 2004; Garfinkel 1992; Gopher and Gophna 1993; Lovell *et al.* 2007): each of them may originate from a variable range of communities, or may reflect different degrees of community mobility. Thus, the fact that the ceramic assemblages of a site like Tel Tsaf seem to be different from those of Abu Hamid, and are characterized in particular by specific painted ceramics (Garfinkel *et al.* 2007; Gophna and Sadeh 1988–9), is consistent with the hypothesis of a chrono-cultural period, the early 5th millennium, marked by a progressive and differential increase in ceramic production, communities and interactions whose consequence would have been a growth of technological diversity at the scale of the southern Levant.

Conclusions

The techno-petrographic approach proves particularly relevant for a description of the ceramic assemblages in terms of traditions and therefore learning networks and communities of practice. When these communities use datable material resources it enables us to characterize cultural horizons – that is, periods during which a set of communities coexisted and interacted. The relevance of the approach lies also in the integration of the technological and morpho-stylistic features. The latter are a strong expression of cultural templates or norms. Combining technological and morpho-stylistic attributes proves to be particularly useful for interpreting ceramics in socio-cultural terms.

Our techno-petrographic analysis as applied to the Abu Hamid ceramic assemblage suggests that in the early 5th millennium cal BC there was great diversity in technological practices at the meso-regional scale. This diversity is in fact characteristic of the transitional period prior to the Beer Sheva–Ghassulian culture and reflects the diversity of the communities of the time. The traces of disparate communities on the one site suggest interactions which presage the Beer Sheva–Ghassulian culture. More techno-petrographic data are required to better define the 5th millennium cal BC cultural landscape and, by extension, the function of each site at a macro-regional scale.

Acknowledgments

This research project was funded by grants from the French Ministry of Foreign Affairs-DGCID (Mission Archéologique Franco-Jordanienne de Tell Abu Hamid). We would like to express our deepest gratitude to our friend Dr Zeidan Kafafi, co-director of the Abu Hamid expedition, for all the fruitful discussions on 6th–4th millennia pottery we had either in the field or at Irbid in the basements of Yarmouk University as well as at Nanterre in the Maison de l'Archéologie et de l'Ethnologie. Dr Ziad el Saad, then Dean of the Faculty of Archaeology and Anthropology of Yarmouk University, is gratefully acknowledged for his hospitality, as is Dr Fawwaz al Khreysheh, then Director General of the Department of Antiquities of Jordan, for delivering the authorization to ship samples for analyses. We are grateful to Gabriel Humbert (IFPO) for his constant help. Photographs have been taken by Hossein Debajah (Yarmouk University, FAA), thanks to whom the Phase II Abu Hamid ceramic assemblage has been extensively documented (photographed).

References

Ali, N. (2005) *The Development of Pottery Technology from the Late Sixth to the 5th millennium BC in Northern Jordan. Ethno- and Archaeological Studies: Abu Hamid as a Key Site* Oxford: BAR Int. Ser. 1422.

Arnold, D. E. (1985) *Ceramic Theory and Cultural Process.* Cambridge: Cambridge University Press.

Banning, E. B. (2002) Consensus and debate on the Late Neolithic and Chalcolithic of southern Levant. *Paléorient* 28, 143–55.

Banning, T. (2007) Wadi Rabah and related assemblages in the southern Levant: interpreting radiocarbon evidence. *Paléorient* 33, 77–101.

Blackham, M. (2002) *Modeling Time and Transition in Prehistory: The Jordan Valley Chalcolithic (5500–3500 BC).* Oxford: BAR Int. Ser. 1027.

Braun, E. (2004) *Early Beth Shan (Strata XIX–XIII): G. M. Fitzgerald's Deep Cut on the Tell.* Philadelphia, PA: University of Pennsylvania Museum.

Bril, B. (2002) L'apprentissage de gestes techniques: ordre de contraintes et variations culturelles. Pp. 113–50 in B. Bril and V. Roux (eds), *Le geste technique. Réflexions méthodologiques et anthropologiques*. Ramonville Saint-Agne: Editions érès.

Burton, M. and Levy, T. E. (2001) The Chalcolithic radiocarbon record and its use in southern Levantine archaeology. *Radiocarbon* 43, 1223–46.

Clarke, D. L. (1978) *Analytical Archaeology*, 2nd edn. London: Methuen.

Courty, M.-A. (1994) Le cadre paléogéographique des occupations humaines dans le bassin du Haut Khabour (Syrie du nord-est). Premiers résultats. *Paléorient* 20, 21–59.

Courty, M.-A. (2001) Micro-facies analysis assisting archaeological stratigraphy. Pp. 205–39 in P. Goldberg, V. T. Holliday and R. Ferring (eds), *Earth Science and Archaeology*. New York: Plenum Publishing Co.

Creswell, R. (1996) *Prométhée ou Pandore? Propos de technologie culturelle*. Paris: Kimé.

Degoy, L. (2006) La variabilité céramique en Andhra Pradesh: regard sur des productions céramiques indiennes entre histoire, sociologie et transformations économiques. Unpublished thesis, Université de Paris-X.

Dietler, M., and Herbich, I. (1998) Habitus, techniques, style: an integrated approach to the social understanding of material culture and boundaries. Pp. 232–69 in M. T. Stark (ed.), *The Archaeology of Social Boundaries*. Washington DC and London: Smithsonian Institution Press.

Dollfus, G. (1993) Recent researches at Abu Hamid. *Annual of the Department of Antiquities of Jordan* 37, 241–63.

Dollfus, G. and Kafafi, Z. (eds) (1988) *Abu Hamid, village du 4e millénaire de la vallée du Jourdain*. Amman: Economic Press.

Gallay, A. (2007) The decorated marriage jars of the inner delta of the Niger (Mali): essay of archaeological demarcation of an ethnic territory. *The Arkeotek Journal* 1, 1 (www.thearkeotekjournal.org).

Garfinkel, Y. (1992) *The Pottery Assemblages and the Sha'ar Hagolan and Rabah Stages at Munhata (Israel)*. Cahiers du Centre de Recherche Français de Jérusalem 6. Paris: Association Paléorient.

Garfinkel, Y. and Miller, M. A. (2002) *Sha'ar Hagolan, volume 1. Neolithic Art in Context*. Oxford: Oxbow Books.

Garfinkel, Y., Ben-Shlomo, D., Freikman, M. and Vered, A. (2007) Tel Tsaf: the 2004–2006 excavation seasons. *Israel Exploration Journal* 57, 1–33.

Gelbert, A. (2003) *Traditions céramiques et emprunts techniques dans la vallée du fleuve Sénégal*. Paris: éditions de la MSH, éditions Epistèmes (bilingual cdrom, www.arkeotek.org).

Gilead, I. (1990) The Neolithic–Chalcolithic transition and the Qatifian of the northern Negev and Sinai. *Levant* 22, 47–63.

Gopher, A. and Gophna, R. (1993) Cultures of the eighth and seventh millenia BP in the southern Levant: a review for the 1990s. *Journal of World Prehistory* 7, 297–353.

Gophna, R. and Sadeh, S. (1988–9) Excavations at Tel Tsaf: An early Chalcolithic site in the Jordan Valley. *Tel Aviv* 15–16, 3–36.

Gosselain, O. P. (2000) Materializing identities: an African perspective. *Journal of Archaeological Method and Theory* 7, 187–218.

Gosselain, O. P. (2008) Mother Bella was not a Bella. Inherited and transformed traditions in southwestern Niger. Pp. 150–77 in M. Stark, B. Bowser and L. Horne (eds), *Breaking Down Boundaries, Cultural Transmission and Material Culture*. Tucson, AZ: Arizona University Press.

Hourani, F. (2002) Le cadre paléogéographique des premières sociétés agricoles dans la vallée du Jourdain. Etude de l'impact des évènements climatiques de l'Holocène ancien sur la dynamique des peuplements. Unpublished PhD thesis, Paris-Grignon Institut National Agronomique.

Hourani, F. and Courty, M. A. (1997) L'évolution morpho-climatique de 10500 à 5500 BP dans la vallée du Jourdain. *Paléorient* 23, 95–106.

Kafafi, Z. (2001) *Jebel Abu Thawwab (Er-Rumman), Central Jordan. The Late Neolithic and Early Bronze Age I Occupations*. Monographs of the Institute of Archaeology and Anthropology 3. Berlin: ex oriente.

Kaplan, J. (1958) Excavations at Wadi Rabah. *Israel Exploration Journal* 8, 149–60.

Kaplan, J. (1972) The Wadi-Rabah culture – Twenty years after. *Bulletin of the Haaretz Museum* 14, 23–9.

Kerner, S. (2001) *Das Chalkolithikum in der südlichen Levante. Die Entwicklung handwerklicher Specialisierung und ihre Beziehung zu gesellschaftlicher komplexität*. Orient-Archäologie 8. Rahden/Westf.: Verlag Marie Leidorf GmbH.

Lave, J. and Wenger, E. (1991) *Situated Learning: Legitimate Peripheral Participation*. Cambridge: Cambridge University Press.

Livingstone Smith, A. (2000) Processing clay for pottery in northern Cameroon: social and technical requirements. *Archaeometry* 42, 21–42.

Lovell, J. (2001) *The Late Neolithic and Chalcolithic Periods in the Southern Levant. New Data from the Site of Teleilat Ghassul, Jordan*. Monographs of the Sydney University Teleilat Ghassul Project 1. Oxford: BAR Int. Ser. 974.

Lovell, J., Kafafi, Z. and Dollfus, G. (1997) A preliminary note on the ceramics from the basal levels of Abu Hamid. Pp. 361–9 in H.-G. Gebel, Z. Kafafi and G. Rollefson (eds), *Prehistory of Jordan II. Perspectives from 1997*. Berlin: ex oriente.

Lovell, J., Dollfus, G. and Kafafi, Z. (2004) The middle phases at Abu Hamid and the Wadi Rabah horizon. Pp. 263–74 in F. al-Khraysheh, K. 'Amr, H. Taher and S. Khouri (eds), *Studies in the History and Archaeology of Jordan* 8. Amman: The Department of Antiquities of Jordan.

Lovell, J., Dollfus, G. and Kafafi, Z. (2007) The ceramics of the Late Neolithic and Chalcolithic: Abu Hamid and the burnished tradition. *Paléorient* 33/1, 51–76.

Manning, S. W. (2007) Preface. Beyond dates to chronology: rethinking the Neolithic–Chalcolithic Levant. *Paléorient* 33/1, 5–10

Mayor, A. (2006) Traditions céramiques et histoire du peuplement dans la Boucle du Niger (Mali) au temps des empires précoloniaux. Unpublished PhD thesis, Université de Genève.

Philip, G. and Baird, D. (eds) (2000) *Ceramics and Change in the Early Bronze Age of the Southern Levant*. Sheffield: Sheffield Academic Press.

Renfrew, C. (1972) *The Emergence of Civilization*. London: Methuen.

Roux, V. (2003) Ceramic standardization and intensity of production: quantifying degrees of specialization. *American Antiquity* 68, 768–82.

Roux, V. (2007) Ethnoarchaeology: a non-historical science of reference necessary for interpreting the past. *Journal of Archaeological Method and Theory* 14/2, 153–78.

Roux, V. and Courty, M. A. (1998) Identification of wheel-fashioning methods: technological analysis of 4th–3rd millenium BC oriental ceramics. *Journal of Archaeological Science* 25, 747–63.

Roux, V. and Courty, M. A. (2005) Identifying social entities at a macro-regional level: Chalcolithic ceramics of south Levant as a case study. Pp. 201–14 in A. Livingstone Smith,

D. Bosquet and R. Martineau (eds), *Pottery Manufacturing Processes: Reconstitution and Interpretation*. Oxford: BAR Int. Ser. 1349.

Roux, V. and Courty, M. A. (2007) Analyse techno-pétrographique céramique et interprétation fonctionnelle des sites: un exemple d'application dans le Levant Sud Chalcolithique. Pp. 153–67 in A. Bain, J. Chabot, and M. Mousette (eds), *La mesure du passé: contributions à la recherche en archéométrie (2000–2006)*. Oxford: BAR International Series 1700.

Rye, O. S. (ed.) (1981) *Pottery Technology. Principles and Reconstruction*. Manuals on Archaeology. Washington DC: Taraxacum Press.

Shennan, S. J. (ed.) (1989) *Archaeological Approaches to Cultural Identity*. London: Unwin Hyman.

Shennan, S. J. and Wilkinson, J. R. (2001) Ceramic style change and neutral evolution: a case study from Neolithic Europe. *American Antiquity* 66, 577–93.

Stark, M. (ed.) (1998) *The Archaeology of Social Boundaries*. Washington DC: Smithsonian Institution Press.

10. Developmental Trends in Chalcolithic Copper Metallurgy: A Radiometric Perspective

Aaron N. Shugar and Christopher J. Gohm

Introduction

The Chalcolithic period of the southern Levant (*c.*4500–3600 BC) was a time of significant technological sophistication and rich cultures, perhaps best represented by the remains associated with the 'Beer Sheva' culture of the northern Negev. In comparison with the earlier Late Neolithic period, the Chalcolithic period is characterized by extensive population growth, diverse architectural traditions, shifting settlement patterns, the establishment of religious sanctuaries and the growth and advancement of craft industries (Levy 1986; Gilead 1988; Mazar 1992, 59–90; Levy 1995). Most prominent among these craft industries is copper metallurgy, which appeared suddenly and contemporaneously across the region and has been the subject of numerous scientific and art-historical discussions. As Levy and Shalev indicate, 'the small proportion of surviving metal tools to stone tools, as well as the economic investment involved in metal production, emphasizes the special role of metal tools in the Chalcolithic communities of southern Palestine' (Levy and Shalev 1989, 365). The great advances made in copper metallurgy during this period of time are of pivotal importance for our understanding of both the ancient cultures of the Chalcolithic period as well as the later developments in the copper industry in Early Bronze Age society.

Previous studies have demonstrated that Chalcolithic metallurgists produced two classes of artefacts: simple 'utilitarian' tools cast in an open mould, such as axes, adzes and awls; and more complex 'prestige' items produced using the 'lost-wax' technique, such as standards, maceheads, crowns and vessels (Levy and Shalev 1989, 355–9; Shalev 1999). These artefacts have been excavated at numerous Chalcolithic sites in the southern Levant (Figure 1.1), and nearly 600 artefacts have been brought to light (Table 10.1), over two-thirds of which originated from the Nahal Mishmar hoard (Bar-Adon 1980).

Generally, these two classes of artefact are thought to be differentiated by morphology as well as composition. Items with a simple shape were, for the most part, made of relatively pure copper, while complex/ornate artefacts were cast with an unique alloy with varying high levels of arsenic (up to 8.2%), antimony (up to 22.6%), and nickel (up to 8.27%), along with lower levels of other impurities, such as lead, iron, tin, bismuth and silver (Levy and Shalev 1989, 359; Shalev 1991, 415–16; Shalev 1995, 111–14).

Owing to the relatively homogenous nature of the period's ceramic assemblage (Amiran 1969, 22–34; Garfinkel 1999, 200–96) it has been difficult to tease out any chronological or developmental patterns relating to the emergence of these two classes of artefacts. However, owing to the substantial increase of scholarly interest in the field of radiometry (*e.g.*, see Weinstein 1984; Joffe and Dessel 1995; Burton and Levy 2001; Blackham 2002), the present quantity and, more importantly, quality of radiocarbon determinations from Chalcolithic sites has made such an investigation feasible.

The purpose of this study is to address possible technological developments in the Chalcolithic copper industry over time through correlations between archaeo-metallurgical analyses of copper-based artefacts and radiocarbon determinations from contexts best associated with such finds. It is hypothesized that this investigation will result in the recognition of meaningful patterns relating to changing trends in artefact compositions over time, suggesting that the Chalcolithic copper industry was as dynamic as the period itself. The long-standing compositional dichotomy between utilitarian goods and prestige objects may need to be reassessed, as several scholars have recently suggested (Tadmor *et al.* 1995, 143–5; Namdar 2002, 114; Segal and Kamenski 2002, 161).

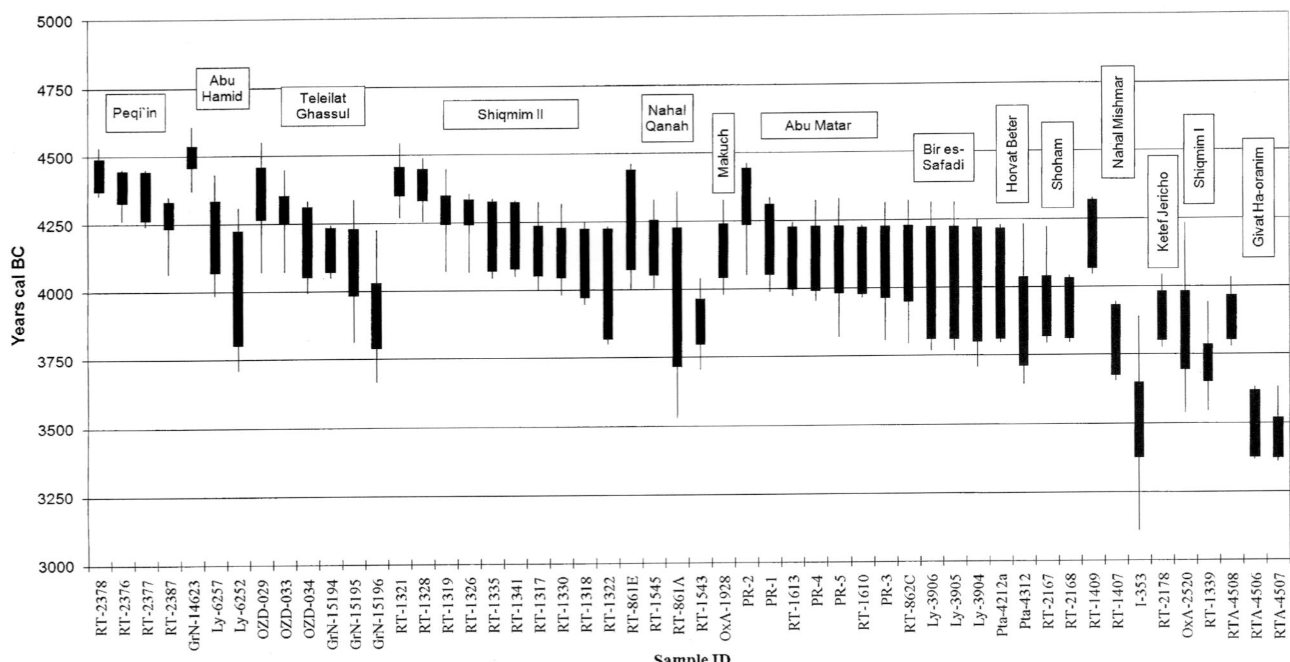

Figure 10.1 Radiometric data from Chalcolithic sites where copper artefacts have been found (thick bar = 1 sigma range, thin bar = 2 sigma range)

Site	^{14}C *Dated*	*Crucible Frags*	*Furnace Frags*	*Slag*	*Ore*	*Axe/ Chisel*	*Awl*	*Macehead*	*Standard*	*Crown*	*Misc.*	***Total***
Abu Hamid	Yes						2				1	**3**
Abu Matar	Yes	Yes	Yes	Yes	Yes	1	1	4	1		4	**11**
Arad		Yes		Yes			1					**1**
Azor						2						**2**
Bir es-Safadi	Yes	Yes		Yes	Yes	3	1				1	**5**
Gilat	Yes				Yes		1	1				**2**
Giv'at ha-Oranim					Yes	6	2	4	3	2	2	**19**
Horvat Beter	Yes			Yes	Yes						2	**2**
Ketef Jericho	Yes					2		1				**3**
Makuch	Yes					5	1		1			**7**
Meser						5	1					**6**
Nahal Ashan								1				**1**
Nahal Lahat								1				**1**
Nahal Mishmar	Yes					16	1	256	118	10	16	**417**
Nahal Qanah	Yes			Yes	Yes	1			1	1	8	**11**
Nahal Ze'elim						1		3				**4**
Nevatim		Yes		Yes	Yes		1					**1**
Neve Noy	Yes	Yes	Yes	Yes	Yes	2	3		2	1	2	**10**
Palmachim									1		3	**4**
Peqi'in	Yes					2			2		3	**7**
Shiqmim	Yes	Yes	Yes?	Yes	Yes	5	12	3	2	1	2	**25**
Shoham	Yes					1						**1**
Tall al-Magass		Yes		Yes	Yes		2				1	**3**
Teleilat Ghassul	Yes			Yes	Yes	3	8				1	**12**
Umm Qatafa											1	**1**

Table 10.1 Site information and artefact counts

Defining 'alloy'

The term 'alloy' implies a deliberate manipulation of the composition of the metal in an attempt to achieve certain properties, whether those properties are physical or aesthetic in nature. Questions of interest relating to the Chalcolithic peoples who undertook copper smelting in the Levant are whether or not they intentionally produced alloyed copper (with arsenic, antimony and nickel) and whether they were aware of the specific properties of such complex alloyed copper. How can we objectively address these elusive aspects of ancient metallurgy?

Initial investigators looking into the purposeful alloying of early arsenical copper chose rather arbitrary values for the weight per cent required to define the process as intentional alloying. Tylecote (1991) chose a value of 2%, while others have chosen 1% (Northover 1989). What seems clear now is that the amount of arsenic needed to produce meaningful changes in the resulting metal is a rather minimal 0.5% (Lechtman 1996). The general investigation of arsenical copper artefacts has shown that the alloying of copper with arsenic is mainly related to the beneficial properties that arsenic provides. These include the following properties: deoxidization of the metal, hardening of the metal to allow greater working before it fractures, the alteration of the colour to an increasingly silvery hue depending on the amount of arsenic present in the alloy, the decreasing of the melting temperature of the metal, and improving casting (Northover 1989; Budd and Ottaway 1991).

Arsenic-rich prills are distinctive for their shiny silvery colour, which makes them easy to identify and select (Merkel *et al.* 1994, 221). A colour difference is clearly visible between copper with as little as 1% arsenic and copper without arsenic. This would allow for separation of copper based on composition. The result is a collection of two or more distinct groupings of copper with increasingly silvery hues which can be remelted and cast into the appropriate item, utilitarian un-alloyed or prestigious alloyed.

The copper–arsenic phase diagram shows that at as little as 5% arsenic the melting temperature drops from 1083 ºC to around 1000 ºC. This would allow faster initial melting of the alloy and provide a subsequent longer pour time for casting. Arsenical copper would have been very useful for the Chalcolithic smiths who required a long pour time for the molten metal to work its way into the complex lost wax casting designs.

Based on these technical observations of arsenical copper, we would propose that the purposeful alloying of copper and arsenic would occur when there were visible changes to the resulting metal, which, based on experimentation, is at approximately 1 wt% as suggested by Northover (1989).

Methodology

In order for a correlation between radiocarbon dates and artefacts from a given site to have any meaning in terms of reconstructing Chalcolithic technology, a well-defined and consistently followed methodology is a prerequisite. In addition, clearly articulated caveats are vital, as is a thorough understanding of the nature of radiometric data (van der Plicht and Bruins 2001).

First and foremost, it must be stated that the radiometric evidence from a site at which copper artefacts have been found does not necessarily relate *directly* to the *production* of the artefact, as these objects could obviously have been in use for a lengthy period. However, given the lack of other chronological indicators for dating an occupational level or deposit in the Chalcolithic period, these determinations are of utmost importance and require consideration. For the purpose of this study the assumption of a close correlation between the production of a copper artefact and the use and disposal of said artefact relatively soon after is necessary.

Recently, many radiocarbon samples have been processed and published from Levantine sites, yet not all belong to the occupational or depositional phases associated with copper-based artefacts. 'Relevant' dates, defined here as those obtained from samples originating from stratigraphic contexts best associated with such finds, are exclusively used for the purposes of this study. In other words, determinations from pre- and post-Chalcolithic contexts are not considered, nor are those from Chalcolithic contexts which are earlier or later than phases to which copper artefacts have been attributed. In the case of sites where the original stratigraphic interpretations have been brought into question, such as Abu Matar, Bir es-Safadi/Neve Noy, Horvat Beter and Shiqmim (Gilead 1994), only the most current and reliable dates are considered. Radiocarbon determinations from sites where artefacts have been found only in secondary contexts contribute little to the research objective and are also discounted.

Determinations from prior to 1985 are not considered, as most of the dates that cover an exceptionally wide range of calibrated years were measured early in the history of the technique (for example, see the results in Weinstein 1984) and have proved to be somewhat unreliable. For example, dates from the site of Teleilat Ghassul, measured in 1977, proved to be inaccurate by several centuries, as they were measured prior to the discovery of 'non-uniformities in the shape of the hand made glass vials used for measurements in one of the liquid scintillation counters' (Bourke *et al.* 2001, 1219). Recent dates with standard deviations of over 150 years are also not considered, unless they are especially relevant and occur in the same locus or building as deposited artefacts, a situation that occurs only at Nahal Qanah and Nahal Mishmar. All the relevant dates are presented on a region-by-region basis, recalibrated using CALIB v5.0.1 software and the INTCAL04 dataset (Stuiver and Reimer 1993).

Sub-period	*Upper limit (cal BC)*	*Lower limit (cal BC)*
A	4499	4300
B	4299	4100
C	4099	3900
D	3899	3700
E	3699	3500
F	3499	3300

Table 10.2 Arbitrary sub-periods of the Late Chalcolithic

Both 1 and 2 sigma ranges are presented in the graphs, but because of the restricted time frame of the period and the great variability of the 2 sigma ranges, 1 sigma ranges are used for the purpose of site-by-site comparisons. For the purpose of the overall interpretation, these 1 sigma ranges are considered representative (at 68% confidence) of the most likely date range in which the charcoal samples were deposited, and by inference and assumption (see above), the rough time frame for the deposition of each artefactual assemblage. As 1 sigma ranges are considered to be reliable indices of such time frames, in this study cumulative probability distributions, *i.e.* 100%, are used to make the data more robust.

As any comparison between two or more radiocarbon date ranges is a problematic endeavor, attested to by past errors resulting in the possible misinterpretation of occupational sequences (Gilead 1994, 3–8), the individual ranges from a given site must be considered independently unless they can be proven to be statistically similar or manipulated in a meaningful and methodologically sound construct. Following the approach adopted by Gilead regarding the radiocarbon dates from the Beer Sheva area (Gilead 1994, 3), pooled means are considered representative as long as the assemblage proves to be statistically the same based on a χ^2 test at 95% confidence with CALIB v5.0.1 (Stuiver and Reimer 1993, 227). In the event that pooled means were not viable, the maximum and minimum extremes of all sample ranges are used as parameters for dating any given site, as the true date of the sample (and hence the rough date of the finds) could fall anywhere within that range.

In an attempt to further define the occupation histories of each site an arbitrary ranking system is utilized in which sites are assigned to sub-periods based on the chronological spread of each assemblage's radiocarbon ranges through consideration of their maximum, minimum and most frequent range distributions (Table 10.2). These sub-periods are A (45th–44th centuries cal BC), B (43rd–42nd centuries cal BC), C (41st–40th centuries cal BC), D (39th–38th centuries cal BC), E (37th–36th centuries cal BC) and F (35th–34th centuries cal BC). While overlap between these sub-periods is inevitable, they are assigned based on the frequency of radiocarbon years within each and the bulk 'presence' of the resultant ranges. For example, a radiocarbon range of 4368 and 4214 cal BC would be assigned to the A/B sub-period, while a range of 4068 and 3960 cal BC would be considered as belonging exclusively to the C sub-period. To elaborate, with the first sample, the range would be considered as belonging to sub-period B more than sub-period A, as the majority of the range determination falls within the B parameters (85 years) rather than the A parameters (68 years). This relationship is presented, using bold typeface, as A/**B**, indicating that the bulk of the range fell within sub-period B.

The integration of the radiometric data and the metallographic/chemical analyses from each of these sites is presented on a region-by-region basis, beginning from the northern extent of the study area and proceeding southwards. These regional divisions provide a sense of the spatial distribution of artefact types and their associated compositions in addition to their relative chronological position.

Before beginning our survey of these integrations a few comments about the variety of contexts in which these artefacts have been found are warranted. It is worth noting that the collections of Chalcolithic metal finds come from two different types of deposit: excavated materials found on site and hoards of material found in caches. The differences between these finds can create potential issues when considering the chemical composition of the collection of materials with regard to their potential production. Metal artefacts are very hardy and long-lasting. Some can be passed down through generations and be discarded many years after their initial production. For artefacts found on site, however, as seen at Abu Matar, Shiqmim and Neve Noy, a tighter connection, based on compositional comparisons with these production sites, along with stylistic similarities, can be made between these 'on-site' objects and the production centres than can be said for artefacts found in hoards.

Hoards are placed in a specific location for a variety of reasons, from sacred storage for ritual purposes to safekeeping storage in case of potential enemy attack and possible storage for long-distance trade and exchange (for examples, see *World Archaeology* 20/2, 1988). The arguments for trade and safekeeping have been used to describe why the Nahal Mishmar hoard might have been placed where it was (Moorey 1988; Tadmor 1989). In addition, it has also been suggested that the Nahal Mishmar hoard was a collection of religious offerings brought yearly to the En Gedi temple by Chalcolithic metalsmiths (Ussishkin 1980), but this theory has been disputed in more recent years (I. Gilead, pers. comm.).

The geographical regions of metallurgical finds

Copper artefacts dating to the Chalcolithic period have been unearthed at numerous settlement sites and burial contexts, from as far north as Peqi'in to the southernmost sites of the Beer Sheva cluster. In order to bring structure to the ensuing integration of radiocarbon dates and metallurgical

Site	*Relevant samples*	*^{14}C date*	±	*1 sigma upper*	*1 sigma lower*	*2 sigma upper*	*2 sigma lower*	*Sub-periods represented*	*Reference*
Peqi'in	RT-2376	5510	45	4445	4330	4454	4264	A	Segal *et al.* 1998, 709–11
Peqi'in	RT-2377	5490	55	4443	4263	4451	4244	**A**/B	Segal *et al.* 1998, 709–11
Peqi'in	RT-2378	5615	45	4490	4371	4533	4356	A	Segal *et al.* 1998, 709–11
Peqi'in	RT-2387	5410	50	4334	4236	4351	4066	A/**B**	Segal *et al.* 1998, 709–11
Shoham	RT-2167	5160	55	4041	3820	4221	3796	**C**/D	Segal and Carmi 1996, 88
Shoham	RT-2168	5140	50	4033	3811	4042	3799	**C**/D	Segal and Carmi 1996, 88

Table 10.3 Radiocarbon determinations from the upper Galilee and coastal plain regions

analyses the geographical regions of the southern Levant are discussed separately in a roughly north–south order, with exclusive reference to only those sites where copper artefacts have been found. These regions include Upper Galilee, the coastal plain, the central hill country, the Jordan Valley, the eastern Negev and Wadi Arabah, and finally the western Negev. The radiocarbon determinations from each site and their associated chronological implications for the copper finds are discussed within this framework.

Upper Galilee

The only copper artefacts from the region of Upper Galilee originate from the karstic cave known as Peqi'in, discovered and excavated in 1995 as part of a salvage project (Gal *et al.* 1997a; 1997b). Although occupied prior to the period in question, Peqi'in was primarily used for burial purposes in the Chalcolithic, as is made evident by numerous ossuaries and grave goods. Seven copper artefacts were discovered in the cave, including standards, chisels, beads and a 'flower-shaped' object (Gal *el al.* 1997a, 15; 1997b, 23). Recent analyses of the standards and chisels from the site through Inductively Coupled Plasma-Atomic Emission Spectrometry (ICP-AES) have demonstrated that both the simple and complex artefacts were made of relatively pure copper (D. Segal, Y. Goren and A. Kamenski, pers. comm.). Of a total of 22 radiocarbon samples collected from Peqi'in (Segal *et al.* 1998, 709–11), 4 originated from burial contexts (Table 10.3), and can be considered representative of the use of the cave during the Chalcolithic period (RT-2376, 2377, 2378 and 2387). These samples cluster well between the 45th and 43rd centuries cal BC, but are not statistically the same and cannot be used to determine a pooled mean. Sub-period A is best represented at Peqi'in, although there is some evidence of use into sub-period B.

The coastal plain

Excavations at four sites along the Levantine coastal plain, including Shoham, Azor, Palmachim and Meser, report the discovery of Chalcolithic copper artefacts. Radiocarbon data are available only from the site of Shoham, which was excavated between 1994 and 1996 (Gophna and Feldstein 1998, 72–3). At this site excavators unearthed Chalcolithic and Early Bronze Age remains from six karstic caves, one of which contained a copper chisel in a Chalcolithic context as yet unanalysed. Two radiocarbon determinations from Shoham (RT-2167 and 2168; Table 10.3) suggest that the area was inhabited or utilized for burials between the late 41st and 39th centuries cal BC (Segal and Carmi 1996, 89). These samples proved to be statistically the same after testing with CALIB 4.4.2, which provided a pooled mean ranging between 4035 and 3825 cal BC (1 sigma; 5149 ± 37 years BP). Sub-period C is best represented at Shoham, with some evidence for use extending into the early years of sub-period D.

Copper artefacts from the Chalcolithic/Early Bronze Age transitional settlement of Meser, excavated in 1956 and 1957, include five axes/adzes and one awl (Dothan 1957; 1959b), and two chisels are reported from the Chalcolithic burial site of Azor, excavated between 1957 and 1958 (Perrot 1961, fig. 12; Miron 1992, pl. 1.12). These assemblages have not yet been metallurgically investigated. At Palmachim, a Chalcolithic cemetery consisting of burial caves partially reused in the Early Bronze I, four artefacts were reported from the 1968–1971 excavations (Gophna and Lifschitz 1980): two miscellaneous items, a small hook and an elaborate standard, the last of which proved to contain significant levels of arsenic and antimony (8.28% and 8.58% respectively) when analysed by Atomic Absorption Spectroscopy (AAS) (Gophna and Liphschitz 1980, 8, note 22).

The central hill country

Three sites in the central hill country, Umm Qatafa, Giv'at ha-Oranim and Nahal Qanah, have provided examples of copper-based artefacts; the latter two of these sites have provided radiocarbon dates. Finds from Umm Qatafa, a cave site in use in during the Chalcolithic period and earlier, are limited to a single ring, which has not been metallurgically analysed (Neuville and Mallon 1931, 32; Perrot 1992, 100–1).

More substantial are the finds from Giv'at ha-Oranim, excavated in 1997 as part of a salvage project (Oren and Scheftelowitz 1999; Scheftelowitz and Oren 2004). In total, 19 artefacts were found among the subterranean complexes, graves, storage pits and caves at the site; these included standards, crowns, awls, maceheads, axes/

Site	*Relevant samples*	*^{14}C date*	*±*	*1 sigma upper*	*1 sigma lower*	*2 sigma upper*	*2 sigma lower*	*Sub-periods represented*	*Reference*
Giv'at ha-Oranim	RTA-4506	4690	40	3617	3375	3630	3368	E/**F**	Carmi 2004, 227–40
Giv'at ha-Oranim	RTA-4507	4675	50	3518	3372	3631	3360	E/**F**	Carmi 2004, 227–40
Giv'at ha-Oranim	RTA-4508	5105	50	3967	3804	4033	3780	C/**D**	Carmi 2004, 227–40
Nahal Qanah	RT-861A	5150	190	4228	3716	4359	3531	B/**C**/D	Carmi and Segal 1992, 125
Nahal Qanah	RT-861E	5440	100	4440	4074	4462	4000	A/**B**/C	Carmi and Segal 1992, 125
Nahal Qanah	RT-1543	5090	75	3965	3798	4040	3707	C/**D**	Segal and Carmi 1996, 88
Nahal Qanah	RT-1545	5340	57	4257	4055	4329	4006	**B**/C	Segal and Carmi 1996, 88

Table 10.4 Radiocarbon determinations from the central hill country

chisels and smaller miscellaneous items (Namdar 2002, 54). Metallurgical analyses of many of these artefacts (by ICE-AES and Scanning Electron Microscopy/SEM-WDS) provided evidence for complex artefacts containing low levels of arsenic and antimony (<1% each), as well as those containing higher levels of these elements (up to 6.12% and 11.85% respectively) (Namdar 2002, 69–70). One particular complex casting, macehead #97–3470, was completely unalloyed, while one simple tool, chisel #97–3484, contained 1.3% arsenic.

Recent radiocarbon determinations from the site provide valuable chronological pegs for this impressive and diverse collection (Table 10.4). The three samples (RTA-4506, RTA-4507 and RTA-4508) are not statistically the same, and instead span much of the first half of the 4th millennium cal BC, from the 40th through to the 34th centuries. The sub-period best represented by the ^{14}C samples is F, suggesting that Giv'at ha-Oranim was one of the latest sites in the southern Levantine Chalcolithic period.

Excavations between 1986 and 1990 at Nahal Qanah cave, in use during the Neolithic, Chalcolithic and Early Bronze periods, resulted in the discovery of 15 copper-based artefacts (Gopher and Tsuk 1996). Found primarily in the cave's 'Main Hall', 'Passage' and 'Copper Room' areas, these include eight sections of copper wire, decorative fragments (possibly crowns or standards), miscellaneous fragments, an axe and a standard (Gopher and Tsuk 1996, 30). Metallurgical analysis of the standard, an unidentifiable 'lump' and a decorative fragment by Electron Probe Micro-Analysis (EPMA) and AAS resulted in the detection of significant levels of arsenic and antimony, while analysis of a section of wire suggested that it was composed of relatively pure copper, as only 0.09% arsenic was detected (Shalev 1996, tab. 7.1 and tab. 7.2.).

In total, eight radiocarbon determinations are available from Nahal Qanah (Carmi and Segal 1992, 125; Segal and Carmi 1996, 88), three of which originate from Chalcolithic contexts and have standard deviations of less than 150 years (RT-861E, 1543 and 1545; Table 10.4). These samples suggest that the cave was in use over a long period of time, with ranges extending between the 45th and 38th centuries cal BC. The copper artefacts may have been in use/deposited at any time during that period. One additional date (RT-861A) deserves mention despite its higher standard deviation, as it originated from the same locus as a decorative fragment and an unidentifiable lump, both of alloyed copper (Grave III). This determination provides a range between the 43rd and the 38th century BC, suggesting a slightly later date for these arsenical pieces. The samples from Nahal Qanah are not statistically the same, and so a pooled mean cannot aid in clarifying its occupation history. Based on the bulk presence of radiocarbon years from the samples, the best-attested sub-period is B, but sub-period C is also well attested.

The Jordan Valley

Numerous copper artefacts dating to the Chalcolithic period have also been found at sites in the vicinity of the Jordan valley, both in the north as well as in the southern areas near the Dead Sea. Fortunately, all of these sites have been radiocarbon dated, making them particularly relevant to this study (Table 10.5).

Several copper artefacts were unearthed over the course of the joint Jordano-French expedition (including Yarmouk University, the CNRS and IFAPO) to Abu Hamid between 1986 and 1992 (Dollfus and Kafafi 1988). At this important well-stratified site Chalcolithic deposits were identified in Phase III (Area A levels 2d–a and 1c–a), which was characterized for the most part by mudbrick rectilinear architecture, while earlier Wadi Rabah-like deposits and late Yarmoukian features were found in deeper levels (Phase II, levels 3e–a and Phase I, levels 5b–a and 4, respectively) (Lovell *et al.* 2004, 263–5; Lovell *et al.* 2007). Copper finds include two corroded awls and an unidentified object (Dollfus and Kafafi 1988, 48; Kerner 2001, 136). These have been analysed by Hauptman (2000), who found that they are composed of pure copper, aside from one awl which exhibits slight increases in nickel and silver content.

Despite numerous radiocarbon determinations from Abu Hamid there are unfortunately few samples which originate from clean Phase III contexts. Two samples previously assigned to Phase III/Upper Levels (Ly-6252 and Ly-6253; Lovell *et al.* 2004, Table 10.2) have been recently reinterpreted as belonging to Phase II, and two other samples believed to originate from Phase III levels (GrN-17496 and GrN-17497) are from mixed concentrations

Site	*Relevant samples*	*^{14}C date*	±	*1 sigma upper*	*1 sigma lower*	*2 sigma upper*	*2 sigma lower*	*Sub-periods represented*	*Reference*
Abu Hamid	Ly-6257	5385	90	4335	4072	4432	3987	A/**B**/C	Lovell *et al.* 2007
Abu Hamid	Ly-6252	5180	110	4225	3804	4308	3713	B/**C**/D	Lovell *et al.* 2007
Abu Hamid	GrN-14623	5670	40	4539	4459	4610	4372	**Pre-A/A**	Lovell *et al.* 2007
Ketef Jericho	RT-2178	5125	60	3983	3804	4044	3777	C/**D**	Segal and Carmi 1996, 90
Makuch	OxA-1928	5310	80	4241	4043	4327	3979	**B**/C	Housley 1994, 65
Teleilat Ghassul	GrN-15194	5330	25	4235	4072	4244	4051	**B**/C	Neef 1990
Teleilat Ghassul	GrN-15195	5270	100	4231	3986	4336	3814	B/**C**	Neef 1990
Teleilat Ghassul	GrN-15196	5110	90	4031	3790	4225	3667	C/**D**	Neef 1990
Teleilat Ghassul	OZD-029	5524	88	4459	4266	4550	4074	**A**/B	Bourke *et al.* 2001, 1219–20
Teleilat Ghassul	OZD-033	5454	58	4353	4254	4449	4076	**A**/B	Bourke *et al.* 2001, 1219–20
Teleilat Ghassul	OZD-034	5342	71	4311	4054	4334	3997	A/**B**/C	Bourke *et al.* 2001, 1219–20

Table 10.5 Radiocarbon determinations from the Jordan Valley

of organic material and do not lend themselves easily to interpretation (Lovell *et al.* 2007). One date from a standing section (GrN-14623) does appear to originate from a Phase III context (level 2a), and two others from a Phase II context found with significant intrusive Phase III material (Ly-6252 and Ly-6257) may also relate to the Chalcolithic occupation. Based on these three dates, the Phase III levels of Abu Hamid (Table 10.5) appear to date to the broad range between the 46th and 39th centuries cal BC. These determinations are not statistically the same, and the time frame best represented by the distribution of radiocarbon years is sub-period B, while sub-period C is also well attested.

Both simple (axes/chisels) and complex artefacts (a macehead) were unearthed at Ketef Jericho during the Israel Antiquities Authority's 'Operation Scroll' in 1993, all of which originated from the 'Cave of the Sandal' and were deposited in burial contexts (Eshel and Zissu 1995). Analysis of these finds by means of ICP-AES demonstrated that they were all composed of relatively pure copper, without any traces of arsenic or antimony (Segal and Kamenski 2002, 159). A single radiocarbon sample from the Chalcolithic use of the cave (RT-2178; Table 10.5) yielded a date between the 40th and 39th centuries cal BC (Segal and Carmi 1996, 90), with the best-attested sub-period being D.

Chalcolithic remains were also discovered in the Lower Wadi Makuch over the course of the Hebrew University's Judean Desert Cave Survey in 1987 (Agur *et al.* 1990), and seven copper artefacts were identified in one of the five excavated caves (Cave 6). These finds included simple 'utilitarian' tools such as axes, chisels and an awl, as well as a single complex standard which has not been chemically investigated. Analyses of the simple artefacts by means of EPMA and AAS has demonstrated that they all contained insignificant amounts of arsenic and antimony, therefore supporting the previously proposed model of simple (pure) versus complex (alloyed) (Shalev 1991, tab. 5; Shalev 1995, 112). One radiocarbon date from the Lower Wadi Makuch which may relate to the use of this cave (OxA-1928) yielded a range between the 43rd and 41st centuries cal BC (Housley 1994, 65), with the best-attested sub-period being B (Table 10.5). Perhaps future analysis of the standard from Cave 6 may shed more light on the development of the industry in this region in the late 5th millennium.

The final site in the southern Jordan valley of relevance to this study is the type-site of the 'Ghassulian' culture, Teleilat Ghassul. Excavated by three different projects – 1929–1938 and 1959–1960 (Pontifical Biblical Institute) (Mallon *et al.* 1934; North 1961), 1967–1977 (British School of Archaeology in Jerusalem and University of Sydney) (Hennessy 1969; 1982), and 1994–1999 (University of Sydney) (Bourke 1997; 2002) – Teleilat Ghassul has a complex stratigraphic history spanning the Late Neolithic and Chalcolithic periods (Lovell 2001, 19–28). A total of 12 simple tools has been unearthed at the site, including axes, awls and a small hook (Mallon *et al.* 1934, 75; Lee 1973, 281), all of which originated from the lengthy Chalcolithic occupation of the site (Level IV, Phases D–A). None of these artefacts have been metallurgically investigated.

Befitting its station as a type-site for the period, Teleilat Ghassul has undergone extensive radiometric investigation. Of a total of 34 radiocarbon dates published for the entire occupational history of the site (Bourke *et al.* 2001; Bourke *et al.* 2004), a selection of six relevant samples from Chalcolithic contexts (GrN-15194, 15195, 15196, OZD-029, 033 and 034) indicate that the site was occupied between the 45th and 38th centuries cal BC (Table 10.5). Unfortunately, these dates contribute little to the dating of the finds, which could have been in use or deposited at any time within that range. These determinations are not statistically the same, and the sub-period best represented by these six determinations is B, suggesting that the time frame between the 43rd and 42nd centuries cal BC was one of significant activity at the site.

Site	*Relevant samples*	^{14}*C date*	±	*1 sigma upper*	*1 sigma lower*	*2 sigma upper*	*2 sigma lower*	*Sub-periods represented*	*Reference*
Nahal Mishmar	ARP-201a	5375	55	4328	4077	4335	4052	A/**B**/C	Aardsma 2001, 1250
Nahal Mishmar	ARP-201b	5475	60	4433	4256	4457	4086	**A**/B	Aardsma 2001, 1250
Nahal Mishmar	ARP-212	5520	50	4446	4334	4459	4263	A	Aardsma 2001, 1250
Nahal Mishmar	ARP-213a	6020	55	4986	4844	5191	4777	**Pre-A**	Aardsma 2001, 1250
Nahal Mishmar	ARP-213b	5724	47	4652	4497	4687	4462	**Pre-A**/A	Aardsma 2001, 1250
Nahal Mishmar	ARP-213c	6020	60	4993	4841	5196	4730	**Pre-A**	Aardsma 2001, 1250
Nahal Mishmar	BM-140	5390	150	4355	4043	4541	3814	A/**B**/C	Weinstein 1984, 335
Nahal Mishmar	I-285	4780	100	3653	3379	3772	3358	**E**/F	Weinstein 1984, 335
Nahal Mishmar	I-353	4760	120	3648	3375	3891	3110	**E**/F	Bar-Adon 1980, 86
Nahal Mishmar	RT-1407	4990	70	3934	3676	3945	3656	C/**D**/E	Carmi and Segal 1992, 131
Nahal Mishmar	RT-1409	5355	55	4320	4069	4328	4049	A/**B**/C	Carmi and Segal 1992, 131
Nahal Mishmar	W-1341	4880	250	3960	3370	4244	2945	C/**D**/**E**/F	Weinstein 1984, 335

Table 10.6 Radiocarbon determinations from Nahal Mishmar

The eastern Negev and Wadi Arabah

Four sites in the eastern Negev have yielded copper-based artefacts, including the famous site of Nahal Mishmar (Cave 1/The Cave of the Treasure), where a hoard of more than 400 metal artefacts was discovered (Bar-Adon 1980). Excavations carried out in this cave between 1960 and 1962 demonstrated that it was occupied during the Chalcolithic period (Stratum III), as well as in the Iron Age (Stratum II) and Bar-Kokhba periods (Stratum I). Based on the excavator's observation that the inhabitants of Cave 1 dug over 2 m into earlier deposits to hide the hoard in a small niche, it is widely accepted that that the artefacts were hidden towards the end of the cave's occupation (Bar-Adon 1980, 7).

This well-known assemblage includes both simple and complex artefacts, a great number of which have been metallurgically analysed (Key 1980; Shalev and Northover 1993; Tadmor *et al.* 1995). These analyses have demonstrated that the majority of complex items were composed of a complex arsenic/antimony/nickel alloy, and that simple tools were made of relatively pure copper. However, several of the complex artefacts from this assemblage, including several standards and maceheads, were found to contain little to no arsenic or antimony (Tadmor *et al.* 1995, tab. 2). A recent study carried out by the authors will shed further light on the varying compositions detected in the Nahal Mishmar assemblage, as the entire collection at the Israel Museum has been analysed using a portable X-ray florescence (XRF) device (Shugar, pers. comm.).

Radiometric evidence from Nahal Mishmar (Cave 1) is complicated, as dates both old and new offer contradictory information (Table 10.6). For the most part, these contradictions are related to the dating of the reed mat in which the hoard was wrapped (ARP-series, BM-140, I-285 and W-1341, the last three of which are included here for comparative purposes only, as they were measured very early in the history of the technique and may not be entirely reliable). These nine dates suggest that the mat was an ancient heirloom repaired occasionally over time, as they 'spread out in at least three groups over a millennium or more … and that such repairs may be responsible for the divergent ^{14}C ages from different portions of the mat' (Aardsma 2001, 1251–3).

Owing to the incredible variations between these determinations the date of the reed mat contributes little to the present discussion, and instead other samples from Cave 1 should be considered. A sample from another reed mat (RT-1407) yielded a date between the 40th and 37th centuries cal BC, while a sample from a possible loom fragment (RT-1409) appears to date between the 44th and 41st centuries cal BC (Carmi and Segal 1992, 131). A third date originating from the haft of one of the copper standards (I-353), between the 40th and 34th centuries cal BC, also deserves mention despite its age (measured in the 1960s) (Weinstein 1984, 335). These determinations are not statistically the same, and the sub-periods best represented by these three dates are D followed by E, suggesting significant activity at Nahal Mishmar from the 39th to the 36th centuries cal BC (there is also a concentration of radiocarbon years in sub-period B, but these are strongly outweighed by those of D and E). Based on these determinations and the stratigraphic context of the hoard itself, it would be very difficult to push the date of the hoard's deposition earlier than the first quarter of the 4th millennium cal BC (a conclusion also reached by Moorey (1988, 173)).

Excavations at Nahal Ze'elim (Cave 49) in 1960 also resulted in the discovery of copper artefacts, including three maceheads and an axe (Aharoni 1961). Analyses of these artefacts demonstrated that the maceheads contained high levels of arsenic and antimony, while the axe consisted of relatively pure copper (Notis *et al.* 1991; Shalev and Northover 1993, tab. 1). At Tall al-Magass, a transitional

Site	*Relevant samples*	^{14}*C date*	±	*1 sigma upper*	*1 sigma lower*	*2 sigma upper*	*2 sigma lower*	*Sub-periods represented*	*Reference*
Abu Matar	PR-1	5340	80	4311	4053	4336	3991	A/**B**/C	Shugar 2000, 71
Abu Matar	PR-2	5470	80	4444	4237	4462	4055	**A**/B	Shugar 2000, 71
Abu Matar	PR-3	5230	80	4227	3964	4315	3808	B/**C**	Shugar 2000, 71
Abu Matar	PR-4	5270	80	4229	3992	4325	3956	**B**/C	Shugar 2000, 71
Abu Matar	PR-5	5260	90	4229	3982	4329	3821	**B**/C	Shugar 2000, 71
Abu Matar	RT-1610	5250	55	4225	3981	4233	3968	**B**/C	Segal and Carmi 1996, 93
Abu Matar	RT-1613	5275	55	4228	3999	4242	3974	**B**/C	Segal and Carmi 1996, 93
Bir es-Safadi	Ly-3906	5190	100	4226	3811	4314	3770	B/**C**/D	Perrot 1987, 18
Bir es-Safadi	Ly-3905	5190	100	4226	3811	4314	3770	B/**C**/D	Perrot 1987, 18
Bir es-Safadi	Ly-3904	5170	110	4223	3800	4251	3710	B/**C**/D	Perrot 1987, 18
Bir es-Safadi	RT-862C	5220	105	4231	3952	4323	3796	B/**C**	Carmi and Segal 1992, 125
Horvat Beter	Pta-	5180	70	4218	3812	4229	3798	B/**C**/D	Rosen and Eldar 1993, 24
Horvat Beter	Pta-4312	5100	130	4039	3713	4232	3647	C/**D**	Rosen and Eldar 1993, 24

Table 10.7 Radiocarbon determinations from Abu Matar, Bir es-Safadi/Neve Noy and Horvat Beter

Site	*Relevant samples*	^{14}*C date*	±	*1 sigma upper*	*1 sigma lower*	*2 sigma upper*	*2 sigma lower*	*Sub-periods represented*	*Reference*
Shiqmim II	RT-1317	5330	50	4239	4055	4325	4004	**B**/C	Carmi and Segal 1992, 124
Shiqmim II	RT-1318	5240	65	4225	3972	4252	3949	B/**C**	Carmi and Segal 1992, 124
Shiqmim II	RT-1319	5450	60	4352	4247	4449	4072	A/**B**	Carmi and Segal 1992, 124
Shiqmim II	RT-1321	5570	65	4456	4352	4542	4272	**A**	Carmi and Segal 1992, 124
Shiqmim II	RT-1322	5190	75	4224	3819	4232	3800	B/**C**/D	Carmi and Segal 1992, 124
Shiqmim II	RT-1326	5420	50	4335	4244	4357	4070	A/**B**	Carmi and Segal 1992, 124
Shiqmim II	RT-1328	5520	60	4448	4332	4487	4257	**A**	Carmi and Segal 1992, 124
Shiqmim II	RT-1330	5300	60	4231	4046	4317	3984	**B**/C	Carmi and Segal 1992, 124
Shiqmim II	RT-1335	5370	65	4328	4072	4338	4046	A/**B**/C	Carmi and Segal 1992, 124
Shiqmim II	RT-1341	5370	40	4325	4079	4331	4055	A/**B**/C	Carmi and Segal 1992, 125
Shiqmim I	OxA-	5060	140	3984	3696	4233	3537	C/**D**/E	Levy 1992, 352
Shiqmim I	RT-1339	4940	70	3786	3651	3943	3545	**D**/E	Carmi and Segal 1992, 124

Table 10.8 Radiocarbon determinations from Shiqmim

Chalcolithic/Early Bronze Age site in the Wadi Arabah, excavations in 1985 and 1990 resulted in the discovery of copper artefacts (awls) as well as evidence of copper production in the form of crucible smelting (Khalil 1987; 1995; Khalil and Riederer 1998). Other finds from the eastern Negev include a macehead from Nahal Lahat (Alon and Gilead 1986, 78) and an awl from Arad (Amiran 1978, 9), neither of which has been analysed. Unfortunately, radiocarbon determinations are not yet available for these four important sites.

The western Negev

The Chalcolithic sites in the western Negev are of particular importance to this study, as extensive evidence for copper metallurgy has been discovered in the region. Aside from the three primary sites in the region, Shiqmim, Abu Matar and Bir es-Safadi/Neve Noy, all of which have been subject to radiometric investigations (Tables 10.7–10.8) and will be discussed in more detail, copper artefacts have also been found at four other sites in the region. Artefacts from Nahal Ashan (Goren 1995, 296, 303), Gilat (Alon 1977; Alon and Levy 1989) and Nevatim (Shugar 2000, tab. 3.01) are limited to one or two examples of maceheads and awls, none of which have been analysed aside from a single awl from Gilat (98.9% Cu and 0.97% As, detected by EPMA) (Shalev 1995, 112). Radiocarbon determinations are not available from Nahal Ashan or Nevatim, while eight samples from Gilat (Burton and Levy 2001, 1244) contribute little to the present discussion, as the complex casting from the site (a macehead) was found in a secondary context (Alon 1977, 63).

Excavations at the settlement site of Horvat Beter between 1953 and 1954 resulted in the discovery of copper ore, slag and two unidentifiable artefacts, all of which were associated with the latest architectural phase (Stratum I) (Dothan 1959a, 32). The site was reinvestigated in 1982, and two new radiocarbon determinations (Pta-4212a and

4312) suggested that the settlement was occupied between the 42nd and 38th centuries BC (Table 10.7) (Rosen and Eldar 1993, 24–5). These samples are statistically the same, with a χ^2 test yielding a pooled mean of 5162 ± 62 BP, or between 4043 and 3815 cal BC. The sub-period best represented at Horvat Beter is C.

Excavations at the site of Abu Matar between 1952 and 1954 by the French National Scientific Research Centre resulted in the discovery of numerous copper-based artefacts and three principal production centres consisting of anvils, ore fragments, ovens and crucibles (Perrot 1955, 79; Golden *et al.* 2001). Reinvestigation of the site in 1990 and 1991 as part of a salvage project identified three other areas of copper production (Gilead *et al.* 1994, 98–9), and further research into these remains has resulted in the identification of a two-stage process model for metallurgical production at the site, including initial furnace smelting followed by crucible remelting (Shugar 2000). Additionally, arsenical copper prills were also identified in the production remains from Abu Matar, which is the first evidence in the southern Levant suggesting that the complex arsenical artefacts exemplified by the finds from Nahal Mishmar may be of local manufacture (Shugar 2000, 204).

Compositional investigations of the artefacts from Abu Matar were carried out on a bead and an axe, both of which contained minute traces of arsenic (0.023% and 0.22% respectively), suggesting that they were composed of relatively pure copper (Hauptmann 1989, tab. 14.4). An early analysis of the standard from Abu Matar indicated that it contained 12% arsenic (Key 1980), an extremely high percentage which may be the result of an erroneous analysis, evidence of which has already been documented for other results through recent re-analysis (Shalev and Northover 1993, 40–5).

Radiometric evidence from Abu Matar, all of the samples of which were collected from one of its copper-producing areas (Table 10.7), suggests that copper production took place at the site between the 44th and 40th centuries cal BC (Segal and Carmi 1996, 93; Shugar 2000, 71). Testing of the Abu Matar dates demonstrates that they are statistically the same, providing a pooled mean of 5291 ± 27 BP, calibrated between 4227 and 4047 cal BC (1 sigma). The sub-period best represented by this pooled mean is B, suggesting extensive metallurgical activity at the site as early as the 43rd or 42nd centuries cal BC.

Excavations between 1954 and 1960 at the site of Bir es-Safadi, located immediately south of Abu Matar, also yielded several copper-based artefacts, including axes, awls and a macehead (Perrot 1968; 1984, 80–7; 1990). The eastern extension of the site, an area which was named Neve Noy after the modern suburb being built over the remains, was excavated in 1983 as part of a salvage project (Eldar and Baumgarten 1985). Copper-based artefacts were discovered during these excavations as well; these included standards, awls and a possible crown fragment, as well as remains associated with copper production (Eldar and Baumgarten 1985, 137).

Recent analyses of several simple and complex artefacts from the Neve Noy collection by means of SEM has resulted in the discovery that both artefact types were composed of relatively pure copper. Radiocarbon determinations from Bir es-Safadi and Neve Noy (Ly-3904, 3905, 3906 and RT862C; tab. 7) cluster tightly between the late 43rd and 39th centuries cal BC, suggesting that it was roughly contemporary with its sister settlement Abu Matar (Perrot 1987, 18; Carmi and Segal 1992, 125). These dates were also statistically the same, yielding a pooled mean of 5193 ± 52 BP, calibrated between 4047 and 3957 cal BC (1 sigma). The sub-period best represented by the Neve Noy determinations is C, although sub-period B is also strongly attested.

Large-scale excavations at Shiqmim, a long-lived settlement site roughly 18 km downstream from Abu Matar, took place over the course of three project 'Phases', from 1977 to 1985 (Phase I), from 1987 to 1989 (Phase II) and in 1993 (Phase III) (Levy and Alon 1987; Levy *et al.* 1991; Levy *et al.* 1996). Three main occupational phases were identified, including 'Early' (BP IV–III), 'Main' (BP II) and 'Late' (BP I) phases (Levy 1992, 350–3; Burton and Levy 2001, 1235–7).

A total of 14 artefacts was discovered during the Phase I excavations at the site. These included simple tools from BP II, such as axes, awls and a bead, as well as simple and complex artefacts from BP I, such as awls and a standard (Levy and Alon 1987, 161–79). Analysis of the utilitarian artefacts from both periods indicated that they were made of pure copper, and the standard from BP I was also relatively pure, containing a mere 0.86% arsenic and 0.45% antimony (Shalev and Northover 1987, 368). An alloyed macehead was also found during the Phase I excavations, and although it was from an isolated probe (Upper Village) that has not been linked with any building phase, it has been suggested that it was 'discarded there during the last phases of occupation at the site' (*i.e.*, Shiqmim BP I; Shalev *et al.* 1992, 64).

Additional artefacts were unearthed during the Phase II and III excavations, although their stratigraphic contexts have not yet been published in full detail (see Levy 1995, fig. 3, for the location of most of these finds). A total of 11 artefacts was discovered, which included both simple tools and prestige goods, the majority of which appear to originate from the rectilinear structures at the site (BPs II and I) and have not been analysed. Analyses of a macehead and standard by EPMA resulted in the identification of significant levels of arsenic and antimony (Shalev 1995, tab. 1), although the stratification of these finds remains unclear. Again, an alloyed macehead was discovered outside the main excavation area, which the excavators suggest belonged to a Shiqmim II deposit (Levy *et al.* 1996, 108; Golden *et al.* 2001, 958).

Several areas associated with the production of pure copper tools were also exposed over the course of the excavations; these were characterized by fragments of ore, crucibles and slag, and have been attributed to both the 'Main' (BP II) and 'Late' (BP I) phases of occupation (Levy and Alon 1987, 163, 177; Shalev and Northover 1987, 361–4).

A substantial repertoire of radiocarbon determinations is available from Shiqmim. Many of them can be correlated to the metallurgical finds from Shiqmim II and I (Table 10.8). A total of 10 determinations from Shiqmim which can be correlated to the 'Main' phase of occupation (BP II) yielded dates between the 45th and 39th centuries cal BC (Carmi and Segal 1992, 124–5). The samples from Shiqmim II are not statistically the same, and therefore should not be used to create a pooled mean. Sub-period B is the best represented among these 10 samples, although sub-period C is also well attested.

Only two determinations (RT-1339 and OxA-2520) with standard deviations of less than 150 years are available for the occupation of Shiqmim I, providing a range between the 40th and 37th centuries cal BC (Table 10.8) (Carmi and Segal 1992, 124; Levy 1992, 352). These two samples are statistically the same and testing provided an pooled mean date of 4964 ± 63 BP, which yields a calibrated date between 3797 and 3658 cal BC (1 sigma). Sub-period D is the best represented by this pooled mean for Shiqmim I.

Based on the final publication of the Phase I excavations and the archaeometallurgical analyses of the finds (Levy and Alon 1987; Shalev and Northover 1987), it appears that unalloyed prestige goods were largely limited to Shiqmim I contexts. Of particular importance would be the further analysis of prestige goods from clear Shiqmim II contexts in order to determine if any examples of unalloyed complex artefacts can be identified, as occur at the slightly later sites of Bir es-Safadi/Neve Noy, Ketef Jericho and Giv'at ha-Oranim.

Interpretation

Based on the correlation between archaeometallurgical analyses and contextually related radiometric data considered at the highest confidence interval (2 sigma range, 95% confidence), a considerable amount of overlap between the dates of relevant samples can be seen (Figure 10.1). This overlap limits the reliability of such a correlation in terms of reconstructing developmental or changing trends associated with Chalcolithic copper metallurgy, as both alloyed and unalloyed finds appear to be roughly contemporary. However, by decreasing the confidence interval to the 1 sigma range and assigning relative sub-periods to each individual site, significant patterns do begin to emerge (Figure 10.1 and Table 10.9). It is possible to make some preliminary interpretations based on the research conducted to date regarding these apparent 'changing trends' in artefact composition, which can be tested as future information becomes available. New radiocarbon determinations, for example, are still needed to enhance the reliability of the sub-period designations for poorly dated sites such as Makuch, Horvat Beter, Shoham and Ketef Jericho. New data from Shiqmim I

Site	No. of relevant ^{14}C samples	1 sigma upper (max.)	1 sigma lower (min.)	Attested sub-period(s)	Best represented sub-period	No. of artifacts analyzed	Total no. of analyses	'Pure' tools	Alloyed tools	'Pure' prestige	Alloyed prestige
Peqi'in	4	4490	4236	A/B	A	4	4	Yes	No	Yes	No
Abu Hamid	3	4539	3804	Pre-A/A/B/C/D	B	3	3	Yes	No	No	No
Teleilat Ghassul	6	4459	3790	A/B/C/D	B	0	0	n.y.d.	n.y.d.	n.y.d.	n.y.d.
Shiqmim II	10	4456	3819	A/B/C/D	B	10	15	Yes	No	No	Yes
Nahal Qanah	4	4440	3716	A/B/C/D	B	4	7	Yes	No	No	Yes
Makuch	1	4241	4043	B/C	B	6	7	Yes	No	n.y.d.	n.y.d.
Abu Matar	7	4227	4047	A/B/C	B	3	3	Yes	No	No	Yes
Bir es-Safadi/Neve Noy	4	4047	3957	B/C/D	C	9	23	Yes	No	Yes	Yes
Horvat Beter	2	4043	3815	B/C/D	C	0	0	n.y.d.	n.y.d.	n.y.d.	n.y.d.
Shoham	2	4035	3825	C/D	C	0	0	n.y.d.	n.y.d.	n.y.d.	n.y.d.
Nahal Mishmar	3	4320	3375	A/B/C/D/E/F	D	64	91	Yes	No	Yes	Yes
Ketef Jericho	1	3983	3804	C/D	D	3	3	Yes	No	Yes	No
Shiqmim I	2	3797	3658	D/E	D	2	3	Yes	No	Yes	Yes
Giv'at ha-Oranim	3	3967	3372	C/D/E/F	F	19	40	Yes	Yes	Yes	Yes

Table 10.9 Chronological distribution of unalloyed and alloyed artefacts at sites that have been radiocarbon dated. The increased precision of ranges from Abu Matar, Bir es-Safadi, Horvat Beter, Shoham and Shiqmim I are the result of pooled means. The sequences of all other sites are represented by the maximum and minimum ranges from their radiometric assemblage, within which the deposits probably date. All sites are categorized according to sub-period(s) and ranked according to the sub-period best represented

will surely add to our understanding of that important site and its metallurgical remains in the early 4th millennium cal BC.

Radiometric evidence from the northern site of Peqi'in suggests that the copper artefacts deposited in the burial contexts there (*i.e.*, as grave goods) were of an early date, with the best-represented sub-period being A, or between the 45th and 44th centuries cal BC. The finds from this early site were entirely of relatively pure copper and included both utilitarian goods and complex castings. In comparison with the finds from sites best represented by the B sub-period, the results from Peqi'in are extremely anomalous.

Analyses of artefacts from the production centres of Abu Matar and Shiqmim, as well as the more northern sites of Nahal Qanah and Makuch, were in remarkable congruence with the long-standing dichotomy of alloyed prestige goods versus unalloyed tools (Levy and Shalev 1989, 355–9; Shalev 1991). These sites are well dated by numerous ^{14}C determinations to the late 5th millennium cal BC (particularly the 43rd and 42nd centuries), and it appears that during this time frame the Beer Shevan and possibly the Ghassulian Chalcolithic cultures were capable of sophisticated metallurgical processes with advanced material control.

While the early finds from Peqi'in are especially noteworthy, and could represent the first evidence of a developmental trend from the production of unalloyed prestige goods to alloyed prestige goods, one must keep in mind the nature of the site (*i.e.* a burial context with grave goods) and its geographic isolation from the southern cultures. Additional evidence is clearly needed for this early period in the north, as it is difficult to determine whether the results from Peqi'in are linked to an early northern tradition or perhaps even to technological choice relating to mortuary consumption (rather than consumption as tools or status symbols in daily life). It is likely that these questions must await further investigation into early Chalcolithic remains in this region.

Complex castings such as standards, maceheads and crowns continued to be produced throughout the Chalcolithic period, and examples of these copper artefacts alloyed with arsenic and antimony occur from sub-period B through to F (*i.e.*, from the 43rd to the 35th centuries cal BC). Perhaps the best attestations of these alloyed goods are the complex castings from the Nahal Mishmar hoard, as well as the well-known collections from Nahal Qanah and Shiqmim.

Interestingly, around the turn of the fifth to fourth millennia, identified in this scheme as sub-period C, relatively pure prestige objects begin to appear (Table 10.9). The first unalloyed standards appear in the south at Bir es-Safadi/Neve Noy during this time (Shugar and Gohm forthcoming; SEM analysis of standard 82–1174 yielded a result of 100% copper, while standard 82–1175 yielded a result of 97.87% copper, 1.3% iron, 0.475% sulphur and 0.36% aluminium), and unalloyed or weakly alloyed prestige goods continue to appear in sub-periods D, E and F, including maceheads from Ketef Jericho, standards and maceheads from Nahal Mishmar, a standard from Shiqmim I and a macehead from Giv'at ha-Oranim.

The evidence also suggests that utilitarian tools were made of pure copper throughout the Chalcolithic period, with the only exception being a small chisel from Giv'at ha-Oranim. As perhaps the latest site included in this study, dating roughly to the mid 4th millennium cal BC, the presence of an alloyed tool there is unique but not surprising. At this terminal stage in the period, which was severely troubled and possibly violent (Levy 1995, 241–3; for evidence of macehead wounds see Dawson *et al.* 2003), older prestige goods were probably recycled for useful copper.

The exclusive utilitarian/pure copper and prestige/alloyed copper dichotomy previously identified clearly requires revision (Key 1980; Levy and Shalev 1989; Shalev 1991), as it is now clear that complex castings were occasionally produced with relatively pure copper, especially late in the period. Indeed, Chalcolithic metallurgists appear to have produced both alloyed and unalloyed complex artefacts in the early 4th millennium cal BC. Conversely, aside from the early and distant site of Peqi'in, the majority of middle to late 5th millennium cal BC prestige goods appear to be intentionally alloyed, and occurrences of unalloyed prestige goods are few and far between.

Interestingly, the 'simple' versus 'complex' distinction appears to hold true for finds dating between the 44th and 42nd centuries cal BC, where it is perhaps indicative of a 'golden age' of sophisticated alloying methods and abundant resources. Later in the period complex artefacts were cast with either pure copper, weakly alloyed copper or strongly alloyed copper, which in turn attests to a further increase in technological sophistication. This shift from exclusively alloyed complex items to this new wide variety later in the period may be related to advancements in furnace efficiency and achievable temperatures. These advancements would enable the metallurgists to effectively cast complicated *unalloyed* copper objects owing to the extended casting time available prior to the metal's solidification. Problems relating to the acquisition of suitable alloying materials may also be related to this changing trend, but this remains to be demonstrated.

The integration of radiometric evidence and archaeometallurgical analyses suggests that during the second half of the 5th millennium cal BC copper metallurgy flourished in the eastern and western Negev regions (previously noted in Levy and Shalev 1989, 360–1), and that the earliest full-scale processing took place at Abu Matar, contemporary with crucible remelting at Shiqmim (Shugar 2000). It is likely that the majority of the early copper artefacts included in this study were produced at one of these two production centres. Petrographic studies of lost wax mould remnants found in objects from the later sites of Nahal Mishmar (Y. Goren, pers. comm.) and Giv'at ha-Oranim (Namdar 2002, 114–15) point towards sources in the Shephelah, supplying further evidence for local production in the southern Levant and perhaps hinting at the location of a new copper-producing 'heartland' later in the Chalcolithic.

This potential shift of copper production northwards from the Beer Sheva valley towards the Shephelah fits nicely into the known alterations that occur in the region, with new settlements at the start of the Early Bronze Age in the Shephelah and the demise of the Ghassulian villages. Along with this cultural change we see dramatic alterations in the metal artefacts being produced. These changes include alterations in the style, size, colour and chemical composition of copper artefacts (Shalev 1994, 633). As Shalev indicates (1994, 636) the Early Bronze Age brought about a significant change in the nature of craft specialization for the copper industry.

Conclusion

Owing to the imprecision of many earlier radiocarbon determinations and the relative scarcity of samples obtained from contexts directly associated with deposited copper-based artefacts, this correlation between radiocarbon dates and specific finds yielded no *conclusive* results regarding changes in artefact compositions over time. However, it is possible with reduced confidence to observe a shifting trend from the frequent use of arsenic/antimony alloying early in the Chalcolithic to its more sporadic use later in the period. By the end of the Chalcolithic period it appears that the ancient metallurgists produced both pure and alloyed tools and prestige goods, but it should be noted that for the most part tools remained predominantly 'pure' and prestige goods were predominantly 'alloyed'.

The identification of these trends may or may not have been influenced by strong variations in sample size between early contexts and late contexts. For example, while only 26 artefacts have been analysed from sub-period B contexts (including sites such as Shiqmim II, Nahal Qanah, Makuch and Abu Matar), 97 artefacts have been analysed from sub-period C, D, E and F contexts (including Nahal Mishmar, Giv'at ha-Oranim and others). It is indeed possible that the appearance of pure prestige goods in these late assemblages is directly related to the disproportionate ratio between sample sizes, and it is true that only a handful of complex casts from early contexts have been analysed. However, it can be said with certainty that every analysed prestige good from an early context, aside from the anomalous Peqi'in, has proved to be alloyed, and that this has been demonstrated across three different assemblages. Further analyses of early prestige goods are clearly needed to reinforce the results obtained here (*e.g.*, standards from Makuch and Shiqmim II), and the results must remain preliminary because of these factors.

The changes in the industry elucidated by this study may account for a significant portion of the compositional variability identified in previous investigations, and a statistical investigation of past metallographic and chemical analyses may help clarify this problematic aspect. Reasons for this shift require further study, and a wide variety of social, economic and political aspects of Chalcolithic cultures needs to be considered. Was the apparent increase in the frequency of unalloyed prestige goods in the 4th millennium cal BC related to a decline in the availability of raw materials needed to produce alloys or simply to a shift in technological choice? Was the initial sophistication of the industry in the south the result of a development from earlier northern traditions (*i.e.*, Peqi'in), or are the two industries completely unrelated? What influence did the emergence of more complex systems of social and political organization (*i.e.*, rank societies – chiefdoms; see Levy 1995) have on the industry, and what was the relationship between their collapse and the observed trends? What role did external stimuli play in these developments, if any? How do these changes relate to developments in the metallurgical industry of the subsequent Early Bronze Age, when alloyed prestige goods disappear and new types of tools and weapons begin to be produced (Shalev 1994, 633–6)? These and other important questions require the attention of future studies.

This hypothetical model requires further testing, and new AMS radiocarbon determinations associated with reliable provenance information and further archaeometallurgical investigations, as mentioned above, are sorely needed. Limitations in sample size need to be addressed, but this must await future analyses and archaeological discovery. One possible refinement that may aid in elucidating the problems encountered in this study would be the use of Bayesian statistics, which would greatly assist in dating deposits from multi-period sites. This study is part of an ongoing research project geared towards addressing issues involving the development of copper metallurgy in the Chalcolithic, and a comprehensive analysis of copper-based artefacts from the Israel Museum collection will be forthcoming.

Acknowledgements

We would like to graciously acknowledge the financial support provided by the Social Sciences and Humanities Research Council of Canada for this ongoing research project (Grant No. 410-2002-0996). We would also like to thank the Israel Antiquities Authority and the Israel Museum for allowing the archaeometallurgical sampling of artefacts from the Neve Noy assemblage, as well as the analysis of their entire Chalcolithic copper collection by means of a portable XRF. Thanks must also be expressed to Prof. S. Shalev for providing copper samples from his previous research for retesting, to Prof. I. Gilead for his valuable comments provided over the course of this research project, and to Oxford Instruments for allowing the use of their X-MET3000TX handheld XRF.

References

Aardsma, G. E. (2001) New radiocarbon dates for the reed mat from the Cave of the Treasure, Israel. *Radiocarbon* 43, 3, 1247–54.

Agur, B., Arobes, B. and Patrich, Y. (1990) Judean Desert, Cave Survey –1986/1987. *Excavations and Surveys in Israel* 7/8, 92–5.

Aharoni, Y. (1961) Expedition B. *Israel Exploration Journal* 11, 11–24.

Alon, D. (1977) A Chalcolithic temple at Gilath. *Biblical Archaeologist* 40, 63–5.

Alon, D. and Gilead, I. (1986) Nahal Lahat Cave. *Excavations and Surveys in Israel* 4, 78.

Alon, D. and Levy, T. E. (1989) The archaeology of cult and the Chalcolithic sanctuary at Gilat. *Journal of Mediterranean Archaeology* 2, 163–221.

Amiran, R. (1969) *Ancient Pottery of the Holy Land.* Jerusalem: Massada.

Amiran, R. (1978) *Early Arad: The Chalcolithic and Early Bronze City I, First–Fifth Seasons of Excavations, 1962–1966.* Jerusalem: Israel Exploration Society.

Bar-Adon, P. (1980) *The Cave of the Treasure: The Finds from the Caves in Nahal Mishmar.* Jerusalem: Israel Exploration Society.

Beck, P. (1989) Notes on the style and iconography of the Chalcolithic hoard from Nahal Mishmar. Pp. 39–53 in A. Leonard and B. Williams (eds), *Essays in Ancient Civilization Presented to Helene J. Kantor*. Chicago: The Oriental Institute.

Blackham, M. (2002) *Modeling Time and Transition in Prehistory: The Jordan Valley Chalcolithic (5500–3500 BC)*. Oxford: BAR Int. Ser. 1027.

Bourke, S. J. (1997) The urbanization process in the south Jordan valley: renewed excavations at Teleilat Ghassul 1994/1995. Pp. 249–59 in G. Bisheh, M. Zaghloul, I. Kehrberg (eds), *Studies in the History and Archaeology of Jordan* 6. Amman: The Department of Antiquities of Jordan.

Bourke, S. J. (2002) The origins of social complexity in the southern Levant: new evidence from Teleilat Ghassul, Jordan. *Palestine Exploration Quarterly* 134, 2–27.

Bourke, S. J., Lawson, E., Lovell, J., Hua, Q., Zoppi, U. and Barbetti, M. (2001) The chronology of the Ghassulian Chalcolithic period in the southern Levant: new ^{14}C determinations from Teleilat Ghassul, Jordan. *Radiocarbon* 43, 3, 1217–22.

Bourke, S. J., Zoppi, U., Meadows, J., Hua, Q. and Gibbons, S. (2004) The end of the Chalcolithic period in the south Jordan Valley: new ^{14}C determinations from Teleilat Ghassul, Jordan. *Radiocarbon* 46/1, 315–23.

Budd, P. and Ottaway, B. S. (1991) The properties of arsenical copper alloys: implications for the development of eneolithic metallurgy. Pp. 132–42 in P. Budd, B. Chapman, C. Jackson, R. Janaway and B. Ottaway (eds), *Archaeological Sciences 1989*. Oxford: Oxbow Books.

Burton, M. and Levy, T. E. (2001) The Chalcolithic radiocarbon record and its use in southern Levantine archaeology. *Radiocarbon* 43/3, 1233–46.

Carmi, I. (2004) ^{14}C analysis. Pp. 227–40 in N. Schftelowtiz and R. Oren (eds), *Giv'at Ha-Oranim: A Chalcolithic Site near Nahal Beit Arif.* Tel Aviv: Sonia and Marco Nadler Institute of Archaeology, Tel Aviv University.

Carmi, I. and Segal, D. (1992) Rehovot radiocarbon measurements IV. *Radiocarbon* 34/1, 115–32.

Dawson, L., Levy, T. E. and Smith, P. (2003) Evidence of interpersonal violence at the Chalcolithic village of Shiqmim (Israel). *International Journal of Osteoarchaeology* 13, 115–19.

Dollfus, G. and Kafafi, Z. (1988) *Abu Hamid, village du 4e millénaire de a Vallée du Jourdain*. Amman: Economic Press.

Dothan, M. (1957) Excavations at Meser, 1956: preliminary report on the first season. *Israel Exploration Journal* 7, 217–28.

Dothan, M. (1959a) Excavations at Horvat Beter (Beersheba). *`Atiqot* 2, 1–42.

Dothan, M. (1959b) Excavations at Meser, 1957: preliminary report on the second season. *Israel Exploration Journal* 9, 13–29.

Eldar, I. and Baumgarten, Y. (1985) Neve Noy: a Chalcolithic site of the Beer-Sheba culture. *Biblical Archaeologist* 48, 134–9.

Eshel, H. and Zissu, B. (1995) Ketef Jericho, 1993. *Israel Exploration Journal* 45, 292–8.

Gal, Z., Smithline, H. and Shalem, D. (1997a) A Chalcolithic burial cave in Peqi'in, Upper Galilee. *Israel Exploration Journal* 47, 145–54.

Gal, Z., Smithline, H. and Shalem, D. (1997b) Peqi'in. *Excavations and Surveys in Israel* 16, 22–4.

Garfinkel, Y. (1999) *Neolithic and Chalcolithic Pottery of the Southern Levant*. Qedem 39, Jerusalem Institute of Archaeology, The Hebrew University of Jerusalem.

Gilead, I. (1988) The Chalcolithic period in the Levant. *Journal of World Prehistory* 2/4, 397–443.

Gilead, I. (1994) The history of the Chalcolithic settlement in the Nahal Beer Sheva area: the radiocarbon aspect. *Bulletin of the American Schools of Oriental Research* 296, 1–13.

Gilead, I., Rosen, S. A. and Fabian, P. (1994) Horvat Matar (Bir Abu Matar) – 1990/1991. *Excavations and Surveys in Israel* 12, 97–9.

Golden, J., Levy, T. E. and Hauptmann, A. (2001) Recent discoveries concerning Chalcolithic metallurgy at Shiqmim, Israel. *Journal of Archaeological Science* 28, 951–63.

Gopher, A. and Tsuk, T. (eds) (1996) *The Nahal Qanah Cave: Earliest Gold in the Southern Levant*. Monograph Series of the Institute of Archaeology 12. Tel Aviv: Institute of Archaeology.

Gophna, R. (1968) Palmachim (notes and news). *Israel Exploration Journal* 18, 132–3.

Gophna, R. and Feldstein, A. (1998) Shoham (South). *Excavations and Surveys in Israel* 18, 72–3.

Gophna, R. and Lifshitz, S. (1980) A Chalcolithic burial cave at Palmachim. *`Atiqot* 14, 1–8.

Goren, Y. (1995) Shrines and ceramics in Chalcolithic Israel: the view through the petrographic microscope. *Archaeometry* 37, 287–305.

Hauptmann, A. (1989) The earliest periods of copper metallurgy in Feinan, Jordan. Pp. 119–35 in A. Hauptmann, E. Pernicka and G. A. Wegner (eds), *Old World Archaeometallurgy*. Der Anschnitt, Zeitschrift für Kunst und Kultur im Bergbau 7. Bochum: Deutsches Bergbaumuseum.

Hauptmann, A. (2000) *Zur frühen Metallurgie des Kupfers in Fenan, Jordanien*. Der Anschnitt, Beiheft 11. Bochum.

Hennessy, J. B. (1969) Preliminary report on a first season of excavations at Teleilat Ghassul. *Levant* 1, 1–24.

Hennessy, J. B. (1982) Teleilat Ghassul and its place in the archaeology of Jordan. Pp. 55–8 in A. Hadidi (ed.), *Studies in the History and Archaeology of Jordan* 1. Amman: Department of Antiquities of Jordan.

Housley, R. A. (1994) Eastern Mediterranean chronologies: the Oxford AMS contribution. Pp. 55–73 in O. Bar-Yosef and R. S. Kra (eds), *Late Quaternary Chronology and Paleoclimates of the Eastern Mediterranean*. Tucson, AZ: University of Arizona.

Joffe, A. H. and Dessel, J. P. (1995) Redefining chronology and terminology for the Chalcolithic of the southern Levant. *Current Anthropology* 36, 507–18.

Kerner, S. (2001) *Das Chalkolithikum in der südlichen Levante: die Entwicklung handwerklicher Spezialisierung und ihre Beziehung zu gesellschaftlicher Komplexität*. Rahden: Leidorf.

Key, C. A. (1980) The trace-element composition of the copper and copper alloys artifacts of the Nahal Mishmar hoard. Pp. 238–43 in P. Bar-Adon (ed.), *The Cave of the Treasure: The Finds from the Caves in Nahal Mishmar*. Jerusalem: Israel Exploration Society.

Khalil, L. (1987) Preliminary report on the 1985 season of excavation at el-Maqass-'Aqaba. *Annual of the Department of Antiquities of Jordan* 31, 481–3.

Khalil, L. (1995) The second season of excavation at al-Magass-'Aqaba, 1990. *Annual of the Department of Antiquities of Jordan* 39, 65–79.

Khalil, L. and Riederer, J. (1998) Examination of copper metallurgical remains from a Chalcolithic site at el-Magass, Jordan. *Damaszener Mitteilungen* 10, 1–9.

Lechtman, H. (1996) Arsenic bronze: Dirty copper or chosen alloy? A view from the Americas. *Journal of Field Archaeology* 23/4, 477–514.

Lee, J. (1973) Chalcolithic Ghassul: New Aspects and Master Typology. Unpublished PhD thesis, Hebrew University, Jerusalem.

Levy, T. E. (1986) The Chalcolithic period. *Biblical Archaeologist* 49, 82–108.

Levy, T. E. (1992) Radiocarbon chronology of the Beersheva culture and Predynastic Egypt. Pp. 345–56 in E. C. M. van den Brink (ed.), *The Nile Delta in Transition 4th–3rd Millennium BC*. Jerusalem: Israel Exploration Society.

Levy, T. E. (1995) Cult, metallurgy and rank societies – Chalcolithic period (ca. 4500–3500 BCE). Pp. 226–44 in T. E. Levy (ed.), *The Archaeology of Society in the Holy Land*. London: Leicester University Press.

Levy, T. E. and Alon, D. (1987) Excavations in the Shiqmim village. Pp. 153–218 in T. E. Levy (ed.), *Shiqmim I: Studies Concerning Chalcolithic Societies in the Northern Negev Desert, Israel (1982–1984)*. Oxford: BAR Int. Ser. 356.

Levy, T. E. and Shalev, S. (1989) Prehistoric metalworking in the southern Levant: archaeometallurgical and social perspectives. *World Archaeology* 20/3, 352–72.

Levy, T. E., Alon, D., Goldberg, P., Grigson, C., Smith, P., Holl, A., Buikstra, J. E., Shalev, S., Rosen, S. A., Ben Itzhak, S. and Beb Yosef, A. (1991) Proto-historic investigations at the Shiqmim Chalcolithic village and cemetery: interim report on the 1987 season. Pp. 29–46 in W. E. Rast (ed.), *Preliminary Reports of ASOR-Sponsored Excavations 1982–89*. Baltimore, MD: Johns Hopkins University.

Levy, T. E., Alon, D. and Holl, A. (1996) Shiqmim – 1993. *Excavations and Surveys in Israel* 15, 106–8.

Lovell, J. L. (2001) *The late Neolithic and Chalcolithic Periods in the Southern Levant: New Data from the Site of Teleilat Ghassul, Jordan*. Monographs of the Sydney University Teleilat Ghassul Project 1. Oxford: BAR Int. Ser. 974.

Lovell, J. L., Dollfus, G. and Kafafi, Z. (2004) The middle phases at Abu Hamid and the Wadi Rabah horizon. Pp. 263–74 in F. al-Khraysheh, K. 'Amr, H. Taher and S. Khouri (eds), *Studies in the History and Archaeology of Jordan* 8. Amman: The Department of Antiquities of Jordan.

Lovell, J. L., Dollfus, G. and Kafafi, Z. (2007) The ceramics of the Late Neolithic and Chalcolithic: Abu Hamid and the burnished tradition. *Paléorient* 33/1, 51–76.

Mallon, A., Koeppel, R. and Neuville, R. (1934) *Teleilat Ghassul I, 1929–32*. Rome: Institut Biblique Pontifical.

Mazar, A. (1992) *Archaeology of the Land of the Bible, 10,000–586 BCE*. New York: Doubleday.

Merkel, J. F., Shimada, I., Swann, C. P. and Doonan, R. (1994) Pre-Hispanic copper alloy production at Batán Grande, Peru: Interpretation of the analytical data from ore samples. Pp. 199–227 in D. A. Scott and P. Meyers (eds), *Archaeometry of Pre-Columbian Sites and Artifacts*. Los Angeles, CA: The Getty Conservation Institute.

Miron, E. (1992) *Axes and Adzes from Canaan*. Prahistorische Bronzefunde, Band 19. Stuttgart: Steiner Verlag.

Moorey, P. R. S. (1988) The Chalcolithic hoard from Nahal Mishmar, Israel, in context. *World Archaeology* 20/2, 171–89.

Namdar, D. (2002) The Copper Industry in the Chalcolithic Period in Israel: The Findings from the Site of Give'at-Ha'oranim. Unpublished MA dissertation, Department of Archaeology and Ancient Near Eastern Civilizations, Tel Aviv University (Hebrew).

Neef, R. (1990) Introduction, development and environmental implications of olive culture: the evidence from Jordan. Pp. 295–306 in S. Bottema (ed.), *Man's Role in the Shaping of the Eastern Mediterranean Landscape*. Rotterdam: A. A. Balkema.

Neuville, R. and Mallon, A. (1931) Les débuts de l'age des métaux dans les grottes du désert de Judée. *Syria* 12, 24–47.

North, R. (1961) *Ghassul 1960 excavation report*. Rome: Pontifical Biblical Institute.

Northover, J. P. (1989) Properties and use of arsenic-copper alloys. Pp. 111–17 in A. Hauptmann, E. Pernicka and G. A. Wagner (eds), *Old World Archaeometallurgy*. Der Anschnitt Beiheft 7. Bochum.

Notis, M. R., Moyer, H., Barnisin, M. A. and Clemens, D. (1991) A mace head from a cave in N. Seelim. *Institute of Archaeo-Metallurgical Studies* 17, 4.

Oren, R. and Scheftelowitz, N. (1999) Giv'at Oranim (Nahal Bareqet). *Hadashot Arkheologiyot – Excavations and Surveys in Israel* 110, 48–50.

Perrot, J. (1955) The excavations at Tell Abu Matar, near Beersheba. *Israel Exploration Journal* 5, 17–40, 73–84, 167–89.

Perrot, J. (1961) Une tombe à ossuaires du IVe millenaire à Azor, pres de Tel-Aviv. *`Atiqot* 3, 1–83.

Perrot, J. (1968) La Préhistoire palestinenne. *Supplement au Dictionaire de la Bible*, cols 286–446.

Perrot, J. (1978) *Syrie-Palestine I: des origines a l'age du bronze*. Archaeologia Mundi. Genève: Les Éditions Nagel.

Perrot, J. (1984) Structures d'habitat, mode de vie et environnement, les villages souterrains des pasteurs de Beershéva, dans le sud d'Israel, au IVe millénaire avant l'ère chrétienne. *Paléorient* 10/1, 75–96.

Perrot, J. (1987) Introduction. Pp. 15–18 in C. Commenge-Pellerin (ed.), *La poterie d'Abou Matar et de l'Ouadi Zoumeili (Beershéva) au IVe millénaire avant l'ère chrétienne.* Les Cahiers du centre de recherche Français de Jérusalem 3. Paris: Association Paléorient.

Perrot, J. (1990) Introduction. Pp. xi–xiii in C. Commenge-Pellerin (ed.), *La poterie de Safadi (Beershéva) au IVe millénaire avant l'ère chrétienne.* Les Cahiers du centre de recherche Français de Jérusalem 5. Paris: Association Paléorient.

Perrot, J. (1992) Umm Qatafa and Umm Qala'a: two 'Ghassulian' caves in the Judean Desert. *Eretz-Israel* 23, 100–11.

Plicht, J. van der and Bruins, H. J. (2001) Radiocarbon dating in Near-Eastern contexts: confusion and quality control. *Radiocarbon* 43/3, 1155–66.

Rosen, S. A. and Eldar, I. (1993) Horvat Beter revisited: the 1982 salvage excavations. *`Atiqot* 22, 13–27.

Scheftelowitz, N. and Oren, R. (2004) *Giv'at Ha-Oranim: A Chalcolithic Site near Nahal Beit Arif.* Salvage Excavation Reports 1. Tel Aviv: Sonia and Marco Nadler Institute of Archaeology, Tel Aviv University.

Segal, D. and Carmi, I. (1996) Rehovot radiocarbon date list V. *`Atiqot* 29, 79–106.

Segal, D. and Kamenski, A. (2002) Chalcolithic copper objects from cave VIII/28. *`Atiqot* 41/2, 157–61.

Segal, D. and Carmi, I., Galm, Z., Smithline, H. and Shalem, D. (1998) Dating a Chalcolithic burial cave in Peqi'in, Upper Galilee, Israel. *Radiocarbon* 40/2, 707–12.

Shalev, S. (1991) Two different copper industries in the Chalcolithic culture of Israel. Pp. 413–24 in J.-P. Mohen and C. Éluère (eds), *Découverte du Métal.* Paris: Picard.

Shalev, S. (1994) The change in metal production from the Chalcolithic period to the Early Bronze Age in Israel and Jordan. *Antiquity* 68, 630–7.

Shalev, S. (1995) Metals in ancient Israel: archaeological implications of chemical analysis. *Israel Journal of Chemistry* 35, 109–16.

Shalev, S. (1996) Metallurgical and metallographic studies. Pp. 155–63 in A. Gopher and T. Tsuk (eds), *The Nahal Qanah Cave: Earliest Gold in the Southern Levant.* Monograph Series of the Institute of Archaeology 12. Tel Aviv: Institute of Archaeology.

Shalev, S. (1999) Recasting the Nahal Mishmar hoard: experimental archaeology and metallurgy. Pp. 295–9 in A. Hauptmann, E. Pernicka, T. Rehren and U. Yalcin (eds), *The Beginnings of Metallurgy.* Der Anschnitt, Beiheft 9. Bochum: Dt. Bergbau-Museum.

Shalev, S. and Northover, P. J. (1987) Chalcolithic metal and metalworking from Shiqmim. Pp. 357–71 in T. E. Levy (ed.), *Shiqmim I: Studies Concerning Chalcolithic Societies in the Northern Negev Desert, Israel (1982–1984).* Oxford: BAR Int. Ser. 356.

Shalev, S. and Northover, P. J. (1993) The metallurgy of the Nahal Mishmar hoard reconsidered. *Archaeometry* 35, 35–47.

Shalev, S., Goren, Y., Levy, T. E. and Northover, P. J. (1992) A Chalcolithic mace head from the Negev, Israel: technological aspects and cultural implications. *Archaeometry* 34/1, 63–71.

Shugar, A. N. (2000) Archaeometallurgical Investigation of the Chalcolithic Site of Abu Matar, Israel: A Reassessment of Technology and its Implications for the Ghassulian Culture. Unpublished PhD thesis, Institute of Archaeology, University College London.

Stuiver, M. and Reimer, P. J. (1993) Extended ^{14}C data base and revised CALIB 3.0 14C age calibration program. *Radiocarbon* 35.1, 215–30.

Tadmor, M. (1989) The Judean desert treasure from Nahal Mishmar: a Chalcolithic traders' hoard? Pp. 249–62 in J. Albert Leonard and B. B. Williams (eds), *Essays in Ancient Civilization Presented to Helene J. Kantor.* Chicago, MI: Oriental Institute of the University of Chicago.

Tadmor, M., Kedem, D., Begemann, F., Hauptmann, A., Pernicka, E. and Schmitt-Strecker, S. (1995) The Nahal Mishmar hoard from the Judean desert: technology, composition, and provenance. *`Atiqot* 27, 95–148.

Tylecote, R. F. (1991) Early copper base alloys; natural or man-made. Pp. 213–22 in C. Eluere and J.-P. Mohen (eds), *Decouverte du Metal.* Paris: Picard.

Ussishkin, D. (1980) The Ghassulian shrine at En-Gedi. *Tel Aviv* 7, 1–44.

Weinstein, J. M. (1984) Radiocarbon dating in the southern Levant. *Radiocarbon* 26/3, 297–366.

11. Canaanean Blades in Chalcolithic Contexts of the Southern Levant?

Ianir Milevski, Peter Fabian and Ofer Marder

Introduction

In keeping with the theme of this volume – culture, chronology and the Chalcolithic of the southern Levant (Lovell and Rowan, this volume) – in this paper we confront the problematic aspects of 'type fossils': that is, the static ascription of particular artefact types to precise chronological or socio-cultural frameworks. Our particular concern is with the probable Chalcolithic origins of a distinctive techno-typological artefact: the Canaanean blade.

It is widely accepted that Canaanean blades are a hallmark of the Early Bronze Age (henceforth EBA) in the southern Levant (Rosen 1997, 46–65). The EBA is distinguished from the Chalcolithic in terms of modes of production and different regional entities (de Miroschedji 1986; Braun 1996), which we describe as different archaeological cultures (*i.e.* systems of settings of artefacts and settlements in a discrete region and time) (Trigger 1989, 156ff; Gilead, this volume). Therefore, this case study not only involves traditional typological definitions, but also addresses the character of transitions both in chronological and technological terms.

Transitions

The transition between the final phase of the Chalcolithic, often termed the Ghassulian/Beer Sheva culture (4400–3800/3600 BC) and the Early Bronze I (3600–2900 BC) has been a subject of archaeological research for some time (*e.g.*, Kenyon 1965, 54ff; Perrot 1968, 439). In spite of the fact that these periods are recognized as separate entities, some scholars advocated continuity in aspects of the material culture (*e.g.*, Amiran 1977, 54–6; 1992) while others have emphasized the differences between the periods (*e.g.*, Hanbury-Tenison 1986, 102–3; Gophna 1995, 269–72). Joffe *et al.* (2001, 9) emphasize that the Chalcolithic completes a long tradition and trajectory that began in the Palaeolithic and is replaced by the EB I and thus a line must be drawn between both periods. Gilead (1993) argues for significant discontinuity between the Chalcolithic and the EB I on the basis of radiocarbon dates. On the other hand, Braun (1996) notes that, based on the material culture, the hiatus following the Chalcolithic is more pronounced in the north, while in the south the gap has considerably lessened in light of recent excavations (Gophna 2004). Nonetheless, the accepted wisdom of a considerable difference in material culture has prompted searches for a missing link (Braun 1989; this volume), while others have employed ethnography to examine the transition (*e.g.*, Gazit 2002). Some argue for 'transitional assemblages' that are, in fact, admixtures, as proof of a transitional period – for instance, the appearance of Chalcolithic and EB I finds altogether (see Golani 2004; Golani *et al.*, this volume).

Transitions have been defined in several ways: by 'transition' we mean the change from one state or form to another, but also the period when this change occurs. In structural-analytical archaeology terms a transition is 'the change that occurs when an attribute, entity or vector is acted upon some factor' (Clarke 1978, 495). Unless we are dealing with clear historical discontinuities, the first and final states will be different, but will contain some similar, continuous elements – that is, elements in the later state borrowed from the earlier. This process can be seen as the opposite of a revolution (*i.e.*, the replacement of a socio-economic formation, a change of a cultural entity or the overthrow of a regime and its replacement with another) (*cf.* Bar-Yosef 2005). However, most transitions result in changes that can be clearly perceived as breaks in historical continuities. These transitions bear the contradictions between the socio-economic forces of the earlier and the later entities or socio-cultural frameworks (Hodder 1989, 57–60, 80).

The transition between different historical periods has

been the subject of numerous studies (*e.g.*, Anderson 1996; Weber 1976). Even in very early phases of prehistory, where processes occurred very slowly, transitions can be observed (*e.g.*, Hovers and Kuhn 2006). There are transitions that are the result of a gradual local transformation, called by Belfer-Cohen and Goring-Morris (2003, 278) '*in situ* transitions'. By contrast, *abrupt transitions* may result from external factors, such as the Hellenistic conquest and colonization of Asia, which led to new social, economic and technological developments in the Near East (*e.g.*, Preaux 1978; Briant 1987), or the conquest and colonization of America by the Spanish empire, which pushed new social, economic and technological developments (*e.g.*, Peña 1970). In our case, the transition concerns two chrono-typological late prehistoric entities in the same territory (Figure 1.1). Both entities constitute different socio-economic formations, but the precise character of the continuities and disjunctures between both periods is the key to understanding the transition between them.

Canaanean blades as a case study

Here we present a case study focused upon the nature of the flint assemblages and we specifically address the occurrence of Canaanean blades in Chalcolithic contexts. Previous discussions of flint technology and transfers of technology across the Chalcolithic–EBA transition have focused upon tabular scrapers (Rosen 1983c; 1997, 71–80), but other flint types see changes; examples include the technique of sickle blade manufacture (Rosen 1997, 44–50). Chalcolithic blades are relatively short and thin in comparison with Canaanean blades, with variable cross sections (generally triangular in shape) and without regularity on the ridges. Fine denticulation is common on one of the working edges. During the Chalcolithic, backing and truncation is usually abrupt (Figure 11.1.1–8) (Hermon 2003, 273–4). In the Beer Sheva region the raw material consists of flint wadi pebbles derived primarily from Judean Cenomanian-Turonion or Senonian-Eocene varieties, originating with different sources through the wadis (Gilead *et al.* 1995, 226; Gilead *et al.* 2004, 252; Rowan 2006, 509) (Figure 11.1.9). In this region, one of the most commonly used materials for blade production is the pebble-banded flint. In the hill country and the Shephelah most of the raw materials, brecciated flint or semi-translucent chalcedony, are local (Hermon 2003).

Canaanean blades are the result of a specialized blade technology. Some decades ago, Neuville (1930) was the first define this technology, while Rosen (1983a; 1983b; 1997, 46–60) provided the first in-depth study of its typological characteristics and distribution. A preliminary technological study of cores from Har Haruvim (Figure 1.1) was conducted by Shimelmitz *et al.* (2000). Canaanean technology is prismatic and intended for blade production. Cores are large single platform blocks worked on one to three faces, some of them with cortex (Figure 11.2) and the raw material is generally restricted to fine-grained Eocene nodules, even though coarse-grained blades were also found. The most common tool produced from Canaanean blades (Figure 11.3) is the Canaanean sickle segment, but there are also retouched blades, plain blades and other tools on Canaanean blanks. For the sake of unity we will refer to all Canaanean blades as one category.

The technology of Canaanean blades is therefore completely different to Chalcolithic blade technology, although backing appears in a few cases (Rosen 1997, 48; Zbenovich 2004, 70). Furthermore, the entire system of raw material procurement, production and distribution of Canaanean blades differs, including the core sources and multiple stages of blade distribution (see Milevski 2005, 110–42). It seems that during the EBA full-time specialists/craftspeople were responsible for Canaanean blade production, while in the Chalcolithic period specialists produced sickle blades on only a part-time basis (Gilead *et al.* 2004; Winter 2006). This has important implications: it seems that Canaanean blades and sickle blades were frequently used as burial offerings, which is indicative of their significant value within EBA society; by contrast, Chalcolithic sickle blades were not used for this purpose (Marder 2005).

A number of suggestions regarding Canaanean blades in Chalcolithic contexts, including examples from Gilat (Rowan and Levy 1994; *cf.* Rowan 2006), Shoham (North) (van den Brink and Gophna 2005), and Gat Guvrin (Nahal Komem) (Khalaily and Hermon 1998; forthcoming), have appeared in recent years. In addition we will add Horvat Qarqar (South), recently excavated by P. Fabian, and the site of Afridar, Area E (Golani 2004), where the mixture of Chalcolithic and EB I remains, including Canaanean blades, has been utilized to create a transitional Chalcolithic/EB I phase or to pre-date the EB I.

These examples may represent the final phase of the Chalcolithic, given that transitional examples would be likely. In this paper three possibilities are suggested to explain the phenomenon of Canaanean blades within Chalcolithic contexts (Figure 11.4):

1) Canaanean blades are an integral part of the Chalcolithic assemblages. If this is true we are dealing with a transitional case where elements considered the hallmark of one culture or period (EBA) appear in the previous culture (Chalcolithic). In this case there should be an intersection in the material culture of the final phase of the Beer Sheva/Ghassulian culture and the material culture of the beginning of the EB I.
2) The appearance of the Canaanean blades within Chalcolithic (Beer Sheva/Ghassulian culture) contexts is the result of post-depositional and/or site formation processes occurring at multi-period deposits.
3) Canaanean blades appear at the end of the Chalcolithic (a late stage of the Beer Sheva/Ghassulian culture) as sporadic finds within well-defined contexts, potentially within a limited region (in this case, the central-southern region).

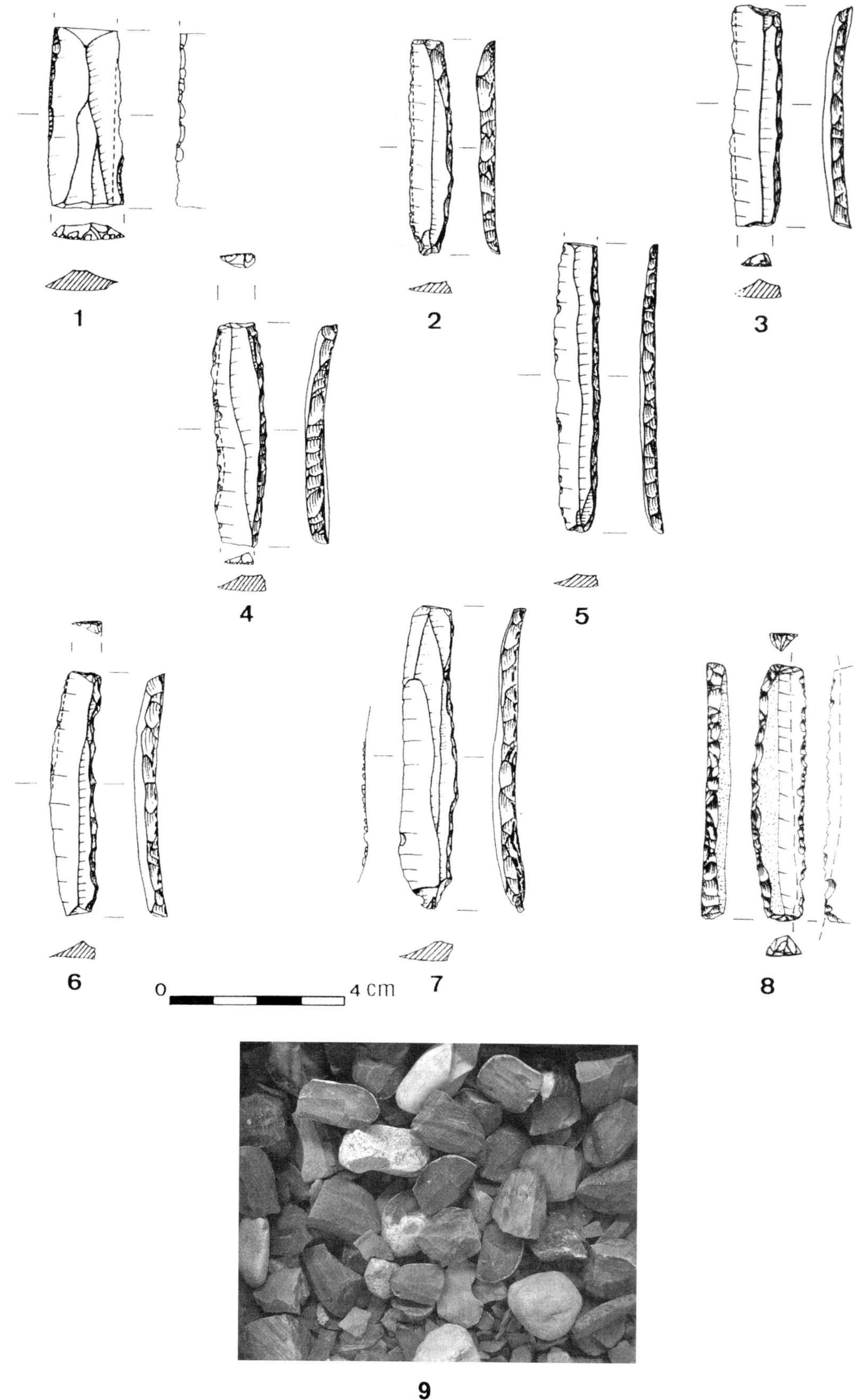

Figure 11.1 Chalcolithic blades (1–8) and cores (9). 1–7: Grar (after Gilead et al. *1995, fig. 5.18). 8: Shoham (N) (after Marder 2005, fig. 10.4.8). 9: Beit Eshel blade cores and limestone pebbles (after Gilead* et al. *2004, fig. 7)*

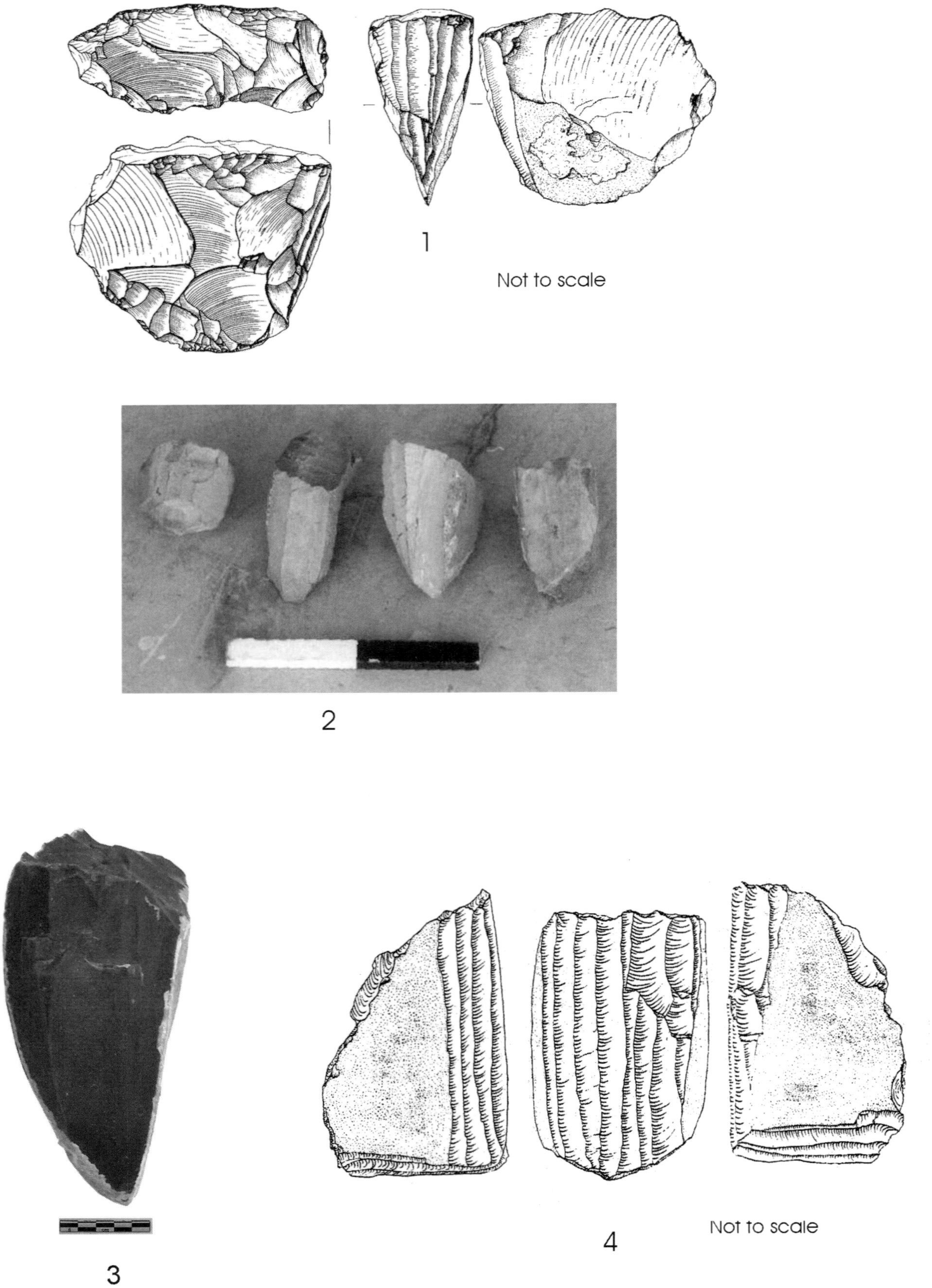

1

Not to scale

2

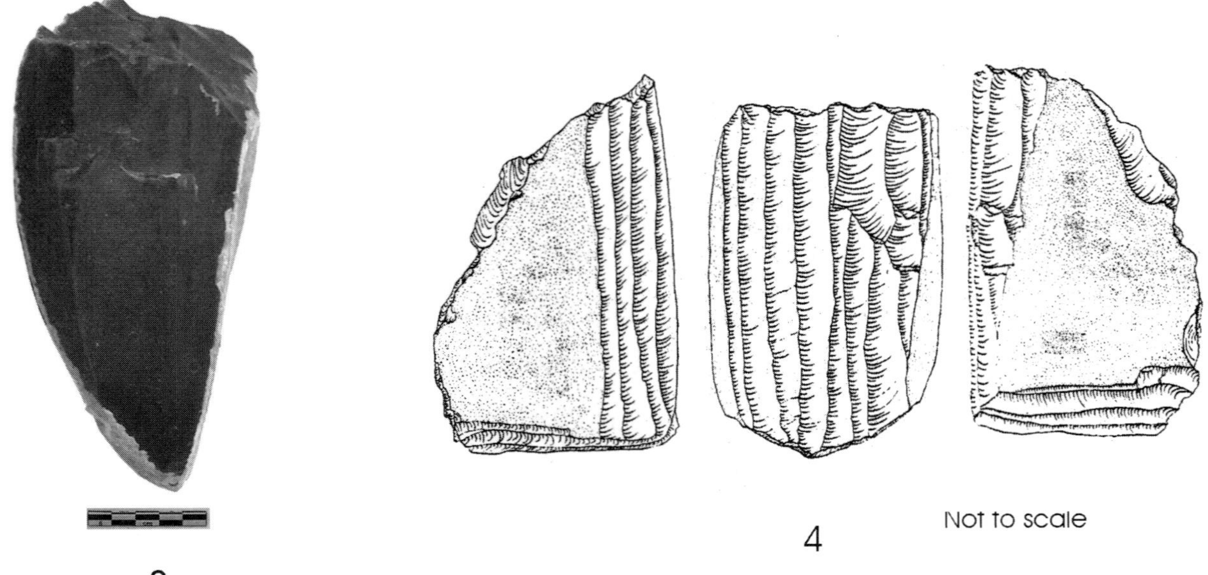

Not to scale

4

3

Figure 11.2 Canaanean cores. 1: Har Haruvim (after Shimelmitz et al. *2000, fig. 3). 2: Har Haruvim (courtesy of the Ramat Hashofet Museum). 3: Fazael (courtesy of the IAA). 5: Tel Halif (after Futato 1996, fig. 4.3)*

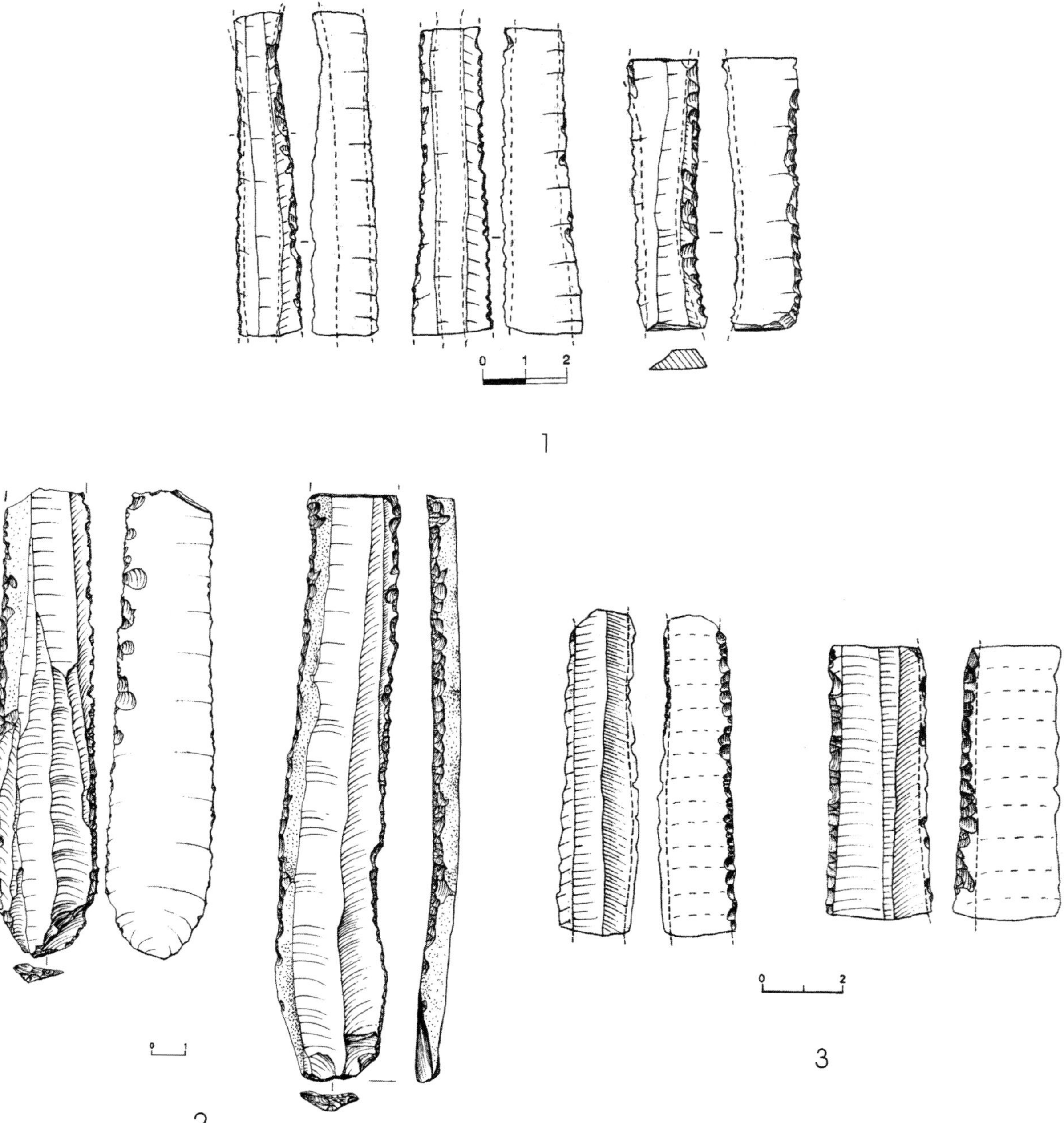

Figure 11.3 Canaanean blades. 1: Canaanean sickle blades from Horvat Illin Tahtit (after Marder et al. *1995, fig. 8.5–7). 2: Canaanean retouched blades from Afridar, Area J (after Zebenovich 2004, fig. 7). 3: Canaanean sickle blades from Arad, stratum III (after Schick 1978, Pl. 85: 6–7.9)*

Case studies

In order to examine the above possibilities, we will briefly present the cases of Horvat Qarqar, Gilat, the Cave of the Warrior, Gat Guvrin, Shoham and Ashkelon Afridar (in chronological order) below.

Horvat Qarqar

The Chalcolithic cemetery of Horvat Qarqar (South) was excavated recently by P. Fabian as a salvage project of the Israel Antiquities Authority (IAA) (Permit A-4635/2006); it is located 4 km south of Nahal Lachish (Figure 1.1). The cemetery includes at least 20 burial caves, 2 of which contained Canaanean blades. Cave 4 includes two burial phases: both phases contained pottery considered 'Ghassulian', while the later phase contains later Chalcolithic burial vessels. On the upper floor of this later phase, one Canaanean blade (Figure 11.5.1) segment was

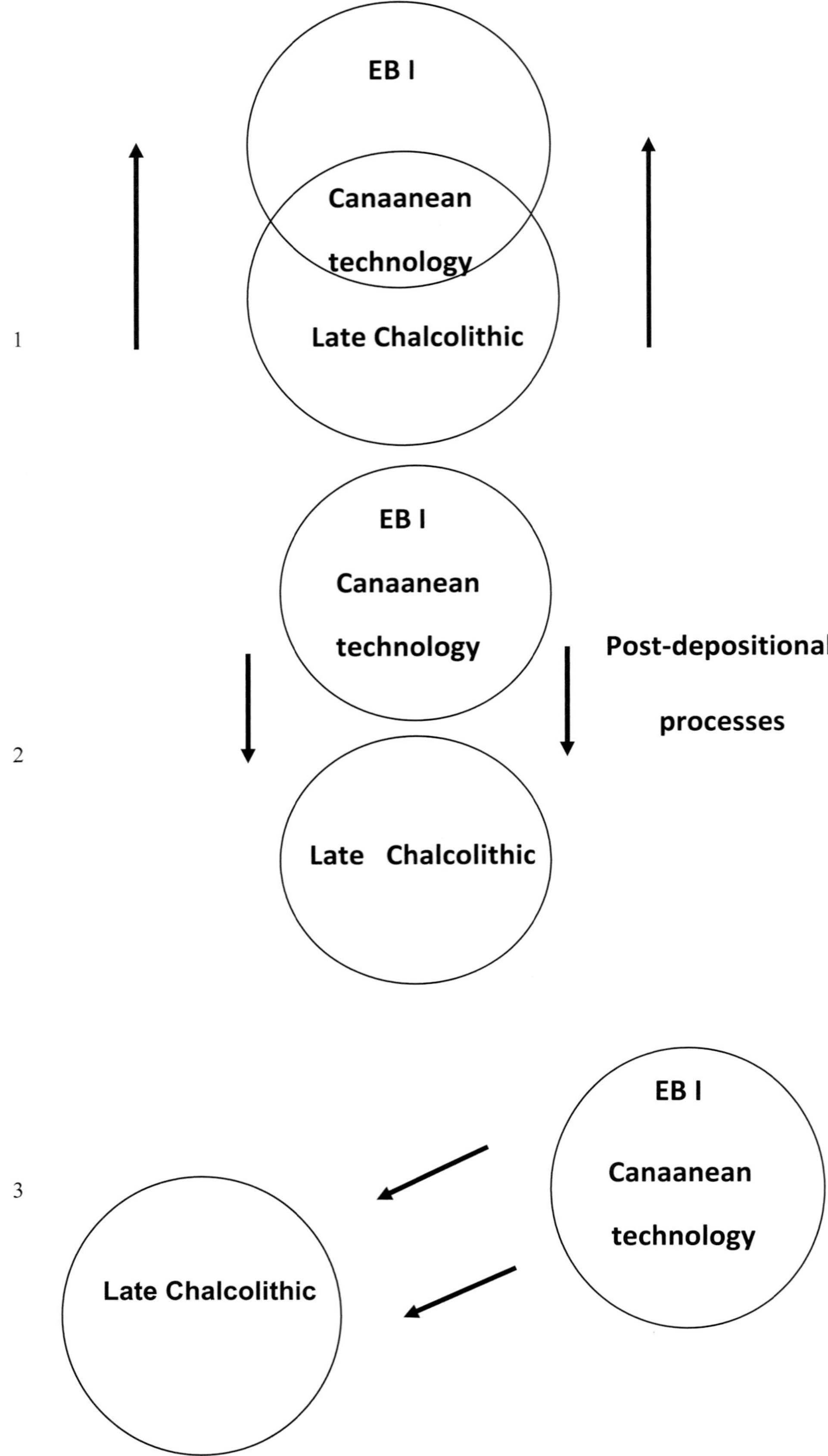

Figure 11.4 The appearance of Canaanean blades within Chalcolithic contexts

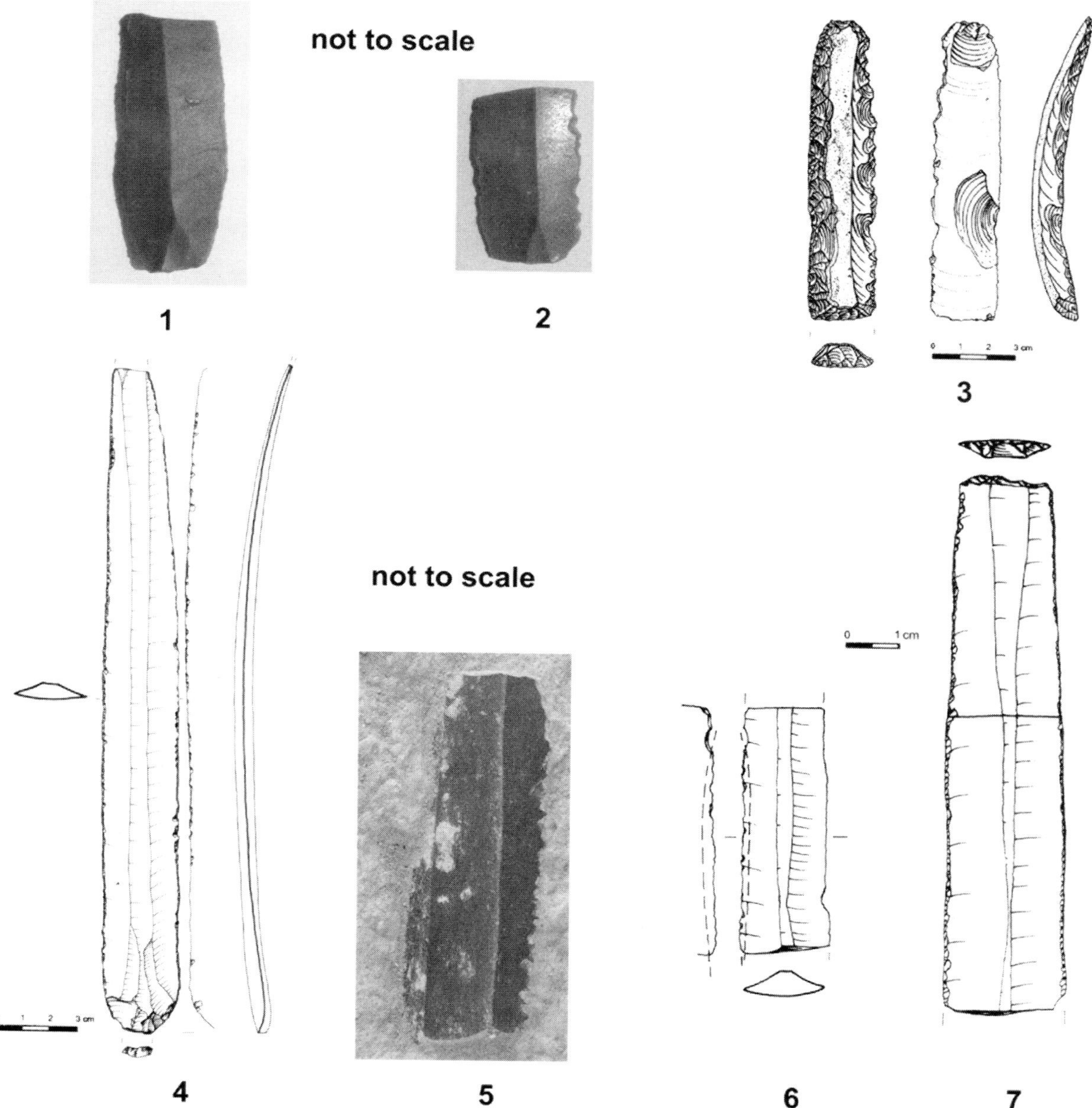

Figure 11.5 Canaanean and prismatic blades.1–2: Horvat Qarqar (South) (courtesy of IAA). 3: Gilat (after Rowan 2006, fig. 11.13:3). 4: Cave of the Warrior (after Oshri and Schick 1998, fig. 12.2). 5: Gat Guvrin (courtesy of the IAA). 6–7: Shoham (North) (after Marder 2005, fig. 10.4: 1–2)

found (Locus 413). In the other cave, Cave 10, a Canaanean sickle blade (Figure 11.5.2) was found on the floor (Locus 1001). These blades were apparently deposited with the burials but, because the caves remained open after the burial, we cannot rule out the possibility that the blades were deposited at some point after the Chalcolithic – that is, during the EBA. For instance, at Mazor West (Milevski 2007) a cache of Canaanean blades was found in Cave B2. In this cave the main remains are dated to the Chalcolithic although some EB I pottery was also found. Given that the research at Horvat Qarqar (South) is in a preliminary stage it is possible that the segments are intrusive.

Gilat

The well-known Chalcolithic site of Gilat, located on the northern bank of Nahal Zoumeili in the northern Negev (Figure 1.1) and interpreted as a sanctuary by the excavators (Alon and Levy 1989; Levy 2006), produced lithics relevant to our discussion. It was clear that the site was not occupied during the EBA in any of the four strata (Levy 2006). The earliest stratum (IV) begins in the Chalcolithic; Stratum I is represented by disturbed topsoil with a rich assemblage of Chalcolithic artefacts and occasional artefacts from modern periods (Levy 2006, 139). Most of the radiocarbon dates (Levy 2006, table 5.3) fall between 4900 and 4000 cal BC; however, some of them (*e.g.*, RT-2058) fall into the EB I. The relevant sample was obtained from Stratum IIC and seems to be intrusive. It must be stressed that no EBA pottery was reported.

Blades found at Gilat in the 1987 and 1990–1 seasons were published as 'proto-Canaanean' (Rowan and Levy 1994) (Figure 11.5.3). To these additional blades were added in the 1992 season (Rowan 2006). Following a re-examination (Rowan 2006, 514–51), the 'proto-Canaanean' segments were clearly described as prismatic. As noted by Rowan (2006), the prismatic blades from Gilat were not used as sickle blades but for some other function, although a few have polish or sickle sheen. It is clear that, while the blades under discussion differ from the typical Chalcolithic blades, they are not Canaanean blades.

Cave of the Warrior

A cave located in the lower part of Wadi el-Makkukh was discovered during a survey of rock shelters in the area (Figure 1.1). Excavation revealed a burial dated via associated artefacts to the 4th millennium BC (Schick 1998). In light of the fact that pottery was not found, the author (Schick 1998) did not assign this cave, which was termed the 'Cave of the Warrior', to the Chalcolithic or to the EBA. Together with osteological remains, textiles, basketry, sandals, weapons and other objects, a long Canaanean blade (Figure 11.5.4) was found in association with the burial (Oshri and Schick 1998). The only chronological indicator for the Canaanean blade is the ^{14}C date of the reed mat and other artefacts associated with the blade. While the calibrated age range of the objects in the burial corresponds to 3912–3777 BC, the reed mat is dated to 3764–3645 cal BC (Jull *et al.* 1998). This last date represents the very end of the Chalcolithic or the beginning of the EB I.

Gat Guvrin

The site of Gat Guvrin, located in the coastal plain (Figure 1.1), was excavated over several seasons by J. Perrot (1961), H. Khalaily (Khalaily and Hermon 1998; forthcoming) and P. Fabian of the IAA (Permit A-4432/2005). One of the excavators (H. Khalaily) has argued that some of the Canaanean blades, found in pits together with Chalcolithic pottery, are backed. This has been argued to be proof of a Chalcolithic–EB I transitional form (Khalaily and Hermon 1998; forthcoming). While the Canaanean cores, blades and debitage are made of high-quality Eocene flint, the typical Chalcolithic backed blades found at Gat Guvrin (Figure 11.5.5) are made of local flint encountered in cobbles and a flint that originated in the northern Negev.

The new excavations by P. Fabian, and the previous information from Perrot's excavations, indicate that the upper layers of the site, dated to the EB I, have been largely destroyed by post-depositional activities such as deep ploughing or mole-rat burrowing. Most of the Canaanean blades appear in the upper part of the Chalcolithic contexts and are hardly present in the lower contexts. In both Perrot's and Fabian's excavations pottery sherds dated to the EB I were found in the upper phases of the excavation and in EBA pits that cut into the Chalcolithic layers. It seems that pits dated early in the Chalcolithic did not contain any Canaanean blades, and Canaanean cores were found only in the topsoil.

Shoham (North)

At Shoham (North) four caves were excavated within a salvage project of the IAA in the Ayalon basin (Figure 1.1) (van den Brink and Gophna 2005). A group of Canaanean blades (*e.g.*, Figure 11.5.6–7) were found within a Chalcolithic context radiocarbon dated to *c.*4000 cal BC in Cave 4 (van den Brink and Gophna 2005, 21–5). In addition, Chalcolithic sickle blade segments were found (*e.g.*, Figure 11.1.8). It must stressed that an EB I layer exists in the cave; the authors describe some pits dated to the EB I as cutting the Chalcolithic layer. Although the excavators did not definitively argue that the Canaanean blades were Chalcolithic, they suggested that an association with the early layer was a possibility (van den Brink and Gophna 2005, 170). However, it seems most probable that the Canaanean blades do not belong to the Chalcolithic layer, but were deposited after the Chalcolithic use of the cave (Marder 2005, 147).

Ashkelon/Afridar

Salvage excavations in the marina of Ashkelon Afridar Area E (Figure 1.1) were conducted over four seasons: the first season was directed by Z. Wallach (unpublished, Permit A-2139/1994), the second, third and fourth seasons by A. Golani, and the third season by A. Golani and I. Milevski (Golani and Milevski 1997; Golani 2004).

For the most part the remains are dated to the first half of the 4th millennium BC, with later occupation dated to the Late Roman, the Byzantine and the Islamic periods. The primary features exposed were pits containing ancient refuse and abundant objects associated with metallurgical activities. The central component of the finds, including pottery, Canaanean blades and other flint artefacts and stone tools, and the date of the site were assigned to the EB I (Golani 2004). Utilizing radiocarbon dates of samples found within the refuse pits, Golani (2004) concluded that the EB I must be re-dated to an earlier period, or that the site represented a 'transitional phase' between the Chalcolithic and the EB I (Golani 2004, 46–8). Some of the dates belong to the end of the Chalcolithic (*i.e.*, they are in the range of 4000–3700 years cal BC) and others belong to the beginning of the EB I (in the range of 3700–3500 years cal BC) (Segal and Carmi 2004). Unfortunately, the final report does not significantly address the fact that the pits contained early EB I artefacts as well as numerous Chalcolithic finds, including pottery (Golani

2004, 39–42), flint tools (Zbenovich 2004, 65–6) and basalt bowls (Rowan 2004, 88–94). Furthermore, at all the adjacent sites at Ashkelon, Afridar, Areas F, G and J (Khalaily 2004, Braun 2004, Baumgarten 2004) show clear Chalcolithic cultural material finds different from the EB I material (pottery, flints, basalt vessels). It would appear that of Area E do not represent a 'transitional phase' (nor do they provide evidence for an earlier dating of the EB I, and thus an earlier date for the Canaanean blade), but the mixture of at least two different assemblages in refuse pits that contained artefacts that were in use for centuries (*contra* Golani 2004, 46–8).

Discussion

There remains a possibility that Canaanean blades appear at the very end of the Chalcolithic as sporadic finds within well-defined contexts in the centre of the country (possibility 3 in Figure 11.4). Given the current data, however, we argue that the appearance of the Canaanean blades within Chalcolithic contexts is most likely to be the result of post-depositional processes – that is, the blades are intrusive in those contexts (possibility 2 in Figure 11.4). It seems that in most of the sites (*e.g.*, Gat Guvrin, Shoham (North)) post-depositional activities influenced the interpretation of the finds. In the case of Gilat it is now clear that the prismatic blades are not Canaanean blades; the example from the 'Cave of the Warrior' must thus be considered one of the earliest Canaanean blades.

Canaanean blade technology, which includes raw material procurement, production and distribution, was part of a different tradition to that of Chalcolithic blade production (Rosen 1997, 44–50; Milevski 2005, 110–42), and the main Chalcolithic settlement sites of the Negev do not contain Canaanean blades or Canaanean cores, or even Eocene raw material. Additionally, in the Chalcolithic sites of the Golan and the Galilee no Canaanean blades were found as integral parts of Chalcolithic assemblages (Noy 1998). Moreover, we might expect that if Canaanean technology was part of Chalcolithic material culture we would find some 'hybrid' forms within the Chalcolithic industry, such as Canaanean sickle blades produced by Chalcolithic blade technology or short irregular Chalcolithic blank blades produced by Canaanean technology. As far as we know, there are no such examples within the assemblages discussed above.

Canaanean blades which appear with Chalcolithic artefacts may come from sites that lie on the transition between both entities at around 3600 BC in a limited region of the southern Levant. It appears that the phenomenon of the contact between the last Chalcolithic sites and Canaanean technology, if it existed, was restricted to a certain region which includes the centre-south of the country at sites dated to the very end of the Chalcolithic and the beginning of the EB I. If Chalcolithic communities continued to exist at this point they may have acquired the Canaanean blades from the EBA producers. The possibility that Canaanean blades occurred *in situ* within Chalcolithic mortuary contexts may highlight the social value of the new Canaanean technology. The reason for Canaanean blades appearing in tombs during the end of the Chalcolithic might, then, be related not only to the utilitarian aspect of the new blades (being better than the old Chalcolithic blades) but to their prestige value as luxury goods (*cf.* Levy 1995, 240–1).

The possibility that Canaanean blades may be found in Chalcolithic deposits introduces new questions regarding the disintegration of the Chalcolithic culture and the onset of the EB I. The EBA communities certainly acquired some techniques from the previous period, including backing of Canaanean blades and the exploitation of tabular flint for the production of scrapers. Continuity from the Chalcolithic to the EB I in basalt vessel production is also evident, although there is a clear change in style and probably function(s) in several types of vessels (Braun 1990; Rowan 1998).

In order to define the relationship between the Chalcolithic and the EB I in relation to Canaanean blades in particular, we require more extensive and well-stratified excavations, together with meticulous site formation analyses. At this stage it is clear that the technology and the economic system related to the production of Canaanean blades was not directly borrowed from Chalcolithic blade production. Until Canaanean blades are found in single-period Chalcolithic deposits (and preferably not caves), the question remains unsolved (van den Brink and Gophna 2005, 170), but the possibilities are intriguing and careful and open-minded investigation of the transition itself may provide new avenues for research.

Acknowledgements

The authors wish to thank Isaac Gilead, Hamoudi Khalaily, Thomas E. Levy, Yorke M. Rowan and the Centre de Recherche Français de Jerusalem for permitting us to utilize unpublished and published information from their excavations. Special thanks are owed to Isaac Gilead, Steve Rosen and Jaimie L. Lovell for offering valuable comments on a first draft of this paper. Yorke M. Rowan and Jaimie L. Lovell helped with the English editing of the text.

Additional note

While this paper was in press, new data for Canaanean blades from Chalcolithic Fazael 2 were published (Bar and Winter 2010). Fazael 2 is located in the Jordan Valley, 200 m from Fazael 5 and 500 m from Fazael 4, both EB I sites (Bar 2008, 321–9). Fazael 2 has three strata, 2 and 3 are dated to the Chalcoltithic Ghassulian period. The Canaanean finds include blades and blade cores, mainly from Stratum 2, ca. 30 cm below top soil, Stratum 1 (Bar and Winter 2010, fig. 7.2.6). The radiocarbon dates are in the range of 4,000 cal BC, characteristic of the middle part of the Ghassulian, not the end of this period, as the excavator's claim (Bar and Winter 2010, 35, fig. 2). Fazael is located on Eocene sources and it is highly likely that a workshop or workshops existed at the site. Canaanean cores were found in the area dispersed on topsoil (Milevski 2005, 105–6, fig. 10:3). We are cautious about ascribing the Canaanean finds from Fazael 2 to the Chalcolithic, and suggest that they may be the result of EB I activity in open spaces between the different house agglomerations.

References

Alon, D. and Levy, T. E. (1989) The archeology of cult and the Chalcolithic sanctuary at Gilat. *Journal of Mediterranean Archaeology* 2, 163–221.

Amiran, R. (1977) Pottery from the Chalcolithic site near Tell Delhamiya and some notes on the character of the Chalcolithic–Early Bronze I transition. *Eretz-Israel* 13, 48–56 (Hebrew with English summary).

Amiran, R. (1992) The development of the cult stand from the Chalcolithic period through the Early Bronze I, II and III periods. *Eretz-Israel* 23, 72–5 (Hebrew with English summary).

Anderson, P. (1996) *Passages from Antiquity to Feudalism*. New York: W. W. Norton.

Bar, S. (2008) The Pattern of Settlement in the Lower Jordan Valley and the Sesert Firnges of Samaria during the Late Chalcolithic Period and Early Bronze Age 1. Unpublished PhD Thesis, Haifa University.

Bar, S. and Winter, H. (2010) Canaanean flint blades in Chalcolithic context and the possible onset of the transition to the Early Bronze Age: A case study from Fazael 2. *Tel Aviv* 37, 33–47.

Bar-Yosef, O. (2005) On the nature of transitions and revolutions in prehistory. *Mitekufat Haeven. Journal of the Israel Prehistoric Society* 35, 469–83.

Baumgarten, Y. (2004) An Excavation at Asqelon, Afridar – Area J. *`Atiqot* 45, 161–184.

Belfer-Cohen, A. and Goring-Morris, A. N. (2003) Final remarks and epilogue. Pp. 274–80 in A. N. Goring-Morris and A. Belfer-Cohen (eds), *More than Meets the Eye. Studies on Upper Palaeollithic Diversity in the Near East*. Oxford: Oxbow Books.

Braun, E. (1989) The transition from the Chalcolithic to the Early Bronze Age in northern Israel and Transjordan. Is there a missing link? Pp. 7–28 in P. de Miroschedji (ed.), *L'urbanisation de la Palestine à l'âge du Bronze ancien. Bilan et perspectives des recherches actuelles*. Oxford: BAR Int. Ser. 527i.

Braun, E. (1990) Basalt bowls of the EBI horizon in the southern Levant. *Paléorient* 16, 87–95.

Braun, E. (1996) Cultural Diversity and Change in the Early Bronze I of Israel and Jordan. Unpublished PhD thesis, Tel Aviv University.

Braun, E. (2004) *Early Beth Shan (Strata XIX–XIII). G. M. FitzGerald's Deep Cut on the Tell.* University Museum Monograph 121. Philadelphia, PA: University of Pennsylvania Museum of Archaeology and Anthropology.

Briant, P. (1987) *De la Grece à l'Orient: Alexandre le Grand.* Paris: Gallimard.

Brink, E. C. M. van den and Gophna, R. (2005) *Shoham (North). Late Chalcolithic Burial Caves in the Lod Valley, Israel.* Israel Antiquities Authority Reports 27. Jerusalem.

Bunimovitz, S. (2001) Chronological separation, geographical segregation, or ethnic demarcation? Ethnography and the Iron Age low chronology. *Bulletin of the American Schools of Oriental Research* 322, 1–10.

Clarke, D. L. (1978) *Analytical Archaeology.* New York: Columbia University Press.

Futato, E. M. (1996) Early Bronze III Canaanean Blade/Scraper Cores from Tell Halif, Israel. Pp. 61–74 in J. D. Seger (ed.), *Retrieving the Past. Essays on Archaeological Research and Methodology in Honor of Gus W. Van Beek*. Winona Lake, IN: Eisenbrauns.

Gazit, D. (2002) The transition from the Chalcolithic period to the Early Bronze Age: an analogy to a known historical situation. Pp. 155–8 in E. C. M. van den Brink and E. Yannai (eds), *In Quest of Ancient Settlements and Landscapes. Archaeological Studies in Honour of Ram Gophna*. Tel Aviv: Ramot Publishing.

Gilead, I. (1993) Sociopolitical organization in the northern Negev at the end of the Chalcolithic. Pp. 82–97 in A. Biran and J. Aviram, *Biblical Archaeology Today 1990. Pre-Congress Symposium: Population, Production and Power*. Proceedings of the Second International Congress on Biblical Archaeology, Jerusalem, 1990. Jerusalem: Israel Exploration Society.

Gilead, I., Hershman, D. and Marder, O. (1995) The flint assemblages from Grar. Pp. 223–80 in I. Gilead (ed.), *Grar: A Chalcolithic Site in the Northern Negev.* Beer-Sheva VIII. Beersheva: Ben-Gurion University of the Negev.

Gilead, I., Marder, O., Khalaily, H., Fabian, P., Abadi, Y. and Yisrael, Y. (2004) The Beit Eshel Chalcolithic flint workshop in Beer Sheva: a preliminary report. *Mitekufat Haeven. Journal of the Israel Prehistoric Society* 34, 245–63.

Golani, A. (2004) Salvage excavations at the Early Bronxe Age site of Ashqelon, Afridar – Area E. *`Atiqot* 45, 9–62.

Golani, A. and Milevski, I. (1997) Ashqelon, Afridar (A). *Excavations and Surveys in Israel* 19, 83*.

Gophna, R. (1995) Early Bronze Age Canaan: some spatial and demographic observations. Pp. 269–80 in T. E. Levy (ed.), *The Archaeology of Society in the Holy Land.* London: Leicester University Press.

Gophna, R. (2004) Excavations at Ashqelon, Afridar – Introduction. *`Atiqot* 45, 1–8.

Hanbury-Tenison, J. W. (1986) *The Late Chalcolithic to Early Bronze I Transition in Palestine and Transjordan.* Oxford: BAR Int. Ser. 311.

Hermon, S. (2003) Socio-Economic Aspects of Chalcolithic (4500-3600 BC) Societies in the Southern Levant. Unpublished PhD thesis, Ben Gurion University of the Negev.

Hodder, I. (1989) *Reading the Past. Current Approaches to Interpretation in Archaeology*. Cambridge: Cambridge University Press.

Hovers, E. and Kuhn, S. L. (2006) *Transitions Before the Transition. Evolution and Stability in the Middle Paleolithic and Middle Stone Age*. New York: Springer.

Joffe, A. H., Dessel, J. P. and Hallote, R. (2001) The 'Gilat Woman': female iconography, Chalcolithic cult, and the end of southern Levantine prehistory. *Near Eastern Archaeology* 64, 9–23.

Jull, A. J. T., Donahue, D. J., Carmi, I. and Segal, D. (1998) Radiocarbon dating of finds. Pp. 110–11 in T. Schick, *The Cave of the Warrior. A 4th millennium Burial in the Judean Desert*. Israel Antiquites Authority Reports 5. Jerusalem.

Kenyon, K. M. (1965) *Archaeology in the Holy Land*. London: Benn.

Khalalily, H. (2004) An Early Bronze Age Site at Asqelon, Afridar – Area F. *`Atiqot* 45, 121–59.

Khalaily, H. (forthcoming) Excavations at Gat-Govrin (Nahal Komem): a late Chalcolithic site in the northern Negev. *`Atiqot*.

Khalaily, H. and Hermon, S. (1998) New excavations at Nahal Komem (Gat Guvrin). *Abstracts of the Israel Society of Prehistory Annual Meeting. December 1998*. Beersheva.

Levy, T. E. (1995) Cult, metallurgy and rank societies – Chalcolitithic period (ca. 4500–3500 BCE). Pp. 226–68 in T. E. Levy (ed.), *The Archaeology of Society in the Holy Land.* London: Leicester University Press.

Levy, T. E. (2006) *Archaeology, Anthropology and Cult. The Sanctuary at Gilat, Israel.* London: Equinox Publishing.

Marder, O. (2005) The flint assemblages. Pp. 141–8 in E. C. M. van den Brink and R. Gophna (eds), *Shoham (North). Late Chalcolithic Burial Caves in the Lod Valley, Israel.* Israel Antiquities Authority Reports 27. Jerusalem.

Marder, O., Braun, E. and Milevski, I. (1995) The flint assemblage of Lower Horvat `Illin: some technical and economnic considerations. *`Atiqot* 27, 63–93.

Milevski, I. (2005) Local Exchange in Early Bronze Age Canaan. Unpublished PhD thesis, Tel Aviv University.

Milevski, I. (2007) Mazor (West). *Hadashot Arkhelogiyot – Excavations and Surveys in Israel* 119. http://www.hadashot-esi.org.il/report_detail_eng.asp?id=571&mag_id=112 (accessed 20 January 2010).

Miroschedji, P. de (1986) Céramiques et mouvements de population: le cas de la Palestine au IIIe millénaire. Pp. 10–46 in M. Th. Barrelet and J. C. Gardin (eds), *A propos des interprétations archéologiques de la poterie: questions ouverte*. Memoire 64. Paris: Editions Recherche sur les Civilizations.

Neuville, R. (1930) Notes de préhistoire palestinienne. *Journal of the Palestine Oriental Society* 10, 193–221.

Noy, T. (1998) Flint artefacts. Pp. 269–332 in C. Epstein, *The Chalcolithic Culture of the Golan*. Israel Antiquities Authority Reports 4. Jerusalem.

Oshri, A. and Schick, T. (1998) The lithics. Pp. 59–62 in T. Schick, *The Cave of the Warrior. A 4th millennium Burial in the Judean Desert.* Israel Antiquities Authority Reports 5. Jerusalem.

Peña, M. (1970) *Antes de Mayo: formas sociales del trasplante español al Nuevo Mundo.* Buenos Aires: Fichas.

Perrot, J. (1961) Gat-Govrin. *Israel Exploration Journal* 11, 76.

Perrot, J. (1968) *La préhistoire palestinienne*. Supplément au Dictionnaire de la Bible. Paris: Gabalda.

Preaux, C. (1978) *Le monde hellénistique: la Grèce et l'Orient de la mort d'Alexandre à la conquête romaine de la Grèce (323–146 av. J.-C.).* Paris: Press Universitaires de France.

Rosen, S. A. (1983a) The Lithics in Bronze and Iron Ages in Israel. Unpublished PhD thesis, University of Chicago.

Rosen, S. A. (1983b) The Canaanean blade and the Early Bronze Age. *Israel Exploration Journal* 33, 15–29.

Rosen, S. A. (1983c) The tabular scraper trade: a model for material cultural dispersion. *Bulletin of the American School of Oriental Research* 249, 79–86.

Rosen, S. A. (1997) *Lithics After the Stone Age. A Handbook of Stone Tools from the Levant.* Walnut Creek, CA: AltaMira Press.

Rowan, Y. M. (1998) Ancient Distribution and Deposition of Prestige Objects: Basalt Vessels during Late Prehistory in the Southern Levant. Unpublished PhD thesis, University of Texas at Austin.

Rowan, Y. M. (2004) The ground stone assemblage from Ashqelon, Afridar – Area E. *`Atiqot* 45, 85–96.

Rowan, Y. M. (2006) The chipped stone assemblage at Gilat. Pp. 507–74 in T. E. Levy (ed.), *Archaeology, Anthropology and Cult. The Sanctuary at Gilat, Israel.* London: Equinox Publishing.

Rowan, Y. M. and Levy, T. E. (1994) Proto-Canaanean blades of the Chalcolithic period. *Levant* 26, 167–74.

Schick, T. (1978) Flint implements, Strata V–I. Pp. 58–64 in R. Amiran, U. Paran, Y. Shiloh, R. Brown, Y. Tsafrir and A. Ben-Tor, *Early Arad. The Chalcolithic Settlement and the Early Bronze City*. Jerusalem: Israel Exploration Society.

Schick, T. (1998) *The Cave of the Warrior. A 4th millennium Burial in the Judean Desert.* Israel Antiquities Authority Reports 5. Jerusalem.

Segal, D. and Carmi, I. (2004) Rehovot radiocarbon date list VI. *`Atiqot* 48, 123–48.

Shimelmitz, R., Barkai, R. and Gopher, A. (2000) A Canaanean blade workshop at Har Haruvim, Israel. *Tel Aviv* 27, 3–22.

Trigger, B. (1989) *A History of Archaeological Thought.* Cambridge: Cambridge University Press.

Weber, M. (1976) *The Protestant Ethic and Spirit of Capitalism.* London: George Allen and Unwin.

Winter, R. (2006) Stone Tool Production Areas in the Southern Levant during the Proto-Historic Periods: Definitions and Social Meaning. Unpublished MA dissertation, Ben-Gurion University of the Negev, Beersheva (Hebrew).

Zbenovich, V. (2004) The flint assemblage from Ashqelon, Afridar – Area E. *`Atiqot* 45, 63–84.

12. The Transition from Chalcolithic to Early Bronze I in the Southern Levant: A 'Lost Horizon' Slowly Revealed

Eliot Braun

Introduction

This paper considers as axiomatic that, beginning with the end of the Epipalaeolithic period, the well-watered zones of the southern Levant have been continuously populated by humans, *contra* Perrot's (1972, 404; 2001, 25) postulation of an '*hiatus palestinien*'. A corollary to this axiom is that never within that time span was the region devoid of sedentary human populations. It further proposes that these late prehistoric populations have been documented by abundant evidence within the archaeological record revealed to date, and that as archaeological exploration increases, so will evidence for them increase.

It follows that given constant human presence, no chrono-cultural unit recognized by archaeologists (*i.e.*, cultures, periods, phases, horizons, *etc.*) was devoid of contacts with those immediately preceding and succeeding it. Such arbitrarily defined units are constructs imposed onto the archaeological record in order to study one or more segments of a chronological continuum in human experience. Accordingly, this paper regards all populations living within the region, at least from the Epipalaeolithic period until the present, as having received and transferred some portion of a 'cultural burden'. It further maintains that such transmission is observable in material-culture artefacts unearthed within the archaeological record of the region.

Specifically, this work attempts to outline the existence of evidence that links the material culture of the Late Chalcolithic period (henceforth LC) with that of the Early Bronze I period (henceforth EB I). This evidence has tended to be ignored or minimized by scholars; indeed, the definitions of these periods as separate entities (LC and EB I), *ipso facto*, parochialize their attributes by arbitrarily defining their parameters to emphasize disparity.

Combined with a poor understanding of the internal sequences of the Chalcolithic and EB I horizons, differences perceived between the material-cultural manifestations of these chrono-cultural entities have been greatly magnified in earlier studies. In turn this has led to a kind of self-fulfilling prophecy: a selective, commonly shared perception of the archaeological record that confirms a particular view. As a young student I recall earnest discussion of such matters; while one serious scholar (Elliott 1978, 52) even suggested another virtual hiatus in occupation of the southern Levant between the LC and the EB I.

In order to redress what I understand to be an imbalance in comprehension of the archaeological record, this paper virtually ignores the existence of some truly great differences between the material cultures of the LC and the EB I and seeks to summarize information, much of which has only recently come to light, which indicates a far greater degree of continuity between these periods than has been hitherto perceived.

The transition from the LC to the EB I – a survey of scholarly opinion

Formerly, evidence of transmission of the cultural burden from the LC to the EB I eluded discernment because of profound lacunae in our knowledge of the archaeological record. Given the quantitative degree of systematic excavation that had taken place in many areas up until little more than a decade ago, it is not surprising that earlier generations of archaeologists perceived a thoroughgoing break in material culture between these periods, especially when it was emphasized by a major shift in settlement patterns, although few scholars seem to have agreed with Elliott's radical interpretation. A number of scholars' views on the subject of the transmission of the cultural burden are of particular interest.

The views of Kathleen Kenyon

Kenyon (1970, 82–3) was, understandably, given available information, somewhat vague about the idea of transition between the LC (her 'Upper Chalcolithic') and the EB I (her Proto-Urban). At one time she suggested that Chalcolithic peoples, whom she termed 'Ghassulians', were newcomers to the region, invaders bringing with them different traditions which they did not pass on, stating it thus:

> So far evidence of Ghassulian occupation has never been found in the lower levels of any of the sites which subsequently became a town. Their settlements seem simply to have died out. The recognizably Ghassulian forms of pottery and flint implements do not have their descendants in the forms of the Early Bronze Age. The origins of the town builders of the Early Bronze Age must be sought elsewhere. (Kenyon 1970, 82)

In a revised, posthumous version of her *Archaeology of the Holy Land*, Kenyon's (1979, 64–5) thesis that the Ghassulians were basically a group of 'self-centred' immigrants who 'penetrated' the region and mixed little with additional 'groups of diverse origin', whom she believed to be the indigenous descendants of inhabitants of Sha'ar Hagolan and Pottery Neolithic B Jericho, was reiterated. Those non-Ghassulian groups, she intimated, explained any evidence of cultural continuity which she apparently understood from the archaeological record.

Although the specific information that prompted Kenyon's recognition of continuity is unclear, I suspect it may lie particularly within the realm of ceramic typology and some rather compelling morphological parallels that exist between Late Neolithic ceramics and early EB I vessels (Braun 2004, 39–42), but which are not shared by normative LC pottery types. These typological similarities remain a conundrum, but at Jericho they led the excavator and her colleague (Kenyon and Holland 1983, xxxiii) to postulate what they perceived as a 'transitional phase between the PNB and PU periods' (PNB = Pottery Neolithic B; PU = Proto-Urban = early EB I), but which they deliberately avoided labelling Chalcolithic. Kenyon, rather understandably, could not well reconcile such a transition between these chrono-cultural entities, and her discussion of available ^{14}C dates left her with what she termed 'a nasty long period to fill' (Kenyon 1979, 64). She does not appear to have been cognizant of any real transfer of even part of the cultural burden from the LC to the early EB I in her interpretations.

The views of Roland de Vaux

In his overview of developments in the Neolithic and Chalcolithic periods, Roland de Vaux (1970) agreed with Kenyon as to the intrusive nature of the Chalcolithic culture, but, perhaps because of the time at which he wrote, he was far more firm in his characterization of the parochial nature of Chalcolithic culture, stating: 'The Ghassul-Beersheva culture, which made its appearance without any preliminaries, disappeared without any sequel' (de Vaux 1970, 529–32).

The views of Ruth Amiran

Amiran (1977) claimed evidence for a transition on the basis of interpretations of different aspects of material culture, intuitively inferring transition from a number of objects purportedly derived from the site of Delhamiyah on the banks of the Jordan River, not far south of the Sea of Galilee. In a later work (1985, 108) she stated:

> The essence of the thesis I shall attempt to prove in this paper is that the Early Bronze culture evolved from the Chalcolithic culture, there being no sharp break between the two periods, and that such a development does not exclude or does not conflict with the existence of clear diacritical features of each of these two cultures.

However, her ideas appear to be based on an assumption that the EB I was a rather short period, a view no longer tenable (Braun 2001b) and which virtually negates the reasoning behind her thesis. Indeed, lacking much information on the internal chronology of the EB I, she (1969, 35–57) seems to have virtually ignored it when dealing with this subject, probably because most of the pottery then known was derived from mortuary contexts that yielded no reliable chronological information.

One example of Amiran's idea of transition was supposedly in LC to EB I occupation sequences, particularly at such sites as Tel Kitan and Small Tel Malhata. In both those instances the EB I sites date to considerably advanced phases of the period (Tel Kitan probably dates to the very end of the EB I, *c.*3000 BC; Braun in press b), hundreds of years after all Chalcolithic occupation ceased. Amiran's additional suggestions of supposed evidence for an LC–EB I transition, based on foreign associations with the Uruk culture and Egypt, suffer from the same problem, a lack of chronological proximity.

Nevertheless, Amiran had a remarkable eye for form in artefacts and she was among the first to note continuity in ceramics and basalt bowl production. It would be interesting to examine a still unpublished jar from the site of Abu Hof, touted by her as heralding the body shape and incipient ledge handles of the EB I (Amiran 1985, 111). Similar evidence from other sites (see below) to no little extent verifies Amiran's claim for transition between the LC and the EB I.

The views of Jack Hanbury-Tenison

Hanbury-Tenison (1986, 117–18) hypothesized a 'Post-Ghassulian Chalcolithic' phase considered transitional from the LC to the EB I, but his short list of sites where it is claimed to have been observed remains less than convincing. His synthesis, based on the archaeological record of published and unpublished excavations could, however, martial only rather meagre evidence for such a period.

Hanbury-Tenison's claims for such a phase at Tell es-Shuna are apparently based on his understanding of de Contenson's (1960a; 1960b; 1961) and Mellaart's (1962) brief descriptions of soundings there, and possibly from viewing material from later excavations not yet or then only recently published (Gustavson-Gaube 1985; 1986). He also included Zeita/Gat Guvrin in his list, citing it as the 'perfect transitional site' based on his understanding of a surface collection and a ceramic assemblage from excavations (pers. comm.) at a then virtually unpublished (except for two brief notes; Perrot 1961; 1962) site. However, subsequent recent excavations at Zeita have yielded evidence of a Chalcolithic level (Perrot n.d.) and material superimposed upon it that was obviously not *in situ*. Notably, the site has been deep ploughed and Zeita (Nahal Qoman) is now known to have yielded evidence of an Early Chalcolithic level with semi-subterranean houses overlain by barely discernible remains of early EB I activity (Khalaily 2002; Commenge 2006, 437–8; I. Milevski and H. Khalaily pers. comm.; Braun and van den Brink 2008, 647–9). Obviously there is no suggestion for continuity between these occupations and hence no evidence for a 'transition', merely a mixing of artefacts from two chronologically distant and distinct periods.

Wadi Ghazzeh, Site H, also claimed by Hanbury-Tenison to belong to this same period, demonstrably has several phases of occupation, one of which is quite early EB I, and another that is somewhat later in the period (Yekutieli 2001, 665) as well as pottery types associated with Level C at Tel Erani (Macdonald 1932, Pl. XXXVII, 2 and 3 stranded handles in lower corner) that is dated to quite advanced phases of EB I (Braun 2010a; Braun in press a; see also below). Together, the different phases evident in the architectural remains at the site yielded a mixed artefact assemblage not very useful for chronological determinations. Whether the earliest phase is equivalent to Hanbury-Tenison's 'Post-Ghassulian Chalcolithic' is unclear because it is difficult to state precisely which material derived from it. Notably, some objects might be identified with such a phase and are paralleled at Afridar, Area G (Braun and Gophna 2004), which yielded evidence of the initial phases of the EB I.

Level 3 in a cave at Azor, and Installation C above it, were also claimed by Hanbury-Tenison to exhibit post-Ghassulian Chalcolithic utilization. However, those deposits represent a range of utilizations of uncertain duration. The Level 3 assemblage is well placed in the LC, but Installation C seems to be a mixed bag, with a rather long chronological range indicated by its ceramic assemblage, which includes some very early EB I pottery such as Gray Burnished Ware (GBW) (Perrot and Ladiray 1980, fig. 75, 8–9, and other vessels (Perrot and Ladiray 1980, fig. 73, 13, fig. 74, 19, 22, 30) of an advanced phase of the EB I known as the Erani C horizon, which are dated to the time of Tomb U-j in Abydos Egypt, at least a century before the end of the EB I (Braun and van den Brink 1998).

Although Hanbury-Tenison appears to have been intuitively correct in his discernment of a phase between the LC and the early EB I (his 'Post Ghassulian Chalcolithic') and his idea of 'gradual transition rather than abrupt change' (Hanbury-Tenison 1986, 251), nowhere did he specifically substantiate his claim for the 'Post Ghassulian Chalcolithic' by defining its parameters and then demonstrating its existence within the archaeological record. For example, his and others' interpretations (Hanbury-Tenison 1986, 129; Betts and Helms 1992, 7) of 'Tell Umm Hammad/ Proto-Urban D Ware' as evidence of transmission of Chalcolithic pot types to an advanced phase of the EB I (Hanbury-Tenison's early EB Ib), a notion apparently derived from the work of Helms (1984a; 1984b) at the type site, has not been corroborated. 'Tell Umm Hammad Ware' is now known to have appeared in a well-advanced phase of the EB I (Helms 1992, 107), and the association remains unclear (Bar 2010).

Hanbury-Tenison's (1986, 251–5) 'Post Ghassulian Chalcolithic' was actually rather sparsely documented, its discussion really only an addendum to a large catalogue of data, some of it containing serious errors (Braun 1987). Definition of this phase was then based on a poorly revealed and poorly understood archaeological record, emphasized by a lack of material with which to illustrate it, as indicated by the extreme poverty of illustrations in the volume. Nevertheless, although many of Hanbury-Tenison's claims remain undocumented and unsubstantiated, and some are based on misinterpretations, his perspicacious observation (1986, 135) that 'The strong signs of continuity in the plain wares are unmistakable.' seems to have been based on a good understanding of pottery from sites in the central Jordan valley. That observation may be best understood in light of Gustavson-Gaube's (1985; 1986) and later Betts and Helm's (1992) ceramic seriations at Tell es-Shuna (particularly Stages 1–4) and their claim of continuity in ceramic traditions (Helm 1992, 136–47).

The views of Rivka Gonen

Gonen (1992, 79–80) claimed both the beginning and especially the end of the Chalcolithic to be so poorly understood that she declared their origins to be nothing less than 'mysterious'. Reviewing earlier works of other scholars, she suggested only minimal transfer of the cultural burden between the Chalcolithic and the EB I, arguing that, with the exception of some 'basic ceramic forms', EB I newcomers 'started from scratch' (*sic*!), while virtually ignoring the level of technology evidenced in their material culture.

The views of Amnon Ben-Tor

Ben-Tor understood something of the transference of the cultural burden from the LC to the EB I, but was less than precise as to the mechanics. For him (1992, 82–3), the Chalcolithic 'disappears under unclear circumstances and a new epoch in the history of Palestine begins'. He suggested changes so rapid and far-reaching that they should be understood as 'revolutionary'. By contrast, he perceived the end of the Chalcolithic period to have been an 'extended process', with the material culture of that period making major contributions to that of the EB I, the latter period evidencing a mixture of those and new elements, especially in its pottery repertoire (Ben-Tor 1992, 95–6).

The present author's views

In my contribution to the Emmaüs conference (de Miroschedji 1989) in 1985, I drew conclusions for evidence of transition between the LC and the EB I that emphasized lines of continuity in material culture for the northern region of the southern Levant (Braun 1989a). However, I was then only able to base my argument on comparanda for material-culture artefacts from Yiftahel (Stratum II) and a rather poorly understood 'horizontal sequence' of the LC and EB I derived from analysing a number of sites spread out over a rather large geographic region. I was at that time, and remain, less mystified than Gonen, although I was then neither privy to the ceramic sequences of the Jordan valley sites nor able to view material from them, and so remained unaware of any LC–EB I sequence at any given site. Indeed, it was believed then that there was no such site, although later, based on my intuitive understanding of the earliest EB I pottery I had encountered (which seemed to be too different from LC pottery to be very proximal to it in time) I postulated the existence of a transitional LC–EB I phase that I rather whimsically labelled 'the lost horizon' (Braun 1996). Unfortunately, I was, and remain, unsure of precisely what constitutes the LC in the northern region.

Later, when my work centred in the southern region, I encountered additional support for the hypothesis of LC–EB I continuity in details of material culture at initial EB I sites at Palmahim Quarry and Afridar Area G (Braun 2001a; Braun and Gophna 2004, 96). The clinching argument for proving this hypothesis, however, remained elusive, although supporting circumstantial evidence was impressive as the internal sequence of EB I was slowly becoming understood (Braun 1997; 2001b; Braun and van den Brink 1998). Still missing, however, was even one single, sizable occupational sequence with architectural remains that bridged the LC–EB I transition. That was to appear in a region which was, until quite recently, virtually *terra incognita* for the periods under discussion, the Shephelah (the inland plain and piedmont of central Israel), as a result of rather dubious benefits of contemporary building activity.

A terminological caveat

Before beginning discussion of details of this newly revealed part of the archaeological record, I wish to inform the reader that I personally eschew any hard and fast terminology for EB I periodization except when citing others, preferring instead to merely append descriptive terms such as early or initial. I especially reject terminology prevailing in the literature which subdivides EB I into only two phases, EB IA and EB IB (or any similar designations) because it fails to recognize a major bifurcation in EB I material culture between the northern and southern regions and evidence for at least three phases for the former region and probably four for the south-west region (*e.g.*, Yekutieli 2000; 2001). Such a rigid, two-part framework for periodization obscures new information (Braun in press b) on a sequence derived from decades of painstaking excavation and research by scholars.

Review of the evidence for continuity from the LC to the EB I

Modi'in-Buchman: a major element in a 'missing link'

Recently E. C. M. van den Brink (2004) has unearthed a continuous LC–EB I sequence on 'Hill B' in the Buchman neighbourhood of Modi'in in central Israel. It is an important segment of the once-'missing link' for the southern region between these periods. Seven superimposed strata, with no evidence for abandonment, were encountered there. While the ceramic assemblages of this site are not yet published, the evidence of architecture is indicative of the transition from the Chalcolithic to the EB I.

Architectural traditions

Modi'in Buchman Stratum 7, the earliest occupation at the site, although exposed in only a limited area, is known to date to the LC (van den Brink 2007). The significant exposures of Strata 6–4 are dated to the LC on the basis of well-preserved ceramic finds recovered *in situ* in clear association with rectilinear architectural remains. Notably, buildings of Strata 6 and 5 share the same orientation, but a partially superimposed broadroom structure unearthed in Stratum 4 has a different orientation. Stratum 3, dated to the EB I on the basis of associated ceramics found *in situ*, includes a jar with indented ledge handles and a type of pithos bearing rope-like design with close parallels in Stratum II at Yiftahel (*e.g.*, Braun 1997, 105–6, figs 9.15–9.19). Stratum 3 lacks curvilinear architecture, the norm for early EB I sites (Braun 1997, 104–5), but does have a rectilinear broadroom that quite significantly shares the orientation of its predecessor in Stratum 4, which is an indication of continuity of traditions. Only in the following early EB I occupation was the more normative early EB I curvilinear tradition of architecture introduced (see below). Thus, Stratum 3 at Modi'in Buchman represents the first really good evidence in the southern Levant for a transitional LC–EB I phase.

The succeeding occupation (Stratum 2) is particularly noteworthy for the presence of a long large curvilinear structure with a well-defined portal, stone pavers and a door socket *in situ*, features paralleled in several of the

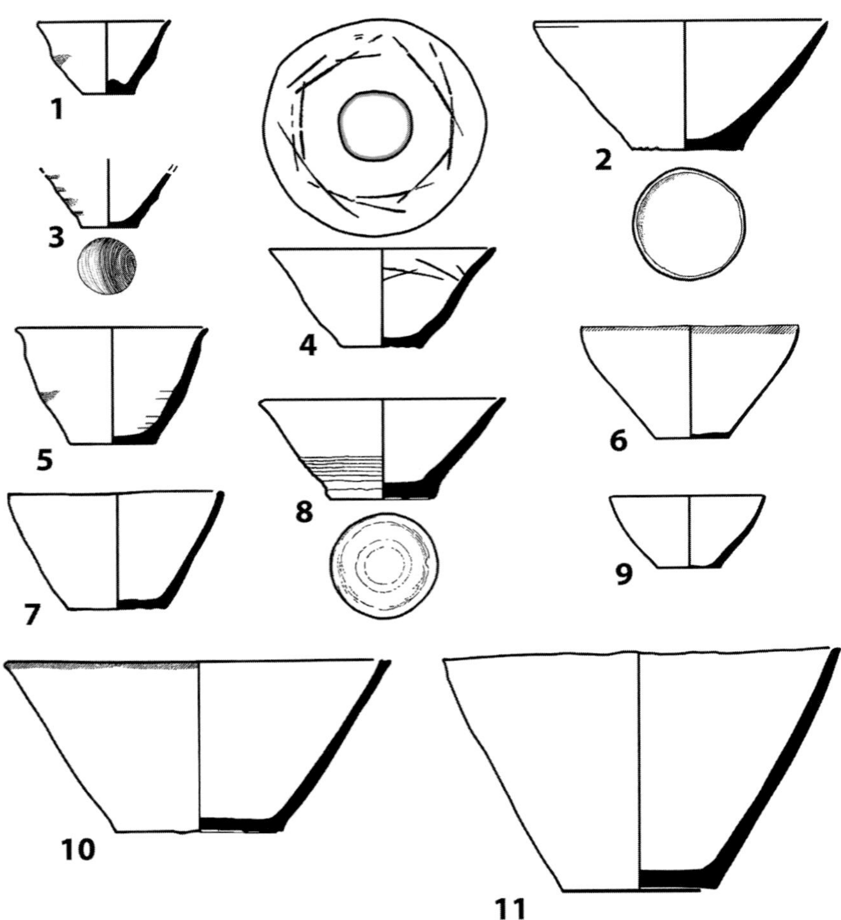

Figure 12.1 Early EB I and LC straight-walled bowls. 1–5, Early EB I bowls from southern sites. 1: Afridar Area G (after Braun and Gophna 2004, fig. 17.6); 2: Palmahim Quarry 3 (courtesy of the Israel Antiquities Authority); 3: Afridar Area G (after Braun and Gophna 2004, fig. 15.1); 4: Nizzanim Stratum 5 (after Yekutieli and Gophna 1994, fig. 12.5); 5: Afridar Area G (after Braun and Gophna 2004, fig. 17.9). 6–11, LC bowls from LC sites. 6: Abu Matar (after Commenge-Pellerin 1987, fig. 45.3); 7: Safadi (after Commenge-Pellerin 1990, fig. 21.4); 8: Safadi (after Commenge-Pellerin 1990, fig. 21.2); 9: Abu Matar (after Commenge-Pellerin 1987, fig. 45.11); 10: Safadi (after Commenge-Pellerin 1990, fig. 24.8); 11: Giv'at ha-Oranim (after Scheftelowitz and Oren 2004, fig. 3.3, 4)

curvilinear houses in Stratum II at Yiftahel and other contemporary or nearly contemporary occupations, as at Palmahim Quarry and Ashkelon Afridar Area G (Braun 1997, 29–42, 103–4; 2001a; Braun and Gophna 2004). The Stratum 2 building at Modi'in is probably associated with a nearby small free-standing circular structure, another feature found in Stratum II at Yiftahel and other sites such as Pithat Ha-Yarmuk, where they probably date to roughly contemporary occupations (Braun 1989b, fig. 18). Such circular structures were not innovative, but have a long history in the southern Levant which can be seen, for example, in an early phase of the Chalcolithic at Tel Tsaf (Garfinkel *et al.* 2007, fig. 6) and at Teleilat Ghassul (Koeppel *et al.* 1940, pl. 1) in a Chalcolithic context. Poorly preserved remains of another, superimposed, occupation at Modi'in (Stratum 1) yielded pottery assigned by the excavator to the EB IA, but still ascribable to an early phase within the period. Excavations at 'En Esur (Yannai 2006, 34) reflect a similar break in architectural traditions between the LC and the EB I, so at best it seems they indicate only a modicum of continuity between these periods. However, other aspects of material culture, which indicate more than a minimum of continuity, somewhat alter the perception of a break in traditions.

Continuity in ceramic traditions

A study of early EB I ceramics indicates data which support the idea of transference of the cultural burden, and which belie the existence of any major gap or hiatus in occupation between these chrono-cultural periods (Braun 1989a; Betts and Helms 1992, 136–7). Ceramic analysis provides some important insights into the process and suggests an altered paradigm for the entire cultural event known as EB I. Its early phases owe a considerable debt to Chalcolithic traditions, while its later phases break almost completely

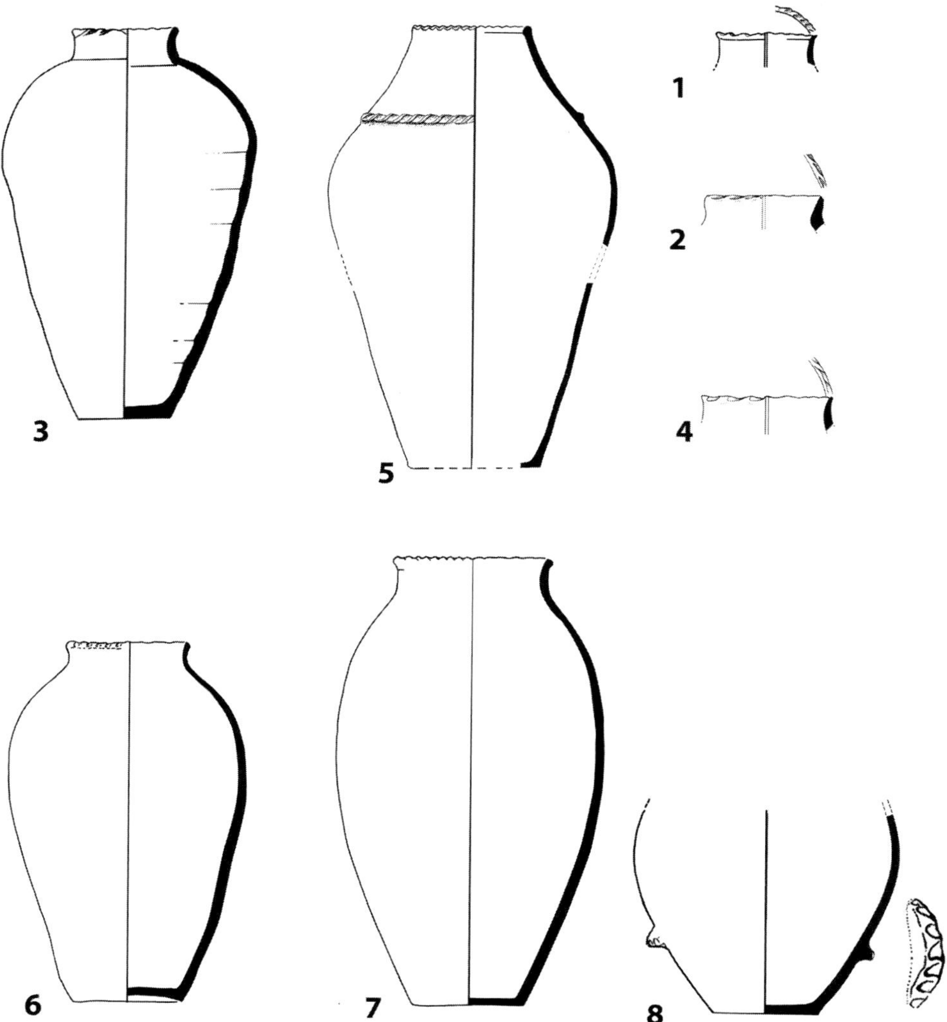

Figure 12.2 Early EB I and LC pithoi. 1–5, Early EB I. 1: Nizzanim Stratum 5 (after Yekutieli and Gophna 1994, fig. 12.5); 2: Afridar, Area G (after Braun and Gophna 2004, fig. 19.10); 3: Afridar Area J (after Baumgarten 2004, fig. 15.5); 4: Afridar Area J (after Braun and Gophna 2004, fig. 19.10); 5: Modi'in, Stratum 3 (Earliest EB I occupation) (courtesy of E.C.M. van den Brink and the Israel Antiquities Authority). 6–7, LC. 6: Giv'at ha-Oranim (after Scheftelowitz and Oren 2004, fig. 3.15.1); 7: Giv'at ha-Oranim (after Scheftelowitz and Oren 2004, fig. 3.15.2); 8: Ben Shemen cave (after Perrot and Ladiray 1980, fig. 129.8)

with them, perhaps as a result of the evolution of a new social reality related to the rise of hierarchical and complex social systems (Braun in press b; 2010b).

Modes of pottery production and morphological preferences

Specialized LC methods of pottery production, which have left tell-tale visual elements on pots and many fragments thereof, are best known from the large, well-published and extensively studied assemblages of Abu Matar and Bir es-Safadi (Commenge-Pellerin 1987; 1990). When compared with the earliest EB I pottery they attest to the ideological proximity of early EB I potters to their LC predecessors with regard to such aspects as Roux's (2005, 211) '*chaîne opératoire*' and mental templates expressed in vessel morphology and techniques of decoration. Traditional LC potters' methods were continued by early EB I potters, who often practised them with notably less skill, especially in the production of small to medium-sized vessels.

Some outstanding LC ceramic types (Figure 12.1.5–11) and primary and secondary morphological features also associated with early EB I assemblages are: 1) forms such as the straight-walled bowl, erroneously called 'V'-shaped despite its distinctly flat base (*e.g.*, Figure 12.1.1–4); 2) pithoi with wide shoulders and relatively small bases (*e.g.*, Figure 12.2.1–5); 3) the copious use of incisions or rope-like or pie-crust decoration on walls of vessels and especially on and just below rims (*e.g.*, Figures 12.2.1–7, 12.4.3, 12.5.1, 3–4); 4) the obvious use of the tournette or wheel for thinning and shaping of straight-walled bowls (Roux and Courty 1997; Roux 2003, 15–21; *e.g.*, Figure

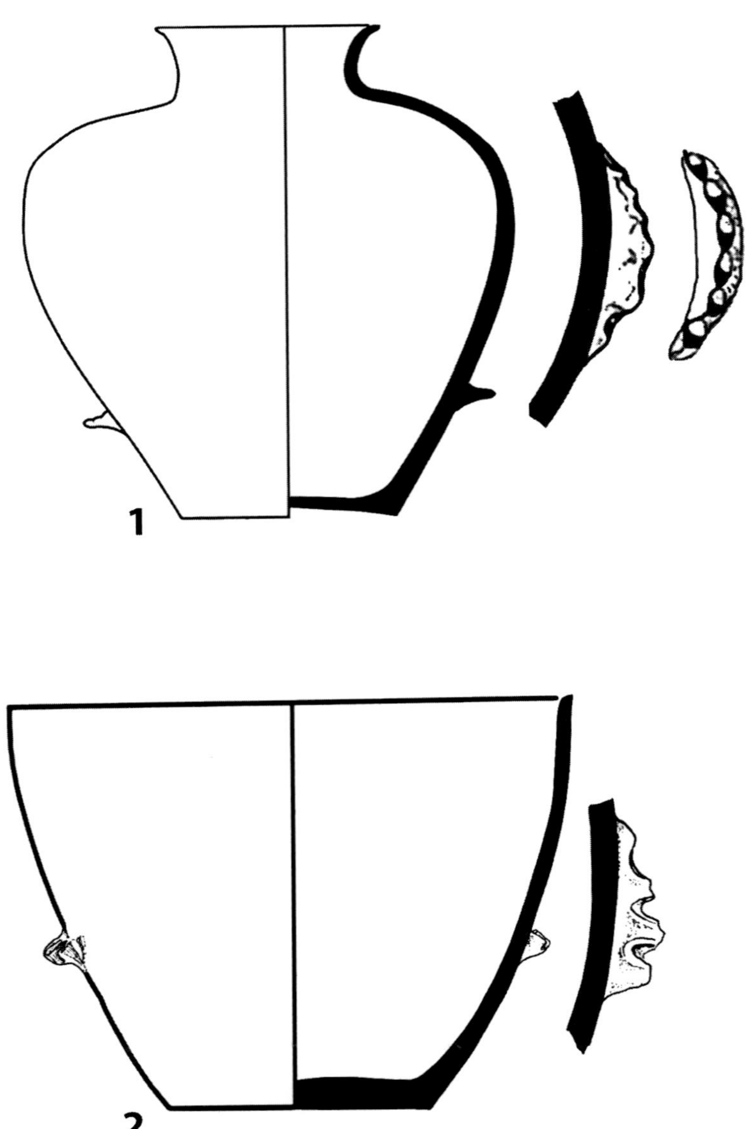

Figure 12.3 LC Jars with ledge handles. 1: Giv'at ha-Oranim (after Scheftelowitz and Oren 2004, fig. 3.14.1); 2: Mazor, burial cave (courtesy I. Milevski and the IAA)

12.1.3, 5); and 5) the manner in which lumps of clay were affixed to wheels or tournettes (Braun 2000, 125; *e.g.*, Figure 12.1.2, 8) and removed, leaving tell-tale traces.

Comparison of the small bowl production of early EB I potters with that of their LC predecessors (*e.g.*, Figure 12.1.6–9) evinces a notable diminution in the level of skills in the later period (*e.g.*, Figure 12.1.1–5). These latest examples are considerably coarser in finish and often in the quality of fabric, possibly owing to choices in raw materials and/or diminished pyro-technological expertise. Since such features are not associated with the ceramics of the more advanced phases of the EB I their disappearance over time suggests a change in modes of ceramic production probably associated with altered arrangements in social organization during the EB I (Braun in press b). In addition, the evidence of ceramic sequences from the Jordan valley sites of Tell es-Shuna and Tell Umm Hammad suggest that, as cited above, quotidian, common pot types appear to have been produced throughout the transition. There is also evidence there for a localized tradition of splash and drip style (SDS) of painting (Hanbury-Tenison 1986, 135; Braun 1996, 182–3; Braun 2010b) that apparently transcends these periods.

Continuity in ceramic morphology

The ledge handle

Ledge handles with indented, striated or wavy edges were, until very recently, thought to be unknown in Chalcolithic contexts, rather being an EB I innovation: *i.e.*, the perfect *fossile directeur* for the latter period. That is yet another

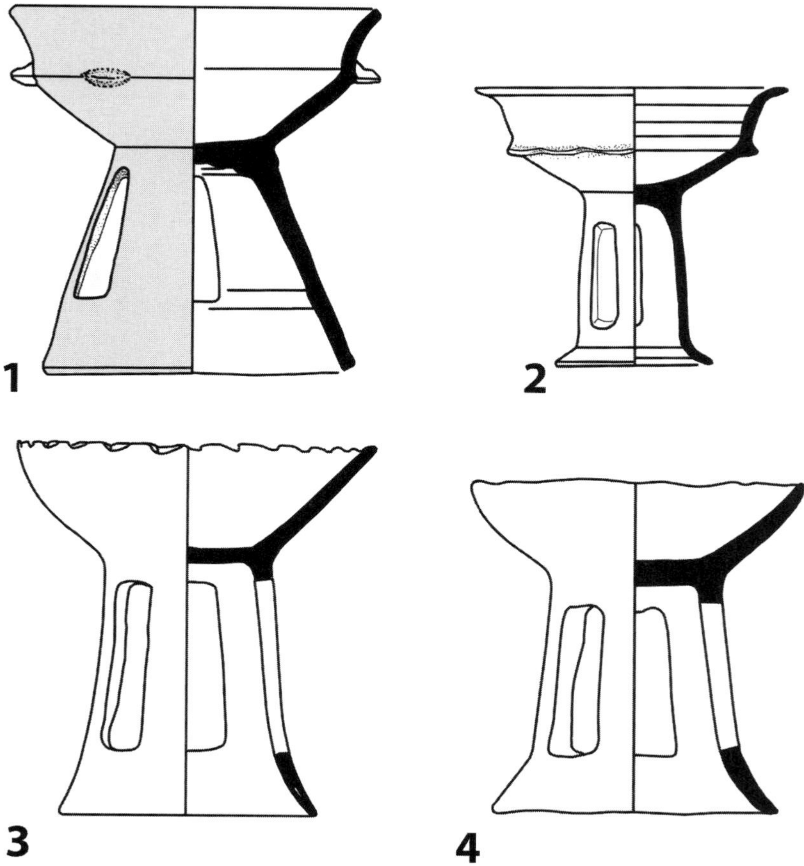

Figure 12.4 Early EB I and LC fenestrated pedestalled bowls. 1–4, Early EB I and LC. 1: Yiftahel (after Braun 1997, fig. 9.4.1) (Red slipped); 2: Yiftahel (after Braun 1997, fig. 9.4.2) (Gray Burnished Ware); 3: Azor Tomb (after Perrot and Ladiray 1980, fig. 70.1); 4: Azor Tomb (after Perrot and Ladiray 1980, fig. 70.2)

sacred archaeological concept that must be abandoned at least partially in light of new information indicating that it was primarily a regional LC phenomenon associated with the Shephelah, although one example from a Chalcolithic context at Teleilat Ghassul (Bourke *et al.* 1995, fig. 9.11) seems to presage its arrival.

The most convincing evidence of the LC appearance of this highly stylized appendage derives from excavations at Giv'at ha-Oranim (Scheftelowitz and Oren 2004, fig. 3.14.1–2, fig. 3.18.1–4; Figure 12.3.1) and Mazor (Figure 12.3.2) in the Shephelah, where they are found on complete vessels as well as in the form of sherds. The two complete vessels from Giv'at ha-Oranim appear to be more EB I than LC in their morphology, except for the exceptionally low positioning (below the mid-point) of the indented ledge handles, a trait known from LC pithoi (*e.g.*, Figure 12.2.8, 12.3). At Mazor, I. Milevski (2007) unearthed a small cache of burial deposits in a Late Chalcolithic cave context devoid of any evidence of EB I material culture; the deposits included several complete vessels, each with two full blown opposing scalloped or indented ledge handles. These discoveries essentially confirm an LC ascription for two additional vessels, also with similar ledge handles, from nearby Ben Shemen (Perrot and Ladiray 1980, fig. 129.8–9), which also contains EB I pottery (Perrot and Ladiray 1980, fig. 132.21–28), as well as some analogous appendages on LC vessels from nearby Shoham (Commenge 2005, figs 6.30.1, 6.32) and possibly on a pithos from a pit unearthed in bedrock below the bulldozed early EB I site at Palmahim Quarry (Braun 2001a). More recently, such appendages were also found on a jar utilized for an infant burial beneath the LC site of Sheikh Diab 2 in the Fazael valley, a small tributary of the Jordan valley approximately 20 km north of Jericho (Bar 2008).

Thus it is now quite clear that one of the hallmarks of the EBA, the wavy edged ledge handle, is actually an innovation of Chalcolithic potters and was readily adopted by LC peoples in the Shephelah and beyond, who passed it along to their early EB I successors as part of the cultural burden. Information currently available suggests that such contacts were likely to have taken place primarily in the central, western region; for the present, there is only rare definitive evidence of the ledge handle in the LC ceramic sequences of other regions, although it would not be surprising were new discoveries to challenge this observation.

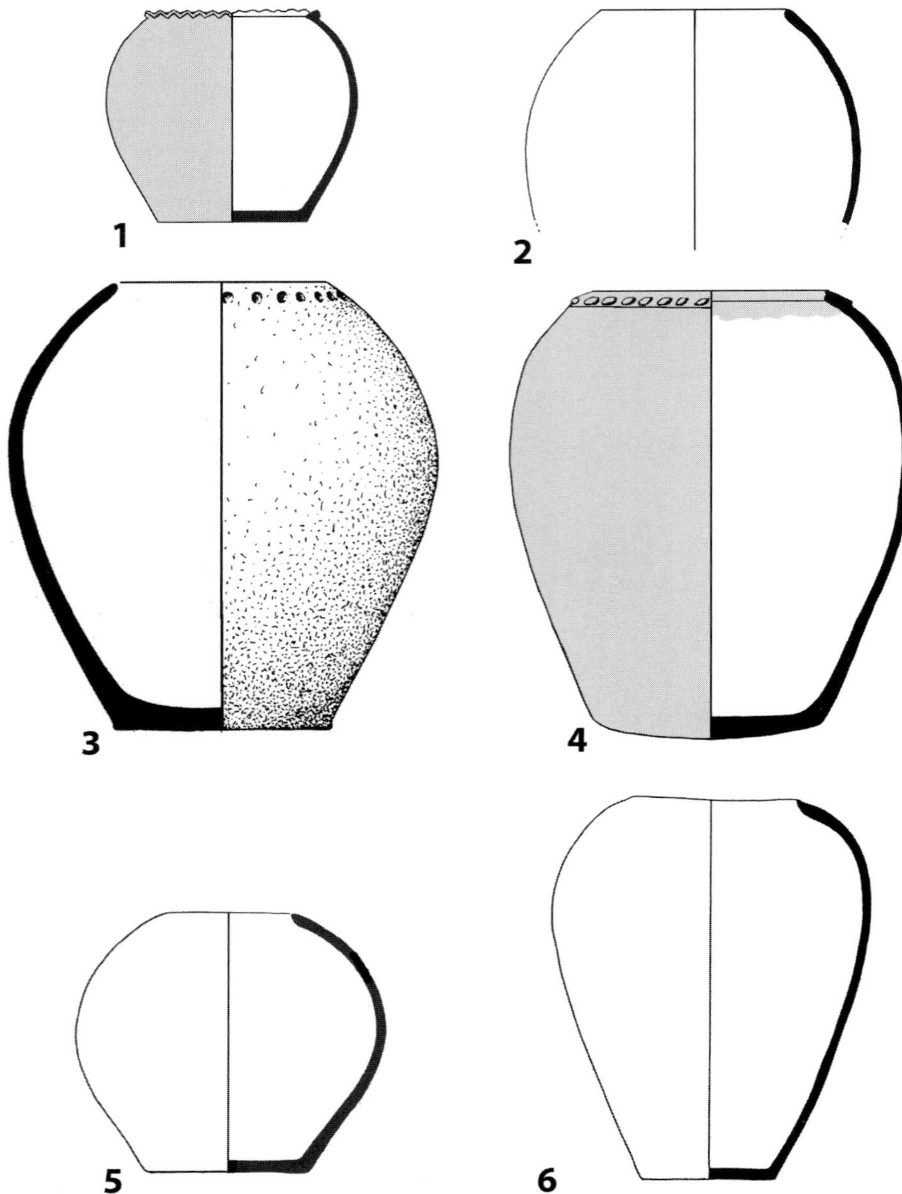

Figure 12.5 Early EB I and LC holemouths. 1–4, EB I. 1: Yiftahel (after Braun 1997, fig. 9.8.2); 2: Nizzanim Stratum 5 (after Yekutieli and Gophna 2004, fig. 12.5); 3: Wadi Fidan 4 (courtesy of Adams 1999, fig. 5.11); 4: Tel Te'o Stratum V (Eisenberg et al. 2001, fig. 7.5,11). 5–6, LC. 5: Safadi (after Commenge-Pellerin 1990, fig. 46.4); 6: Safadi (after Commenge-Pellerin 1990, fig. 46.6)

The fenestrated pedestalled bowl

This highly distinctive and idiosyncratic vessel type is clearly a carryover form from the LC, in which period it was made from stone and pottery (Figure 12.4.3, 4; *e.g.*, Scheftelowitz and Oren 2004, 43, figs 3.7, 8). Vessels sharing the rather tall LC characteristics of the type are common in early EB I assemblages in the northern region, where they were often fashioned of GBW and related or analogous fabrics, and with morphological variations (*e.g.*, Figure 12.4.1–2), but I know of only one example belonging to the same generic family from a southern context: a small, squat vessel from Tell en Nasbeh (Wampler 1947, pl. 52.1156). The disappearance of this type, by the 'En Shadud phase (Braun in press b), a developed but not very late phase of EB I in which GBW was still present, seems also related to major changes in social organization which affected pottery production and distribution (Braun 2010b).

A special case: pottery from the arid zones of the southern Levant

Information from the more southerly regions, especially

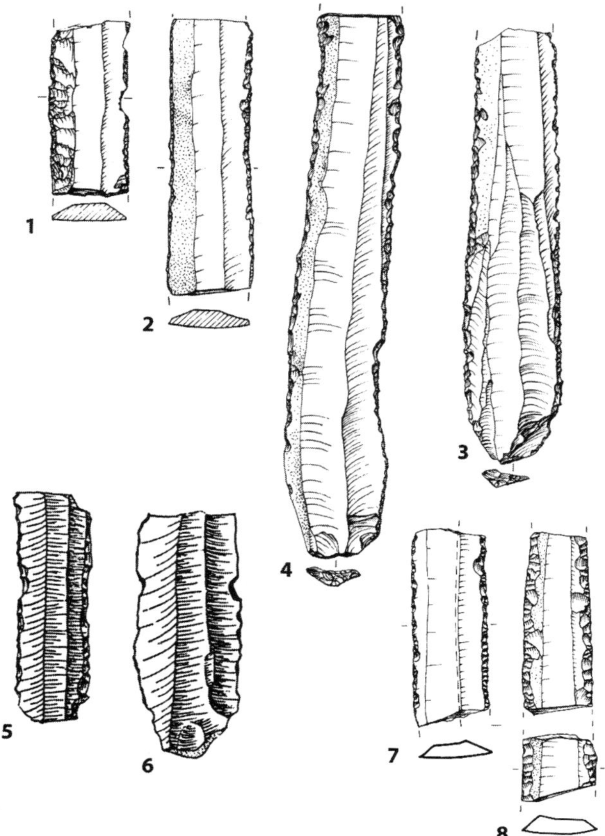

Figure 12.6 Early EB I and LC Canaanean or prismatic blades. 1–4, Early EB I. 1: Afridar Areas G and J (after Zbenovich 2004, fig. 3.2); 2: Afridar Areas G and J (after Zbenovich 2004, fig. 3.3); 3: Afridar Areas G and J (after Zbenovich 2004, fig. 7.2); 4: Afridar Areas G and J (after Zbenovich 2004, fig. 7.1). 5–8, LC. 5: Giv'atayim Tomb 3 (after Sussman and Ben-Arieh 1966, fig. 6.5); 6: Giv'atayim Tomb 3 (after Sussman and Ben-Arieh 1966, fig. 6.8); 7: Giv'at ha-Oranim (after Scheftelowitz and Oren 2004, fig. 7.4.3); 8: Giv'at ha-Oranim (after Scheftelowitz and Oren 2004, fig. 7.4.2)

east of the Great Rift Valley, where pottery has been found in relatively small quantities, suggests that it was a somewhat rare utilitarian commodity at sites such as Tell Magass. Types associated with LC and early EB I contexts are devoid of many of the idiosyncratic features that allow for specific chrono-cultural associations (Adams 1999, 51–2). The pottery from Wadi Fidan 4, originally thought by the excavators to be Chalcolithic (Adams and Genz 1995), is now believed to date to early EB I, as demonstrated by the presence of holemouths with decorated rims (Figure 12.5.3; compared to LC types, *e.g.*, Figure 12.5.5–6) and other artefacts, including a small impressed ledge handle (Adams and Genz 1995, fig. 4.5), Canaanean blades and cortex-bearing tabular flint scrapers. Adams' revised chrono-cultural association for the overall assemblage from this site emphasizes the continuity of ceramic styles in this region. The presence of a number of seemingly archaic features (usually indicative of Late Neolithic and Early Chalcolithic repertoires) in the ceramic assemblage – including vessels with large knobs (Adams and Genz 1995, fig. 3.2; Adams 1999, figs. 5.08:2, 5.17:3) and mat-impressions, explained as idiosyncratic, local elements (Adams and Genz 1995, fig. 4.7; Adams 1999, figs. 5.09.1, 3, 5) – notwithstanding, the same assemblage also includes some LC-type ceramic objects. Non-EB I types are: 1) deep, almost vertically walled open vessels, bowls and cups (Adams and Genz 1995, fig. 3.4–6; Adams 1999, fig. 5.09.3, 6, 8–13, 5.09.1–5); 2) a deep thin-walled holemouth with non-decorated, tapering rim (Adams 1999, fig. 5.09.7); and 3) a cylindrically pierced vertical lug handle (Adams and Genz 1995, fig. 4.4). Based on most available evidence one could interpret this site as LC, transitional LC–EB I or early EB I. Neither the presence of ledge handles at the site nor the presence of Canaanean blades in the assemblage negate an LC chrono-cultural ascription for this site (see below), although available dates suggest the last option (Adams 1999, 112) as the most likely.

Chipped stone technology and typology

There is some slight, albeit convincing, evidence that Canaanean ('prismatic') blade production (Khalaily 2002;

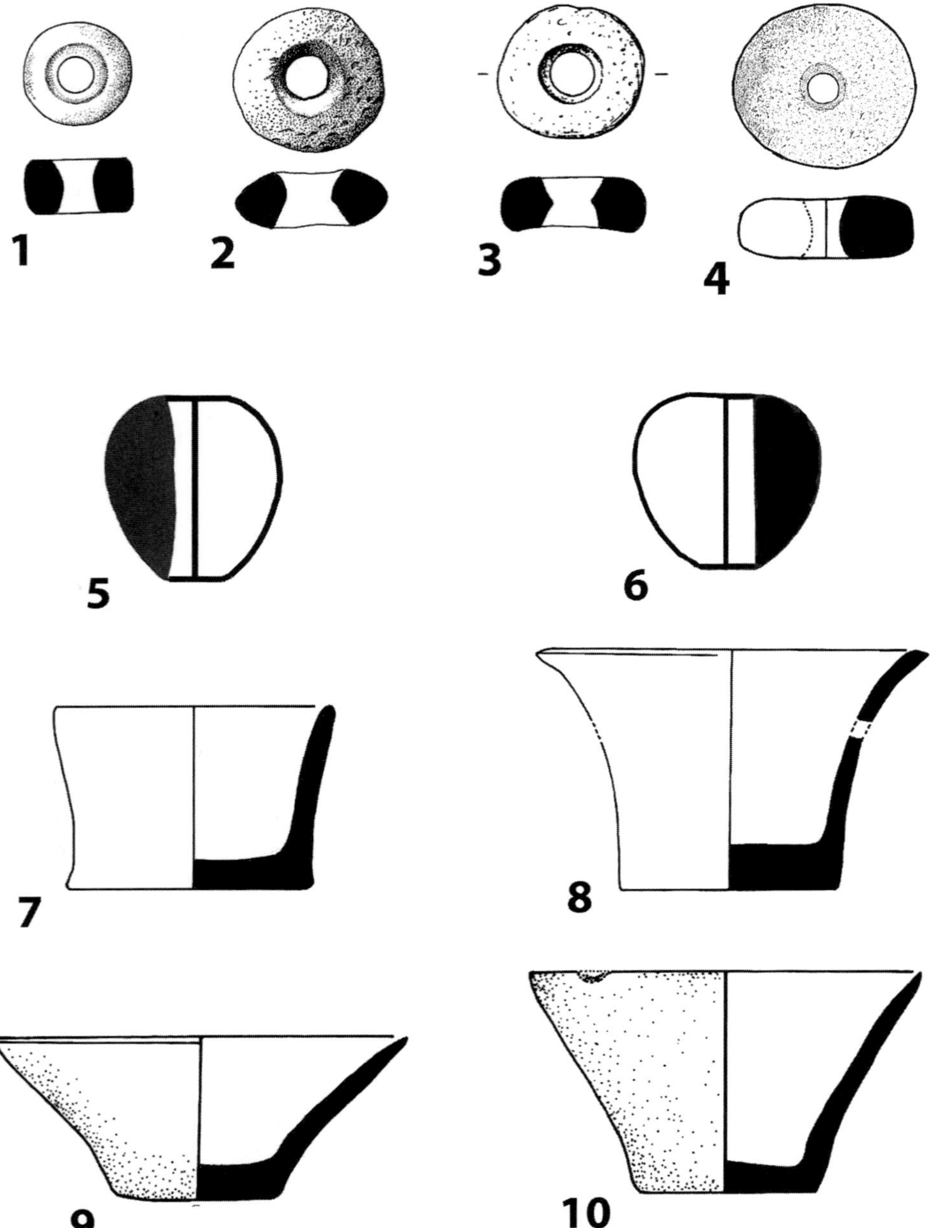

Figure 12.7 Early EB I and LC ground stone objects. 1–2, Early EB I. 1: Spindle whorl, Afridar Area F (after Khalaily 2004, fig. 23.8); 2: Spindle whorl, Yiftahel (after Braun 1997, fig. 12.12.2). 3–4, LC. 3: Spindle whorl, Giv'at ha-Oranim (after Scheftelowitz and Oren 2004, fig. 6.2.4); 4: Spindle whorl, Nahal Mishmar (after Bar-Adon 1980, ill. 57.3). 5, EB I. 5: Stone macehead, Tomb C, Bâb edh-Dhra^c (after Rast and Schaub 1989, fig. 118.4). 6, LC. 6: Stone macehead, Benei Beraq tomb (after Kaplan 1963, fig. 9.14). 7–8, Early EB I. 7: Bowl, Afridar Area F (after Khalaily 2004, fig. 23.1); 8: Bowl, Yiftahel (after Braun 1990, fig. 2.4). 9–10, LC. 9: Bowl, Safadi (after Braun 1990, fig. 2.1); 10: Bowl, Abu Matar (after Braun 1990, fig. 2.2)

Milevski *et al.*, this volume) began in the LC, which provides additional evidence for continuity between the LC and the EB I. The major distinction between these periods appears to be in terms of the scope of production and distribution, which was vastly more widespread in the EB I than in the LC.

Canaanean technology: the Canaanean or prismatic blade

Hanbury-Tenison (1986, 147–8) suggested that Canaanean blades (Figure 12.6) first appeared in the Chalcolithic period, but his observations were based on a number of mixed assemblages from Azor and Zeita (see above), as well as Magas (*i.e.*, Tell Magass, a site that arguably may be dated to either the LC or the early EB I; Adams 1999,

52). Idiosyncratically, he also equated all blades having trapezoidal sections with Canaanean or 'prismatic' blades (*contra* Rosen 1997, 46), which does not take into account technological methods of manufacture associated with a particularly skilful type of craft specialization, nor what appears to have been an extensive system of distribution of these items demonstrably associated with EB I (Rosen 1983). None of the blades chosen by Hanbury-Tenison (1986, fig. 31) from Teleilat Ghassul, Tell el Farah North *grotte* U and sites in the Pella region and in Wadi Fidan seems well enough preserved to be definitively identified as the product of such technology and to illustrate his thesis, although evidence from other sites seems to do so.

Rowan (2006, 514–15, table 11.15) has noted 18 examples (the lowest quantity of any tool type at the site) of what he interprets as evidence for this technology (labelled 'proto-Canaanean') from purely Chalcolithic contexts at Gilat (*contra* Oshri and Schick 1998, 61). Seventeen of them derive from stratified contexts ranging from Stratum 3A to Stratum 1, definitively indicating that the type made its primary appearance prior to early EB I. But, as noted by Rowan, these blades may have fulfilled functions somewhat different from those found in EB contexts. Four blades produced by this technology (similarly labelled) discovered in excavations at Giv'at ha-Oranim (Barkai 2004, 90, 93–4, fig. 6,7–8), were found in clear Chalcolithic contexts, while six Canaanean blades as well as fragments of a Chalcolithic ossuary were recovered in Cave 3 at Giv'atayim (Sussman and Ben-Arieh 1966, fig 6.5–9, 11, fig. 6.5–6) that yielded no evidence of post-Chalcolithic activity. Additional claims for the presence of these distinctive blades in LC contexts have been made for Zeita (also called Nahal Qomem; Khalaily 2002), Cave 4 at Shoham and Cave 1 at Sha'ar Efrayim (van den Brink and Gophna 2005, 170), but these last three sites also indicate definitive EB I utilization. An exceptionally large flint knife from a tomb in the Judean desert, identified as the product of Canaanean technology and dated to sometime within the first quarter of the 4th millennium BC (Oshri and Schick 1998), further indicates the existence of such technology within the generally accepted time span of the LC, although the unusually large size of the object distinguishes it from most Canaanean blades.

In a recent lecture Y. Paz (Tel Aviv University), reporting on a late prehistoric site at Yesodot (just north-west of modern Beth Shemesh at the eastern edge of the central Shephelah), noted an occupation which he ascribes to an LC–EB I transitional chrono-cultural phase in which the pottery was recognizably Chalcolithic, but which yielded a flint tool kit that includes a rather large number of Canaanean blades. Not surprisingly, architectural traditions associated with this phase were rectilinear. This discovery may well be another segment of the 'missing link' between the LC and the EB I, but we will have to wait for some definitive publication for more specific information with which to evaluate such a claim. Some few Canaanean blades are also associated with the late Chalcolithic occupation at Fazael 2, a site that yielded LC ceramics including vessels with wavy-line ledge handles (see above; Bar and Winter 2010).

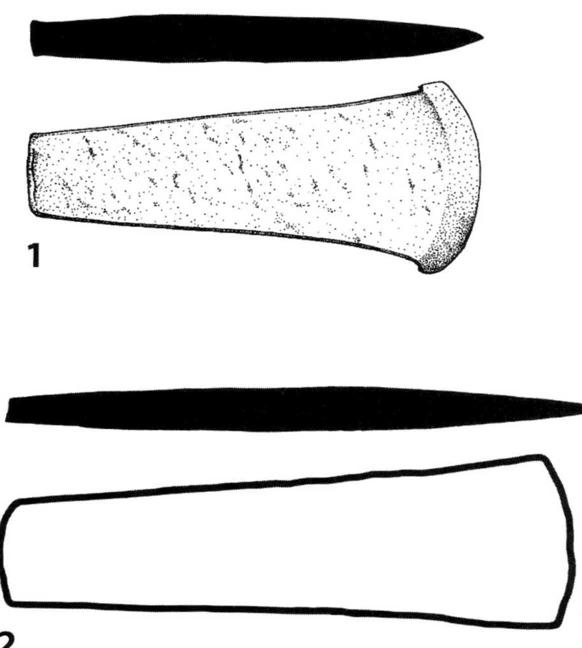

Figure 12.8 Early EB I and Chalcolithic copper tools. 1: Copper axehead, Yiftahel (after Braun 1997, fig. 11.3.2); 2: Copper chisel, Nahal Mishmar (after Bar-Adon 1980, 113, no. 164)

Tabular scrapers

It has long been recognized that tabular scrapers first appeared during the Chalcolithic period and continued to be manufactured and used throughout EB I and well into the EB II. While it is quite certain that this tradition involved specialized production associated with geological sources that would probably not have required the labour of their recipients in the well-watered zones of the southern Levant (from whence they have been recovered; *e.g.*, Marder *et al.* 1995, 79–82 and references therein, figs. 11–13), it does imply groups actively engaged in their production and distribution remained in position and in contact with consumers throughout the period of transition from the LC to the EB I. Thus, the appearance of this blade type in LC as well as EB I contexts may be understood as evidence of a probable conduit by means of which the cultural burden was passed on.

Ground stone technology and morphology

Elsewhere (Braun 1990; 1997) I have noted the similarity between the morphology of some LC basalt bowls, with their flat bases, deep wells and flaring sides (*e.g.*, Figure 12.7.9–10), and those derived from EB I contexts (*e.g.*,

Figure 12.7.7–8). Indeed, the very fact that EB I artisans chose to engage in the labour-intensive task of shaping this hard stone, as well as the relative skill exhibited in many examples of their craft, indicates not merely a transference of basic morphological templates, but also a sophisticated degree of technology (*i.e.*, craft specialization) that could not have arisen independently. Such skills could only have been passed on from one chrono-cultural horizon to the next.

EB I piriform maceheads in stone (*e.g.*, Figure 12.7.5; Sass 2000, fig. 12.22.8–11) may well have been influenced by metal and stone prototypes from Chalcolithic contexts (*e.g.* Figure 12.7.6; Bourke 2001, fig. 4.19.1, 7, 8; Scheftelowitz and Oren 2004, fig. 4.8), although the somewhat simple shape is eminently practical and the later examples may have resulted from independent development. The ubiquitous basalt spindle whorls found at EB I sites (*e.g.*, Figure 12.7.1–2; Braun 1997, fig. 12.2.1–2; Sass 2000, fig. 12.17.3) also appear to be the continuation of an LC type (*e.g.*, Figure 12.7.3–4).

Metallurgy

The earliest evidence for copper utilization and probably production from ores in the southern Levant (Tadmor *et al.* 1995, 145) is associated with LC contexts. The existence of a local copper industry at Wadi Fidan 4 (Adams 1999, 154) in the early EB I should be understood as additional evidence of continuity. It is unclear, however, whether the morphology of these rather simple, utilitarian axes and adzes of the latter period (*e.g.* Figure 12.8.1, Shalev and Braun 1997, 94) should be attributed to Chalcolithic prototypes (*e.g.* Figure 12.8.2) or merely to functional considerations. Probably there are elements of both these influences inherent in the forms of these tools.

Shells

The penchant of Chalcolithic people for shell bracelets of *Lambis truncata* (Bar-Yosef Mayer 2002a; 2002b, 131–3; 169, 171, 175–6) was apparently shared by their EB I successors and perhaps remained popular with south Levantine peoples into EB II. It is too highly coincidental to be feasible that demands for these bracelets, and the associated craft specialization which produced them from elaborate mollusc shells, were independent developments in both periods. These objects should be understood as additional evidence for the transference of the cultural burden between the LC and the EB I.

Mortuary traditions

A general lack of good information on early EB I mortuary behaviour is due to the relatively few examples of burials and an equally impoverished record of publication on inhumation strategies in this period. Most dated examples (by the association of GBW) are in caves, such as tombes 3, 5 and 8 at Tell el Farah North (de Vaux and Steve 1949, 104, 123, 133–4, fig. 2, pl. 6), which appear to have been intermittently used over many generations. In the largest sense early EB I tombs seem to continue several general aspects of Chalcolithic mortuary practices in the use of caves for multiple burials over time for successions of individuals with the addition of grave goods, albeit without the ossuaries that are often encountered in LC tombs (*e.g.*, Perrot and Ladiray 1980, 128–30; van den Brink and Gophna 2005, 161). One notable instance of possible continuity was found in a Chalcolithic burial cave (Cave 1) at Sha'ar Efrayim, which was reused by EB I peoples who left some GBW as grave goods (van den Brink and Gophna 2005, 169; van den Brink 2005). It is the only indubitable example of such early EB I re-utilization of a Chalcolithic mortuary context (there is also late EB I utilization of the same cave), although just how early in the LC–EB I sequence GBW attests to remains unclear. While there is additional evidence for GBW found in cave contexts primarily associated with activity in the LC (van den Brink and Gophna 2005, 169), their association beyond mere knowledge and utilization of the same locations for burial is unclear. Other examples of secondary utilization of burial contexts, such as most of those cited by Perrot and Ladiray (1980, 127) and Hanbury-Tenison, are associated with advanced phases of the EB I and so do not argue well for continuity.

Jar burials, relatively rare in EB I, are known from a handful of sites including Tel Te'o (Eisenberg *et al.* 2001, 39), Nizzanim (Yekutieli and Gophna 1994, 166–7), Beth Yerah (Paz 2006, 89), Tel Kabri (Scheftelowitz 2002, 28–9) and possibly Afridar Area G, although this last is probably dated to the Chalcolithic period (Braun and Gophna 2004, 198). EB I jar burials may be considered a continuation of a relatively rare tradition of intra-site burials in jars, especially of infants, in the Chalcolithic period, as at Teleilat Ghassul (Mallon *et al.* 1934, 48–9; Lee 1973, 332), Sheikh Diab 2 (see above) and at a site on Nahal Besor (Perrot 1962, 390). Golani (2005a) claims an EB I infant jar burial at Afridar Area L, but he has previously failed to recognize the presence of Chalcolithic remains in another area at that site (Braun and Gophna 2004, 219–25 and especially note 37), and so its date remains enigmatic.

Cists, tumuli and other similar constructions in the EB I cemetery at Ala-Safat, Jordan (Stekelis 1961), are very close in concept to megalithic structures in the Chalcolithic cemetery of Adeimeh (Stekelis 1935, 39–68). They attest to the continuity of some traditions within certain segments of the population of the southern Levant. Similar types of structures may be found up and down the Great Rift Valley and throughout the arid zones of the southern and eastern regions (*e.g.*, Clark 1979). Golani (2005b) found cist burials of this period at Ashkelon Barnea which are similar to 'ladder burials' found in a Chalcolithic cemetery at Palmahim (Gorzalczany 2006), but we must wait for more detailed publication of the associated material culture to be sure of evidence for continuity.

External influences: the Egyptian connection

Evidence that external influences could have engendered and/or enhanced transference of the cultural burden from LC to EB I in the southern Levant is found at the Delta site of Ma'adi (modern Cairo). The site, probably contemporary with both the LC and the early EB I (Braun and van den Brink 2008, 649, 656–9; van den Brink and Braun 2008), is remarkable for evidencing two unusual dwellings, both of which are believed to be south Levantine in inspiration. One is a Chalcolithic-type subterranean dwelling (Rizkana and Seeher 1989, 51), while the other is a stone-built sub-rectangular broadroom (Hartung *et al.* 2003, 155–67, abb. 3, tafel 34) with affinities to EB I houses.

Most imported and south Levantine ceramics and similar morphological types from the site of Ma'adi (*i.e.*, Ware V, Rizkana and Seeher 1987, 73–7, pls 72–75) appear to be dated to the early EB I on morphological grounds. Their lug handles have rounded sections and were applied as coils in apposition to the bodies of these vessels rather than having been applied as knobs with triangular sections that were pierced circularly, as is most often the case with LC lugs (Braun in press b). One bowl is even morphologically similar to some GBW examples. In addition, the presence of tabular scrapers (Rizkana and Seeher 1988, 29–30, pls 49–67), Canaanean blades (Rizkana and Seeher 1988, 35–6, pls 74–6), basalt bowls (Rizkana and Seeher 1988, pl. 109, 1–8) and spindle whorls (Rizkana and Seeher 1988, 52, pl. 95, 17–22) also indicates south Levantine associations. By contrast, ceramic comparanda for Egyptian material culture suggest a longer chronological range for the duration of Ma'adi, bolstered by sets of dates derived from ^{14}C determinations, which traverse the generally accepted time span between the LC and the EB I (Rizkana and Seeher 1989, 81–3; Caneva *et al.* 1989, 289–90; Seeher 1990, 154–5; Tutundžić 2001; 2002). Thus, Ma'adi, and other contemporary Egyptian communities in contact with the southern Levant may have acted as repositories of Chalcolithic traditions and knowledge, and perhaps even as filters through which they were transferred to early EB I peoples of the southern Levant.

The desert dwellers responsible for the construction of the *nawamis* tombs of southern Sinai (Bar-Yosef *et al.* 1977, 86–8; Bar-Yosef Mayer 2002a, 176) appear to have successfully made the transition from LC to EB I, possibly without even being aware of the momentous changes that occurred in the well-watered zones of the southern Levant. The tombs they left, which yielded the few grave goods, are evidence of continuity in occupation for even a marginal, arid region, and one of the possible conduits for transference of the cultural burden. So too are finds in early EB I contexts at Afridar (Braun and Gophna 2004, 212–13; Khalaily 2004, 142; Braun and van den Brink 2008, 652–3) and the eastern Sahara of a scarcely understood type of ceramic artefact, the 'Clayton ring' (Riemer and Kuper 2000). 'Clayton rings', often incised with potter's marks, are slightly tapering ceramic tubes open at both ends that are found in direct association with flat, pierced discs (often found inside the tubes). They attest to the movement of objects and ideas over long distances and perhaps through long spans of time, by shadowy means, probably involving semi-nomadic populations that have left few additional traces in the archaeological record of the region. They may also have been responsible for the importation of Nilotic shells (*Chambardia rubens acruata*), prized for their nacreous, 'mother of pearl' surfaces, throughout LC and early EB I, to sites in the southern region of the southern Levant (Braun and van den Brink 2008, 646–9).

Summary

As our knowledge of the archaeological record increases, and gaps in understanding are filled, it becomes incrementally obvious that the landscape of the well-watered zones of the southern Levant was never, at least during the last 10 millennia, devoid of human populations. Concurrently, there seems to have also been abundant activity in arid zones, perhaps even throughout that entire span of time.

Although 'cultures', as defined by archaeologists (*i.e.*, recognized 'chrono-cultural units), came and went, none disappeared without something of it being transferred to the succeeding 'culture'. These 'cultures' evolved and changed through natural processes and with increments from whatever sources they came into contact with. Each in its turn was transmogrified through processes that were at once continuous and cumulative. It is apparent that changes occurred at varying rates and it is only when degrees of what might be termed 'critical masses' of 'incontestable visibility' were reached are archaeologists wont, or even able to discern them in the archaeological record and then define them. Disagreements between scholars as to how to periodize some entities, based as they must be on sets of mute artefacts, indicate just how subjective an exercise defining a chrono-cultural entity may sometimes be.

There is, however, virtually no disagreement that 'incontestable visibility' of a new chrono-cultural unit was attained very shortly after the decline of the LC. Major changes in ceramic styles, architectural traditions and technology used to create chipped-stone artefacts were easily detected by pioneering researchers, who used them to define EB I as a chrono-cultural phenomenon distinct from and later than Chalcolithic. However, scholarship tended to emphasize a rupture in the smooth flow of evolution through time and to ignore or dismiss a mass of data which indicates no little degree of continuity between the material culture of LC and that of EB I.

The evidence, for the present, suggests that changes at the end of the Chalcolithic period progressed rapidly, which would explain easily perceived disparities between LC and EB I and why a gap once seemed so apparent. Such rapid change also accounts for the lack of much evidence for a transitional phase in the archaeological record.

Better understanding deriving from an expanded knowledge of the archaeological record indicates a far greater degree of continuity in traditional methods of ceramic and metal production and approaches to ground stone production and flint knapping than previously discerned. Even in the realm of architectural and mortuary traditions there is evidence for at least a modicum of continuity between the LC and the EB I. The distinctions between them are becoming somewhat blurred, enough to leave the question of the cultural ascription of Tell Magass open and that of Wadi Fidan 4 to be determined by radiocarbon data.

Collation of all these data, some new, some old, informs us that the EB I peoples did not merely 'start from scratch', but received an excellent head start from their Chalcolithic predecessors. It remains for us to continue to reveal and better interpret the archaeological record, to try and discern the thin thread that bound LC peoples and their traditions to their EB I successors, so as to better understand the human condition in the southern Levant *circa* the middle of the 4th millennium BC. For, despite the somewhat prosaic material culture of EB I, it was a vital link in passing the cultural burden down from the village societies to the urbanized cultures of the 3rd millennium BC and beyond.

Acknowledgements

I am extremely grateful to E. C. M. van den Brink (IAA), for his willingness to share unpublished data from his excavations at Modi'in and for his comments on earlier drafts of this paper. I am also grateful to H. Khalaily and I. Milevski (IAA) for their generosity in sharing with me information on their fieldwork at the sites of Zeita/Gat Guvrin and Mazor. R. Adams kindly allowed me to reproduce an illustration from his PhD thesis and offered some important insights into the Wadi Fidan sites. Thanks are also due to an unknown reader of an earlier draft of this paper for invaluable observations and suggestions, and to all the scholars who have taken the trouble to publish the results of their work that has so enriched our understanding of the archaeological record of the 4th millennium BC.

References

Adams, R. B. (1999) The Development of Copper Metallurgy during the Early Bronze Age of the Southern Levant: Evidence from the Faynan Region, Southern Jordan. Unpublished PhD thesis, University of Sheffield.

Adams, R. B. and Genz, H. (1995) Excavations at Wadi Fidan 4. A Chalcolithic village complex in the copper ore district of Feinan, southern Jordan. *Palestine Exploration Quarterly* 127, 9–20.

Amiran, R. K. (1969) *Ancient Pottery of the Holy Land. From its Beginnings in the Neolithic Period to the End of the Iron Age*. Jerusalem and Ramat Gan: Massada Press.

Amiran, R. K. (1977) Pottery from the Chalcolithic site near Tell Delhamiya and some notes on the character of the Chalcolithic–Early Bronze I transition. *Eretz-Israel* 13, 48–56 (Hebrew with English summary).

Amiran, R. K. (1985) The transition from the Chalcolithic to the Early Bronze Age. Pp. 108–12 in J. Aviram and A. Biran (eds), *Biblical Archaeology Today*. Jerusalem: The Israel Exploration Society.

Bar, S. (2008) The Pattern of Settlement in the Lower Jordan Valley and the Desert Fringes of Samaria during the Late Chalcolithic and Early Bronze Age I Periods. Unpublished PhD thesis, University of Haifa (Hebrew).

Bar, S. (2010) Early Bronze Age I 'Umm Hammad Ware': A Study in Regionalism. *Palestine Exploration Quarterly* 142/2, 82–94.

Bar, S. and Winter, H. (2010) Canaanean Flint Blades in Chalcolithic Context and the Possible Onset of the Transition to the Early Bronze Age: A Case Study from Fazael 2. *Tel Aviv* 37, 33–47.

Bar-Adon, P. (1980) *The Cave of the Treasure. The Finds from the Caves in Nahal Mishmar*. Jerusalem: The Israel Exploration Society.

Barkai, R. (2004) Chapter 7. The Chalcolithic lithic assemblage. Pp. 87–109 in N. Scheftelowitz and R. Oren (eds), *Giv'at Ha-oranim. A Chalcolithic Site*. Salvage Excavation Reports 1. Tel Aviv: Sonia and Marco Nadler Institute of Archaeology, Tel Aviv University.

Bar-Yosef, O., Belfer, A., Goren, N. and Smith, P. (1977) The nawamis near `Ain Huderah (eastern Sinai). *Israel Exploration Journal* 27/2, 65–88.

Bar-Yosef Mayer, D. (2002a) The shells of the nawamis in southern Sinai. Pp. 166–80 in H. Buitenhuis, A. M. Choyke, M. Mashkour and A. H. Al-Shiyab (eds), *Archaeozoology of the Near East V. Proceedings of the Fifth International Symposium on the Archaeozoology of Southwestern Asia and Adjacent Areas*. Groeningen: ARC Publicaties 62.

Bar-Yosef Mayer, D. (2002b) Egyptian–Canaanite interaction during the 4th and 3rd millennia BCE. The shell connection. Pp. 129–35 in E. C. M. van den Brink and T. E. Levy (eds), *Egypt and the Levant. Interrelations from the 4th through the Early 3rd Millennium BCE*. London: Leicester University Press.

Baumgarten, Y. Y. (2004) An excavation at Ashqelon, Afridar–Area J. *`Atiqot* 45, 161–84.

Ben-Tor, A. trans. by R. Greenberg (1992) The Early Bronze Age. Pp. 81–124 in A. Ben-Tor (ed.), *The Archaeology of Ancient Israel*. New Haven, CT: Yale University Press.

Betts, A. V. G. and Helms, S. (1992) Conclusion. Pp. 136–47 in A. V. G. Betts (ed.), *Excavations at Tell Um Hammad. The Early Assemblages (EBI–II)*. Edinburgh: Edinburgh University Press.

Bourke, S. J. (2001) The Chalcolithic period. Pp. 107–62 in B. MacDonald, R. Adams and P. Bienkowski (eds), *The Archaeology of Jordan*. Sheffield: Sheffield Academic Press.

Bourke, S. J., Seaton, P. L., Sparks, R. T., Lovell, J. L. and Mairs, L. D. (1995) A first season of renewed excavation by the University of Sydney at Tulaylat al-Ghassul. *Annual of the Department of Antiquities of Jordan* 39, 31–63.

Braun, E. (1987) Review of *The Late Chalcolithic to Early Bronze Transition in Palestine and Transjordan* by J. W. Hanbury-Tenison. *Mitekufat Haeven* 20, 187–90.

Braun, E. (1989a) The transition from the Chalcolithic to the Early Bronze Age in Northern Israel and Transjordan. Is there a missing link? Pp. 7–28 in P. de Miroschedji (ed.), *L'urbanisation de la Palestine à l'âge du Bronze ancien:*

bilan et perspectives des recherches actuelles (Actes du Colloque d'Emmaüs, 20–24 octobre 1986). Oxford: BAR Int. Ser. 527 (1).

Braun, E. (1989b) The problem of the apsidal house. New aspects of Early Bronze I domestic architecture in Israel, Jordan and Lebanon. *Palestine Exploration Quarterly* 121, 1–43.

Braun, E. (1990) Basalt bowls of the EBI horizon in the Southern Levant. *Paléorient* 16, 87–95.

Braun, E. (1996) Cultural Diversity and Change in the Early Bronze I of Israel and Jordan: Towards an Understanding of the Chronological Progression and Patterns of Regionalism in Early Bronze I Society. Unpublished PhD thesis, Tel Aviv University.

Braun, E. (1997) *Yiftah'el: Salvage and Rescue Excavations at a Prehistoric Village in Lower Galilee, Israel*. Israel Antiquities Authority Reports 2. Jerusalem.

Braun, E. (2000) Area G at Afridar, Palmahim Quarry 3 and the earliest pottery of Early Bronze I. Part of the missing link. Pp. 113–28 in G. Philip and D. Baird (eds), *Breaking with the Past. Ceramics and Change in the Early Bronze Age of the Southern Levant*. Sheffield: Sheffield Academic Press.

Braun, E. (2001a) Post mortem: a late prehistoric site at Palmahim Quarry. *Bulletin of the Anglo-Israel Archaeological Society* 18, 17–28.

Braun, E. (2001b) Proto and Early Dynastic Egypt and Early Bronze I–II of the southern Levant. Uneasy ^{14}C correlations. *Radiocarbon* 43, 1202–18.

Braun, E. (2004) *Early Beth Shan (Strata XIX–XIII). G. M. FitzGerald's Deep Cut on the Tell*. University Museum Monograph 121. Philadelphia, PA: University of Pennsylvania Museum of Archaeology and Anthropology.

Braun, E. (2010a) South Levant Early Bronze Age chronological correlations with Egypt in light of the Narmer *serekhs* from Tel Erani and Arad: New interpretations. *British Museum Studies in Ancient Egypt and Sudan* 13: 25–48. (http://www.britishmuseum.org/research/online_journals/bmsaes/issue_13/braun.aspx). accessed 8/12/10.

Braun, E. (2010b) Social development in Early Bronze Age I of the southern Levant: reflections on evidence for different modes of ceramic production. Pp. 233–52 in S. A. Rosen and V. Roux (eds), *Techniques and People: Anthropological Perspectives on Technology in the Archaeology of the Proto-historic and Early Historic Periods in the Southern Levant* (Mémoires et travaux du Centre de Recherche Français à Jérusalem; archéologie et sciences de l'antiquité et du Moyen Âge 9) Paris: De Brocard.

Braun, E. (in press a) On some South Levantine Early Bronze Age Ceramic 'Wares' and Styles. *Palestine Exploration Quaterly*.

Braun, E. (in press b) Early Bronze I pottery. In S. Gittin (ed.), *The Pottery of Israel and its Ancient Neighbors*. Jerusalem: The Israel Exploration Society and the Israel Antiquities Authority.

Braun, E. and Brink, E. C. M. van den (1998) Some comments on the late EBI sequence of Canaan and the relative dating of Tomb U-j at Umm el Ga'ab and Graves 330 and 787 from Minshat Abu Omar with imported ware: the view from Egypt and Canaan. *Egypt and the Levant* 7, 71–95.

Braun, E. and Brink, E. C. M. van den (2008) Appraising south Levantine–Egyptian interaction: recent discoveries from Israel and Egypt. Pp. 643–88 in B. Midant-Reynes and Y. Tristant (eds), *Egypt at Its Origins 2. Proceedings of the International Conference 'Origin of the State. Predynastic and Early Dynastic Egypt', Toulouse (France), 5th–8th September, 2005*. Leuven: Peeters.

Braun, E. and Gophna, R. (2004) Salvage excavations at Afridar in Area G. *'Atiqot* 45, 185–242.

Brink, E. C. M. van den (2004) Khirbet Hadat–Modi'in (Buchman). License #A/4069–04/01: Evaluation and assessment of salvage excavations at Modi'in-Buchman, Southeast Precinct, Hills 'B' and 'C', Fall/Winter 2004. Unpublished Ms, Jerusalem, Israel Antiquities Authority Archives.

Brink, E. C. M. van den (2005) Sha'ar Efrayim. *Hadashot Arkheologiyot – Excavations and Surveys in Israel* 117. http://www.hadashot-esi.org.il/report_detail_eng.asp?id=170&mag_id=110 (accessed 23 November 2009).

Brink, E. C. M. van den (2007) Modi'in, Horbat Hadat and Be'erit (A). *Hadashot Arkheologiyot – Excavations and Surveys in Israel* 119. http://www.hadashot-esi.org.il/report_detail_eng.asp?id=484&mag_id=112 (accessed 23 November 2009).

Brink, E. C. M. van den and Braun, E. (2008) Foreign relations. Introduction. Pp. 637–41 in B. Midant-Reynes and Y. Tristant (eds), *Egypt at Its Origins 2. Proceedings of the International Conference 'Origin of the State. Predynastic and Early Dynastic Egypt', Toulouse (France), 5th–8th September, 2005*. Leuven: Peeters.

Brink, E. C. M. van den and Gophna, R. (2005) *Shoham (North), Late Chalcolithic Burial Caves in the Lod Valley, Israel*. Israel Antiquities Authority Reports 27. Jerusalem: IAA.

Caneva, I., Frangipane, M. and Palmieri, A. (1989) Excavations at Maadi. Pp. 287–91 in L. Krzyzaniak and M. Kobusiewicz (eds), *Studies in African Archaeology 2*. Poznan: Poznan Archaeological Museum.

Clark, V. A. (1979) Investigations in a prehistoric necropolis near Bab edh-Dhra[c]. *Annual of the Department of Antiquities of Jordan* 23, 57–76.

Commenge, C. (2005) The late Chalcolithic pottery. Pp. 51–97 in E. C. M. van den Brink and R. Gophna (eds), *Shoham (North). Late Chalcolithic Burial Caves in the Lod Valley, Israel*. Israel Antiquities Authority Reports 27. Jerusalem: IAA.

Commenge, C. (2006) Gilat's ceramics. Cognitive dimensions of pottery production. Pp. 394–506 in T. E. Levy (ed.), *Archaeology, Anthropology and Cult. The Sanctuary at Gilat, Israel*. London: Equinox.

Commenge-Pellerin, C. (1987) *La poterie d'Abou Matar et de l'Ouadi Zoumeili (Beersheva) au ive millénaire avant l'ère chrétienne*. Paris: Association Paléorient.

Commenge-Pellerin, C. (1990) *La poterie de Safadi (Beersheva) au ive millénaire avant l'ère chrétienne*. Paris: Association Paléorient.

Contenson, H. de (1960a) Three soundings in the Jordan Valley. *Annual of the Department of Antiquities of Jordan* 4–5, 12–98.

Contenson, H. de (1960b) La chronologie relative du niveau le plus ancien de Tell esh Shuna (Jordanie) d'après le decouvertes recentes. *Mélanges de l'Université Saint Joseph* 37, 57–75.

Contenson, H. de (1961) Remarques sur le chalcolithique récent de Tell esh-Shuneh. *Revue Biblique* 68, 546–56.

Eisenberg, E., Gopher, A. and Greenberg, R. (2001) *Tel Te'o: A Neolithic, Chalcolithic, and Early Bronze Age Site in the Hula Valley*. Israel Antiquities Authority Reports 13. Jerusalem: IAA.

Elliott, C. (1978) The Ghassulian Culture in Palestine. Origins, influences and abandonment. *Levant* 10, 37–54.

Garfinkel, Y., Ben-Shlomo, D., Freikman, M. and Vered, A. (2007) Tel Tsaf. The 2004–2006 excavation seasons. *Israel Exploration Journal* 57/1, 1–33.

Golani, A. (2005a) Ashqelon, Ha-Tayyasim St. *Hadashot Arkheologiyot – Excavations and Surveys in Israel* 117. http://www.hadashot-esi.org.il/report_detail_eng.asp?id=282&mag_id=110 (accessed 23 November 2009).

Golani, A. (2005b) Ashqelon, Barnea' B–C. *Hadashot Arkheologiyot – Excavations and Surveys in Israel* 117. http://www.hadashot-esi.org.il/report_detail_eng.asp?id=134&mag_id=110 (accessed 23 November 2009).

Gonen, R. trans. R. Greenberg (1992) The Chalcolithic period. Pp. 40–80 in A. Ben-Tor (ed.), *The Archaeology of Ancient Israel*. New Haven, CT: Yale University Press.

Gorzalczany, A. (2006) Palmahim. *Hadashot Arkheologiyot – Excavations and Surveys in Israel* 118. http://www.hadashot-esi.org.il/report_detail_eng.asp?id=312&mag_id=111 (accessed 23 November 2009).

Gustavson-Gaube, C. (1985) Tell esh-Shuna North 1984. A preliminary report. *Annual of the Department of Antiquities of Jordan* 29, 43–87.

Gustavson-Gaube, C. (1986) Tell esh-Shuna North 1985. A preliminary report. *Annual of the Department of Antiquities of Jordan* 30, 69–113.

Hanbury-Tenison, J. W. (1986) *The Late Chalcolithic to Early Bronze I Transition in Palestine and Transjordan*. Oxford: BAR Int. Ser. 311.

Hartung, U., el-Gelil, M. A., von den Driesch, A., Fares, G., Hartmann, R., Hikade, T. and Ihde, C. (2003) Vorbericht über neue Untersuchungen in der prädynastischen Siedlung von Maadi. *Mitteilungen des Deutschen Archáologischen Instituts Abteilung Kairo* 59, 149–95, Tafeln 33–7.

Helms, S. W. (1984a) Excavations at Tell Umm Hammad Esh-Sharqiya in the Jordan valley, 1982. *Levant* 16, 35–54.

Helms, S. W. (1984b) The land behind Damascus. Urbanism during the 4th millennium in Syria/Palestine. Pp. 15–31 in T. Khalidi (ed.), *Land Tenure and Social Transformation in the Middle East*. Beirut: American University in Beirut.

Helms, S. W. (1992) The pottery typology. Pp. 39–118 in A. V. G. Betts (ed.), *Excavations at Tell Um Hammad 1982–1984. The Early Assemblages (EBI–II)*. Edinburgh: Edinburgh University Press.

Kaplan, J. (1963) Excavations at Benei Beraq, 1951. *Israel Exploration Journal* 13/4, 300–12.

Kenyon, K. M. (1970) *Archaeology of the Holy Land*, 3rd edn. New York and Washington DC: Praeger.

Kenyon, K. M. (1979) *Archaeology of the Holy Land*, 4th edn. London: Ernest Benn.

Kenyon, K. M. and Holland, T. A. (1983) *Excavations at Jericho* 5. London: British School of Archaeology in Jerusalem.

Khalaily, H. (2002) Naḫal Qomem, A-2968. *Hadashot Arkheologiyot* 114, 85*–86*.

Khalaily, H. (2004) An Early Bronze Age site at Ashqelon, Afridar – Area F. *`Atiqot* 45, 121–60.

Koeppel, R., Senes, H., Murphy, W. and Mahan, G. S. (1940) *Teileilat Ghassul II. Compe rendu des fouilles l'Institut Biblique Pontifical 1932–1936. Planches*. Rome: Institut Biblique Pontifical.

Lee, J. R. (1973) Chalcolithic Ghassul. New Aspects and Master Typology. Unpublished PhD thesis, Hebrew University of Jerusalem.

Macdonald, E. (1932) *Prehistoric Fara, Beth Pelet II*. London: The British School of Archaeology in Egypt.

Mallon, A. S. J., Koeppel, S. J. and Neuville, R. (1934) *Teleilat Ghassul* I. Rome: Pontifical Biblical Institute.

Marder, O., Milevski, I. and Braun, E. (1995) The flint assemblage of lower Horvat `Illin. Some technical and economic considerations. *`Atiqot* 27, 63–93.

Mellaart, J. (1962) Preliminary report of the archaeological survey in the Yarmouk and Jordan valleys. *Annual of the Department of Antiquities of Jordan* 6–7, 126–57.

Milevski, I. (2007) Mazor (West). *Hadashot Arkheologiyot* 119: http://www.hadashot-esi.org.il/report_detail_eng.asp?id=571&mag_id=112 (Accessed 8/12/10).

Miroschedji, P. de (ed.) (1989) *L'urbanisation de la Palestine à l'âge du Bronze ancien: bilan et perspectives des recherches actuelles* (Actes du Colloque d'Emmaüs, 20–24 octobre 1986). Oxford: BAR Int. Ser. 527 (1–2).

Oshri, A. and Schick, T. H. (1998) The lithics. Pp. 59–62 in T. Schick, *The Cave of the Warrior. A 4th millennium Burial in the Judean Desert*. Israel Antiquities Authority Reports 5. Jerusalem: The Archeological Staff Officer of Judea and Samaria.

Paz, S. (2006) Area SA. The Stekelis–Avi-Yonah excavations (Circles Building), 1945–1946. Pp. 53–104 in R. Greenberg, E. Eisenberg, S. Paz and Y. Paz (eds), *Bet Yerah. The Early Bronze Age Mound. Volume I. Excavation Reports, 1933–1986*. Israel Antiquities Authority Reports 30. Jerusalem: IAA.

Perrot, J. (n.d.) *Recherche à Oumm Qatafa–Ouadi Zoumeili–Patish-Gerar–O. Zeita–O. Ghazzeh. Complémentaires aux fouilles de Beershéva (1949–1961)*. Comptes-rendus de la mission archéologique Français en Israël. Vol. I. (internal publication).

Perrot, J. (1961) Gat Guvrin (notes and news). *Israel Exploration Journal* 11, 76.

Perrot, J. (1962) Gat-Govrin. *Revue Biblique* 69, 387–8.

Perrot, J. (1972) Préhistoire Palestinienne—prémices. In L. Pirot, A. Robert, H. Cazelles and A. Feuillet (eds), *Dictionnaire de la bible (Supplément)*, cols. 286–446. Paris: Letouzey et Ané.

Perrot, J. (2001) Réflexions sur l'état des recherches concernant la préhistoire récente du proche et du Moyen-Orient. *Paléorient* 26/1, 5–28.

Perrot, J. and Ladiray, D. (1980) *Tombes à ossuaires de la région côtière palestinienne au ive millénaire avant l'ère chrétienne*. Mémoires et travaux du Centre de Recherches Préhistoriques Français de Jérusalem 1. Paris: Association Paléorient.

Riemer, H. and Kuper, R. (2000) Clayton rings. Enigmatic ancient pottery in the eastern Sahara. *Sahara* 12, 91–101.

Rizkana, I. and Seeher, J. (1987) *Maadi I. The Pottery of the Predynastic Settlement*. Archäologische Veröffentlichungen 64. Deutsches Archäologisches Institut, Abteilung Kairo. Mainz am Rhein: Philipp von Zabern.

Rizkana, I. (1988) *Maadi II. The Lithic Industries of the Predynastic Settlement*. Archäologische Veröffentlichungen 65. Deutsches Archäologisches Institut, Abteilung Kairo. Mainz am Rhein: Philipp von Zabern.

Rizkana, I. (1989) *Maadi III. The Non-Lithic Small Finds and the Structural Remains of the Predynastic Settlement*. Archäologische Veröffentlichungen 80. Deutsches Archäologisches Institut, Abteilung Kairo. Mainz am Rhein: Philipp von Zabern.

Rosen, S. A. (1983) The Canaanean blade and the Early Bronze Age. *Israel Exploration Journal* 33, 15–29.

Rosen, S. A. (1997) *Lithics After the Stone Age. A Handbook of Stone Tools from the Levant*. Walnut Creek, CA: Altamira Press.

Roux, V. (2003) A dynamic systems framework for studying technological change: application to the emergence of the potter's wheel in the southern Levant. *Journal of Archaeological Method and Theory* 10/1, 1–30.

Roux, V. (2005) Pottery manufacturing processes: Reconstitution and interpretation. Pp. 201–13 in A. L. Smith, D. Bosquet and R Martineau (eds), *Acts of the XIVth UISPP Congress, University of Liège, Belgium, 2–8 September 2001*. Oxford: BAR Int. Ser. 1349.

Roux, V. and Courty, M.-A. (1997) Les bol élaborés au tour d'Abu Hamid. Rupture technique au 4e millénaire avant J.-C. dans le Levant-Sud. *Paléorient* 23/1, 25–43.

Rowan, Y. M. (2006) The chipped stone assemblage at Gilat. Pp. 507–74 in T. E. Levy (ed.), *Archaeology, Anthropology and Cult. The Sanctuary at Gilat, Israel*. London: Equinox.

Sass, B. (2000) The small finds. Pp. 349–423 in I. Finkelstein, D. Ussishkin and B. Halpern (eds), *Megiddo III. The 1992–1996 Seasons*. Tel Aviv University Monograph Series 18. Tel Aviv: The Sonia and Marco Nadler Institute of Archaeology, Tel Aviv University.

Schaub, R. T. and Rast, W. E. (1989) *Bâb edh-Dhrâ*ᶜ*. Excavations in the Cemetery Directed by Paul W. Lapp (1965–67)*. Reports of the Expedition to the Dead Sea Plain, Jordan 1. Winona Lake, IN: Eisenbrauns.

Scheftelowitz, N. (2002) Stratigraphy, architecture and tombs. Pp. 19–90 in A. Kempinski, N. Scheftelowitz and R. Oren (eds), *Tel Kabri. The 1986–1993 Excavation Seasons*. Tel Aviv University Monograph Series 20. Tel Aviv: The Sonia and Marco Nadler Institute of Archaeology, Tel Aviv University.

Scheftelowitz, N. and Oren, R. (2004) *Giv'at Ha-oranim. A Chalcolithic Site*. Salvage Excavation Reports 1. Tel Aviv: Sonia and Marco Nadler Institute of Archaeology, Tel Aviv University.

Seeher, J. (1990) I. Abhandlungen. Maadi–eine prĕdynastische Kulturgruppe zwischen Obergägypten und Palästina. Pp. 123–56 in *Praehistorische Zeitschrift* (*Herausgegeben von Niels Bantelmann, Bernard Hansel, Michael Müller-Wille*). Band 65, Heft 2. Berlin and New York: Walter de Gruyter.

Shalev, S. and Braun, E. (1997) The metal objects from Yiftah'el II. Pp. 92–6 in E. Braun (ed.), *Yiftah'el. Salvage and Rescue Excavations at a Prehistoric Village in Lower Galilee, Israel*. Israel Antiquities Authority Reports 2. Jerusalem: IAA.

Stekelis, M. (1935) *Les monuments mégalithiques de Palestine*. Archives de l'Institut de paleontology humaine, mémoire 1. Paris: Masson et Cie Editeurs.

Stekelis, M. (1961) *La necropolis megalítica de Ala-Safat, Transjordania*. Monografia 1. Barcelona Diputación Provincial de Barcelona, Instituto de Prehistoria y Arqueologia.

Sussman, V. and Ben-Arieh, S. (1966) Ancient Burials in Giv'atayim. *`Atiqot* 3, 27–39, *4 (Hebrew with English summary).

Tadmor, M., Kedem, D., Begemann, F., Hauptmann, A., Pernicka, E. and Schmitt-Strecker, S. (1995) The Nahal Mishmar hoard from the Judean desert. Technology, composition, and provenance. *`Atiqot* 27, 95–148.

Tutundžić, S. P. (2001) The Ghassulian traits of domestic animal figurines at Maadi. *Journal of Serbian Archaeological Society* 17, 77–89.

Tutundžić, S. P. (2002) Painted pottery at Maadi and the Ghassulian tradition. *Journal of Serbian Archaeological Society* 18, 63–86.

Vaux, R. M. de (1970) Palestine during the Neolithic and Chalcolithic periods. Pp. 498–535 in I. E. S. Edwards, C. J. Gadd and N. G. L. Hammond (eds), *Cambridge Ancient History*, 3rd edn, vol. 1, part 1. Cambridge: Cambridge University Press.

Vaux, R. M. de and Steve, A. M. (1949) La deuxième campagne de fouilles de Tell el-Far'ah, près Naplouse. *Revue Biblique* 56, 102–38.

Wampler, J. C. (1947) *Tell en-Nasbeh II. The Pottery. Excavated under the Direction of the Late William Frederic Badé*. Berkeley, CA, and New Haven, CT: The Palestine Institute of Pacific School of Religion and the American Schools of Oriental Research.

Yannai, E. (2006) *'En Esur ('Ein Asawir) I. Excavations at a Proto-historic Site in the Coastal Plain of Israel*. Israel Antiquities Authority Reports 31. Jerusalem: IAA.

Yekutieli, Y. (2000) Early Bronze Age I pottery in southwestern Canaan. Pp. 129–52 in G. Philip and D. Baird (eds), *Ceramics and Change in the Early Bronze Age of the Southern Levant*. Sheffield: Sheffield Academic Press.

Yekutieli, Y. (2001) The Early Bronze Age IA of southwestern Canaan. Pp. 659–88 in S. R. Wolff (ed.), *Studies in the Archaeology of Israel and Neighboring Lands in Memory of Douglas L. Esse*. Studies in Ancient Oriental Civilization No. 59/ASOR Book Series No. 5. Chicago, MI, and Atlanta, GA: The Oriental Institute.

Yekutieli, Y. and Gophna, R. (1994) Excavations at an Early Bronze Age site near Nizzanim. *Tel Aviv* 21, 162–85.

Zbenovich, V. G. (2004) The flint assemblages from Ashqelon, Afridar – Areas G and J. *`Atiqot* 45, 263–78.

13. The End of the Chalcolithic Period (4500–3600 BC) in the Northern Negev Desert, Israel

Margie M. Burton and Thomas E. Levy

Introduction

The end of the Chalcolithic period (*c.*4500–3600 cal BC) in the southern Levant is marked by a clear disjunction in settlement patterns and material culture. Across a broad region from the Mediterranean coast to the eastern side of the Jordan valley, and from the Golan south to Sinai, many large sites were abandoned and generally shared economic and ideological features disappeared. The Chalcolithic–Early Bronze I (EB I) horizon has been drawn by archaeologists to mark this dramatic change. As research has progressed, geographically and, to varying degrees, temporally restricted 'culture groups' have been defined and assigned to the Chalcolithic (*e.g.*, Amiran 1969, 22; Epstein 1998; Gilead 1994; 1995, 473–6) or EB I (*e.g.*, Braun 1989; 1996; 2000; Gophna 1998, 272). Such groupings are based on observed sub-regional differences in material culture which may reflect important differences in economy and social structure (Childe 1929; Clarke 1978, 299–300; Renfrew 1984a, 33–9). However, ethnoarchaeological and historical studies (*e.g.*, Hodder 1978; 1982; Moore and Romney 1994; Welsch *et al.* 1992) remind us that the people who gave rise to the material record existed within social continua that spanned both time and space and that cultural boundaries shift through time (Holl and Levy 1992). With this reality, it is perhaps not surprising that static constructions of southern Levantine culture history, which have emphasized material differences between defined chrono-cultural entities, have largely failed to explain cultural shifts or to further illuminate proposed reasons for what has been called the Chalcolithic 'collapse' (Joffe 1993; Levy 1998).

A useful approach for sorting out the geographic, social and small-scale chronological factors that may contribute to culture change (*e.g.* Parkinson 2006, 50), is to look for evidence of diachronic similarities across sites, sets of sites or regions. Along these lines and within the southern Levantine context, E. Braun (1989; 1996; 2000; this volume; see also Dessel 1991; 2001; Yekutieli 2001) has productively documented continuities in late Chalcolithic and initial EB I materials that indicate the social links between these two cultural periods. In this paper a similar but explicitly quantitative approach is used to investigate the end of the Chalcolithic period in the northern Negev Desert of Israel. First, the chronology for the final phase of settlement in this sub-region is reviewed and refined with new ^{14}C dates from Shiqmim, one of the largest northern Negev Chalcolithic sites. Second, ceramic assemblage data from Shiqmim and other selected Chalcolithic and initial EB I (here designated 'EB IA') sites are analysed using statistical methods developed for biological population studies. The results facilitate an interpretation of archaeological sites as points within social networks. When combined with independent chronological data, these networks can be seen to shift during the first quarter of the 4th millennium under the influences of social, economic and environmental factors which are discussed in the final section of the paper. The diachronic quantitative approach, coupled with improved chronological resolution, helps to move us closer to identifying local agents of change.

Chronology of final Chalcolithic settlement

Evidence of the latest Chalcolithic occupation of the northern Negev desert comes from the site of Shiqmim in the Beer Sheva valley. This large (*c.*10 hectares) agricultural village has three main architectural phases (Levy *et al.* 1991) and, at the present time, more ^{14}C dates (n = 43) than any other Chalcolithic site in its sub-region. It was Shiqmim's extensive radiocarbon record that led researchers (*e.g.* Burton and Levy 2001, 1237; Lovell 2002, 94) to posit the northern Negev as one of the last bastions of Chalcolithic culture, enduring until *c.*3500

Sample[1]	*Year/area/locus and basket*	*Context*	*Uncalibrated BP*	*Calibrated BC (2 sigma)*[2]	*Probability*
Beta-161863	1987/North trench/L.270 B.0525	Negative pit impressions, Sq. L7	5780 ± 100	4900–4350	95.4
RT-859E	1987/North trench/L.211 B.0328	Fill, Sq. K10	5390 ± 180	4600–3750	95.4
RT-859D	1987/North trench/L.216 B.0323	Fill, Sq. K10	5370 ± 180	4600–3750	95.4
Beta-161868	1989/J/L.3259 B.Z56	Circular stone feature, Sq. M12	5460 ± 90	4460–4040	95.4
Beta-161865	1988/P/L.536 B.81XX	Deep ashy pit, Sq. G10	5440 ± 80	4450–4050	95.4
RT-554A	1982	Room 1, floor 1	5250 ± 140	4400–3700	95.4
RT-1341	1989/J/L.3256 B.Z569	Pit, stone-lined, Sq. L12	5370 ± 40	4330–4220	51.7
				4210–4050	43.7
Beta-161871	1989/J/L.3267 B.Z605	Ash pit/hearth, Sq. L12	5300 ± 80	4330–4280	6.8
				4270–3970	88.6
RT-859C	1987/North trench/L.210 B.0317	Fill, Sq. K11	5080 ± 180	4350–3500	95.4
Beta-161875	1993/Z/L.5004 B.C38	Ash pit, Sq. T1–2/S1–2	5280 ± 70	4320–4290	2.3
				4270–3960	93.1
Beta-161866	1988/P/L.561 B.8164	Ash pit in baulk, Sq. G10	5270 ± 70	4320–4290	1.6
				4270–3960	93.8
Beta-161874	1993/D/L.4112 B.A280	Hearth removal, Sq. Q13	5270 ± 70	4320–4290	1.6
				4270–3960	93.8
Beta-161870	1989/J/L.3263 B.Z611	Ash pit/hearth, Sq. L12	5270 ± 70	4320–4290	1.6
				4270–3960	93.8
Beta-161876	1993/E/L.5029 B.C69	Hearth, Sq. A14	5300 ± 50	4260–3980	95.4
Beta-161867	1989/J/L.3258 B.Z56	Ash, Sq. K12	5130 ± 70	4250–3700	95.4
Beta-161869	1989/J/L.3261 B.Z604	Pit in smelter, Sq. K12	5250 ± 50	4240–4190	13.1
				4180–3960	82.3
Beta-161864	1988/Y/L.429 B.7260	Stone circle/hearth, Sq. L10	5220 ± 70	4240–3930	90.9
				3880–3800	4.5
Beta-161872	1989/J/L.3311 B.Z807	Ash layer, Sq. K12	5220 ± 70	4240–3930	90.9
				3880–3800	4.5

[1] All samples consisted of charcoal
[2] OxCal version 3.10, IntCal04.14c, Reimer *et al.* 2004

Table 13.1 ^{14}C dates from the final phase (Stratum I) at Shiqmim

cal BC. However, at the time of the previous syntheses very few dates were available from the final occupation phase (Stratum I) at Shiqmim (Burton and Levy 2001, 1236). Furthermore, a number of the Shiqmim dates had large standard deviations, in some cases as much as 180 years (Burton and Levy 2001, 1243–4). Thirteen recently processed ^{14}C dates from Stratum I (Table 13.1: Beta-161863 to -161872, and Beta-161874 to -161876; Burton 2004, 657, appendix 5.1) are more precise, with none extending later than 3700 cal BC at the 95% confidence interval (OxCal version 3.10, IntCal04.14c, Reimer *et al.* 2004). Most suggest a *terminus* by between 4000 and 3800 cal BC, a few centuries earlier than previously thought. Abandonment of Shiqmim by 3800 cal BC would significantly decrease the temporal 'gap' between the end of Chalcolithic occupation in the northern Negev and the Jordan valley. Substantive Chalcolithic habitation of the latter sub-region is thought to have ended by *c.*4000 cal BC based on recent revisions to the chronology of Teleilat Ghassul (Bourke *et al.* 2001, 1221, fig. 2). The new, earlier, dates for Shiqmim's abandonment also appear to diminish the possibility of asymmetric colonization or conquest of northern Negev Chalcolithic communities by a centralized Egyptian entity (*cf.* Joffe 1993, 37; Joffe *et al.* 2001, 17), an influence not thought to be significant until after *c.*3500 BC (Braun 2004, 518; de Miroschedji 2002, 39–44, table 2.1).

The ^{14}C dates and cultural material from Shiqmim further indicate that, within the northern Negev sub-region, habitation of the Beer Sheva valley may have continued for some time after the decline of Chalcolithic settlement along the Nahal Grar to the north. Although the major sites of Grar (Gilead 1989; 1995) and Abu Hof Village (Alon 1961; Burton 2004, 98–159) lack adequate radiometric records, relative cross-dating based on ceramic typological parallels with Teleilat Ghassul (primarily an abundance of 'cigar-shaped' cornets, *cf.* Gilead and Goren 1995, 158) suggest that the main thrust of Nahal Grar Chalcolithic occupation occurred within a time frame of *c.*4400 to 4000 cal BC (Burton 2004, 103; *cf.* Gilead 1995, 479). Two relatively late ^{14}C dates (RT-2058, Burton and Levy 2001, 1244; and RT-860B, Carmi and Segal 1992, 125) have come from the Chalcolithic cult site of Gilat on the Nahal Patish, which flows south of the Nahal Grar. However, these two dates are now thought to be related to disturbed contexts. The remaining six ^{14}C determinations for Gilat indicate activity within the three or four centuries centred on 4500 cal BC (Levy and Burton 2006, 864, table appendix 2.2). More radiocarbon dates are still needed from Gilat and other sites to clarify these relationships (Avner and Carmi 2001). However, this time frame appears to correspond with the initial settlement of Shiqmim (Levy and Burton 2006, 865, fig. appendix 2.2). All of the recently emerging comparative material continues to affirm the relatively late persistence of the Shiqmim settlement both within its own sub-region and across sub-regions, while tending to diminish the absolute temporal disparity among these.

Other northern Negev sites with 'Chalcolithic-style' assemblages have been identified along the Nahal Tillah, a north-easterly branch of the Nahal Grar. These are mostly small habitation loci with ephemeral architecture or natural cave occupations (*e.g.* Abu Hof Cave, part of the Nahal Tillah/Halif Terrace project; Levy *et al.* 1997, 43). Some of the excavated portions of the Halif Terrace show continuous occupation into the EB I (Alon and Yekutieli 1995; Dessel 1991, 2001; Levy *et al.* 1997; Seger 1983; 1987; 1990; 1991; Seger *et al.* 1990; Yekutieli 2001). Researchers have described the cultural material, mainly pottery, from the early strata at these sites as representing a 'degenerated' or 'Terminal' Chalcolithic stage (Dessel 1991, 88, 92; Joffe and Dessel 1995). A single ^{14}C date from the Nahal Tillah/Halif Terrace Stratum IV excavations by Levy and Alon (Beta-167478, 5030 ± 40 BP, Burton 2004, 334) places the basal Chalcolithic level at 3950–3710 cal BC (2-sigma, OxCal version 3.10, IntCal04.14c, Reimer *et al.* 2004). Such a date, late in the Chalcolithic period, is generally consistent with previous assessments of the cultural material. It does not, however, rule out some relatively brief period of contemporaneity with final-phase Shiqmim. The directly superimposed EB IA level, Stratum IIIb, at Nahal Tillah/Halif Terrace (Levy *et al.* 1997, 7, table 1) may correspond to absolute dates of *c.*3700 to 3500 cal BC (Burton 2004, 335; Yekutieli 2000, 130, table 8.3), perhaps coincident with EB IA occupations at Afridar Area G (Braun 2001, 1290, table 2) and Ashkelon Afridar Area E (Golani and Segal 2002, 146, 150; Segal and Carmi 1996, 91) on Israel's coastal plain. Across the Arava, small EB IA villages engaged in copper metallurgy, such as Wadi Fidan 4 in Jordan's Faynan district, have yielded somewhat later but overlapping dates (*c.*3600 to 3400 cal BC, Adams and Genz 1995, 19; Levy 2007; Levy *et al.* 2001, 169). The sites of Tall al-Magass and Tall Hujayrat al-Ghuzlan, near the Wadi al-Yutum north-east of Aqaba, revealed material-culture assemblages similar to Wadi Fidan 4 (Khalil and Eichmann 1999, Khalil and Eichmann 2001). The architecture and material culture of all these EB IA occupations differs from that of large northern Negev Chalcolithic sites such as Grar, Abu Hof Village, Shiqmim and others in the Beer Sheva valley so that they can be clearly recognized as representing distinct, though in some cases probably emergent, cultural traditions.

Taken together, the additions to and refinements of the radiometric record discussed above clarify the absolute chronology of northern Negev Chalcolithic site abandonment and EB IA site establishment. The dates now suggest that final abandonment of the Beer Sheva valley took place no later than *c.*3800 cal BC, not *c.*3500 cal BC as previously thought (Burton and Levy 2001, 1236–7; Lovell 2002, 93–4). However, some sites lack ^{14}C dates and the picture remains complex. On a technical level, it should be recognized that ^{14}C dates alone are unlikely to resolve differences in site establishment or abandonment within an approximately 200-year time interval (Blackham 2002, 26, 29–32 points out that radiocarbon dates are more properly referred to as 'time placement dates'). Therefore, it may be difficult or impossible to reject hypotheses of site contemporaneity based on sets of radiocarbon dates. On an interpretive level, it is necessary to entertain the possibility, or even likelihood, that not all northern Negev Chalcolithic sites were established or abandoned at the same time. This does not mean that they did not share phases of occupational contemporaneity. The lack of clear breaks in the Chalcolithic radiocarbon record as a whole suggests a continuous stream of time (Blackham 2002, 24–5; Burton and Levy 2001, 1232) during which there may have been a waxing and waning of Chalcolithic settlement centres (*cf.* Blackham 2002, 21; for a previous recognition of sub-phasing during the northern Negev Chalcolithic see Gilead 1994; 1995, 479–80). Communities typically cycle through asynchronous phases of establishment, expansion and decline and this can be expected to lead to accumulations of overlapping time placement dates.

In terms of overall sub-regional population change, it is still possible to conclude, based on changes in the numbers and sizes of sites, that the northern Negev experienced demographic decline following the Chalcolithic cultural period (*cf.* Gophna 1998, 269). However, the relative severity of absolute population decrease is difficult to assess because the Chalcolithic archaeological record probably conflates multiple events of site settlement and abandonment over the course of its thousand-year time frame. Difficulties in recognizing phases of population mobilization and dispersal that may have followed large-site abandonments have probably also contributed to the sense of catastrophic demographic decline. For example, prior reconstructions of population decrease in the Halif Terrace vicinity following the end of the 'Chalcolithic', calculated with the presumption of continuous occupation over broad areas (Alon and Yekutieli 1995, 184), may be incorrect owing to the scattered nature of settlement and some cases of imprecise temporal attribution of habitation sites. The improved chronology of EB IA site occupation and Chalcolithic site abandonment afforded by the increasing number and precision of ^{14}C dates shows that there was no significant chronological 'gap' in the northern Negev, although there was a shift in the geographic focus of settlement (Levy and van den Brink 2002). The radiometric record thus helps to outline the time and direction of demographic change at the end of the Chalcolithic, but it does so in only a general and relative way that cannot, taken alone, address the processes that led to change.

Ceramic 'connectivity' as a material correlate of social interaction and movement

Demographic shifts imply social group movement and transitioning patterns of interaction between and within social groups. Possible movements and new social interactions which can provide the impetus for cultural change can be assessed through comparative examination of cultural material. When archaeological assemblages are very similar from site to site, or when they include artefacts traceable to other points of origin, it is possible to infer some form of social interaction across time and space (Renfrew 1984a, 36–7). Scholars have pointed out the various ways in which constructed archaeological culture groups do not accurately correspond to human social groups (for discussions of the relationship between 'archaeological cultures' and the social groups that generate them see, for example, Clarke 1978, 249, 269–72; Hodder 1978, 1982; Renfrew 1984a, 33–9). Nonetheless, tests of congruence in material assemblages are still the primary available means for tracing pre- and proto-historic movements of people, goods and/or ideas (*e.g.*, Parkinson 2006). The concept of 'connectivity' – a relationship of relative similarity between populations measured in terms of detectable traits – has been used in a parallel way in biological population studies (*e.g.*, Hellberg *et al.* 2002, Thorrold *et al.* 2002) to reconstruct patterns of recruitment and evolutionary sequences for organisms. This is different from the notion of cultural connectivity being explored in deep-time studies of cultural interaction in the southern Levant (LaBianca and Scham 2006); however, it has the potential to provide a method for testing cultural connectivity models. In the biological population approach 'connectedness' is presumed to arise through interaction or exchange between populations without *a priori* knowledge of the mechanism through which transmission of traits occurs. Very similar populations or species are said to have a high degree of connectivity and therefore are thought to be closely related. Connectivity measures may be used to arrange closely related populations as branches on phylogenetic 'trees' that reflect varying levels of interaction between groups.

By applying connectivity measures and clustering techniques commonly employed in the construction of phylogenetic trees (PHYLIP, Felsenstein 1989, 1995) to archaeological site assemblages, it is possible to quantitatively assess the relative level of interaction between sites. The example presented in this paper uses ceramic characteristics of vessel type and technology (expressed as assemblage frequencies in Table 13.2) for selected northern Negev Chalcolithic sites (Abu Hof Village; Shiqmim and its 'hamlets' Mezad Aluf, Shiqmim Dorom and Shiqmim Mizrah), sites/strata that have been identified as 'Terminal' Chalcolithic (Nahal Tillah/Halif Terrace Stratum IV, Abu Hof Cave), and EB IA sites/strata in the northern Negev (Nahal Tillah/Halif Terrace Stratum IIIb) and Jordan's Faynan copper-ore district (Wadi Fidan 4 Village) (Figure 1.1; see Figure 13.1 for examples of key ceramic types used in this study; see Blackham 2002, 89–97, and Parkinson 2006 for other examples of diachronic quantitative analyses of social interaction using ceramic assemblages). Pottery from these sites has been shown by petrographic analysis to be overwhelmingly the product of local potters (Abu Hof: Gilead and Goren 1989; Shiqmim: Goren and Gilead 1987; Nahal Tillah/Halif Terrace: Levy *et al.* 1997, 35–8; Wadi Fidan 4: Adams 1998, 114) and may therefore be assumed to reflect the needs and production traditions of the site inhabitants. All of the assemblages used in this analysis were excavated by Levy and colleagues between 1987 and 1997 using similar excavation methods, and all material was typed, recorded and summarized by the same analysts (see also Burton 2004). Thus the dataset may be considered internally consistent and amenable to comparative analysis (*cf.* Bourke and Lovell 2004, 181).

The connectivity analysis proceeded by, first, calculating 'genetic distances' between assemblages using Cavalli-Sforza's Chord measure (a mathematical algorithm that assumes all differences between populations arise from random processes occurring at a constant rate through time). Second, the UPGMA (Unweighted Pair Group Method with Arithmetic mean) method of clustering was used to generate branch lengths (based on the 'genetic distances') that connect assemblages and construct a 'tree' (Figure 13.2). This procedure serves to quantitatively formalize similarities among pottery assemblages. The results have been drawn as a phenogram with scaled branch lengths in Figure 13.3.

It should be noted with respect to the phenogram that while the UPGMA protocol constructs a rooted tree, the presumption of a common 'root' or 'ancestral' assemblage is in this case purely fictitious and probably false. What is relevant to the identification of social interaction is that the primary division among the assemblages (Node 1) is along geographic lines, setting the Wadi Fidan 4 Village assemblage east of the Arava valley apart from all of the northern Negev assemblages. Wadi Fidan 4 Village pottery is distinct from both Chalcolithic and early EB IA pottery in the northern Negev, suggesting that social contact between the two areas was extremely limited or was not expressed in shared ceramic traditions. Historical studies (*e.g.*, Welsch *et al.* 1992) show that geographic distance is an important factor in assemblage variation presumably because greater distance limits communication and exchange in sedentary village-level societies. Linguistic factors may be as important as distance in moderating cultural exchange (*e.g.*, Moore and Romney 1994). In this light, the major junction at Node 1 may be interpreted as possible evidence that linguistic differences or other elements of ethnicity played a role in limiting the sharing of material culture between social groups in the northern Negev and southern Jordan.

The second break (Node 2) reflects the significant disjunction in pottery type frequencies and ceramic technology that marks the Chalcolithic–EB IA horizon in the northern Negev. It is possible to conclude that Node

Vessel type	*AHVL*[1]	*Shiqmim Village*[2]	*Shiqmim Mizrah*[2]	*Shiqmim Dorom*[2]	*Mezad Aluf*[2]	*NT IV*[3]	*NT III/IIIB*[3]	*Abu Hof Cave*[3]	*Wadi Fidan 4*[4]
	n = 763	*n* = 17550	*n* = 79	*n* = 223	*n* = 75	*n* = 253	*n* = 523	*n* = 31	*n* = 433
Bowl/basin	55.6	76.7	71.0	76.0	72.0	81.4	79.2	71.0	34.4
Cornet	21.7	0.0	0.0	0.0	0.0	0.4	0.4	3.2	0.0
Holemouth jar	12.8	13.3	21.0	16.0	12.0	7.1	8.8	9.7	31.6
Necked jar/pithos	8.0	7.2	7.0	8.0	12.0	7.1	10.1	16.1	33.0
Churn	1.2	2.2	1.0	0.0	4.0	0.8	0.0	0.0	0.0
Pedestal vessel	0.2	0.2	0.0	0.0	0.0	0.0	0.0	0.0	0.0
Other	0.5	0.4	0.0	0.0	0.0	3.2	1.5	0.0	1.0
Total	**100.0**	**100.0**	**100.0**	**100.0**	**100.0**	**100.0**	**100.0**	**100.0**	**100.0**
Technology[5]									
Wheel-made	50	70	70	70	70	70	40	70	0
Hand-made	50	30	30	30	30	30	60	30	100
Total	**100**	**100**	**100**	**100**	**100**	**100**	**100**	**100**	**100**
Inclusions									
Inorganic	100	100	100	100	100	96	72	100	100
Organic	0	0	0	0	0	4	28	0	0
Total	**100**	**100**	**100**	**100**	**100**	**100**	**100**	**100**	**100**

Source: Burton 2004
[1] 114, table 4.2
[2] 185, 263, tables 5.2, 5.21
[3] 403, 406, 412, tables 6.15, 6.17, 6.18
[4] 454, table 7.3
[5] Estimate based on per cent of bowl rim sherds with rilling multiplied by proportion of bowl rim sherds in the assemblage

Table 13.2 Ceramic frequency data (based on diagnostic sherd counts) used for PHYLIP analysis (Source: Burton 2004, 633, table 10.2)

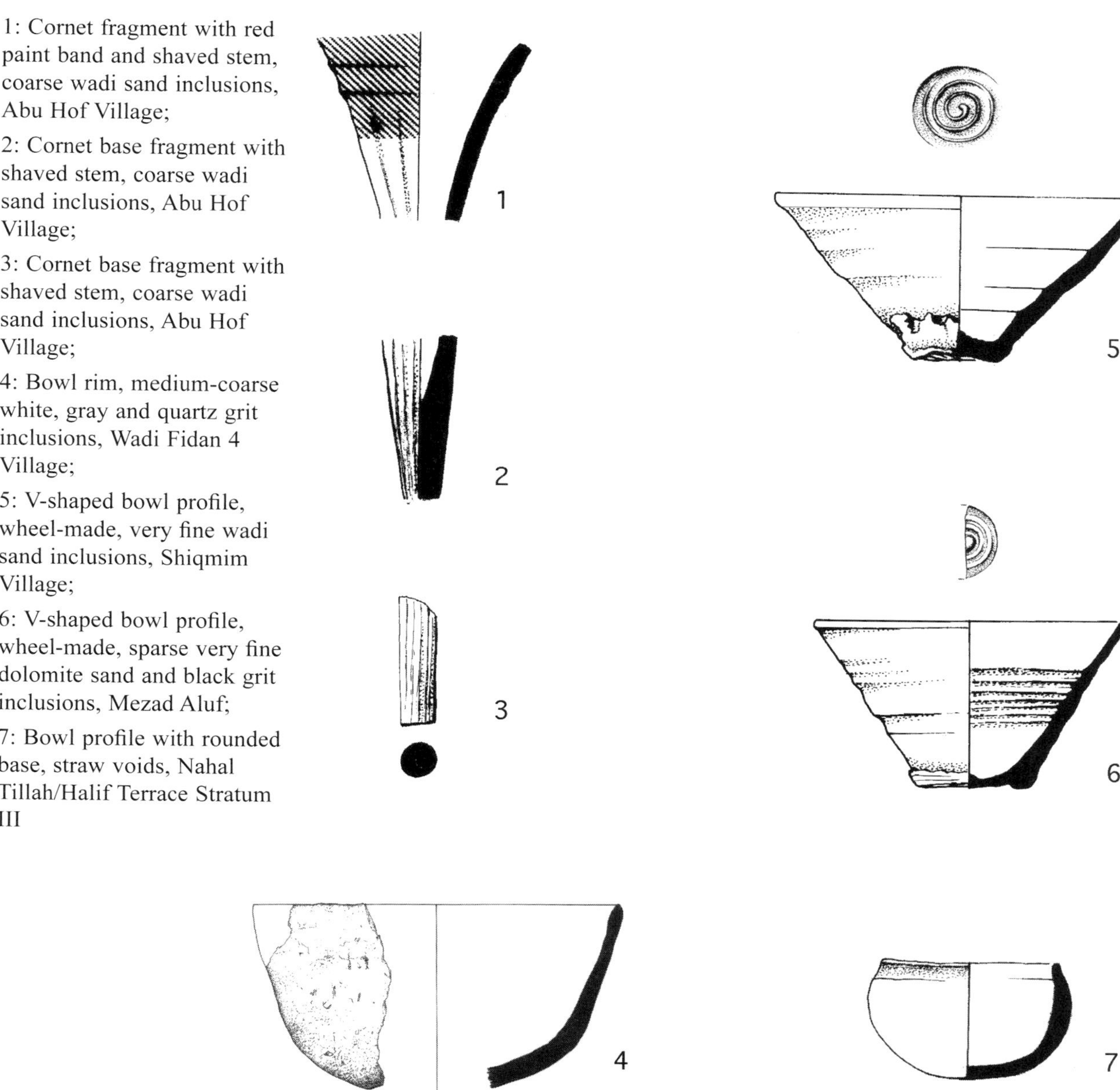

Figure 13.1 Selected examples of ceramic types used in this study

2 represents an abrupt temporal, rather than a geographic, disjunction because Nahal Tillah/Halif Terrace Stratum III/IIIb stratigraphically overlies Nahal Tillah/Halif Terrace Stratum IV.

The third major branch point in the phenogram is at Node 3. This divergence reflects the considerable difference between the Abu Hof Village assemblage and assemblages from the Beer Sheva valley sites and basal strata at other habitation sites within the Halif Terrace vicinity. Cross-dating with Teleilat Ghassul (Burton 2004, 103) and ^{14}C dates from Beer Sheva valley Chalcolithic sites (Burton and Levy 2001, 1243–4) suggests that the origins of this disjunction with respect to the Shiqmim cluster of sites are primarily socio-geographic (though some temporal component cannot be entirely discounted), since the Nahal Grar and Nahal Beer Sheva settlements appear to have coexisted for some period of time. It is notable that Nahal Tillah/Halif Terrace Stratum IV and Abu Hof Cave show a very high degree of ceramic connectivity with the Beer Sheva valley Chalcolithic assemblages, despite the large

```
9 Populations
Neighbor-Joining/UPGMA method version 3.573c
UPGMA method
Negative branch lengths allowed
```

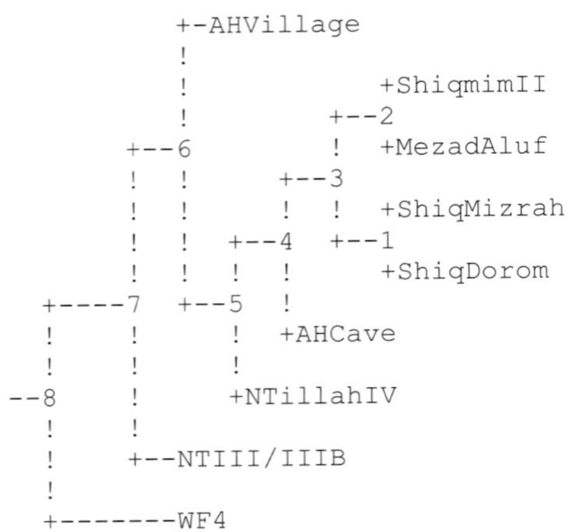

```
          +-AHVillage
          !
          !           +ShiqmimII
          !        +--2
       +--6        !  +MezadAluf
       !  !     +--3
       !  !     !  !  +ShiqMizrah
       !  !  +--4  +--1
       !  !  !  !     +ShiqDorom
  +----7  +--5  !
  !    !     !  +AHCave
  !    !     !
--8    !     +NTillahIV
  !    !
  !    +--NTIII/IIIB
  !
  +-------WF4
```

Between	And	Length
8	7	0.08424
7	6	0.01937
6	AHVillage	0.03355
6	5	0.02065
5	4	0.00367
4	3	0.00532
3	2	0.00190
2	ShiqmimII	0.00200
2	MezadAluf	0.00200
3	1	0.00210
1	ShiqMizrah	0.00180
1	ShiqDorom	0.00180
4	AHCave	0.00923
5	NTillahIV	0.01290
7	NTIII/IIIB	0.05292
8	WF4	0.13716

Figure 13.2 Output of UPGMA clustering program (PHYLIP version 3.57C, J. Felsenstein 1995) using Cavalli-Sforza Chord measures for Chalcolithic and EB IA ceramic assemblages (Source: Burton 2004, 634, fig. 10.1)

geographic distance between them (*c*.30 km). Conversely, Nahal Tillah/Halif Terrace Stratum IV and Abu Hof Cave show a low level of connectivity with Abu Hof Village only 2 km away. This result would seem to violate the general rule that 'geographic propinquity' correlates with similarities in material cultural (Welsch *et al.* 1992; Moore and Romney 1994). One way to explain the anomaly is to posit an event of relatively long-distance population movement from the Beer Sheva valley to the Halif Terrace. If this were coupled with small-scale chronological variation suggested by the ^{14}C dates discussed above, significant social interaction between the Abu Hof Village population and inhabitants of Abu Hof Cave and Nahal Tillah/Halif Terrace Stratum IV would have been precluded (*cf.* Parkinson 2006, 52). Alternatively, rigid social barriers may have prevented a sharing of pottery production traditions within a 2 km radius. By way of contrast, the extremely close temporal and spatial relationships between the Shiqmim Village 'centre' and the neighbouring smaller 'hamlets' of Mezad Aluf, Shiqmim Mizrah and Shiqmim Dorom (Levy *et al.* 2006) are clearly reflected in the very short branch lengths that link them. These Beer Sheva valley sites seem to have been part of a distinctive, socially coherent sub-regional settlement system during the Chalcolithic period (Levy *et al.* 2006).

In summary, certain patterns of social interaction and population movement at the Chalcolithic–EB IA horizon may be inferred from the ceramic 'connectivities' depicted in the UPGMA phenogram and site chronologies. Given ^{14}C dates presented above that place Shiqmim's abandonment and initial occupation of the Halif Terrace within the same time interval (*c*.3900–3700 BC), the substantive ceramic differences observed within a *c*.2 km radius in the Halif Terrace vicinity may imply the arrival of distinctive social groups from the Beer Sheva valley (consistent with similar proposals made by Alon and Yekutieli 1995, 176–8; Dessel 1991, 92; 2001, 109; Yekutieli 2001; 2002) at a time late in the occupational history of Abu Hof Village. Though not explicitly tested here, it is possible that some social

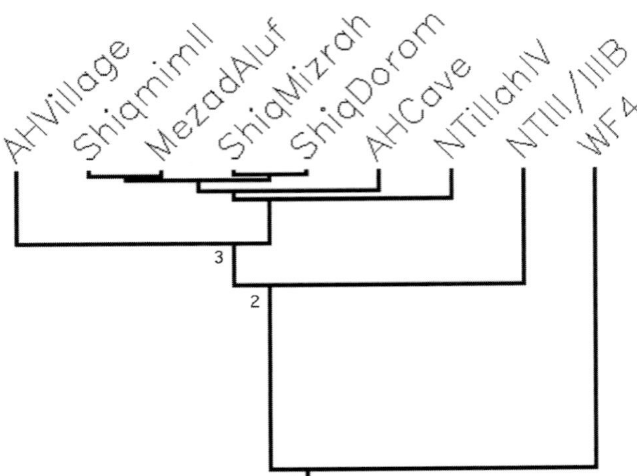

Figure 13.3 UPGMA phenogram with scaled branch lengths for Chalcolithic and EB IA ceramic assemblages (Source: Burton 2004, 635, fig. 10.2)

groups may have continued further on toward the Judean desert (*cf.* Bar-Adon 1980). Pathways of migration out of the Beer Sheva valley northward and westward toward the Mediterranean coastal plain have also been suggested based on continuities in material culture (Braun 2001; Golani and Segal 2002). Additionally, movements of people from the Beer Sheva valley toward the Nile delta at the end of the Chalcolithic period are supported by locally made northern Negev-style pottery at Buto Ia dated to the first quarter of the 4th millennium BC (Commenge and Alon 2002, 146; Faltings 2002, 166–7). Informal social and exchange networks across the northern Negev, Mediterranean coastal plain, northern Sinai and the Egyptian delta have been documented as existing well before the Chalcolithic *dénouement* (Bar-Yosef Mayer 2002; Goren and Fabian 2002; Joffe 1993, 33; de Miroschedji 2002; Perrot and Ladiray 1980; Yekutieli 2002). These hypothesized population movements thus seem to follow previously established routes. Such demographic patterns may be typical of post-collapse population translocations: a similar case is noted by Cordell (2000) in the Pueblo Southwest, where migrations away from large sites affected by the chaotic precipitation regime of 1200–1400 AD followed pre-existing exchange networks.

If social groups from Shiqmim had moved southward and eastward toward Jordan's Faynan copper-ore district at the close of the Chalcolithic, a pattern of ceramic similarities might be expected with that sub-region. The pottery data do not support such a pathway of social interaction, even though the northern Negev–Faynan route must have been travelled during the late Chalcolithic to provide the copper ore for metal production at sites like Shiqmim, Mezad Aluf, Abu Matar and Bir es-Safadi (Golden *et al.* 2001; Hauptmann 1989; Levy and Shalev 1989). In spite of the evidenced ore extraction activity, extensive surveys of the Faynan region indicate an absence of settlement during the Beer Sheva valley Chalcolithic (Levy *et al.* 2001). In the EB IA, Faynan sites show some elements of a mutually shared ceramic tradition with the Transjordan and eastern Dead Sea areas (*cf.* Schaub and Rast 2000, 88) while seeming to have been largely isolated from influence from western Palestine (*cf.* Braun 1996, 187; Gophna 1998, 272). This situation apparently extended back in time to at least the Chalcolithic period (*cf.* Bourke 2002; Lovell 2001, 51). The implication is that the *main* axis for proto-historic movement of people and material goods in what is today Jordan was north–south along the eastern side of the Dead Sea and the Arava valley. A possible pathway of social interaction away from Chalcolithic Teleilat Ghassul (*cf.* Prag 2000, 98) and toward the Faynan at the beginning of the EB IA is supported by some parallels in pottery decorative techniques (Burton 2004, 481–3), but this remains speculative and additional evidence is needed. In contrast, at the close of the Chalcolithic, archaeologically visible social groups from the Beer Sheva valley do not appear to have moved toward the source of the copper that had been a unique aspect of their economy. Given the lack of contemporary occupation and later material culture incongruity, the northern Negev–Faynan copper-ore route during the Chalcolithic may be interpreted as representing a long-distance exploitation of a natural resource rather than a pathway of symbiotic exchange and social interaction.

Social and economic processes in northern Negev Chalcolithic devolution

What were the reasons behind the cultural and demographic shifts that occurred at the end of the Chalcolithic period? The demise of Chalcolithic culture generally has been explained recently in terms of gradually unfolding pan-regional factors. For example, Joffe *et al.* (2001, 9) characterized the southern Levantine Chalcolithic period as a transitional phase 'at the end of a long stream of tradition that began in the Palaeolithic'. This explanatory paradigm draws attention to the roots of Chalcolithic iconography and sources of power in symbols of the Late Natufian and Neolithic periods, and further to the duality of public versus private and elite versus household spheres in early village societies that circumscribed innovative responses to new challenges. Lovell (2002) emphasized regional ecological and economic forces in explaining the Chalcolithic–EBA transition. She argued that general environmental deterioration and trading networks shaped new subsistence strategies and settlement patterns that focused on olive cultivation. Certainly these are important causal factors. The limitations inherent in Chalcolithic organizational structures, the failure by elites to develop new, broadly based sources of social and economic power, and regional environmental and subsistence change probably all contributed to the decline of southern Levantine Chalcolithic societies.

However, such panoptic explanations remain prime-mover models that are too simplistic to address acknowledged sub-regional variability in the timing of site abandonment (*cf.* Lillios 1993, 117–18). The different trajectories of decline and abandonment observed in different southern Levantine sub-regions can only be understood through investigation of more localized parameters of social change. In particular, the course of social evolution and devolution of Israel's northern Negev has been recognized as notably divergent from other areas of Chalcolithic settlement (Burton and Levy 2001, 1237; Levy 1998, 241; Lovell 2001, 51; Lovell 2002, 90, 92–5). One aspect of this divergence is chronological. As recounted in this paper, chronological data establish the relatively late *dénouement* of the northern Negev Chalcolithic sites and their close temporal relationship to neighbouring initial EB I sites. A second aspect of the divergence is related to the unique material culture of the northern Negev Chalcolithic. This material culture suggests a social trajectory characterized by increasing economic complexity probably linked to the initial emergence of 'chiefdom' (or 'ranked' or 'intermediate-level') societies within this particular sub-region of the southern Levant during the Chalcolithic time frame (*c.*4500–3500 BC) (Levy 1998, 2007). The ceramic connectivity analysis presented in the preceding section examined some of the spatial patterns in the transfer of the northern Negev Chalcolithic 'cultural burden' (Braun, this volume) following site abandonment. The results implied pathways of interaction and possible population movement at the close of the Chalcolithic that evidenced a marked shift in the geographic focus of settlement northwards out of the Beer Sheva valley. The demographic shift was accompanied by decreased investment in permanent architecture and declines in forms of craft specialization within the sub-region (*e.g.*, Alon and Yekutieli 1995; Braun 1996, 4, 12–28; Dessel 1991, 92; 2001, 109; Joffe 1993, 41; Levy 1998, 241–2; Yekutieli 2001, 678–9). In total, the material record across the Chalcolithic–EB IA horizon in the northern Negev has been widely recognized as consistent with defined archaeological correlates of social collapse (*cf.* Renfrew 1984b).

A number of environmental, social and economic factors have been proposed to explain the northern Negev collapse, including climate change, attenuation of the socio-political organization, commercialization and warfare (Joffe 1993, 36–7; Levy 1998, 241–3). It remains difficult to sort out precise sequences of events in this proto-historic time frame and, therefore, cause and effect in a situation that was probably complex. However, refinements in the dating of Beer Sheva valley site abandonment and the ceramic connectivity study presented in this paper highlight two particular social and economic processes that may have been involved in the demise of northern Negev Chalcolithic communities. These scenarios of change, outlined below, are not mutually exclusive. Furthermore, while not unrelated to events that were occurring in other parts of the region, the processes cited must be understood as operating within the specific social context of the northern Negev and particularly the Beer Sheva valley, where Chalcolithic culture endured the longest. General pan-regional factors, such as the trend toward more arid climatic conditions around the end of the Chalcolithic period supported by geomorphology and other palaeoenvironmental evidence (Goldberg and Rosen 1987; Goldberg 1987), are in these reconstructions viewed as stressors whose impact is contingent upon society's ability to respond and adapt (*cf.* Rosen and Rosen 2001, 546).

Loss of control over metal production and trade

First, based on observable patterns in the archaeological data, Beer Sheva valley Chalcolithic society may be best described as an emerging 'simple chiefdom' (Earle 1991, 3) at the cusp of its demise. Control over the production and exchange of staple goods and/or prestige goods is considered key to the economic power that underlies political power in chiefdoms (Earle 1997, 7). Existence of a 'prestige-good chiefdom' in the Beer Sheva valley by the end of the Chalcolithic period is indicated by apparent 'elite' control over copper production and distribution (Golden 2010; Levy 1998, 240–1; Levy 2007). Evidence for elite control includes copper-smelting activities located within the confines of courtyards associated with the largest buildings at Shiqmim, a cache of prestige copper objects in a foundation deposit associated with a public building, a copper macehead found within a 'corporate'-scale building and the sub-regional spatial restriction of metallurgical production that entailed the interregional importation of copper ore (Golden *et al.* 2001, 952, 961–2). The sum total of this evidence suggests that a primary economic foundation of political power was control over an elaborate technology and the acquisition of foreign goods and raw materials (*cf.* Commenge and Alon 2002, 147; Joffe *et al.* 2001, 17; Levy 1998, 240). Chalcolithic metallurgy focused on the production of exotic objects made with non-local alloyed copper (*e.g.*, Bar-Adon 1980), and these objects may have circulated in a gift-giving system among late-5th-millennium BC elite groups (Levy 1998, 240–1). 'Pure' copper implements produced at Beer Sheva valley sites using ore from southern Jordan were probably also prestige goods, given their extreme rarity in the Chalcolithic tool kit (Levy 2007, 51).

However, the power of Chalcolithic elites may have been limited and only weakly institutionalized (*cf.* Joffe *et al.* 2001, 17), as there is little evidence for restricted spatial distributions of classes of material culture other than metals. Exchange relationships and transportation routes to obtain complex 'natural' alloys for metal castings (currently unknown, Golden *et al.* 2001, 961) and ores from Faynan (Levy 1998; Levy *et al.* 2001) and Timna (Rothenberg and Merkel 1998) were therefore critical. A breakdown in the raw material supply network would have been a serious blow to elite authority. Similarly, loss of social control over the metallurgical process would also have had a destabilizing effect. Knowledge of the technology itself may have proved difficult to restrict, as smelting had to be conducted outdoors. Evidence of metallurgical production at the small satellite site Mezad Aluf (Golden *et al.* 2001, 959) indicates that copper-tool production was not confined to territorial centres in the Beer Sheva valley even during the Chalcolithic. Its later total geographic and social dislocation is proven by substantive evidence of production at Wadi Fidan 4 Village in the EB IA (Adams and Genz 1995, Levy *et al.* 2001). This site, in the Faynan copper-ore district, shows no significant ceramic or other material culture linkages with the Beer Sheva valley Chalcolithic. Whether the local condition of technological decentralization within the Shiqmim site cluster was responsible for the eventual loss of control or was symptomatic of it cannot be ascertained from currently available data. However, deprivation of an essential source of power that had been dependent on long-distance exchange and control of technological knowledge seems to be the most plausible direct 'trigger' for the collapse of Beer Sheva valley societies, given the chronological evidence and the inherently limited political strategy (*cf.* Earle 1997, 5–7, 9–10) by which authority and status appear to have been established and maintained. The low level of northern Negev–Faynan social interaction suggested by the ceramic connectivity measures may be indicative of the tenuous, secretive or even hostile nature of the Chalcolithic copper-ore supply network. An analogous case may be found in the cycling of Early Bronze Age (1700–1300 BC) chiefdoms in the Thy region of Denmark (Earle 1997, 197–200), where possible disruptions in the long-distance trade of metal for the production of status-materializing bronze swords and other metal objects have been linked to socio-political instability and ultimate demise.

Competitive involution

Available archaeological evidence is also consistent with a second social process pertinent to understanding northern Negev Chalcolithic collapse. P. Kirch (1991) has described the notion of competitive involution among chiefly leaders as a spiralling competition for the means and relations of production in a circumscribed environment that can ultimately lead to ecological failure and societal disintegration. As illuminated by C. Commenge and D. Alon (2002, 144–5), Beer Sheva valley communities of the late Chalcolithic seem to have had very limited interregional exchange in pottery and ground stone palettes compared to earlier settlement sub-phases within the northern Negev (perhaps reciprocally, Bourke 2002 also suggests extremely limited 'foreign' exchange in the Jordan valley at Late Chalcolithic Teleilat Ghassul). The spatial restriction of metallurgical production within the northern Negev sub-region toward the end of the Chalcolithic is further evidence of isolation, either intentional and politically driven, or a result of chrono-geographic accident.

Regardless of the factors that led to isolation, a cycle of increasing demands on agricultural production within a circumscribed territory for the purposes of feeding a growing population and accumulating wealth for the acquisition and production of 'prestige' copper goods could have led to human-induced environmental decline. Environmental damage caused by human activities – in this case, intensified production – could have occurred independently from the general climatic drying trend suggested by palaeoenvironmental evidence (Goldberg 1987; Goldberg and Rosen 1987). It is also possible that general climatic drying stimulated a social response to increase surplus production further to manage risk associated with perhaps fluctuating and marginally adequate water resources (*cf.* Levy 1998, 226, 241). If so, environmental decline in the Beer Sheva valley may have been the outcome of interactions between general climate change and social forces.

Efforts toward surplus agricultural production and centralized storage, though not apparent in ceramic vessel distributions at Shiqmim (Burton 2004, 276), may be reflected in the many subterranean room complexes at Late Chalcolithic Beer Sheva valley 'territorial centres' such as Shiqmim, Abu Matar and Safadi, especially those with evidence of silo storage pits and grain-processing equipment (Levy 1993, 68; Levy 2007; Witten 2006; Witten *et al.* 1995). The widespread use of these subterranean storage facilities at the large settlement centres may indicate that these societies had developed some of the economic aspects of 'staple finance chiefdoms' (Earle 1997, 209–10). Competition among territorial centres within the Beer Sheva valley for the primary productive resource – land for grazing and agriculture – has been demonstrated by means of a spatial analysis of soil types and overlapping site catchment zones (Levy *et al.* in prep., see also discussion in Levy 1993, 68). Possibly resulting inter- or intra-societal conflict is suggested by some recently published skeletal remains (Dawson *et al.* 2003), 'destruction layers' comprised of ashy, burnt fill within some structures at Shiqmim (Levy 1993, 71–2, table 1; Levy and Alon 1987, 164, 166), and the violent imagery evoked by ground stone and prestige copper maceheads (Levy 1993, 68–71). Meanwhile, pre-existing tensions between egalitarian and hierarchical ideologies (*cf.* Joffe *et al.* 2001, 17; see also Earle 1997, 5–7; for an ethnographic example see Leach 1954), perhaps exemplified in the paradoxical distributions of technologically sophisticated ceramic and metallurgical products – the former abundant and uniformly distributed (Burton 2004, 253), the latter rare and restricted – would have made elite authority inherently unstable. A combination of failing crops and weakened political organization may have prompted social groups to splinter and move north, away from the Beer Sheva valley and toward the better-watered, less-degraded Shephelah, as suggested by the ceramic connectivity measures. In this scenario it is unnecessary to invoke external causes such as abrupt, severe climate shifts or foreign incursions (*e.g.*, Joffe 1993, 37; Joffe *et al.* 2001, 17; Levy 1998, 242–3; Lovell 2002, 90) to explain social collapse. The Beer Sheva valley Chalcolithic societies may have simply imploded because of inherent contradictions in the social structure and internal processes of escalating competition set in motion by power-seeking individuals.

Summary

The definition and sequencing of 'culture groups', while providing the archaeologist with convenient nameable analytical entities, is not sufficient to explain the processes that lead to cultural transitions. Mechanisms that promote differentiation in material culture may be chronological, geographic or social in nature. Therefore, only precise chronologies and an understanding of social networks can implicate local processes of social and economic change, which operate within general pan-regional conditions. In this study, ceramic connectivity was used to measure degrees of social interaction among Chalcolithic and EB IA sites; this was combined with ^{14}C data that helped to establish the timing of site occupation and abandonment.

It was possible thereby to assess the relative intensity of social links between Chalcolithic and EB IA sites and to trace the course of probable population movement and cultural influence out of the northern Negev's Beer Sheva valley to other parts of the Negev and beyond. Particularly important social and economic processes that may have prompted these demographic shifts include the loss of control over copper metallurgy and competitive involution. These processes were specific to the northern Negev social context and were affected, but not determined, by general pan-regional factors of climate change and socio-economic adaptation (*cf.* Lovell 2002; Joffe *et al.* 2001). Future progress in understanding the Chalcolithic–EB I transition in the southern Levant will probably depend on focused sub-regional studies of local social and economic parameters and interactions that span the cultural horizon. In general, approaches that utilize some form of diachronic quantitative analysis in conjunction with anthropological models as a basis for explanation appear most likely to advance our understanding of cultural transitions in pre- and proto-history.

Acknowledgements

The authors would like to thank Dr Aviram Biran, Dr David Ilan and the staff of the Nelson Glueck School of Biblical Archaeology at the Hebrew Union College – Jewish Institute of Religion, Jerusalem, for their support in carrying out the Shiqmim and Nahal Tillah/Halif Terrace pottery analyses. Ms Anna Eirikh-Rose, Hebrew University, Jerusalem, assisted with the Shiqmim pottery analysis, and Dr Russell Adams, Ithaca College, New York, helped to make the Wadi Fidan 4 Village pottery available for study. Professor Ron Burton, Scripps Institution of Oceanography, University of California, San Diego, assisted with the connectivity and phenogram analysis. Ms Noga Z'evi drew the Abu Hof Village, Shiqmim, Mezad Aluf, and Nahal Tillah/Halif Terrace pottery, and students supervised by Dr Adams drew the Wadi Fidan 4 Village pottery included here. Their contributions are much appreciated. The Shelby White-Leon Levy Publication Fund provided funding for post-excavation artefact analysis for Shiqmim and we gratefully acknowledge the Fund's generosity. Margie Burton thanks also the Wenner-Gren Foundation for Anthropological Research (Pre-doctoral Grant #6496) for financial support for the Shiqmim, Nahal Tillah/Halif Terrace and Wadi Fidan 4 Village pottery analyses.

References

Adams, R. B. (1998) The Development of Copper Metallurgy During the Early Bronze Age of the Southern Levant: Evidence from the Feinan Region, Southern Jordan. Unpublished PhD thesis, University of Sheffield.

Adams, R. and Genz, H. (1995) Excavations at Wadi Fidan 4: a Chalcolithic village complex in the copper ore district of Feinan, Southern Jordan. *Palestine Exploration Quarterly* 127, 8–20.

Alon, D. (1961) Early settlements along the Nahal Grar and Nahal Patish. *Mibifnim* 24, 87–96.

Alon, D. and Yekutieli, Y. (1995) The Tel Halif Terrace 'Silo Site' and its implications for the Early Bronze Age I. *`Atiqot* 27, 149–89.

Amiran, R. (1969) *Ancient Pottery of the Holy Land*. Jerusalem: Massada Press.

Avner, U. and Carmi, I. (2001) Settlement patterns in the southern Levant deserts during the 6th–3rd millennia BC: a revision based on ^{14}C dating. *Radiocarbon* 43, 1203–16.

Bar-Adon, P. (1980) *The Cave of the Treasure*. Jerusalem: Israel Exploration Society.

Bar-Yosef Mayer, D. (2002) Egyptian–Canaanite interaction during the fourth and third millennia BCE: the shell connection. Pp. 129–38 in E. C. M. van den Brink and T. E. Levy (eds), *Egypt and the Levant. Interrelations from the 4th through the Early 3rd Millennium BCE*. London: Leicester University Press.

Blackham, M. (2002) *Modeling Time and Transition in Prehistory: The Jordan Valley Chalcolithic (5500–3500 BC)*. Oxford: BAR Int. Ser. 1027.

Bourke, S. J. (2002) Teleilat Ghassul: foreign relations in the late Chalcolithic period. Pp. 154–64 in E. C. M. van den Brink and T. E. Levy (eds), *Egypt and the Levant. Interrelations from the 4th through the Early 3rd Millennium BCE*. London: Leicester University Press.

Bourke, S. J. and Lovell, J. L. (2004) Ghassul, chronology and cultural sequencing. *Paléorient* 30/1, 179–82.

Bourke, S. J., Lawson, E. M., Lovell, J., Hua, Q., Zoppi, U. and Barbetti, M. (2001) The chronology of the Ghassulian Chalcolithic period in the southern Levant: new ^{14}C determinations from Teleilat Ghassul, Jordan. *Radiocarbon* 43/3, 1217–22.

Braun, E. (1989) The transition from the Chalcolithic to the Early Bronze Age I in northern Israel and Transjordan: is there a missing link? Pp. 7–27 in P. de Miroschedji (ed.), *L'Urbanisation de la Palestine a l'Age du Bronze Ancien, Bilan et Perspectives des Recherches Actuelle*. Oxford: BAR Int. Ser. 527(I).

Braun, E. (1996) Cultural Diversity and Change in the Early Bronze I of Israel and Jordan: Towards an Understanding of the Chronological Progression and Patterns of Regionalism in Early Bronze I Society. Unpublished PhD thesis, Tel Aviv, Tel Aviv University.

Braun, E. (2000) Area G at Afridar, Palmachim Quarry 3 and the earliest pottery of Early Bronze Age I: part of the 'missing link'. Pp. 113–28 in G. Philip and D. Baird (eds), *Ceramics and Change in the Early Bronze Age of the Southern Levant*. Sheffield: Sheffield Academic Press Ltd.

Braun, E. (2001) Proto, Early Dynastic Egypt, and Early Bronze I–II of the Southern Levant: Some uneasy ^{14}C correlations. *Radiocarbon* 43/3, 1279–95.

Braun, E. (2004) Egypt and the southern Levant in the late 4th millennium BCE: shifting patterns of interaction. *`Atiqot* 45, 511–21.

Burton, M. (2004) Collapse, Continuity, and Transformation: Tracking Proto-historic Social Change Through Ceramic Analysis. Case Studies of Late 5th–Early 4th Millennium Societies in the Southern Levant. Unpublished PhD thesis, University of California, San Diego.

Burton, M. and Levy, T. E. (2001) The Chalcolithic radiocarbon record and its use in southern Levantine archaeology. *Radiocarbon* 43/3, 1223–46.

Carmi, I. and Segal, D. (1992) Rehovot radiocarbon measurements IV. *Radiocarbon* 34/1, 115–32.

Childe, V. G. (1929) *The Danube in Prehistory*. Oxford: Clarendon Press.

Clarke, D. L. (1978) *Analytical Archaeology*. New York: Columbia University Press.

Commenge, C. and Alon, D. (2002) Competitive involution and expanded horizons: Exploring the nature of interaction between northern Negev and lower Egypt (*c*.4500–3600 BC). Pp. 139–53 in E. C. M. van den Brink and T. E. Levy (eds), *Egypt and the Levant. Interrelations from the 4th through the Early 3rd Millennium BCE*. London: Leicester University Press.

Cordell, L. (2000) Aftermath of chaos in the Pueblo southwest. Pp. 179–93 in G. Bawden and R. M. Reycraft (eds), *Environmental Disaster and the Archaeology of Human Response*. Albuquerque, NM: Maxwell Museum of Anthropology.

Dawson, L., Levy, T. E. and Smith, P. (2003) Evidence of interpersonal violence at the Chalcolithic village of Shiqmim (Israel). *International Journal of Osteoarchaeology* 13, 115–19.

Dessel, J. P. (1991) Ceramic Production and Social Complexity in 4th millennium Canaan: A Case Study from the Halif Terrace. Unpublished PhD thesis, The University of Arizona, Tucson.

Dessel, J. P. (2001) The relationship between ceramic production and sociopolitical reconfiguration in fourth-millennium Canaan. Pp. 99–118 in S. R. Wolff (ed.), *Studies in the Archaeology of Israel and Neighboring Lands in Memory of Douglas L. Esse*. Studies in Ancient Oriental Civilization 59. Chicago, MI: The Oriental Institute of the University of Chicago.

Earle, T. (1991) The evolution of chiefdoms. Pp. 1–15 in T. Earle (ed.), *Chiefdoms: Power, Economy, and Ideology*. Cambridge: Cambridge University Press.

Earle, T. (1997) *How Chiefs Come to Power: The Political Economy in Prehistory*. Stanford, CA: Stanford University Press.

Epstein, C. (1998) *The Chalcolithic Culture of the Golan*. Jerusalem: Israel Antiquities Authority.

Faltings, D. A. (2002) The chronological frame and social structure of Buto in the 4th millennium. Pp. 165–72 in E. C. M. van den Brink and T. E. Levy (eds), *Egypt and the Levant. Interrelations from the 4th through the Early 3rd Millennium BCE*. London: Leicester University Press.

Felsenstein, J. (1989) PHYLIP – Phylogeny Inference Package (Version 3.2). *Cladistics* 5, 164–6.

Felsenstein, J. (1995) *PHYLIP (Phylogeny Inference Package) version 3.57C*. Distributed by the author. Department of Genetics, University of Washington, Seattle.

Gilead, I. (1989) Grar: a Chalcolithic site in the Northern Negev, Israel. *Journal of Field Archaeology* 16, 377–94.

Gilead, I. (1994) The history of the Chalcolithic settlement in the Nahal Beer Sheva area: the radiocarbon aspect. *Bulletin of the American Schools of Oriental Research* 296, 1–13.

Gilead, I. (1995) *Grar, A. Chalcolithic Site in the Northern Negev*. Studies by the Department of Bible and Ancient Near East 7. Beersheva, Israel: Ben Gurion University of the Negev Press.

Gilead, I. and Goren, Y. (1989) Petrographic analyses of fourth-millennium BC pottery and stone vessels from the northern Negev, Israel. *Bulletin of the American Schools of Oriental Research* 275, 5–14.

Gilead, I. and Goren, Y. (1995) The pottery assemblages from Grar. Pp. 137–232 in I. Gilead (ed.), *Grar: A Chalcolithic Site in the Northern Negev*. Studies by the Department of Bible and Ancient Near East 7. Beersheva, Israel: Ben-Gurion University of the Negev Press.

Golani, A. and Segal, D. (2002) Redefining the onset of the Early Bronze Age in southern Canaan: new evidence of ^{14}C dating from Ashkelon Afridar. Pp. 135–54 in E. C. M. van den Brink and Yannai, E. (eds), *In Quest of Ancient Settlements and Landscapes. Archaeological Studies in Honour of Ram Gophna*. Tel Aviv: Ramot Publishing, Tel Aviv University.

Goldberg, P. (1987) The geology and stratigraphy of Shiqmim. Pp. 35–9 in T. E. Levy (ed.), *Shiqmim I: Studies Concerning Chalcolithic Societies in the Northern Negev Desert, Israel*. Oxford: BAR Int. Ser. 356.

Goldberg, P. and Rosen, A. M. (1987) Early Holocene palaeoenvironments of Israel. Pp. 23–33 in T. E. Levy (ed.), *Shiqmim I: Studies Concerning Chalcolithic Societies in the Northern Negev Desert, Israel*. Oxford: BAR Int. Ser. 356.

Golden, J. (2010) *Dawn of the Metal Age*. London: Equinox.

Golden, J., Levy, T. E. and Hauptmann, A. (2001) Recent discoveries concerning Chalcolithic metallurgy at Shiqmim, Israel. *Journal of Archaeological Science* 28, 951–63.

Gophna, R. (1998) Early Bronze Age Canaan: some spatial and demographic observations. Pp. 269–81 in T. E. Levy (ed.), *The Archaeology of Society in the Holy Land*. New York: Facts on File.

Goren, Y. and Fabian, P. (2002) *Kissufim Road: A Chalcolithic Mortuary Site*. Israel Antiquities Authority Reports 16. Jerusalem.

Goren, Y. and Gilead, I. (1987) Petrographic analysis of pottery from Shiqmim: a preliminary report. Pp. 411–18 in T. E. Levy (ed.), *Shiqmim I: Studies Concerning Chalcolithic Societies in the Northern Negev Desert, Israel*. Oxford: BAR Int. Ser. 356.

Hauptmann, A. (1989) Ancient copper production in the area of Faynan, Khirbet en-Nahas, and Wadi el-Jariye, Wadi Arabah, Jordan. Pp. 7–16 in S. J. Fleming and H. R. Schenk (eds), *History of Technology: The Role of Metals*. MASCA Research Papers in Science and Archaeology 6. Philadelphia, PA: University of Pennsylvania.

Hellberg, M. E., Burton, R. S., Neigel, J. E. and Palumbi, S. R. (2002) Genetic assessment of connectivity among marine populations. *Bulletin of Marine Science* 70/1 Supplement, 273–90.

Hodder, I. (1978) Simple correlations between material culture and society: A review. Pp. 3–24 in I. Hodder (ed.), *The Spatial Organization of Culture*. Pittsburgh, PA: University of Pittsburgh Press.

Hodder, I. (1982) *Symbols in Action: Ethnoarchaeological Studies of Material Culture*. Cambridge: Cambridge University Press.

Holl, A. F. C. and Levy, T. E. (eds) (1992) *Spatial Boundaries and Social Dynamics: Case Studies from Food-Producing Societies*. Ann Arbor, MI: International Monographs in Prehistory.

Joffe, A. H. (1993) *Settlement and Society in the Early Bronze Age I and II, Southern Levant: Complementarity and Contra-*

diction in a Small-Scale Complex Society. Monographs in Mediterranean Archaeology 4. Sheffield: Sheffield Academic Press.

Joffe, A. H. and Dessel, J. P. (1995) Redefining chronology and terminology for the Chalcolithic of the southern Levant. *Current Anthropology* 36, 507–18.

Joffe, A. H., Dessel, J. P. and Hallote, R. S. (2001) The 'Gilat Woman': female iconography, Chalcolithic cult, and the end of southern Levantine prehistory. *Near Eastern Archaeology* 64, 9–23.

Khalil, L. A. and Eichmann, R. (1999) Archaeological survey and excavation at the Wadi al-Yutum and Tall al-Magass Area – Aqaba (ASEYM) – a preliminary report on the first season of 1998. *Annual of the Department of Antiquities Jordan* 43, 501–20.

Khalil, L. A. and Eichmann, R. (2001) Archaeological survey and excavation at the Wadi al-Yutum and Magass Area – Al-'Aqaba (ASEYM): a preliminary report on the second season in 2000. *Annual of the Department of Antiquities of Jordan* 45, 195–204.

Kirch, P. V. (1991) Chiefship and competitive involution: the Marquesas Islands of eastern Polynesia. Pp. 119–45 in T. Earle (ed.), *Chiefdoms: Power, Economy, and Ideology*. Cambridge: Cambridge University Press.

LaBianca, O. and Scham, S. (eds) (2006) *Connectivity in Antiquity – Globalization as Long-Term Historical Process*. London: Equinox.

Leach, E. (1954, repr. 1993) *Political Systems of Highland Burma: A Study of Kachin Social Structure*. London School of Economics Monographs on Social Anthropology 44. London: The Athlone Press.

Levy, T. E. (1993) Production, space, and social change in protohistoric Palestine. Pp. 63–82 in A. Holl and T. E. Levy (eds), *Spatial Boundaries and Social Dynamics: Case Studies from Food-Producing Societies*. Ann Arbor, MI: International Monographs in Prehistory.

Levy, T. E. (1998) Cult, metallurgy, and rank societies – Chalcolithic period (*c*.4500–3500 BCE). Pp. 226–44 in T. E. Levy (ed.), The *Archaeology of Society in the Holy Land*. New York: Facts on File.

Levy, T. E. (2007) *Journey to the Copper Age – Archaeology in the Holy Land*. San Diego, CA: San Diego Museum of Man.

Levy, T. E. and Alon, D. (1987) Excavations in the Shiqmim village. Pp. 153–218 in T. E. Levy (ed.), *Shiqmim I: Studies Concerning Chalcolithic Societies in the Northern Negev Desert, Israel*. Oxford: BAR Int. Ser. 356.

Levy, T. E. and Brink, E. C. M. van den (2002) Interaction models, Egypt and the Levantine periphery. Pp. 3–38 in E. C. M. van den Brink and T. E. Levy (eds), *Egypt and the Levant. Interrelations from the 4th through the Early 3rd Millennium BCE*. London: Leicester University Press.

Levy, T. E. and Burton, M. (2006) Radiocarbon dating of Gilat. Pp. 863–6 in T. E. Levy (ed.), *Archaeology, Anthropology, and Cult: The Sanctuary at Gilat, Israel*. London: Equinox.

Levy, T. E. and Shalev, S. (1989) Prehistoric metalworking in the southern Levant: archaeometallurgical and social perspectives. *World Archaeology* 20, 352–72.

Levy, T. E., Alon, D., Grigson, C., Holl, A., Goldberg, P., Rowan, Y. and Smith, P. (1991) Subterranean Negev settlement. *National Geographic Research & Exploration* 7/4, 394–413.

Levy, T. E., Alon, D., Rowan, Y. M., Brink, E. C. M. van den, Grigson, C., Holl, A., Smith, P., Goldberg, P., Witten, A. J., Kansa, E., Moreno, J., Yekuteili, Y., Porat, N., Golden, J., Dawson, L. and Kersel, M. (1997) Egyptian–Canaanite interaction at Nahal Tillah, Israel (*ca*.4500–3000 BCE): an interim report on the 1994–1995 excavations. *Bulletin of the American Schools of Oriental Research* 307, 1–51.

Levy, T. E., Adams, R. B., Witten, A. J., Anderson, J., Arbel, Y., Kuah, S., Moreno, J., Lo, A. and Wagonner, M. (2001) Early metallurgy, interaction, and social change: the Jabal Hamrat Fidan (Jordan) research design and 1998 archaeological survey: preliminary report. *Annual of the Department of Antiquities of Jordan* 45, 159–87.

Levy, T. E., Burton, M. M. and Rowan, Y. M. (2006) Chalcolithic hamlet excavations near Shiqmim, Negev Desert, Israel. *Journal of Field Archaeology* 31/1, 41–60.

Levy, T. E., Rowan, Y. M. and Burton, M. M. (eds) (in prep.) *Desert Chiefdom: Dimensions of Subterranean Settlement and Society in Israel's Negev Desert (ca.4500–3600 BC) Based on New Data from Shiqmim*. London: Equinox.

Lillios, K. T. (1993) Regional settlement abandonment at the end of the Copper Age in the lowlands of west-central Portugal. Pp. 110–20 in C. M. Cameron and S. A. Tomka (eds), *Abandonment of Settlements and Regions: Enthoarchaeological and Archaeological Approaches*. Cambridge: Cambridge University Press.

Lovell, J. L. (2001) *The Late Neolithic and Chalcolithic Periods in the Southern Levant. New Data from the Site of Teleilat Ghassul, Jordan*. Oxford: BAR Int. Ser. 974.

Lovell, J. L. (2002) Shifting subsistence patterns: some ideas about the end of the Chalcolithic in the southern Levant. *Paléorient* 28/1, 89–102.

Miroschedji, P. de (2002) The socio-political dynamics of Egyptian–Canaanite interaction in the Early Bronze Age. Pp. 39–57 in E. C. M. van den Brink and T. E. Levy (eds), *Egypt and the Levant. Interrelations from the 4th through the Early 3rd Millennium BCE*. London: Leicester University Press.

Moore, C. C. and Romney, A. K. (1994) Material culture, geographic propinquity, and linguistic affiliation on the north coast of New Guinea: a reanalysis of Welsch, Terrell, and Nadolski (1992). *American Anthropologist* 96/2, 370–96.

Parkinson, W. A. (2006) Tribal boundaries: stylistic variability and social boundary maintenance during the transition to the Copper Age on the Great Hungarian Plain. *Journal of Anthropological Archaeology* 25, 33–58.

Perrot, J. and Ladiray, D. (1980) *Tombes a ossuaires de la region cotiere palestinienne au IVe millenaire avant l'ere chretienne*. Paris: Association Paléorient.

Prag, K. (2000) Tell Iktanu, south Jordan valley: Early Bronze Age I ceramics. Pp. 91–9 in G. Philip and D. Baird (eds), *Ceramics and Change in the Early Bronze Age of the Southern Levant*. Sheffield: Sheffield Academic Press.

Reimer, P. J., Baillie, M. G. L., Bard, E., Bayliss, A., Beck, J. W., Bertrand, C., Blackwell, P. G., Buck, C. E., Burr, G., Cutler, K. B., Damon, P. E., Edwards, R. L., Fairbanks, R. G., Friedrich, M., Guilderson, T. P., Hughen, K. A., Kromer, B., McCormac, F. G., Manning, S., Bronk Ramsey, C., Reimer, R. W., Remmele, S., Southon, J. R., Stuiver, M., Talamo, S., Taylor, F. W., Plicht, J. van der and Weyhenmeyer, C. E. (2004) IntCal04 terrestrial radiocarbon age calibration, 0–26 kyr BP. *Radiocarbon* 46, 1029–58.

Renfrew, C. (1984a) Space, time, and polity. Pp. 30–53 in C.

Renfrew (ed.), *Approaches to Social Archaeology*. Cambridge, MA: Harvard University Press.

Renfrew, C. (1984b) Systems collapse as social transformation. Pp. 366–89 in C. Renfrew (ed.), *Approaches to Social Archaeology*. Cambridge, MA: Harvard University Press.

Rosen, A. M. and Rosen, S. A. (2001) Determinist or not determinist? Climate, environment, and archaeological explanation in the Levant. Pp. 535–49 in S. R. Wolff (ed.), *Studies in the Archaeology of Israel and Neighboring Lands in Memory of Douglas L. Esse*. Studies in Ancient Oriental Civilization 59. Chicago, MI: The Oriental Institute of the University of Chicago.

Rothenberg, B. and Merkel, J. (1998) Chalcolithic, 5th millennium BC, copper smelting at Timna – new radiocarbon dating evidence for Timna site 39. *Institute for Archaeo-Metallurgical Studies* 20, 1–3.

Schaub, R. T. and Rast, W. E. (2000) The Early Bronze Age I stratified ceramic sequences from Bab edh-Dhra'. Pp. 73–90 in G. Philip and D. Baird (eds), *Ceramics and Change in the Early Bronze Age of the Southern Levant*. Sheffield: Sheffield Academic Press.

Segal, D. and Carmi, I. (1996) Rehovot radiocarbon date list V. *`Atiqot* 29, 79–106.

Seger, J. D. (1983) Investigations at Tell Halif, Israel, 1976–1980. *Bulletin of the American Schools for Oriental Research* 252, 1–23.

Seger, J. D. (1987) Tel Halif – 1986. *Excavations and Surveys in Israel* 5, 45–6.

Seger, J. D. (1990) Tel Halif – 1987. *Excavations and Surveys in Israel* 7–8, 69–71.

Seger, J. D. (1991) Tel Halif – 1989. *Excavations and Surveys in Israel* 9, 67–8.

Seger, J. D., Baum, B., Borowski, O., Cole, D. P., Forshey, H., Futato, E., Jacobs, P. F., Laustrup, M., O'Conner-Seger, P. and Zeder, M. (1990) The Bronze Age settlements at Tell Halif: Phase II excavations, 1983–1987. In W. E. Rast (ed.), *Bulletin of the American Schools for Oriental Research* 26 Supplement, 1–32.

Thorrold, S. R., Jones, G. P., Hellberg, M. E., Burton, R. S., Swearer, S. E., Neigel, J. E., Morgan, S. G. and Warner, R. R. (2002) Quantifying larval retention and connectivity in marine populations with artificial and natural markers. *Bulletin of Marine Science* 70/1 Supplement, 291–308.

Welsch, R. L., Terrell, J. and Nadolski, J. A. (1992) Language and culture on the north coast of New Guinea. *American Anthropologist* 94/3, 568–600.

Witten, A. (2006) *Handbook of Geophysics and Archaeology*. London: Equinox.

Witten, A., Levy, T. E., Ursic, J. and White, P. (1995) Geophysical diffraction tomography: new views on the Shiqmim prehistoric subterranean village site (Israel). *Geoarchaeology* 10, 97–118.

Yekutieli, Y. (2000) Early Bronze Age I pottery in southwestern Canaan. Pp. 129–52 in G. Philip and D. Baird (eds), *Ceramics and Change in the Early Bronze Age of the Southern Levant*. Sheffield: Sheffield Academic Press.

Yekutieli, Y. (2001) The Early Bronze Age IA of southwestern Canaan. Pp. 659–88 in S. R. Wolff (ed.), *Studies in the Archaeology of Israel and Neighboring Lands in Memory of Douglas L. Esse*. Studies in Ancient Oriental Civilization 59. Chicago, MI: The Oriental Institute of the University of Chicago.

Yekutieli, Y. (2002) Settlement and subsistence patterns in north Sinai during the 5th to 3rd millennia BCE. Pp. 422–36 in E. C. M. van den Brink and T. E. Levy (eds), *Egypt and the Levant. Interrelations from the 4th through the Early 3rd Millennium BCE*. London: Leicester University Press.

14. The Later Prehistory of the Southern Levant: Issues of Practice and Context

Graham Philip

Introduction

The workshop published here was intended to improve our understanding of the developments during the 6th to the mid 4th millennia BC. Accordingly, it was focused upon two key transitions. The first, the transition from the final phase of the Neolithic to the early phase of the Chalcolithic, is now generally dated to the early 5th millennium cal BC. The second, that from the Chalcolithic to the initial phases of the Early Bronze Age, falls in the early centuries of the 4th millennium BC. The intervening period is occupied by a developed phase of the Chalcolithic often termed the 'Ghassulian Culture' (Bourke 2008, for a recent summary). The second transition has recently been termed the 'End of Prehistory' (Joffe *et al.* 2001), and there is now a range of evidence which suggests that Early Bronze Age communities were organized along rather different lines from their predecessors (Philip 2008).

Participants were asked to provide ways to move beyond traditional debates, and ask new questions concerning developments in the 5th and 4th millennia cal BC. The editors have invited me to review the extent to which these hopes have come to fruition, and to consider the range of ideas that have emerged from discussion. I will also consider areas within which progress is less apparent, and make some suggestions as to why this might be. In addition, I will try to place the periods concerned, and some of the issues raised by the papers in this volume, in a wider context. In pursuing this I will make some brief comparisons between work on the later prehistory of the southern Levant and both research on earlier and later periods in the region and current research on prehistoric societies elsewhere in the Middle East. I will also suggest that we might usefully consider new types of narrative and touch upon issues arising from current archaeological practice and possibilities apparent from current developments in the wider field of prehistoric archaeology.

The later prehistory of the southern Levant: regional context and disciplinary impact

The discovery shortly after World War II of convincing evidence for early agricultural settlements at sites such as Jarmo and Jericho placed Near Eastern prehistory firmly within a global-scale narrative: that of the emergence of agriculture. Since then, the growing quantity and quality of the primary evidence for early sedentary communities in the southern Levant (*e.g.*, Bar-Yosef and Gopher 1997; Byrd 2005; Finlayson and Mithen 2007; Kenyon and Holland 1981; 1982; 1983) and the existence of an ample supply of accessible summary literature (Bar-Yosef and Meadow 1995; Kuijt 2000; Rollefson 2001; Simmons 2007) has ensured the region's place in global prehistories (Clark 1977; Mithen 2003; Scarre 2005).

The region's later prehistory has received far less attention. In contrast to Aceramic Neolithic communities, which receive extensive discussion, the Ceramic Neolithic does not feature in the accounts of Mithen (2003) or Watkins (2005), both of which are set within major volumes intended to provide a global overview. In practice, as far as general accounts are concerned, discussion of the later prehistory of the Middle East has traditionally been dominated by the Mesopotamian evidence. This trend is exemplified by Matthews (2005), whose account of the 'rise of civilization in southwest Asia', is in effect a follow-on to Watkins (2005), yet makes no mention of the Levant prior to the Bronze Age. This is no real surprise given the number of substantial region/period overviews of the Mesopotamian evidence published in recent years (*e.g.*, Algaze 2004; 2008; Rothman 2001; 2004; Pollock 1999; Charvàt 2002; Matthews 2000; 2003). Collectively, these accounts provide a rich source of information, much of which has been arranged around a series of important themes (*e.g.*, the development of complex societies, the growth of bureaucracy, urbanization and the scale and form of long-distance contact) which allow the mass of data to be arranged in a comprehensible manner. In addition, the last two or three years have seen the publication of thematic volumes addressing topics such as prehistoric ceramics (Nieuwenhuyse 2007) and textiles (Breniquet 2008). This material has contributed greatly to the impact that Mesopotamian archaeology has had in shaping the understanding of the development of complex societies among the wider subject community.

The later prehistory of the Levant was, of course, accorded more detailed discussion by Mellaart (1975, 227–43). However, in keeping with the aims of this still-fundamental text, his discussion was largely focused upon the description of material assemblages and their space–time systematics and generalized consideration of regional interaction. Such dedicated volumes are rare, however, and the later prehistory of the southern Levant has more often been covered in multi-period regional accounts, which generally prioritize the evidence for the 2nd and 1st millennia BC. The latter is, of course, of interest to a wide audience, including biblical scholars, Egyptian archaeologists, ancient historians and specialists in the ancient Aegean and Mediterranean. The very titles of many such volumes (Kenyon 1979; Mazar 1990; Ben-Tor 1992; Levy 1995), which reverberate with terms such as 'Holy Land', 'Land of Israel', and 'bible' or 'biblical' serve to cast the later prehistory of the region as a kind of extended prologue, something to be covered almost through a sense of obligation.

Why does the evidence from the southern Levant 'drop out' of wider narratives towards the end of the Aceramic Neolithic? Admittedly Mesopotamia covers a much larger area and there have been numerous research projects working there in recent decades. However, the southern Levant is a well-studied region and, while excavations have been fewer in total than in Mesopotamia, they are more densely distributed across the landscape and the material is generally more accessible for study. Moreover, I would suggest that in terms of data – for example, the final publication of recent field projects (*e.g.* Barker *et al.* 2008; Garfinkel and Miller 2002; Garfinkel and Dag 2008; Scheftelowitz and Oren 2004; van den Brink and Gophna 2005) and the availability of palaeoeconomic and palaeoenvironmental data – the Levant is quite well served (*e.g.* Hill 2006; Hunt *et al.* 2007; Kuijt *et al.* 2007; Rosen 2006). Despite this, however, the evidence from the region has played relatively little part in wider debates.

An obvious answer is that as far as the southern Levant is concerned, the Ceramic Neolithic and Chalcolithic periods fall between what have been arguably the two main foci of archaeological research in recent years. The first of these, early sedentism and the domestication of plants and animals, with all its implications for social and economic organization, is related primarily to the study of Aceramic Neolithic societies, and is thus focused upon the 7th millennium cal BC and earlier. The second, the development of complex societies, early states and urbanism, has tended to focus on the 4th and 3rd millennia BC, with discussion of the evidence from earlier periods focused upon the perceived south and north Mesopotamian 'cores'.

But the gap is not only a temporal one. Researchers working on early sedentary communities and those studying complex societies have each created not just a dense network of data but also a set of theories and concepts through which debate has been conducted, and themes around which the mass of evidence can be organized. Through this process our understanding of these periods has been modified substantially in recent decades. However, the period between, which is the subject of this volume, appears to lack a group of unifying themes of the kinds which provide strong research cores for these other areas. Thus, it sits to some extent within an intellectual 'gap' between these lively fields of debate and, as the editors observe, 'scholarly discussion has often prioritized the definition and redefinition of "archaeological cultures", and matters of chronology and terminology' (Introduction). In this light it is telling that the 'chiefdom' concept, first introduced to discussions of Levantine prehistoric societies more than 20 years ago (Levy 1986) still remains the closest thing to an anthropological framework in common usage.

Nomenclature

As regards the intellectual 'gap' mentioned above, the terminology used for the Neolithic and Chalcolithic periods is a case in point. Many of the key themes, such as domestication and the social and conceptual implications of sedentism, can usefully be investigated across extensive territories (Colledge *et al.* 2005; Colledge and Conolly 2007; Hodder 2007; Larson *et al.* 2007; Watkins 2004). Accordingly, the main phase terminologies associated with the Aceramic Neolithic are applied Levant-wide despite the existence of regional distinctions in material culture (*e.g.*, Kozlowski and Aurenche 2005). Equally, for the Early Bronze Age a set of successive chronological phases numbered EBA I–IV is employed across the southern Levant (except for the arid zones – Rosen, this volume), and less consistently in south and west Syria (compare Braemer 2002, 10, tab. 3, and Mazzoni 2002 with Akkermans and Schwarz 2003, 215, 236).

However, in the case of the Ceramic Neolithic and Chalcolithic of the southern Levant, the material has traditionally been discussed in terms of a number of chrono-stratigraphic units defined on the basis of material culture. These are generally equated with traditional 'archaeological cultures', and remain at the heart of even recent overviews, most of which are substantially devoted to their characterization and the clarification of their chronological relationships (Garfinkel 1993; Gopher 1995; Gopher and Gophna 1993; Gilead, this volume). From these accounts it is apparent that these cultures provide not only the basic organizational structure for the data, but also a key element of the research vocabulary.

The 'Archaeological Culture' as a mode of analysis

From the standpoint of a researcher working in a British university, one of the most striking elements of the papers in this volume is the extent to which a normative or essentialist notion of the 'Archaeological Culture' (Childe 1956, 123) continues to play a central role in discussion. Some papers seek to identify and refine archaeological cultures (*e.g.*, Gilead, Kafafi, this volume), others refer to 'type-fossils' as characteristic of a particular chronological or cultural phase (Milevski *et al.*, this volume), while some cite population movements as explanations for the appearance of new material (Golani and Nagar, this volume). All of these approaches are consistent with classic culture-historical practice, and while some claim to conceive of cultures mainly as units for organizing the data, many contributors at least implicitly follow Childe (1933, 198), who stated that 'Culture is a social heritage; it corresponds to a community sharing common traditions, common institutions and a common way of life.' Many contributions to this volume (*e.g.*, Milevski *et al.*; Gilead; Roux *et al.*; Rosen) refer less directly to Childe, than to Clarke's reformulation of the concept of the archaeological culture (Clarke 1978, 247), which allowed for material-culture distributions which were overlapping but not congruent. However, the widely recognized problems with the whole concept of the archaeological culture (Trigger 1968, 530; also see Shennan 1994, 5–14, for a more recent summary of critiques, with references) go largely unremarked.

As Trigger (1978, 86) has pointed out, the culture-historical approach grew out of the need to classify the space–time variability that was apparent within the archaeological record, a statement consistent with the views of several contributors. The initial phase of prehistoric research in the Middle East brought to light a past for which no ready interpretational framework existed (Wengrow 2006, 190), and which was therefore partly defined by the absence of a range of features (*e.g.*, writing, cities) which were readily observed among later societies in the region. Given this situation, it is no surprise that scholars adopted the standard disciplinary practices of the mid 20th century AD (see below).

Despite its limitations culture history continues to be the preferred analytical framework within many regional traditions (Ucko 1995, 5), suggesting that it produces outcomes sufficiently useful to make it 'fit for purpose' in the eyes of many users. However, Ucko (1995, 11) also notes that its persistence cannot be attributed to the same reasons in each case. Among those he lists are: a focus upon the collection, organizing and ordering of data; a desire to create models of the past that support present-day identity claims or which provide 'unproblematic' narratives for those seeking to write a national 'prehistory'; a general suspicion of theory. The present account will, hopefully begin to explore the particular reasons for its persistence in the southern Levant. Reading Gilead's (this volume) contribution, one might suspect that a desire to retain the place of artefact data at the very centre of analysis has played an important part.

Cultures as legacy

In this particular case, I would suggest that the tenacity of 'cultures' within accounts of the Ceramic Neolithic and Chalcolithic results from a combination of factors. Firstly, at the time when pioneering scholars such as Stekelis (1950–51; 1972), de Vaux (1966; 1971), Perrot (1968) and Kenyon (1960) were laying the foundations of our knowledge of the later prehistory of the Levant, the concept of the 'archaeological culture' was current within archaeology, and widely employed by authorities such as Childe (Rowan and Lovell, this volume, with further references). In the Middle East generally, prehistory was a relatively late addition to an archaeological tradition that had taken shape around the evidence – tombs, palaces and tablets – of the ancient civilizations of Egypt and Mesopotamia (Wengrow 2006, 189). This characterization is also apt for the situation in the southern Levant, where a relatively small group of prehistorians worked within a disciplinary field dominated by scholars dealing with the archaeology of the Bronze and Iron Ages. For the latter, the notion of bounded archaeological cultures appeared compatible with a historical narrative expressed largely in terms of the rise and fall of regional and 'ethnic' polities, the reconstructions of which sought to characterize broad regional phenomena. In this situation, a normative approach to the material evidence appeared eminently suitable.

It should be no surprise, then, that material culture was used to define chrono-stratigraphic groups which were generally equated with 'archaeological cultures', and that, following Childe (*e.g.* 1956, 135), these were taken as representative of past societies. In addition, a particularly striking feature of later prehistoric material assemblages in the region was pottery, a body of material which offers real scope for the incorporation of variability and so lends itself very well to classification on stylistic grounds. This was, of course, the very practice which underlay the definition of cultural units. However, as Anfinset *et al.* (this volume) observe, the focus on pottery may have led scholars to neglect other aspects of the evidence.

Many of the basic culture-groups, such as the Yarmoukian (Stekelis 1950–51, 1972), Wadi Rabah (Kaplan 1958a; 1958b) and the Ghassulian (Neuville 1930), entered the discussion many decades ago, and were defined on the basis of what is now best termed 'legacy data': that is, material much of which is now viewed as unreliable for reasons such as suspect stratigraphy, selective reporting of finds, a focus on painted ceramics to the neglect of undecorated material, inadequate publication, and weak stratigraphic or chronological control. It should come as no surprise, therefore, that despite a continuing emphasis on the role of ceramic typology it has not always been easy to incorporate more recent evidence within older frameworks. Thus attempts during the 1980s by Hanbury-Tenison (1986) and Helms (1987, also in Betts 1992) to demonstrate continuity across the Chalcolithic–EB transition were ultimately frustrated not only by inadequacies in the dataset, but also by the fact that the organizational units which provided the vocabulary for debate were themselves inextricably bound to existing interpretations.

Aspects of current practice

Scholars have continued to define new 'cultures' such as the Besorian (Gilead 2007) and the 'Qatifian' (Goren 1990), although the latter has not found universal acceptance (Bourke 2007, 29). Moreover, the contributions to this volume highlight the fact that the Wadi Rabah Culture, while defined by Kaplan (1958a; 1958b) half a century ago, and still prominent in the literature, has proved difficult to discuss in a way that is acceptable to the research community as a whole. Nor do the various 'cultures' comprise units that are directly comparable. Some – the 'Ghassulian', for example – are deemed to embrace sites and phases across much of the southern Levant, while others, such as the Besorian (Gilead 2007) or the recently proposed 'Esurian' (Yannai 2006, 275), are more confined in both space and time. The resulting mosaic of entities and variants presents scholars with a framework that is very different from that provided by the overarching regional units identified in both earlier and later periods.

Also relevant is Rosen's observation (this volume) that arid zone cultures, previously defined on the basis of distinct chipped-stone 'industries', may well be the result of particular techniques of lithic analysis. He further observes that, while the 'Timnian' of the Negev can be said to conform to Clarke's (1978) definition of an 'archaeological culture', the two ends of this very long temporal trajectory are quite different, and there is no reason to assume the maintenance of a single distinct 'Timnian' identity throughout.

Clearly the widespread retention of the culture concept does pose certain problems. The relevant issues have been usefully summarized by Johnson (1999, 16–17), who notes that when artefacts are taken to express cultural norms, this leads to the definition of groups of an idealized nature. Firstly, the resulting focus upon difference emphasizes the peculiarities of individual cultures, rendering it hard to identify and discuss elements that are shared between cultures. Secondly, normative cultures tend to be viewed as relatively stable entities, and so when a period of time is presented as a succession of cultures, it can be hard to discuss change and transition, except in terms of the replacement of one unit by another.

This second issue is particularly apparent in articles which focus upon demonstrating the differences between cultural groups (*e.g.*, Gilead 2007; this volume), and is implicit in others. One result, as Johnson (1999, 16–17) observes, is the creation of the kind of poorly defined transitional periods that represent a major focus of this volume. While often no more than the boundary zone between two arbitrarily defined and highly abstracted cultural units, such 'transitions' are often viewed as periods of instability and rapid change. However, this view has tended to reduce the visibility of change *within* 'better-defined' periods, a point recently made by Campbell (2007) with respect to the archaeological units commonly used in discussions of Mesopotamian prehistory.

The importance of type-sites to the definition of 'cultures' is underscored by the use of nomenclature such as Ghassul(ian), Timna(in) and Besor(ian). However, the role of type-sites in setting the expectations of a later prehistoric 'culture' is crucial. In fact, some are poorly dated, some were poorly excavated or published, while others produced quite small datasets, with the resulting material-cultural entities created by the addition of supposedly representative material from yet other sites (for further discussion see Clarke *et al.* 2007, 14). Campbell and Fletcher (2010, 80) have argued recently for Neolithic North Mesopotamia that 'a very restricted group of classic type sites in Iraq fundamentally influenced the chronological divisions across northern Mesopotamia', and go on to point out that 'if we accept that our traditional chronological structure is created by the slightly random choice of the initial range of excavated sites, then there is at least a possibility that questions which are generated by that structure may be misleading.' In this light, Lovell's suggestion (2001, 50) that Teleilat Ghassul, type-site for the supposedly well-defined Ghassulian, may itself be atypical, might argue that we would do well to review some of our core assumptions.

Anfinset *et al.* (this volume) highlight another problem when they note that practice in the southern Levant generally conforms to what Dobres (1999, 13) terms 'normative research', in that site-specific patterns of artefact variability are employed to describe ways of life on a regional scale. This process is facilitated by the prevalence of 'cultures' which act as an intermediary 'black box', allowing analysis to jump from the detailed material culture record to more generalizing statements. Two particular outcomes of this process are of concern. Firstly, by becoming 'cultures', what were ostensibly classificatory entities are treated akin to active agents, and become the building blocks around which narratives are constructed (Pluciennik 1999, 660). Secondly, by framing our narratives around high-level abstractions, we risk losing sight of the variability present within the primary data.

The result has been that our organizational units have come to shape not only our terminology but also scholarly expectations, the very questions asked by researchers, and the narrative structures deployed in writing accounts of Levantine prehistory. However, if, as Burton and Levy (this volume) argue, 'communities typically cycle through asynchronous phases of establishment, expansion and decline', and excavations tend to produce more data from some occupational phases than others, then the culture model risks creating macroscalar narratives through the combination of evidence drawn from quite different stages of the developmental trajectories of individual sites.

While the foregoing suggests that interpretation has in many respects adhered to traditional modes, the field of Levantine prehistory has certainly been open to external influences and has witnessed a substantial uptake of new methodological developments such as geophysical survey and palaeoenvironmental investigations. It is useful to try to understand how this situation came about, and why approaches currently favoured in Americanist archaeology, or the more theoretical end of European and Mediterranean prehistory, perhaps exemplified by the *European Journal of Archaeology* or the *Journal of Mediterranean Archaeology*, appear to have had a limited impact in the region. Of course, a full-scale analysis of the issue lies beyond the scope of the present paper, so I will restrict myself to making a few specific observations.

Some pointers might be drawn from a recent paper by Bernbeck and Pollock (2004, 338–40) who have argued that two distinct research traditions can be distinguished among foreign archaeologists working in the Middle East. The first, which they term 'Europeanist', is characterized by a close interest in historical problems and often finds expression through long-term projects based upon a single site or region. Such approaches accept that knowledge is built incrementally, and that the accumulation of evidence is itself of value, even if a considerable amount of this may appear of limited immediate use. The second tradition, which they term 'Americanist' (perhaps better termed 'Anglo-Saxon' as it applies also to projects funded from British, Canadian and Australian sources), is more closely allied to the social sciences. Research tends to be problem-orientated, with an interest in processes or structures. Importantly, data collection is designed to address specific research questions, often of a type likely to be relevant to a range of researchers, including an audience beyond others working in that specific sub-discipline or region. Fieldwork projects are often of limited duration and more focused, and the results are expected to have an impact upon the field which is apparent within a limited time scale.

Using the terms of Bernbeck and Pollock (2004, 340) the approaches favoured by many archaeological projects in the region, including locally based ones and those run in collaboration with overseas institutions, are aligned with the 'Europeanist' model. Its historical orientation fits well with local agendas, while researchers involved in long-term field projects are well positioned to gain a genuinely detailed knowledge of the regional material culture: the high priority assigned to long-term excavations at major Bronze and Iron Age tell sites is a case in point. However, the kind of theoretical literature noted above, while integral to 'Anglo-Saxon' research frameworks, is perhaps of less obvious value to scholars working within traditions where priorities differ.

Cultures and transitional periods

Some contributors (*e.g.*, Milevski *et al.*, this volume) appear to conceive of periods as comprising distinct entities characterized, if not by cultural norms, then by specific socio-economic structures as a result of which material-cultural preferences are shaped. Gilead's remark (this volume) that the transition between the 'Besorian' and the 'Ghassulian' is marked by 'a profound technological, typological and aesthetic change' provides a good illustration. Clearly if the data are organized into cultures, then the change detectable within the material record must be understood as that between cultures, which are seen as periods of stasis separated by 'transitions' – for example, that from the Chalcolithic to the EB I period. These are exactly the problems raised by Johnson (1999, 16–17). Moreover, groups of material that appear to share elements of both earlier and later cultures, which thus conflict with expectations, can be dismissed as 'mixed'.

However, Braun (this volume) and van den Brink (this volume) have now documented sufficient elements of continuity between the Late Chalcolithic and early EB I to show that the assemblage generally understood as 'early EB I' took shape gradually during the earlier part of the 4th millennium cal BC. Moreover, those features which were to become most distinctive of the period can be shown to have appeared at slightly different temporal points in the process. This suggests that, rather than seeing one culture as replacing another, we would do better to view the changes detectable in the archaeological record as evidence for complex, multidimensional transformations of relationships between people, with their environment and with a range of material resources. This suggestion builds upon the idea that 'culture' is not fixed, but is constantly being brought into existence through daily practice, much of which is mediated through the use of material objects (DeMarrais *et al.* 1996).

Returning to the matter of the Chalcolithic–EBA transition, it seems that the issue is likely to be resolved not through discussion and debate but by acquisition of new data, in particular from the early and mid 4th millennium cal BC deposits at sites such as Ashkelon Afridar and Modi'in (Braun and Gophna 2004; Braun, this volume; van den Brink, this volume). Van den Brink (this volume) notes that the various phases of occupation at individual sites provide merely synchronic snapshots of slightly different points within a continuum of development. It should be obvious, therefore, that models which seek to assign such snapshots to one or other of a limited number of large-scale chrono-stratigraphic units will reduce the explanatory potential of the evidence by replacing the continuity present in the data with a break created by the model itself.

That said, while the evidence in favour of gradual change appears increasingly plausible, in order to demonstrate such changes convincingly we need to be more explicit about the nature of the contexts from which key material derives. Researchers must also be sensitive to the degree to which residual material may complicate the situation on sites with long occupational sequences (Peltenburg 2003, 258). Thus, while excavation reports now increasingly include an appendix containing descriptions of the individual contexts or loci, it is not always clear to what extent this evidence has informed the discussion of artefactual data, which are all too often still presented by phase or stratum rather than by individual deposit.

Chronology and the use of radiometric dating

The region/period overviews of the late 20th century (*e.g.*, Gopher and Gophna 1993; Hanbury-Tenison 1986; Stager 1992) were held back by the lack of a *reliable* absolute chronology. However, a growing corpus of good radiometric dates linked to sound stratigraphic sequences at sites such as Teleilat Ghassul (Bourke 2007, 26), Wadi Ziqlab (Banning 2007a) and Tell Abu Hamid (Lovell *et al.* 2007, 57–9), and sites in the Wadi Beer Sheva (Burton and Levy, this volume), means that the absolute chronology of the Ceramic Neolithic and Chalcolithic is now much clearer than was the case even a decade ago.

Radiometric evidence now indicates that material termed Chalcolithic is unlikely to continue much beyond 3800 cal BC (Bourke *et al.* 2004; Burton and Levy 2001; Burton and Levy, this volume), and that the material assemblages taken to characterize the initial phase of the EB I were in use by 3600–3500 cal BC at Afridar (Segal and Carmi 2004, 119–20, Braun and Gophna 2004, 220–4) and Tell es-Shuna (Bronk-Ramsey *et al.* 2002, 83–4). Rosen (this volume) has shown, using radiocarbon evidence, that various elements traditionally lumped under the term 'Timnian' appeared at different times. Thus he demonstrates not only the extent of diachronic variability within steppe lithic assemblages but also the contemporaneity of quite distinct material-culture assemblages in the Mediterranean and steppe zones. We may soon be able to test Bourke's suggestion (2007, 28) that regions within the Mediterranean zone might also have developed at rather different speeds.

However, despite recent discussion (Banning 2007b), there are substantial variations in the ways in which radiocarbon dates are used by contributors. It is important that scholars are aware of problems inherent in the manipulation and grouping of radiometric dates if we are to exploit the full potential of the growing date-corpus. When dealing with groups of dates we should note the cautionary remarks of Bronk-Ramsey (2005) to the effect that 'Combination of dates should clearly only be carried out if there is good reason to assume that the events being dated all occurred within a short period ("short" here implies small in comparison to the errors associated with the dating methods).' The danger inherent in averaging dates, in particular when done without a clear understanding of the chronological and contextual relationships between the various samples, has been well illustrated by Millard and Wilkinson (1999). Given the nature of averaging as a procedure, it is unsurprising that the outcome is diagrams which show the dates for each archaeological culture forming a distinct cluster, clearly separated from the dates from earlier and later cultures (*e.g.*, Gilead, this volume, Figure 2.3). In fact, the apparently stable bounded entities which emerge are simply a product of the methods used, as the averaging procedure does to dates what the creation of normative cultures does to artefactual data. Such a procedure can hardly stand as a validation of the existence of cultures.

Related criticisms can be levelled at the treatment of dates by Shugar and Gohm (this volume). Radiocarbon dates should be combined only if (a) there is some *a priori* reason to believe that they represent the same point in time, and (b) they are statistically indistinguishable. The fact that dates satisfy condition (b) is not sufficient in itself to justify this procedure. The method of assigning sites to 200-year sub-periods on the basis of radiocarbon dates also appears problematic (Shugar and Gohm, this volume, Table 10.2). The calibrated date is a probability distribution and the range (whether expressed at 1 or 2 sigma) is simply not a reliable means of deciding which of the bicenturies it is most likely to belong to. For example, RTA-4506, the first date in Shugar and Gohm's Table 10.4 (this volume), has when calibrated a 95% range of 3630 to 3368 BC, and so apparently a near-equal split of 130 years before 3500 and 132 years after 3500. However, the probability plot shows that around two-thirds of the probability falls after 3500 cal BC. Moreover, many of these sites are complex and long-lived and even when dateable material is closely associated with metal artefacts this would date not their production and use, but their final deposition.

Banning *et al.* (this volume) demonstrate, using a Bayesian approach (Buck *et al.* 1996; Philip and Millard 2000), how one might undertake a sophisticated diachronic study of localized developments using less than ideal datasets. In a similar way, Banning (2007a) has used Bayesian analysis of radiocarbon dates to establish the chronological positions of a variety of archaeological 'entities', including both traditional 'cultures' and individual phases at specific sites, some of which had previously proved hard to place on material-culture grounds alone. The construction of chronologies on the basis of radiometric dates, rather than through claimed material-culture parallels, renders it possible to establish the temporal relationships between individual stratigraphic units without the circularity inherent in typology-based schemes. The recognition of this fact is the first step towards moving discussion away from pre-determined chrono-stratigraphic blocks and towards viewing the evidence from individual sites and regions in all its complexity and contradiction. Bayesian analyses are an invaluable aid to the systematic comparative analyses of archaeological evidence at the inter-site scales, that are necessary if we wish to write macroscalar accounts without recourse to traditional 'cultures'.

Of particular value will be the opportunity to examine separately the chronological development of different components of activity and material culture. This will allow us to assess whether changes in different fields of action were genuinely contemporary, and whether these might indeed form closely linked 'clusters' of activity. It will also allow us to investigate the degree of variability between synchronous communities, the significance of differential rates of development around the region and the relative timing of different communities' decisions regarding specific technical or material innovations. In effect, it will allow us to ask more sophisticated questions by accessing a richer and more complex range of archaeological evidence.

Towards an alternative framework

My own view is that we need to move away from working with pre-defined chrono-stratigraphic units and focus attention on the transformation of material culture through human action. However, this is best argued through a consideration of the possible value of alternative approaches to the south Levantine dataset. In this context it is possible to identify a number of issues which, if examined in detail, might provide rather more finely textured interpretations.

Environment and subsistence practices, while studied and reported, have not always been well integrated with the wider discussion of community structure, organization and social reproduction. It is striking, for example, that few of the contributors (but see Roux *et al.*, this volume) have explored the implications for human activity of recent environmental evidence (Brooks 2006; Robinson *et al.* 2006; Rosen 2006). Of course, archaeologists should be wary of resorting to environmental determinism, but Rosen (this volume) demonstrates that, while the environment sets certain constraints upon the range of behavioural possibilities consistent with sustainability, the record of human groups in the arid zone is not lacking in internal variability. In practice, a community's response to an environmental threat such as drought, or to a new opportunity will almost certainly be contingent upon a set of very localized concerns, including the way that the threat is perceived (*e.g.*, as a regular, if unfortunate, event, as opposed to, say, an act of divine retribution), and the degree to which the responses available are attractive to the community's main internal groupings. Consequently, there may be considerable diversity in the form and timing of different communities' responses to a particular opportunity or threat.

The very divergence of these responses may be an important driver of change. Some communities within a region might respond to a period of localized drought by changing cropping patterns or investing in improved water management technology, some might choose to retain their traditional ways and adjust population levels to reduced yields, while others might fission, forming smaller groups and adopting a more extensive resource procurement strategy. While there may be several workable responses to such a challenge, the particular route taken is likely to involve changes in the nature of the relationships of the community concerned with the landscape. Moreover, when the period of drought ended, the members of the various communities might find that, as a result of their divergent strategies, they were in rather different positions with respect to their levels of access to key resources.

The relevance of the above is that during the period from the 6th to the 4th millennium cal BC communities in the southern Levant had to engage with a range of new opportunities, any one of which had the potential to cascade change through society. These included the cultivation of olives and the production of olive oil (Lovell 2008 for a recent overview), the increasing adoption of woollen textiles *via* the appearance of wool-bearing sheep (Grigson 2006; Levy *et al.* 2006b), the growing availability of copper (Golden *et al.* 2001; Shugar 2001) and the domestication of the donkey (Grigson 1995; 2006, 224). The period also saw the appearance of both substantial individual settlements such as Teleiliat Ghassul and settlement concentrations such as that along the Wadi Beer Sheva (see Bourke 2008, 114–17).

If we set aside cultures and instead imagine a mosaic of communities, each grappling with a complex range of possibilities, we might think that the kinds of development noted above would form useful entry points for the investigation of change. By way of an example, it seems reasonable to enquire what the demonstrable changes in settlement size and subsistence regimes might have meant for the relationship between people, animals and land. Changes in crops and herd structures would surely imply changes in the valuation of different tracts of terrain and in patterns of access to resources such as land and water, a point made recently by Philip (2003) with respect to changes in the economy detectable during the later 4th millennium cal BC.

Another obvious gap is in the appreciation of the relationship between people and livestock in shaping past societies. In addition to their obvious role within food systems, domestic animals provide an important link between human groups at both intra- and inter-community scales. Robb (2004, 135–6) makes the interesting point that in prehistoric communities the herd of domestic livestock controlled by many individual households would have been too small to be demographically viable over the long term, necessitating a larger biological herd comprised of various smaller social herds, with livestock circulating between households. This situation would have been especially pronounced in the case of resource-intensive species such as cattle, animals which are present at many sites in the southern Levant, albeit in varying proportions. Thus cattle may have played an important role in social relations well beyond their apparent value for subsistence and traction.

In a related issue, scholars have rarely considered the social and political implications of evidence pointing to the very variable role of pig as a source of meat at Chalcolithic and EB I sites (but see Anfinset *et al.*, this volume; Croft

1994; Grigson 2007). Domestic pigs tend to live close to a settlement, unlike caprines, which are amenable to being herded across the landscape. Thus the contrast between the manner in which each species is best managed and the relationship between herding practices and matters of territory and distance may have given them very different social values, perhaps even ideological characteristics. These processes are likely to have contributed, alongside local environmental affordances, to the shaping of social attitudes to meat consumption within different communities. If the great predominance of caprine remains and virtual absence of pig bone in what appear to be EB I cultic deposits at Megiddo (Wapnish and Hesse 2000) are indicative of the dietary preferences of the gods, one might wonder what this meant for the status of those communities wherein pig-raising and pork consumption featured strongly. A discussion along these lines opens up a range of interesting ways to integrate studies of environment and economy with matters of status and ideology among past communities.

Scales of analysis and the role of communities

While the distinctive nature of the Chalcolithic material culture attested in the Jaulan is now well documented (Epstein 1998), and its place as one of several regional Chalcolithic variants widely remarked (Gonen 1992; Levy 1995; Kerner 2001), the significance of this difference has been less thoroughly explored. If, for example, Chalcolithic copper objects circulated in the context of some kind of prestige-goods system (Kerner 2001; Levy 1986; 1995), then the virtual absence of such artefacts from excavated settlements in the Jaulan (Epstein 1998) might suggest that that these communities differed markedly from contemporary societies elsewhere in the region, both internally and in the way in which extra-regional relationships were conducted. To echo the work of John Barrett (1994) on prehistoric communities in Britain, we might ask what the evidence can tell us about the way in which communities in the Jaulan responded to the challenges posed to them by the particular natural and social environment of their upland landscape, how this compared with the behaviour of contemporary groups in the various lowland environments, and how communities related to each other. We would also wish to understand the time-trajectories of individual communities in terms of their changing relationship with the natural and material world. In this way we may begin to distinguish between elements of change that were constituted at a local level, and those which were spatially more extensive.

When 'cultures' become the actors, as in many macroscalar narratives (Pluciennik 1999, 660), then the story of individual communities becomes part of, and is effectively submerged within, a common narrative. As our data take the form of interlinked sets of evidence generally drawn from individual space–time loci, it seems almost perverse to abandon specifics at an early stage in the process of interpretation. Pluciennik (1999) argues that the source material necessary for the construction of microscalar narratives is best sought at the level of individual sites (or occupational phases), and that this approach requires us to emphasize the historically specific, and thus investigate the small-scale localized events from which larger patterns might be constructed. Thus, if our narrative framework and analyses are set exclusively at the macroscale, then our interpretations will be restricted to this scale. If, however, we wish to produce more nuanced narratives, developed from the bottom up, we need to think not in terms of 'cultures', but in terms of a mosaic of communities, each grappling with a complex range of possibilities. These communities would have existed within variably composed local clusters linked by dense, routine interaction, but also by a multi-scalar set of more dispersed networks (in both spatial and temporal terms) mediated through a complex range of persons and materials.

An example of such an approach is that of Hodder (2006) at Çatalhöyük; he provides a richly textured account of an individual community in its own terms with only modest reference to contemporary sites. Core to his interpretative framework is the concept of agency. In fact, Barrett (2000, 63) has suggested that narratives which mark the passing of time without referring to agency work at a level of abstraction in which 'economic processes operate without labour, ideologies arise without the struggle to maintain belief'. In practice, few sites excavated in the southern Levant have benefited from either the exceptional preservation encountered at Çatalhöyük or the level of support required to facilitate the scale and highly intensive nature of that particular excavation.

However, that said, I am not certain that current archaeological practice in the region is suited to such high-density analysis, although the southern Levant is far from unique in this regard. In fact, a recent overview of practice in British prehistory (Jones 2002, 51) has pinpointed a number of issues which appear germane to the southern Levant. Among other things, Jones observes that it is the normal practice in excavation reports for stratigraphy, architecture and the various classes of finds to be presented in separate chapters: these are often, necessarily, the work of different specialists, who may devote much effort to reviewing parallels from other sites. However, detailed spatial and contextual analysis at the site level is less common. The result is that the various facets of the artefactual data from a particular project are not necessarily reviewed within a site-specific framework. Rather, they are dislocated from their contexts to become artefacts in the abstract, with analysis generally taking the form of comparison with 'related' objects recovered from a selection of sites covering relatively extensive intervals of time and space. This practice is a key element in facilitating 'normative research' and is linked to the perceived need to produce the kind of generalizing macroscalar accounts in which 'archaeological cultures' feature prominently. The outcome, however, is that artefact patterning at a regional scale may be discussed without a clear understanding of the detailed contextualization of the material at individual sites.

Clearly these practices are historically contingent and reflect the expectations of the intellectual environment within which they were formed. However, the way in which we organize and present our data impacts upon the way in which archaeology can be 'written' at a synthetic level – for example, by rendering some forms of interpretation relatively straightforward (*e.g.* inter-site or regional ceramic comparisons), but making other modes of analysis more difficult to develop.

In the case of the southern Levant, we lack knowledge on some very basic topics, such as the social and economic implications of the palpable differentiation of communities by size, function and local subsistence possibilities. Such investigations might be viewed as the prime function of long-term research excavations such as those at Gilat (Levy *et al.* 2006b), Teleilat Ghassul (Bourke 2002; 2007), Shiqmim (Levy 1987) or Sha'ar Hagolan (Garfinkel and Miller 2002), all of which have provided large quantities of high-quality evidence. Yet, as Rowan and Lovell (this volume) observe, some of the most important data to emerge in recent years have come from salvage excavations such as Afridar (Braun and Gophna 2004), Modi'in (van den Brink, this volume), Yiftahel (Braun 1997) and Peqi'in (Gal *et al.* 1997). The fact that new research questions are being addressed through salvage archaeology has parallels in contemporary Britain. There, fieldwork in lowland landscapes in response to the activities of developers has highlighted the scale of prehistoric settlement away from the areas traditionally favoured by long-term research projects (Bradley 2007). In the case of the Levant, the growing impact of the evidence from salvage projects might indicate that the questions which appeal to research funding agencies, or the issues around which researchers have designed their projects, have been able to address some gaps in our knowledge more effectively than others.

Approaches to material culture

Boivin (2004, 66–7), citing examples from anthropology, points out how the properties of material objects can shape the form of social schemes. In a specific example, Roux *et al.* (this volume) note how changes in the form of material culture and production techniques would have impacted upon a wide range of activities, including the procurement of raw materials, the organization of labour, the timing and perceived status of different activities and the range of skills and facilities required. To take another instance, the replacement of chipped stone by metal for cutting tools might be expected to have had ramifications not just for the relative values of the different materials; it would have impacted upon the relative status assigned to particular forms of labour, but also the importance of the connections through which different resources were obtained, and thus the strength and orientation of different social networks and the relative status associated with participation in these. The infrequency with which such issues were addressed by contributors to the volume might be seen as symptomatic of the grip of the 'archaeological culture', which both sets the questions and provides the vocabulary with which answers can be constructed.

If we seek to move away from 'cultures' we will need to modify the way in which we approach artefact data, and if we wish to build regional narratives from the bottom up there is a need for detailed inter-site material-culture studies. However, these must go beyond simple typological comparisons, to assemble and interpret the variable evidence for matters of manufacture, context and consumption. We need to understand the spatial and chronological extents of specific artefact styles, but also how these are expressed in terms of raw materials and technology in different contexts. This does not mean, however, that we should produce only the occasional definitive study accompanied by a massive *corpus*. Rather, we require a continuing and flexible engagement with the evidence, as it is such information that will allow us to begin to investigate the networks of knowledge and communication which underpinned much past behaviour. The need to interpret past societies through the medium of their objects requires us to consider the cultural logic which brought these remains into being, a point expounded many years ago by Shanks and Tilley (1987), among others. Jones (2002, 25) has argued that a potentially useful way to do this is by 'tacking back and forth between the material evidence and our theoretically informed notions of how human society is reproduced ... and to thus develop a web of meaning, building up connections and networks of significance between objects and concepts and practices'.

This might indeed be a useful way to move forward, as even where striking and spatially extensive similarities are evident in the material record, attempts to consider their significance remain few. Spatially extensive networks for the circulation of items of material culture (and probably other things too) clearly existed (Commenge 2006; Roux *et al.*, this volume; Rutter and Philip 2008). These have generally been discussed in terms of prestige goods and craft specialists, with reference to concepts drawn from the general anthropological literature (Kerner 2001; Levy 1986; 1995). However, such explanations sit rather uncomfortably with the apparent absence of such material in many parts of the region (Bourke 2008, 137). Not only do the spatial extents of the various networks remain poorly defined, but we have little understanding of the significance of the *specific* subset of material which circulated within them, even though this may have been of great importance to the communities involved. The lack of attention to these matters may reflect the belief that normative cultures are based upon shared ideas, and that, as Johnson (1999, 65) points out, once the existence of a particular culture is accepted, its specific form and its continued reproduction in that form need no further explanation.

One of the most debilitating aspects of ceramic studies

in the southern Levant has been the tendency to focus analysis upon shape typology and decoration, the primacy of which was established at a time in which ceramics provided the main basis for chronological assignment (*e.g.*, Albright 1932; Wright 1937). However, a wide range of approaches are now available through which material-culture assemblages can be assessed and compared (Chilton 1999), and this without recourse to over-generalized concepts such as 'specialization' (Dessel and Joffe 2000, 48).

Ways in which the ceramic data might be used to consider inter-community relationships at moderate spatial scales have been explored by Roux *et al.* (this volume) and Burton and Levy (this volume). The latter seek to comprehend change among sites in a particular sub-region by mapping quantified ceramic data against a radiometric dating framework. The aim is to compare material-culture assemblages – mainly ceramics – between sites and to investigate to what extent patterns of similarity and difference can be attributed to chronology, physical distance and inter-community connectivity. While the greater use of quantified material-culture studies is to be encouraged, this does raise the issues of sample size and the quality and comparability of contexts. Sherd material from contexts such as domestic middens can provide valuable evidence on ways in which material culture was mobilized and consumed as an aspect of routine household practices (Chesson 2000, 366). However, despite an extensive literature on the subject in American archaeology in particular (*e.g.* Schiffer 1987), the relationship – particularly in quantified terms – between refuse deposits and 'living' household assemblages remains poorly understood in Levantine archaeology.

Communities of practice

There has been growing understanding within the social sciences in recent years that what Giddens (1984) has termed the 'practical consciousness', which informs people's daily routines, is key to comprehending the ways in which people both constructed, and were in turn shaped by, their social and material worlds (Gosselain 1999; 2000; Hodder and Cessford 2004). The techno-petrographic approach employed by Roux *et al.* (this volume) draws upon such practice-based approaches, and is focused upon manufacturing processes, and the sequence of actions known as the *chaînes opératoires* (Lemonnier 1993), which allows them to address the relationship between people and objects through the way they are produced, the selection and acquisition of raw materials, manufacturing techniques and the social relations that underlie their production. Because of the socialized nature of learning, the transmission of technical skills associated with the acquisition of particular bodily techniques is believed to encapsulate important symbolic considerations (Dobres 2000) and thus allow the identification of what Lave and Wenger (1998) term 'communities of practice'. These are groups of people who share a common interest and learn how to further this more effectively through regular interaction – although learning may be an incidental outcome that accompanies other social processes.

The value of this approach is that it provides a means to assess the structure of the ceramic assemblage from Abu Hamid by providing data on the diversity of fabrics, their likely provenance and the relationships between vessel form, petrography and technical procedures. While the case study examines temporal change at Abu Hamid, the method also offers a way in which assemblages from different sites can be compared across many dimensions: the physical distribution of vessels, the transmission of practical knowledge, the organizational dynamics of production and acquisition and the variable relationships between different components of sites' ceramic assemblages.

The complexity of ceramic procurement evidenced at Abu Hamid Phase II (Roux *et al.*, this volume) indicates the risks inherent in assuming as a default option that the assemblage from a single site is, by and large, of local production. It demonstrates that the ceramic assemblage from a particular site should not be treated as a unified package diagnostic of a 'culture' but as componential and highly contingent. Such complex systems of ceramic consumption might well account for the diversity apparent in Late Neolithic/Early Chalcolithic ceramic assemblages in the region, confirming the view that bounded and homogenous ceramic regions, when these exist, require specific explanation (Philip and Baird 2000, 22).

Using this approach, it is possible to assess the nature of individual assemblages and their relationships both to earlier practices in that locality and to wider communities of practice. By showing that the ceramics from Abu Hamid Phase III belong to a different, technologically more homogenous and spatially more extensive tradition than their predecessors (Roux *et al.*, this volume), it is possible to argue for the development by the mid 5th millennium cal BC of widespread communities of practice in the sphere of ceramic production. This is almost certainly one of the elements which underlies what has been termed the 'Ghassulian culture'. The value of a technological approach is further underscored by Braun's revealing observation (this volume) that, despite certain changes of vessel form, early EB I ceramic production was in many respects a de-skilled version of Chalcolithic technology.

The object

Another area of interest is the way that we approach artefacts themselves: this is a discussion that might usefully draw upon recent work on materiality. One useful development from our standpoint has been the understanding that the assignation of the meaning of an artefact is not fixed once and for all, but is created to some extent by context. What this implies is that, while things are bound up within human affairs, people in turn use objects to create and structure social relations. Thus the archaeological record is composed of objects whose relationships with people, and with other artefacts, are changing constantly according to the contexts within which they are being used and thus understood or interpreted. In this light, meanings are rarely 'received' but are constantly remade through practice, what has been called 'the materialization of culture' (DeMarrais 2004, 11–12) – in effect, the way in which objects intervene in social relationships. As material culture is embedded in shared practices and understandings, webs of interaction between the social and the material are generated, creating elements of coherence which we can detect through archaeology.

A simple example would be the way in which the shaping of small lumps of clay into crude representations of animals allowed these to perform a role in rituals associated with hunting (Freikman and Garfinkel 2009), in effect forming a link between the hopes and desires of would-be hunters and the spirits. Of course, other situations will be more complex, with artefacts exchanged between people and thus coming to represent specific relationships or events. As objects may be exchanged a number of times they thus come to carry a complex range of memories and associations – in effect, a biography. In this way, two superficially similar items may come to have very different meanings, and thus to intercede quite differently in the field of human actions. It is probably worth exploring how these ideas might be developed in the context of the data from the southern Levant.

When we discuss exchange networks, we need to consider not just the familiar broad-scale patterns; we must also examine microscalar evidence for local consumption practices (Bradley and Edmonds 1993). A case in point is the basalt vessels which occur at numerous sites in the southern Levant in the Chalcolithic and the EB I periods (Braun 1990; Rowan *et al.* 1999). It is hard to identify a particular task that could *only* have been undertaken (in a strictly functional sense) using a basalt vessel, rather than in one made in wood, pottery or some locally available stone. Therefore, it is clear from the outset that the significance of basalt vessels is almost certainly bound up with a complex understanding of materials in which 'value' or 'significance' would have been influenced by factors such as availability, place of origin, the human relationships involved in their acquisition or transmission and local traditions regarding matters of 'appropriateness'.

To focus upon the situation in the EB I in particular, Schaub (2008, 279–82) has observed that the majority of vessels from Bab edh-Dhra' belong to a single type, and that, in contrast to the wider regional pattern, these were found in mortuary rather than settlement contexts. Moreover, while vessels from sites elsewhere in the southern Levant were generally made using raw materials from sources located in North Jordan or the Jaulan, examples from the southern Ghor appear to have been sourced mainly from local basalt outcrops on the Kerak plateau (Philip and Williams-Thorpe 1993; 2001; Rutter *et al.* 2003). In a study of stone axes in the British Neolithic, Bradley (2000, 86) has argued that, in addition to the functional properties of the rock, a range of social factors also contributed to the choice of axe source, and there is evidence to suggest that place of origin may have been an important element in the past categorization of material culture (Arnold 1971, 27; Bradley and Edmonds 1993). In this light, it is not unlikely that the source of basalt vessels may have influenced their perceived qualities and associations, thus contributing to their creation of a distinct 'identity'.

Thus while basalt vessels are widely distributed across the southern Levant during both the Chalcolithic and EB I periods, the combined evidence of context and geochemistry indicates the existence of quite specific practices at Bab edh-Dhra' during the EB I period, which were presumably embedded within a localized knowledge system. This is exactly the kind of information that can be obscured by large-scale studies of the kind that presume the existence of both an integrated distribution network and a universal system of meaning.

An approach of this type might have potentially interesting implications for our understanding of aspects of Chalcolithic-period metal artefacts, in particular those produced using complex ternary alloys and which generally appear in distinctive forms (Levy and Shalev 1989, 355–9; Shalev 1999; Shalev and Northover 1993; Tadmor *et al.* 1995). It is generally believed that these artefacts moved through prestige exchange networks of some sort (Kerner 2001; Levy 1986; 1995), and would therefore have been closely involved in shaping social relations and social reproduction. To accept this, however, is not to suggest that the significance of these objects remained the same at all times. As Shugar and Gohm (this volume) demonstrate, examples have been recovered from various places and contexts, including burials, settlements and a large hoard at Nahal Mishmar, which included both complete and fragmentary pieces.

Working with data from the Copper Age of south-east Europe, John Chapman (2000, 99–104) has suggested a new way of understanding the use and deposition of metal objects, among other categories of artefact. He argues (Chapman 2000, 5) for 'the creation, maintenance and development of social relations through the enchainment and accumulation of personalised objects'. As I read it, by 'enchainment' he means that two individuals wishing to establish some form of social relationship agree on a specific artefact appropriate to that particular relationship and break it into two or more parts, with each participant in the relationship retaining a part as a marker of the relationship. Parts may be further divided in the process of the establishment of different relationships, or passed on to a different person, and are kept separate until such time as the relationship is reconstituted. In this way items of material culture, or parts thereof, come to materialize relationships between people.

He also suggests that what are often termed 'hoards' might be connected to the notion of the fragmentation of 'sets' of artefacts (Chapman 2000, 46–7). According to this scheme, sets are seen as integrally related groups of individual elements. These too can be enchained, but not as fragments of an artefact, but as individual elements drawn from a set. However, hoards, particularly in the case of valuable materials such as metal, may also indicate the development of a different concept, that of status gained through accumulation (Chapman 2000, 130), and underscores the notion that an object derives meaning from form, material and context. As the notion of enchainment can be applied to fragments, individual objects and groups or sets of artefacts, this may provide us with a new framework through which we might not only consider Chalcolithic metalwork, but also revisit various elements of material culture, including those which are loosely grouped under the heading 'prestige goods'.

The significance of these artefacts is likely to have varied according to context, with a particular object valued and understood differently when in circulation, and when in the possession of a specific individual or group. In addition, the meaning assigned to specific artefacts may have varied according to shifts in the way in which different parts of the human age–gender life course were constructed and represented (Sofaer Deverenski 2000, 401). Value may have been further distinguished depending upon whether the object was in the possession of a named individual, formed part of a hoard, or was associated with the dead – that is, within a tomb. In fact, the prominence of 'secondary interments', a practice which required regular access to burial places for, among other things, the manipulation and structured deposition of human remains (Chesson 2007, 117; Joffe 2003), might suggest that objects associated with the dead could have taken part in social transactions, including their movement back to the world of the living. In short, rather than visualizing a single class of 'prestige' metalwork, we might do better to view it as a material resource deployed flexibly according to specific needs and circumstances. Finally, the potential for metal artefacts to be recycled gives them a very different notion of 'value', perhaps even a different construction of materiality from contemporary artefacts made from materials like stone and ivory. In short, the evidential value of artefacts is maximized not when they are considered as cultural indicators, or 'type-fossils', but when they are treated as material resources which could be deployed actively within various fields of practice.

The distinctive 'ladder' burials identified at Ashkelon Barnea have encouraged Golani and Nagar (this volume) to try to identify the source of an immigrant group. However, using a practice-based approach, one might look beyond formal similarities and differences to consider how changes in burial might indicate the transformation of cultural practices to reflect new social or organizational principles, given the specific material resources available within the landscape of the coastal plain. Superficially, at least, these cemeteries appear very different from 'typical' late EB I cave burials in the region – those from Azor (Ben-Tor 1975), for example. Philip has suggested (2008, 209–10) that one of the key differences between Chalcolithic and EB I societies was the replacement of portable artefacts as sources of power by agricultural products, the generation of which rested upon access to land, water and labour. As such, the multiple successive burials of the EBA have been interpreted as a materialization of the kinship groups (Chesson 2003, 2007; Philip 2003; 2008) which are believed to have underpinned rights to land and to have constituted the basis of extra-household labour units.

Viewed in this light, the linked chains of adult burials documented at Ashkelon Barnea (Golani and Nagar, this volume) might be understood as representing a formative stage in the materialization of kinship, expressed in a form that was compatible with the material affordances of the coastal plain. It is interesting to note, therefore, that the total of 19 interments spread over 10 cists included within the ladder is broadly consistent with the maximum number of individuals interred within any single EB I tomb at Bab edh-Dhra' – Tomb A 71, with 19 burials (see Schaub and Rast 1989, 183, table 4, 233; table 10 for details). Also of note is the fact that in some cases the built stone burial structures which occur in various parts of the southern Levant (and the parallels to which are noted by Golani and Nagar, this volume) are linked by low walls running between individual structures (Mortensen and Thuesen 2007, 109–10; Swauger 1966, 106–7), suggesting that individual burial receptacles were linked to some kind of larger burial landscape.

Equally, there has been little consideration of the way in which societies reproduce themselves through the operation of social memory, although the issue has been explored in both Neolithic and EBA contexts (Chesson 1999; 2001; 2007; Kuijt 2008). Work on mortuary practices in the British Neolithic and in the Balkans (*e.g.*, Chapman 2000, 144–5; Fowler 2002) raises the possibility that the carefully managed disarticulated remains which are found in many Chalcolithic and EB I burials might point to the dead human body having played a role in the mediation of social relations. In fact, it is quite possible that the disarticulation and selective curation evident in the EB I burials at Bab edh-Dhra', for example (Chesson 2007, 117–18), echoes anthropological and archaeological evidence for skeletal remains remaining actively involved in the world of the living (Campbell *et al.* 2003, 123–4; Kansa and Campbell 2004).

Concluding thoughts

Rowan and Lovell (this volume) remark that 'culture history is the platform upon which current archaeological research [in the southern Levant] is discussed'. I have sought to indicate above how the continuing central position of 'cultures' works to deny space to alternative approaches. As a result, the later prehistory of the southern Levant has remained relatively insular as a research field, and has not always been able to address effectively the kind of research questions that are of interest to wider scholarship. While

Bintliff (2008, 162) wisely cautions against the tendency to view 'the development of archaeological theory in stadial evolutionary terms, with the replacement of misguided approaches by superior ones on a generational or decadal level', I believe that in this case there is a genuine need for change, and that this cannot simply be dismissed as bending to current academic fashion.

I am aware that not all of the participants at the Madrid meeting will agree with my remarks. Some, I know, share many of my interests and concerns, some will find parts of value, while others will disagree strongly: divergence of views is appropriate in an academic discipline. It is, of course, highly desirable that regional specialists should seek to build the depth of the dataset by the collection, analysis and publication of new evidence and by detailed comparative analysis. However, I have suggested above that the way in which this is done has a greater impact upon the wider utility of that evidence than has generally been acknowledged.

Wengrow observes (2006, 194) that in much of the western scholarly tradition the ancient Middle East tends to be presented as a stage in global history – surely a perfect example of the suppression of difference to create a macroscalar narrative. As a result, the Middle East has not always been considered as consisting of separate places, each with a distinctive temporal development and encompassing multiple trajectories of social and cultural change. In fact, the later prehistory of the southern Levant provides an excellent instance of a very distinct regional trajectory, one that differs in many respects from those documented for both north and south Mesopotamia (Greenberg 2002, 2–3; Joffe 1993, 58–61; Philip 2008, 161–6). That this is the case appears, at least to me, to offer a way to develop research questions that will interest not only those already working in the region, but a significant swathe of the wider research community. In this way the later prehistory of the southern Levant could make an important contribution to wider debates, thus raising its profile within the discipline and, one might hope, seeing an increase in the flow of research funds.

However, if we are to capitalize on this opportunity there must be some reorientation within Levantine prehistory. While disputes over definitions and units of analysis will never go away, in part because they refer to real issues, we must also make a greater effort to ask the kind of questions which are likely to be of interest to a wider section of the discipline. Data of the quantity and quality of those from the southern Levant are exactly what is needed in order to facilitate the exploration of alternative narratives. However, this will require researchers to address the evidence using concepts that are meaningful to scholars working in other areas, and to frame their discussion around topics of broad and current interest. This will constitute a significant challenge, as it will require a degree of change in both research priorities and practices; the potential rewards, however, could be substantial.

Acknowledgement

I am grateful to my colleague Dr Andrew Millard for his helpful advice on the averaging of radiocarbon dates.

References

Akkermans, P. M. M. G. and Schwartz, G. M. (2003) *The Archaeology of Syria*. Cambridge: Cambridge University Press.

Albright, W. F. (1932) *The Excavations at Tell Beit Mirsim, I. The First Three Campaigns*. New Haven, CT: American Schools of Oriental Research.

Algaze, G. (2004) *The Uruk World System: The Dynamics of Early Mesopotamian Civilization*. Chicago, MI: University of Chicago Press.

Algaze, G. (2008) *Ancient Mesopotamia at the Dawn of Civilization. The Evolution of an Urban Landscape*. Chicago, MI: University of Chicago Press.

Arnold Dean, E. (1971) Ethnomineralogy of Ticul, Yucatan potters: etics and emics. *American Antiquity* 36, 20–40.

Banning, E. B. (2007a) Wadi Rabah and related assemblages in the Southern Levant: interpreting the radiocarbon evidence. *Paléorient* 33, 77–102.

Banning, E. B. (2007b) Introduction. Time and tradition: problems of chronology in the 6th–4th millennia in the Levant and Greater Mesopotamia. *Paléorient* 33, 11–14.

Barker, G. W., Gilbertson, D. D. and Mattingly, D. J. (eds) (2008) *Archaeology and Desertification: The Wadi Faynan Landscape Survey, Southern Jordan*. Levant Supplementary Series. Oxford: Oxbow Books.

Barrett, J. (1987) Contextual archaeology. *Antiquity* 61, 468–73.

Barrett, J. (1994) *Fragments from Antiquity: An Archaeology of Social Life in Britain, 2900–1200 BC*. Oxford: Blackwell.

Barrett, J. (2000) A thesis on agency. Pp. 61–9 in M.-A. Dobres and J. E. Robb (eds), *Agency in Archaeology*. London: Routledge.

Bar-Yosef, O. and Gopher, A. (eds) (1997) *An Early Neolithic Village in the Jordan Valley. Part 1 The Archaeology of Netiv Hagdud*. Bulletin (American School of Prehistoric Research) 43. Cambridge, MA: Peabody Museum of Archaeology and Ethnology, Harvard University.

Bar-Yosef, O. and Meadow, R. (1995) The origins of agriculture in the Near East. In T. D. Price and A. B. Gebauer (eds), *Last Hunters, First Farmers: New Perspectives on the Prehistoric Transition to Agriculture*. Santa Fe, NM: School of American Research Press.

Ben-Tor, A. (1975) *Two Burial Caves of the Proto-Urban Period at Azor, 1971: The First Season of Excavations at Tel Yarmuth 1970*. Jerusalem: The Hebrew University.

Ben-Tor, A. (ed.) (1992) *The Archaeology of Ancient Israel*. New Haven, CT: Yale University Press.

Bernbeck, R. and Pollock, S. (2004) The political economy of archaeological practice and the production of heritage in the Middle East. Pp. 335–52 in L. Meskell and R. W. Preucel (eds), *A Companion to Social Archaeology*. Oxford: Blackwell.

Betts, A. V. G. (ed.) (1992) *Excavations at Tell Um Hammad, 1982–1984: The Early Assemblages (EBI–II)*. Edinburgh: Edinburgh University Press.

Bintliff, J. L. (2008) History and continental approaches. Pp. 147–64 in A. R. Bentley, H. D. G. Maschner and C. Chippindale (eds), *Handbook of Archaeological Theories*. Lanham, MD: Altamira Press.

Boivin, N. (2004) Mind over matter? Collapsing the mind–matter dichotomy in material culture studies. Pp. 63–72 in E. DeMarrais, C. Gosden and C. Renfrew (eds), *Rethinking Materiality: The Engagement of the Mind with the Material World*. Cambridge: McDonald Institute for Archaeological Research.

Bourke, S. J. (2002) The origins of social complexity in the southern Levant: new evidence from Teleilet Ghassul, Jordan. *Palestine Exploration Quarterly* 134, 2–27.

Bourke, S. J. (2007) The Late Neolithic/Early Chalcolithic transition at Teleilat Ghassul: context, chronology and culture. *Paléorient* 33, 15–32.

Bourke, S. J. (2008) The Chalcolithic period. Pp. 109–60 in R. Adams (ed.), *The Archaeology of Jordan: A Reader*. London: Equinox.

Bourke, S. J., Zoppi, U., Meadows, J., Hua, Q. and Gibbins, S. (2004) The end of the Chalcolithic period in the south Jordan valley: new ^{14}C determinations from Teleilat Ghassul, Jordan. *Radiocarbon* 46, 315–24.

Bradley, R. (2000) *An Archaeology of Natural Places*. London: Routledge.

Bradley, R. (2007) *The Prehistory of Britain and Ireland*. Cambridge: Cambridge University Press.

Bradley, R. and M. Edmonds (1993) *Interpreting the Axe Trade*. Cambridge: Cambridge University Press.

Braemer, F. (2002) La céramique du Bronze ancien en Syrie du Sud. Pp. 9–21 in M. Al-Maqdissi, M. Valérie and C. Nicolle (eds), *Céramique de l'âge du bronze en Syrie. 1, La Syrie du sud et la vallée de l'Orontes*. Bibliothèque archéologique et historique (Institut français d'archéologie du Proche-Orient) 161. Beyrouth: Institut français d'archéologie du Proche-Orient.

Braun, E. (1990) Basalt bowls of the EBI horizon in the southern Levant. *Paléorient* 16, 87–96.

Braun, E. (1997) *Yiftah'el: Salvage and Rescue Excavations at a Prehistoric Village in Lower Galilee, Israel*. Jerusalem: Israel Antiquities Authority.

Braun, E. and Gophna, R. (2004) Excavations at Ashqelon, Afridar – Area G. *`Atiqot* 45, 185–241.

Breniquet, C. (2008) *Essai sur le tissage en Mésopotamie: Des premières communautés sédentaires au milieu du IIIe millénaire avant J.-C.* Paris: De Boccard.

Brink, E. C. M. van den and Gophna, R. (2005) *Shoham (North) Late Chalcolithic Burial Caves in the Lod Valley, Israel*. Jerusalem: Israel Antiquities Authority.

Bronk Ramsey, C. (2005) OxCal Program v3.10 University of Oxford Radiocarbon Accelerator Unit http://www.rlaha.ox.ac.uk/oxcal/arch_cmb.htm#radiocarbon (accessed 23 November 2009).

Bronk Ramsey, C., Higham, T. F. G., Owen, D. C., Pike, A. W. G. and Hedges, R. E. M. (2002) Radiocarbon dates fron the Oxford AMS system: Archaeometry datelist 31. *Archaeometry* 44/3 (supplement 1), 1–149.

Brooks, C. (2006) Cultural responses to aridity in the Middle Holocene and increased social complexity. *Quaternary International* 151, 29–49.

Buck, C. E., Cavanagh, W. G. and Litton, C. D. (1996) *Bayesian Approach to Interpreting Archaeological Data*. Chichester: John Wiley.

Burton, M. and Levy, T. E. (2001) The Chalcolithic radiocarbon record and its use in southern Levantine archaeology. *Radiocarbon* 43, 1233–46.

Byrd, B. F. (2005) *Early Village Life at Beidha, Jordan: Neolithic Spatial Organization and Vernacular Architecture: The Excavations of Mrs. Diana Kirkbride-Helbaek*. Oxford: Oxford University Press.

Campbell, S. (2007) Rethinking Halaf chronologies. *Paléorient* 33, 103–36.

Campbell, S. and Fletcher, A. (2010) Questioning the Halaf–Ubaid transition. Pp. 69–83 in R. Carter and G. Philip (eds), *Beyond the Ubaid: Transformation and Integration in the Late Prehistoric Societies of the Middle East*. Chicago, MI: The Oriental Institute.

Campbell, S., Carter, E. and Gauld, S. (2003) Elusive complexity: new data from late Halaf Domuztepe in south central Turkey. *Paléorient* 29, 117–33.

Chapman, J. (2000) *Fragmentation in Archaeology*. London: Routledge.

Charvàt, P. (2002) *Mesopotamia before History*. London: Routledge.

Chesson, M. S. (1999) Libraries of the dead. *Journal of Anthropological Archaeology* 18, 137–64.

Chesson, M. S. (2000) Ceramics and daily life in the EBA household: form, function and action in residential compounds at Tell el-Handaquq, south Jordan. Pp. 365–78 in G. Philip and D. Baird (eds), *Ceramics and Change in the Early Bronze Age of the Southern Levant*. Sheffield: Sheffield Academic Press.

Chesson, M. S. (2001) Embodied memories of place and people: death and society in an early urban community. Pp. 100–13 in M. Chesson (ed.), *Social Memory, Identity and Death: Ethnographic and Archaeological Perspectives on Mortuary Rituals*. American Anthropological Association 10. Arlington, VA.

Chesson, M. S. (2003) Households, houses, neighborhoods and corporate villages: modelling the Early Bronze Age as a house society. *Journal of Mediterranean Archaeology* 16, 79–102.

Chesson, M. S. (2007) Remembering and forgetting in Early Bronze Age mortuary practices on the southeastern Dead Sea Plain, Jordan. Pp. 109–40 in N. Laneri (ed.), *Performing Death. Social Analyses of Funerary Traditions in the Ancient Near East and Mediterranean*. University of Chicago Oriental Institute Seminars 3. Chicago, MI: The Oriental Institute.

Childe, V. G. (1933) Races, peoples and cultures in prehistoric Europe. *History* 18, 193–203.

Childe, V. G. (1956) *Piecing Together the Past. The Interpretation of Archaeological Data*. London: Routledge & Kegan Paul.

Chilton, E. S. (ed.) (1999) *Material Meanings. Critical Approaches to the Interpretation of Material Culture*. Salt Lake City, UT: The University of Utah Press.

Clark, G. (1977) *World Prehistory: A New Perspective*. Cambridge: Cambridge University Press.

Clarke, D. L. (1978) *Analytical Archaeology*. London: Academic Press.

Clarke, J., McCartney, C. and Wasse, A. (2007) *On the Margins of Southwest Asia. Cyprus During the 6th to 4th millennia BC*. Oxford: Oxbow Books.

Colledge, S. and Conolly, J. (eds) (2007) *The Origins and Spread of Domestic Plants in Southwest Asia and Europe*. Walnut Creek, CA: UCL Institute of Archaeology/Left Coast Press.

Colledge, S., Conolly, J. and Shennan, S. (2005) The evolution of Neolithic farming from SW Asian origins to NW European limits. *European Journal of Archaeology* 8, 137–56.

Commenge, C. (2006) Chapter 10. Gilat's ceramics. Cognitive dimensions of pottery production. Pp. 394–506 in T. E. Levy (ed.), *Archaeology, Anthropology and Cult: The Sanctuary at Gilat, Israel*. London: Equinox.

Croft, P. (1994) Some preliminary comments on the animal remains from the first three seasons at Shuna: preliminary report on the third (1993) season of excavations at Tell esh-Shuna North. *Levant* 26, 130–1.

DeMarrais, E. (2004) The materialization of culture. Pp. 11–22 in E. DeMarrais, C. Gosden and C. Renfrew (eds), *Rethinking Materiality: The Engagement of the Mind with the Material World*. Cambridge: McDonald Institute for Archaeological Research.

DeMarrais, E., Castillo, L. J. and Earle, T. K. (1996) Ideology, materialization and power strategies. *Current Anthropology* 37, 15–31.

Dessel, J. P. and Joffe, A. H. (2000) Alternative approaches to Early Bronze Age pottery. Pp. 31–58 in G. Philip and D. Baird (eds), *Ceramics and Change in the Early Bronze Age of the Southern Levant*. Sheffield: Sheffield Academic Press.

Dobres, M.-A. (1999) Of paradigms and ways of seeing: artifact variability as if people mattered. Pp. 7–23 in E. S. Chilton (ed.), *Material Meanings. Critical Approaches to the Interpretation of Material Culture*. Salt Lake City, UT: The University of Utah Press.

Dobres, M.-A. (2000) *Technology and Social Agency*. Oxford: Blackwell.

Epstein, C. (1998) *The Chalcolithic Culture of the Golan*. Jerusalem: Israel Antiquities Authority.

Finlayson, B. and Mithen, S. (eds) (2007) *The Early Prehistory of Wadi Faynan, Southern Jordan: Archaeological Survey of Wadis Faynan, Ghuwayr and al-Bustan and Evaluation of the Pre-pottery Neolithic A Site of WF16*. Levant Supplementary Series 4. Oxford: Oxbow Books.

Fowler, C. (2002) Body parts: personhood and materiality in the earlier Manx Neolithic. Pp. 47–69 in Y. Hamilakis, M. Pluciennik and S. Tarlow (eds), *Thinking Through the Body: Archaeologies of Corporeality*. New York: Kluwer/Plenum.

Freikman, M. and Garfinkel, Y. (2009) The zoomorphic figurines from Sha'ar Hagolan: hunting magic practices in the Neolithic Near East. *Levant* 41, 5–17.

Gal, Z., Smithline, H. and Shalem, D. (1997) A Chalcolithic burial cave in Peqi'in, Upper Galilee. *Israel Exploration Journal* 47, 145–54.

Garfinkel, Y. (1993) The Yarmoukian Culture in Israel. *Paléorient* 19, 115–34.

Garfinkel, Y. and Dag, D. (2008) *Neolithic Ashkelon*. Jerusalem: Institute of Archaeology, The Hebrew University of Jerusalem.

Garfinkel, Y. and Miller, M. A. (eds) (2002) *Sha'ar Hagolan. Vol. 1, Neolithic Art in Context*. Oxford: Oxbow Books.

Giddens, A. (1984) *The Constitution of Society: Outline of the Theory of Structuration*. Cambridge: Polity Press.

Gilead, I. (2007) The Besorian: a Pre-Ghassulian cultural entity. *Paléorient* 33, 33–50.

Golden, J., Levy, T. E. and Hauptmann, A. (2001) Recent discoveries concerning Chalcolithic metallurgy at Shiqmim, Israel. *Journal of Archaeological Science* 28, 951–64.

Gonen, R. (1992) The Chalcolithic period. Pp. 40–80 in A. Ben-Tor (ed.), *The Archaeology of Ancient Israel*. New Haven, CT: Yale University Press.

Gopher, A. (1995) Early pottery-bearing groups in Israel – the Pottery Neolithic period. Pp. 205–21 in T. E. Levy (ed.), *The Archaeology of Society in the Holy Land*. Leicester: Leicester University Press.

Gopher, A. and Gophna, R. (1993) Cultures of the eighth and seventh millennia BP in the southern Levant: a review for the 1990s. *Journal of World Prehistory* 7, 297–354.

Goren, Y. (1990) The 'Qatifian Culture' in southern Israel and Transjordan: additional aspects for its definition. *Israel Journal of Prehistory* 23, 100–12.

Gosselain, O. P. (1999) In pots we trust – the processing of clay and symbols in sub-Saharan Africa. *Journal of Material Culture* 4, 205–30.

Gosselain, O. P. (2000) Materializing identities: an African perspective. *Journal of Archaeological Method and Theory* 7, 187–217.

Greenberg, R. (2002) *Early Urbanizations in the Levant: A Regional Narrative*. London: Leicester University Press.

Grigson, C. (1995) Plough and pasture in the early economy of the southern Levant. Pp. 245–68 in T. E. Levy (ed.), *The Archaeology of Society in the Holy Land*. Leicester: Leicester University Press.

Grigson, C. (2006) Farming? Feasting? Herding? Large mammals from the Chalcolithic of Gilat. Pp. 215–319 in T. E. Levy (ed.), *Archaeology, Anthropology and Cult: The Sanctuary at Gilat, Israel*. London: Equinox.

Grigson, C. (2007) Culture, ecology and pigs from the 5th to the 3rd millennium BC. Pp. 83–108 in U. Albarella, F. Dubney, A. Eruyrick and P. Rowley-Conwy (eds), *Pigs and Humans. 10,000 Years of Interaction*. Oxford: Oxford University Press.

Hanbury-Tenison, J. W. (1986) *The Late Chalcolithic – Early Bronze I Transition in Palestine and Transjordan*. Oxford: BAR Int. Ser. 311.

Helms, S. W. (1987) Jawa, Tell um Hamad and the EBI/late Chalcolithic landscape. *Levant* 19, 49–81.

Hill, J. B. (2006) *Human Ecology in the Wadi al-Hasa: Land Use and Abandonment Through the Holocene*. Tucson, AZ: University of Arizona Press.

Hodder, I. A. (1991) *Reading the Past. Current Approaches to Interpretation in Archaeology*. Cambridge: Cambridge University Press.

Hodder, I. A. (2006) *Çatalhöyük: the Leopard's Tale Revealing the Mysteries of Turkey's Ancient 'Town'*. London: Thames & Hudson.

Hodder, I. A. (2007) Çatalhöyük in the context of the Middle Eastern Neolithic. *Annual Review of Anthropology* 36, 105–210.

Hodder, I. A. and Cessford, C. (2004) Daily practice and social memory at Çatalhöyük. *American Antiquity* 69, 17–40.

Hunt, C. O., Gilbertson, D. D. and El-Rishi, H. A. (2007) An 8000-year history of landscape, climate, and copper exploitation in the Middle East: the Wadi Faynan and the Wadi Dana National Reserve in southern Jordan. *Journal of Archaeological Science* 34, 1306–38.

Joffe, A. H. (1993) *Settlement and Society in the Early Bronze I and II Southern Levant*. Sheffield: Sheffield Academic Press.

Joffe, A. H. (2003) Slouching towards Beersheva: Chalcolithic mortuary practices in local and regional context. Pp. 45–67 in

B. A. Nakhai (ed.), *The Near East in the Southwest. Essays in Honor of William G Dever*. Boston, MA: American Schools of Oriental Research.

Joffe, A. H., Dessel, J. P. and Hallote, R. S. (2001) The 'Gilat Woman': female iconography, Chalcolithic cult, and the end of southern Levantine prehistory. *Near Eastern Archaeology* 64, 8–23.

Johnson, M. (1999) *Archaeological Theory: An Introduction*. Oxford: Blackwell.

Jones, A. (2002) *Archaeological Theory and Scientific Practice*. Cambridge: Cambridge University Press.

Kansa, S. W. and Campbell, S. (2004) Feasting with the dead? A ritual bone deposit at Domuztepe, south eastern Turkey (c.5550BC). Pp. 2–13 in S. Jones O'Day (ed.), *Proceedings of the 9th ICAZ Conference Durham 2002, Vol. 1 Behaviour Behind Bones*. Oxford: Oxbow Books.

Kaplan, J. (1958a) Excavations at Wadi Rabah. *Israel Exploration Journal* 8, 149–60.

Kaplan, J. (1958b) Excavations at Teluliot Batashi, Nahal Soreq. *Eretz Israel* 5, 9–24.

Kenyon, K. M. (1960) *Archaeology in the Holy Land*. London: Benn.

Kenyon, K. M. (1979) *Archaeology in the Holy Land*, 4th edn. London: Benn.

Kenyon, K. M. and Holland, T. A. (1981) *Excavations at Jericho. Vol. 3, The Architecture and Stratigraphy of the Tell*. London: British School of Archaeology in Jerusalem.

Kenyon, K. M. and Holland, T. A. (1982) *Excavations at Jericho. Vol. 4, The Pottery Type Series and Other Finds*. London: British School of Archaeology in Jerusalem.

Kenyon, K. M. and Holland, T. A. (1983) *Excavations at Jericho. Vol. 5, The Pottery Phases of the Tell and Other Finds*. London: British School of Archaeology in Jerusalem.

Kerner, S. (2001) *Das Chalkolithikum in der südlichen Levante die Entwicklung handwerklicher Spezialisierung und ihre Beziehung zu gesellschaftlicher*. Rahden: Leidorf.

Kozlowski, S. K. and Aurenche, O. (2005) *Territories, Boundaries and Cultures in the Neolithic Near East*. Oxford: BAR Int. Ser. 1362.

Kuijt, I. (ed.) (2000) *Life in Neolithic Farming Communities: Social Organization, Identity, and Differentiation*. Fundamental Issues in Archaeology. New York: Kluwer Academic/Plenum.

Kuijt, I. (2008) The regeneration of life: Neolithic structures of symbolic remembering and forgetting. *Current Anthropology* 49, 171–98.

Kuijt, I., Finlayson, B. and MacKay, J. (2007) Pottery Neolithic landscape modification at Dhra'. *Antiquity* 81, 106–18.

Larson, G., Albarella, U., Dobney, K., Rowley-Conwy, P., Schibler, J., Tresset, A., Vigne, J. D., Edwards, C. J., Schlumbaum, A., Dinu, A., Balacsescu, A., Dolman, G., Tagliacozzo, A., Manaseryan, N., Miracle, P., Van Wijngaarden-Bakker, L., Masseti, M., Bradley, D. G. and Cooper, A. (2007) Ancient DNA, pig domestication, and the spread of the Neolithic into Europe. *Proceedings of the National Academy of Sciences of the United States of America* 104/15, 276–81.

Lave, J. and Wenger, E. (1998) *Communities of Practice: Learning, Meaning, and Identity*. Cambridge: Cambridge University Press.

Lemonnier, P. (1993) Introduction. In P. Lemonnier (ed.), *Technological Choices. Transformation in Material Cultures since the Neolithic*. London: Routledge.

Levy, T. E. (1986) Archaeological sources for the history of Palestine – the Chalcolithic period. *Biblical Archaeologist* 49, 82–108.

Levy, T. E. (1987) *Shiqmim I – Studies Concerning Chalcolithic Societies in the Northern – Negev Desert, Israel (1982–1984)*. Oxford: BAR Int. Ser. 356.

Levy, T. E. (ed.) (1995) *The Archaeology of Society in the Holy Land*. London: Leicester University Press.

Levy, T. E. and Shalev, S. (1989) Prehistoric metalworking in the southern Levant: archaeometallurgical and social perspectives. *World Archaeology* 20, 352–72.

Levy, T. E., Alon, D., Rowan, Y. M. and Kersel, M. (2006a) The sanctuary sequence excavations at Gilat 1975–77, 1989, 1990–92. Pp. 95–212 in T. E. Levy (ed.), *Archaeology, Anthropology and Cult. The Sanctuary at Gilat, Israel*. London: Equinox.

Levy, T. E., Conner, W., Rowan, Y. and Alon, D. (2006b) The intensification of production at Gilat: textile production. Pp. 705–38 in T. E. Levy (ed.), *Archaeology, Anthropology and Cult. The Sanctuary at Gilat, Israel*. London: Equinox.

Lovell, J. (2001) *The Late Neolithic and Chalcolithic Periods in the Southern Levant. New Data from the Site Teleilat Ghassul, Jordan*. Oxford: BAR Int. Ser. 974.

Lovell, J. (2008) Horticulture, status and long range trade in Chalcolithic southern Levant: early connections with Egypt. Pp. 741–62 in B. Midant-Reynes and Y. Tristant (eds), *Egypt at its Origins 2. Proceedings of the International Conference 'Origin of the State. Predynastic and Early Dynastic Egypt', Toulouse (France), 5th–8th September, 2005*. Leuven: Peeters.

Lovell, J., Dollfus, G. and Kafafi, Z. (2007) The ceramics of the Late Neolithic and Chalcolithic: Abu Hamid and the burnished tradition. *Paléorient* 33, 51–76.

Matthews, R. (2000) *The Early Prehistory of Mesopotamia, 500,000 to 4,500 BC*. Turnhout: Brepols.

Matthews, R. (2003) *The Archaeology of Mesopotamia: Theories and Approaches*. London/New York: Routledge.

Matthews, R. J. (2005) The rise of civilization in Southwest Asia. Pp. 432–71 in C. Scarre (ed.), *The Human Past. World Prehistory and the Development of Human Societies*. London: Thames & Hudson.

Mazar, A. (1990) *Archaeology of the Land of the Bible 10,000–586 BCE*. New York: Doubleday.

Mazzoni, S. (2002) The ancient Bronze Age pottery production in north-west Syria. Pp. 69–79 in M. Al-Maqdissi, M. Valérie and C. Nicolle (eds), *Céramique de l'âge du bronze en Syrie. 1, La Syrie du sud et la vallée de l'Orontes*. Bibliothèque archéologique et historique 161. Beyrouth: Institut français d'archéologie du Proche-Orient.

Mellaart, J. (1975) *The Neolithic of the Near East*. London: Thames & Hudson.

Millard, A. R. and Wilkinson, T. (1999) Comment on 'AMS radiocarbon dates from the Predynastic Egyptian cemetery, N7000, at Naga–ed-Dêr' by S. H. Savage. *Journal of Archaeological Science* 26, 339–41.

Mithen, S. (2003) *After the Ice Age: A Global Human History 20,000–5000 BC*. London: Weidenfeld & Nicolson.

Mortensen, P. and Thuesen, I. (2007) Investigating Conder's Circle at 'Ayn Jadida near Mount Nebo. Pp. 451–6 in M. Lavento, P. Kouki, S. Silvonen, H. Ynnilä and M. Huotari (eds), *Studies in the History and Archaeology of Jordan* 9. Amman: The Department of Antiquities of Jordan.

Neuville, R. (1930) Notes de préhistoire palestinienne. *Journal of the Palestine Oriental Society* 10, 114–21.

Nieuwenhuyse, O. (2007) *Plain and Painted Pottery. The Rise of Late Neolithic Ceramic Styles on the Syrian and Northern Mesopotamian Plains*. Turnhout: Brepols.

Peltenburg, E. (2003) Post-colonisation settlement patterns: settlement trends in the Late Neolithic-Chalcolithic transition. Pp. 257–76 in E. Peltenburg (ed.), *The Colonisation and Settlement of Cyprus: Investigations at Kissonerga-Mylouthkia 1976–1996. Lemba Archaeological Project III.1.* Studies in Mediterranean Archaeology 70, 4. Sävedalen: Åströms Förlag.

Perrot, J. (1968) La prehistoire palestinienne. *Supplément au Dictionnaire Archéologique de la Bible* 8, 285–446.

Philip, G. (2003) The Early Bronze Age of the southern Levant: a landscape approach. *Journal of Mediterranean Archaeology* 16, 103–31.

Philip, G. (2008) The Early Bronze Age I–III. Pp. 161–226 in R. Adams (ed.), *The Archaeology of Jordan: A Reader*. London: Equinox.

Philip, G. and Baird, D. (2000) Early Bronze Age ceramics in the southern Levant: an overview. Pp. 3–30 in G. Philip and D. Baird (eds), *Ceramics and Change in the Early Bronze Age of the Southern Levant*. Sheffield: Sheffield Academic Press.

Philip, G. and Millard, A. R. (2000) Khirbet Kerak ware in the Levant: the implications of radiocarbon chronology and spatial distribution. Pp. 279–96 in C. Marro (ed.), *Chronologies des pays du Caucase et de l'Euphrate aux IVème–IIIème millénaires*. Paris: Boccard.

Philip, G. and Williams-Thorpe, O. (1993) A provenance study of Jordanian basalt vessels of the Chalcolithic and Early Bronze Age I periods. *Paléorient* 19, 51–63.

Philip, G. and Williams-Thorpe, O. (2001) The production and consumption of basalt artifacts in the southern Levant during the 5th–4th millennia BC: a geochemical and petrographic investigation. Pp. 11–30 in A. R. Millard (ed.), *Proceedings of Archaeological Sciences 1997*. Oxford: BAR Int. Ser. 939.

Pluciennik, M. (1999) Archaeological narratives and other ways of telling. *Current Anthropology* 40, 653–78.

Pollock, S. (1999) *Ancient Mesopotamia: The Eden That Never Was*. Cambridge: Cambridge University Press.

Robb, J. E. (2004) The extended artifact and the monumental economy. A methodology for material agency. Pp. 131–9 in E. DeMarrais, C. Gosden and C. Renfrew (eds), *Rethinking Materiality: The Engagement of the Mind with the Material World*. Cambridge: McDonald Institute for Archaeological Research.

Robinson, S. A., Black, S., Sellwood, B. W. and Valdes, P. J. (2006) A review of palaeoclimates and palaeoenvironments in the Levant and Eastern Mediterranean from 25,000 to 5,000 years BP: setting the environmental background for the evolution of human civilisation. *Quaternary Science Review* 25, 1517–41.

Rollefson, G. O. (2001) The Neolithic period. Pp. 67–105 in B. MacDonald, R. Adams and P. Beinkowski (eds), *The Archaeology of Jordan*. Sheffield: Sheffield Academic Press.

Rosen, A. M. (2006) *Civilizing Climate: The Social Impact of Climate Change in the Ancient Near East*. Lanham, MD: Altamira Press.

Rothman, M. S. (ed.) (2001) *Uruk Mesopotamia and its Neighbours: Cross-Cultural Interactions and their Consequences in the Era of State Formation*. SAR advanced seminar series. Santa Fe, NM: School of American Research Press.

Rothman, M. S. (2004) Studying the development of complex society: Mesopotamia in the late fifth and fourth millennia BC. *Journal of Archaeological Research* 12, 75–119.

Rowan, Y. M., Brink, E. C. M. van den and Braun, E. (1999) Pedestalled basalt bowls of the Chalcolithic: new variations (mortuary evidence from late prehistoric cultures of the southern Levant). *Israel Exploration Journal* 49, 161–83.

Rutter, G. P. and Philip, G. (2008) Beyond provenance analysis: the movement of basaltic artifacts through a social landscape. Pp. 343–58 in Y. M. Rowan and J. E. Ebeling (eds), *New Approaches to Old Stones: Recent Studies of Ground Stone Artifacts*. London: Equinox.

Rutter, G. P., Pearson, D. G., Philip, G., Day, J. M. D. and Ottley, C. J. (2003) The use of ICP-MS in provenancing igneous stone artifacts: examples from the southern Levant. Pp. 209–18 in G. Holland and S. Tanner (eds), *Plasma source mass spectroscopy*. London: Royal Society of Chemistry.

Scarre, C. (ed.) (2005) *The Human Past. World Prehistory and the Development of Human Societies*. London: Thames & Hudson.

Schaub, R. T. (2008) Basalt bowls in Early Bronze IA shaft tombs at Bab edh-Dhra': placement, production and symbol. Pp. 277–84 in Y. M. Rowan and J. E. Ebeling (eds), *New Approaches to Old Stones: Recent Studies of Ground Stone Artefacts*. London: Equinox.

Schaub, R. T. and Rast, W. E. (1989) *Bab edh-Dhra. Excavations in the Cemetery Directed by Paul W. Lapp (1965–67)*. Winona Lake, IN: Eisenbrauns.

Scheftelowitz, N. and Oren, R. (eds) (2004) *Giv'at ha-Oranim: A Chalcolithic Site*. Emery and Claire Yass Publications in Archaeology, Salvage Excavation Reports. Tel Aviv: Tel Aviv University.

Schiffer, M. B. (1987) *Formation Processes of the Archaeological Record*. Albuquerque, NM: University of New Mexico Press.

Segal, D. and Carmi, I. (2004) Determination of age using the ^{14}C method on archaeological samples from Ashqelon, Afridar – Area E. *`Atiqot* 45, 119–20.

Shalev, S. (1999) Recasting the Nahal Mishmar hoard: experimental archaeology and metallurgy. Pp. 295–300 in A. Hauptmann, E. Pernicka, T. Rehren and U. Yalçin (eds), *The Beginnings of Metallurgy*. Der Anschnitt 9. Bochum: Deutschen Bergbau-Museum.

Shalev, S. and Northover, P. J. (1993) The metallurgy of the Nahal Mishmar hoard reconsidered. *Archaeometry* 35, 35–47.

Shanks, M. and Tilley, C. (1987) *Reconstructing Archaeology: Theory and Practice*. Cambridge: Cambridge University Press.

Shennan, S. J. (1994) Introduction: archaeological approaches to cultural identity. Pp. 1–32 in S. J. Shennan (ed.), *Archaeological Approaches to Cultural Identity*. London and New York: Routledge.

Shugar, A. N. (2001) Archaeometallurgical Investigation of the Chalcolithic Site of Abu Matar, Israel: A Reassessment of Technology and its Implications for the Ghassulian Culture. Unpublished PhD thesis, University College London.

Simmons, A. H. (2007) *The Neolithic Revolution in the Near East. Transforming the Human Landscape*. Tucson, AZ: University of Arizona Press.

Sofaer Derevenski, J. (2000) Rings of life: the role of early metalwork in mediating the gendered life course. *World Archaeology* 31, 389–409.

Stager, L. E. (1992) The periodization of Palestine from Neolithic through Early Bronze times. Pp. 22–41 in R. W. Ehrich (ed.), *Chronologies in Old World Archaeology*. Chicago: University of Chicago Press.

Stekelis, M. (1950–51) A new Neolithic industry: the Yarmukian of Palestine. *Israel Exploration Journal* 1, 1–19.

Stekelis, M. (1972) *The Yarmukian Culture of the Neolithic Period*. Jerusalem: Magnes Press.

Swauger, J. L. (1966) Dolmen studies in Palestine. *Biblical Archaeologist* 29, 106–14.

Tadmor, M., Kedem, D., Begemann, F., Hauptmann, A., Pernicka, E. and Schmitt-Strecker, S. (1995) The Nahal Mishmar hoard from the Judean desert: technology, composition, and provenance. *`Atiqot* 27, 95–148.

Trigger, B. G. (1968) Major concepts of archaeology in historical perspective. *Man* n.s. 3/4, 527–41.

Trigger, B. G. (1978) *Time and Traditions: Essays in Archaeological Interpretation*. Edinburgh: Edinburgh University Press.

Ucko, P. (1995) Introduction: archaeological interpretation in a world context. Pp. 1–27 in P. Ucko (ed.), *Theory in Archaeology. A World Perspective*. London: Routledge.

Vaux, R. de (1966) Palestine during the Neolithic and Chalcolithic periods. *Cambridge Ancient History*, vol. 1, 499–538. Cambridge: Cambridge University Press.

Vaux, R. de (1971) Palestine in the Early Bronze Age. *Cambridge Ancient History*, vol. 1, part 2, 208–37. Cambridge: Cambridge University Press.

Wapnish, P. and Hesse, B. (2000) Mammal remains from the Early Bronze sacred compound. Pp. 429–62 in I. Finkelstein, D. Ussishkin and B. Halpern (eds), *Megiddo III: the 1992–1996 seasons*. Tel Aviv: Institute of Archaeology Tel Aviv University.

Watkins, T. (2004) Architecture and theatres of memory in the Neolithic of southwest Asia. Pp. 97–106 in E. DeMarrais, C. Gosden and C. Renfrew (eds), *Rethinking Materiality: The Engagement of the Mind with the Material World*. Cambridge: McDonald Institute for Archaeological Research.

Watkins, T. (2005) From foragers to complex societies in southwest Asia. Pp. 200–33 in C. Scarre (ed.), *The Human Past. World Prehistory and the Development of Human Societies*. London: Thames & Hudson.

Wengrow, D. (2006) The idea of prehistory in the Middle East. Pp. 187–97 in R. Layton, S. Shennan and P. Stone (eds), *A Future for Archaeology*. London: UCL Press.

Wright, G. E. (1937) *The Pottery of Palestine from the Earliest Times to the End of the Early Bronze Age*. New Haven, CT: American Schools of Oriental Research.

Yannai, E. (2006) *'En Esur ('Ein Asawir) 1: Excavations at a Proto-historic Site in the Coastal Plain of Israel*. Jerusalem: Israel Antiquities Authority.

Index